YALE ORIENTAL SERIES

BABYLONIAN TEXTS

VOLUME XVII

YALE ORIENTAL SERIES • BABYLONIAN TEXTS VOL. XVII

TEXTS FROM THE TIME OF NEBUCHADNEZZAR

BY

DAVID B. WEISBERG

INCLUDING

21 PLATES BY RAYMOND P. DOUGHERTY

NEW HAVEN AND LONDON, YALE UNIVERSITY PRESS, 1980

Published with assistance from the
Yale Babylonian Collection and the
Henry Englander-Eli Mayer Publication
Fund of the Hebrew Union College-
Jewish Institute of Religion.

Set in Monotype Scotch type
by Heritage Printers, Inc., Charlotte, N.C.
Printed in the United States of America by
The Murray Printing Co., Westford, Mass.

Library of Congress Cataloging in Publication Data

Weisberg, David B.
Texts from the time of Nebuchadnezzar

(Yale oriental series: Babylonian texts; v. 17)
Includes indexes.
1. Assyro-Babylonian language-texts. 2. Names, Personal—Assyro-Babylonian. 3. Names, Geographical—Assyro-Babylonian. 4. Nebuchadnezzar II, King of Babylonia, d. 562 B.C. I. Dougherty, Raymond Philip, 1877–1933. II. Title. III. Series.
PJ3711.Y3 vol. 17 [PJ3725] 492′.1s [492′.1]
ISBN 0-300-02338-3 79-16038

TO

PROFESSOR ABRAHAM SACHS

CONTENTS

Preface	ix
Abbreviations	xiii
Introduction	xv
Classified Catalogue	1
Descriptive Catalogue	5
Indices	
Personal Names	26
Geographical Names	
Cities, Towns, Forts, Gates, Wharves, Regions	74
Rivers, Canals, Seasonally Inundated Areas	76
Concordance of Museum Numbers	77
Comments and Collations to Copies Autographed by Raymond Philip Dougherty	81
Autographed Texts	Plates I–CLIV

PREFACE

The completion of a volume such as this must inevitably owe much to many friends and colleagues, both in and out of the field of Assyriology.

I was privileged to spend many pleasant hours in Rhode Island with Professor Abraham Sachs, benefiting from his careful criticism and superb guidance. It is a great pleasure to acknowledge his contribution to this volume, and to dedicate this work to him.

During 1973/74, two generous grants made it possible for me to travel to Europe to study with specialists in the field. Under the auspices of the American Association of Theological Schools, I was able to work with Professor Dr. Herbert Petschow at the Leopold Wenger Institut für antike Rechtsgeschichte und Papyrusforchung in Munich for a period of four months. I would like to thank Professor Petschow, who gave so freely of his time, for his constructive criticism and encouragement during my visit to Munich.

In the spring of 1974, a grant from the International Research and Exchanges Board for travel to the Soviet Union enabled me to visit Moscow, Leningrad, and Yerevan, where I derived much advantage from cooperation with Soviet colleagues. To Professor I. M. Diakonoff, of the Institut Vostokovedeniya, Leningrad, Professor G. K. Sarkisian of Yerevan, and Professor I. S. Klotschkoff of the Institut Vostokovedeniya of Moscow I owe much for their kind help during my visit.

To Professor M. Dandamayev, of the Institut Vostokovedeniya in Leningrad, with whom I spent many wonderful hours reviewing the material in this book and learning from his vast erudition, a great debt is owed. Professor Dandamayev patiently answered many queries by mail, as well, during the course of the preparation of this work.

A special word of thanks is due to Professor Marvin A. Powell, Jr., of Northern Illinois University, DeKalb, for collations made during the spring of 1977, when I was unable to travel to Yale. Dr. Elizabeth R. Jewell, Assistant Curator of the Babylonian Collection, Dr. Piotr Michalowski, now of the University of California at Los Angeles, and Dr. Mark E. Cohen were most kind to me during my visits to New Haven and greatly aided in the preparation of the texts by their work in the Collection.

Ms. Ulla Kasten, Museum Editor of the Babylonian Collection, was of great assistance in the preparation of the volume for the press. I record here, with gratitude, her role in expediting its publication. Ms. Laurie Pearce, a student at Yale University, was kind enough to assist, in the winter of 1976/77, in the preparation of the plates copied by Professor Dougherty. The keen eye and first-rate editorial experience of Mrs. Jane Isay, of the Yale University Press, enhanced the appearance of this book. She and Mr. Charles Grench, for whose help I am grateful, ably edited this book.

Professor George Cameron, of the University of Michigan, discussed with me the section of the Introduction dealing with the problem of the three Nebuchadnezzars. He offered important advice on how to deal with this material. I am happy to express my gratitude to him here.

On two occasions, while he was visiting the British Museum, Professor Erle V. Leichty, of the University of Pennsylvania, patiently collected material for me bearing upon years 0 and 1 of the Nebuchadnezzars and of Darius I. For his efforts on my behalf I am pleased to take this opportunity to thank him here.

My colleagues, Drs. Samuel Greengus and Matitiahu Tsevat, were ever ready to listen to problems and give useful suggestions. I thank them for their help.

To three deans at Hebrew Union College, Kenneth D. Roseman, Herbert C. Brichto, and Kenneth E. Ehrlich, I would like to express my profound gratitude. They made it possible to obtain help in the form of student aid in typing and filing. Further help was forthcoming through the efforts of Dean Brichto; acknowledgment is hereby made to Mrs. Lester A. Jaffe, through whose generosity a grant was obtained from the Lester A. Jaffe Research Fund, which greatly aided in the completion of the manuscript. In addition, I would like to thank the Hebrew Union College Publications Committee and its chairman, Dr. Michael Meyer, who generously made available a grant from the Henry Englander-Eli Mayer Publication Fund of the Hebrew Union College-Jewish Institute of Religion.

Typing of the front matter of the manuscript was done by several graduate students at the Hebrew Union College. This job was begun by the Rev. John C. Ralls. On 13 June 1975 we were shocked to learn of his untimely passing. His loss is keenly felt. The work was continued by Mr. Gary Huber and then by Ms. Mary B. Diamond. She is responsible for the typing of the manuscript Proper Name Index, the Classified and Descriptive Catalogues, and for the layout of the texts on the plates. Her patient and diligent work in preparing and checking the manuscript is here gratefully acknowledged. The manuscript of the Introduction, Geographical Index, and list of Comments and Collations to Copies Autographed by Raymond Philip Dougherty were typed by Ms. Ruth J. Deemy, a graduate student in Assyriology. The care with which she worked resulted in increased accuracy in the text of this volume. Ms. Barbara Sniderman was of great help in the final stages of work on the manuscript and in correcting the galleys and page proof.

Rabbi Benjamin Lefkowitz, Dr. Karen Nemet-Nejat, and Father Gregory Tajchman, O.F.M., made important contributions to the Indices.

Work during the summer months was carried on under grants from the National Endowment for the Humanities at the Yale Babylonian Collection. For these and for his constant encouragement, I express my deep indebtedness to Professor William W. Hallo, Curator of the Babylonian Collection at Yale. This book owes more to him than could possibly be stated in any preface. I take pride in the fact that I was his first student at Yale, and I take pleasure in thanking him publicly for the ceaseless and generous help that he characteristically gave me and his other students.

Finally, I express my love for Ophra.

GRASS ISLAND
JULY 1977

D. B. W.

ABBREVIATIONS

ABL	R. F. Harper, *Assyrian and Babylonian Letters*, London and Chicago, 1892–1914
AfO	*Archiv für Orientforschung*, 1926–
AHw.	W. von Soden, *Akkadisches Handwörterbuch*, Wiesbaden, 1959–
AJSL	*American Journal of Semitic Languages and Literatures*, 1895–1941
ASAW	Abhandlungen der Sächsischen Akademie der Wissenschaften zu Leipzig
ASSF	Acta Societatis Scientiarum Fennicae
BSOAS	*Bulletin of the School of Oriental and African Studies*, 1917–
CAD	*The Assyrian Dictionary of the Oriental Institute of the University of Chicago*, Chicago, 1956–
Cocquerillat, *Palmeraies*	Denise Cocquerillat, *Palmeraies et Cultures de l'Eanna d'Uruk (559–520)*, Ausgrabungen der Deutschen Forschungsgemeinschaft in Uruk-Warka 8, Berlin, 1968
DB	Darius, Behistun
GCCI	R. P. Dougherty, *Goucher College Cuneiform Inscriptions* 1, New Haven, 1923; 2, New Haven, 1933
HG	J. Kohler et al., Hammurabi's Gesetz. P. Koschaker and A. Ungnad, "Verwaltungsurkunden," *HG*, volume VI, Leipzig, 1923
JCS	*Journal of Cuneiform Studies*, 1947–
JNES	*Journal of Near Eastern Studies*, 1942–
Moore, *Mich. Coll.*	E. W. Moore, *Neo-Babylonian Documents in the University of Michigan Collection*, Ann Arbor, 1939
Moore, *Neobab. Documents*	E. W. Moore, *Neo-Babylonian Business and Administrative Documents*, Ann Arbor, 1935
NBC	Nies Babylonian Collection
Nbk.	J. N. Strassmaier, *Inschriften von Nabuchodonosor*, Leipzig, 1889
Nbn.	J. N. Strassmaier, *Inschriften von Nabonidus*, Leipzig, 1889
OLZ	*Orientalistische Literaturzeitung*, 1898–
Or. NS.	*Orientalia*, New Series, 1932–

Parker and Dubberstein	R. A. Parker and W. H. Dubberstein, *Babylonian Chronology 626* B.C.–A.D. *75*, Providence, 1956
Petschow, *Pfandrecht*	H. Petschow, *Neubabylonisches Pfandrecht*, ASAW Phil.-Hist. Kl. 48/1, Berlin, 1956
RA	*Revue d'assyriologie et d'archéologie orientale*, 1886–
"Royal Women"	David B. Weisberg, "Royal Women of the Neo-Babylonian Period," *XIX*e *Rencontre Assyriologique Internationale*, Paris, 1971
RPD	Raymond Philip Dougherty
San Nicolò, *Prosopographie*	M. San Nicolò, *Beiträge zu einer Prosopographie neubabylonischer Beamten der Zivil-und-Tempelverwaltung*, SBAW II, 2, Munich, 1941
SBAW	Sitzungsberichte der Bayerischen Akademie der Wissenschaften
von Soden, *Syllabar*	W. von Soden, *Das akkadische Syllabar*, AnOr 27; 2nd ed., AnOr 42, Rome, 1967
Stamm, *Namengebung*	J. J. Stamm, "Die akkadische Namengebung," *MVAG* 44 (1939), Darmstadt, 1968
Tallqvist, *NBN*	K. Tallqvist, *Neubabylonisches Namenbuch* ..., ASSF 32/2, Helsinki, 1905
TCL	*Textes cunéiformes du Louvre*, G. Contenau, volume 12, Paris, 1927
TuM	*Texte und Materialien der Frau Professor Hilprecht Collection of Babylonian Antiquities im Eigentum der Universität Jena*, O. Krückmann, II/III, Leipzig, 1933
UET	*Ur Excavations, Texts*. H. Figulla, volume IV, London, 1949
Ungnad, *NRVG*	A. Ungnad, *Neubabylonische Rechts- und Verwaltungsurkunden, Glossar*, Leipzig, 1937
VAB	*Vorderasiatische Bibliothek*, Leipzig, 1907
Wörterbuch der Mythologie	D. O. Edzard, "Mesopotamien: Die Mythologie der Sumerer und Akkader," *Wörterbuch der Mythologie*, Stuttgart, 1965
YBC	Yale Babylonian Collection
YOS	*Yale Oriental Series, Babylonian Texts*, New Haven and London, 1915–
ZA	*Zeitschrift für Assyriologie*, 1886–
ZDMG	*Zeitschrift der Deutschen Morgenländischen Gesellschaft*, 1846–

INTRODUCTION*

Some years ago, the late Ferris J Stephens, the then Curator of the Yale Babylonian Collection, called me into his office and showed me 21 plates containing cuneiform copies by the late R. P. Dougherty. These texts, all from the Yale Babylonian Collection, and numbering 84[1], represented the beginning of a volume of texts dating to the time of Nebuchadnezzar. The preparation of this volume had been interrupted by the death of Professor Dougherty on 13 July 1933 (*AfO* 9 [1933-34], p. 156).

Together with these plates, there existed some notes in rough form prepared by the late Arch Tremayne, author of *YOS* 7, which indicated that at one time he had contemplated picking up where Professor Dougherty had left off and perhaps completing the volume. The notes covered about seven texts in transliteration as well as a list of YBC numbers by year of Nebuchadnezzar's rule. Either Dougherty or Tremayne had prepared this list to facilitate the preparation of the copies. However, it seems that Dr. Tremayne did not carry his work on these texts beyond this point.

Professor Stephens asked me if I would like to continue the project begun so many decades earlier and to see the work to its completion. To this I readily agreed, though it was not until some years later, indeed until after the death of Professor Stephens himself, that I was able to begin concentrated work on the Nebuchadnezzar texts. The work has continued for the past seven years; summers, with the exception of 1971, were spent in Connecticut copying, and winters, with the exception of 1973/74, were spent in Cincinnati reading, studying the texts, and preparing the indices.

During these years, thanks to the encouragement of the Curator of the Yale Babylonian Collection, Professor William W. Hallo, I copied an additional 285 texts, which, together with the previously mentioned 84, form the corpus of 369 legal and administrative texts of this volume. The major part of two summers (1975 and 1976) was devoted to collating both the Dougherty material and the texts I had copied.

The arrangement on the plates is as follows: my copies, organized along lines evident from the Classified Catalogue, are given first; these are followed by the original plates of Professor Dougherty. The Dougherty copies have been untouched, except for the addition of plate, text, and line numbers, and the notations for "Obverse," "Lower Edge," etc. The results of my collations of the Dougherty texts are presented sepa-

*Parts of this Introduction were read at the meeting of the American Oriental Society on 26 April 1977, in Ithaca, New York, and at the Seventh World Congress of Jewish Studies on 10 August 1977, in Jerusalem.

1. His numbers actually ran to 88, but when errors due to misnumbering are removed, there remain 84.

rately in the section entitled Comments and Collations to Copies Autographed by Raymond Philip Dougherty. Some general comments to these texts are given below.

The craftsmanship and skill in the production of his cuneiform copies are evident on every line copied by Professor Dougherty. The signs are beautifully drawn, and many excellent readings were obtained by him from damaged surfaces or difficult-to-make-out lines.

There is some evidence that Professor Dougherty did not get a chance to review his own work before his death. At the top of what is now plate CLIV, the copyist scribbled the penciled notation, "rough draft." On one text, 289:6–10, where the text is broken, there is no shading at the conclusion of the four lines where the signs are missing. Another text, 307, is marked with two separate text numbers (in Dougherty's original numbers, 22 and 23), the former text, according to this numbering, containing only one line. In the same text, lines 9f. are omitted. All these errors would undoubtedly have been discovered had the copyist lived to collate his own work.

As for my own copies, the following should be mentioned: differences in style can be noted; these are due to the evolution of my technique during the years the texts were copied.[2] Most of the copies were drawn larger than life-size; however some are made on a 1:1 scale.[3]

The texts in the present volume are mostly from the Yale Babylonian Collection, though there is a group from the Nies Babylonian Collection. The latter group numbers 65 texts.

Regarding the dating: most of the texts copied were written from 605 to 581 B.C. This is equivalent to years 0 (Accession) to 24 of the reign of Nebuchadnezzar II. However, the texts in this volume do not exhaust the number of texts from these years in either the Yale or the Nies collections. Moreover, the range of dates in the present volume is wider than the above limits. Texts with broken dates are included because there was some prosopographic, stylistic, or other cogent reason to assume a connection with other included texts. Texts entirely without dates are included for the same reason. A text such as 9 in the present collection is included for historical reasons, and will be discussed below.[4] There are additional texts that deserve special mention here, namely, those dating to the Achaemenid rather than the Chaldean period. According to currently accepted reckoning, they date to either 522 or 521 B.C.[5] Professor Dougherty included a group of these in his early plates (those dating

2. A similar observation was made by the late Professor J. J. Finkelstein; see the Introduction to his volume, *YOS* 13.

3. The texts copied on a 1:1 ratio or very close thereto are: 16, 19, 27, 36, 38–41, 43, 45, 46, 51, 63–65, 70–75, 77, 80–82, 85, 87, 88, 90, 91, 93–96, 99, 104, 107, 111, 112, 116, 118–120, 124, 127, 130, 136, 141–147, 153, 155–157, 160, 167, 168, 171, 172, 177, 180, 183, 184, 186, 187, 189, 191, 193, 197, 198, 200, 205, 206, 208–211, 217, 218, 226, 230, 231, 233, 234, 236, 242–244, 247, 248, 257, 260, 265, 268, 270, 271, 282, and 285.

4. See p. xix, which mentions the novel date, "The Lady-of-Uruk, King of Babylon."

5. See pp. xix–xxvi for a brief review of the problem of the three Nebuchadnezzars of the seventh and sixth centuries B.C.

to Nebuchadnezzar years 0 and 1), and I also included a small number. The historical problem posed by these dates will be touched upon below. One text comes from Nabopolassar year 9 (92).

The majority of the texts in the present volume stems from Uruk.[6] In addition, either through explicit mention or through other means such as prosopography, texts can be assigned to Sippar, Opis, Babylon, Borsippa, Nippur,[7] and Larsa. Some can be assigned to a number of small villages, several of which are definitely suburbs of Uruk, and others of which are probably not;[8] closer identification of the latter at this time is not possible.

Besides the copies, the volume contains a Classified Catalogue organized along lines suggested by Koschaker,[9] Ungnad,[10] and Figulla,[11] and a Descriptive Catalogue on the model of that in *YOS* 13, by the late J. J. Finkelstein.

There are indices of personal and geographical names. The former contains approximately 2,500 separate names, many of them not previously known. The Personal Name Index is arranged in chronological order within each entry, rather than in alphabetical order. The date for each name is included with the entry, in the hope that scholars wishing to do prosopographic studies on the names of this period can easily use the material herein.[12] Some further remarks on prosopography will be made below.

Some new words in the present volume are pointed out in the transliterations in the Descriptive Catalogue. Several examples are: an object of bronze brought to the "work-house" (261:1 and 3); several objects together with X silver received and brought to GN (278:1–5); five objects of or from the *kabsarru*, received by a smith (in addition to a quantity of iron) (310:2–5); an object of iron brought to Babylon (344:1).

An unidentifiable object occurs as a *Verfallpfand*, to be forfeited in case of failure to pay;[13] it is once spelled *uḫ-ḫu-ul* (16:3) and once *uḫ-ḫu-lu-ul* (16:6). A similar term may occur listed with weapons in text 269:2: GIŠ.BAN *ul-ḫu-ul-lu* . . .

Text 246, dated to Nebuchadnezzar 8 (597 B.C.), is introduced by the words *šuqulti arīti ša* [d]*Nanā*, and lists fourteen different items, all of gold, many of them unknown to me. The word *šuqultu* itself denotes some object of bronze in Nbn. 1052 and may be connected with the verb *šaqālu*, "to weigh out," though that seems unlikely. The text is an important addition to our knowledge about the jewelry of the gods and should be treated with the subject, "The Golden Garments of the Gods."[14]

6. Geographical Names are given in the Descriptive Catalogue, and in a separate list on pp. 74–76.
7. The reading EN.LÍL.KI in 320:14 is unsure.
8. See Cocquerillat, *Palmeraies*, plates 3a and 3b.
9. See Koschaker, *HG* VI, pp. 155ff. and M. San Nicolò, "Beiträge zur Rechtsgeschichte im Bereiche der keilschriftlichen Rechtsquellen," (Oslo, 1931), p. 133.
10. With M. San Nicolò, in *Neubabylonische Rechts- und Verwaltungsurkunden* I (Leipzig, 1935), p. III.
11. H. H. Figulla, *UET* IV (The British Museum, 1949), pp. 9–15.
12. There are affinities with names from *GCCI* 1 and Strassmaier's *Nbk*, for example.
13. Petschow, *Pfandrecht*, pp. 119–124.
14. See A. L. Oppenheim, *JNES* 8 (1949), pp. 172–93.

A frequently attested figure among these tablets is a man named *Tukulti-*^{d}*Marduk,* descendant of *Kudurri,* a ^{h}*rē'i ginê* official. *Tukulti-*^{d}*Marduk* is attested in eleven different texts coming from Uruk and its environs from the years 592 to 581 B.C. Seven other attestations are available: four from *GCCI* 1 and three from the tablet collection of the Oriental Institute.[15] The dates range from 588 to 569 B.C. What emerges from a study of the texts in which *Tukulti-*^{d}*Marduk* occurs is an invaluable set of links with other personnel connected with Eanna at Uruk (such as *Kiribtu* son of ^{d}*Bēl-ibnî*) and a picture of the cattle industry there from the years 592-569, a twenty-three-year period. This is a welcome addition to the material amassed by San Nicolò in his series of articles "Materialien zur Viehwirtschaft in den neubabylonischen Tempeln."[16]

The famous *Ṣillā* son of ^{d}*Inninna-šum-uṣur,* descendant of *Kidin-*^{d}*Marduk,* a scribe well known from documents coming from the last quarter of the sixth century and important for dating texts at that period of time, is attested in our volume fifteen times.[17] In many cases it is possible because of prosopographic links to establish firm dating for figures mentioned in parallel documents otherwise without secure dates.

Numbers 35, 37, 286-300 form a welcome addition to the collection of documents relating to the work of the general leaser *Gimillu apilšu ša* ^{d}*Inninna-šum-ibnî* (see Cocquerillat, *Palmeraies,* pp. 43 and 58f.) as well as to the *ēmidu* ("tax-assessor") *Gimillu apilšu ša Aḫulap-*^{d}*Ištar apil Ḫunzû.* The latter is probably identical with the *ēmidu* of the same name in A. Pohl, *Analecta Orientalia* 8 (Rome, 1933), 30:2. See H. Petschow, "Imittu," in *Reallexikon der Assyriologie* (Berlin, 1976) 5/1, pp. 69b, 70a.

Here is a sampling of personal names belonging to slaves occurring in this collection: ^{d}*Bunene-kibsu-ab-uṣur, Linuḫ-libbi-*^{d}*Ištar, Manna-akī-Arbail,* ^{d}*Nabû-šuzibanni,* ^{d}*Nanā-kiširat, Rikis-kalama-*^{d}*Bēl, Ša-*^{d}*Nanā-ba-ni, Ša-*^{d}*Nanā-udu (-ú-du), Ša-Šapirti, Tukulti-*^{d}*Ištar, and* ^{f}*Tuqnā.*

Two brief orthographic notes: in 101:1 we have the following spelling: 3 LÚ.BAD ⌈UDU.X⌉ SÁ.DUG$_4$, which I translate as "3 cadavers of X *satukku*-sheep." The spelling LÚ.BAD for *pagru,* is, to my knowledge, previously unattested in Neo-Babylonian economic documents. (See *AHw.* 809a–b.)

In 45:11–16 there occurs a list of numbers followed by *ša* plus various other signs that do not seem to make sense, and seem to be unrelated to the balance of the text, which is a list of *imittu*-obligations dealing with barley. It is conjectured that these are doodles of a kind not unknown elsewhere in Neo-Babylonian and in cuneiform generally.

I should like to make some comments arising out of this work that bear upon chronological and larger historical perspectives from 605 to 521 B.C. One interesting

15. See Personal Name Index, p. 70n.
16. *Or.* NS. 17 (1948), 18 (1949), 20 (1951), 23 (1954), and 25 (1956).
17. Personal Name Index, pp. 65f.

sidelight is the appearance in one of the texts of a hitherto unknown son of Nebuchadnezzar II. Text 142 is a record of withdrawal of barley for sick people (*ana marṣūtu*). Line 19 of the text reads: 5 BÁN [1]É.AN.NA.LUGAL.URÙ A LUGAL. There is no way of determining for the present whether or not this text is from Uruk, yet it is interesting to see that the prince's name is *Eanna-šar-uṣur*, so it may presumably come from that city. The text dates to 587 B.C.

Text 9 is dated to a place called ÍD *ḫar-ri šá* [1]MU-*a* and deals with the hire of a woman *šerku*. It has the fascinating date: [d]GAŠAN *ša* UNUG.KI LUGAL TIN.TIR.KI. The precise date is *Abu* 15 year 43, in Julian terms, perhaps 29 August, 562 B.C. Now at this particular time, Nebuchadnezzar II was officially still alive and ruling, the latest date so far known being 8 October, 562 (*TCL* XII, 58, Parker and Dubberstein, p. 12). Yet it is conceivable that he died earlier. Cautious scribes continued to date to him even after his death, waiting prudently to see who his successor would be. One, however, may have tipped his hand and opted for a dating to The Lady-of-Uruk, "King" of Babylon.

In an article written one hundred years ago, W. St. Chad Boscawen seems to have been the first to make a clear distinction among contract tablets mentioning a king named Nebuchadnezzar. Boscawen distinguished between those texts to be assigned unquestionably to Nebuchadnezzar II [ruled 605–562] and those assigned either to Nebuchadnezzar III [*Nidinti-*[d]*Bēl* son of *Kin-zēr*, who ruled, according to present theories, for two months and ten days in the autumn of 522] or Nebuchadnezzar IV [*Araḫu* son of [d]*Ḫaldita*, who ruled, according to present theories, for three months and two days in the autumn of the following year, 521 B.C.].[18] Boscawen referred to the Behistun Inscription where Darius mentions two usurper kings each of whom took the name of "Nebuchadnezzar son of Nabonidus" and ruled briefly during his (Darius's) first year. Boscawen identified the figures mentioned in the contract tablets under consideration in his article with those who lived during Achaemenid rule in Babylonia.

During the first few decades of the twentieth century, the problem received the attention of scholars in this country and abroad,[19] and a consensus developed about

18. "Babylonian Dated Tablets and the Canon of Ptolemy," *Transactions of the Society of Biblical Archaeology* 6 (1878), p. 31. See improved readings offered by von Voigtlander, *The Bisitun Inscription of Darius the Great: Babylonian Version* (below, n. 25), pp. 19f. and 55, and pp. 37 and 60.

19. Note the following: F. H. Weissbach, *ZDMG* 61 (1907), p. 730; Weissbach, "Zur neubabylonischen und achämenidischen Chronologie," *ZDMG* 62 (1908), esp. pp. 635–39; A. Poebel, "The Names and the Order of the Old Persian . . . Months . . . " *AJSL* 54–55 (1937–38), pp. 130–41; Poebel, "The Chronology of Darius' First Year" *AJSL* 54–55, pp. 142–65; pp. 285–314; A. T. Olmstead, *AJSL* 54–55, pp. 392–416; Waldo H. Dubberstein, *AJSL* 54–55, pp. 417–19; Walther Hinz, "Das erste Jahr des Grosskönigs Dareios," *ZDMG* 92 (1938), pp. 136–73; Poebel, "The Duration of the Reign of Smerdis . . . " *AJSL* 56 (1939), pp. 121–45; Richard A. Parker, "Persian and Egyptian Chronology," *AJSL* 58 (1941), pp. 285–301; George G. Cameron, "Darius and Xerxes in Babylonia," *AJSL* 58, pp. 314–25; 96 (1942), pp. 326–31; Richard T. Hallock, "The 'One Year' of Darius I," *JNES* 19 (1960), pp. 36–39; F. M. Th. De Liagre Böhl, "Die babylonischen Prätendenten zur Anfangszeit des Darius (Dareios) I," *Bibliotheca Orientalis* 25 (1968), pp. 150–53. A. Shahpur Shahbazi, "The 'One Year' of Darius Re-examined," *BSOAS* 35 (1972), pp. 609–14;

how best to place these kings. The consensus has been ably summarized in Parker and Dubberstein's indispensable "Babylonian Chronology 626 B.C.–A.D. 75."[20]

Among the texts prepared for the present study there are 38 that directly bear upon the problem of the three Nebuchadnezzars. These include all that are dated to the accession year or to year one of Nebuchadnezzar (putting aside for a moment *which* Nebuchadnezzar). (There is general agreement that all texts dated after Arahsamnu 22, year 1 of Nebuchadnezzar must be dated to Nebuchadnezzar II on the basis of the traditional criteria.[21]) The 38 texts have been sorted out and arranged according to regnal years of

1. Nebuchadnezzar II (accession year and year one);

2. Nebuchadnezzar III (there seems to be one text dating to this reign according to the prevailing criteria) and

3. Nebuchadnezzar IV (year one).

The dates, geographical names, and titles are given in the list below.

Now the following criteria must be taken into account in discussing the problem:

1. The date formulae of the contract tablets, including day-month-year and geographical name;[22]

2. The titulary of the kings as found in the documents;[23]

3. The prosopography of the figures mentioned in the contracts;[24] and

4. The material of the Behistun Inscription, especially in Sections 16, 18, 19, 20, 49, 50, 51, and 52.[25]

As I worked through the relevant scholarship, however,[26] several problems continued to trouble me about the methods used to distinguish between the three Nebuchadnezzars.

---

and Jack Martin Balcer, "The Date of Herodotus IV. 1 Darius' Scythian Expedition," *Harvard Studies in Classical Philology* 76 (1972), pp. 99–132, esp. n. 41 [2nd part]. Prof. J. D. Bing of the University of Tennessee discussed this article with me. I am grateful for his help.

20. *Brown University Studies* 19 (Providence: Brown University Press, 1956), pp. 14–17.

21. See below, notes 22–25.

22. *TCL* 12, 22, and 23 (with Moore, *Neo-Babylonian Documents* [Ann Arbor: University of Michigan Press, 1935], p. 284 at note to text 22;); *Nbk.* 1–18; Dhorme, *RA* 25 (1928), Nos. 1 and 2; *TuM* 2–3: 6 and 150.

23. F. X. Kugler, *Sternkunde und Sterndienst* (Münster: Aschendorff, 1909–10), pp. 403–05.

24. Weissbach, *ZDMG* 62 (1908), p. 636; Ungnad, *ZA* 19 (1905–6), p. 416 n. 1.; and *OLZ* 10 (1907), pp. 464f.; Cameron, *AJSL* 58 (1941), p. 318, n. 23. Also, San Nicolò, *Prosopographie* (Munich, 1941), p. 26, n 38. There are, unfortunately, no personal names in common with our list.

25. In L. W. King and R. C. Thompson, *The Sculptures and Inscriptions of Darius the Great on the Rock of Behistun in Persia,* (1907); Weissbach, "Die Keilinschriften der Achämeniden," *VAB* 3 (Leipzig: Hinrichs, 1911); Roland G. Kent, "Old Persian," *American Oriental Series* vol. 33 (New Haven, 1953); M. A. Dandamayev, "Persien unter den ersten Achämeniden (6. Jahrhundert v. Chr.)," *Beiträge Zur Iranistik* 8, translated by Heinz-Dieter Pohl (Wiesbaden, 1976); Warren C. Benedict and Elizabeth von Voigtlander, "Darius' Bisitun Inscription, Babylonian Version, lines 1–29," *JCS* 10 (1956), pp. 1ff.; Elizabeth von Voigtlander, *The Bisitun Inscription of Darius the Great: Babylonian Version,* "Corpus Inscriptionum Iranicarum," part I, vol. II, texts I (1978), a study of DB Babylonian version, based upon Professor George Cameron's 1957 squeezes.

26. In general for the classical and Persian sources, see Edouard Will, *Le Monde Grec et l'Orient* (Paris, 1972), pp. 13f., nn. 1–2. This and other references are due to the kind help of Professor Getzel Cohen of the University of Cincinnati.

I am accepting as a working hypothesis the position that there *were* two historic figures, Nebuchadnezzar III and Nebuchadnezzar IV, who ruled around 522–520 B.C., though I have doubts about the criteria that have been used to support this position, and even about the tenability of the position itself. Further research may disprove the prevailing theories, and perhaps other writers may find additional indicators.[27]

Though this is not the place to enter into a full-scale review of the problem,[28] some elements of my reservations can be set forth:

1. The Date Formulae

An accepted observation concerning the date formulae is that "it is now quite clear that all tablets assignable to this [Achaemenid] period which belong to Nebuchadnezzar III are dated to the 'accession year of Nebuchadnezzar.' "[29] The balance of the tablets assignable to this period dated to "Nebuchadnezzar, year 1"[30] are assignable to Nebuchadnezzar IV.

The reconstruction by Professor Poebel that seeks to summarize in tabular form the dates of Darius's accession and first years and mesh these with the known dates of Nebuchadnezzar (III) and Nebuchadnezzar (IV) is presented by him in his epoch-making study, "The Duration of the Reign of Smerdis, the Magian, and the Reigns of Nebuchadnezzar III and Nebuchadnezzar IV," in *AJSL* 56 (1939).[31] Poebel concludes: "A glance at this chronologically arranged table shows that the two groups of Nebuchadnezzar tablets in the left column fit like the cogs of a cogwheel into two corresponding gaps of the Darius dates in the right column. . . ."[32]

Note, however, that there are four dates in the present collection which according to Poebel's criteria would be assigned to Nebuchadnezzar IV that conflict with his dates of Darius I:

286	V	16	1	Nebuchadnezzar
35	V	18	1	Nebuchadnezzar
287	V	24	1	Nebuchadnezzar
288	V	26	1	Nebuchadnezzar

These texts all stem from Uruk and its environs and seem to destroy at least a part of the symmetry that is evident in Poebel's chart on p. 135.

27. I am indebted to Professor J. A. Brinkman, who graciously discussed the problem with me and suggested this formulation. Naturally, the opinions expressed herein are my own.

28. So many new texts aside from those in this volume have come to light that a truly definitive study must await their full elucidation.

29. Cameron, "Darius and Xerxes in Babylonia," *AJSL* 58 (1941), pp. 316f.

30. *AJSL* 58, p. 318.

31. Pp. 134–36.

32. *AJSL* 58, p. 136.

2. The Titulary

In his section "Königstitel," F. X. Kugler remarks, "Der Titel 'König von Babel' . . . ist der einzige, . . . welchen die Herrscher von Nabonassar bis Nabonid inkl. führen. Mit Cyrus beginnt die Reihe der Herrscher, die sich *šar mātāti* 'König der Länder' nennen."[33] The problem of these two titles as used by Cyrus and Cambyses cannot concern us here,[34] though this is of great interest and importance.

Most interesting is a new date, 162 (YBC 3437). The text, dealing with the disbursement of dates to two groups of men, is dated to I/30/18 Nebuchadnezzar, LUGAL KUR.KUR. A text dated to May 587 B.C. with the title *šar mātāti* would seem to show that Kugler's criterion that this title was used only *after* Cyrus II should now be modified.

3. Prosopography

Aside from the observations made by Boscawen noted above,[35] arguments cited by Weissbach, Ungnad, and Cameron[36] seem to me to be cogent, and in fact form the main reason for my hesitancy to tamper as of yet with the accepted theory on Nebuchadnezzar IV.

However, there are arguments that might be cited in criticism of this position. But these should be presented in fuller form elsewhere.

An intriguing and crucial point by way of the prosopography centers about the name of a man mentioned in text 8 dated to Borsippa, VIII/24/0 Nebuchadnezzar. The name of the man in question is *Mušēzib-^{d}Bēl*, son of *Zēr-Babili*, descendant of ^{1}*At-ta-ba-ni*. In 1944, Professor Goetze made reference to our text (YBC 9163) in a footnote. He considered it to be from the time of Nebuchadnezzar III; indeed it was the only one from the reign of that monarch in the Yale Collection cited by him. In his words, "this tablet is assigned here because of its shape and script."[37]

If Professor Goetze is right, then the date for this text, a lease of land (ŠE. NUMUN *ana errešūtu . . . iddin*), would be 522.

I communicated some doubts concerning this dating to Professor M. Dandamayev, who graciously responded with a very appealing insight. He compared our figure with a certain *Mušēzib-^{d}Bēl*, son of *Zēr-Babili*, descendant of ^{1}DINGIR-*ta*-DÛ, who appears with some frequency in texts "that cover the period between 545–510 B.C., all from Borsippa or its suburbs. So it is likely that Goetze was right to consider YBC 9163 as a text belonging to the time of Nebuchadnezzar III."[38] Professor Dandamayev

33. *Sternkunde und Sterndienst*, II (Münster, 1909–10), p. 203.

34. See William H. Shea, "An Unrecognized Vassal King of Babylon in the Early Achaemenid Period," *Andrews University Seminary Studies* 9 (1971), pp. 51–67; 99–128; 10 (1972), pp. 88–117 and 147–78.

35. See n. 18, above.

36. See n. 24, above.

37. *JNES* 3 (1944), p. 45, n. 20.

38. Correspondence dated 23 August, 1976.

read the name of the ancestor *Ilūta-bani* and suggested that the reading in our case (text 8) might perhaps also be ¹DINGIR-*ta-ba-ni* instead of ¹*At-ta-ba-ni*. Collation by Dr. Elizabeth Jewell, Assistant Curator of the Babylonian Collection, revealed that in both places in the text in which the name occurs, it is definitely not DINGIR, but *at-ta-ba-ni*. If Professor Dandamayev's insight is correct, then we would have to assume an error of the scribe in lines 3 and 11 of text 8.

A further suggestion regarding this figure comes from Professor Abraham Sachs. Professor Sachs offers the opinion that the name ¹DINGIR-*ta*-DÙ/*ba-ni* may be nothing more than a variant, due to dissimilation, of ¹*at-ta-ba-ni* (perhaps *Atta-bāni* > *Anta-bāni* [under the influence of Aramaic *'ant?*—DBW]). Names with *atta* as a component are known.[39] On the assumption that the name is Semitic (it does not seem to be Persian), it may mean "You (m. sg.) are the Creator/Beautiful." If the two names are in fact variants of each other, then Professor Goetze's original identification of the king with the Achaemenid rather than the Chaldean ruler seems supported.

4. The Material in the Behistun Inscription

Professor Goetze used to say that it takes big guns to shoot down a tradition, and we must apply that cautious criterion here. In his inscription Darius actually mentions the two "pretenders," yet some doubts about the material presented in the Behistun Inscription might be raised.

Basically, I think these doubts have been alluded to best by R. T. Hallock. They revolve about the notion of the use of propaganda: "Let it be said that Poebel's attention to detail is awe-inspiring. But his basic assumption is naive. He believes that the purpose of the narrative is simply to communicate facts, and he has a compulsion to defend the literal veracity of Darius."[40] Hallock's objections to Poebel's reconstruction of the events of "The 'one year' of Darius I" concern the possibility of fitting all the events recorded in the Behistun Inscription for that year into the logical framework.

My own doubts stem from a different perspective. It is my suspicion that the gap in the attested Nebuchadnezzar documents from *Kislimu* in an accession year (presumably 522 B.C.) until *Ululu* in a first year (incidentally, there was an intercalary *Addaru* in 521 B.C.) will be narrowed by the discovery of new documents. This fact will render it unlikely that there were actually two kings with the name Nebuchadnezzar in the Achaemenid period.[41] Then, however, we would be forced to the conclusion that Darius is lying in his Behistun Inscription. For it is only there that we read of the existence of two kings named Nebuchadnezzar in 522/1.

The implications of this fact, and details as to the outlines of this reconstruction must await a future study. An Introduction such as this is not the proper place for such

39. See Stamm, *Namengebung* sub *atta*.
40. *JNES* 19 (1960), p. 39.
41. See above, p. xxi, for the beginning of this process.

an elaborate set of data; and the reconstruction itself will depend partially upon texts from outside the present volume only now coming to light.[42]

New evidence from titles, prosopography, and hopefully, new dates to fill in the gap during Darius's first year will surely enable us to draw the picture more clearly when all this evidence can be evaluated.

TABLE 1

Texts from year 0 *and year* 1 *arranged according to kings*

		Text	*Locale**	*Date*		*Royal title*
		I.	Nebuchadnezzar II accession year (605–604)			
	1.	153	?	12 *Ulu*	0	LUGAL E.KI [Goetze, *JNES* 3 (1944), p. 44] Canal names: *Nār* ^{d}*Amurri*, ^{d}*Banitu*
	2.	113	———	[*ultu Taš*	0]	LUGAL TIN.TIR.KI [*Ibid.*]
	3.	56	———	1 *Araḫ*	0	LUGAL TIN.TIR.KI
	4.	29	(Uruk)	2 *Araḫ*	0	LUGAL TIN.TIR.KI
605	5.	126	(Uruk)	27 *Kis*	0	LUGAL TIN.TIR.KI [IX 29 Dar. defeats Nbk III Parker-Dubberstein, *Chronology*, p. 15] l. 11: IGI ^{d}GAŠAN *ša* UNUG.KI
604	6.	11	(Uruk)	22 *Add*	0	LUGAL TIN.TIR.KI [Note spring month] witnesses + l. 4
	7.	54	URU KAL-*gu-gu*	4 *Šab.*	0	LUGAL TIN.TIR.KI

42. Since the completion of this Introduction, several groups of relevant texts have come to my attention.

Professor Erle V. Leichty, of the University Museum of the University of Pennsylvania, is currently preparing a catalogue of the texts from Sippar (Abu Habbah) in the British Museum, a collection that numbers more than 35,000 Neo-Babylonian texts. A minimum of 90 percent of these come from the É.BABBARA archive; others are from Babylon, Dilbat, and Uruk. So far, he has listed 20,000. Of this latter number, Professor Leichty has noted close to 100 that are dated to either Nebuchadnezzar year 0 or year 1 or Darius year 0 or year 1. Their museum numbers range from BM 49209 to 92735. Professor Leichty has kindly brought these to my attention.

A second additional source of texts is the other collections housed at the Yale Babylonian Collection. I have recently discovered approximately ten additional unpublished texts dating to Nbk. 0 or Nbk. 1 (but none as yet of Darius). One of these, NCBT (Newell Collection of Babylonian Tablets) 364, available in photograph, is one of the earliest "Nbk. IV" dates listed so far by Parker and Dubberstein in their "Babylonian Chronology" (p. 16). It is dated to V/26/1 (4 September 521) at Uruk. There are nine more texts, four of which are available in preliminary copy, and five of which must await further study. All of the texts that have some geographical name are clearly from Uruk and vicinity, an unfortunate occurrence, since aside from the Sippar texts mentioned above, we still fail to have a clear-cut cross-section of texts on which we might make some sounder historical judgment.

These texts and others, yet unstudied, undoubtedly will influence the outcome of the discussion on the Nebuchadnezzars.

*All texts except for 8, which comes from Borsippa, seem to come from Uruk and its environs. See Poebel, *AJSL* 56 (1939), p. 138.

II. Nebuchadnezzar II year 1 (604–603)

		Text	*Locale*	*Date*		*Royal title*
	1.	50	————	18 *Nis*	1	LUGAL TIN.TIR.KI [Note spring month, after Nebuchadnezzar IV.]
	1a.	199	————	24 *Duz*	1	LUGAL E.KI
	2.	301	————	15 *Ulu*	1	LUGAL TIN.TIR.KI
	3.	302	Uruk	16 *Taš*	1	LUGAL TIN.TIR.KI
	4.	245	(Uruk)	24? *Taš*	1	LUGAL E.KI [Deals with *daššu* of ^{d}*Innin* UNUG.KI]
	5.	160	————	5 *Araḫ*	1	LUGAL E.KI
	6.	247	————	10 *Araḫ*	1	LUGAL E.KI
	7.	52	————	25 *Araḫ*	1	LUGAL TIN.TIR.KI
	8.	62	————	16 *Kis*	1	LUGAL E.KI [Note spring month]
603	9.	102	————	4 *Add*	1	LUGAL E.KI [Note spring month]
	10.	198	(Uruk)	18 *Add*	1	LUGAL TIN.TIR.KI [^{d}*Nabû-nadin-šumi* was *šatammu* in 604.]
	11.	28	————	22 *Add*	1	LUGAL TIN.TIR.KI [Note spring month]
	12.	47	————	5 [X]	1	LUGAL TIN.TIR.KI [Trace of month: ]

III. Nebuchadnezzar III accession year (fall, 522 B.C.)

1.	8	Borsippa	There is only one text from the 2 months and 10 days in *Taš* - *Araḫ* - *Kis* Yr. 0 with the title that includes the phrase LUGAL KUR.KUR. 24 *Araḫ*	0

IV. Nebuchadnezzar IV year 1 (fall, 521 B.C.)

1.	286	*Gadēti*	16 *Abu*	1	LUGAL E.KI *u* KUR.KUR
2.	35	^{al}KUR.BAD	18 *Abu*	1	LUGAL E.KI *u* KUR.KUR
3.	287	*Uruk*	24 *Abu*	1	LUGAL E.KI *u* KUR.KUR
4.	288	^{al}*Nāru eššu*	26 *Abu*	1	LUGAL E.KI *u* KUR.KUR
5.	289	GARIN *naḫallum*	2 *Ulu*	1	LUGAL E.KI *u* KUR.KUR
6.	290	^{al}KÁ *asurritu*	3 *Ulu*	1	LUGAL E.KI *u* KUR.KUR
7.	291	*al šakillatu*	8 *Ulu*(?)	1	LUGAL E.KI *u* KUR.KUR
8.	292	^{al}*naḫallum*	13 *Ulu*(!)	1	LUGAL E.[KI] *u* KUR.KUR
9.	293	*Bitqa ša* ^{d}*Bēl-ēṭir šiḫi ša* ^{d}*Bēlit ša Uruk*	3 *Taš*	1	LUGAL E.KI *u* KUR.KUR

	Text	*Locale*	*Date*		*Royal title*
10.	294	*Bitqa ša* ^{d}*Bēl-ētir šiḫi ša* ^{d}*Bēlit ša Uruk*	3 *Taš*	1	LUGAL E.KI *u* KUR.KUR [Same day as above.]
11.	295	*Bitqa ša* ^{d}*Bēl-ēṭir šiḫi ša* ^{d}*Bēlit ša Uruk*	3 *Taš*	1	LUGAL E.KI *u* KUR.KUR [Same day as above.]
12.	296	*Bitqa ša* ^{d}*Bēl-ēṭir šiḫi ša* ^{d}*Bēlit ša Uruk*	5 *Taš*	1	LUGAL E.KI *u* KUR.KUR
13.	297	*Bitqa ša* ^{d}*Bēl-ēṭir eqlu ša* ^{d}*Nanā šiḫi ša* ^{d}*Bēlit ša Uruk*	5 *Taš*	1	LUGAL E.KI [Note absence of KUR.KUR] [Same day as above.]
14.	298	*Bitqa ša* ^{d}*Bēl-ēṭir šiḫi ša* ^{d}*Bēlit ša Uruk*	6 *Taš*	1	LUGAL KUR.KUR [Note absence of E.KI] [Day later]
15.	299	*Kār Eanna ālu ša* ^{d}*Anu-aḫ-ēreš*	24 ⌈X⌉	1	LUGAL E.KI *u* KUR.KUR [Trace: ]
16.	300	*eqlāti ša Kišād nār Bitqa*		1	LUGAL E.KI *u* KUR.KUR [Note *Gimillu* A *Inninna-šum-ibnî.*]
17.	37	*ālu* [X.X . . .] *ša Nad-na*-A KUR-*šu* ^{d}*Bēlit ša Uruk*	[X X]	1	[LUGAL E.KI *u*] ⌈KUR.KUR⌉

CLASSIFIED CATALOGUE

A. Family rights	
I. Adoption of children	1
B. Sales	
I. of houses	2, 3, 322
II. of land	303
III. of office (*isqu*) [contained in document recording loan]	4
C. Lease, rent, and hire	
I. Lease of property	
(a) of a house	5
(b) of land	6, 7, 8
(c) of boat	302
II. Hire of labor	9
D. Inheritance	348
E. Partnership in business	10
F. Documents concerning debts	
I. Loans of money	
(a) to be repaid in silver	
1. free of interest for a short time, afterwards interest	11, 13, 14
2. interest specified, payable immediately	327, 337, 361
3. payable on demand or specified interest	315
4. interest unspecified, with pledge	
a. of real estate	12, 15, 336, 338, 340
b. of slave	357
c. *uḫḫulu* (*Verfallpfand*)	16
5. interest specified, with pledge	17
(b) to be repaid in kind (*Lieferungskauf*)	
1. interest unspecified	18, 19

2. according to prevailing rate when loan falls due	20, 21, 22, 23
II. Loans of barley or produce	24, 25, 26, 27, 28
III. Guarantee for appearance of PN	29, 319, 359
IV. Order to settle an account	30
V. Record of repayment (*Datio in solutum*)	31
G. Court documents	
I. Relinquishment of a claim	358
II. Penalty for withholding property	32
III. Lawsuit concerning slave	320
IV. Farmer's oath	33
V. Damaged; penalty, witnesses and date preserved	34
H. Documents dealing with estimated yield of date groves (*Imittu*)	35–38, 286–99
I. Lists of various kinds	
I. Names only	39
II. Names with assorted items listed together	363
III. Names of men, "responsibility" of other men	40
IV. *Imittu* lists noting obligations of several parties	
(a) dealing with dates	41, 42, 300, 364
(b) dealing with barley and emmer	43–45
J. Imposts	
I. *ešru* and *šibšu*	46
II. *telītu*	47, 360
K. Administrative transactions	
I. Livestock and by-products	
(a) the cattle industry	
1. receipts (IGI-*ir*) and lists of cattle	48–54, 313, 345, 346
2. cattle at the disposal of (*ina* IGI)	55
3. receipts and withdrawal of cattle carcasses (*pagri*)	56–61, 328
4. cattle hides for various purposes	62–65
(b) the sheep industry	
1. receipts of sheep	66–77
2. sheep *ina paqdu ša* PN	78
3. sheep at the disposal of	79–84
4. sheep "set aside" (*parsu*),	

"inspected" (*amru*),	
"disbursed" (GURU$_9$),	
"sent" (*šubul*) and other	85–92, 321
5. receipts of sheep carcasses	93–102, 342
6. wool[43]	
a. receipt	103
b. at disposal of	104
c. weighed out	105–07, 339, 352
d. withdrawals	108–12, 332, 356
e. assorted	113–18
(c) ass, *irbu*	119
(d) doves, receipt	120
II. Agricultural produce	
(a) barley	
1. receipts	121–24, 306, 318, 343
2. at the disposal of	125–27, 330
3. withdrawals	128–47, 362, 365, 367
4. for various other and assorted purposes	148–57, 325, 353
(b) dates	
1. receipts	158–60, 309
2. withdrawals	161–68
3. other and assorted purposes	169–73, 317
(c) sesame	
1. receipts	314, 326
2. withdrawals	174–77
3. other and assorted purposes	178–80, 366
(d) emmer wheat	
1. withdrawals	181, 182
2. for other purposes	183, 184
(e) oil	
1. receipts	185, 308
2. withdrawal	186
(f) flour	
1. withdrawals	187, 188
(g) unspecified "measures" or "rations"	
1. receipt	189
2. at the disposal of	190, 191
3. withdrawals	192, 193, 355
4. other	334
III. Salt	
(a) receipt	312

43. In all but explicitly cultic context; for other documents see sub V: "Sacred garments and paraphernalia."

(b) withdrawals	194, 350
IV. Silver	
(a) receipts	195–200
(b) at the disposal of (*ina pani*); given (SUM-*in*, and other complements); combined (also with *maṭû* and *našû*)	201–22, 311, 323, 333, 349
(c) withdrawals (*našû*)	223–30[44], 331, 341, 369
(d) brought to (*šubul*) various parties	231–33
(e) other (no verb or verb broken away)	234–44, 324
V. Sacred garments and paraphernalia	
(a) golden garments and paraphernalia	245–48, 347
(b) wool and linen items	
1. receipts	249, 250, 301, 307
2. at the disposal of	251–54, 305
3. withdrawals	255, 329
4. other	256
VI. Bronze	
(a) receipts	257, 258
(b) at the disposal of smith and others	259–61, 351
VII. Iron and products of iron	
(a) receipts by smith	262–65, 310
(b) at the disposal of smith	266, 304, 368
(c) withdrawal	344
VIII. Weapons	
(a) at the disposal of	267–69, 316, 335
(b) withdrawal	270
(c) brought (*šubul*)	271
IX. Bricks	
(a) "given"	272, 273
(b) inventory and verb unspecified	274–76
X. Miscellaneous and assorted	277–83
L. Destroyed	284, 285

44. 230: gold.

DESCRIPTIVE CATALOGUE

Text	*Museum Number*	*Month*	*Day*	*Year*	*Year B.C.*	*Description*
1	NBC 4813	*Add*	20	22	582	Uruk, adoption of children; IM. DUB DUMU-*ú-tu* . . . *ik-nu-ku-'*.
2	YBC 6936	*Araḫ*	24	17	588	Uruk, sale of house; *ṭup-pi* É *ki-šub-ba-'* . . . ŠÁM É-[*šú*] . . . *ma-ḫir*.
3	YBC 7424	*Add*	9	3	601	Uruk, sale of house; *ṭup-pi* É *ep-šú* ⌈*sip-pu*⌉ [*rak-su* . . .] É *rug-gu-bi* G[IŠ.IG *u* GIŠ *sik-kur*]; cf. 2.
4	YBC 3733	*Nis*	25	16	589	Babylon, loan containing sale of office; IM.DUB *is-qu ina* IGI ᵈU.GUR *u* ᵈEREŠ.KI. GAL . . . *im-ḫur-ru*.
5	YBC 9139	*Abu*	17	13	592	Babylon, lease of house for a year; *i-di* É *a-na* PN *i-nam-din*.
6	NBC 4853	*Sim*	23	21	584	Kar Eanna, lease of land from Eanna for planting date palms; *qaq-qar a-na za-qí-pu-tu* [*i*]*d-da-áš-ši*; dialogue document.
7	YBC 9205	*Šab*	10	3	601	Uruk, lease of land from Eanna for date cultivation; A.ŠÀ *šá* GN *i-din-nu-u-šú*; dialogue document.
8	YBC 9163	*Araḫ*	24	0	522	Borsippa, lease of land; ŠE. NUMUN . . . *a-na er-re-šu-ú-tu* . . . *id-din* (Nbk. III).
9	YBC 4071	*Abu*	15	43	562	*Nār Ḫarri šá* ¹MU-*a*, hire of woman *šerku*; ᶠPN . . . *ina pa-ni* PN . . . *ú-šá-az-za-at* . . . KÙ.BABBAR . . . *i-nam-din*; dated to: ᵈGAŠAN

Text	Museum Number	Month	Day	Year	Year B.C.	Description
						šá UNUG.KI LUGAL TIN.TIR.KI.
10	YBC 9283	[X]	23	11	594	Uruk, record concerning capital venture—mostly damaged.
11	YBC 9182	*Add*	22	0	604	Loan of money to be repaid in silver; interest-free for a short time; afterwards interest; KÙ.BABBAR *šá* PN *ina* UGU PN_2 UD.1.KÁM [*šá* M]N *i-nam-din.*
12	YBC 9183	*Kis*	9	5	600	Uruk, loan of money to be repaid in silver (interest destroyed); [*mim-mu-šú š*]*á* URU *u* EDIN *ma-la ba-šu-*[*ú maš-ka-*]*nu šá* PN.
13	YBC 3714	*Abu*	4	17	588	Babylon, loan of money to be repaid in silver; interest-free for a short time, afterwards interest of $23\frac{1}{3}$ percent.
14	YBC 7053	*Nis*	15	[X]	[X]	⸢Uruk,⸣ loan of money to be repaid in silver; interest-free for a short-time, afterwards interest; UD-*mu* 4 SÌLA ŠE.BAR *man-da-at-ta i-nam-din.*
15	YBC 9562	*Abu*	25	17	588	Uruk, loan of money to be repaid in silver; *Nutzpfand*: É *šá* PN *ina lìb-bi áš-bi maš-ka-nu. šá* É *i-*⸢*di* É *ya-a-nu* ḪAR.RA⸣ [KÙ.BABBAR *ya-a-nu?*].
16	YBC 9312	*Nis*	10	21	584	Loan of money to be repaid in silver; interest unspecified, with pledge of *uḫ-ḫu-ul* (*uḫ-ḫu-lu-ul*). Scribe is debtor.
17	YBC 9404	*Add*	23	2	602	Uruk, loan of money to be repaid in silver; interest specified (20 percent), with pledge.
18	YBC 7362	*Teb*	17	13	591	Loan of money to be repaid in barley; interest unspecified.
19	YBC 7365	*Šab*	12	21	583	Larsa, loan of money (NÌ.GA ^{d}UTU *u* ^{d}*a-a*) to be repaid in barley; interest unspecified.

Text	Museum Number	Month	Day	Year	Year B.C.	Description
20	YBC 9572	*Ulu*	15	14	591	Borsippa, loan of money to be repaid in dates according to prevailing rate when loan falls due; . . . *ki-i la it-tan-nu a-ki-i* KI.LAM *šá* MN *ina qaq-qar in-nam-din-nu* ZÚ.LUM.MA *i-nam-din.*
21	YBC 9597	*Šab*	11	13	591	Uruk, loan of money to be repaid in barley according to prevailing rate when loan falls due.
22	YBC 9123	*Sim*	20	4	601	Uruk, loan of money to be repaid in kind according to prevailing rate when loan falls due plus 9 *qa* per shekel of silver.
23	YBC 8816	*Add* II	9	17	587	Babylon, loan of money to be repaid in barley according to prevailing rate (*ina* 1 GÍN 2 BÁN ŠE.BAR) when loan falls due.
24	YBC 9198	*Add*	29	19	585	Uruk, loan of barley, interest unspecified. Scribe is surety for part of loan.
25	NBC 6176	*Šab*	15	18	586	Uruk, loan of barley, interest unspecified.
26	YBC 3701	*Šab*	2	9	595	Uruk, loan of cress seed (ŠE.NUMUN *saḫ-lu-ú*) interest unspecified.
27	YBC 9241	*Šab*	24	15	589	Loan of barley; *pu-ut na-š*[*u-ú?*] *šá* GUD *a-na* UGU-*ḫi* 1 GUR 1 PI *i-nam-din.*
28	YBC 7398	*Add*	22	1	603	*Ḫuṣṣēti ša* ᵈ*Bēl*, loan of barley (interest possibly broken away).
29	YBC 9131	*Araḫ*	2	0	605	Uruk, guarantee for appearance of PN with penalty for nonfulfillment; PN *pu-ut* PN_2 . . . *na-áš-ši.*
30	YBC 3422	*Duz*	26	2	603	Opis, order to settle an account concerning goats; *ina* MN PN . . . NÍG.ŠID *šá* ÙZ.ME . . . *ip-pu-uš.*

Text	Museum Number	Month	Day	Year	Year B.C.	Description
31	YBC 3820	*Šab*	22	16	588	*Ḫuṣṣētu ša Baba*, record of repayment, É *šá* PN . . . *pa-ni* PN$_2$ *ku-um* (X silver) . . . *pa-ni-šú id-dag-gal*; datio in solutum.
32	YBC 4103	*Aya*	15	19	586	Babylon, court document—penalty for withholding sheep to be paid to Lady-of-Uruk when witnesses have confirmed this; 1-*en* 30 PN . . . *i-nam-din*.
33	YBC 9177	*Kis*	20	19	586	Kar Eanna, court document, farmer's oath that no one will act secretly; *man-m*[*a*] *a-na pa-ši-ru il-ta-k*[*a-an*] 1-*en* 30 *i-nam-di-in*.
34	YBC 3442	*Ulu*	7	10	595	Uruk, court document—mostly destroyed.
35	YBC 4066	*Abu*	18	1	521	URU KUR.BAD, document dealing with estimated yield (*imittu*) of date grove; 14 GUR ZÚ.LUM.MA ZAG.LU A.ŠÀ . . . ina UGU-*ḫi* PN . . . *ina* ITI.DU$_6$ ZÚ.LUM.MA . . . *i-nam-din*.
36	YBC 4110	*Ulu*	[X+]8	21	584	URU KUT-*ta-a-in*, *imittu* document; cf. 35.
37	YBC 7400	[X]	[X]	1	521	Uruk, *imittu* document; cf. 35.
38	YBC 8860	*Ulu* II	16	21	584	Uruk, *imittu* document; cf. 35.
39	NBC 4785	*Duz*	17	19	586	List of men.
40	YBC 4010	*Taš*	9	21	584	Names of men "responsibility" of other men; *pu-ut* EN.NUN-*ti šá gab-bi-šú-nu na-šú-ú*.
41	NBC 4924	*Ulu*	12	12	593	*Imittu* list dealing with dates noting obligations of several parties; ⌈ZÚ.LUM.MA⌉ *i-mit-ti* . . .
42	YBC 9643	*Nis?*	8	19	586	Two-dimensional *imittu* list dealing with dates noting obligations of several parties; ZÚ.LUM.MA ZAG *šá* LÚ.NU.KIRI$_6$.MEŠ *šá* GN.

Text	Museum Number	Month	Day	Year	Year B.C.	Description
43	NBC 4770	*Nis*	10	15	590	Two-dimensional *imittu* list dealing with barley and emmer; ŠE.BAR ZÍZ.A.AN ZAG *šá* GN.
44	YBC 9164	*Teb*	24	16	588	Two-dimensional *imittu* list dealing with barley and dates noting obligations of several parties; ŠE.BAR ⌈ZÚ.LUM. MA?⌉ . . . *šá* GN.
45	NBC 4886	*Nis*	27	2	603	*Imittu* list; from DAG.KI. GUŠKIN, cf. 43.
46	NBC 4803	[X]	3	3	602	Imposts; GIŠ *ma-šiḫ šá* ŠE. BAR *šá eš-re-e ù šib-šú šá qaq-qar*-ME *šá* É.AN.NA PN *u* PN_2 *šá* UGU-*ḫi eš-re-e* IGI-*ú*.
47	YBC 9634	⌈X⌉	5	1	603	Impost list; *te-lit šá* MN.
48	YBC 9361	*Araḫ*	14	16	589	Receipt (IGI-*ir*) of ⌈GUD *tap*-⌉ *ṭi-ri*.
49	YBC 9059	*Araḫ*	5	11	594	Receipt of cattle.
50	YBC 9532	*Nis*	18	1	604	Receipt of oxen for *ḫarû*-ceremony.
51	YBC 8822	[X]	[X]	[X+]6	[X]	Receipt of 5-year-old trained ox.
52	YBC 9495	*Araḫ*	25	1	604	List of cattle.
53	NBC 4887	*Kis*	2	20	585	List of cattle.
54	YBC 9649	*Šab*	4	0	604	Two-dimensional list of cattle deliveries.[45]
55	YBC 3436	*Nis*	9	19	586	Unblemished cattle (ÁB.GUD. ḪI.A *ta-mi-ma-a-t*[*a*]) at the disposal of (*ina* IGI) PN.
56	YBC 9427	*Araḫ*	1	0	605	Receipt of cattle carcass after accounts had been drawn up; *pag-ru* EGIR *e-piš* NÍG.ŠID PN IGI-*ir*.
57	YBC 6886	*Šab*	9	11	593	Receipt of cow carcass.
58	YBC 8794	*Abu*	18	18	587	Receipt of ox carcass.
59	YBC 9637	*Ulu*	22	17	588	Receipt of cow carcass.
60	YBC 9602	*Aya*	1	18	587	Receipt of cow carcass and plow.

45. See Levine, *JAOS* 85 (1965), p. 316.

Text	Museum Number	Month	Day	Year	Year B.C.	Description
61	YBC 9321	*Šab*	3	4	600	Receipt of ox carcass.
62	YBC 8827	*Kis*	16	1	604	Receipt of cattle-hides (KUŠ. TAB.BA.ME).
63	NBC 4728	⌈X⌉	22	9	596	Receipt of cattle-hides after accounts had been drawn up.
64	NBC 4635	*Abu*	5	13	592	Dyed cattle-hides for tents (KUŠ *du-uš-šu-ú*-ME *a-na za-ra-ti*) at the disposal of PN.
65	NBC 4643	*Araḫ*	10	4	601	Cattle-hides for coloring (*a-na* KUŠ *ši-in-du*) at the disposal of PN.
66	YBC 8812	*Kis*	26	14	591	Sheep sent to (*šu-bu-ul*) *šatammu* in Opis, received by PN.
67	YBC 9375	*Add* II	30	14	590	Receipt of sheep?
68	YBC 9612	*Kis?*	⌈X⌉	16	589	Receipt of sheep *a-na pa-ra-su šá* MN.
69	YBC 9592	*Teb*	20	23	581	Receipt of sheep.
70	YBC 9378	*Šab*	17	21	583	Receipt of sheep.
71	YBC 9421	*Araḫ*	7	21	584	Receipt of sheep.
72	YBC 9481	*Duz*	15	21	584	Receipt of sheep.
73	NBC 4628	*Duz*	11	23	582	Receipt of sheep.
74	NBC 4822	*Duz*	24	2	603	Receipt of sheep, *irbu* of PN; goats and wool.
75	NBC 6129	*Teb*	27	3	601	Receipt of sheep.
76	NBC 4807	*Šab*	10[+X]	21	583	Receipt of sheep.
77	YBC 9473	*Ulu*	5	22	583	Receipt of sheep.
78	YBC 9430	*Sim*	20	13	592	Sheep *ina* IGI PN *u* PN_2 *paq-du*.
79	YBC 9127	*Araḫ*	27	18	587	Sheep, with some in the hair, (*lu-ub-bu-uš-tú*) at the disposal of PN.
80	YBC 9482	*Sim*	24	21	584	Sheep at the disposal of PN.
81	NBC 4660	*Duz*	29	13	592	Sheep at the disposal of PN.
82	NBC 4809	*Add*	10	14	590	Sheep and goats at the disposal of PN.
83	YBC 9334	*Add*	25	18	586	Sheep and goats at the disposal of PN.
84	YBC 8832	[X]	8	13	592	Sheep at the disposal of PN.
85	NBC 4701	*Nis*	11	23	582	Lambs "set aside" (*par-su*).
86	YBC 9376	*Aya*	30	16	589	Sheep "inspected" (*am-ra*).

Text	Museum Number	Month	Day	Year	Year B.C.	Description
87	YBC 6915	[X]	9	[X+]6	(after 599)	Withdrawal of sheep ($GURU_9$).
88	YBC 9563	*Taš*	22	16	589	Withdrawal of sheep.
89	YBC 8824	*Kis*	26	16	588	Sheep and small cattle sent ([*šu-*]⌈*bul*⌉) to *qīpu* and *šatammu*.
90	NBC 4662	*Kis*	3	21	584	Lambs and ducks (UZ.TUR. MUŠEN.ME) sent by PN for *kinūnu*-festival.
91	YBC 9555	*Araḫ*	1	16	589	Note concerning sheep.
92	YBC 9616	*Taš*	8	9	617	Note concerning sheep. Time of Nabopolassar.
93	YBC 9623	*Šab*	22	21	583	Receipt of sheep carcass (*pag-ra*).
94	YBC 9443	*Duz*	23	22	583	Receipt of sheep carcass.
95	YBC 9419	*Šab*	6	22	582	Receipt of sheep carcass.
96	NBC 4615	*Teb*	18	21	583	Receipt of sheep carcasses.
97	YBC 8789	*Araḫ*	6	16	589	Receipt of sheep carcasses.
98	YBC 9377	*Abu*	13	26	579	Receipt of sheep carcasses.
99	NBC 4617	*Šab*	29	22	582	Receipt of sheep carcasses.
100	YBC 9624	*Add*	19	22	582	Receipt of sheep carcasses.
101	YBC 9615	*Araḫ*	22	22	583	Receipt of three LÚ.BAD ⌈UDU.X⌉ sheep carcasses.
102	YBC 9065	*Add*	4	1	603	Receipt of sheep carcasses.
103	YBC 9454	*Duz*	12[+X]	2	603	Receipt of wool (SÍG).
104	YBC 9581	*Šab*	1	20	584	Wool (SÍG SAG, *ta-kil-tum*) at the disposal of PN.
105	YBC 8808	*Sim*	23	13	592	Wool weighed out (PN *iḫ-ti-iṭ*).
106	NBC 4816	*Sim*	17	11-29(?)	594-576(?)	Wool weighed out.
107	NBC 4691	*Sim*	29	12	593	Wool weighed out.
108	YBC 9415	*Sim*	10	13	592	Withdrawal of wool.
109	YBC 8805	*Taš*	17	14	591	Withdrawal of wool.
110	YBC 9465	*Duz*	2	19	586	Withdrawal of wool.
111	YBC 9492	*Šab*	11	17	587	Withdrawal of wool.
112	YBC 9369	*Abu*	29	21	584	Withdrawal of blue-dyed wool (SÍG ZA.GÌN.KUR.RA).
113	YBC 4170	*Taš*	(none)	0	605	Wool given for barley and dates ⌈*pap-*⌉*pa-su i-na maš-šar-tu*$_4$*-šú-nu šá ul-tu* MN . . . ⌈SUM-⌉

Text	Museum Number	Month	Day	Year	Year B.C.	Description
						na. Deviations between computation and text are indicated by *sic* in margin of copy.
114	YBC 9433	*Duz*?	1	22	583	Wool, baskets, and various other commodities, including 5 LÚ. ÌR.É.GAL.MEŠ, at the disposal of PN.
115	NBC 4605	*Kis*	5	5	600	Wool at the disposal of PN for silver; partially to purchase gold and lambs; balance of silver to Eanna.
116	NBC 4648	*Sim*	21	13	592	Wool, lead, small cattle?, myrrh, antimony-paste, utensils, [SÍG.]ḪI.A, *a-ba-ru*, GIŠ.GÍN.A.NI, UDU *pa-ṭir*, ŠIM.SIS EN *gu-ra-bi*, ŠIM. BI.⌈ZI.?DA? EN⌉ *gu-ra-bi*, ⌈*ú*-⌉*di-e*.
117	YBC 16299	[X]	[X]	[X]	[X]	Purchase of wool and [X] . . . [X] UD LUGAL *ḫi-it-pu* UD. [X.KÁM . . .].
118	NBC 4752	*Šab*	10	22	582	Wool (mostly destroyed).
119	YBC 7410	*Abu*	20	18	587	Ass, *ir-bi šá* PN.
120	YBC 8828	*Sim*	10	5	600	Receipt of 85 doves (TU.KUR$_4$. MUŠEN [X.X]).
121	YBC 9485	*Aya*	6	12	593	Receipt of barley (ŠE.BAR).
122	YBC 9262	*Šab*	2	3	601	Receipt of barley.
123	YBC 8778	*Aya*	5	19	586	Receipt of barley.
124	NBC 4721	*Add*	9	3	601	Receipt of barley.
125	YBC 9568	*Duz*	27	17	588	Barley at the disposal of PN.
126	YBC 4003	*Kis*	29	0	605	Barley at the disposal of PN to purchase sheep.
127	NBC 4629	*Šab*	22	17	587	Barley at the disposal of PN.
128	YBC 9596	*Araḫ*	22	13	592	Withdrawal of barley *ina* UD. ME *šá* PN.
129	YBC 9610	*Abu*	12	14	591	Withdrawal of barley NÍG. ḪI.A *šá* ERÍN.ME *šá* É. GUR$_7$.
130	YBC 8820	*Duz*	10	17	588	Withdrawal of barley for limestone and pitch, (*a-bat-tum u* A.ESÍR).

Text	Museum Number	Month	Day	Year	Year B.C.	Description
131	YBC 6898	*Abu*	18	18	587	Withdrawal of barley, part of PN's still outstanding (KÁ-*ti*) maintenance allowance.
132	YBC 9413	*Šab*	11	12	592	Withdrawal of barley.
133	YBC 9635	*Taš*	8	17	588	Withdrawal of barley for flour.
134	YBC 9354	*Ulu*	8	18	587	Withdrawal of barley for cattle fodder (*bal-lum šá* GUD. MEŠ).
135	YBC 9463	*Add*	22	14	590	Withdrawal of barley.
136	YBC 9663	*Taš*	14	19	586	Withdrawal of barley.
137	YBC 9586	*Ulu*	9	16	589	Withdrawal of barley by PN from his son's maintenance.
138	YBC 8810	*Add*	24	16	588	Withdrawal of barley *a-na za-bil-la-ni a-na* GN.
139	YBC 9561	*Kis*	15	17	588	Withdrawal of barley for bread and utensils? (*mu-ra-*⌈X⌉[XX?][*murammû*?]).
140	YBC 8817	*Taš*	20	18	587	Withdrawal of barley.
141	YBC 9613	*Aya*	23	[X]	[X]	Withdrawal of barley *ina* UD. MEŠ LÚ MU-*ú-tu*.
142	NBC 4682	*Aya*	25	18	587	Withdrawal of barley for sick people (*a-na . . . mar-ṣu-tu*); l. 19: ⌈5 BÁN⌉ ¹É.AN.NA. LUGAL.URÙ A LUGAL.
143	NBC 4614	*Taš*	20	20	585	Withdrawal of barley.
144	NBC 4922	*Nis*	7	15	590	Withdrawal of barley.
145	NBC 4698	*Araḫ*	28	22	583	Withdrawal of barley.
146	NBC 4923	[X]	13	17	588 (609? Nbp.)	Withdrawal of barley for tithe? (*a-na eš-*⌈*ri*?-⌉[*e*]). Deviations from the rule that the first quantity is twelve times the second are not expressly indicated in the copy.
147	NBC 8354	*Kis*	6	17	588	Withdrawal of barley.
148	YBC 9565	*Aya*	22	15	590	Barley for [. . .].
149	YBC 9295	*Aya*	21	15	590	Barley distributed to 12 men.
150	YBC 9383	*Ulu*	1	19	586	Barley, income *šá* MU.19. KÁM.
151	YBC 9168	*Araḫ*	28	19	586	Barley *ir-bi šá* MU.19.KÁM *ina bi-rit* KAR *ù kar-mu*.
152	NBC 4823	*Aya*	(none)	19	586	Barley and cress (*saḫ-li-e*) . . .

Text	Museum Number	Month	Day	Year	Year B.C.	Description
						ZAG *šá* LÚ *da-li-iá šá* ÍD *ḫar-ri šá* [1]*gub-ba-a.*
153	NBC 4746	*Ulu*	12	0	605	Barley[. . .].
154	YBC 9348	*Šab*	25	20	584	Barley delivered into storehouse (*šá a-na* É.NÌ.GA SUM-*na*).
155	YBC 9659	*Araḫ*	8	19	586	List of names with numbers of measures given to LÚ.Ì. SUR.MEŠ.
156	NBC 4633	*Add* II	12	17	587	Barley given for flour.
157	YBC 8795	*Araḫ*	23	5	600	Barley [. . .].
158	YBC 9412	*Abu*	2	18	587	Receipt of dates.
159	YBC 8802	*Ulu*	5	18	587	Receipt of dates and silver.
160	NBC 4668	*Araḫ*	5	1	604	Receipt of dates.
161	YBC 9456	*Add*	4	17	587	Withdrawal of dates for "days" of Nisanu.
162	YBC 3437	*Nis*	30	18	587	Withdrawal of dates; dated to [d]AG.NÌ.DU.URÙ LUGAL KUR.KUR.
163	YBC 8801	*Šab*	29	19	585	Withdrawal of Dilmun dates.
164	YBC 9599	*Taš*	20	18	587	Withdrawal of dates and barley, *ni-ḫi-is-*⌜*tú*?⌝.
165	YBC 9598	*Kis*	10	18	587	Withdrawal of dates.
166	YBC 4175	*Šab*	26	15	589	Withdrawal of dates for four deities.
167	YBC 9390	*Nis*	7	22	583	Withdrawal of dates IGI [d]URÙ. INIM-*su*.
168	NBC 4740	*Araḫ*	11	22	583	Withdrawal of dates.
169	YBC 3430	*Add*	15	15	590	Dates (mostly broken).
170	YBC 9493	*Araḫ*	24	18	587	Dates given for work in the temple É.TÙR.KALAM.
171	NBC 4677	*Šab*	3	14	590	Dates given for [. . .].
172	NBC 4902	*Araḫ*	9	7	598	Dates *maš-šar-ti šá* MN, for four deities.
173	NBC 4825	*Ulu*	1	18	587	Withdrawal of Dilmun dates for UD.ÈŠ.ÈŠ.
174	YBC 9512	*Araḫ*	19	13	592	Withdrawal of sesame (ŠE.GIŠ. Ì) for sweetcakes (*a-na mut-ta-*⌜*qu*⌝)
175	YBC 9529	*Kis*	1	17	588	Withdrawal of sesame for sweetcakes for *eššešu* festival

Text	Museum Number	Month	Day	Year	Year B.C.	Description
						(*a-na mut-ta-*⌈*qu*⌉ *šá* 8 UD.ÈŠ.ÈŠ.MEŠ *šá* MN).
176	YBC 9450	*Šab*	15	17	587	Withdrawal of sesame for É *ḫi-il-ṣu*.
177	YBC 9620	*Šab*	22	21	583	Withdrawal of sesame.
178	YBC 9359	*Araḫ*	[X]	11	594	Sesame *ina maššartu ša* MN.
179	YBC 9487	*Taš*	27	17	588	Sesame subtracted (*in-da-ṭi-ma*).
180	NBC 4814	*Teb*	19	22	582	Sesame given.
181	YBC 9426	*Abu*	21	14	591	Withdrawal of emmer wheat (ŠE.ZÍZ.A.AN) balance of the "days" of PN.
182	YBC 6891	*Aya*	23	17	588	Withdrawal of emmer wheat.
183	YBC 9381	*Nis*	23	[X]	[X]	Emmer wheat *ina maššarti ša* MN.
184	NBC 4901	*Ulu*	28?	9	596	Emmer wheat for barley [. . .]
185	YBC 9357	*Šab*	[X]	2	602	Receipt of oil (Ì.GIŠ).
186	NBC 4687	*Šab*	29	22	582	Withdrawal of oil *ana nu-úr šá* TA GUD.MEŠ.
187	YBC 3440	*Add*	14	15	589	Withdrawal of flour and fodder.
188	YBC 11527	*Add*	1	19	585	Withdrawal of fine flour (*si-il-t*[*i*]).
189	NBC 4699	*Add*	10	13	591	Receipt of ŠUK.ḪI.A *šá* MN.
190	YBC 9391	*Abu*	19	11	594	Unspecified ŠUK.ḪI.A at the disposal of PN.
191	NBC 4727	*Aya*	28	4	601	Unspecified "measures" (*ma-š*⌈*iḫ*⌉) at the disposal of PN.
192	YBC 9505	*Ulu*	22?	5	600	Withdrawal of six unspecified measures for six months, beginning in *Nisanu*.
193	YBC 9279	*Taš*	19	21	584	Withdrawal of GIŠ *ma-ši-ḫu gu-uq-qù-ú*.
194	YBC 9515	*Nis*	11	14	591	Withdrawal of salt (MUN.Ḫ[I.A]).
195	YBC 9468	*Taš*	25	2	603	Receipt of silver for various purchases.
196	YBC 9440	*Abu*	28	22	583	Receipt of silver, balance (*ri-ḫi-it* KÙ.BABBAR).
197	NBC 4659	*Kis*	6	13	592	Receipt of silver.
198	NBC 4768	*Add*	18	1	603	Receipt of silver.
199	YBC 9632	*Duz*	24	1	604	Receipt of silver for 3 cattle.

Text	Museum Number	Month	Day	Year	Year B.C.	Description
200	NBC 4788	*Aya*	22	3	602	Receipt of silver.
201	YBC 9050	*Araḫ*	16	6	599	Silver at the disposal of PN.
202	YBC 11665	*Add* II	11	17	587	Silver at the disposal of [PN] for baskets? (*za-bi-lu*).
203	YBC 9288	*Kis*	9	18	587	Silver, amount due, at the disposal of PN, for bitumen (*ku-pur*).
204	YBC 9382	*Aya*	12	16	589	[Silver]at the disposal of PN.
205	YBC 11517	*Šab*	30	[X]	[X]	Silver at the disposal of PN to purchase straw (*a-na ti-ib-ni*).
206	NBC 4760	*Taš*	22	23	582	Silver at the disposal of seven(?) persons.
207	YBC 9630	*Add*	[X]	16	588	Silver at the disposal of PN.
208	YBC 9073	*Aya*	9	21	584	Silver at the disposal of PN.
209	YBC 9429	*Šab*	23	21	583	Silver at the disposal of various parties to purchase: UDU *par-rat šá ki-na-a-a-ta*, ŠE.GIŠ.Ì *pe-ṣu-tú*, *mu-mar-ri-tum*, UDU *tup-šik šá sil-li*, ŠE.BAR.
210	YBC 9474	*Šab*	4	22	582	Silver at the disposal of PN given for blue wool.
211	YBC 9506	[X]	19	[X+?]16	589 (579?, 569?)	Silver given for reed bundles GI *gu-zu-ul-lu*, and *šil-ta-ḫi*.
212	YBC 9629	*Duz*	25	12	593	Silver given to PN for work on quay (*dul-li šá ka-a-ri*).
213	YBC 9622	*Duz*	7	15	590	Silver given to LÚ.KÙ.TIM.
214	YBC 11514	*Aya*	24	18	587	Silver given for various purposes.
215	NBC 4715	*Add*	16	14	590	Silver given to several parties.
216	YBC 9350	*Kis*	10	22	583	Silver given to PN *a-na pa-áš-šu-ru šá* [X X X].
217	NBC 4947	*Šab*	9	12	592	Record of refinement of silver.
218	NBC 4708	*Aya*	30	14	591	Record of refinement of silver.
219	YBC 11315	*Duz*	16	14	591	Silver given for purchase, and withdrawn.
220	YBC 9554	*Add*	21	17	587	Silver given to several people for various purposes, partly for acquiring wool.
221	YBC 8791	*Nis*	16	18	587	Record of withdrawal of silver

Text	Museum Number	Month	Day	Year	Year B.C.	Description
						šá ri-ḫa-a-ta a-na LUGAL *iš-šu-ú* and maintenance for a sailor.
222	YBC 8826	*Duz*	18	18	587	Withdrawal of silver partly to purchase fine beer (KAŠ.SAG).
223	YBC 9488	*Ulu*	23	14	591	Withdrawal of silver to acquire wool.
224	YBC 9558	*Add*	12	18	587	Withdrawal of silver as wages (*i-di-šú* PN *it-ta-ši*).
225	YBC 8811	*Aya*	9	14	591	Withdrawal of silver which three people had brought to *qīpu*.
226	YBC 9145	*Duz*	4	17	588	Withdrawal of silver as wages.
227	YBC 9579	*Araḫ*	15	17	588	Withdrawal of silver for(?) wool, barley.
228	YBC 9501	*Šab*	18	18	586	Withdrawal of silver from PN's maintenance.
229	YBC 9627	*Abu*	24	17	588	Withdrawal of silver to purchase full-weight iron (AN.BAR *gam-ru*), spades (MAR.MEŠ AN.BAR), and other iron tools (*kám-ma-a-ta* AN.BAR).
230	YBC 9275	*Ulu*	12	21	584	Withdrawal of 1 23/24 shekels of gold for 17½ shekels of silver, and withdrawal of other commodities from the treasury.
231	NBC 6180	*Teb*	18	19	585	Silver withdrawn and brought to *qīpu*.
232	YBC 9340	*Add*	18	16	588	Silver, balance on account, brought to PN.
233	YBC 9522	*Add*	15	16	588	Silver brought to PN and PN_2 for barley and limestone (*a-bat-tum*).
234	NBC 4700	*Šab*	11	22	582	Silver *ina* KÙ.BABBAR *šá ir-bi* for straw (*ti-ib-ni*) and wood beam(s) (GIŠ.Ù[R]) for roofing a sheep-shed (*a-na ṣu-ul-lul šá* É UDU.NITÁ).
235	YBC 9484	*Duz*	28	12	593	Note concerning silver balance, ⌈*a-na*⌉ *dul-li šá ka-a-ri*.

Text	Museum Number	Month	Day	Year	Year B.C.	Description
236	YBC 6866	*Kis*	10	14	591	Note concerning silver.
237	YBC 9439	*Araḫ*	12	2	603	Note concerning silver.
238	YBC 11500	[X]	29	10	595	Note concerning silver (mostly destroyed).
239	YBC 6892	*Araḫ*	10	16	589	Note concerning silver and barley.
240	YBC 11511	*Šab*	15	16	588	Note concerning silver(?) for repairs (*a-na bat-qa*).
241	YBC 9331	*Sim*	10	2	603	Note concerning silver for four workmen on temple tower (*e-piš dul-lu šá* É *ziq-qur-rat*).
242	YBC 9595	*Sim*	15	21	584	Note concerning silver and gold, *ir-bi šá* [1d]EN.MU.GAR-*un* A-*šú šá* [1d]AG-*pir-la-'*.
243	NBC 4654	*Abu*	20	23	582	Note concerning silver and barley(?) for workers.
244	NBC 4647	(none)	(none)	17	588	Note concerning silver, *ri-ḫi-it* KÙ.BABBAR . . . *ir-bi šá* LUGAL.
245	YBC 9408	*Taš*	24?	1	604	Receipt of gold and golden *da-áš-šú* of the standard ([d]URÌ. GAL-*lum*) of [d]INNIN UNUG.KI.
246	YBC 9646	*Abu*	1	8	597	List of ornamental jewelry(?) (*šu-qul-ti a-ri-ti*) *šá* [d]*na-na-a*.
247	NBC 4931	*Araḫ*	10	1	604	*Ḫulātu*-stones (NA_4.ZA.NIM) for a necklace (*a-na* GÚ.ME) and [. . .] at the disposal of PN.
248	NBC 4726	*Šab*	26	21	583	Golden ornaments from the garments of the gods given to goldsmiths for cleaning.
249	YBC 9363	*Ulu*	13	5	600	Receipt of white thread (⌈TÚG⌉ *mi-iḫ-ṣu* BABBAR-*ú*) and sacred garments by weaver.
250	YBC 6864	[X]	17	10	595	Receipt of linen cult-curtain(s) (GADA . . . *bu-lu-ú*).
251	YBC 9575	*Aya*	15	19	586	GADA *šal-ḫu*-ME-garments for cleaning (*a-na zi-ku-tu*) at the disposal of PN and PN_2.
252	YBC 9425	*Teb*	19	5	599	*Ḫa-at-ḫu-ri-e-ta*-dye for garment of goddess, at the disposal of PN.

Text	Museum Number	Month	Day	Year	Year B.C.	Description
253	YBC 9272	*Aya*	2	4	601	Wool colored with mineral blue dye and wool *šá* KUR *ya-a-ma-nu* at the disposal of PN.
254	YBC 9342	*Sim*	22	17	588	Scarlet wool (SÍG.GAN.ME. DA.KUR.RA) at the disposal of PN.
255	YBC 9396	*Taš*	26	18	587	Withdrawal of TÚG.KUR.RA garment.
256	YBC 16300	[X]	[X]	[X]	[X]	Items for or list of weavers and fullers *šá* É ^{d}*bi-ru-*[*u-a?*].
257	YBC 9157	*Nis*	16	21	584	Receipt of bronze (UD.KA. BAR).
258	YBC 9589	*Aya*	24	13	592	Receipt of ŠEN UD.KA.BAR.
259	YBC 9618	*Sim*	29	22	583	Bronze and 2 *kal-la-nu šá* GIŠ *zi-ba-ni-tum* at the disposal of smith.
260	YBC 9392	*Abu*	22	22	583	Bronze at the disposal of smith.
261	YBC 9569	*Sim*	14	12	593	Bronze utensils: *mu-nak-ki-ti*, *gul-gul-lum*, at the disposal of PN.
262	YBC 8830	*Abu*	2	17	588	Receipt of iron (AN.BAR *gam-ru*) and 1 axe (*qul-mu-u*) by smith.
263	YBC 6893	*Sim*	13	3	602	Receipt of iron and 2 *kak-kab-ti* by smith.
264	YBC 6896	*Abu*	25	18	587	Receipt of iron and GÍR AN. BAR.ME by smith.
265	YBC 9625	*Šab*	17	17	587	Receipt of iron and 2 *ḫa-lil-a-nu* AN.BAR by smith.
266	YBC 6875	*Aya*	7	14	591	Iron at the disposal of smith.
267	YBC 9483	*Araḫ*	10	17	588	Bows (GIŠ.BAN.MEŠ) at the disposal of PN and PN_2.
268	NBC 4634	*Add*	14	22	582	Quiver (KUŠ *til-lu rak-su*) and handcuffs (GIŠ.$ŠU^{II}$ AN. BAR) at the disposal of PN.
269	YBC 9422	*Šab*	6	22	582	Quiver, GIŠ.BAN *ul-ḫu-ul-lu* . . . arrows (GI *šil-ta-ḫu*) at the disposal of PN.
270	NBC 4661	*Abu*	10	12	593	Withdrawal of iron dagger (GÍR AN.BAR) and iron.
271	NBC 4644	*Šab*	7	22	582	Quiver, lances (*az-ma-ra-ni-e*), and arrows 'brought.'

Text	Museum Number	Month	Day	Year	Year B.C.	Description
272	YBC 9461	*Teb*	20	17	587	Bricks (*a-gur-rum*) given to PN.
273	YBC 9462	*Nis*	22	16	589	Bricks given to PN.
274	YBC 4061	*Kis*	25	18	586	Inventory taken of bricks (177,000 *a-gur-ru šá* É.AN.NA *ina* É.NÌ.GA.MEŠ . . . PN *u* PN_2 . . . *is-ni-qu*).
275	YBC 9166	*Sim*	[X]	18	587	Note concerning bricks.
276	YBC 9508	*Duz*	24	6	599	Note, probably concerning bricks.
277	YBC 9546	*Abu*	9	16	589	Withdrawal of baskets (*zab-bi-la-nu*).
278	YBC 9349	*Add*	20[+X]	16	588	Receipt and withdrawal of sundry items: 8-*ta áš-la-a-ta*, . . . 10 *zab-bi-*⌈*la-*⌉*nu* . . .
279	YBC 9336	*Šab*	29	2	602	Receipt of *na-an-gu*, GIŠ *at-ma-nu šá* [. . .], *un-qa-a-ti*.
280	YBC 6899	*Duz*	10	18	587	Boat cranes? (*mu-še-li-il-i šá* GIŠ.MÁ) at the disposal of PN.
281	YBC 9401	*Ulu*	9	19	586	Withdrawal of sesame and bronze bands for kettledrums (*rik-si li-li-si* UD.KA.BAR).
282	NBC 4671	*Ulu*	10	11	594	Receipt of [. . .].
283	YBC 9307	*Duz*/ *Taš*?	15	14	591	If he does not turn over the ox he must return the field that has been put under cultivation; *ki-i* GUD *la it-tan-nu* ŠE.NUMUN DÙ-*šú i-tur-ru*.
284	YBC 8787	*Nis*	8	17	588	(destroyed)
285	YBC 8797	*Aya*	29	13	592	(destroyed)
286	YBC 4049	*Abu*	16	1	521	URU *ga-di-e-ti*, *imittu* document; cf. 35.
287	YBC 7386	*Abu*	24	1	521	KAR! É.AN.NA, *imittu* document; cf. 35.
288	YBC 4045	*Abu*	26	1	521	URU ÍD *eš-šú*, *imittu* document; cf. 35.
289	YBC 3700	*Ulu*	2	1	521	GARIN *na-ḫal-lum*, *imittu* document; cf. 35.
290	YBC 4050	*Ulu*	3	1	521	URU KÁ *a-sur-ri-tum*, *imittu* document; cf. 35.
291	YBC 3790	*Ulu*?	8	1	521	URU *šá-kil-lat*, *imittu* document; cf. 35.

Text	Museum Number	Month	Day	Year	Year B.C.	Description
292	YBC 4093	*Ulu*	13	1	521	URU *na-ḫal-lum*, *imittu* document; cf. 35.
293	YBC 3806	*Taš*	3	1	521	*Bit-qa šá* [1d]EN.SUR, *imittu* document; cf. 35.
294	YBC 3825	*Taš*	3	1	521	See 293.
295	YBC 3736	*Taš*	3	1	521	See 293.
296	YBC 4058	*Taš*	5	1	521	See 293.
297	YBC 3799	*Taš*	5	1	521	See 293.
298	YBC 4077	*Taš*	6	1	521	See 293.
299	YBC 4125	[X]	24	1	521	KAR É.AN.NA, *imittu* document; cf. 35.
300	YBC 4025	(none)	(none)	1	521	*Imittu* list noting obligations of several parties; ZÚ.LUM. MA *i-mit-ti* A.ŠÀ.MEŠ *šá* GÚ ÍD *bit-qa*, cf. 41.
301	YBC 6938	*Ulu*	15	1	604	Receipt of wool and linen garments of the gods by PN and PN_2.
302	YBC 3792	*Taš*	16	1	604	Lease of boat for one month; GIŠ.MÁ *šá* PN . . . *a-na* 12 GÍN KÙ.BABBAR *a-na i-di-šú a-na* NÌ.GA É.AN.NA *id-din*.
303	YBC 6944	*Araḫ*	25	2	603	Babylon, sale of land; 3 KÙŠ GI.MEŠ A.ŠÀ *ki-šub-bu-u* KI-*tim ku-*⌈*ma-*⌉*ru šá qé-reb* KÁ.DINGIR.RA.KI; cf. 2.
304	YBC 9534	*Abu*	17	2	603	Iron *šá* URU *ṣi-im-mir* at the disposal of smith.
305	YBC 9584	*Taš*	4	3	602	Blue wool and NA_4-*gab-bu-ú* for sacred garments at the disposal of weavers.
306	YBC 9287	*Teb*	25	3	601	Receipt of barley; measured out by (*in-daš-ḫi*) the *qallu* of the *qīpu*.
307	YBC 9451	*Šab*	27	3	601	Receipt of garments of wool and linen *šá a-na* [d]PALIL *šá* URU *ú-*[X X] SUM-*na* by launderers.
308	YBC 9305	*Šab*	23[+X]	4	600	Receipt of oil (X *né-sep* X SÌLA Ì.GIŠ).
309	YBC 9587	*Araḫ*	18	5	600	Receipt of Dilmun dates by PN.

Text	Museum Number	Month	Day	Year	Year B.C.	Description
310	YBC 8837	*Duz*	11	6	599	Receipt of iron and *ma-aq-qa*, *mu-ṣi-bi-it*, *ṣi-ṣi-ib-ti*, *ba-at-qu-ú* and *ú-ra-šú* by smith, cf. 262–65.
311	YBC 9504	*Šab*	16	6	598	Silver at the disposal of PN and PN_2.
312	YBC 9303	*Add*	8	8	596	Receipt of salt (MUN.ḪI.A).
313	YBC 3542	*Araḫ*	[X]	3	602	Sippar, list of offerings; ⌈GUD⌉ [*šuk-lu-lu* UDU.] BABBAR. GAL $SILA_4$ KUR.GI. MUŠEN UZ.TUR.MUŠEN $TU.KUR_4$.MUŠEN.
314	YBC 3793	*Kis*	23	4	601	Receipt of sesame.
315	YBC 4108	*Add*	14	6	598	Loan of money, payable on demand (UD-*mu šá . . . ir-ri-šu-šú . . . i-*⌈*nam-*⌉*din*) or specified interest (20 percent).
316	YBC 9289	*Ulu*	4	8	597	Weapons, cases with arrows, *ana* LÚ.ERIN.ME *šá* KÁ. É.GAL, at the disposal of PN.
317	YBC 9207	*Teb*	⌈29⌉	7	597	Dates *šá* PN, PN_2 *u* PN_3 (and) silver *ina* GUB-*zu šá* PN_4 *u* PN_5 *a-mi-ir*.
318	YBC 9311	*Sim*	27	10	595	Receipt of barley, 12-month allocation for LÚ *ši-rak*-MEŠ.
319	YBC 9519	*Teb*	3	8	596	Guarantee for appearance of PN; cf. 29.
320	YBC 9245	*Kis*	21	10	595	Lawsuit concerning slave: returned to PN; PN *it-ti* PN_2 *di-i-ni i-dib-bu-ub-ma* LÚ *qal-la šá* PN *i-tu-ru*.
321	YBC 9261	*Add*	6	6	598	Sheep, *irbu*, set aside (*par-su*); cf. 85.
322	YBC 6940	*Taš*	3	9	596	Uruk, sale of house as *nudunnû*; *ṭup-pi* É *ab-tu šá na-pa-ṣu ù e-pi-šu . . .* É PN *šá a-na* SAL PN_2 DUMU.SAL-*šú a-na nu-dun*ₓ (=DIN-)*nu-ú id-di-nu*.
323	YBC 9160	*Šab*	2	12	592	Note concerning silver to purchase seed (ŠE.NUMUN) and fodder (*bal-lu šá* GUD. MEŠ).

Text	Museum Number	Month	Day	Year	Year B.C.	Description
324	YBC 9435	*Kis*	20	12	593	Note concerning silver *a-na ḫu-ṣa-bu ina* NÍG.GA.
325	YBC 4027	*Nis*	21	8	597	Barley and emmer given to workmen as their allowance (*a-na* 30 ERÍN.ME *ku-um* ŠUK.ḪI.A.MEŠ-*šú-nu šá* 8 ITI.MEŠ . . . *i-nam-din*).
326	YBC 9464	*Teb*	18	11	593	Receipt of sesame *šá* LÚ.ENGAR.ME.
327	YBC 9152	*Kis*	21	11	594	Loan of money, interest specified (six shekels on one mina), payable immediately.
328	YBC 9329	*Teb*	23	11	593	Withdrawal of cattle carcasses and receipt of cattle; cf. 56–61.
329	YBC 6854	*Duz*	6	12	593	Withdrawal of sacred garments to Babylon; 1 SÍG *na-ba-su* 1 TÚG GÚ.È *šá kám-mu* . . . PN GIŠ [sic!] MÁ.LAḪ$_4$ *it-ti* PN$_2$ *a-na* TIN.TIR.KI *it-ta-ši*.
330	YBC 6904	*Teb*	30	12	592	Barley at the disposal of PN for cattle-fodder.
331	YBC 9367	*Add*	22	12	592	Withdrawal of silver.
332	YBC 8799	*Šab*	23	12	592	Withdrawal of wool for allowance.
333	YBC 9633	*Araḫ*	26	11	594	Silver for repairs (*a-na bat-qa šá* GIR$_4$) at the disposal of PN.
334	YBC 9600	*Ulu*	30	11	594	Note concerning an allocation (ŠUK.ḪI.A.ME *šá* MN) for two men.
335	YBC 9360	*Add*	16	12	592	Case and iron dagger at the disposal of PN.
336	YBC 4057	*Araḫ*	17	11	594	Borsippa, loan of money, interest unspecified, with *Generalhypothek*; cf. 15. Duplicate of 338.
337	YBC 4053	*Abu*	7	9	596	Uruk, loan of money, interest specified, payable immediately.
338	YBC 4044	*Araḫ*	17	11	594	Duplicate of 336.
339	YBC 9146	*Duz*	6	12	593	12 minas of wool worth 3 shekels

Text	Museum Number	Month	Day	Year	Year B.C.	Description
						of silver weighed out for purchase of bow.
340	YBC 3697	*Sim*	22	11	594	Uruk, loan of money, interest unspecified, with pledge of real estate; cf. 15.
341	YBC 9175	*Šab*	16	12	592	Withdrawal of silver, balance, as allocation of MN for 17 LÚ *ki-zu-ú*-ME *šá* LÚ *qí-i-pi*.
342	YBC 9384	*Sim*	27	12	593	Receipt of sheep carcasses (*mi-i-tu*); cf. 93–102.
343	YBC 9573	*Duz*	2	12	593	Receipt of barley for LÚ *um-man-nu*.
344	YBC 9389	*Duz*	3	12	593	Note concerning *ma-šá-ri* AN. BAR *šá* KI.NE.NE.
345	YBC 9552	*Add*	6	12	592	Receipt of UDU.NITÁ.MEŠ *gi-ni-e* for deities.
346	YBC 9458	*Add*	20	10	594	Receipt of GUD.NINDÁ.MEŠ for deities.
347	YBC 9538	*Add*	1	12	592	Gold from GIŠ *šad-du*-receptacle for repairs given for GIŠ. DUL.DUL and GIŠ.KA × ŠE.
348	YBC 3735	*Šab*	25	13	591	Uruk, inheritance, partition of estate between two brothers; *ṭup-pi* ḪA.LA *šá* PN *u* PN_2 A.MEŠ *šá* PN_3 *it-ti a-ḫa-meš i-zu-zu*.
349	YBC 9528	*Add* II	5	24	590	Silver for arrows and spices (*ri-iq-qa*) at the disposal of PN.
350	YBC 9409	*Sim*	6	12	593	Withdrawal of salt for two deities.
351	YBC 9518	*Aya*	6	12	593	Bronze vats (*ki-ir-ri*-MEŠ, *sap-pu*-MEŠ. *zu-us-qu-ú* of UD. KA.BAR *a-na gur-ru-ú nap-ta-nu*) at the disposal of PN; cf. 259–61.
352	YBC 9591	*Sim*	8	12	593	Wool weighed out to purchase cress (*saḫ-li-e*) and as allocation, cf. 105–07.
353	YBC 9459	*Sim*	12	13	592	Barley given to PN.
354	YBC 8814	*Šab*	26[+X]	12	592	Silver for reeds (GI.MEŠ) and beer (KAŠ) given to PN and PN_2.

Text	*Museum Number*	*Month*	*Day*	*Year*	*Year B.C.*	*Description*
355	YBC 9626	*Duz*	13	12	593	Withdrawal of unspecified "measures."
356	YBC 9405	*Sim*	18	12	593	Withdrawal of wool, allocation for 20 men.
357	YBC 3854	*Nis*	12	13	592	Borsippa, loan of silver, interest unspecified, with pledge of slave (PN, LÚ *qal-la-šú*, *maš-ka-nu šá* PN_2 *a-di* PN_2 KÙ.BABBAR-*šú in-niṭ-ṭi-ru*).
358	YBC 9150	*Nis*	10	14	591	URU *a-ma-nu*, court document—relinquishment of a claim for sheep; *ul i-ta-ri-ma* PN *it-ti* PN_2 . . . *ina* UGU-*ḫi* U_8.UDU.ḪI.A . . . *ul i-díb-bu-ub* PN *e-ṭir*.
359	YBC 9654	*Teb*	9	15	589	URU *na-mar sa-par-ra-a-ta*, guarantee for appearance of PN; cf. 29.
360	YBC 4189	*Aya-Šab*		14	591-590	Six-column impost list; gold, income, given for silver and "expenses"; KÙ.GI *ir-bi šá a-na* KÙ.BABBAR SUM-*nu u a-na te-lit i-lu-ú*; cf. 47.
361	YBC 4123	*Araḫ*	5	16	589	Loan of silver, interest specified (20 percent) payable immediately.
362	YBC 9653	*Šab*	12	14	590	Withdrawal of barley for *šerkū* (LÚ PA.KAB.DU).
363	YBC 9514	*Sim*	19	14	591	List of names with notations (people *šá* GIŠ.MÁ *i-pe-eḫ-ḫu-*[*ú*], and *šá* ⌈*i-du*-⌉*ru* 10 GIŠ *ḫu-ṣa-bi i-zab-bil-lu*).
364	YBC 9234	*Ulu*	28	11	594	*Imittu* list; cf. 41.
365	YBC 9388	*Add* II	26	14	590	Withdrawal of barley for birds (*iṣ-ṣur*) and *dullu*.
366	YBC 9500	*Šab*	2	15	589	Sesame for oil given to PN's.
367	YBC 9455	*Sim*	16	15	590	Withdrawal of barley by PN.
368	YBC 9346	*Nis*	22	14	591	Iron for *dullu* at the disposal of smith.
369	YBC 9322	*Add*	21	14	590	Withdrawal of silver.

INDICES

PERSONAL NAMES

In this Index of Personal Names elements of names are taken as independent units and as such supersede alphabetization of full words. For example, *Ša-^{d}Nabû-šū* precedes *Šadunu*; all *Marduk-* names precede *Marduka*. All names beginning in *Ili-* precede those beginning *Ilī-*.

When a Sumerogram is written, the Index transcribes it into Akkadian without an ending, for example, *^{d}Adad-aḫ-erība*, *^{d}Adad-šum-iddin*, and *Aḫ-ittabši*. But if in the original, the noun is spelled out syllabically, no adjustment is made between transliteration and transcription. The names are rendered as closely as possible to the original spellings. For example, there are three separate groups of names beginning *^{d}Innin-*, *^{d}Inninna-*, and *^{d}Inninni-*. One result is that there will be separate entries for *Arad-^{d}Innin* and *Arad-^{d}Inninna*; for *Arrab* and *Arrabi*; for *Babutti* and *Babutu*; *Eriši* and *Erišu*; *Kurî* and *Kurû*; *Marduk* and *Marduku*. The reader may notice a few exceptions to this practice, as in nouns ending in a consonant cluster which would be difficult to render without a "proper" case-ending, e.g., *aplu*.

Whenever the text has only PN$_1$ *mār* PN$_2$, PN$_2$ is arbitrarily but consistently identified as the ancestor of PN$_1$ because it is normally impossible to distinguish between father and ancestor in this ambiguous formulation.

Abbreviations: a., ancestor; *a.*, ancestor, in the formula PN A PN$_2$ (possibly a father); br., brother; daught., daughter; desc., descendant; f., father; h., husband; m., mother; s., son; w., wife; wit., witness.

Determinatives: ^{d}, DINGIR (god); ^{f}, feminine, ^{h}, denotes occupation, ^{l}, masculine.

A.[X.X], f. of *Kudurri*, desc. of *Epeš-ili*, 360 iii 2.

*Ab-bi-*ZU (^{l}AD-*bi*-ZU), f. of *^{d}Nabû-šum-ēreš*, 2:6.

Ab-lūmur (^{l}AD-*lu-mur*) (585) desc. of *^{d}Nanā-ēreš*, 143:8.

^{l}AD.⸢X.⸣[X] (587), 131:2.

^{d}Adad-aḫ-erība (^{ld}IM.ŠEŠ.⸢SU⸣) *a.* of *Rīmūt*, 360 iv 3.

^{d}Adad-bēl-kinātum (^{ld}IM.EN-*ki-na-tum*) f. of *Ilī-dibbē*, 19:3.

^{d}Adad-šum-iddin (^{ld}⸢IM.⸣MU.MU) (590) desc. of *^{d}Nanā-ēreš*, 149:7.

Aḫ-ibnî (^{l}ŠEŠ.DÙ-*i*) a. of *^{d}Nabû-aḫḫē-uballiṭ* and *^{d}Marduk-zēr-ibnî*, 32:11.

Aḫ-iddin (^{l}ŠEŠ.MU) (521) h. of *^{f}Burāšu*, 300:17.

Aḫ-ilia (^{l}ŠEŠ.DINGIR-*a-a*) (601) desc. of *Manna-kī-ili*, 75:5.

Aḫ-ittabši (^{l}ŠEŠ-*it-tab-ši*)
1. (594) s. of *Rīmūt*, 336:8 and 338:8.
2. f. of *^{d}Nanā-uṣalli*, 1:28.

Aḫ-lūmur (^{I}ŠEŠ-*lu-mur*)
1. (592) desc. of ^{d}*Nabû-aḫḫē-iddin*, 354:2.
2.[46] (^{I}ŠEŠ.IGI) (591), 360 iii 10.
3.[46] (^{I}ŠEŠ.IGI) (588, possibly Nbp., 609) desc. of ^{d}*Nabû-aḫ*-⌈X⌉, 146:18.
4. (583), 70:4.
5. f. of *Aplā*, desc. of *Supē-*^{d}*Bēl*, 12:13.
6. f. of ^{d}*Nabû-banî-aḫ*, 137:3.

Aḫ-rāmu (^{I}ŠEŠ-*ra-mu*) *a.* of *Balṭiya*, 358:1.

Aḫ-ša (^{I}ŠEŠ-*šá*) (589), 166:9.

Aḫ-šu (^{I}ŠEŠ-*šú*) *a.* of ^{d}*Marduk-šum*-[X], 53:2.

Aḫ-šunu (^{I}ŠEŠ-*šú-nu*) (590), 215:2.

Aḫ-[X.X], *a.* of *Tadan*, 44:5.

Aḫḫē-lūmur (^{I}ŠEŠ.MEŠ.IGI) *a.* of *Zēriya*, 146:17.

Aḫḫē-⌈X⌉, f. of ^{d}*Bēl-ušallim*, 23:4.

Aḫḫēa (^{I}ŠEŠ.MEŠ-*e-a*)
1. f. of ^{d}*Nergal-ēpuš*, 31:3.
2. f. of ^{d}*Nabû-zēr-iqīša*, desc. of *Kurî*, 6:1.
3. *a.* of *Šum-ukīn*, 53:5.

Aḫḫēšā (^{I}ŠEŠ.MEŠ-*šá-a*)
1. (604), 52:9.
2. f. of *Aplā*, 16:2.
3. (^{I}ŠEŠ-*e-šá-a*) *a.* of *Aplā*, 320:11, 14; and of *Zēr-iqīša*, line 12.
4. *a.* of *Marduk*, 79:10.

Aḫḫēšu (^{I}ŠEŠ.MEŠ-*šú*) *a.* of ^{d}*Nabû-šum-ukīn*, 53:3.

Aḫulap-^{d}*Ištar* (^{I}*a-ḫu-lap-*^{d}15)
1. (589) s. of ^{d}*Nabû-zēr-ibnî*, 88:1.
2. f. of *Gimillu*, desc. of *Ḫunzû*, 35:14; 286:16; 287:15; 288:14; 289:14; 290:15; 291:18; 292:16; 293:15; 294:14; 295:14; 296:16; 297:15.

Aḫūtu (^{I}ŠEŠ-*tú*) (589) ^{h}*puṣāya*, 359:2, 4, 6.

Amēl-^{d}*Ea* (^{I}LÚ.^{d}BE)
1. *a.* of *Zēriya*, 234:4.
2. a. of *Mušēzib-*^{d}*Bēl* and *Balāṭsu*, 302:10.
3. a. of ^{d}*Nabû-uballiṭ* and *Ina-Esaggil-zēr*, 302:11.
4. a. of ^{d}*Nabû*-[X.X] and ^{d}*Ea-šum*-[X], 154:6.

Amēl-^{d}*Nabû* (^{I}LÚ.^{d}AG)
1. (603) desc. of *Amēl-*^{d}*Nanā*, 241:3; possibly identical with 146:37 (588 or Nbp., 609).
2. (596) s. of ^{d}*Bēl-aḫḫē-erība*, 322:38.
3. (588, possibly Nbp., 609) desc. of ^{d}*Nabû-aḫ-iddin*, 146:12.
4. (588, possibly Nbp., 609) desc. of *Amēl-*^{d}*Nanā*, 146:37; possibly identical with 241:3 (603).
5. (586) s. of ^{d}*Šamaš-iddin*, br. of *Silim-*^{d}*Bēl*, 25:3.

Amēl-^{d}*Nanā* (^{I}LÚ-^{d}*na-na-a*)
1. (601) s. of (A) *Arrab*, 314:18; and (A-*šú šá*) 308:7 (600).
2. (591) desc. of *Nadna-aplu*, 363:8.
3. (590) ^{h}*atû*, a *šerku*, 362:13.
4. (590) desc. of *Talli*, ^{h}*atû*, a *šerku*, 362:12.
5. (590) ^{h}*aškappu*, a *šerku*, 362:7, 26.
6. (588, possibly Nbp., 609) desc. of *Ibnā*, 146:38.
7. (588) desc. of *Riḫēti*, 125:2.
8. (588) desc. of *Rē'û*, 89:2.
9. (588, possibly Nbp., 609) *a.*'s name broken, 146:31.
10. (587) desc. of *Tabnēa*, 222:2.
11. (586) desc. of *Zākir*, 110:3.
12. (year destroyed) f.'s name broken, wit., 14:17.
13. *a.* of *Amēl-*^{d}*Nabû*, 241:4; possibly identical with 146:37.
14. *a.* of *Amēl-*^{d}*Nabû*, 146:37; possibly identical with 241:4.

46. ŠEŠ.IGI (= *Aḫ-lūmur*) following Figulla, *UET* IV p. 16, and assuming IGI = *lu-mur*, and against Dougherty *GCCI* 1 Index.

15. *a.* of *Banitušu*, 316:4.
16. *a.* of ^{d}*Nabû-*⸢X.X-⸣*ilī*, wit., 337:13.
17. *a.* of ^{d}*Nabû-ušallim*, 146:20.

Amēl-⸢X.⸣A (591), 225:1.

Amēl-^{d}[X.X.X] (589), 169:2.

Ammeni-ili (^{1}*am-me-ni-*DINGIR) *a.* of *Iqīša-*^{d}*Innin*, wit., 337:12.

Ammi-ili (^{1}*am-mi-*DINGIR) f. of ^{d}*Bēl-iqbî*, desc. of *Ḫanab*, 2:31.

^{d}*Amurru-ušēzib* (^{1d}KUR.GAL-*ú-še-zib*) (586), 274:17.

Ana-^{d}*Innin-taklak* (^{1}*ana-*^{d}INNIN-*tak-lak*) (588), 147:2.

^{d}*Anu-aḫ-ēreš* (^{1d}60.ŠEŠ.KÁM) (521) in KAR.É.AN.NA URU *šá* . . . , 299:19 and 287:19.

^{d}*Anu-aḫ-iddin* (^{1d}*a-num-*ŠEŠ.MU) f. of ^{d}*Marduk-šum-uṣur*, 29:2.

^{d}*Anu-apla-iddin* (^{1d}*a-nu-*DUMU.UŠ.MU) (604) s. of *Ardiya*, desc. of *Kurî*, 302:1.

^{d}*Anu-ēṭir* (^{1d}*a-num*?-SUR) f. of *Arad-*^{d}*Bēl*, desc. of *Iddin-*^{d}*Papsukkal*, 8:5.

^{d}*Anu-ibnî* (^{1d}*a-nu-*DÙ) (605), 126:14.

^{d}*Anu-lē'ī* (^{1d}60.GIŠ.DA) (588) possibly f., 226:3.

^{d}*Anu-šum-ibnî* (^{1d}60.MU.DÙ)
1. (605) desc. of ^{1}[^{d}X-]*ēṭir*, 113:45.
2. f. of ^{d}*Šamaš-uballiṭ*, desc. of ^{h}*Bā'iru*, 286:7.

^{d}*Anu-usippi* (^{1d}*a-num-ú-sip-pi*) (601) s. of ^{d}*Bēl-ibnî*, desc. of ^{h}*Šangû-parakki*, wit., 22:9.

^{d}*Anu-zēr-ušabšî* (^{1d}60.NUMUN.BE) (521) s. of *Marduk*, desc. of *Gimil-*^{d}*Nanâ*, wit.; 35:16 (^{1d}60.NUMUN.GÁL-*ši*); 286:18; 288:15; 290:16; 291:16; 292:16; 293:19; 296:15; and 298:17.

^{d}*Anu-*⸢X.⸣[X.X] (586) s. of ^{d}*Nabû-šum-ibnî*, wit., 25:8.

Apkallu (^{1}NUN.ME)
1. (^{1}*ap-kal-lum*) (603) ^{h}*errešu*, 45:5.
2. (597), 325:25.
3. *a.* of ^{d}*Bēl-iddin*, 301:20.
4. *a.* of ^{d}*Šamaš-šum-uṣur*, 360 i 15 and 19:15.

Aplā (^{1}A-*a*)
1. (603) desc. of ^{h}*Paḫḫāru*, 303:4.
2. (600) s. of *Aḫ-lūmur*, desc. of *Supē-*^{d}*Bēl*, 12:13.
3. (599) s. of *Ubar*, desc. of ^{h}*Šangû-*^{d}*Ninurta*, 276:9.
4. [47](596) ^{h}*ša-ṭabtī-šu*, 312:3.
5. (595) s. of *Dadīa*, 34:9.
6. (595), 26:7.
7. (594) desc. of *Aḫḫēšā*, 320:11, 14.
8. (591) desc. of ^{d}*Bēl-ammeni*, wit., 358:14.
9. (591) desc. of ^{d}*Gula-zēr-ibnî*, br. of *Bulluṭ*, 360 iv 29.
10. (591) desc. of ^{d}*Marduk-šum-ibnî*, 360 v 31.
11. (591), 181:2.
12. (588) s. of ^{d}*Marduk-nāṣir*, desc. of *Nādin-*^{d}*Marduk*, wit., 2:30.
13. (588) desc. of ^{d}*Nabû-šum-*⸢X⸣, 267:5.
14. (588) ^{h}U.MUG, 226:2.
15. (587), 173:4; possibly same man in line 7.
16. [48](586) s. of *Nēšu*, 155:6.
17. (584) s. of *Iqīšā*, desc. of *Irani*, wit., 36:9.
18. (584) s. of *Aḫḫēšā*, 16:2, 5, 7, 11.
19. (583) desc. of ^{d}*Bēl-šar-erība*, 76:7.
20. (583), 76:9.
21. (521), 300:8.
22. f. of ^{d}*Bēl-ibnî*, 41:7.

47. ^{h}*Ša-ṭabtīšu* may possibly belong with *Gimillu*; or may possibly be an ancestral name and not a professional designation.

48. ⸢*ap-*⸣*la-a;* also possible: ⸢*ṣil-*⸣*la-a*.

23. f. of ^{d}*Bēl-rīb*-[X], desc. of *Iddin-*^{d}*Papsukkal*, 27:7.
24. f. of *Eṭir-*^{d}*Bēl*, desc. of *Arrabti*, 38:7; and 33:15.
25. f. of *Gimillu*, 274:16.
26. f. of *Pān-*^{d}*Nabû-adaggal*, 40:5; and 142:16.
27. f. of ^{d}*Innin-šum-ēreš*, desc. of *Kurî*, 336:19; and 338:20.
28. f. of ^{d}*Marduk-mukallim*, desc. of *Balti-*^{d}*Sîn*, 5:16.
29. f. of *Mīnu-īpuš-ilī*, 40:23.
30. f. of *Mušēzib-*^{d}*Bēl*, desc. of *Arrabti*, 6:22 and 360 ii 10.
31. f. of ^{d}*Nabû-lē'ī*, 4:18.
32. f. of ^{d}*Nabû-mukīn-zēr*, desc. of *Ili-bānû*, 20:5; 327:3; 272:2; and 273:2.
33. f. of ^{d}*Nabû-mušētiq-ṣēti*, 176:4.
34. f. of ^{d}*Nabû-šum-iddin*, desc. of *Kurû*, 322:34.
35. f. of *Nadna-aplu*, desc. of *Kurî*, 12:9.
36. f. of *Nadna-aplu*, 24:2.
37. f. of *Silim-*^{d}*Bēl*, 57:2.
38. f. of *Silim-*^{d}*Bēl*, 121:3.
39. f. of ^{d}*Šamaš-marṣa-uṣur*, desc. of *Danni-*^{d}*Adad*, 303:12, 39.
40. f. of *Ṭab-*^{d}*Marduk*, desc. of *Ekur-zākir*, 30:15.
41. *a.* of *Pān-*^{d}*Nabû-adaggal*, 40:5; and 142:16.
42. *a.* of ^{d}*Šamaš-šum-ukīn*, 19:13.

Aplā-banunu (^{1}A-*a-ba-nu-nu*) (593), 328:13.

Appunu (^{1}*ap-pu-nu*) (600) s. of *Nadan-apli*, 115:7.

Aqara (^{1}*a-qar-a*, possibly ^{1}*a-qar*-A)
1. (601) s. of ^{d}*Nabû-lē'ī*, 308:10 (^{1}KAL-*a*) (600); and 314:15.
2. (591), 236:2.
3. (^{1}KAL-*a*) (588), 227:5.
4. [49]*a.* of ^{d}*Nergal-nāṣir*, 159:5 (^{1}KAL-*a*); 193:5; 306:6; and 360 v 35.

Aqriya (^{1}*aq-ri-iá*) (521) s. of ^{d}*Nabû-dala'*, 295:16.

Arad-^{d}*Anu* (^{1}ÌR-^{d}*a-nu*) (521), 300:8.

Arad-^{d}ÁŠ.ŠÚ (582) [s. of] *Balāṭu*, [desc. of] *Arad-*^{d}*Nabû*, 271:4.

Arad-^{d}*Banīti* (^{1}ÌR.^{d}DÙ-*ti*) (593), 343:12.

Arad-^{d}*Bēl* (^{1}ÌR.^{d}EN)
1. (589), 166:3, 9, 11, 12, 13.
2. (522) s. of ^{d}*Anu-ēṭir*, desc. of *Iddin-*^{d}*Papsukkal*, 8:5, 8.

Arad-^{d}*Gula* (^{1}ÌR-^{d}*gu-la*) f. of ^{d}*Nabû-riḫti-uṣur*, 23:3.

Arad-^{d}*Innin* (^{1}ÌR.^{d}INNIN)
1. (598) s. of *Kunā*, wit., 315:9.
2. (588) s. of *Šadunu*, 13:3.
4. (year destroyed), 141:3.

Arad-^{d}*Inninna* (^{1}ÌR.^{d}INNIN-*na*)
1. (605) f.'s name broken, 29:11.
2. (597), 325:7.
3. (594) broken context, 282:2.
4. (590) desc. of ^{d}*Nabû-zēr-ukīn*, 149:4.
5. (588, possibly Nbp., 609) desc. of ^{1}[X-] ^{d}*Nabû*-⌈X.X⌉, 146:27.
6. (588), 233:4.
7. (582) s. of *Rīmūt*, 1:29.
8. f. of *Nā'id-*^{d}*Ištar*, 287:17; and 299:17.
9. *a.* of *Silim-*^{d}*Bēl*, 360 vi 13.
10. a. of ^{d}*Šamaš*-[X] and ^{d}*Bēl-ēṭir*, 145:4.

Arad-^{d}*Inninni* (^{1}ÌR-^{d}*in-nin-ni*)
1. (588) desc. of *Kunā*, 179:3.
2. f. of *Ibnî-*^{d}*Ištar*, 41:5.

Arad-^{d}*Marduk* (^{1}ÌR.^{d}AMAR.UTU)
1. (605), 113:39.
2. (605) desc. of ^{d}*Marduk-šum-iddin*, 113:46.
3. (586), 55:6.

49. ^{d}*Nergal-nāṣir* s. of *Aqara* appears in *GCCI* 1, 20:4, dated to Nbk. 4.

Arad-^{d}Nabû (^{1}ÌR.^{d}AG)
1. (587) ^{h}*mar šipri ša Pān-^{d}Nabû-lūmur*, 275:13.
2. (585), 188:5.
3. (582), 243:9.
4. f. of *Balāṭu*, 15:13′.
5. *a.* of *^{d}Bēl-aḫ-ušabši*, 224:4.
6. a. of *Arad-^{d}*ÁŠ.ŠÚ and *Balāṭu*, 271:6.

Arad-^{d}Nanā (^{1}ÌR-^{d}*na-na-a*)
1. (591) s. of *^{d}Nabû-šum*-[X.]⸢X⸣, 348:23.
2. (590) ^{h}*nuḫatimmu šá* LÚ.ḪAB. GUD.MEŠ(?), a *šerku*, 362:19.
3. (588) ^{h}*aškappu*, 233:2.
4. (587), 134:5.
5. f. of *Balāṭsu*, 177:3; and 178:3.
6. *a.* of *^{d}Nabû-ušabši*, 39:8.

Arad-^{d}Ninurta (^{1}ÌR.^{d}MAŠ) (586), 152:4.

Arad-^{d}Šamaš (^{1}ÌR.^{d}UTU) (521) s. of *Šulā*, wit., 292:14.

Arad-^{d}⸢X.⸣[X?] (588), 139:5.

Ardā (^{1}ÌR-*a*)
1. (601) s. of *^{d}Nanā-ēreš*, 7:1, 11.
2. (590) ^{h}*atû*, a *šerku*, 362:11.
3. f. of *Iddin-^{d}Nabû*, desc. of *Kidin-^{d}Marduk*, 360 ii 7.
4. [50]f. of *Kudurri* and *Iqīša-^{d}Marduk*, desc. of *Rīmi-^{d}Anu*, 357:18, 19.
5. f. of *^{d}Nanā-ēreš*, 314:5, 13; and 308:12.
6. f. of *^{d}Nanā-ēreš*, 3:18.

Ardaya (^{1}ÌR-*a-a*) f. of *Iqīša-^{d}Marduk* and *^{d}Ea-zēr-iqīša*, 4:4.

Ardiya (^{1}ÌR-*ya*)
1. (587) desc. of *^{d}Nabû-rēma-iškun*, 142:17.
2. (587) desc. of *Šula*, 165:4.
3. (585) desc. of *^{d}Nabû*-⸢X-⸣*ša*, 143:10.
4. (^{1}ÌR-*ya*) (521) s. of *^{d}Šamaš-uballiṭ*, 290:5, 13.
5. (^{1}ÌR-*iá*) (521) desc. of *Šullum*, 300:22.
6. f. of *^{d}Anu-apla-iddin*, desc. of *Kurî*, 302:1.
7. [51]f. of *Kudurri*, desc. of *Rēmānu*, 4:21.
8. f. of *^{d}Nanā-aḫ-iddin*, 296:6.
9. *a.* of *^{d}Nanā-karābi*, 300:27.
10. *a.* of *Silim-^{d}Bēl*, 360 iii 19.

Ardu-eššu (^{1}ÌR-*eš-šu*) (562), 9:13.

Arrab (^{1}*ár-rab*)
1. (600), 157:3.
2. f. of *^{d}Bēl-aḫḫē-iqīša*, 37:16.
3. a. of *Amēl-^{d}Nanā*, 308:8 (*ár-ra-bi*); 314:18; possibly same *a.* as 308:4.
4. a. of *^{d}Nanā-aḫ-iddin*, 308:4 (*ár-ra-bi*); 314:9; possibly same *a.* as 308:8.

Arrabi (^{1}*ár-ra-bi*) (601) s. of *Balāṭsu*, 314:14; and 308:9 (600).
for *Arrabi*, *a.* (308:8) see sub *Arrab* (314:18).
for *Arrabi*, *a.* (308:4) see sub *Arrab* (314:9).

Arrabti (^{1}*ar*/*ár-rab-ti*)
1. a. of *Mušēzib-^{d}Bēl* and *Aplā*, 360 ii 11; and 6:22.
2. a. of *Eṭir-^{d}Bēl* and *Aplā*, 33:15 (*ár-rab-tú*); and 38:7.

Aššur-killanni (^{1}AN.ŠÁR-*ki-la-an-ni*) *a.* of *Kalb*-⸢X-⸣*a-a*, 28:10.

Aššur-māt-tuqqin (^{1}AN.ŠÁR.KUR-*tuq-qin*) (562) s. of *^{d}Nabû'ā*, 9:3.

^{h}*Atkuppu* (LÚ.AD.KID) a. of *Tukulti-^{d}Marduk* and *Zēr-ukīn*, 5:15.

Attabani (^{1}*at-ta-ba-ni*)
1. a. of *Mušēzib-^{d}Bēl* and *Zēr-Bābili*, 8:3.
2. a. of ⸢X.⸣⸢X-⸣^{d}*Marduk* and *Šum-ukīn*, 8:11.

Atû (LÚ.NI.DUḪ)

50. Same as *Ardiya* (^{1}ÌR-*iá*) in 4:21.
51. Same as *Ardā* (^{1}ÌR-*a*) in 357:18, 19.

1. [52]a. of ^{d}*Bēl-aḫḫē-iddin*, 360 iv 23.
2. *a.* of ^{d}*Nabû-aḫḫē-[iddin]*, 136:4.
Ayarum (^{1}*a-a-ru-um*) *a.* of *Eanna-riṣua*, 142:9.
A[X.X], f. of *Kudurri*, desc. of *Epeš-ili*, 360 iii 2.

Ba?-⌈ar?-⌉[X] (601) s. of *Nadna-aplu*, desc. of ^{h}*Šangû-parakki*, wit., 22:12.
Baba (^{1}*ba-ba*) in GN (588), 31:15.
Babilaya (^{1}TIN.TIR.KI-*a-a*) (588, possibly Nbp., 609) desc. of ^{d}*Nanā-ēreš*, 146:6.
Babiya (^{1}*ba-bi-iá*)
1. (596) s. of ^{d}*Nabû-zēr-ukīn*, desc. of *Dūr-*^{d}*Marduk*, 322:32.
2. (582), 180:9.
3. f. of ^{d}*Nergal-ušallim*, 55:9.
Babūtti (^{1}*ba-bu-ut-ti*) a. of *Nādin* and *Marduk*, 323:14; and 361:15 (^{1}*ba-bu-tú*).
Babutu (^{1}*ba-bu-tu*) a. of *Šamaš-mukīn-apli* and *Šangû-nādin-šum*, 286:18.
^{h}*Bā'iru* (LÚ ŠU.KU$_{6}$)
1. a. of ^{d}*Nabû-zēr-ukīn* and ^{d}*Ea-zēr-iqīša*, 22:11.
2. a. of ^{d}*Šamaš-uballiṭ* and ^{d}*Anu-šum-ibnî*; ^{d}*Šamaš-zēr-iddin* and ^{d}*Ištar-aḫ-iddin*, 286:6 and 7.
3. a., (son's name broken) and of *Tabnēa*, 6:18.
Balaṭ (^{1}*ba-laṭ*)
1. (604), 52:8.
2. f. of ^{d}*Nergal-uballiṭ*, 306:3.
3. *a.* of ⌈X.X-⌉*ṣi-gil*(?), 52:10.
Balāṭsu (^{1}*ba-laṭ-su* or ^{1}TIN-*su*)
1. (603) s. of ^{d}*Nabû-zēr-iddin*, 195:5.
2. (after 599) desc. of ^{d}*Nabû-karābi*, 87:13.
3. (598) desc. of [^{d}X-]*ēpuš*, 172:4.
4. (594) desc. of *Arad-*^{d}*Nanā*, 177:3 (583); 178:3.
5. (594) desc. of ^{d}*Bēl-ēṭir*, 320:5.
6. (594), 10:8.
7. (591) desc. of *Bēlā*, 20:12.
8. (588) s. of ^{d}*Bēl-aḫḫē-iddin*, 15:11′.
9. (588, possibly Nbp., 609), 146:33.
10. (586), 42:5; possibly same as line 6, desc. of ^{d}*Nabû-zēr-iddin*.
11. f. of *Arrabi*, 308:9; and 314:14.
12. f. of ^{d}*Bēl-aḫḫē-erība*, 11:2; and 358:2.
13. f. of *Gimillu*, ^{h}*bā'iru*, 4:22.
14. f. of *Mušēzib-*^{d}*Bēl*, desc. of *Amēl-*^{d}*Ea*, 302:10.
15. f. of *Nādin*, desc. of *Sukallē*(?), 26:13.
16. f. of ^{d}*Nanā-ēreš*, 322:35.
17. *a.* of *Gimillu*, 159:11.
Balāṭu (^{1}*ba-la-ṭu*)
1. (605), 126:23.
2. (599), 276:2.
3. (595) s. of *Šumā*, desc. of *Iddin-*^{d}*Papsukkal*, wit., 26:11; 32:13 (586); 33:12 (586).
4. (593) s. of *Šumā*, 351:5.
5. (592) desc. of *Kudurri*, 84:1.
6. [53](592) s. of *Šumā*, desc. of *Iddin-*^{d}*Nergal*, 323:12.
7. (592), 128:2.
8. (589), 166:6.
9. (588) s. of *Arad-*^{d}*Nabû*, scribe, 15:13′.
10. (585) desc. of ^{d}*Bēl-ēpuš*, 163:3.
11. (585) desc. of *Imbā*, 53:8.
12. (^{1}TIN) (521) s. of *Ṣillā*, wit., 291:15.
13. f. of *Arad-*^{d}ÁŠ.ŠÚ, desc. of *Arad-*^{d}*Nabû*, 271:5.

52. Possibly same *a.* as in 324:2 (*a.* of ^{d}*Nabû-aḫḫē-iddin*) and 360 iv 34 (*a.* of ^{d}*Nabû-aḫḫē-iddin*).
53. Possibly the same man as 33:12; ancestor there: *Iddin-*^{d}*Papsukkal*. There is no evidence (cf. *Wörterbuch der Mythologie*, pp. 109, 118), that ^{d}*Nergal* = ^{d}*Papsukkal*. Yet it remains tempting because the man in 323:13 is definitely the same as the one in 33:13 (^{d}*Šamaš-zēr-iqîša*).

14. f. of ^{d}*Marduk-šapik-zēr*, desc. of *Miṣir*, 294:15.
15. f. of ^{d}*Marduk-šum-uṣur*, 31:1.
16. f. of ^{d}*Nusku-nāṣir*, 28:12.
17. f. of *Rīmūt*, 124:3.
18. f. of *Tabnēa*, 65:3.
19. *a.* of ^{d}*Nabû-ēṭir*, 363:4.
20. *a.* of ^{d}*Nabû-muk-ki-e-lip*, 39:6.
21. *a.* of *Nādin*, scribe, 358:17.
22. *a.* of *Zēriya*, 108:4.
23. *a.* of *Zēriya*, 360 ii 6.

Balti-^{d}*Sîn* (^{1}TÉŠ.^{d}ŠEŠ.KI) a. of ^{d}*Marduk-mukallim* and *Aplā*, 5:17.

Balṭiya (^{1}*bal-ṭi-ya*)
1. (591) desc. of *Aḫ-rāmu*, 358:1, 4, 6.
2. *a.* of *Lāqīpi*, 77:3.

Baniya[54]
1. (^{1}*ba-ni-ia*) (594) desc. of ^{d}*Bēl-rē'ī*, 320:6.
2. (^{1}DÙ-*ia*) (521), 300:36.
3. (^{1}DÙ-*ia*) *a.* of *Ḫaḫḫuru*, 300:24.

Banitušu (^{1}DÙ-*tu-šú*)
1. (597) desc. of *Amēl-*^{d}*Nanā*, 316:4.
2. (593) s. of ^{d}*Šamaš-ēreš*, 41:8.

^{f}*Banunatum* (SAL *ba-nu-na-tum*) (583), 209:12.

Banunu (^{1}*ba-nu-nu*) (year destroyed) s. of ^{d}*Nergal-ušallim*, desc. of ^{d}*Sîn-tabnî*, wit., 14:15.

Bariḫi-ili (^{1}*ba-ri-ḫi*-DINGIR) a. of ^{d}*Nabû-mukīn-*[*apli*] and ^{d}*Nabû-*[X.X], 27:11.

Barsipayu (LÚ BÁR.SÍP.KI) *a.* of ^{d}*Bēl-lē'ī*, 201:2.

Basiya
1. (^{1}*ba-si-iá*) (521) desc. of *Liširu*, 300:16.
2. (^{1}*ba-si-ya*) a. of ^{d}*Šamaš-iddin* and *Kāṣir*, 298:6.

^{d}*Bau-iqīša*
1. (^{1d}*ba-ú-*BA-*šá*) (588) s. of *Pir'u*, 13:13.
2. (^{1d}KÁ.⸢BA?-⸣[*šá*?]) (585) *a.*'s name broken, ^{h}*mar šipri ša amēli ša pān ekalli*, 231:9.

Bazulim (?) (^{1}⸢*ba-zu-lim*⸣) f. of ^{d}*Bēl-ušallim*, 41:12.

⸢*Ba*-X.⸣[X] (605), 113:30.

Ba-[X.X.X] (year broken), 117:4′.

^{d}*Bēl-aḫ-iddin* (^{1d}EN.ŠEŠ.MU)
1. (595) s. of *Šullumu*, wit., 34:7.
2. (584) s. of ^{d}*Bunene-ibnî*, desc. of ^{h}*Naggāru*, scribe, 36:12.
3. f. of ^{d}*Bēl-zēr*, desc. of ^{h}*Šangû-*^{d}*Innin-Bābili*, 276:7.
4. f. of *Rīmūt*, 245:4.
5. f. of *Rīmūt*, 54:10.
6. f. of *Zēriya*, 270:3.
7. *a.* of ^{d}*Nabû-šum-iddin*, 40:19.
8. *a.* of ^{d}*Šamaš-zēr-iqīša*, 119:3.
9. a. of *Ibnî-*^{d}*Innin*, 42:4.

^{d}*Bēl-aḫ-ušabši* (^{1d}EN.ŠEŠ.⸢GAL-*ši*⸣) (586) desc. of *Arad-*^{d}*Nabû*, 224:3.

^{d}*Bēl-aḫ-*[X] (^{1d}EN.ŠEŠ.[X]) (601) desc. of *Mudammiq-māti*, br. of ^{d}*Marduk-zēr-ibnî*, 75:4.

^{d}*Bēl-aḫḫē-erība* (^{1d}EN.ŠEŠ.MEŠ/ME.SU)
1. (604) s. of *Balāṭsu*, ^{h}*rab būlu*, 11:1, 9; 358:2, 4 (591).
2. (594) s. of *Šāpik*, 340:5.
3. (591) s. of ^{d}*Nabû-ušēzib*, desc. of ^{h}*Šangû-*⸢X.X⸣, 348:21.
4. (587) desc. of *Ḫabil-kīnu*, 142:14.
5. (587) desc. of *Šarranu*, 60:3.
6. (583) desc. of *Zērūtu*, 196:3.
7. f. of *Amēl-*^{d}*Nabû*, 322:38.
8. f. of ^{d}*Nabû-aḫḫē-iddin*, 5:4.
9. f. of ^{d}*Nabû-šum-iddin*, desc. of *Sippē*, 303:35.

54. Sp. ^{1}DÙ-*iá* are read *Baniya* (cp. ^{1}*ba-ni-ia*); sp. ^{1}DÙ-*a* are read *Ibnā* (cp. ^{1}*ib-na-a*); sp. ^{1}DÙ.DN are read *Ibnî*-DN (cp. *ib-ni-*^{d}*iš-tar*).

10. (^{1d}EN.PAB.ME.SU) *a.* of ^{d}*Nabû-šar-aḫḫēšu*, 314:8; 308:2.
11. *a.* of *Nadna-aplu*, 143:4.

^{d}*Bēl-aḫḫē-iddin* (^{1d}EN.ŠEŠ.MEŠ.MU)
1. (603) s. of *Ilī-bānî*, desc. of ^{h}*Rē'ī-sisē*, 303:6, 13.
2. (597) s. of *Marduku*, 317:3.
3. (591) desc. of ^{h}*Atû*, 360 iv 23.
4. f. of *Balāṭsu*, 15:12′.
5. f. of ^{d}*Innin-šum-uṣur*, desc. of ^{h}*Šangû-*^{d}*Innin-Bābili*, scribe, 357:20.
6. *a.* of ⌜*Šākin-*⌝*šum*, 193:5, 9; 360 iii 41′.

^{d}*Bēl-aḫḫē-iqīša* (^{1d}EN.ŠEŠ.ME.BA-*šá*)
1. (600) s. of *Tabnēa*, 115:9.
2. (521) s. of *Arrab*, 37:16.

^{d}*Bēl-ammeni* (^{1d}EN-*am-me-ni*) a. of *Aplā*, wit., 358:14.

^{d}*Bēl-apla-uṣur* (^{1d}EN.A.URÙ) a., descs.' names broken, 6:17.

^{d}*Bēl-banû* (^{1d}EN.DÙ): Read ^{d}*Bēl-ibnî*, q.v.

^{d}*Bēl-bulliṭanni* (^{1d}EN.TIN-*an-ni*) *a.* of *Eṭir-*^{d}*Bēl*, 230:3.

^{d}*Bēl-ēpuš* (^{1d}EN.DÙ-*uš*)
1. (599) desc. of ⌜X.X-⌝*ši*, 310:7.
2. (593) s. of *Bulluṭa*, 41:4.
3. (592) desc. of *Bulluṭa*, 354:1.
4. (584), 40:20.
5. (year destroyed), 205:3.
6. f. of ^{d}*Nabû-tabnî-uṣur*, desc. of ^{d}*Sîn-tabnî*; scribe; 359:14.
7. *a.* of *Balāṭu*, 163:4.

^{d}*Bēl-ēreš* (^{1d}EN.KÁM)
1. (604) s. of *Kunā*, desc. of *Ekur-zākir*, 11:11.
2. (593) desc. of *Ḫašdiya*, 355:3.
3. f. of ^{d}*Marduk-šum-ibnî*, 311:4.
4. (^{1d}EN.PIN-*eš*) f. of ^{d}*Nabû-ušallim*, desc. of [*Taqīš-*]^{d}*Gula*, 14:3.
5. f. of *Nādin*, 54:7.
6. f. of *Zēriya* and ^{d}*Nabû-aḫḫē-iddin*, 294:6.
7. *a.* of *Nādin*, 53:4.

^{d}*Bēl-erība* (^{1d}EN.SU) (582) s. of ^{d}*Nanā-uṣalli*, h. of ^{f}*Bēlitsunu*, 1:1, 9, 12, 15.

^{d}*Bēl-ēṭir* (^{1d}EN.SUR)
1. (594) s. of ^{d}*Bēl-usat*, desc. of *Gaḫal*, 340:11.
2. (585) a.'s name broken, 231:8.
3. (584), 16:6.
4. in GN: *bitqu ša* . . . (521); 293:22; 294:19; 295:19; 296:18; 297:19; 298:21.
5. f. of *Mukīn-zēr*, desc. of ^{h}*Šangû-*^{d}*Adad*, 361:13.
6. f. of ^{d}*Šamaš-*[X], desc. of *Arad-*^{d}*Inninna*, 145:4.
7. *a.* of *Balāṭsu*, 320:5.

^{d}*Bēl-ēṭir-napšāti* (^{1d}EN.SUR.ZI.ME) (605), 113:47.

^{d}*Bēl-ibnî*[55] (^{1d}EN.DÙ)
1. (601) s. of *Kudurri*, desc. of *Kurî*, br. of *Ibnî-*^{d}*Ištar* (line 32), wit., 3:30.
2. (600) f.'s name broken, 115:1.
3. (594) br. of ^{d}*Nergal-ašared*, s. of ^{d}*Nabû-iqbî*, desc. of *Ili-banû*, 327:4.
4. (594) s. of ^{d}*Nabû-zēr-ibnî*, 333:3.
5. (593) s. of *Aplā*, 41:7.
6. (591) s. of ^{d}*Bēl-iddina*, 18:9.
7. (587) ^{h}*mar-šipri ša Mušallim-*^{d}*Marduk*, 111:2.
8. (585) s. of ^{d}*Nabû-ušēzib*, 24:7.
9. f. of ^{d}*Anu-usippi*, desc. of ^{h}*Šangû-parakki*, 22:10.
10. f. of *Bēlšunu*, 30:17.
11. f. of ^{d}*Nergal-ušallim*, 14:18.
12. f. of ^{d}*Šamaš-aḫḫē-erība*, 288:6.
13. *a.* of ^{d}*Ininna-zēr-ušabši*, 259:6.
14. *a.* of *Kiribtu*, 71:7.

55. This reading is to be preferred over ^{d}*Bēl-banû* since Tallqvist has a reading ^{1d}EN-*ib-ni* (RPD reads ^{d}*Bēl-ibnî*, too).

15. *a.* of ^{d}*Nabû-ušabši*, 146:39.

^{d}*Bēl-ibnî*-[X] (^{1d}EN.DÙ.[X]) (582), 206:8.

^{d}*Bēl-iddin* (^{1d}EN.MU)
1. (605) desc. of ^{d}*Sîn-iddin*, 126:18.
2. (604) s. of ^{d}*Sîn-ēreš*, desc. of *Ibnî-ilī*, 302:9.
3. (604) s. of ^{d}*Marduk-aḫ-iddin*, 62:7.
4. (604) desc. of *Apkallu*, ^{h}*išparu*, 301:20.
5. (603) s. of ^{d}*Nabû-iddin*, scribe, 30:19.
6. (594) s. of *Rāši-ili*, desc. of *Kudurānu*, wit., 336:13 and 338:14.
7. (594) s. of ^{d}*Nabû-zēr-iddin*, wit., 336:18 and 338:19.
8. (582), 180:12.
9. (521) desc. of *Ḫašdiya*, 300:7.
10. f. of ^{d}*Bēl-šum-iškun*, desc. of *Kurî*, 357:6.
11. f. of ^{f}*Bēlitsunu*, 1:3.
12. f. of *Nadna-aplu*, 30:18.
13. f. of *Šum-iddin*, 41:11.
14. f. of *Šum-uṣur*, 1:26.

^{d}*Bēl-iddina* (^{1d}EN.SUM-*na*)
1. f. of ^{d}*Bēl-ibnî*, 18:10.
2. f. of *Nadna-aḫ*, 348:24.

^{d}*Bēl-iqbî* (^{1d}EN-*iq-bi*)
1. (591) desc. of ^{d}*Šamaš-uballiṭ*, wit., 358:16.
2. (590) ^{h}*išparu*, a *šerku*, 362:4, 28.
3. (588) s. of *Ammi-ili*, desc. of *Ḫanab*, wit., 2:31.

^{d}*Bēl-iqīša* (^{1d}EN.BA-*šá*) *a.* of *Kinā*, 300:13.

^{d}*Bēl-kuṣuranni* (^{1d}EN-*ku-ṣur-an-ni*) (595), 318:2.

^{d}*Bēl-lē'i* (^{1d}EN.DA)
1. (599) desc. of *Barsipayu*, 201:1.
2. (592), 105:4.
3. (582), 180:17.
4. f. of *Mukīn-zēr*, desc. of *Šumāti*, 13:12.
5. f. of ^{d}*Nabû-ēṭir-napšāti*, desc. of *Šigua*, 7:13; 323:11.
6. *a.* of ^{d}*Nanā-iddin*, 40:4.
7. *a.* of ^{d}*Nergal-uballiṭ*, 187:9.

^{d}*Bēl-nādin-apli*
1. (^{1d}EN-*na-din*-A) (588) f.'s name destroyed, ^{h}*errēšu*, 44:9.
2. (^{1d}EN-*na-din*-DUMU.UŠ) (586) s. of *Iddin*-^{d}*Marduk*, desc. of *Nūr*-^{d}*Sîn*, 32:12.

^{d}*Bēl-nāṣir* (^{1d}EN.PAB)
1. (590), 43:6.
2. f. of *Iddin*-^{d}*Marduk*, desc. of ^{h}*Nappāḫu*, 11:3.
3. f. of *Kudurri*, 253:4.
4. f. of *Mušallim*-^{d}*Marduk*, 31:5.
5. (^{1d}EN-*na-ṣir*) *a.* of ^{d}*Nergal-ušallim*, 107:4.

^{d}*Bēl-nibšari* (^{1d}EN-*ni-ib-šá-ri*) f. of ^{d}[X-]*ušallim*, a.'s name broken, 20:3.

^{d}*Bēl-nuḫšu* (^{1d}EN-*nu-uḫ-šú*) *a.* of ^{d}*Nanā-aḫ-iddin*, 241:2.

^{d}*Bēl-rē'ī* (^{1d}EN.⌈SIPA⌉) *a.* of *Baniya*, 320:6.

^{d}*Bēl-rīb*-[X] (^{1d}EN-*ri-ib*-[X]) (589) s. of *Aplā*, desc. of *Iddin*-^{d}*Papsukkal*, wit., 27:6.

^{d}*Bēl-šar-erība* (^{1d}EN.MAN.SU) *a.* of *Aplā*, 76:7.

^{d}*Bēl-šar-uṣur* (^{1d}EN.LUGAL.URÙ) f. of *Mušēzib*-^{d}*Bēl*, 5:15.

^{d}*Bēl-šum-iškun* (^{1d}EN.MU.GAR-*un*)
1. (603), 74:9.
2. (598), 172:6.
3. (592) s. of ^{d}*Bēl-iddin*, desc. of *Kurî*, ^{h}*šakin-ṭēmi Uruk*, 357:5.
4. (591) f.'s name broken, wit., 21:10.
5. [56](584) s. of ^{d}*Nabû-pir-la'*, 242:3.
6. f. of ^{d}*Marduk-ēṭir*, desc. of *Dabibi*,

56. See "Royal Women," pp. 451ff.

ʰṭupšar Eanna, 7:18; 201:4 (only f. listed); and 309:5 (only f. listed).
   7. f. of ᵈMarduk-nāṣir, desc. of Dabibi, 315:1.

ᵈBēl-tabnī-il (⌈ᴵᵈEN?-⌉tab-ni-il) a. of Ša-ᵈNabû-šū, 39:4.

ᵈBēl-uballiṭ (ᴵᵈEN.TIN-iṭ)
   1. (598) a.'s name broken, 172:5.
   2. (590) master of Rikis-kalamma-ᵈBēl, 215:4.
   3. (582) desc. of Buṣu, 216:4 (year destroyed); and 234:5.
   4. f. of ᵈNabû-erība, desc. of ʰRabbānû, 38:8.
   5. f. of Tabnēa, desc. of Ibnî-ᵈSîn, 32:3.
   6. a. of Labāši, 40:11.
   7. a. of ᵈNergal-ušēzib, 149:2.

ᵈBēl-udūa (ᴵᵈEN-ú-du-ú-a) (591), 348:10.

ᵈBēl-ukīn⁵⁷ (ᴵᵈEN.GUB) f. of ᵈ[X-]gāmil, 155:5.

ᵈBēl-upaḫḫir (ᴵᵈEN.NIGIN-ir)
   1. ⁵⁸(591) s. of Rīmūt, ʰnappāḫu, 266:2.
   2. (588) ʰpaḫḫāru, 133:2; and 353:2 (592).
   3. ⁵⁸(587?) ʰnappāḫu, 265:4.
   4. f. of ᵈBēl-zēr-ibnî, desc. of Nanaḫu, 36:11.
   5. f. of ᵈNabû-apla-iddin, 315:10.

ᵈBēl-usat (ᴵᵈEN-ú-sat)
   1. f. of ᵈBēl-ēṭir, desc. of Gaḫal, 340:12.
   2. f. of Gimillu, desc. of Ekur-zākir, 11:13.
   3. f. of Nadna-aplu, 41:10.
   4. a. of ᵈMarduk-šum-līšir and Rīmūt, 6:23.

ᵈBēl-ušallim (ᴵᵈEN.GI)
   1. (605) s. of ᴵ[X.]⌈X.X-⌉zēr, 29:12.
   2. (604) s. of ᵈNabû-šar-uṣur, 50:5.
   3. (602) s. of Šāpik, desc. of ᵈŠamaš-⌈X.X⌉, scribe, 17:15.

   4. (593) s. of Bazulim(?), 41:12.
   5. (589) s. of Ezū-pāšir, wit., 359:9.
   6. (587) s. of Aḫḫē-⌈X⌉, 23:4.
   7. f. of ᵈMarduk-šum-līšir, desc. of Mušituq, 4:17.
   8. f. of ᵈNabû-balāṭsu-iqbî, 183:5.
   9. f. of ᵈNabû-lē'î, desc. of ⌈ᵈNergal-līšir⌉, 154:3.
   10. f. of ᵈŠamaš-zēr-iqīša, desc. of Kurî, 33:14; and 323:13.
   11. a., desc.'s name broken, 118:2.

ᵈBēl-ušēzib (ᴵᵈEN-ú-še-zib) (588) desc. of ᵈNabû-ēreš, 44:7.

ᵈBēl-zēr-ibnî (ᴵᵈEN.NUMUN.DÙ) (584) s. of ᵈBēl-upaḫḫir, desc. of Nanaḫu, 36:10.

ᵈBēl-zēr-iddin (ᴵᵈEN.NUMUN.MU) a. of Mušēzib, 8:12.

ᵈBēl-zēr-uṣur (ᴵᵈEN.NUMUN.PAB) (521) s. of Ṣillā, wit., 37:15.

ᵈBēl-zēr (ᴵᵈEN.NUMUN)
   1. (599) s. of ᵈBēl-aḫ-iddin, desc. of ʰŠangû-ᵈInnin-Bābili, 276:7.
   2. f. of Šum-ukīn, 23:12.

ᵈBēl-⌈X.X⌉ (601) s. of ᴵ⌈X.X⌉⌈X-⌉zēr, desc. of Ekur-zākir, wit., 22:13.

ᵈBēl-[X.X], f. of Ṣillā, 23:10.

ᵈBēl-[X.X] (587) desc. of ᴵ⌈X.X⌉⌈X.⌉GI, 142:21.

Bēlā (ᴵEN-a-a) a. of Balāṭsu, 20:13.

ᶠBēlitsunu (SAL be-lit-su-nu) (582) daughter of ᵈBēl-iddin, w. of ᵈBēl-erība, 1:2, 9, 12, 15.

Bēliya (ᴵEN-ia) f. of ᵈNabû-šum-iddin, 30:1.

Bēlšunu (ᴵEN-šú-nu)
   1. (605), 113:58.
   2. (603) s. of ᵈBēl-ibnî, 30:17.
   3. (603) s. of ᵈNabû-[X.X], ʰerrēšu, 45:8.
   4. (600) f.'s name broken, 115:15.

---

57. Reading of PN unsure.
58. Possibly same man.

5. (590), 369:3.
6. (587) s. of *Ša-^{d}Nabû-šū*, 220:2.
7. (586) s. of *Lū-aḫūa*, ^{h}*rē'ī ša* ^{d}*Bēlit ša Uruk*, 32:1, 5.
8. (599[+X]) desc. of *Zēr-ukīn*, 51:2.
9. f. of ^{d}*Marduk-šum-uṣur*, desc. of *Kurî*, 26:12.

Bibea (^{1}*bi-bi-e-a*) (589), 86:4.

Būdi-īli (^{1}*bu-*⌈*di-*DINGIR⌉) (586), 152:2.

Bulluṭ (^{1}*bul-luṭ*) (591) s. of ^{d}*Gula-zēr-ibnî*, br. of *Aplā*, 360 iv 29.

Bulluṭa (^{1}*bul-luṭ-a*)
1. [59](589) desc. of ^{d}*Nanā-ibnî*, 68:3.
2. (521) ⌈desc. of?⌉ ^{d}*Nabû-nāṣir*, 37:5.
3. f. of ^{d}*Bēl-ēpuš*, 41:4.
4. f. of ^{d}*Nabû-erība*, 41:6.
5. f. of *Zērūtu*, 41:3.
6. *a.* of ^{d}*Bēl-ēpuš*, 354:2.
7. [60]*a.* of *Ibāššî-ili*, 91:5.
8. *a.* of ^{d}*Nabû-zēr-ibnî*, 326:5.

Bulta[X?] (^{1}*bul-ta*[X?]) in GN ^{a1}*Asurritum ša* . . . , (521), 37:2.

^{d}*Bunene-ibnî* (^{1d}*bu-ne-ne-*DÙ) f. of ^{d}*Bēl-aḫ-iddin*, desc. of ^{h}*Naggāru*, scribe, 36:13.

^{d}*Bunene-kibsu-ab-uṣur* (^{1d}*bu-nin-ni-kib-su-*AD*-ú-ṣur*) (year broken) ^{h}*qalla ša* ^{d}*Nabû-ušallim*, 14:7.

^{f}*Burāšu* (SAL *bu-ra-šu*) (521) wife of *Aḫ-iddin*, 300:17.

Buṣu (^{1}*bu-ṣu*) *a.* of ^{d}*Bēl-uballiṭ*, 216:5; and 234:5.

Dabibi (^{1}*da-bi-bi*)
1. a. of *Kabti-ili-^{d}Marduk*, and ^{d}*Nergal-šum-uṣur*, 5:13.
2. a. of ^{d}*Marduk-ēṭir*, and ^{d}*Bēl-šum-iškun*, 7:19.
3. a. of ^{d}*Marduk-nāṣir*, and ^{d}*Bēl-šum-iškun*, 315:2.
4. a. of ^{d}*Marduk-šum-ibnî*, and *Zēriya*, 18:12.
5. a. of ^{d}*Nabû-mīta-uballiṭ*, and *Nadna-aplu*, 18:2.
6. a. of ^{d}*Nabû-*[X.X.X.X.X.X], and *Nadna-aplu*, 28:2.

Dadīa (^{1}*da-di-ía*) f. of *Aplā*, 34:10.

Dan-ilī (^{1}*da-an-*DINGIR.MEŠ) (562), 9:10.

Danni-^{d}Adad (^{1}KAL.^{d}IŠKUR) a. of ^{d}*Šamaš-marṣa-uṣur*, and *Aplā*, 303:12, 22, 39.

Danni-^{d}Nergal
1. (^{1}KAL.^{d}U.GUR) (604) s. of *Erišu*, 160:4.
2. (^{1}*dan-ni-*^{d}U.GUR) f. of *Isinnaya*, 72:3; and 98:3 (^{1}*dan-nu-*^{d}U.GUR).

Diḫaum (^{1}⌈*di-*⌉*ḫa-um*) (594) ^{h}*rab-qanāta*, 320:1.

Dūr-^{d}Marduk (^{1}BÀD.^{d}AMAR.UTU) a. of *Babiya*, and ^{d}*Nabû-zēr-ukīn*, 322:32.

Dūru-ṣīru-^{d}Marduk (^{1}BAD.MAḪ.^{d}AMAR.UTU) (593) desc. of *Kudurri*, ^{h}*rē'ī satukki*, 78:2 (592) no *a.* listed; 84:8 (592); 101:2 (583); 342:3.

^{d}*Ea-bēl-ilī* (^{1d}*é-a-*EN.DINGIR.MEŠ) f. of *Tabnēa*, 18:8.

^{d}*Ea-ilūtu-bāni* (^{1d}BE.DINGIR*-tu-*DÙ) a. of ^{d}*Nabû-šum-iškun* and *Puḫḫuru*, 5:2.

^{d}*Ea-iqbî*[61] (^{1d}BE*-iq-bi*) (587) ^{h}*Šangû Bābili*, 127:2.

^{d}*Ea-šum-ibnî* (^{1d}BE.MU.DÙ) f. of ^{d}*Nergal-tēšī-ēṭir*, desc. of ^{h}*Šangû-parakki*, 17:4.

^{d}*Ea-šum-*[X] (^{1d}BE.⌈MU.⌉[X]) f. of ^{d}*Nabû-*[X.X], desc. of *Amēl-^{d}Ea*, 154:5.

^{d}*Ea-ukīn* (^{1d}BE.GUB) *a.* of ^{d}*Šamaš-uballiṭ*, 146:16.

59. Possibly same man as *GCCI* 1, 3:6 (year 1; same *a.*;) text deals with animal hides.
60. [A ^{1}*bul-*]*luṭ-a*; also possible: [A ^{1}*mar-*]*duk-a*.
61. For ^{d}BE = ^{d}*Ea*, see *TuM* 2–3, 185:7 and 8.

^{d}*Ea-zēr-iqīša* (^{1d}BE.NUMUN.BA-*šá*)
1. (603) s. of *Šulā*, 30:13.
2. (589) s. of *Ardaya*, br. of *Iqīša-*^{d}*Marduk*, 4:4, 9.
3. f. of ^{d}*Nabû-zēr-ukīn*, desc. of ^{h}*Bā'iru*, 22:11.
4. *a.* of ^{d}*Nabû-ušdu-uṣur*, 142:13.

Eanna-līpi-uṣur (^{1}É.AN.NA-*li-pi*-PAB)
1. (601) s. of *Rīmūt*, desc. of ^{d}*Sîn-lēq-unnini*, 122:6 (no a. listed); 319:14 (596); 350:5 (^{1}É.AN.NA-*li-i-pi*-PAB) (no a. listed) (593).
2. (592) ^{h}*aškappu*, 64:3.

Eanna-rišua (^{1}É.AN.NA-*ri-ṣu-ú-a*) (587) desc. of *Ayarum*, 142:8.

Eanna-šar-uṣur (^{1}É.AN.NA.LUGAL.URÙ) (587) *mār šarri*, 142:19.

Eanna-šum-ibnî (^{1}É.AN.NA.MU.DÙ) f. of *Pir'u*, 302:12.

Eanna-šum-lišir (^{1}É.AN.NA.MU.GIŠ) (582), 180:11.

Eda-ēṭir (^{1}AŠ.SUR) *a.* of ^{d}*Nabû-bēl-šumāti*, 360 iv 29.

Egibi (^{1}*e-gi-bi*)
1. a. of ^{d}*Marduk-ēṭir*, and ^{d}*Nabû-aḫḫē-iddin*, 360 v 48.
2. a. of ^{d}*Nabû-balāṭsu-iqbî*, and *Iqīša-*^{d}*Marduk*, 4:24.
3. a. of [^{1d}X-]*aḫḫē-iqīša*, and *Eṭir-*^{d}*Marduk*, 6:21.

Ekur-zākir (^{1}É.KUR-*za-kir*)
1. a. of ^{d}*Bēl-ēreš*, and *Kunā*, 11:12.
2. a. of ^{d}*Bēl-*⌈X.X⌉, and [X.X]⌈X-⌉*zēr*, 22:13.
3. a. of *Gimillu*, and ^{d}*Bēl-usat*, 11:14.
4. a. of ^{d}*Nabû-bānî-aḫ*, and *Ibnā*, 33:17, and 38:11.
5. a. of ^{d}*Nabû-ēṭir-napšāti*, and *Šum-ukīn*, 2:39.
6. a. of ^{d}*Nabû-udammiq* and ^{d}*Nabû-zēr-ukīn*, 7:17.
7. a. of ^{d}*Nergal-ina-tēšî-ēṭir* and ^{d}*Nabû-iddin*, 11:18.
8. a. of (broken) and *Ḫašdia*, 17:14.

^{d}*Enlil-aḫḫē-iddin* (^{1d}50.PAB.MEŠ.MU) (594) desc. of ^{d}*Ninurta-bānî*, 320:9.

Epeš-ili (^{1}DÙ-*eš*-DINGIR) a. of *Kudurri* and A.[X.X], 360 iii 3.

Erība-^{d}*Marduk* (^{1}SU.^{d}AMAR.UTU)
1. (605), 113:56.
2. (594) desc. of ^{d}*Ninurta-iqīša*, 320:3.

Erībšu (^{1}TU-*šú*) *a.* of ^{d}*Šamaš-*⌈X.⌉A-*iddin*, 142:18.

Eriši (^{1}*eri*[URU-]*ši*) *a.* of ^{d}*Nabû-šum-ēreš*, 363:6; possibly *a.* of ^{d}*Inninna-zēr-ušabši*, (line 7).

Erišu (^{1}*e-ri-šu*) f. of *Danni-*^{d}*Nergal*, 160:5.

Etellu (^{1}*e-tel-lu*$_4$)
1. (587) f.'s name destroyed, 275:6, 19.
2. (583) s. of *Rīmūt*, 19:11.

Etelpi (^{1}*e-tel-pi*) *a.* of *Mukīn-zēr*, 149:1.

Eṭēru (^{1}*e-ṭè-ru*) f. of ^{d}*Marduk-erība*, and *Iddin-*^{d}*Marduk*, 31:9, 11.

Eṭir-^{d}*Bēl* (^{1}KAR.^{d}EN)[61a]
1. (587) ^{h}*nappāḫu*, 264:4.
2. (584) s. of *Aplā*, desc. of *Arrabti*, 38:6; in 33:14 (586) a.'s name spelled *ár-rab-tú*.
3. (584) desc. of ^{d}*Bēl-bulliṭanni*, 230:3.
4. *a.* of ^{d}*Ištar-aḫḫē-uṣur*, 143:3.
5. *a.* of ^{d}*Nabû-šum-iddin*, 360 iv 10.

Eṭir-^{d}*Marduk* (^{1}KAR.^{d}AMAR.UTU)[61b] f. of [^{1d}X-]*aḫḫē-iqīša*, desc. of *Egibi*, 6:21.

Eṭir-⌈X⌉ (^{1}SUR.⌈X⌉) (588), 182:4.

Ezū-pāšir (^{1}*e-zu-*(*u-*)*pa-šir* /*šìr*)
1. f. of ^{d}*Bēl-ušallim*, 359:9.
2. f. of ^{d}*Innin-zēr-ibnî*, 326:8.
3. *a.* of *Nēšu*, 314:7.

Gaḫal (^{1}*ga-ḫal*) a. of ^{d}*Bēl-ēṭir* and ^{d}*Bēl-usat*, 340:12.

^{h}*Gallābu* (LÚ ŠU.I) a. of *Kinā* and *Rāši-ili*, 360 ii 5.

Gilānu (^{1}*gi-la-nu*) in the phrase *ina bīt*

61a. Or: *Mušēzib-*^{d}*Bēl*, *q.v.* (p. 49); cp. #2 here with #4 there.
61b. Or: *Mušēzib-*^{d}*Marduk*.

Gilānu in an *imittu* document (586), 42:8.

Gimil-apli (^{l}ŠU.A) (589?) desc. of ^{d}*Nabû-uballiṭ*, 211:4.

Gimil-^{d}*Gula* (^{l}ŠU-^{d}*gu-la*) (586) s. of ^{d}*Nabû-zēr-ušabši*, scribe, 25:11.

Gimil-^{d}*Nanā* (^{l}ŠU-^{d}*na-na-a*)
1. (595) s. of *Šūzubu*, scribe, 26:16.
2. a. of ^{d}*Anu-zēr-ušabši* and *Marduk*, 35:16; 286:19; 288:15; 290:16; 291:17; 292:16; 293:19; 296:15; 297:16; and 298:18.
3. a. of *Iddin-*^{d}*Nabû* and *Šākin-šum*, 13:16.
4. a. of *Marduk* and *Nadna-aplu*, 336:15; and 338:16.
5. a. of *Mušēzib-*^{d}*Bēl* and ^{d}*Nergal-iddin*, 17:2.
6. a. of ^{d}*Nabû-aḫḫē-ušallim* and *Kalum*, 2:34; 361:18.
7. a. of ^{d}*Nabû-nādin-šum*, KA.LU.MAŠ, and ^{d}*Inninni-šum-uṣur*, 12:12, 15.
8. a. of ^{d}*Nabû-zēr-ukīn* and ^{d}*Nergal-uballiṭ*, 323:15.
9. a. of ^{d}*Nanā-ēpuš* and *Mukīn-zēr*, 2:32.
10. (^{l}*gi-mil-*^{d}*na-na-a*) a. of *Šulā* and *Nādin*, 348:26.

Gimillu (^{l}ŠU)
1. (605) desc. of ^{d}*Nabû-šum-iddin*, 113:44.
2. (604) s. of ^{d}*Bēl-usat*, desc. of *Ekur-zākir*, 11:13.
3. (603) desc. of *Kunā*, 198:6.
4. (598) 321:5.
5. [62](596) desc. of ^{h}*Ša-ṭabtišu*, ^{h}*mar šipri ša Aplā*, 312:2.
6. (591) desc. of *Mukīn-zēr*, 360 v 4.
7. (591) desc. of *Zēriya*, 360 v 25.
8. (591) 181:2.
9. (589) s. of *Balāṭsu*, ^{h}*bā'iru*, wit., 4:21.
10. (588) desc. of *Labāši*, 229:5.
11. (587) desc. of *Balāṭsu*, 159:10.
12. (586) s. of *Aplā*, 274:16.
13. (584) desc. of *Zēriya*, 193:3, 7.
14. [63](521) s. of *Aḫulap-*^{d}*Ištar*, desc. of *Ḫunzû*, 35:14; 286:16 wit.; 287:15; 288:14; 289:14; 290:15; 293:18; 294:16; 295:15; 296:14; 297:14; 298:16; 299:15.
15. [64](521) s. of ^{d}*Inninna-šum-ibni*, ^{h}*ša muḫḫi sūti ša* ^{d}*Bēlit ša Uruk*, 35:4; 37:4; 286:4; 287:4; 288:4; 289:3; 290:4; 291:5; 292:4; 293:6; 294:4; 295:4; 296:4; 297:4; 298:4; 299:5; 300:3.
16. (521), 300:20.
17. f. of ^{d}*Marduk-apla-uṣur*, 24:10.
18. f. of ^{d}*Nanā-ēreš*, 287:16; 288:16; 289:16; 292:15; 299:16.
19. f. of ^{d}*Nergal-ana-bītišu*, 34:9.
20. *a.* of ^{d}*Marduk-zēr-līšir*, 44:6.
21. *a.* of ^{d}*Nabû-nāṣir*, 360 v 19.
22. *a.* of ^{d}*Nergal-ušallim*, 143:5.

Gubbā (^{l}*gub-ba-a*) in GN (586), 152:14, 21.

^{d}*Gula-zēr-ibni*, f. of *Aplā* and *Bulluṭ*, 360 iv 30.

Guzanu (^{l}*gu-za-nu*)
1. (605) ^{h}*naggāru*, 126:23.
2. (605), 126:9, 21.
3. (521) desc. of ^{d}*Marduk-ēṭir*, 300:9, 19.
4. *a.* of *Itti-*^{d}*Šamaš-balāṭu*, 300:30.

Gu-[X.X] (589), 187:3.

62. The ancestral name ^{h}*Ša-ṭabtišu* may belong with *Aplā* or may possibly be a professional designation and not an ancestral name.

63. Same man mentioned in I, 2 δ1659:9 (Pushkin Museum), VII.2. Nbk 1.KÁM.

64. Same man mentioned in I, 2 δ1659:4 (Pushkin Museum).

Ḫabaṣiru (^{1}*ḫa-ba-ṣi-ru*) (605), 113:8.
Ḫabil-kīnu (^{1}*ḫa-bil*-GIN) *a.* of ^{d}*Bēl-aḫḫē-erība*, 142:15.
Ḫab?-bu-nu (605), 153:5.
Ḫaḫḫuru (^{1}*ḫa-aḫ-ḫu-ru*)
1. (590), 144:3.
2. (521) desc. of *Baniya*, 300:24.
Ḫalia (^{1}*ḫa-li-iá*) (585) desc. of *Ibā*, 53:7.
^{f}*Ḫāmmā* (SAL *ḫa-am-ma-a*) (596) daughter of *Ṣillā*, desc. of ^{d}*Nanā-uballiṭ*, 322:11, 15, 19, 25, 44.
Ḫammili-ili (^{1}*ḫa-am-mi-li*-DINGIR) (596) s. of *Iddin-*^{d}*Nabû*, 322:14, 18, 25, 43.
Ḫanab (^{1}*ḫa-nab*) a. of ^{d}*Bēl-iqbî* and *Ammi-ili*, 2:31.
^{f}*Ḫanina'* (SAL *ḫa-ni-na-'*) (562) SAL PA.KAB.D[U-]*ti*, 9:1.
Ḫanunu (^{1}*ḫa-nu-nu*) (592) ^{h}*rē'ū*, 189:6.
Ḫarīṣ (^{1}*ḫa-ri-iṣ*) *a.* of *Nurānu*, 76:10.
Ḫaṣabdu (^{1}*ḫa-ṣab-du*) f. of *Ṣilliya*, 19:4.
Ḫašdā (^{1}*ḫaš-da-a*) (583) desc. of ^{d}*Nabû-ēreš*, 76:6.
Ḫašdiya[65] (^{1}*ḫaš-di-ya*)
1. (602) desc. of *Ekur-zākir*, 17:13.
2. in GN (597), 325:3.
3. (593) s. of *Ḫimmit*, 41:15.
4. (586) s. of ^{d}*Nanā-ēreš*, 155:1.
5. *a.* of ^{d}*Bēl-ēreš*, 355:3.
6. *a.* of ^{d}*Bēl-iddin*, 300:7.
Ḫa-[X.X] (604), 52:9.
Ḫimmit (^{1}*ḫi-im-mit*) f. of *Ḫašdiya*, 41:15.
Ḫišurinīlu (^{1}*ḫi-šu-ri-ni-i-lu*) (562) s. of *Šalammanu-ilī*, 9:12.
⸢*Ḫi*-⸣[X.X.X.X.X] (589), 169:4.
Ḫunzû (^{1}*ḫu-un-zu-ú*)
1. a. of *Gimillu* and *Aḫulap-*^{d}*Ištar*, 35:15; 286:16; 287:15; 288:14; 289:14; 290:15; 293:18; 294:16; 295:15; 296:14; 297:15; 298:17; 299:15.
2. a. of ^{d}*Innin-aḫḫē-iddin* and *Rīmūt*, 26:15.
3. a. of *Kudurri* and *Mukīn-zēr*, 7:12; 319:12.
4. a. of *Šāpiku* and ^{d}*Nabû-zēr-uṣur*, 3:31.
5. a. of ^{d}*Marduk-apla-uṣur* and *Šāpik*, 3:33.

For all *Ia-* names, see *Ya-*.
Ibā (^{1}*i-ba-a*)
1. *a.* of *Ḫalia*, 53:7.
2. *a.* of ^{d}*Nabû-šum-ukīn*, 53:9.
Ibaššî-ili ([^{1}*i-ba-*]⸢*áš*-⸣*ši*-DINGIR) (589) desc. of *Marduka* (also possible: *Bulluṭa*), 91:4.
Ibnā[66] (DÙ-*a*)
1. (601) desc. of *Marduk*, 306:5.
2. (601) s. of ^{d}*Šamaš-iddin*, scribe, 22:14.
3. (599) (^{1}*ib-na-a*) s. of *Marduk*, 201:5.
4. (589) (^{1}*ib-na-a*) ^{h}*ṣāḫitu*, 366:2, 4.
5. (588, possibly Nbp., 609), 146:22.
6. f. of ^{d}*Nabû-bānî-aḫ*, desc. of *Ekur-zākir*, 33:16; 38:10.
7. *a.* of *Amēl-*^{d}*Nanā*, 146:38.
8. *a.* of ^{d}*Inninna-šum-uṣur*, 360 vi 22.
9. *a.* of ^{d}*Nanā-ēreš*, 91:2.
10. *a.* of ^{d}*Nergal-ēreš*, 241:7.
11. *a.* (desc.'s name broken), 360 v 20.
Ibnî-ilī (DÙ.DINGIR.MEŠ) a. of ^{d}*Bēl-iddin* and ^{d}*Sîn-ēreš*, 302:9.
Ibnî-^{d}*Innin* (^{1}DÙ.^{d}INNIN)
1. (597) desc. of ^{d}*Nabû-ēreš*, 325:16.
2. (593) s. of *Mukīn-zēr*, 41:16.
3. (590), 144:2.
4. (587) desc. of *Nadna-aplu*, 142:5.
5. (586) desc. of ^{d}*Bēl-aḫ-iddin*, ^{h}*nukarribu*, 42:4, 5.
Ibnî-^{d}*Ištar* (^{1}*ib-ni-*^{d} *iš-tar* or ^{1}DÙ.^{d}15)
1. (601) s. of *Kudurri*, desc. of *Kurî*,

65. ^{1}*Ḫaš-di-ya* names read: *Ḫašdiya*, not *Tardiya*, cp. *GCCI* 2, 96:1, 6 *Ḫaš-áš-da-a*.
66. Possibly *Ibna-aplu*.

br. of ^{d}*Bēl-ibnî* (l. 30), wit., 3:32.
2. (601) s. of ^{d}*Nabû-zēr-ukīn*, desc. of ^{h}*Pūṣāya*, wit., 3:34.
3. (594) s. of *Iqīšā*, possibly br. of ^{d}*Marduk-nāṣir*, wit., 10:11.
4. (593) (^{1}DÙ-^{d}*iš-tar*) s. of *Arad-*^{d}*Inninni*, 41:5.
5. (587) desc. of ^{d}*Nabû-ušēzib*, 159:9.
6. (587), 173:8.
7. (586) s. of ^{d}*Nabû-zēr-ukīn*, desc. of ^{h}*Šatammu*, scribe, 32:15.
8. f. of *Nadna-aplu*, 295:17; 300:39.

Ibnî-^{d}*Nabû* (^{1}DÙ.^{d}AG)
1. (589) s. of ^{d}*Nabû-ēpuš*, 88:3.
2. (586), 251:3.
3. (582), 243:4.

Ibnî-^{d}*Sîn* (^{1}DÙ.^{d}30) a. of *Tabnēa* and ^{d}*Bēl-uballiṭ*, 32:4.

Iddin-aḫšu (^{1}MU.ŠEŠ-*šu*) (594–576 possible), 106:8.

Iddin-^{d}*Amurru* (^{1}MU.^{d}KUR.GAL) (521), 300:7.

Iddin-^{d}*Bēl* (^{1}MU.^{d}EN) (605), 113:48.

Iddin-ili[67] (*it*/*d*-[*ti*/*din*-]DINGIR) *a.* of *Nadna-aplu*, 227:2.

Iddin-^{d}*Inninna* (^{1}MU.^{d}INNIN-*na*)
1. (591) desc. of ^{d}*Nabû-zēr-iddin*, 194:4.
2. (590) ^{h}*naggāru*, a *šerku*, 362:6, 26.

Iddin-^{d}*Marduk* (^{1}MU.^{d}AMAR.UTU)
1. (604) s. of ^{d}*Bēl-nāṣir*, desc. of ^{h}*Nappāḫu*, 11:3.
2. (588) s. of *Eṭēru*, probably the brother of ^{d}*Marduk-erība* (line 9), 31:11.
3. (584), 40:17.
4. f. of ^{d}*Bēl-nādin-apli*, desc. of *Nūr-*^{d}*Sîn*, 32:12.
5. f. of *Zēriya*, 12:2.

Iddin-^{d}*Nabû* (^{1}MU.^{d}AG)
1. (596) s. of *Šākin-šum*, desc. of *Gimil-*^{d}*Nanā*, scribe, 13:15 (588, Babylon); 337:15 (a. not listed, Uruk).
2. (591) s. of *Arda*, desc. of *Kidin-*^{d}*Marduk*, 360 ii 7.
3. (589) desc. of ^{d}*Nergal-ušallim*, 97:2.
4. (586) s. of ^{d}*Nabû-šum-ēreš*, 25:1.
5. f. of *Ḫammili-ili*, 322:14, 18.
6. *a.* of *Ṭāb-šār-Eanna*, 175:8; 182:8; 188:8.

Iddin-^{d}*Nergal* (^{1}MU.^{d}U.GUR)
1. f. of *Nadna-aplu*, 74:8.
2. f. of *Isinnaya*, 99:6.
3. f. of ^{d}*Nabû-šum-ibnî*, 326:2.
4. a. of *Balāṭu* and *Šumā*, 323:12.

Iddin-^{d}*Papsukkal* (^{1}MU.^{d}PAB. SUKKAL)
1. a. of *Arad-*^{d}*Bēl* and ^{d}*Anu-ēṭir*, 8:6.
2. a. of *Balāṭu* and *Šumā*, 26:11; 32:14; 33:13.
3. a. of ^{d}*Bēl-rīb-*[X] and *Aplā*, 27:7.
4. a. of *Mušēzib-*^{d}*Marduk* and ^{d}*Nabû-kēšir*, 357:2.
5. a. of *Šumā* and ^{d}*Nabû-šum-iddin*, 336:2 and 338:2; 357:12 and 15.

Iddinunu (^{1}SUM-*nu-nu*) (582), 243:5.

Idūa (^{1}*i-du-ú-a*) f. of ⌜^{d}⌝[X-]*šum-ibnî*, 15:11′.

Ili-ana-bīti-šu (^{1}DINGIR-*a-na-É-šú*) f. of ^{d}*Nabû-*[X-]*binanni*, 292:6.

Ili-bānî-aḫ (^{1}DINGIR.DÙ.ŠEŠ) (600) f.'s name broken, 115:13.

Ili-banû (^{1}DINGIR-*ba-nu*)
1. [68]a. of ^{d}*Bēl-ibnî*, ^{d}*Nergal-ašared*, and ^{d}*Nabû-iqbî*, 327:5.
2. [68]a. of *Marduk* and *Saggil*, 327:13.
3. a. of ^{d}*Nabû-mukīn-zēr* and *Aplā*, 20:6; 272:2 (^{1}DINGIR.DÙ); 273:3.

Ili-danni (^{1}DINGIR-*dan-ni*) (583) ^{h}*rē'ū ša Aplā*, 76:8.

67. Possibly *Itti-ili*.
68. These may be the same ancestor.

Ilī-bānî (¹DINGIR.MEŠ-*ba-ni*) f. of ᵈ*Bēl-aḫḫē-iddin*, desc. of ʰ*Rē'ī-sisē*, 303:13.
Ilī-dibbē (¹DINGIR.MEŠ-*díb-bi-e*)
1. (583) s. of ᵈ*Adad-bēl-kinātum*, 19:3.
2. (521), 300:21.
Ilī-iddin (¹DINGIR.MEŠ.MU) *a.* of ᵈ*Šamaš-ēreš*, 300:15.
Imbā (¹*im-ba-a*) *a.* of *Balāṭu*, 53:8.
ᶠ*Ina-Eanna-lūmur* (SAL *ina*-É.AN.NA-*lu*-[*mur*?]) (591) slave-girl, 348:8.
Ina-Esaggil-zēr (¹*ina*-É.SAG.ÍL.NUMUN) f. of ᵈ*Nabû-uballiṭ*, desc. of *Amēl*-ᵈ*Ea*, 302:11.
Ina-qībi-ᵈ*Bēl* (¹*ina-qí-bi*-ᵈEN) (591) desc. of *Nadna-aplu*, ʰ*kizū ša šarri*, 358:8.
Ina-qībi-ᵈ*Nabû-lišlim* (¹*ina-qí-bi*-ᵈAG-*liš-lim*) (591), desc. of ᵈ*Nabû-šum-ukīn*, 363:9.
Ina-qībit-ᵈ*Bēl-nūr* (¹*ina-qí-bit*-ᵈEN.ZALAG) (591) ʰ*nappāḫu*, 368:3.
Ina-ṣilli-ᵈ*Bēl* (¹*ina*-GIŠ.MI.ᵈEN) (585) desc. of *Zēr-Bābili*, 143:11; 40:7 (584).
Ina-ṣilli-ᵈ*Nanā* (¹*ina*-GIŠ.MI-ᵈ*na-na-a*)
1. (597), 325:22.
2. (592) s. of *Nišānu*, 189:2; 360 i 51′ (591).
3. (591) desc. of ᵈ*Nanā*-[X], 363:2.
4. (590) ʰ*atû ša bāb nēribu*, a *šerku*, 362:14.
5. (588, possibly Nbp., 609), *a.*'s name broken, 146:41.
6. (587) desc. of ᵈ*Nabû-ēpiš*, 142:20.
7. (582), 180:14.
Ina-ṣilli-ᵈ*Nergal* (¹*ina*-GIŠ.MI.ᵈU.GUR) (584) desc. of *Šullum*, 40:24.
Ina-tēšī-ēṭir (¹*ina*-SÙḪ.SUR)
1. (596) s. of *Šākin-zēr*, desc. of ᵈ*Sîn-lēq-unnini*, 322:33.
2. (596) s. of ᵈ*Nabû-ušabši*, 322:4.
3. f. of ᵈ*Nabû-iddina*, desc. of ᵈ*Sîn-tabnî*, 322:31.
4. f. of ᵈ*Nergal-iddin*, 41:9.
5. f. of *Tabnēa*, 41:13.
6. f. (son's name broken), 155:7.
7. *a.* of *Labāši-ili*, 146:32.
8. *a.* (desc.'s name broken), 107:2.
Iniya[69]
1. (¹IGI-⌜*ni*-⌝*ya*) (586), 152:6.
2. (IGI-⌜*ni*-X⌝) *a.* of ᵈ*Nabû-balāṭsu-iqbî*, 146:7.
ᵈ*Innin-aḫ-iddin* (¹ᵈINNIN.ŠEŠ.MU) (582) s. of ᵈ*Nanā-silim*, br. of ᶠᵈ*Nanā-kiširrat*, 1:5, 10.
ᵈ*Innin-aḫ-uṣur* (¹ᵈINNIN.ŠEŠ.URÙ) (591) desc. of ᵈ*Nabû-šum-ukīn*, 363:10.
ᵈ*Innin-aḫḫē-iddin* (¹ᵈINNIN.ŠEŠ.ME.MU) (595) s. of *Rīmūt*, desc. of *Ḫunzû*, 26:14.
ᵈ*Innin-mukīn-šūm* (¹ᵈINNIN.GUB.MU) (584) s. of ᵈ*Nabû-ušallim*, 16:9.
ᵈ*Innin-riṣūa* (¹ᵈINNIN-*ri-ṣu-ú-a*) (587), 255:3.
ᵈ*Innin-šum-ēreš* (¹ᵈINNIN.MU.KÁM)
1. (594) s. of *Aplā*, desc. of *Kurî*, scribe, 336:19 and 338:20.
2. (589) s. of ᵈ*Nabû-aḫḫē-ušallim*, desc. of *Rēmānu*, 2:10, 17 (588); 4:2, 6, 8, 14.
3. (582), 180:18.
ᵈ*Innin-šum-uṣur* (¹ᵈ*in-nin*-MU.URÙ)
1. (592) s. of ᵈ*Bēl-aḫḫē-iddin*, desc. of ʰ*Šangû*-ᵈ*Innin-Bābili*, scribe, 357:20.
2. (583) desc. of *Mār*-ᵈ*Bēl-dānu*, 168:3.
ᵈ*Innin-zēr-ibnî* (¹ᵈINNIN.NUMUN.DÙ)
1. (¹ᵈ*in-nin*-NUMUN.DÙ) (593) s. of *Ezū-pāšir*, 326:7.
2. (593) desc. of *Iddin*-ᵈ[X], 261:5.
3. (562) s. of *Šulā*, scribe, 9:14.
ᵈ*Innin-zēr-iqīša* (¹ᵈ*in-nin*-NUMUN.BA-*šá*)
1. (596) s. of ᵈ*Nabû-ušallim*, 322:37.

69. Perhaps an abbreviation of DN-*iniya*, Stamm, *Namengebung*, p. 212.

2. (589) s. of ^{d}*Nabû-iqīša*, 361:2.

^{d}*Innin-zēr-ušabši* (^{1d}*in-nin*-NUMUN. GÁL-*ši*) (584), 40:21.

^{d}*Inninna-aḫḫē-iddin* (^{1d}INNIN-*na*-ŠEŠ. ME.MU) (584), 40:18.

^{d}*Inninna-mušēzib* (^{1d}INNIN-*na-mu-še-zib*) (585), 231:13.

^{d}*Inninna-šum-ibnî* (^{1d}INNIN-*na*-MU. DÙ)

1. (521) s. of ^{f}*Sigiti*, 300:5.
2. f. of *Gimillu*, 35:4; 37:4; 287:4; 288:4; 289:3; 290:4; 291:5; 292:4; 293:6; 294:4; 295:4; 296:4; 297:4; 298:4; 299:5; 300:3.
3. *a.* of *Nadna-aplu*, 300:32.

^{d}*Inninna-šum-uṣur* (^{1d}INNIN-*na*-MU. PAB)

1. (605), 113:9.
2. (598) s. of [X] LÚ *na-qid-di*, 311:4.
3. (590) desc. of *Ibnā*, 360 vi 22.
4. (590), 43:7.
5. (588, possibly Nbp., 609) s. of *Ša*-⌈X X?⌉, 146:24.
6. (587), 173:15.
7. (521) s. of ^{d}*Nergal-ušēzib*, desc. of *Kidin*-^{d}*Marduk*, wit., 294:17; 298:19 (a. not listed).
8. (521) s. of ^{d}*Nergal-uṣur*, scribe, 35:17.
9. (521) s. of *Silim-ili*, 299:7, 14.
10. f. of *Ṣillā*, desc. of *Kidin*-^{d}*Marduk*, 37:18; 286:20; 287:18 (no a. listed); 288:17; 289:17 (no a. listed); 290:17; 291:18 (no a. listed); 292:17 (no a. listed); 293:21; 294:18; 295:18; 296:17; 297:18; 298:20 (no a. listed); 299:18 (no a. listed).
11. f. of *Nadna-aplu*, desc. of ^{d}*Sîn-lēq-unnini*, 289:15; 290:14.

^{d}*Inninna-zēr-ibnî* ([^{1d}INN]IN-*na*-NUMUN.DÙ) (601) s. of ^{d}*Nabû-ušallim*, 124:4.

^{d}*Inninna-zēr-iqīša* (^{1d}INNIN-*na*-NUMUN.BA-*šá*) f. of *Rīmūt*, 35:15.

^{d}*Inninna-zēr-ušabši* (^{1d}INNIN-*na*-NUMUN.BAD)

1. (591) possibly s. of *Eriši*, 363:7.
2. (588, possibly Nbp., 609) scribe, 146:26.
3. (583) desc. of ^{d}*Bēl-ibnî*, ^{h}*nappāḫu*, 259:5.

^{d}*Inninna-zēr*-⌈X⌉ (^{1d}INNIN-*na*-NUMUN. ⌈X⌉) (585) ^{h}*qīpi*, 231:12.

^{d}*Inninni-šum-uṣur* (^{1d}*in-nin-ni*-MU. PAB) (600) s. of ^{d}*Nabû-nādin-šum*, desc. of *Gimil*-^{d}*Nanā*, scribe, 12:14.

Iqbā (^{1}*iq-ba-a*)

1. (592) desc. of ^{d}*Šamaš-ilūa*, 197:9.
2. (589) ^{h}*nuḫatimmu*, 166:4, 5, 6, 15.

Iqīšā[70] (^{1}BA-*šá-a*)

1. (605) s. of ^{d}*Nabû-zēr-iddin*, 29:13.
2. (602) ^{h}*išparu*, 305:9.
3. (600) desc. of *Nūr*-^{d}*Šamaš*, 61:5.
4. (599) ^{h}*išparu*, 252:3.
5. (597), 325:13 (^{1}BA-*šá*), 20.
6. (594) desc. of ^{d}*Marduk-šarrašu*, 49:4.
7. (592) ^{h}*išparu*, 258:2.
8. (591), 360 ii 4.
9. (588) ^{h}*išparu*, 254:3.
10. (587), 221:1.
11. f. of *Aplā*, desc. of *Irani*, 36:9.
12. f. of *Ibnî*-^{d}*Ištar* and ^{d}*Marduk-nāṣir*, 10:11, 12.
13. f. of ^{d}*Marduk-nāṣir* (lines 13, 21), and ^{d}*Marduk-zēr-ibnî*, 322:39.
14. f. of ^{d}*Nabû-zēr-ibnî*, 7:15.
15. f. of ^{d}*Šamaš-udammiq*, desc. of ^{h}*Rē'û*, 6:24; 276:11.
16. *a.* of *Itti*-^{d}*Marduk-balāṭu*, 210:5.
17. *a.* of ^{d}*Marduk-ēṭir*, 53:6.

70. Possibly *Iqīša-aplu*.

18. a. of ᵈNabû-zēr-ušabšî, 240:5.
19. (¹BA-šá) a. of ᵈNergal-iddin, 300:29.

Iqīša-ᵈInnin (¹BA-šá-ᵈin-nin) (596) desc. of Ammeni-ili, wit., 337:12.

Iqīša-ᵈMarduk (¹BA-šá-ᵈAMAR.UTU)
1. (592) s. of Ardā, desc. of Rīmi-ᵈAnu, br. of Kudurri, wit., 357:19.
2. (589) br. of ᵈEa-zēr-iqīša, s. of Ardaya, 4:3, 8.
3. f. of ᵈNabû-balāṭsu-iqbî, desc. of Egibi, 4:24.

Irani (¹ir-a-ni) a. of Aplā and Iqīšā, 36:10.

Isinnaya (¹i-sin-na-a-a)
1. (593), 328:2.
2. (584) desc. of Danni-ᵈNergal, 72:3; 80:2 (no f. listed); 98:2 (579).
3. (582) s. of Iddin-ᵈNergal, 99:5.
4. a. of ᵈNabû-aḫ-ēreš, 40:2.
5. a. of Silim-ᵈBēl, 360 iii 20, v 9, vi 6.

Iški-iddinu⁷¹ (¹iš-ki-id-di-nu) (586), 152:8, 9.

ʰIšparu (LÚ UŠ.BAR) a. of Nādin and ᵈNergal-nāṣir, 6:19.

ʰIššakku (¹LÚ.PA.TE.SI) a. of ᵈNabû-šum-līšir and ᵈNabû-ušabšî, 303:33.

ᵈIštar-aḫ-iddin (¹ᵈ15.ŠEŠ.MU) f. of ᵈŠamaš-zēr-iddin, desc. of ʰBā'iru, 286:6.

ᵈIštar-aḫḫē-uṣur (¹ᵈ15.ŠEŠ.MEŠ.URÙ) (585) desc. of Eṭir-ᵈBēl, 143:3.

ᵈIštar-nādin-aḫi (¹ᵈ15-na-[din-]ŠEŠ) (594) s. of Ṣillā, scribe, 10:13.

ᵈIštar-riṣūa (¹ᵈ15-ri-ṣu-ú-a) (591) slave, 348:6.

ᵈIštar-šum-ēreš (¹ᵈ15.MU.K[ÁM]) (601) desc. of [¹X.]BA.[X.X], 65:4.

ᵈIštar-šum-iddin (¹ᵈ15.MU.MU) (588) f.'s name broken, 2:13.

Itti-ᵈAnu-balāṭu (¹KI.ᵈ60.TIN) (605), 113:41.

Itti-ᵈBēl-limmir (¹KI.ᵈEN-li-im-mir) (588), 262:3.

Itti-Eanna-budia (¹KI.É.AN.NA-bu-di-iá)
1. (590) ʰaškappu, a šerku, 362:8, 27.
2. (590) ʰnuḫatimmu, a šerku, 362:20.
3. (588), 147:5.
4. (584) desc. of ᵈNabû-ēpuš, 40:15.

Itti-ili⁷² (¹it/d-[ti/din-]DINGIR) a. of Nadna-aplu, 227:2.

Itti-ᵈMarduk-balāṭu (¹KI.ᵈAMAR.UTU.TIN)
1. (595) s. of ᵈMarduk-[apla?-]iddin, scribe, 34:11.
2. (593), 328:6, 9.
3. (591) desc. of ᵈNabû-[X.X], 360 iii 8.
4. (582) desc. of Iqīšā, 210:4.
5. a. of ᵈNabû-aḫ-iddin, 222:4.

Itti-ᵈNabû-balāṭu (¹KI.ᵈAG.TIN) (605), 113:53.

Itti-ᵈŠamaš-balāṭu (¹KI.ᵈUTU.TIN)
1. (584) s. of ᵈNabû-aḫḫē-iddin, br. of Nā'id-ᵈInnin, 40:9.
2. (521) desc. of Guzanu, 300:30.
3. (521) desc. of Nadna-aḫ, 300:14.
4. (521) desc. of ᵈNabû-aḫḫē-ušallim, 300:10.
5. (521), 300:35.

Itti-ᵈŠamaš-budīa (¹[KI.]ᵈUTU-bu-di-iá) (587), 255:2.

Kabti (¹IDIM-ti) (594–576, possible), 106:6.

Kabti-ili-ᵈMarduk (¹IDIM.DINGIR.ᵈAMAR.UTU) (592) s. of ᵈNergal-šum-uṣur, desc. of Dabibi, 5:12.

Kabtiya (¹IDIM-ya)
1. (582) s. of ᵈNabû-lē'î, desc. of ʰNaggāru, 269:4.
2. a. of ᵈNabû-ušallim, 19:13.

---

71. Possibly to be read ¹mil-ki-iddinu, see Stamm, Namengebung, p. 292 n. 2. See also CAD I, 251b.
72. Possibly Iddin-ili.

Kalbā (^{l}*kal-ba-a*)
1. (589) s. of ^{d}*Šamaš-nāṣir*, desc. of *Nūr-*^{d}*Sîn*, wit., 4:15.
2. (586) desc. of *Zēriya*, 152:19.
3. (521) s. of ^{d}*Nergal-ibnî*, wit., 286:17.
4. (521), 293:2.

Kalb-⸢X-⸣*a-a* (^{l}UR.⸢KU?.⸣⸢X-⸣*a-a*) (603) desc. of *Aššur-killanni*, wit., 28:9.

Kalum (^{l}*ka-lum*) f. of ^{d}*Nabû-aḫḫē-ušallim*, desc. of *Gimil-*^{d}*Nanā*, wit., 2:34 (*ka-lum-mu*); 268:4 (a. not listed); 361:18.

^{l}KA.LU.MAŠ, f. of ^{d}*Nabû-nādin-šum*, desc. of *Gimil-*^{d}*Nanā*, 12:12.

Kāṣir (^{l}*ka-ṣir*) f. of ^{d}*Šamaš-iddin*, desc. of *Basiya*, 298:6.

Kāšid-^{d}*Nabû* (^{l}KUR.^{d}AG) (590), 215:2.

Kidin-^{d}*Marduk* (^{l}*ki-din-*^{d}ŠÚ / -^{d}AMAR.UTU)
1. a. of *Iddin-*^{d}*Nabû* and *Arda*, 360 ii 7.
2. a. of *Nadna-aplu* and *Kudurri*, 2:35.
3. a. of ^{d}*Inninna-šum-uṣur* and ^{d}*Nergal-ušēzib*, 294:17.
4. a. of *Marduk* and *Kunā*, 30:14.
5. a. of *Mukīn-zēr* and *Nadna-aplu*, 336:16 and 338:17.
6. a. of *Mušibšî* and *Zēr-ukîn*, 7:14.
7. a. of *Ṣillā* and *Inninna-šum-uṣur*, 37:18; 286:20; 288:17; 290:17; 293:21; 294:18; 295:18; 296:17; 297:19.

Kidinu (^{l}*ki-di-nu*) (596) desc. of ^{d}*Nabû-aḫ-iddin*, wit., 337:11.

Kinā (^{l}*ki-na-a*)
1. (591) s. of *Rāši-ili*, desc. of ^{h}*Gallābu*, 360 ii 4.
2. (590) ^{h}*nuḫatimmu*, a *šerku*, 362:18.
3. (584) desc. of ^{d}*Nanā-ēreš*, 40:14.
4. (521) desc. of ^{d}*Bēl-iqīša*, 300:13.

Kinunaya (^{l}KI.NE-*na-a-a*) (588, possibly Nbp., 609), 146:5.

Kiribtu (^{l}*ki-rib-ti*) (584) desc. of ^{d}*Bēl-ibnî*, ^{h}*rē'ī satukki*, 71:6; 72:6; 76:17 (583); 94:3 (583).

Kudurānu (^{l}*ku-du-ra-nu*) a. of ^{d}*Bēl-iddin* and *Rāši-ili*, 336:14 and 338:15.

Kudurri (^{l}NÌ.DU)
1. (604) desc. of *Lē'û-zitti*, 199:2.
2. (603) ^{h}*rē'ī satukki*, 102:3; 75:11 (601).
3. (602) ^{h}*išparu*, 305:3.
4. (601) s. of *Mukīn-zēr*, desc. of *Ḫunzû*, 7:12; 319:11 (596).
5. (601) s. of ^{d}*Bēl-nāṣir*, ^{h}*išparu*, 253:4, 9.
6. (601) s. of *Šumā*, desc. of ^{h}*Rē'ī-satukki*, 7:16.
7. (598), 321:4.
8. (593) s. of ^{d}*Nabû-nāṣir*, 235:4.
9. (592) s. of *Ardā*, desc. of *Rīmi-*^{d}*Anu*, wit., 4:20 (589); 357:18.
10. (591) desc. of *Mukīn-zēr*, 360 v 13, f. of ^{d}*Marduk-šum-ibnî* in 360 iii 34′.
11. (591) s. of ^{l}A[X.X], desc. of *Epeš-ili*, 360 iii 2.
12. (590) desc. of ^{d}*Nabû-nāṣir*, 171:2.
13. (589) desc. of ^{d}*Nabû-nāṣir*, 277:2.
14. (587) desc. of ^{d}*Nabû-nāṣir*, 280:3.
15. (583) desc. of ^{d}*Nabû-aḫ-iqīša*, 76:11.
16. f. of *Nadna-aplu*, desc. of *Kidin-*^{d}*Marduk*, 2:35.
17. f. of ^{d}*Bēl-ibnî*, and *Ibnî-*^{d}*Ištar*, desc. of *Kurî*, 3:30 and 32.
18. *a.* of *Šum-uṣur*, 203:4.
19. *a.* of *Balāṭu*, 84:2.
20. *a.* of *Dūru-ṣīru-*^{d}*Marduk*, 342:4.
21. *a.* of ^{d}*Marduk-zēr-ibnî*, 360 vi 30.
22. *a.* of *Rīmūt*, 369:6.
23. a. of *Tukulti-*^{d}*Marduk*, 69:5; 71:6; 76:17; 345:9.

Kulbibi (^{l}*kul-bi-bi*) (605), 113:10.

Kunā (^{l}*ku-na-a*)
1. f. of *Arad-*^{d}*Innin*, 315:9.
2. f. of ^{d}*Bēl-ēreš*, desc. of *Ekur-zākir*, 11:11.

3. f. of *Marduk*, desc. of *Kidin-^{d}Marduk*, 30:14.
4. *a.* of *Arad-^{d}Inninni*, 179:4.
5. *a.* of *Gimillu*, 198:7.
6. *a.* of *^{d}Nabû-šum-iddin*, 332:3.

Kurî (^{1}*ku-ri-i*)
1. a. of *^{d}Anu-apla-iddin* and *Ardiya*, 302:2.
2. a. of *^{d}Bēl-šum-iškun* and *^{d}Bēl-iddin*, 357:6.
3. a. of *^{d}Innin-šum-ēreš* and *Aplā*, 336:20 and 338:21.
4. a. of *Marduk* and *Upaq*, 357:16.
5. a. of *^{d}Marduk-šum-uṣur* and *Bēlšunu*, 26:13.
6. a. of *^{d}Bēl-ibnî*, *Ibnî-^{d}Ištar*, and *Kudurri*, 3:30, 32.
7. a. of *^{d}Nabû-zēr-iqīša* and *Aḫḫea*, 6:1.
8. a. of *Nadna-aplu* and *Aplā*, 12:9.
9. a. of *^{d}Nergal-uballiṭ* and *^{d}Nabû-nāṣir*, 336:17 and 338:18.
10. a. of *^{d}Šamaš-zēr-iqīša* and *^{d}Bēl-ušallim*, 33:14; 323:13.

Kurû
1. (^{1}*ku-ru-ú*) a. of *^{d}Nabû-šum-iddin* and *Aplā*, 322:34.
2. (^{1}⸢KU?-⸣*ru-ú*!?) a. of *Nadna-aplu* and ^{1}[X-]A, 22:2.

^{1}⸢KU.⸣[X.X.X][73] *a.* of [X-]*ibnî*, 279:8.

Labāši (^{1}*la-ba-ši*)
1. (605) s. of *Ṣillā*, 113:16.
2. (591) ^{h}*Bēl-piqitti* of *^{d}Nabû-bēlšunu*, 360 ii 14.
3. (585), 143:13.
4. (584) desc. of *^{d}Bēl-uballiṭ*, 40:11.
5. (521) s. of *^{d}Nanā-aḫ-iddin*, 293:20; 296:16; 297:5.
6. (521) s. of *^{d}Šamaš-ēṭir-šum*, 37:17.
7. f. of *^{d}Nabû-zēr-iddin*, 325:1.
8. *a.* of *Gimillu*, 229:5.
9. *a.* of *^{d}Nergal-ibnî*, 75:6.

Labāši-ili (^{1}*la-ba-ši*-DINGIR) (588, possibly Nbp., 609) desc. of *Ina-têši-ēṭir*, 146:32.

Lāqīp (^{1}*la-qip*)
1. (521) desc. of *^{d}Šamaš-zēr-līšir*, 300:34.
2. f. of *^{d}Nanā-ēreš*, 300:13.

Lāqīpi (^{1}*la-qí-pi*)
1. (585) desc. of *Šalammu*, 143:1.
2. (583) desc. of *Balṭiya*, 77:2.

Lē'û-zitti (^{1}*li-'*-ḪA.LA) a. of *Kudurri*, 199:3.

Libluṭ (^{1}*lib-luṭ*)
1. (605) a.'s name broken, 126:20.
2. (582) desc. of *^{d}Nanā-iddin*, ^{h}*nappāḫu*, 260:4.

Likunu (^{1}*li-ku-nu*) (590) ^{h}*nuḫatimmu*, a *šerku*, 362:23.

Linūḫ-libbi-^{d}Ištar (^{1}*li-nu-uḫ-lìb-bi*-^{d}15) (591) slave, 348:5.

Linūḫ-libbi-^{d}Innin (^{1}*li-nu-uḫ*-ŠÀ-^{d}INNIN) (587) desc. of *^{d}Nabû-mukīn-apli*, 142:25.

Liširu (^{1}*li-ši-ru*) *a.* of *Basiya*, 300:16.

Lītu-ilī (^{1}*li-ti*-DINGIR.MEŠ) (586), 152:12.

Lū-aḫūa (^{1}*lu-ú*-ŠEŠ-*ú-a*) f. of *Bēlšunu*, 32:2.

Lūṣa-ana-nūr-^{d}Šamaš (^{1}*lu-ṣa-ana*-ZALÁG.^{d}UTU) (605), 113:13.

LÚ.ŠU.⸢X.⸣AN, *a.* of ^{1}⸢X.GIŠ⸣, 239:2.

LÚ.⸢X.X⸣, a. of *Nā'id-^{d}Marduk* and *Nādin*, 21:2.

LÚ.⸢X.⸣[X.X], a. of *Šūzubu* and *^{d}Šamaš-erība*, 21:3.

^{d}Madān-aḫḫē-iddin (^{1d}DI.KU$_{5}$.ŠEŠ.MEŠ.MU) f. of *^{d}Šamaš-mukīn-apli*, desc. of *Šigua*, 126:6 (no a. listed); and 302:8.

73. Possibly *Tukulti*-[X.X.X].

^{h}*Maḫḫû* (LÚ.GUB.BA) a. of ^{d}*Šamaš-šum-ukīn* and ^{d}*Nabû-zēr-ukīn*, 336:3 and 338:3; 357:4.

Manna-akī-Arbail (^{1}*man-na*/*nu-a-ki-i-ár*/*ar-ba-il*)

1. (^{1}*man-na-a-ki-i* (erasure)-*4-ìl*-KI) (610) ^{h}*qallu ša* ^{h}*qīpi*, 306:7.
2. (591, 590) ^{h}*Bēl-piqitti ša* ^{h}*qīpi*, 360 ii 12, vi 31.
3. (580), 349:3.

Manna-kī-ili (^{1}*man-na*-⸢*ki*⸣-DINGIR) *a.* of *Aḫ-ilia*, 75:5.

Mannu-akī-ili (^{1}*man-nu-a-ki-i*-DINGIR) (521), 300:18.

Mannu-i-gi-ir-reš[74] (^{1}*man-nu-i-gi-ir*-⸢*reš*⸣) (521), 300:31.

Mār-^{d}*Bēl-dānu*[75] (^{1}DUMU.^{d}EN-*da-nu*)

1. (598), 172:9.
2. *a.* of ^{d}*Innin-šum-uṣur*, 168:3.

Mār-Esaggil-[X.X.X.X][76] (^{1}DUMU. ⸢É.SAG.GIL-⸣[X.X.X.X]) (587), 173:4.

Mār-⸢X.⸣[X-]*ušabši* (^{1}DUMU.É.⸢X.⸣ [X.]GÁL-*ši*) (587), 173:7.

Marduk (^{1}*mar-duk*)

1. (603) s. of *Kunā*, desc. of *Kidin-*^{d}*Marduk*, 30:14.
2. (598) s. of *Upaq*, desc. of *Kurî*, wit., 315:12 (no a. listed); and 357:15 (592).
3. (594) s. of *Nadna-aplu*, desc. of *Gimil-*^{d}*Nanā*, wit., 336:14 and 338:15.
4. (594) s. of *Saggil*, desc. of *Ili-banû*, 327:12.
5. (589), 166:9.
6. (587) desc. of *Aḫḫēšā*, ^{h}*na-qad*, 79:10.
7. f. of ^{d}*Anu-zēr-ušabši*, desc. of *Gimil-*^{d}*Nanā*, wit., 35:16; 286:19; 288:15; 290:16; 291:17; 292:16; 293:19; 296:15; 297:16; 298:18.
8. f. of *Ibnā*, 201:6.
9. f. of *Nādin*, desc. of *Babūtti*, 323:14; 361:15.
10. f. of *Nādin*, 200:2.
11. *a.* of *Ibnā*, 306:5.

^{d}*Marduk-aḫ-iddin* (^{1d}AMAR.UTU.ŠEŠ. MU)

1. f. of ^{d}*Bēl-iddin*, 62:7.
2. f. of ^{d}*Nabû-bēlšunu*, desc. of *Zannea*, 21:15.

^{d}*Marduk-apla-iddin* (^{1d}AMAR.UTU.A. MU)

1. (584), 40:13.
2. f. of *Itti-*^{d}*Marduk-balāṭu*, 34:11.
3. f. of ^{d}*Šamaš-zēr-ibnî*, 2:15, 23.

^{d}*Marduk-apla-uṣur* (^{1d}AMAR.UTU. DUMU.UŠ.URÙ)

1. (601) s. of *Šāpik*, desc. of *Ḫunzû*, wit., 3:33.
2. (594) s. of ^{d}*Nabû-udammiq*, desc. of ^{h}*Purkullu*, scribe, 327:14.
3. (^{1d}ŠÚ.A.PAB) (585) s. of *Gimillu*, scribe, 24:5, 10.

^{d}*Marduk-bēl-ilī* (^{1d}AMAR.UTU.EN. DINGIR.MEŠ) (582) s. of ^{d}*Nabû-nādin-šum*, scribe, 1:31.

^{d}*Marduk-ēreš* (^{1d}AMAR.UTU.KÁM) f. of *Šum-ukīn*, desc. of ^{h}*Naggariya*, 357:17.

^{d}*Marduk-erība* (^{1d}AMAR.UTU.SU)

1. (601) s. of *Šulā*, br. of ^{d}*Nanā-iddin*, 75:9.
2. (600) s. of ^{d}*Nabû-ēreš*, 120:2.
3. (588) s. of *Eṭēru*, probably br. of *Iddin-*^{d}*Marduk* (line 11); 31:9.

74. Cf. *Man-nu-gi-ri-šu* NBN 99a.

75. Freydank, *Spätbabylonische Wirtschaftstexte aus Uruk* (Berlin, 1971), p. 139, reads *Mār-Bēl-Dajānu* since all his names are spelled *da-a-nu*; but the spelling here would seem to indicate *dānu* or *dannu*.

76. Restore possibly [-*ni-bi*] or [-*ri-ṣu-ú-a*].

4. (^{1d}AMAR.UTU-*eri-ba*) f. of *Mukīn-^{d}Marduk*, 201:8.

^{d}Marduk-ēṭir (^{1d}AMAR.UTU.SUR)
1. (603), 74:15.
2. (601) s. of *^{d}Bēl-šum-iškun*, desc. of *Dabibi*, ^{h}*ṭupsar Eanna*, 7:18. (Possibly br. of *^{d}Marduk-nāṣir*, 315:1, also Uruk.)
3. [77](600) s. of *^{d}Bēl-šum-iškun*, perhaps desc. of *Dabibi*, ^{h}*ṭupsar Eanna*, 309:5.
4. [77](599) s. of *^{d}Bēl-šum-iškun*, perhaps desc. of *Dabibi*, 201:3.
5. (591) s. of *^{d}Nabû-aḫḫē-iddin*, desc. of *Egibi*, 360 v 47.
6. (^{1d}AMAR.UTU.KAR-*ir*) (585) desc. of *Iqīšā*, 53:6.
7. f. of *Guzanu*, 300:9, 19.

^{d}Marduk-mukallim (^{1d}AMAR.UTU-*mu-kal-lim*) (592) s. of *Aplā*, desc. of *Balti-^{d}Sîn*, 5:16.

^{d}Marduk-nāṣir (^{1d}AMAR.UTU.PAB)
1. (598) s. of *^{d}Bēl-šum-iškun*, desc. of *Dabibi*, 315:1. (Possibly br. of *^{d}Marduk-ēṭir*, 7:18.)
2. (597), 317:6.
3. (^{1d}AMAR.UTU-*na-ṣir*) (596) s. of *Iqīšā*, 322:13, 20.
4. (594) s. of *Iqīšā*, possibly br. of *Ibnî-^{d}Ištar*, 10:12.
5. (588) s. of *^{d}Nabû-ēṭir*, scribe, 31:14.
6. (^{1d}AMAR.UTU-*na-ṣir*) (586) ^{h}*šanû*, 150:3.
7. (^{1d}ŠÚ.PAB) (583), 209:9.
8. f. of *Aplā*, desc. of *Nādin-^{d}Marduk*, 2:30.
9. *a.* of *^{d}Nabû-šum-līšir*, 143:18.

^{d}Marduk-šākin-šum (^{1d}AMAR.UTU.GAR.MU) (592), 353:3.

^{d}Marduk-šāpik-zēr (^{1d}AMAR.UTU.DUB.NUMUN)
1. (591) desc. of ^{h}*Rē'ī-alpi*, 20:13.
2. (584) s. of *^{d}Marduk-šum-uṣur*, desc. of ^{h}*Rab-bānû*, ^{h}*šatam Eanna*, 6:2, 7.
3. (521) s. of *Balāṭu*, desc. of *Miṣir*, 294:15.

^{d}Marduk-šar-⌈X⌉ (^{1d}⌈ŠÚ.LUGAL.X⌉) (604), *a.*'s name broken, 62:12.

^{d}Marduk-šarranu (^{1d}AMAR.UTU.LUGAL-*a-ni*)
1. (596), 319:1.
2. f. of *^{d}Nabû-zēr-ibnî*, 31:13.
3. f. of *^{d}Šamaš-zēr-iqīša*, 29:1.
4. *a.* of *Iqīšā*, 49:4.

^{d}Marduk-šum-ēreš (^{1d}AMAR.UTU.MU.KÁM) (585) desc. of *^{d}Nabû-šum-iškun*, 53:13.

^{d}Marduk-šum-ibnî (^{1d}ŠÚ./^{d}AMAR.UTU.MU.DÙ)
1. (604), ^{h}*šanû?*, 54:5.
2. (602), 200:2.
3. (598) s. of *^{d}Bēl-ēreš*, 311:3.
4. (591) s. of *Kudurri*, desc. of *Mukīn-zēr*, 360 iii 35′.
5. (591) s. of *Zēriya*, desc. of *Dabibi*, scribe, 18:11.
6. *a.* of *Aplā*, 360 v 31.
7. *a.* of *Rīmūt*, 53:16.

^{d}Marduk-šum-iddin (^{1d}AMAR.UTU.MU.MU) *a.* of *Arad-^{d}Marduk*, 113:46.

^{d}Marduk-šum-līšir (^{1d}AMAR.UTU.MU.GIŠ)
1. (589) s. of *^{d}Bēl-ušallim*, desc. of *Muštuq*, wit., 4:16.
2. (584) s. of *Rīmūt*, desc. of *^{d}Bēl-usat*, 6:23.

^{d}Marduk-šum-uṣur (^{1d}AMAR.UTU.MU.URÙ)
1. (605) s. of *^{d}Anu-aḫ-iddin*, 29:2, 5, 7.
2. (600) s. of *Zērutu*, 115:23.

77. See 7:18.

3. [78](595) s. of *Bēlšunu*, desc. of *Kurî*, wit., 26:12.
4. (594) s. of ^{d}*Nabû-aḫḫē-iddin*, desc. of ^{h}*Rab-bānû*, 340:13.
5. (588) s. of *Balāṭu*, 31:1.
6. f. of ^{d}*Marduk-šāpik-zēr*, desc. of ^{h}*Rab-bānû*, 6:2.
7. f. of *Naptešir*, 2:14, 23.

^{d}*Marduk-šum-*[X] (^{1d}AMAR.UTU.MU.[X]) (585) desc. of *Aḫ-šu*, 53:2.

^{d}*Marduk-šum-*[X] (^{1d}AMAR.UTU.MU.[X]) (584) ^{h}*malāḫu*, 208:1.

^{d}*Marduk-zēr-ibnî* (^{1d}AMAR.UTU.NUMUN.DÙ)
1. (601) desc. of *Mudammiq-māti*, br. of ^{d}*Bēl-aḫ-*[X], 75:3.
2. (596) s. of *Iqīšā*, 322:39.
3. (590) desc. of *Kudurri*, 360 vi 30.
4. f. of ^{d}*Nabû-aḫḫē-uballiṭ*, desc. of *Aḫ-ibnî*, 32:11.
5. f. of *Rīmūt*, 361:11.
6. *a.* of ^{d}*Nabû-ēṭir-napšāti*, 320:8.

^{d}*Marduk-zēr-līšir* (^{1d}AMAR.UTU.NUMUN.GIŠ) (588) desc. of *Gimillu*, 44:6.

^{d}*Marduk-*⌈X.X⌉(^{1d}AMAR.UTU.⌈X.X⌉) *a.* of *Nadna-aplu*, 126:17.

Marduka (^{1}*mar-duk-a*)
1. (590), 43:8.
2. (589) f.'s name broken, desc. of ^{h}*Šangû-*^{d}*Ninurta*, wit., 359:11.
3. (584), 90:6.
4. f. of ^{d}*Nabû-iqīša*, 315:11.
5. f. of *Šum-ukīn*, 90:6.
6. [79]*a.* of *Ibāššî-ili*, 91:5.
7. *a.* of ^{d}*Nergal-dānu*, 138:2.
8. *a.* of *Rāši-ili*, 21:9.

Marduku (^{1}*mar-duk-ú*) f. of ^{d}*Bēl-aḫḫē-iddin*, 317:3.

Milki-iddinu, see sub *Iški-iddinu*.

Miṣir (^{1}*mi-ṣir*) a. of ^{d}*Marduk-šāpik-zēr* and *Balāṭu*, 294:15.

Mīnu-īpuš-ilī (^{1}*mi-nu-ú-i-pu-uš-*DINGIR.MEŠ) (584) desc. of *Aplā*, 40:23.

Mudammiq-māti(?) (^{1}SIG$_{5}$.KUR) *a.* of ^{d}*Marduk-zēr-ibnî* and ^{d}*Bēl-aḫ-*[X], 75:3.

Mukīn-^{d}*Marduk* (^{1}GUB.^{d}AMAR.UTU) (599) s. of ^{d}*Marduk-erība*, 201:7.

Mukīn-^{d}*Nabû* (^{1}GUB.^{d}AG) (590), 144:4.

Mukīn-zēr (^{1}GUB.NUMUN)
1. (594) s. of *Nadna-aplu*, desc. of *Kidin-*^{d}*Marduk*, wit., 336:15 and 338:16.
2. (590) desc. of *Etelpi*, 149:1.
3. [80](589) s. of ^{d}*Bēl-ēṭir*, desc. of ^{h}*Šangû-*^{d}*Adad*, wit., 361:13.
4. (588) s. of ^{d}*Bēl-lē'ī*, desc. of *Šumāti*, wit., 13:12.
5. f. of *Ibnî-*^{d}*Innin*, 41:16.
6. f. of *Kudurri*, desc. of *Ḫunzû*, 7:12; 319:11.
7. f. of ^{d}*Nanā-ēpuš*, desc. of *Gimil-*^{d}*Nanā*, 2:32.
8. *a.* of *Gimillu*, 360 v 4.
9. *a.* of *Kudurri* and ^{d}*Marduk-šum-ibnî*, 360 iii 34′, v 13 (only *Kudurri*).
10. a. of ^{d}*Nanā-iddin*, 149:6.

Mukkēa (^{1}*muk-ki-e-a*) *a.* of ^{d}*Nanā-ēreš*, 300:6.

Multešir See sub *Naptešir*.

Mūru (^{1}*mu-ú-ru*) f. of ^{d}*Nergal-šum-ibnî*, 322:7.

Mušallim-^{d}*Marduk* (^{1}GI.^{d}AMAR.UTU)
1. (603) s. of *Ṣillā*, 30:16.
2. (591) s. of ^{d}*Nabû-ušabšî*, 223:2.
3. (588) s. of ^{d}*Bēl-nāṣir*, 31:5.
4. (588), 232:4.

78. Cp. □ 15475:12, in the Hermitage Collection (591 B.C.) for the same person, a witness in a document concerning agricultural produce. ^{d}*Nabû-aḫḫē-iddin* occurs in both documents as ^{h}*bēl-piqitti*.

79. Also possible: *Bulluṭa*.

80. See also A 32097:30 (594 B.C.), wit.

5. (587) [h]*šā pān ekalli*, 111:3.
6. (587) 173:6.
7. (year destroyed), 141:5.
8. f. of [d]*Nabû-šum-ēreš*, 340:3, 15.
9. f. of [d]*Nabû-šum-ēreš*, desc. of [h]*Šangû-parakki*, 11:15.
10. *a.* of [d]*Nabû-bānî-aḫ*, 39:3.

Mušēzib ([1]*mu-še-zib*)
1. (522) desc. of [d]*Bēl-zēr-iddin*, 8:12.
2. *a.* of [d]*Nabû-aḫ-iddin*, 27:2.

Mušēzib-[d]*Bēl* ([1]*mu-še-zib-*[d]EN)
1. (604) s. of *Balāṭsu*, desc. of *Amēl-*[d]*Ea*, wit., 302:10.
2. (602) s. of [d]*Nergal-iddin*, desc. of *Gimil-*[d]*Nanā*, 17:1.
3. (592) s. of [d]*Bēl-šar-uṣur*, 5:15.
4. (591) s. of *Aplā*, desc. of *Arrabti*, 360 ii 10; 6:22 (584 B.C.).
5. (522) s. of *Zēr-Bābili*, desc. of *Attabani*, 8:2, 4, 9.

Mušēzib-ili ([1]*mu-še-zib*-DINGIR) *a.* of [d]*Nanā-aḫ-iddin*, 314:17.

Mušēzib-[d]*Marduk* ([1]*mu-še-zib-*[d]AMAR.UTU)
1. (592) s. of [d]*Nabû-kēšir*, desc. of *Iddin-*[d]*Papsukkal*, 357:1, 4, 9 (twice).
2. f. of [d]*Nanā-aḫ-iddin*, 308:6.
3. f. of [d]*Nergal-iddin*, 155:3.

Mušibšî ([1]*mu-šib-ši*) (601) s. of *Zēr-ukīn*, desc. of *Kidin-*[d]*Marduk*, wit., 7:14.

Muštuq ([1]*mu-ši-tuq*) a. of [d]*Marduk-šum-līšir* and [d]*Bēl-ušallim*, 4:17.

Mutakkil-[d]*Nabû* ([1][*m*]*u-tak-kil-*[d]AG) (591), 283:4.

[1]*Na-*[X.]⌜X⌝ (521) in GN *adi miṣir ša* . . . , 292:2.

[d]*Nabû-aḫ-ēreš* ([1d]AG.ŠEŠ.KÁM)
1. (592) *a.*'s name broken, 84:5.
2. (584) desc. of *Isinnaya*, 40:2.
3. f. of [d]*Nabû-ēṭir* and *Šum-ukīn*, 70:3.
4. *a.* of [d]*Nanā-ēpuš*, 42:7.
5. *a.* of *Zēriya*, 142:6.

[d]*Nabû-aḫ-iddin* ([1d]AG.ŠEŠ.MU)
1. (597) [h]*nappāḫ siparri*, 325:8.
2. (593) desc. of [d]*Nanā-ēreš*, 356:3; 335:3 (592).
3. (592), 132:2.
4. (590) [h]*malāḫu*, 367:3.
5. (589) desc. of *Mušēzib*, 27:2.
6. (588), 139:3.
7. (588, possibly Nbp., 609), 146:13.
8. (588), 233:5.
9. (587) desc. of *Itti-*[d]*Marduk-balāṭu*, 222:3.
10. (586) s. of *Ša-*[d]*Nabû-šū*, wit., 25:10.
11. (583), 209:3, 5, 7, 10.
12. f. of [d]*Nabû-bēlšunu*, desc. of [d]*Sîn-lēq-unnini*, 2:33.
13. *a.* of *Amēl-*[d]*Nabû*, 146:12.
14. *a.* of *Kidinu*, 337:11.

[d]*Nabû-aḫ-uṣur* ([1d]AG.ŠEŠ.URÙ)
1. f. of [d]*Nabû-ibnî*, 16:10.
2. *a.* of *Nadna-aplu*, 76:4.
3. ([1d]AG.PAB.URÙ) *a.* of [d]*Nergal-ušallim*, 146:19.

[d]*Nabû-aḫ-*⌜X.⌝[X], *a.*, (desc.'s name broken), 227:15.

[d]*Nabû-aḫ-*⌜X⌝, *a.* of *Aḫ-lūmur*, 146:18.

[d]*Nabû-aḫḫē-ēreš* ([1d]AG.ŠEŠ.MEŠ.KÁ[M?]) f. of *Sāsiya*, 19:2.

[d]*Nabû-aḫḫē-erība* ([1d]AG.ŠEŠ.MEŠ.SU) *a.* of [d]*Nanā-aḫ-iddin*, 293:8.

[d]*Nabû-aḫḫē-iddin* ([1d]AG.ŠEŠ.MEŠ.MU)
1.[81] (600) s. of [d]*Nergal-ušallim*, desc.

81. In □ 15475:4: *bēl piqitti* (591); 26:1, 4: no titles (private transaction) (595); 33:6: *šatammu* (596); □ 15531:1: as lender of money (private?) (598); 12:1, 6, 8: as lender of money (private?) (600).

Taking the earliest dates, 600 and 598, in which [d]*Nabû-aḫḫē-iddin* appears as a private lender, you might argue that he has not yet been appointed *šatammu*. But in 596, he already has this title and one year later, in 595, he again appears as a private lender (this time of produce). This illustrates the nature of these archives as being a mixture of public and private documents.

of *Nūr-*^{d}*Sîn,* 12:1, 6, 8; 26:1, 4 (595); 323:8 (592); 361:1, 5, 9, 12 (589); 33:6 (586).
2. (592) s. of ^{d}*Bēl-aḫḫē-erība,* 5:4, 11.
3. (^{1d}AG.PAB.ME.MU) (592), 323:2.
4. (592) desc. of ^{h}*Atû,* 324:1; 360 iv 34 (591).
5. (591) desc. of ^{h}*Šangû-*^{d}*Šamaš,* 360 iv 9.
6. (591), 360 i 25, 43′, 52′ (^{d}AG.PAB.ME.MU).
7. (586) desc. of ^{h}*Atû,* 136:3.
8. (521) s. of ^{d}*Bēl-ēreš,* br. of *Zēriya,* 294:6.
9. f. of *Aḫ-lūmur,* 354:3.
10. f. of *Itti-*^{d}*Šamaš-balāṭu* and *Nā'id-*^{d}*Innin,* 40:10.
11. f. of ^{d}*Marduk-ēṭir,* desc. of *Egibi,* 360 v 47.
12. f. of ^{d}*Marduk-šum-uṣur,* desc. of ^{h}*Rab-bānû,* 340:13.
13. a. of [X.X.X-^{d}]⌜*Bēl*⌝, 226:4.

^{d}*Nabû-aḫḫē-uballiṭ* (^{1d}AG.ŠEŠ.MEŠ.TIN-*iṭ*) (586) s. of ^{d}*Marduk-zēr-ibnî,* desc. of *Aḫ-ibnî* (^{1}ŠEŠ.DÙ-*i*), 32:10.

^{d}*Nabû-aḫḫē-ušallim* (^{1d}AG.ŠEŠ.MEŠ.GI)
1. (603) ^{h}*ša muḫḫi gizzi,* 195:1.
2. (597) ^{h}*erreššì,* 325:17.
3. (591) desc. of ^{d}*Nabû-zēr-ibnî,* 363:3.
4. (590), 369:2.
5. (589) s. of *Kalum,* desc. of *Gimil-*^{d}*Nanā,* wit., 361:18.
6. (589) s. of ^{d}*Nabû-udammiq,* a.'s name broken, wit., 359:10, restoration uncertain.
7. (584), 40:18.
8. (582) desc. of ^{1}[X-]^{d}*Sîn,* 206:4.
9. (582), 180:15.
10. f. of ^{d}*Innin-šum-ēreš,* desc. of *Rēmānu,* 2:10; 4:2.
11. *a.* of *Itti-*^{d}*Šamaš-balāṭu,* 300:10.
12. *a.* of *Šumā,* 40:12.

^{d}*Nabû-apla-iddin* (^{1d}AG.A.MU)
1. (605), 126:16.
2. (^{1d}AG.DUMU.UŠ.MU) (604) desc. of ^{d}*Nabû-zēr-līšir,* ^{h}*išparu,* 301:20.
3. (598) s. of ^{d}*Bēl-upaḫḫir,* wit., 315:10.

^{d}*Nabû-apla-uṣur* (^{1d}AG.A.URÙ) (590), 144:5.

^{d}*Nabû-apla-*⌜X⌝[82] (^{1d}[A]G.⌜A.X⌝) (year destroyed), 205:4.

^{d}*Nabû-balāṭsu-iqbî* (^{1d}AG.TIN-*su-iq-bi*)
1. (594) s. of *Zēr-ibnî,* desc. of *Nūr-*^{d}*Papsukkal,* 327:11.
2. (^{1d}AG.TIN-*su*-E) (593) desc. of *Šulā,* 352:3.
3. (591) s. of ^{d}*Nabû-ēṭir,* desc. of ^{d}*Sîn-lēq-unnini,* scribe, 361:19 (589); 360 ii 8–9 (^{1d}AG.TIN-*su*-E).
4. (589) s. of *Iqīša-*^{d}*Marduk,* desc. of *Egibi,* scribe, 4:23.
5. (^{1d}AG.TIN-*su*-E) (588, possibly 609, Nbp.) desc. of *Iniya,* 146:7.
6. (^{1d}AG.TIN-*su*-E) (522) s. of *Rīmūt,* scribe ^{h}*rē'û ša* ^{d}*Nabû,* 8:14.
7. (year broken) s. of ^{d}*Bēl-ušallim,* 183:4.

^{d}*Nabû-bānî-aḫ* (^{1d}AG.DÙ.ŠEŠ)
1. (591) desc. of ^{d}*Nabû-šum-iškun,* wit., 358:13.
2. (589) s. of *Aḫ-lūmur,* 137:2.
3. (587), 220:5.

---

^{d}*Nabû-nādin-šumi* is listed as *šatammu* in San Nicolò, *Prosopographie* no later than 602/1; in our texts as late as *Ṭebetu* 596, 319:10. ^{d}*Nabû-aḫḫē-iddin* is listed as *šatammu* in *Prosopographie* no earlier than 588/7, in our texts as early as *Kislimu* 595, 33:6. Therefore the office changed hands between January 596 and January 595.

82. If the first part of the name is read correctly, the expected last trace should show either MU or URÙ, but this is not the case.

4. (586) desc. of *Mušallim-*^{d}*Marduk*, 39:3.
5. (584) s. of *Ibnā*, desc. of *Ekur-zākir*, scribe, 38:11; 33:16 (586).
6. (584), 40:20.
7. (582) ⸢LÚ.X.X⸣, 180:8.
8. (582) s. of ^{d}*Šamaš-šum-iddin*, 1:30.

^{d}*Nabû-bēl-aḫḫēšu* (^{1d}AG.EN.PAB.⸢MEŠ-*šu*⸣) (582), 243:6.

^{d}*Nabû-bēl-ilī* (^{1d}AG.EN-*ì-lí*) (588), 232:5.

^{d}*Nabû-bēl-šumāti* (^{1d}AG.EN.MU.MEŠ) (591) desc. of *Eda-ēṭir*, 360 iv 28.

^{d}*Nabû-bēlšunu* (^{1d}AG.EN-*šú-nu*)
1. (591) s. of ^{d}*Marduk-aḫ-iddin*, desc. of *Zannea*, scribe, 21:14.
2. (591), 360 ii 15.
3. (588) s. of ^{d}*Nabû-aḫ-iddin*, desc. of ^{d}*Sîn-lēq-unnini*, wit., 2:33.
4. (587) desc. of *Kudurri*, br. of *Šum-uṣur*, 203:4.
5. (586) desc. of ^{d}*Nabû-šum-ukīn*, 228:2.
6. (582), 180:16.

^{d}*Nabû-bēl-*[X.X] (^{1d}AG.EN.[X.X]) f. of ^{d}*Nabû-šar-*⸢*ḫi*?-⸣*ilāni*, a.'s name broken, 27:9.

^{d}*Nabû-dala'* (^{1d}AG-*da-la-'*) f. of *Aqria*, 295:16.

^{d}*Nabû-dīna-ēpuš* (^{1d}AG.DI.KU_5.DÙ-*uš*) f. of ^{d}*Nabû-ēreš*, 295:6.

^{d}*Nabû-dummiqanni*[83] (^{1d}AG.SIG_5-*ni*) (601), 191:2.

^{d}*Nabû-eḫa-*[X.X] (^{1d}AG-*e-ḫa-*⸢*a*-⸣[X.X]) *a.* of ^{d}*Nergal-*[X],[84] 360 ii 21.

^{d}*Nabû-ēpir-la'* (^{1d}AG-*e-pir-la-'*) f. of *Zēriya*, 82:23.

^{d}*Nabû-ēpiš* (^{1d}AG-*e-piš*) *a.* of *Ina-ṣilli-*^{d}*Nanā*, 142:20.

^{d}*Nabû-ēpuš* (^{1d}AG.DÙ-*uš*)
1. (582) desc. of ^{1}⸢X.X-⸣*ki-*^{d}*Ea*, 234:6.
2. f. of *Ibnî-*^{d}*Nabû*, 88:3.
3. f. of ^{d}*Nabû-tabnî-uṣur*, desc. of ^{d}*Sîn-tabnî*, 3:36.
4. *a.* of *Itti-Eanna-budia*, 40:16.

^{d}*Nabû-ēreš* (^{1d}AG.KÁM)
1. (521) s. of ^{d}*Nabû-dīna-ēpuš*, 295:5, 14.
2. f. of ^{d}*Marduk-erība*, 120:2.
3. *a.* of ^{d}*Bēl-ušēzib*, 44:7.
4. *a.* of *Ḫašdā*, 76:6.
5. *a.* of *Ibnî-*^{d}*Innin*, 325:16.

^{d}*Nabû-erība* (^{1d}AG.SU)
1. (593) s. of *Bulluṭa*, 41:6.
2. (584) s. of ^{d}*Bēl-uballiṭ*, desc. of ^{h}*Rab-bānû*, 38:8.
3. (521) s. of *Zākir*, 287:6, 14.
4. f. of ^{d}*Nergal-ibnî*, desc. of ^{d}*Sîn-nuqunnunu*, 12:10.

^{d}*Nabû-ēṭir* (^{1d}AG.SUR)
1. (591) desc. of *Balāṭu*, 363:4.
2. (591) desc. of *Nadna-aplu*, 360 iii 15.
3. (589) desc. of *Nadna-aplu*, ^{h}*nuḫatimmu*, 166:2, 14.
4. (583) s. of ^{d}*Nabû-aḫ-ēreš*, br. of *Šum-ukīn*, 70:2.
5. (521), 300:37.
6. f. of ^{d}*Marduk-nāṣir*, 31:14.
7. f. of ^{d}*Nabû-balāṭsu-iqbî*, desc. of ^{d}*Sîn-lēq-unnini*, 360 ii 8–9; 361:19.
8. *a.* of ^{d}*Nanā-aḫ-iddin*, 314:6.
9. *a.* of ^{d}*Nergal-dānu*, 146:11.

^{d}*Nabû-ēṭir-napšāti* (^{1d}AG.SUR.ZI.MEŠ)
1. (605) f.'s name broken, 29:10.
2. (603) ^{h}*šanû ša mat tamtim*, 198:2; 360 i 22 (591) (^{1d}AG.KAR.ZI.MEŠ).
3.[85] (601) s. of ^{d}*Bēl-lē'ī*, desc. of *Šigua*, 7:13; 319:13 (596) no f. listed, wit.; 323:10 (592).

83. For the reading of this name, cf. NBN p. 313b.
84. For ^{1d}⸢U.⸣G[UR.X], ^{1d}PA[PSUKKAL...] is also possible.
85. *GCCI* 1, 6:9 *ina* GUB-*zu ša* ^{d}*Nabû-ēṭir-napšāti* A *Šigua*.

4. (596), 184:6.
5. (^{1d}PA-*e-ṭir*-ZI.MEŠ) (594) desc. of ^{d}*Marduk-zēr-ibnî*, 320:8.
6. (592) *a.*'s name broken, 84:3.
7. (592), 105:3.
8. (591), 360 iv 48 (^{1d}AG.KAR.ZI.MEŠ), 50.
9. (588) s. of *Šum-ukīn*, desc. of *Ekur-zākir*, scribe, 2:38.

^{d}*Nabû-ēṭir*-[X.X] (⸢^{1d}AG.SUR?.⸣[X.X]) (date broken), 117:1′.

^{d}*Nabû-gāmil* (^{1d}AG-*ga-mil*)
1. (605), 153:3.
2. (593) s. of *Zēr-ukīn*, 41:17.

^{d}*Nabû-ibnî*
1. (^{1d}AG-⸢*ib!*-⸣*ni*) (591) s. of *Ṣillā*, 18:8.
2. (^{1d}PA.DÙ) (584) s. of ^{d}*Nabû-aḫ-uṣur*, 16:10.

^{d}*Nabû-iddin* (^{1d}AG.MU)
1. f. of ^{d}*Bēl-iddin*, 30:19.
2. f. of ^{d}*Nergal-ina-tēšî-ēṭir*, desc. of *Ekur-zākir*, 11:18.
3. f. of *Ṣillā*, 340:2.
4. *a.* of *Riḫētu*, 43:2.

^{d}*Nabû-iddina* (^{1d}AG.SUM-*na*) (596) s. of *Ina-tēšî-ēṭir*, desc. of ^{d}*Sîn-tabnî*, 322:31.

^{d}*Nabû-iqbî* (^{1d}AG-*iq-bi*) f. of ^{d}*Bēl-ibnî* and ^{d}*Nergal-ašared*, desc. of *Ili-banû*, 327:5.

^{d}*Nabû-iqbî-nadān* (^{1d}AG.E-*na-dan*) (588) s. of *Taḫallu*, 13:14.

^{d}*Nabû-iqīša* (^{1d}AG.BA-*šá*)
1. (598) s. of *Marduka*, wit., 315:11.
2. (589) s. of ^{d}*Nanā-iddin*, 361:3.
3. (587) ^{h}*malāḫi*, 221:6.
4. (585) desc. of ^{d}*Nanā-iddin*, 143:6.
5. f. of ^{d}*Innin-zēr-iqīša*, 361:3.

^{d}*Nabû-iraššî* (^{1d}AG.TUG) f. of ^{d}*Nergal-ibnî*, 24:9.

^{d}*Nabû-karābi* (^{1d}AG.SIZKUR.SIZKUR), *a.* of *Balāṭsu*, 87:14.

^{d}*Nabû-kāṣir* (^{1d}AG.KÁD) (583), 145:3.

^{d}*Nabû-kēšir* (^{1d}AG-*ke-šìr*)
1. (587) desc. of *Zēr-ibnî*, 159:8.
2. (587), 173:10.
3. (582), 210:2.
4. f. of *Mušēzib*-^{d}*Marduk*, desc. of *Iddin*-^{d}*Papsukkal*, 357:2.

^{d}*Nabû-kīna-uballiṭ* (^{1d}⸢AG.GUB.TIN-⸣*iṭ*) (586), 152:18.

^{d}*Nabû-kišar* (^{1d}AG-*ki-šar*) f. of *Šumā*, 293:8.

^{d}*Nabû-lē'i* (^{1d}AG.DA)
1. (603) desc. of ^{1}⸢X.X-⸣*bi*, 45:1.
2. (602), 46:8.
3. (589) s. of *Aplā*, ^{h}*miṣirā*, wit., 4:17.
4. (584) s. of ^{d}*Bēl-ušallim*, desc. of ⸢^{d}*Nergal-līšir*⸣, 154:2.
5. f. of *Aqara*, 308:10; 314:15.
6. f. of *Kabtiya*, desc. of ^{h}*Naggāru*, 269:5.
7. f. of *Zēr-ukīn*, 83:6.

^{d}*Nabû-luddā* (^{1d}AG-⸢*lu-ud-da*⸣) (605), 113:54.

^{d}*Nabû-mīta-uballiṭ* (^{1d}AG.BE.TIN-*iṭ*) (591) desc. of *Nadna-aplu*, and *Dabibi*, 18:1; possibly 28:1 (broken) (603? possibly 593).

^{d}*Nabû-muk-ki-e-lip* (^{1d}AG-*muk-ki-e-lip*)
1. (590) *a.*'s name broken, 43:3.
2. (586) desc. of *Balāṭu*, 39:6.
3. (521) s. of *Nurānu*, 289:5, 13.

^{d}*Nabû-mukīn-apli* (^{1d}AG.GUB.A)
1. (^{1d}AG.GUB.⸢DUMU.UŠ⸣) (596) s. of *Ṣillā*, 322:36.
2. (589) s. of ^{d}*Nabû*-[X.X], desc. of *Bariḫi-ili*, 27:10.
3. (588) s. of *Šulā*, 15:4.
4. *a.* of *Linūḫ-libbi*-^{d}*Innin*, 142:26.

^{d}*Nabû-mukīn-zēr* (^{1d}AG.GUB.NUMUN)
1. (594) s. of *Aplā*, desc. of *Ilī-bānû*, 327:3; 20:5 (591); 273:2 (589); 272:2 (587).
2. (583), 209:13.

^{d}*Nabû-munammir* (^{1d}AG.ZALÁG-*ir*)
1. (589) s. of *Sarriya*, 359:1, 4, 6, 8.

2. a. of ^{d}*Nabû-zēr-ibnî*, 61:3.
^{d}*Nabû-mušētiq-ṣēti* (^{1d}AG-*mu-še-tíq*-UD.DA) (587) s. of *Aplā*, 176:3.
^{d}*Nabû-nādin-aḫi* (^{1d}AG.SUM.ŠEŠ)
1. (605), 113:14.
2. (605), 113:40.
^{d}*Nabû-nādin-šum* (^{1d}AG-*na-din*-MU)
1.[86] (605) ^{h}*šatammu*, 29:4; 30:4, 9 (603); 198:3 (603); 46:13 (602); 7:2, 8 (601); 317:5 (597); 319:10 (596).
2. (600) s. of ^{1}KA.LU.MAŠ, desc. of *Gimil-^{d}Nanā*, 12:11.
3. f. of ^{d}*Ininni-šum-uṣur*, desc. of *Gimil-^{d}Nanā*, 12:15.
4. f. of ^{d}*Marduk-bēl-ilī*, 1:32.
^{d}*Nabû-nā-'id*
1. (^{1d}AG.NÍG.TUG) (603) desc. of *Šarraḫu*, 303:8.
2. (^{1d}AG.I) f. of ^{d}*Nabû-zēr-ukīn*, 25:2; 155:2.
^{d}*Nabû-nāṣir* (^{1d}AG.PAB)
1. (603) s. of ^{d}*Nabû*-[X.]⌈X⌉, ^{h}*errēšu*, 45:7.
2. (601) desc. of *Zabidā*, 75:7; 49:5 (594); 59:2 (588).
3. (596) s. of ^{d}*Nabû-šum-ukīn*, scribe, 322:40.
4. (591) desc. of *Gimillu*, 360 v 19.
5. (590) desc. of ^{d}*Šamaš-iddin*, 149:8.
6. (587) desc. of *Nikkassu*, LÚ.⌈X⌉, 140:3.
7. f. of *Kudurri*, 235:5.
8. f. of ^{d}*Nergal-uballiṭ*, desc. of *Kurî*, 336:17 and 338:18.
9. f. of *Tabnēa*, desc. of ^{h}*Purkullu*, 327:10.
10. f. of *Zigga*, 291:16.
11. *a.* of *Bulluṭa*, 37:6.
12. *a.* of *Kudurri*, 171:2.
13. *a.* of *Kudurri*, 280:3.
14. *a.* of *Kudurri*, 277:2.
15. *a.* (son's name partially destroyed), 212:3.
^{d}*Nabû*-⌈*na*?-⌉[X] (589) s. of *Nadna-ilūtim*, wit., 27:5.
^{d}*Nabû-pir-la'*, (^{1d}AG-*pir-la-'*) f. of ^{d}*Bēl-šum-iškun*, 242:4.
^{d}*Nabû-rē'īšunu* (^{1d}AG.SIPA-*šú-nu*) (605), 113:58.
^{d}*Nabû-rēmanni* (^{1d}AG-*re-man-ni*)
1. (590), 144:1.
2. (588, possibly 609, Nbp.), 146:15.
3. (587), 134:2.
4. (585) desc. of ^{d}*Nanā-ēpuš*, 143:7.
5. (582), 206:7.
^{d}*Nabû-rēma-iškun* (^{1d}AG.ARḪUŠ.GAR-*un*) a. of *Ardiya*, 142:17.
^{d}*Nabû-riḫit-uṣur* (^{1d}AG-*ri-ḫi-it*-PAB) (590), 144:6; 135:6 (^{1d}AG-*ri-ḫi-it*-URÙ).
^{d}*Nabû-riḫti-uṣur* (^{1d}AG-*ri-iḫ!-ti!*-URÙ) (587) s. of *Arad-^{d}Gula*, 23:2.
^{d}*Nabû-riṣūa* (^{1d}AG-*ri-ṣu-ú-a*) (590), 144:7.
^{d}*Nabû-ruṣi* (^{1d}AG-*ru-ṣí*[sic]) (587) desc. of *Rīmūt*, 142:7.
^{d}*Nabû-ṣābit-qātē* (^{1d}AG-*ṣa-bit*-ŠU^{II}) (590), 149:12.
^{d}*Nabû-šar-aḫḫēšu* (^{1d}AG.LUGAL.ŠEŠ.MEŠ-*šú*)
1. (603) s. of *Nādin*, desc. of *Nabutu*, 303:31.
2. (^{1d}AG.LUGAL.PAB.ME-*šú*) (601) desc. of ^{d}*Bēl-aḫḫē-erība*, 314:8; 308:2 (600).
3. f. of ^{d}*Nabû-zēr-iqīša*, 337:10.
^{d}*Nabû-šar-uṣur* (^{1d}AG.LUGAL.URÙ)
1. (590), 43:9.
2. (587) ^{h}*mar šiprišu ša* ^{d}*Nabû-nāṣir*, 140:5.
3. (582), 243:3.

86. For ^{d}*Nabû-nādin-šum* as *šatammu*, see above, n. 81.

4. (^{1d}AG.LUGAL.PAB) f. of ^{d}*Bēl-ušallim*, 50:5.

^{d}*Nabû-šar-*[*ḫi*?-]*ilāni* (^{1d}AG-⸢*šar*$_4$-⸣[*ḫi*?-] DINGIR.MEŠ) (589) s. of ^{d}*Nabû-bēl-*[X.X], a.'s name broken, wit., 27:8.

^{d}*Nabû-šum-ēreš* (^{1d}AG.MU.KÁM)
1. (604) s. of *Mušallim-*^{d}*Marduk*, desc. of ^{h}*Šangû-parakki*, 11:15.
2. (596), 319:2.
3. (594) s. of *Mušallim-*^{d}*Marduk*, scribe, 340:2, 15.
4. (591) desc. of *Eriši*, 363:6.
5. (588) s. of *Šūzubu*, 31:10.
6. (588) s. of *Ab-bi-*⸢ZU⸣, 2:6.
7. (588) desc. of *Ša-*^{d}*Nabû-šū*, 267:3.
8. f. of *Iddin-*^{d}*Nabû*, 25:1.
9. f. of ^{d}*Nergal-uballiṭ*, desc. of ^{h}*Šangû-parakki*, 6:25.

^{d}*Nabû-šum-ibnî* (^{1d}AG.MU.DÙ)
1. (604) desc. of ^{d}*Nabû-šum-*[X], 247:10.
2. (603) s. of ^{1}⸢X-⸣*ba*, scribe, 28:13.
3. (600) desc. of ^{1}⸢X-*e*-X.X⸣, 61:2.
4. (598) s. of ^{d}*Nabû-šum-ušabši*, 315:3.
5. (593) s. of *Iddin-*^{d}*Nergal*, 326:2.
6. (590) ^{h}*kuṭimmu*, 213:4.
7. (590), 360 vi 4, 12.
8. (586) desc. of *Šūzubu*, 123:3.
9. f. of ^{d}*Anu-*⸢X.⸣[X.X], 25:9.
10. f. of ^{d}*Nergal-ušallim*, 359:3.

^{d}*Nabû-šum-iddin* (^{1d}AG.MU.MU)
1. (605), 153:4.
2. (604), 54:4.
3. (603) s. of ^{d}*Bēl-aḫḫē-erība*, desc. of *Sippē*, scribe, 303:34.
4. (603) s. of *Bēliya*, 30:1.
5. (597), 325:7.
6. (596) s. of *Aplā*, desc. of *Kurû*, 322:34.
7. (592) desc. of *Kunā*, 332:2.
8. (591) desc. of *Eṭir-*^{d}*Bēl*, 360 iv 10.
9. (589) s. of ^{d}*Nergal-ušallim*, desc. of *Suḫaya*, wit., 4:19.
10. (584) desc. of ^{d}*Bēl-aḫ-iddin*, 40:19.
11. (year destroyed) s. of [^{1d}X-]*aḫḫē-erība*, 14:16.
12. f. of *Šumā*, desc. of *Iddin-*^{d}*Papsukkal*, 336 and 338:1; 357:11, 14.
13. *a.* of *Gimillu*, 113:44.

^{d}*Nabû-šum-imbi* (^{1d}AG.MU-*im-bi*) (605), 113:51.

^{d}*Nabû-šum-iqīša* (^{1d}AG.MU.BA-[*šá*]) f. of *Šulā*, 364:8.

^{d}*Nabû-šum-irši* (^{1d}AG.MU.TUG-*ši*) (603), 47:4.

^{d}*Nabû-šum-iškun* (^{1d}AG.MU.GAR-*un*)
1. (592) s. of *Puḫḫuru*, desc. of ^{d}*Ea-ilutu-bāni*, 5:1, 6, 7, 8.
2. (589), 27:1.
3. (584) s. of ^{d}*Nabû-zēr-iqīša*, 36:2.
4. *a.* of ^{d}*Marduk-šum-ēreš*, 53:14.
5. *a.* of ^{d}*Nabû-bānî-aḫ*, 358:13.
6. *a.* of ^{d}*Nabû-zēr-ukīn*, 106:2.

^{d}*Nabû-šum-līšir* (^{1d}AG.MU.GIŠ)
1. (^{1d}AG.MU.SI.SÁ) (603) s. of ^{d}*Nabû-ušabši*, desc. of ^{h}*Iššakku*, 303:32.
2. (^{1d}AG.MU.SI.SÁ) (591) *a.*'s name broken, scribe, 20:14.
3. (^{1d}AG.MU.SI.SÁ) (591) s. of ^{d}*Nabû-zēr-ukīn*, br. of *Rīmūt-*^{d}*Nabû*, 348:1, 13.
4. (587), 173:5, 8, 13.
5. (587), 161:3.
6. (586), 42:3.
7. (585) desc. of ^{d}*Marduk-nāṣir*, 143:17.

^{d}*Nabû-šum-ukīn* (^{1d}AG.MU.GUB)
1. (602) s. of ^{d}*Nergal-uballiṭ*, 200:3.
2. (592), 132:4.
3. (589) ^{h}*kuṭimmu*, 204:4.
4. (587), 173:11.
5. (585) desc. of *Aḫḫēšu*, 53:3.
6. (585) desc. of *Ibā*, 53:9.
7. (582), 206:6.

8. (521), 291:2.
9. f. of ^{d}*Nabû-nāṣir*, 322:40.
10. *a.* of *Ina-qībi-*^{d}*Nabû-lišlim*, 363:9.
11. *a.* of ^{d}*Innin-aḫ-uṣur*, 363:10.
12. *a.* of ^{d}*Nabû-bēlšunu*, 228:2.

^{d}*Nabû-šum-uṣur* (^{1d}AG.MU.URÙ)
1. (602) ^{h}*ša muḫḫi ešrê*, 46:8.
2. (590) desc. of ^{d}*Nabû-ušallim*, 149:3.

^{d}*Nabû-šum-ušabšî* (^{1d}AG.MU.GÁL-*ši*) f. of ^{d}*Nabû-šum-ibnî*, 315:3.

^{d}*Nabû-šum-*[X] (^{1d}AG.MU.[X]) (587), 173:3.

^{d}*Nabû-šum-*[X] (^{1d}AG.MU.[X]) *a.* of ^{d}*Nabû-šum-ibnî*, 247:10.

^{d}*Nabû-šum-*[X.]⌈X⌉ (^{1d}AG.MU.[X.]⌈X⌉) f. of *Arad-*^{d}*Nanā*, 348:23.

^{d}*Nabû-šum-*⌈X⌉ (^{1d}AG.MU.⌈X⌉) *a.* of *Aplā*, 267:5.

^{d}*Nabû-šuzibanni* (^{1d}AG-*šu-zib-an-ni*) (594–576 possible) ^{h}*qalla ša Iddin-aḫšu*, 106:7.

^{d}*Nabû-tabnî-uṣur*
1. (^{1d}AG-*tab-ni-ú-ṣur*) (601) s. of ^{d}*Nabû-ēpuš*, desc. of ^{d}*Sîn-tabnî*, scribe, 3:36.
2. (^{1d}AG-*tab-ni-*URÙ) (589) s. of ^{d}*Bēl-ēpuš*, desc. of ^{d}*Sîn-tabnî*, scribe, 359:14.

^{d}*Nabû-*TIN.[X] (^{1d}AG.TIN.[X]) (562) in SIL *ṣi-e-ti* (or: *ḫuṣ* [TAR]-*ṣi-e-ti*) *šá*, 9:19.

^{d}*Nabû-tukulti* (^{1d}AG.KU-*ti*) (590) ^{h}*nuḫatimmu ša* LÚ.ḪAB.GUD.MEŠ, a *šerku*, 362:21.

^{d}*Nabû-uballiṭ* (^{1d}AG.TIN-*iṭ*)
1. (604) s. of *Ina-Esaggil-zēr*, desc. of *Amēl-*^{d}*Ea*, 302:11.
2. *a.* of *Gimil-apli*, 211:4.

^{d}*Nabû-udammiq* (^{1d}AG.KAL)
1. (601) s. of ^{d}*Nabû-zēr-ukīn*, desc. of *Ekur-zākir*, 7:17.
2. f. of ^{d}*Marduk-apla-uṣur*, desc. of ^{h}*Purkullu*, 327:14.
3. (^{1d}AG.SIG$_5$-*iq*) f. of ^{d}*Nabû-aḫḫē-ušallim*, a.'s name broken, 359:10.
4. f. of *Nāṣir*, desc. of ^{h}*Rē'û*, 360 i 42′; 361:16.
5. f., (son's name broken), 359:13.
6. *a.* of ^{d}*Šamaš-iddin*, 300:25.

^{d}*Nabû-ušabšî* (^{1d}AG.GÁL-*ši*)
1. (597), 325:7.
2. (596) s. of ^{d}*Nergal-ušallim*, desc. of *Nūr-*^{d}*Sîn*, 337:1, 8; 13:1, 8, 10 (588).
3. (590) ^{h}*nuḫatimmu ša* LÚ.ḪAB.GUD.MEŠ, a *šerku*, 362:24.
4. (^{1d}AG.TIL) (588, possibly Nbp. 609) desc. of ^{d}*Bēl-ibnî*, 146:39.
5. (586) desc. of *Arad-*^{d}*Nanā*, 39:8.
6. (586), 152:5.
7. (584), 40:6.
8. f. of *Ina-tēšî-ēṭir*, 322:4.
9. f. of *Mušallim-*^{d}*Marduk*, 223:3.
10. f. of ^{d}*Nabû-šum-līšir*, desc. of ^{h}*Iššakku*, 303:32.

^{d}*Nabû-ušallim* (^{1d}AG.GI)
1. (593), 328:2.
2. (588, possibly Nbp. 609) desc. of *Amēl-*^{d}*Nanā*, 146:20.
3. (585), 53:9.
4. (583) desc. of *Kabtiya*, 19:13.
5. (year broken) s. of ^{d}*Bēl-ēreš*, desc. of *Taqīš-*^{d}*Gula*, 14:3, 8.
6. f. of ^{d}*Innin-mukīn-šum*, 16:9.
7. f. of ^{d}*Innin-zēr-iqīša*, 322:37.
8. f. of ^{d}*Inninna-zēr-ibnî*, 124:4.
9. f. of ^{d}*Nanā-iddin*, 249:5; 253:5.
10. f. of *Zēr-Bābili*, desc. of ^{h}*Rē'û*, 361:14.
11. f., son's name destroyed, 346:10.
12. *a.* of ^{d}*Nabû-šum-uṣur*, 149:3.

^{d}*Nabû-ušdu-uṣur*[87] (^{1d}AG-*uš-du-*URÙ) (587) desc. of ^{d}*Ea-zēr-iqīša*, 142:12.

87. Sandhi for *Nabû-išd-uṣur*?

ᵈ*Nabû-ušēzib* (ˡᵈAG-*ú-še-zib*)
1. (597) desc. of ʰ*Ša-nāšīšu*, 317:2.
2. (592) ʰ*qalla ša* ᵈ*Šamaš-šum-ukīn*, 357:8.
3. (591), 360 v 40.
4. (590), a *šerku*, 362:9.
5. f. of ᵈ*Bēl-aḫḫē-erība*, desc. of ʰ*Šangû*-⌈X.X⌉, 348:22.
6. f. of ᵈ*Bēl-ibnî*, 24:8.
7. *a*. of *Ibnî*-ᵈ*Ištar*, 159:10.
8. *a*. of ˡ⌈X-*šunu*⌉, 45:2.

ᵈ*Nabû-yāši* (ˡᵈAG-*ya-a-ši*) *a*. of *Ṣillā*, 115:11; 358:15.

ᵈ*Nabû-zabadu* (ˡᵈAG-*za-ba-du*) f. of *Yāda'*, 35:6.

ᵈ*Nabû-zēr-ibnî* (ˡᵈAG.NUMUN.DÙ)
1. (601) s. of *Iqīšā*, ʰ*rab bānû*, 7:15.
2. (601) s. of ˡᵈ[X-]*nāṣir*, desc. of ʰ*Pūṣāya*, 3:14, 17, 23, 39.
3. (600) desc. of ᵈ*Nabû-munammir*, 61:3.
4. (593) s. of *Bulluṭa*, 326:5.
5. (588) s. of ᵈ*Marduk-šarrašu*, 31:13.
6. f. of *Aḫulap*-ᵈ*Ištar*, 88:2.
7. f. of ᵈ*Bēl-ibnî*, 333:3.
8. *a*. of ᵈ*Nabû-aḫḫē-ušallim*, 363:3.
9. *a*. of *Nadan-apli*, 76:5.
10. *a*. of *Zi'iri*, 358:10.

ᵈ*Nabû-zēr-iddin* (ˡᵈAG.NUMUN.MU)
1. (603) ʰ*nappāḫ parzilli*, 304:4; 263:3 (602); 325:23 (597).
2. (597) s. of *Labāši*, 325:1, 5.
3. (593) ʰ*malāḫu* (text: GIŠ.MÁ.LAḪ₄), 329:5.
4. (591) s. of *Šum-ukīn*, wit., 21:12.
5. (590) a *šerku*, 362:2.
6. (588, possibly Nbp. 609), 146:9.
7. (586), 152:11.
8. f. of *Balāṭsu*, 195:5.
9. f. of ᵈ*Bēl-iddin*, 336:18 and 338:19.
10. f. of *Iqīšā*, 29:13.
11. *a*. of *Balāṭsu*, 42:6.
12. *a*. of *Iddin*-ᵈ*Inninna*, 194:5.
13. *a*. of *Silim*-ᵈ*Bēl*, 149:10.
14. *a*. of *Ṣillā*, 300:11.

ᵈ*Nabû-zēr-iqīša* (ˡᵈAG.NUMUN.BA-*šá*)
1. (596) s. of ᵈ*Nabû-šar-aḫḫēšu*, wit., 337:9.
2. (584) desc. of *Yama'*, 71:2.
3. (584) s. of *Aḫḫēa*, desc. of *Kurî*, 6:1, 9.
4. f. of ᵈ*Nabû-šum-iškun*, 36:3.
5. f. of *Šulā*, 208:5.

ᵈ*Nabû-zēr-līšir* (ˡᵈAG.NUMUN.GIŠ)
1. (589) s. of *Nādin*, desc. of *Rēmānu*, wit., 361:17; 2:37 (588).
2. f. of ᵈ*Nergal-iddin*, 45:6.
3. (ˡᵈAG.NUMUN.SI.SÁ) *a*. of ᵈ*Nabû-apla-iddin*, 301:20.

ᵈ*Nabû-zēr*-⌈*li*?-⌉[X] (ˡᵈAG.NUMUN-⌈*li*-⌉[X]) (605), 126:2.

ᵈ*Nabû-zēr-ukīn* (ˡᵈAG.NUMUN.GUB)
1. (601) s. of ᵈ*Ea-zēr-iqīša*, desc. of ʰ*Bā'iru*, wit., 22:11.
2. (594-576 possible) desc. of ᵈ*Nabû-šum-iškun*, 106:2.
3. (592) s. of ᵈ*Nergal-uballiṭ*, desc. of *Gimil*-ᵈ*Nanā*, 323:15.
4. (591) s. of *Ša*-ᵈ*Nabû-šū*, 348:16.
5. (588) s. of *Ša*-ᵈ*Nabû-šū*, desc. of ᵈ*Šamaš-apla*-⌈*iddin*⌉, wit., 2:36.
6. (586) s. of ᵈ*Nabû-nā'id*, 25:2; 155:2.
7. f. of *Babiya*, desc. of *Dūr*-ᵈ*Marduk*, 322:32.
8. f. of *Ibnî*-ᵈ*Ištar*, desc. of ʰ*Šatammu*, 32:16.
9. f. of *Ibnî*-ᵈ*Ištar*, desc. of ʰ*Pūṣāya*, 3:34.
10. f. of ᵈ*Nabû-šum-līšir* and *Rīmūt*-ᵈ*Nabû*, 348:2, 9.
11. f. of ᵈ*Nabû-udammiq*, desc. of *Ekur-zākir*, 7:17.
12. f. of ᵈ*Šamaš-šum-ukīn*, desc. of ʰ*Maḫḫû*, 336 and 338:3; 357:3.
13. *a*. of *Arad*-ᵈ*Inninna*, 149:4.
14. *a*. of *Ša*-ᵈ*Bēl-dubba*, 143:9.

^{d}*Nabû-zēr-uṣur* (^{1d}AG.NUMUN.URÙ) f. of *Šāpiku*, desc. of *Ḫunzû*, 3:31.

^{d}*Nabû-zēr-ušabši* (^{1d}AG.NUMUN.GÁL-*ši*)
1. (601) s. of *Šumā*, desc. of *Nūr-^{d}Sîn*, wit., 3:29.
2. (593) s. of *Ša-^{d}Nabû-šū*, 326:3.
3. (^{1d}AG.NUMUN.TIL) (588) desc. of *Iqīšā*, 240:6.
4. f. of *Gimil-^{d}Gula*, 25:12.

^{d}*Nabû-zēr-*⸢X⸣ (^{1d}AG.NUMUN.⸢X⸣) (585) *a.*'s name broken, 231:7.

^{d}*Nabû-zēr-*[X] (^{1d}AG.NUMUN.[X]) (583), 168:5.

^{d}*Nabû-*[*x*-]*binanni* (^{1d}AG-[*x-bi-na-an-ni*?⸣ (521) s. of *Ilu-ana-bītišu*, 292:5.

^{d}*Nabû-*⸢X-⸣*iddin* (^{1d}A[G.(X.)]MU) (585) desc. of *Nadna-aplu*, 53:1.

^{d}*Nabû-*⸢X.X-⸣*ilī* (^{1d}AG.⸢X.X.⸣DINGIR.MEŠ) (596) desc. of *Amēl-^{d}Nanā*, wit., 337:13.

^{d}*Nabû-*⸢X-⸣*ša* (^{1d}AG.⸢X-⸣*šá*) *a.* of *Ardiya*, 143:10.

^{d}*Nabû-*⸢X-⸣*ši-*[*ṣi-e*?⸣ (586) desc. of *Tabnēa*, 39:7.

^{d}*Nabû-*[X.X.X.X.X.X][88] (603) s. of *Nadna-aplu*, desc. of *Dabibi*, 28:1.

^{d}*Nabû-*[X.X] (594) s. of ^{d}*Nanā-ēreš*, 190:4.

^{d}*Nabû-*⸢X.⸣[X] (588), *a.*'s name destroyed, 262:6.

^{d}*Nabû-*[X.] (584) s. of ^{d}*Ea-šum-*[X], desc. of *Amēl-^{d}Ea*, 154:4.

^{d}*Nabû-*[X.X] (582) ^{h}*rē'ī satukki*, 100:3.

^{d}*Nabû-*[X.], f. of ^{d}*Nabû-mukīn-apli*, desc. of *Bariḫi-ili*, 27:10.

^{d}*Nabû-*[X.X], f. of *Bēlšunu*, 45:8.

^{d}*Nabû-*[X.]⸢X⸣, f. of ^{d}*Nabû-nāṣir*, 45:7.

^{d}*Nabû-*[X.X], *a.* of *Itti-^{d}Marduk-balāṭu*, 360 iii 8.

^{d}*Nabû-*[X.]⸢X⸣, *a.* of ^{d}*Nanā-ēreš*, 146:34.

^{d}*Nabû'ā* (^{1d}AG-'-A.AN) f. of *Aššur-māt-tuqqin*, 9:3.

Nabutu (^{1}*na-bu-tu*) a. of ^{d}*Nabû-šar-aḫḫēšu*, and *Nādin*, 303:31.

Nadan-apli (^{1}*na-dan-*A)
1. (583) desc. of ^{d}*Nabû-zēr-ibnî*, 76:5.
2. f. of *Appunu*, 115:7.

Nādin (^{1}*na-din*)
1. (604) s. of ^{d}*Bēl-ēreš*, 54:7.
2. (602) s. of *Marduk*, 200:2.
3. (595) s. of *Balāṭsu*, desc. of *Sukallē*(?), 26:13.
4.[89] (592) s. of *Marduk*, desc. of *Babūtti*, 323:14; 361:15, wit., (589).
5. (591) desc. of *Balāṭu*, scribe, 358:17.
6. (585) desc. of ^{d}*Bēl-ēreš*, 53:4.
7.[90] (584) s. of ^{d}*Nergal-nāṣir*, desc. of ^{h}*Išparu*, 6:19; 112:5 (^{h}*išparu* designates profession not a.).
8. f. of ^{d}*Nabû-šar-aḫḫēšu*, desc. of *Nabutu*, 303:31.
9. f. of ^{d}*Nabû-zēr-līšir*, desc. of *Rēmānu*, 2:37; 361:17.
10. f. of *Nā'id-^{d}Marduk*, desc. of LÚ.⸢X.X⸣, 21:1.
11. f. of *Šulā*, desc. of *Gimil-^{d}Nanā*, 348:25.
12. f. of *Šulā*, 31:12.
13. *a.* of ^{d}*Nergal-nikkassi*, 4:5, 12.
14. *a.* of ^{d}*Šamaš-mukīn-apli*, 126:13.

Nādin-^{d}Marduk (^{1}*n*[*a-d*]*in-*^{d}AMAR.UTU) a. of *Aplā* and ^{d}*Marduk-nāṣir*, 2:30.

Nadna-aḫ (^{1}SUM-*na-*ŠEŠ)
1. (597) ^{h}*naggāru*, 325:26.
2. (591) s. of ^{d}*Bēl-iddina*, 348:24.

88. Possibly same man as 18:2 (^{d}*Nabû-mīta-uballiṭ*), though traces do not favor this restoration.

89. Same man: *GCCI* 1, 6:12 (602 B.C.).

90. 1) [*Nā*]*din* A-*šú šá* ^{d}*Nergal-nāṣir* A ^{h}*Išparu* (6:19) appears as witness in *zāqipūtu*-document (584 B.C. - *Simanu*).
2) *Nādin* A-*šú šá* ^{d}*Nergal-nāṣir* ^{h}*išparu* (112:6) carries off wool colored with mineral-blue dye (584 B.C.-*Ab.*).

3. (590), 362:1.
4. *a.* of *Itti-^{d}Šamaš-balāṭu*, 300:14.

Nadna-aplu[91] (SUM-*na*-A)
1. (605) desc. of *^{d}Marduk-*⌈X.X⌉, 126:17.
2. (603) s. of *^{d}Bēl-iddin*, 30:18.
3. (603) s. of *Iddin-^{d}Nergal*, 74:7.
4. (603) s. of *Rīmūt*, 74:12.
5. (601) s. of ^{1}[X-]A, desc. of *Kurû*, 22:1.
6. (600) s. of *Aplā*, desc. of *Kurî*, 12:9.
7. (593) s. of *^{d}Bēl-usat*, 41:10.
8. (588) s. of *Kudurri*, desc. of *Kidin-^{d}Marduk*, wit., 2:35.
9. (^{1}*nad-na*-A) (588) desc. of *Itti-ili* (or: *Iddin-ili*), 227:1 (possibly 12).
10. (^{1}*nad-na*-A) (585) desc. of *Aplā*, 24:1, 4.
11. (585) desc. of *^{d}Bēl-aḫḫē-erība*, 143:4.
12. (583) desc. of *^{d}Nabû-aḫ-uṣur*, 76:4.
13. (521) s. of *Ibnî-^{d}Ištar*, 295:17; 300:39.
14. (521) s. of *^{d}Inninna-šum-uṣur*, desc. of *^{d}Sîn-lēq-unnini*, 289:15; 290:14.
15. (521) s. of *^{d}Inninna-šum-ibnî*, 300:32.
16. (521), 300:35.
17. (521), 37:19.
18. (*nad-na*-A) f. of *Ba*-⌈*ar*?-⌉[X], desc. of *^{h}Šangû-parakki*, 22:12.
19. (*nad-na*-A) f. of *Marduk*, desc. of *Gimil-^{d}Nanā*, 336 and 338:15.
20. (*nad-na*-A) f. of *Mukīn-zēr*, desc. of *Kidin-^{d}Marduk*, 336 and 338:16.
21.[92] (*nad-na*-A) f. of *^{d}Nabû-mīta-uballiṭ*, desc. of *Dabibi*, 18:2; possibly 28:2.
22. f. of [^{1d}X-]*ēṭir*, desc. of *Saggiya*, 6:20.
23. *a.* of *Amēl-^{d}Nanā*, 363:8.
24. *a.* of *Ibnî-^{d}Innin*, 142:5.
25. *a.* of *Ina-qībi-^{d}Bēl*, *^{h}kizû ša šarri*, 358:8.
26.[93] (*nad-na-a*-A) *a.* of *^{d}Ninurta-zēr-iqīša*, 320:7.
27. *a.* of *^{d}Nabû-ēṭir*, 166:2; 360 iii 15.
28. *a.* of *^{d}Nabû-*[X-]*iddin*, 53:1.
29. *a.* of *Silim-^{d}Bēl*, 241:5.
30. *a.* of *^{d}Zababa-šar-uṣur*, 358:12.

Nadna-ilūtim (^{1}*nad-*[*na-*]DINGIR-*tim*), f. of *^{d}Nabû-na-*[X], 27:6.

^{h}Naggariya (LÚ NAGAR-*ya*) a. of *Šum-ukīn* and *^{d}Marduk-ēreš*, 357:17.

^{h}Naggāru (LÚ NAGAR)
1. a. of *^{d}Bēl-aḫ-iddin* and *^{d}Bunene-ibnî*, 36:13.
2. a. of *Kabtiya* and *^{d}Nabû-lē'ī*, 269:4.

Nā'id-^{d}Innin (^{1}I.^{d}INNIN) (584) s. of *^{d}Nabû-aḫḫē-iddin*, br. of *Itti-^{d}Šamaš-balāṭu*, 40:9.

Nā'id-^{d}Ištar
1. (^{1}I-^{d}*iš-tar*) (590) a *šerku*, 362:10.
2. (^{1}IM.TUK.^{d}15) (521) s. of *Arad-^{d}Inninna*, 287:17; 299:17.

Nā'id-^{d}Marduk (^{1}I.^{d}AMAR.UTU)
1. (591) s. of *Nādin*, desc. of LÚ.⌈X.X⌉, 21:1.
2. *a.* of *Silim-^{d}Bēl*, 329:8.

^{d}Nanā-aḫ-ēreš (^{1d}*na-na-a*-ŠEŠ.KÁM)
1. (588, possibly Nbp. 609), 146:14.
2. (584) desc. of *Šumā*, 40:8.

^{d}Nanā-aḫ-iddin (^{1d}*na-na-a*-ŠEŠ.MU)
1. (603) desc. of *^{d}Bēl-nuḫšu*, 241:1.
2. (601) desc. of *Arrab*, 314:9; 308:3 (600).
3. (601) desc. of *Mušēzib-ili*, 314:17.
4. (601) desc. of *^{d}Nabû-ēṭir*, 314:6.
5. (600) s. of *Mušēzib-^{d}Marduk*, 308:5.
6. (592) *^{h}qīpu*, 189:11.

91. All SUM-*na*-A names are here read *Nadna-aplu*.
92. 28:2 *^{d}Nabû-*[X.X.X.X.X.X]: possibly same man as 18:2 though traces do not favor this restoration.
93. Does this spelling indicate a reading *Nadnay(a)*?

7. (586), 152:15.
8. (521) s. of *Ardiya*, 296:5.
9. (521) s. of ^{d}*Nabû-aḫḫē-erība*, 293:8.
10. f. of *Labāši*, 293:20; 296:16; 297:6.

^{d}*Nanā-aḫ-uṣur* (^{1d}*na-na-a*-ŠEŠ.URÙ) (583) desc. of *Ṭāb-Uruk*, 114:6.

^{d}*Nanā-ēpuš* (^{1d}*na-na-a*-DÙ-*uš*)
1. (588) s. of *Mukīn-zēr*, desc. of *Gimil-*^{d}*Nanā*, wit., 2:32.
2. (586) desc. of ^{d}*Nabû-aḫ-ēreš*, 42:7.
3. *a.* of ^{d}*Nabû-rēmanni*, 143:7.

^{d}*Nanā-ēreš* (^{1d}*na-na-a*-KÁM)
1. (601) *ša āl zamē*, 122:5.
2. (601) s. of *Ardā*, 3:18.
3. (601) s. of *Ardā*, 314:4, 12, 20; 308:11 (600).
4. (597), 325:26.
5. (596) s. of *Balāṭsu*, 322:35.
6. (595) ^{h}*puṣāya*, 250:4.
7. (590) ^{h}*puṣāya*, a *šerku*, 362:3.
8. (589) desc. of *Ibnā*, 91:2.
9. (588), 227:16.
10. (588, possibly Nbp. 609) desc. of ^{d}*Nabû*-[X.] ⸢X⸣, 146:34.
11. (587) s. of ^{d}*Nanā-ibnî*, 58:2.
12. (586), 251:3.
13. (521) s. of *Gimillu*, 287:16; 288:16; 289:16; 292:15; 299:16.
14. (521) desc. of *Lāqīp*, 300:12.
15. (521) desc. of *Mukkēa*, 300:6.
16. f. of *Ardā*, 7:1.
17. f. of *Ḫašdiya*, 155:1.
18. f. of ^{d}*Nabû*-[X.X], 190:5.
19. *a.* of *Ab-lūmur*, 143:8.
20. *a.* of ^{d}*Adad-šum-iddin*, 149:7.
21. *a.* of *Babilaya*, 146:6.
22. *a.* of *Kinā*, 40:14.
23. *a.* of ^{d}*Nabû-aḫ-iddin*, 335:3; 356:3.
24. *a.* of ^{d}*Nanā-iddin*, 40:1.
25. *a.* of *Zēriya*, 39:2.
26. *a.* of *Zēriya*, 300:18.

^{d}*Nanā-ibnî* (^{1d}*na-na-a*-DÙ)
1. (588, possibly Nbp., 609) desc. of *Yašukimu*, 146:36.
2. (586), 39:11.
3. f. of *Bulluṭa*, 68:3.
4. f. of ^{d}*Nanā-ēreš*, 58:3.
5. *a.* of ^{d}*Nergal-ibnî*, 146:28.
6. *a.* of ^{d}*Nergal-nāṣir*, 39:1, 10.

^{d}*Nanā-iddin* (^{1d}*na-na-a*-MU)
1. (605) desc. of ^{d}*Šamaš-šum-iddin*, 113:59.
2. (603) ^{h}*išparu*, 103:4.
3. (602) ^{h}*išparu*, 305:3, 6.
4. (601) br. of ^{d}*Marduk-erība*, 75:10.
5. (600) s. of ^{d}*Nabû-ušallim*, ^{h}*išparu*, 249:5; 103:4 (603); 253:5 (601).
6. (590) desc. of *Mukīn-zēr*, 149:6.
7. (588, possibly Nbp., 609) desc. of *Ša-*^{d}*Nabû-šū*, 146:21.
8. (588, possibly Nbp., 609) desc. of ^{1}⸢X-⸣*šu*, 146:10.
9. (584) desc. of ^{d}*Bēl-lē'i*, 40:4.
10. (584) desc. of ^{d}*Nanā-ēreš*, 40:1.
11. f. of ^{d}*Nabû-iqīša*, 361:4.
12. *a.* of *Libluṭ*, 260:5.
13. *a.* of ^{d}*Nabû-iqīša*, 143:6.
14. *a.* of *Rīmūt*, 75:8.

^{d}*Nanā-ilūa* (^{1d}*na-na-a*-DINGIR-*ú-a*)
1. (592), 189:10.
2. (590) ^{h}*išparu*, a *šerku*, 362:5.

^{d}*Nanā-karābi* (^{1d}*na-na-a*-SIZKUR.SIZKUR) (521), desc. of *Ardiya*, 300:27.

^{fd}*Nanā-kiširat* (SAL ^{d}*na-na-a-ki-ši-rat*) (591) slave girl given in inheritance, 348:4.

^{fd}*Nanā-kiširrat*[94] (SAL ^{d}*na-na-a-ki-šìr-rat*) (582) daughter of ^{d}*Nanā-silim*, sister of ^{d}*Innin-aḫ-iddin*, 1:6, 13, 18.

^{d}*Nanā-silim* (^{1d}*na-na-a-si-lim*) f. of

94. *NBN*,159a lists: Nbk. 166:3; 175:2 and 265:12 as *qallatu*.

^{fd}*Nanā-kiširrat* and ^{d}*Innin-aḫ-iddin*, 1:7.

^{d}*Nanā-uballiṭ* (^{1d}*na-na-a*-TIN-*iṭ*) f. of *Ṣillā*, a. of ^{f}*Ḫammā*, 322:10.

^{d}*Nanā-uṣalli* (^{1d}*na-na-a-ú-ṣal-li*)
1. (582) s. of *Aḫ-ittabši*, 1:27.
2. f. of ^{d}*Bēl-erība*, 1:1.

^{fd}*Nanā*-[X.X-]*ḫūa* (SAL ^{d}*na-na-a*-[X.X-]*ḫu-ú-a*) (591) slave girl given in inheritance, 348:7.

^{d}*Nanā*-[X-]*iddin* (^{1d}*na-na-a*-[X.]MU) (584) ^{h}*išparu*, 104:5.

^{d}*Nanā*-[X] (^{1d}*na-na-a*-[X]) (590) ^{h}*nuḫatimmu*, a *šerku*, 362:25.

^{d}*Nanā*-[X] (^{1d}*na-na*-[*a*-X]) (588, possibly Nbp., 609), 146:22.

^{d}*Nanā*-[X] (^{1d}*na-na*-[*a*-X]) *a*. of *Ina-ṣilli*-^{d}*Nanā*, 363:2.

Nanaḫu (^{1}*na-na-ḫu*) a. of ^{d}*Bēl-zēr-ibnî* and ^{d}*Bēl-upaḫḫir*, 36:11.

^{h}*Nappāḫu* (LÚ SIMUG) a. of *Iddin*-^{d}*Marduk* and ^{d}*Bēl-nāṣir*, 11:4.

Naptešir (^{1}⌈NAP-⌉*te-ši-ir*) (588) s. of ^{d}*Marduk-šum-uṣur*, 2:14, 22, 41. [possibly error for *mul-te-šir*]

Nāṣir (^{1}*na-ṣir*)
1. (592), 331:1.
2. (591) s. of ^{d}*Nabû-udammiq*, desc. of ^{h}*Rē'û*, 360 i 42′; 361:16 (589) wit.
3. (587), 173:9.
4. (587), 173:10.
5. (586), 136:2.

Nāṣir-'a-ili (^{1}[*na*-]*ṣir*-'-DINGIR) (591) desc. of *Šumā*, wit., 358:11.

Na-⌈X.⌉[X.X] (^{1}*na*-⌈X.⌉[X.X]) (605), 113:31.

^{d}*Nergal-ana-bītišu*[95] (^{1d}U.GUR-*a*-⌈*na*-É-*šú*?⌉) (595) s. of *Gimillu*, 34:8.

^{d}*Nergal-ašared* (^{1d}U.GUR-*a-šá-red*) (594) br. of ^{d}*Bēl-ibnî*, s. of ^{d}*Nabû-iqbî*, desc. of *Ili-banû*, 327:4.

^{d}*Nergal-dānu* (^{1d}U.GUR-*da-a-nu*)
1. (588, possibly Nbp., 609) desc. of ^{d}*Nabû-ēṭir*, 146:11.
2. (588) desc. of *Marduka*, 138:1.

^{d}*Nergal-ēpuš* (^{1d}U.GUR.DÙ-*uš*)
1. (601) s. of *Rīmūt*, 306:4.
2. (588) s. of *Aḫḫēa*, 31:3.

^{d}*Nergal-ēreš* (^{1d}U.GUR.KÁM) (603) desc. of *Ibnā*, 241:6.

^{d}*Nergal-tēšī-ēṭir* (^{1d}U.GUR.SÙḪ.SUR) (602) s. of ^{d}*Ea-šum-ibnî*, desc. of ^{h}*Šangû-parakki*, 17:3.

^{d}*Nergal-ēṭir* (^{1d}U.GUR.SUR)
1. (603) s. of *Šumā*, desc. of *Ṣāḫit-ginē*, 303:29.
2. f. of *Riḫētu*, 21:13.

^{d}*Nergal-ibnî* (^{1d}U.GUR.DÙ)
1. (601) desc. of *Labāši*, 75:6.
2. (600) s. of ^{d}*Nabû-erība*, desc. of ^{d}*Sîn-nuqunnunu*, 12:10.
3. (588, possibly Nbp., 609), 146:29.
4. (588, possibly Nbp., 609) desc. of ^{d}*Nanā-ibnî*, 146:28.
5. (585) s. of ^{d}*Nabû-iraššî*, 24:9.
6. f. of *Kalbā*, 286:17.

^{d}*Nergal-iddin* (^{1d}U.GUR.MU)
1. (603) s. of ^{d}*Nabû-zēr-līšir*, ^{h}*errēšu*, 45:6.
2. (603) desc. of *Ṣāḫit-ginē*, 303:30.
3. (597), 325:18.
4. (593) s. of *Ina-tēšī-ēṭir*, 41:9.
5. (592) ^{h}*rē'û*, 189:5.
6. (586) s. of *Mušēzib*-^{d}*Marduk*, 155:3.
7. (521) desc. of *Iqīša*, 300:29.
8. (year broken), broken context, possibly ancestor, 14:19.
9. f. of *Mušēzib*-^{d}*Bēl*, desc. of *Gimil*-^{d}*Nanā*, 17:2.
10. f. of ^{d}*Šamaš-ibnî*, 26:3.

^{d}*Nergal-iddina* (^{1d}U.GUR.SUM-*na*) (591) s. of ^{d}*Šamaš-iqīša*, 18:3.

95. Only one other reference in Tallqvist, *NBN*, 161a.

^{d}*Nergal-ina-tēšī-ēṭir* (^{1d}U.GUR-*ina*-SÙḪ.SUR)
1. (604) s. of ^{d}*Nabû-iddin*, desc. of *Ekur-zākir*, scribe, 11:17.
2. (586) desc. of *Zabidā*, 33:2.

⸢^{d}*Nergal-līšir*⸣ ([^{1}]^{d}⸢U.GUR.GIŠ?⸣) a. of ^{d}*Nabû-lē'ī* and ^{d}*Bēl-ušallim*, 154:3.

^{d}*Nergal-nāṣir* (^{1d}U.GUR.PAB)
1. (602), 46:15, 17.
2.[96] (601) desc. of *Aqara*, 306:6; 360 v 35 (591); 159:5, 6 (587); 193:5 (584).
3. (^{1d}IGI.DU.PAB) (593) master of *Rikis-kalamma-*^{d}*Bēl*, 352:7.
4. (592), 128:4.
5. (591) desc. of *Rīmūt*, 363:1.
6. (591), 360 iv 45, 50.
7. (587), 173:10, possibly same man as lines 12 and 17.
8. (587), 164:4.
9. (586), 281:9.
10. (586) desc. of ^{d}*Nanā-ibnî*, 39:1, 10.
11. (584) s. of *Šāpik*, scribe, 16:3, 7, 11, 12.
12. (583), 167:6.
13.[97] f. of *Nādin*, desc. of ^{h}*Išparu*, 6:19 (584); f. of *Nādin*, ^{h}*išparu*, 112:6 (584).
14. *a.*, desc.'s name broken, 39:10.

^{d}*Nergal-nikkassi*[98] (^{1d}U.GUR.NÍG.ŠID) (589) desc. of *Nādin*, 4:5, 12.

^{d}*Nergal-šum-ibnî* (^{1d}U.GUR.MU.DÙ)
1. (596) s. of *Mūru*, 322:7.
2. (596) desc. of *Šullummā*, 337:3.

^{d}*Nergal-šum-uṣur*[99] (^{1d}U.GUR.MU.URÙ) f. of *Kabti-ili-*^{d}*Marduk*, desc. of *Dabibi*, 5:13.

^{d}*Nergal-uballiṭ* (^{1d}U.GUR.TIN-*iṭ*)
1. (601) s. of *Balaṭ*, 306:3.
2. (594) s. of ^{d}*Nabû-nāṣir*, desc. of *Kurî*, wit., 336:16 and 338:17.
3. (589) desc. of ^{d}*Bēl-lē'ī*, 187:9.
4. (584) s. of ^{d}*Nabû-šum-ēreš*, desc. of ^{h}*Šangû-parakki*, scribe, 6:25.
5. f. of ^{d}*Nabû-šum-ukīn*, 200:3.
6. f. of ^{d}*Nabû-zēr-ukīn*, desc. of *Gimil-*^{d}*Nanā*, 323:15.

^{d}*Nergal-uṣur* (^{1d}U.GUR-*ú-ṣur*), f. of ^{d}*Inninna-šum-uṣur*, 35:17.

^{d}*Nergal-ušallim* (^{1d}U.GUR.GI)
1. (594) desc. of ^{d}*Ninurta-erība*, 320:4.
2. (593) desc. of ^{d}*Bēl-nāṣir*, 107:4.
3. (591), 283:3.
4. (589) s. of ^{d}*Nabû-šum-ibnî*, ^{h}*rab qannāta*, 359:2, 5, 7, 8.
5. (588, possibly Nbp., 609) desc. of ^{d}*Nabû-aḫ-uṣur*, 146:19.
6. (586) s. of *Babiya*, 55:9.
7. (585) desc. of *Gimillu*, 143:5.
8. (year destroyed) s. of ^{d}*Bēl-ibnî*, 14:18.
9. f. of *Banunu*, desc. of ^{d}*Sîn-tabnî*, 14:15.
10. f. of ^{d}*Nabû-aḫḫē-iddin*, desc. of *Nūr-*^{d}*Sîn*, 12:1; 26:2; 33:7; 323:8; 361:1.
11. f. of ^{d}*Nabû-šum-iddin*, desc. of *Suḫaya*, 4:19.
12. f. of ^{d}*Nabû-ušabši*, desc. of *Nūr-*^{d}*Sîn*, 13:2; 337:2.
13. f. of *Taqīš-*^{d}*Gula*, desc. of *Nūr-*^{d}*Sîn*, 21:4; 15:3 (no a. listed in 15:3).
14. *a.* of *Iddin-*^{d}*Nabû*, 97:2.

^{d}*Nergal-ušēzib* ([^{1}]^{d}U.GUR-*ú-še-zib*)
1. (600) ^{h}*atû*, 192:4.
2. (596) desc. of *Šullummā*, wit., 337:14.
3. (590) desc. of ^{d}*Bēl-uballiṭ*, 149:2.

96. Also *GCCI* 1, 20:4 (601 B.C.).
97. Note interchangeability of PN A-*šú šá* PN_2 PrN with PN A-*šú šá* PN_2 A LÚ PrN.
98. For NÍG.ŠID in PN's, cp. 140:3 and 149:9, *Nikkassu*.
99. For reading compare the name in Freydank, *Spätbabylonische Wirtschaftstexte*, p. 142a.

4. f. of ^{d}*Inninna-šum-uṣur*, desc. of *Kidin-*^{d}*Marduk*, 294:17; 298:19 (a. not listed).

^{d}*Nergal-u-*[X.X] (^{1d}U.GUR-*ú*-[X.X]) (598), 172:7.

^{d}*Nergal-zēr-ibnî*

1. (^{1d}IGI.DU.NUMUN.DÙ) (605), 113:49.
2. (^{1d}U.GUR.NUMUN.DÙ) (587), 275:2.

⌈^{d}*Nergal-*⌉[X] (^{1d}⌈U.⌉G[UR.X])[100] (591) desc. of ^{d}*Nabû-eḫa-*[X.X], 360 ii 20.

^{d}*Nergal-*[X.X] (585), 188:3.

Nēšu (^{1}*ni-e-šú*)

1. (602), 185:2.
2. (601) desc. of *Ezū-pāšir*, 314:7.
3. f. of *Ap/Ṣil-lā*, 155:6.

Nikkassu (^{1}NÌ.ŠID)

1. *a.* of ^{d}*Nabû-nāṣir*, 140:3.
2. *a.* of *Silim-*^{d}*Bēl*, 149:9.

^{d}*Ninurta-bānî* (^{1d}MAŠ-*ba-ni*), *a.* of ^{d}*Enlil-aḫḫē-iddin*, 320:9.

^{d}*Ninurta-erība* (^{1d}MAŠ.SU)

1. (594) desc. of *Šumā*, 320:2.
2. *a.* of ^{d}*Nergal-ušallim*, 320:4.

^{d}*Ninurta-gāmil* (^{1d}MAŠ-*ga-mil*), *a.* of *Šulā*, 24:3.

^{d}*Ninurta-iqīša* (^{1d}MAŠ.BA-*šá*) *a.* of *Erība-*^{d}*Marduk*, 320:3.

^{d}*Ninurta-šar-uṣur* (^{1d}MAŠ.LUGAL.PAB/URÙ) (605) ^{h}*qīpu*, 29:3; 30:4, 8 (603); 7:2, 7 (601); 319:9 (596); 207:2 (588).

^{d}*Ninurta-zēr-iqīša* (^{1d}MAŠ.NUMUN.BA-*šá*) (594) desc. of *Nadna-aplu*, 320:7.

^{d}*Ninurta-*[X.X.X.X.X.X.X] (^{1d}MAŠ.⌈X.⌉[X.X.X.X.X]) *a.*, desc.'s name broken, 28:4.

Nišānu[101] f. of *Ina-ṣilli-*^{d}*Nanā*, 189:3 (^{1}*ni-šá-a-nu*); 360 i 51′ (^{1}*ni-šá-nu*) (*a.*).

Nūr-^{d}*Bēl-lūmur* (^{1}ZALÁG.^{d}EN-*lu-mur*) (592), 78:3.

Nūr-^{d}*Papsukkal* (^{1}ZALÁG.^{d}PAB.SUKKAL) a. of ^{d}*Nabû-balāṭsu-iqbî* and *Zēr-ibnî*, 327:12.

Nūr-^{d}*Sîn* (^{1}ZALÁG.^{d}30)

1. a. of ^{d}*Bēl-nādin-apli* and *Iddin-*^{d}*Marduk*, 32:13.
2. a. of *Kalbā* and ^{d}*Šamaš-nāṣir*, 4:16.
3. a. of ^{d}*Nabû-aḫḫē-iddin* and ^{d}*Nergal-ušallim*, 12:2; 26:2; 33:7; 323:9; 361:2.
4. a. of ^{d}*Nabû-ušabši* and ^{d}*Nergal-ušallim*, 13:2; 337:2.
5. a. of ^{d}*Nabû-zēr-ušabši* and *Šumā*, 3:29.
6. a. of *Taqīš-*^{d}*Gula* and ^{d}*Nergal-ušallim*, 21:5.

Nūr-^{d}*Šamaš* (^{1}ZALÁG.^{d}UTU) *a.* of *Iqīšā*, 61:5.

Nurānu (^{1}*nu-ra-nu*)

1. (583) desc. of *Ḫarīṣ*, 76:10.
2. f. of ^{d}*Nabû-muk-ki-e-lip*, 289:6.
3. *a.* of *Šum-ukīn*, 76:13.

Nūreya (^{1}ZALÁG-*e-a*)

1. [102] (603), 74:14.
2. f. of *Šum-iddin*, 31:4.
3. (^{1}*nu-re-ya*) f. of *Šumā*, 9:14.

Nūršu-ša-^{d}*Anu* (^{1}ZALÁG-*šú-šá-*^{d}60) (591), 225:2.

Nūr-[X.X.X] (⌈^{1}⌉ZALÁG.[X.X.X]) (586), 152:6.

^{d}*Nusku-nāṣir* (^{1d}PA.KU-*na-ṣir*) (603) desc. of *Balāṭu*, wit., 28:11.

^{h}*Paḫḫāru*[103] (^{1}LÚ.BAḪÁR) *a.* of *Aplā*, 303:4.

100. ^{1d}PA[PSUKKAL. . .] is also possible.
101. This reference shows that A-*šú šá* and A are often identical.
102. Reading unsure.
103. Note upright before PrN.

Pān-^{d}*Nabû-adaggal* (^{1}IGI.^{d}AG-*a-dag-gal*) (584) desc. of *Aplā*, 40:5; 142:16 (587).

Pān-^{d}*Nabû-lūmur* (^{1}IGI.⌈^{d}AG-*lu?-mur?*⌉) (587), 275:13.

Pir'u (^{1}*pir-'u*)
1. (604) s. of *Eanna-šum-ibnî*, scribe, 302:12.
2. f. of ^{d}*Bau-iqīša*, 13:13.

Puḫḫuru (^{1}*pu-uḫ-ḫu-ru*) f. of ^{d}*Nabû-šum-iškun*, desc. of ^{d}*Ea-ilutu-bāni*, 5:2.

^{h}*Purkullu* (LÚ BUR.GUL)
1. a. of ^{d}*Marduk-apla-uṣur* and ^{d}*Nabû-udammiq*, 327:15.
2. a. of *Tabnēa* and ^{d}*Nabû-nāṣir*, 327:10.

^{h}*Pūṣāya*[104] (LÚ.TÚG.BABBAR)
1. a. of *Ibnî-*^{d}*Ištar* and ^{d}*Nabû-zēr-ukīn*, 3:34.
2. a. of ^{d}*Nabû-zēr-ibnî* and [^{1d}X-*nāṣir*], 3:18, 39.

Qurdu-^{d}*Nergal* (^{1}*qur-du-*^{d}U.GUR) (586), 152:17.

^{h}*Rab-bānû* (LÚ GAL.DÙ)
1. a. of ^{d}*Marduk-šāpik-zēr* and ^{d}*Marduk-šum-uṣur*, 6:2.
2. a. of ^{d}*Marduk-šum-uṣur* and ^{d}*Nabû-aḫḫē-iddin*, 340:14.
3. a. of ^{d}*Nabû-erība* and ^{d}*Bēl-uballiṭ*, 38:9.

Rāši-ili
1. (^{1}*ra-šil*) (591) desc. of *Marduka*, 21:9.
2. (^{1}TUK-*ši*-DINGIR) f. of ^{d}*Bēl-iddin*, desc. of *Kudurānu*, 336:13; and 338:14.
3. (^{1}*ra-šil*-DINGIR) (591) f. of *Kinā*, desc. of ^{h}*Gallābu*, 360 ii 4.

^{h}*Rē'ī-alpi* (LÚ SIPA.GUD) *a.* of ^{d}*Marduk-šāpik-zēr*, 20:14.

^{h}*Rē'ī-satukki* (LÚ SIPA SÁ.TUK) a. of *Kudurri* and *Šumā*, 7:16.

^{h}*Rē'ī-sisē* (LÚ.SIPA.ANŠE.KUR.RA) a. of ^{d}*Bēl-aḫḫē-iddin* and *Ilī-bānî*, 303:14.

Rēmānu (*re-ma-nu*)
1. a. of ^{d}*Innin-šum-ēreš* and ^{d}*Nabû-aḫḫē-ušallim*, 4:2, (line 3: dittograph), 6[105] (A *Rēmānu*); 2:11.
2.[106] a. of *Kudurri* and *Ardiya*, 4:21.
3. a. of ^{d}*Nabû-zēr-līšir* and *Nādin*, 2:37; 361:17.

Rēmūtu (^{1}*ri-e-mu-tu*) (588) s. of *Zērūtu*, 15:1.

^{h}*Rē'û* (LÚ.SIPA)
1. f. of *Zēr-Bābili*, 317:4.
2. (^{1}*re-'*) *a.* of *Amēl-*^{d}*Nanā*, 89:2.
3. a. of *Nāṣir* and ^{d}*Nabû-udammiq*, 360 i 43′; 361:16.
4. a. of ^{d}*Šamaš-udammiq* and *Iqīšā*, 6:24; 276:12.
5. a. of *Zēr-Bābili* and ^{d}*Nabû-ušallim*, 361:14.

Riḫēti (^{1}*ri-ḫi-e-ti*) *a.* of *Amēl-*^{d}*Nanā*, 125:3.

Riḫētu (^{1}*ri-ḫi-e-tú*)
1. (591) s. of ^{d}*Nergal-ēṭir*, wit., 21:13.
2. (590) desc. of ^{d}*Nabû-iddin*, 43:2.
3. *a.* of *Silim-*^{d}*Bēl*, 146:8.

Riḫi-^{d}*Adad* (^{1}*ri-ḫi-*^{d}IM) (583) s. of *Ša-*^{d}*Nabû-šū*, 19:5.

Rikis-kalama-^{d}*Bēl* (^{1}TIM.DÙ.A.BI.^{d}EN)
1. (593) ^{h}*qalla ša* ^{d}*Nergal-nāṣir*, 352:6.
2. (590) ^{h}*qalla ša* ^{d}*Bēl-uballiṭ*, 215:3.
3. (583), 145:6.

104. "Whitener" of new and used linen garments in the divine wardrobe (*puṣṣû*). Possibly the reading of LÚ.TÚG.BABBAR(/UD) in NB ancestral names. But the reading may also be *ašlāku*; see *CAD* A/2, 447 discussion section.

105. 4:6 shows PN A PN_2 can sometimes refer to ancestor.

106. Possibly Sandhi sp. for *Rīmi-*^{d}*Anu*, 357:18, 19, q.v.

Rīmi-^{d}*Anu*[107] (*ri-i-mi-*^{d}*a-num*) a. of *Kudurri*, *Ardā* and *Iqīša-*^{d}*Marduk*, 357:18, 19.

Rīmūt (^{1}*ri-mut*)
1. (604) s. of ^{d}*Bēl-aḫ-iddin*, ^{h}*kuṭimmu*, 245:4.
2. (604) s. of ^{d}*Bēl-aḫ-iddin*, 54:9.
3. (604), 52:8.
4. (603) desc. of *Šarru-*^{d}*Bēl*, 45:3.
5. (601) s. of *Balāṭu*, 124:3.
6. (601) desc. of ^{d}*Nanā-iddin*, 75:8.
7. (597), 325:22.
8. (592), 189:4.
9. (591) desc. of ^{d}*Adad-aḫ-erība*, 360 iv 3.
10. (590) desc. of *Šum-ukīn*, 149:5.
11. (590) desc. of *Kudurri*, 369:6.
12. (590) ^{h}*nuḫatimmu*, a *širku*, 362:22.
13. (590), 365:3.
14. (590), 67:2.
15. (589) s. of ^{d}*Marduk-zēr-ibnî*, 361:10.
16. (589?, [X+]16) ^{h}*sa-ba-sin-nu*, 211:7.
17. (588), 2:8.
18. (586), 152:3.
19. (585) desc. of ^{d}*Marduk-šum-ibnî*, 53:16.
20. (582) s. of *Ša-*^{d}*Nabû-šū*, 1:25.
21. (521) s. of ^{d}*Inninna-zēr-iqīša*, 35:15.
22. f. of *Aḫ-ittabši*, 336 and 338:8.
23. f. of *Arad-*^{d}*Inninna*, 1:29.
24. f. of *Eanna-līpi-uṣur*, desc. of ^{d}*Sîn-lēq-unnini*, scribe, 122:6 (no a. listed); 319:15; 350:5.
25. f. of *Etellu*, 19:12.
26. f. of ^{d}*Innin-aḫḫē-iddin*, desc. of *Ḫunzû*, 26:15.
27. f. of ^{d}*Marduk-šum-līšir*, desc. of ^{d}*Bēl-usat*, 6:23.
28. f. of ^{d}*Nabû-balāṭsu-iqbî*, 8:14.
29. f. of *Nadna-aplu*, 74:13.
30. f. of ^{d}*Nergal-ēpuš*, 306:4.
31. *a.* of ^{d}*Bēl-upaḫḫir*, 266:2.
32. *a.* of ^{d}*Nabû-ruṣi*, 142:7.
33. *a.* of ^{d}*Nergal-nāṣir*, 363:1.

Rīmūt-^{d}*Gula* (^{1}*ri-mut-*^{d}*gu-la*) *a.* of *Zēriya*, 360 iv 14.

Rīmūt-ili (^{1}*ri-mut-*DINGIR) (521) ^{h}*til-addaya*, 300:23.

Rīmūt-^{d}*Nabû* (^{1}*ri-mut-*^{d}AG) (591) br. of ^{d}*Nabû-šum-līšir*, s. of ^{d}*Nabû-zēr-ukīn*, 348:2, 20.

Rīmūtu (^{1}*ri-mu-tu*) (591), 66:1.

Saggil (^{1}SAG.GIL) f. of *Marduk*, desc. of *Ili-banû*, 327:13.

Saggillu (^{1}⸢*sag-gíl-*⸣*lu*) f. of [^{1}X.X-]^{d}*Nergal*, 155:4.

Saggiya (^{1}*sag-gi*$_{4}$*-ya*) a. of [^{1d}X-]*ēṭir* and *Nadna-aplu*, 6:20.

Sarriya (^{1}*sa-ar-ri-ya*) f. of ^{d}*Nabû-munammir*, 359:1.

Sāsiya (^{1}*sa-si-ya*) (583) s. of ^{d}*Nabû-aḫḫē-ēreš*, 19:2.

^{f}*Sigiti* (SAL *si-gi-ti*) mother of ^{d}*Inninna-šum-ibnî*, 300:5.

Silim-^{d}*Bēl* (*si-lim-*^{d}EN)
1. (603) desc. of *Nadna-aplu*, 241:5.
2. (593) s. of *Aplā*, 57:2.
3. (593) s. of *Aplā*, 121:1.
4. (593) desc. of *Nā'id-*^{d}*Marduk*, 329:7.
5. (591) desc. of *Ardiya*, 360 iii 18.
6. (591) desc. of *Isinnaya*, 360 iii 20; v 8; vi 5 (590).
7. (590) desc. of ^{d}*Nabû-zēr-iddin*, 149:10.
8. (590) desc. of *Nikkassu*, 149:9.
9. (590) desc. of *Arad-*^{d}*Inninna*, 360 vi 13.
10. (590), 360 vi 4, 10, 12.

107. Possibly same as *Rēmānu*, 4:21, q.v.

11. (588, possibly Nbp., 609) desc. of *Riḫētu*, 146:8.
12. (586) br. of *Amēl-ᵈNabû*, s. of *ᵈŠamaš-iddin*, 25:6.

Silim-ili (*ᴵsi-lim-ìli*) f. of *ᵈInninna-šum-uṣur*, 299:7.

ᵈSîn-ab-ilišu (ᴵᵈ30.AD.DU.DINGIR-*šú*) (605), 113:38.

ᵈSîn-aḫ-iddin (ᴵᵈ30.ŠEŠ.MU) f. of *ᵈŠamaš-iqīša*, 291:7.

ᵈSîn-ēreš (ᴵᵈ30.KÁM)
1. (586), 274:7, 15.
2. f. of *ᵈBēl-iddin*, desc. of *Ibnî-ilī*, 302:9.

ᵈSîn-ēṭir (ᴵᵈ30.SUR) (594–576 possible), 106:5.

ᵈSîn-ibnî (ᴵᵈ30.DÙ) (587), 221:2.

ᵈSîn-iddin (ᴵᵈ30.MU)
1. (591) desc. of *ᵈSîn*-[X.X], 360 iii 7.
2. (562) *ʰqīpi ša Eanna*, 9:5, 8.
3. *a.* of *ᵈBēl-iddin*, 126:18.

ᵈSîn-lēq-unnini (ᴵᵈ30.TI.ÌR)
1. a. of *Eanna-līpi-uṣur* and *Rīmūt*, 319:15.
2. a. of *Ina-tēšî-ēṭir* and *Šākin-zēr*, 322:33.
3.[108] a. of *Nadna-aplu* and *ᵈInninna-šum-uṣur*, 289:15; 290:14.
4. a. of *ᵈNabû-balāṭsu-iqbi* and *ᵈNabû-ēṭir*, 360 ii 9; 361:20.
5. a. of *ᵈNabû-bēlšunu* and *ᵈNabû-aḫ-iddin*, 2:33.

ᵈSîn-nuqunnunu[109] (ᴵᵈ30-*nu-qu-un-nu-nu*), a. of *ᵈNergal-ibnî* and *ᵈNabû-erība*, 12:11.

ᵈSîn-tabnî (ᴵᵈ30-*tab-ni*)
1. a. of *Banunu* and *ᵈNergal-ušallim*, 14:16.
2. a. of *ᵈNabû-iddina* and *Ina-tēšî-ēṭir*, 322:31.
3. a. of *ᵈNabû-tabnî-uṣur* and *ᵈBēl-ēpuš*, 359:15.
4. a. of *ᵈNabû-tabnî-uṣur* and *ᵈNabû-ēpuš*, 3:36.
5. a., son and desc.'s names broken, 17:12.

ᵈSîn-[X.X] (ᴵᵈ30.[X.X]) *a.* of *ᵈSîn-iddin*, 360 iii 7.

Sippē (*ᴵsip-pe-e*) a. of *ᵈNabû-šum-iddin* and *ᵈBēl-aḫḫē-erība*, 303:35.

Suḫaya (*ᴵsu-ḫa-a-a*)
1. (562) s. of *ᴵYatama'a*, 9:11.
2. a. of *ᵈNabû-šum-iddin* and *ᵈNergal-ušallim*, 4:20.

Sukallē? (*ᴵ⌈su?-⌉kál-⌈li-⌉le*) a. of *Nādin* and *Balāṭsu*, 26:14.

Supē-ᵈBēl (*ᴵsu-pi-e-*ᵈEN) a. of *Aplā* and *Aḫ-lūmur*, 12:13.

Ṣāḫit-ginē (ᴵÌ.ŠUR.GI.NA)
1. a. of *ᵈNergal-iddin*, 303:30.
2. a. of *ᵈNergal-ēṭir* and *Šumā*, 303:29.

Ṣillā (*ᴵṣil-la-a*)
1. (600) s. of *ᵈNabû-yāši*, 115:11; 358:15 (591) wit.
2. (596) s. of *ᵈNanā-uballiṭ*, f. of *Ḫāmmā*, 322:10, 15.
3. (594) s. of *ᵈNabû-iddin*, 340:1, 6, 8.
4. (587) s. of *ᵈBēl*-[X.X], wit., 23:10.
5.[110] (587), 214:6.
6.[111] (586) s. of *Nēšu*, 155:6.
7.[112] (521) s. of *ᵈInninna-šum-uṣur*, desc. of *Kidin-ᵈMarduk*, scribe, 37:18; 286:20; 287:18; 288:17; 289:17; 290:17; 291:18; 292:17;

108. Also *TCL* 12, 22:4–5.
109. Perhaps a variant spelling of *ᵈSîn-lēq-unnini*, see *NRVG* p. 23.
110. Reading unsure.
111. *⌈ṣil-⌉la-a*; also possible: *⌈ap-⌉la-a*.
112. PN occurs as scribe in I, 2б1659:13f. (Pushkin Museum) dated to VII/2/Nbk 1.

293:21; 294:18; 295:18; 296:17; 297:18; 298:20; 299:18.
8. (521) desc. of ^d^*Nabû-zēr-iddin*, 300:11.
9. f. of ^d^*Bēl-zēr-uṣur*, 37:15.
10. f. of *Balāṭu*, wit., 291:15.
11. f. of ^d^*Ištar-nādin-aḫi*, 10:13.
12. f. of *Mušallim-*^d^*Marduk*, 30:16.
13. f. of ^d^*Nabû-ibnî*, 18:9.
14. f. of ^d^*Nabû-mukīn-apli*, 322:36.
15. a. of ⌈*Labāši*⌉, 113:16.

Ṣilliya (^1^GIŠ.MI-*ya*) (583) s. of *Ḫaṣabdu*, 19:4.

Ša-^d^*Bēl-dubba* (^1^*šá-*^d^EN-*dub-ba*) (585) desc. of ^d^*Nabû-zēr-ukīn*, 143:9.
Ša-^d^*Nabû-šū* (^1^*šá-*^d^AG-*šú-ú*)
1. (591) ^h^*rab-bulū*, 109:2.
2. (591), 360 iv 24.
3. (588, possibly Nbp., 609), 146:30.
4. (586) desc. of ^d^*Bēl-tabnī-il*, 39:4.
5. (586), 274:18.
6. (586), 152:7.
7. (584) s. of *Šum-iddin*, 36:3.
8. f. of *Bēlšunu*, 220:3.
9. f. of ^d^*Nabû-aḫ-iddin*, 25:10.
10. f. of ^d^*Nabû-zēr-ukīn*, desc. of ^d^*Šamaš-apla-*⌈*iddin*⌉, 2:36.
11. f. of ^d^*Nabû-zēr-ukīn*, 348:17.
12. f. of ^d^*Nabû-zēr-ušabši*, 326:4.
13.[113] f. of *Riḫi-*^d^*Adad*, 19:5.
14. f. of *Rīmūt*, 1:25.
15. f. of ^d^*Šamaš-ēpuš*, 44:8.
16. f. of *Šulā*, 364:3.
17. *a.* of ^d^*Nabû-šum-ēreš*, 267:4.
18. *a.* of ^d^*Nanā-iddin*, 146:21.
19.[114] *a.*, desc.'s name broken, 208:3.

^f^*Ša-*^d^*Nanā-bānî* (SAL *šá-*^d^*na-na-a-ba-ni*) (591) slave-girl given in inheritance, 348:15.
Ša-^d^*Nanā-tašmet* (^1^*šá-*^d^*na-na-a-taš-met*)
1. (597), 325:21.
2. (594), 334:3.
3. (592), 330:3.
4.[115] (590) ^h^*mu-šá-kil alpi*, 362:16; 186:3 (582).

^f^*Ša-*^d^*Nanā-udu* (SAL *šá-*^d^*na-na-a-ú-du*) (591) slave-girl given in inheritance, 348:14.
^h^*Ša-nāšīšu* (LÚ *šá-na-ši-šú*) *a.* of ^d^*Nabû-ušēzib*, 317:2.
^f^*Ša-šapirti* (SAL *šá-šá-pir-ti*) (591) slave-girl given in inheritance, 348:7.
^h^*Ša-ṭabtišu*[116] (LÚ *šá*-MUN-*šú*) *a.* of *Gimillu*, ^h^*mar šipri ša Aplā*, 312:3.
Ša-⌈X.X⌉ (^1^*šá-*⌈X(X?)⌉) *a.* of ^d^*Inninna-šum-uṣur*, 146:24.
Šadunu (^1^*šá-du-nu*)
1. (601) s. of *Ukumu*, 191:3.
2. f. of *Arad-*^d^*Innin*, 13:3.

Šākin-šum (^1^GAR.MU)
1. (591) desc. of ^d^*Bēl-aḫḫē-iddin*, 360 iii 41′; 193:5, 9 (584).
2. f. of *Iddin-*^d^*Nabû*, desc. of *Gimil-*^d^*Nanā* 13:15 (Babylon); 337:15 (*a.*) (Uruk).

Šākin-zēr (^1^GAR.NUMUN) f. of *Ina-tēšī-ēṭir*, desc. of ^d^*Sîn-lēq-unnini*, 322:33.
Šalammu (^1^*šá-lam-mu*) a. of *Lāqīpi*, 143:2.
Šaltu-il, in GN URU É ^1^*šá-al-tu₄*-DINGIR, 290:1.
Šalammanu-ilī (^1^*šá-lam-ma-nu*-DINGIR.MEŠ) f. of *Ḫišurinīlu*, 9:12.
^d^*Šamaš-aḫ-iddin* (^1d^UTU.ŠEŠ.MU)

113. Reading of f.'s name unsure.
114. Reading unsure.
115. *GCCI* 1, p. 53a text 96 (yr. 24), text 166 (yr. 12), same man.
116. Ancestral name "He-who-deals-in-salt" (in text dealing with salt) or possibly a professional designation and not an ancestral name.

1. (605), 113:52.
2. (521), 300:36.

ᵈŠamaš-aḫḫē-erība (¹ᵈUTU.ŠEŠ.MEŠ.SU) (521) s. of ᵈBēl-ibnî, 288:6, 13.

ᵈŠamaš-apla-⌈iddin⌉ (¹ᵈUTU.A-id-[din]) a. of ᵈNabû-zēr-ukīn and Ša-ᵈNabû-šū, 2:36.

ᵈŠamaš-ēpuš (¹ᵈUTU.DÙ-uš) (588) desc. of Ša-ᵈNabû-šū, ʰerrēšu, 44:8.

ᵈŠamaš-ēreš
1. (¹ᵈUTU.PIN-eš) (588, possibly Nbp., 609) a.'s name broken, 146:40.
2. (¹ᵈUTU.KÁM) (521) desc. of Ilī-iddin, 300:15.
3. (¹ᵈUTU.KÁM) f. of Banitušu, 41:8.

ᵈŠamaš-erība (¹ᵈUTU.SU)
1. (601) ʰašlaku, 307:6.
2. (592), 341:4.
3. (588), 2:8.
4. (586) ša-rēši, 151:5.
5. (584), 40:3.
6. (521), 292:2.
7. f. of Šūzubu, desc. of LÚ.[X.][X.X], 21:2.
8. f. of Zērūtu, 257:2.
9. a. of Zērūtu, 148:3.

ᵈŠamaš-ēṭir-šum (¹ᵈUTU.KAR.MU) f. of Labāši, 37:17.

ᵈŠamaš-ibnî (¹ᵈUTU.DÙ) (595) s. of ᵈNergal-iddin, 26:3, 6, 9.

ᵈŠamaš-iddin (¹ᵈUTU.MU)
1. (588, possibly Nbp., 609) ʰaškappu, 146:9.
2. (521) s. of Kāṣir, desc. of Basiya, 298:6.
3. (521) desc. of ᵈNabû-udammiq, 300:25.
4. (521) ʰnuḫatimmu, 300:26.
5. (521), 300:38.
6. f. of Amēl-ᵈNabû and Silim-ᵈBēl, 25:3.
7. f. of Ibnā, 22:14.
8. a. of ᵈNabû-nāṣir, 149:8 (twice).

ᵈŠamaš-ilūa (¹ᵈUTU-i-lu-ú-a) a. of Iqbā, 197:9.

ᵈŠamaš-iqīša (¹ᵈUTU.BA-šá)
1. (521) s. of ᵈSîn-aḫ-iddin, 291:7.
2. f. of ᵈNergal-iddina, 18:4.

ᵈŠamaš-kāṣir
1. (¹ᵈUTU-ka-ṣir) (605), 113:55.
2. (¹ᵈUTU.KÁD) (605), 126:19.

ᵈŠamaš-lē'û (¹ᵈUTU.DA) (521), 300:33.

ᵈŠamaš-marṣa-uṣur (¹ᵈUTU.GIG.URÙ) (603) s. of Aplā, desc. of Danni-ᵈAdad, 303:12, 38.

ᵈŠamaš-mukīn-apli (¹ᵈUTU.GUB.DUMU.UŠ/A)
1. (605) desc. of Nādin, 126:13.
2. (605) ʰaklu, 113:37; 126:12.
3. (604) s. of ᵈMadān-aḫ-iddin, desc. of Šigūa, 302:7; 126:6, a. not listed (605).
4. (521) s. of Šangû-nādin-šum, desc. of Babutu, 286:17.

ᵈŠamaš-nāṣir (¹ᵈUTU-na-ṣir) f. of Kalbā, desc. of Nūr-ᵈSîn, 4:15.

ᵈŠamaš-šum-iddin (¹ᵈUTU.MU.MU)
1. f. of ᵈNabû-bānî-aḫ, 1:30.
2. a. of ᵈNanā-iddin, 113:59.

ᵈŠamaš-šum-ukīn (¹ᵈUTU.MU.GUB)
1. (605), 113:59.
2. (592) s. of ᵈNabû-zēr-ukīn, desc. of ʰMaḫḫû, 357:3, 7, 13; 336 and 338:2, 6, 9, 10 (594).
3. (583) desc. of Aplā, 9:12.

ᵈŠamaš-šum-uṣur (¹ᵈUTU.MU.PAB/URÙ) desc. of Apkallu (591) ʰLarsua, 360 i 14; scribe, 19:14 (583).

ᵈŠamaš-uballiṭ (¹ᵈUTU.TIN-iṭ)
1. (597), 325:7.
2. (588 possibly Nbp., 609) desc. of ᵈEa-ukīn, 146:16.
3. (521) s. of ᵈAnu-šum-ibnî, desc. of ʰBā'iru, 286:7.
4. f. of Ardiya, 290:6.

5. *a.* of ^{d}*Bēl-iqbî*, 358:16.

^{d}*Šamaš-udammiq* (^{1d}UTU.KAL)
1. (599) s. of *Iqīšā*, desc. of ^{h}*Rē'û*, 276:11; 6:24 (584).
2. f. of *Ṭābiya*, 288:5.

^{d}*Šamaš-zēr-ibnî* (^{1d}UTU.NUMUN.DÙ) (588) s. of ^{d}*Marduk-apla-iddin*, 2:15, 23, 42.

^{d}*Šamaš-zēr-iddin* (^{1d}UTU.NUMUN.MU) (521) s. of ^{d}*Ištar-aḫ-iddin*, desc. of ^{h}*Bā'iru*, 286:6, 15.

^{d}*Šamaš-zēr-iqīša* (^{1d}UTU.NUMUN.BA-*šá*)
1. (605) s. of ^{d}*Marduk-šarrašu*, 29:1, 7.
2. (587) desc. of ^{d}*Bēl-aḫ-iddin*, 119:2.
3. (586) s. of ^{d}*Bēl-ušallim*, desc. of *Kurî*, 33:13; 323:13 (592).
4. (year destroyed), 141:4.

^{d}*Šamaš-zēr-līšir* (^{1d}UTU.NUMUN.GIŠ) f. of *Lāqīp*, 300:34.

^{d}*Šamaš-*⸢X.⸣*A-iddin*[117] (^{1d}UTU.⸢X.⸣A.MU) (587) desc. of *Erībšu*, 142:18.

^{d}*Šamaš-*⸢X⸣ (^{1d}UTU.⸢X⸣) (588, possibly Nbp., 609), 146:13.

^{d}*Šamaš-*[X] (^{1d}⸢UTU.⸣[X]) (583) s. of ^{d}*Bēl-ēṭir*, desc. of *Arad-*^{d}*Inninna*, 145:3.

^{d}*Šamaš-*⸢X.X⸣ (^{1d}UTU.⸢X.X⸣) a. of ^{d}*Bēl-ušallim* and *Šāpik*, 17:15.

^{h}*Šangû-*^{d}*Adad* (LÚ É.BAR ^{d}IM) a. of *Mukīn-zēr* and ^{d}*Bēl-ēṭir*, 361:13.

^{h}*Šangû-*^{d}*Innin-Bābili*
1. (LÚ É.BAR.^{d}INNIN TIN.TIR.KI) a. of ^{d}*Bēl-zēr* and ^{d}*Bēl-aḫ-iddin*, 276:8.
2. (LÚ SANGA ^{d}INNIN.TIN.TIR.KI) a. of ^{d}*Innin-šum-uṣur* and ^{d}*Bēl-aḫḫē-iddin*, 357:21.

Šangû-nādin-šum (^{1}É.BAR-*na-din*-MU) f. of ^{d}*Šamaš-mukīn-apli*, desc. of *Babutu*, 286:18.

^{h}*Šangû-*^{d}*Ninurta*
1. (LÚ É.BAR.^{d}MAŠ) a. of *Aplā* and *Ubar*, 276:10.
2. (LÚ SANGA ^{d}MAŠ) a. of *Marduka*, f.'s name broken, 359:11.

^{h}*Šangû-*^{d}*Nusku* (^{1}LÚ É.BAR.^{d}PA.KU) (605), 113:35.

^{h}*Šangû-parakki* (LÚ É.BAR.BÁRA)
1. a. of ^{1}*Ba*?-⸢*ar*?-⸣[X] and *Nadna-aplu*, 22:12.
2. a. of ^{d}*Nergal-tēšī-ēṭir* and ^{d}*Ea-šum-ibnî*, 17:4.
3. (LÚ SANGA.BÁRA) a. of ^{d}*Nabû-šum-ēreš* and *Mušallim-*^{d}*Marduk*, 11:16.
4. (LÚ SANGA.BÁ[RA]) a. of ^{d}*Nergal-uballiṭ* and ^{d}*Nabû-šum-ēreš*, 6:25.
5. a. of ^{d}*Anu-usippi* and ^{d}*Bēl-ibnî*, 22:10.
6. a., desc.'s and f.'s names broken, 22:3.

^{h}*Šangû-*^{d}*Šamaš* (LÚ SANGA ^{d}UTU) *a.* of ^{d}*Nabû-aḫḫē-iddin*, 360 iv 9.

^{h}*Šangû-*⸢X.X⸣, a. of ^{d}*Bēl-aḫḫē-erība* and ^{d}*Nabû-ušēzib*, 348:22.

Šāpik (^{1}*šá-pik*)
1. f. of ^{d}*Bēl-aḫḫē-erība*, 340:5.
2. f. of ^{d}*Bēl-ušallim*, desc. of ^{d}*Šamaš-*⸢X.X⸣, 17:15.
3. f. of ^{d}*Marduk-apla-uṣur*, desc. of *Ḫunzû*, 3:33.
4. f. of ^{d}*Nergal-nāṣir*, 16:3, 12.

Šāpiku (^{1}*šá-pi-ku*) (601) s. of ^{d}*Nabû-zēr-uṣur*, desc. of *Ḫunzû*, wit., 3:31.

Šarra-uṣur (^{1}*šár-ra*-URÙ) (586), 55:7. [Interpretation of signs uncertain]

Šarraḫu (^{1}*šar-ra-ḫu*) *a.* of ^{d}*Nabû-nā'id*, 303:8.

Šarranu (^{1}LUGAL-*a-ni*) *a.* of ^{d}*Bēl-aḫḫē-erība*, 60:4.

117. Possibly ^{d}*Šamaš-apla-iddin*.

Šarru-^{d}*Bēl* (^{1}⌈LUGAL.⌉^{d}EN) *a.* of *Rīmūt*, 45:3.
Šarru-dūri (^{1}LUGAL.BÀD) (562), 9:13.
^{h}*Šatammu* (LÚ ŠÀ.TAM) a. of *Ibnî-*^{d}*Ištar* and ^{d}*Nabû-zēr-ukīn*, 32:16.
Šēlibu (^{1}KA$_{5}$.A) (605), 113:11.
Šigūa (^{1}*ši-gu-ú-a*)
1. a. of ^{d}*Nabû-ēṭir-napšāti* and ^{d}*Bēl-lē'ī*, 7:13; 319:13 (*a.*); 323:11.
2. a. of ^{d}*Šamaš-mukīn-apli* and ^{d}*Madān-aḫ-iddin*, 302:8.
3. a. of *Zēriya* and ^{1}[X-]*gu*-[X.X.X], 276:6.
4. a., desc.'s and f.'s names broken, 6:16.
Ši-⌈*rik-* X.X⌉ (^{1}*ši-*⌈*rik*-X.X⌉) (589), 187:11.
Šulā (^{1}*šu-la-a*)
1. (596) s. of *Šum-ukīn*, 63:6.
2. (594) s. of *Ša-*^{d}*Nabû-šū*, 364:3.
3. (594) s. of ^{d}*Nabû-šum-iqīša*, 364:8.
4. (591) s. of *Nādin* and *Gimil-*^{d}*Nanā*, 348:25.
5. (591), 194:8.
6. (591), 225:2.
7. (588) s. of *Nādin*, 31:12.
8. (587) ^{h}*mandidi*, 158:3.
9. (585) desc. of ^{d}*Ninurta-gāmil*, 24:2.
10. (584) s. of ^{d}*Nabû-zēr-iqīša*, 208:4.
11. f. of *Arad-*^{d}*Šamaš*, 292:14.
12. f. of ^{d}*Ea-zēr-iqīša*, 30:13.
13. f. of ^{d}*Innin-zēr-ibnî*, 9:15.
14. f. of ^{d}*Marduk-erība* and ^{d}*Nanā-iddin*, 75:10.
15. f. of ^{d}*Nabû-mukīn-apli*, 15:4.
16. *a.* of *Ardiya*, 165:5.
17. *a.* of ^{d}*Nabû-balāṭsu-iqbî*, 352:3.
Šullum
1. (^{1}GI) *a.* of *Ardiya*, 300:22.
2. (^{1}*šul-lum*) *a.* of *Ina-ṣilli-*^{d}*Nergal*, 40:24.
Šullummā (^{1}*šul-lum-ma-a*)
1. *a.* of ^{d}*Nergal-šum-ibnî*, 337:3.
2. *a.* of ^{d}*Nergal-ušēzib*, 337:14.
Šullumu (^{1}*šul-lu-mu*) f. of ^{d}*Bēl-aḫ-iddin*, 34:8.
Šum-iddin (^{1}MU.MU)
1. (593) s. of ^{d}*Bēl-iddin*, 41:11.
2. (588) s. of *Nureya*, 31:4.
3. f. of *Ša-*^{d}*Nabû-šū*, 36:4.
4. f. of *Zēr-Bābili*, 47:2.
Šum-ukīn (^{1}MU.GUB)
1. (588), 227:9.
2. (587) s. of ^{d}*Bēl-zēr*, 23:11.
3. (585) desc. of *Aḫḫēa*, 53:5.
4. (584) s. of *Marduka*, 90:5.
5. (583) s. of ^{d}*Nabû-aḫ-ēreš*, br. of ^{d}*Nabû-ēṭir*, 70:2.
6. (583) desc. of *Nurānu*, 76:12.
7. (582), 180:10.
8. (521), 300:8.
9. f. of ^{d}*Marduk-ēreš*, desc. of ^{h}*Naggariya*, 357:17.
10. f. of ^{d}*Nabû-ēṭir-napšāti*, desc. of *Ekur-zākir*, 2:38.
11. f. of ^{d}*Nabû-zēr-iddin*, 21:12.
12. f. of *Šulā*, 63:7.
13. f. of ⌈X.⌉⌈X-⌉^{d}*Marduk*, desc. of *Attabani*, 8:11.
14. *a.* of *Rīmūt*, 149:5.
Šum-uṣur (^{1}MU.URÙ)
1. (587) desc. of *Kudurri*, br. of ^{d}*Nabû-bēlšunu*, 203:3.
2. (582) s. of ^{d}*Bēl-iddin*, 1:26.
3. (582) ^{h}*rē'ī ša immer satukki*, 73:4.
Šumā (^{1}*šu-ma-a*)
1. (^{1}MU-*a*) (605), 113:32.
2. (^{1}MU-*a*) (605) *a.*'s name broken, 113:33.
3. (^{1}MU-*a*) (605), 56:2.
4. (^{1}MU-*a*) (594) s. of ^{d}*Nabû-šum-iddin*, desc. of *Iddin-*^{d}*Papsukkal*, 336 and 338:1, 3, 12 (twice in line 12); 357:11, 14 (592).
5. (584) desc. of ^{d}*Nabû-aḫḫē-ušallim*, 40:12.

6. (562) s. of *Nūreya*, 9:13.
7. (562) in GN ÍD *har-ri šá* ^{1}MU-*a*, 9:16, 21.
8. (521) s. of ^{d}*Nabû-kišar*, 293:8.
9.[118] f. of *Balāṭu*, desc. of *Iddin-*^{d}*Papsukkal*, 26:11 (^{1}*šu-ma-a*); 32:14 (^{1}*šu-ma-a*); 33:12 (^{1}MU-*a*).
10. f. of *Balāṭu*, desc. of *Iddin-*^{d}*Nergal*, 323:12.
11. f. of *Balāṭu*, 351:6.
12. f. of *Kudurri*, desc. of ^{h}*Rē'ī-satukki*, 7:16.
13. f. of ^{d}*Nabû-zēr-ušabši*, desc. of *Nūr-*^{d}*Sîn*, 3:29.
14. f. of ^{d}*Nergal-ēṭir*, desc. of *Ṣahit-ginē*, 303:29.
15. f. of ^{1d}[X.X-]*ilī*, 115:5.
16. *a.* of ^{d}*Nana-ah-ēreš*, 40:8.
17. *a.* of *Nāṣir-'a-ili*, 358:11.
18. *a.* of ^{d}*Ninurta-erība*, 320:2.

Šumāti (^{1}MU.MEŠ) a. of *Mukīn-zēr* and ^{d}*Bēl-lē'ī*, 13:12.

Šūzubu (^{1}*šu-zu-bu*)
1. (591) s. of ^{d}*Šamaš-erība*, desc. of LÚ ⌈X.⌉[X.X], 21:2.
2. f. of *Gimil-*^{d}*Nanā*, 26:17.
3. f. of ^{d}*Nabû-šum-ēreš*, 31:10.
4. *a.* of ^{d}*Nabû-šum-ibnî*, 123:3.

Tabalaya (^{1}*ta-ba-la-a-a*) (593) LÚ 10-*tim*, 339:4.

Tabnēa (^{1}*tab-ni-e-a*)
1. (605), 113:50.
2. (601) s. of *Balāṭu*, 65:3.
3. (601), 314:16.
4. (594) s. of ^{d}*Nabû-nāṣir*, desc. of ^{h}*Purkullu*, 327:9.
5. (593) s. of *Ina-tēšī-ēṭir*, 41:13.
6. (591) s. of ^{d}*Ea-bēl-ilī*, 18:7.
7. (590), 215:1.
8. (588), 147:6.
9. (586) s. of ^{d}*Bēl-uballiṭ*, desc. of *Ibnî-*^{d}*Sîn*, 32:3, 8.
10. f. of ^{d}*Bēl-ahhē-iqīša*, 115:9.
11. f., son's name broken, desc. of ^{h}*Bā'iru*, 6:18.
12. *a.* of *Amēl-*^{d}*Nanā*, 222:2.
13. *a.* of ^{d}*Nabû-*⌈X-⌉*ši-*⌈*ṣi-e?*⌉, 39:7.

Tadan (^{1}*ta-dan*)
1. (588) desc. of *Ah-*[X.X], ^{h}*errēšu*, 44:5.
2. (587), 170:2.

Tahallu (^{1}*ta-hal-lum*) f. of ^{d}*Nabû-iqbî-nadān*, 13:14.

Talim (^{1}*ta-lim*) (605), 113:43.

Talli (^{1}*tal-*⌈*li*⌉), *a.* of *Amēl-*^{d}*Nanā*, ^{h}*atû*, 362:12.

Tammeš-nūri (^{1}*tam-meš-nu-ú-ri*) (586), 152:2.

Taqīš-ša-^{d}*Gula* (^{1}*ta-qiš-*⌈*šá-*⌉^{d}*gu-la*) (603), 47:3.

Taqīš-^{d}*Gula* (^{1}*ta-qiš-*^{d}*gu-la*)
1. (591) s. of ^{d}*Nergal-ušallim*, desc. of *Nūr-*^{d}*Sîn*, 21:4; 15:3 (588).
2. (591), 283:2′.
3. a. of ^{d}*Nabû-ušallim* and ^{d}*Bēl-ēreš*, 14:4.

Taqīšu (^{1}*ta-qí-šú*) (582), 180:13.

Taštibi (^{1}*ta-áš-*⌈*ti-*⌉*bi*) (586), 152:8, 9.

Tukulti-^{d}*Ištar* (^{1}KU-*ti-*^{d}15) (591) slave given in inheritance, 348:6.

Tukulti-^{d}*Marduk* (^{1}KU-*ti-*^{d}AMAR.UTU)
1. (^{1}*tu-kul-ti-*^{d}AMAR.UTU) (592) s. of *Zēr-ukīn*, desc. of ^{h}*Atkuppu*, 5:14.
2.[119] (592) desc. of *Kudurri*, ^{h}*rē'ī ginê*, 345:9; 66:5 (no *a.* listed) (591); 71:5 (584); 72:5 (584); 96:2 (583); 76:16

118. All ^{1}MU-*a* names are spelled *šumā* because of the references in texts 26:11 and 32:14 (*šu-ma-a*) that parallel 33:12 (^{1}MU-*a*). This is contra Figulla, *UET* IV, p. 34b, who reads ^{1}MU.A.

119. The name also occurs in A 4255:7 (588 B.C.); A 4256:2 (583 B.C.); *GCCI* 1, 88:5 (582 B.C.); *GCCI* 1, 50:3 (date broken; not earlier than 582); A 5751:4 (580 B.C.); *GCCI* 1, 216:5 (578 B.C.); and *GCCI* 1, 144:3 (569 B.C.).

(583); 93:2 (no *a.* listed) (583); 70:6 (no *a.* listed) (583); 94:2 (no *a.* listed) (583); 95:2 (no *a.* listed) (582); 69:4 (581).
3. (591), 360 iv 36.
Tukulti-[X.X.X][120] (^{1}⌈KU.⌉[X.X.X]) *a.* of [X-]*ibnî*, 279:8.
^{f}*Tuqnā* (SAL *tuq-na-a*) (591) slave-girl given in inheritance, 348:14.
Tuqnatiya (^{1}*tuq-na-ti-ya*) (582), 206:5.

Ṭāb-Eanna (^{1}DU$_{10}$.GA.É.AN.NA)
1. (592), 81:10.
2. (587), 173:19.
Ṭāb-^{d}Marduk (^{1}DU$_{10}$.GA.^{d}AMAR.UTU) (603) s. of *Aplā*, desc. of *Ekur-zākir*, 30:15.
Ṭāb-šār-Eanna (^{1}DU$_{10}$.GA.IM.É.AN.NA) (588) desc. of *Iddin-^{d}Nabû*, 175:7; 182:7; 188:7 (585).
Ṭāb-šār-^{d}Ištar (^{1}DU$_{10}$.GA.IM.^{d}15) (590), 149:11.
Ṭāb-Uruk (^{1}DU$_{10}$.GA.UNUG.KI)
1. (600) f.'s name broken, 115:3.
2. *a.* of *^{d}Nanā-aḫ-uṣur*, 114:7.
Ṭābiya (^{1}DU$_{10}$.GA-*ya*/*iá*) (521) s. of *^{d}Šamaš-udammiq*, 288:5, 13.

U-[X.X] (^{1}*ú*-[X.X]) f., son's name broken, 38:4.
Ubar (^{1}*ú-bar*) f. of *Aplā*, desc. of *Šangû-^{d}Ninurta*, 276:9.
Ubar-^{d}Nabû (^{1}*ú-bar-*^{d}AG) (588) *ša-rēši*, 207:4.
Ukumu (^{1}*ú-ku-mu*) f. of *Šadunu*, 191:4.
Ululaya (^{1}ITI.KIN-*a-a*) (591) ^{h}*qallu*, 109:4.
Upaq (^{1}*ú-paq*) f. of *Marduk*, desc. of *Kurî*, 357:16; 315:12 (^{1}*ú-pa-qa*) no a. listed.
Uqupu (^{1}*ú-qu-pu*) (605), 113:15.

Yāda' (^{1}*ya-a-da-'*) (521) s. of *^{d}Nabû-zabadu*, 35:6.
Yama' (^{1}*ya-ma!-'*) *a.* of *^{d}Nabû-zēr-iqīša*, 71:2.
Yašukimu (^{1}*ya-šu-*⌈*ki-*⌉*mu*) *a.* of *^{d}Nanā-ibnî*, 146:36.
Yatama' (^{1}*ya-a-tam-ma-'*) f. of *Suḫaya*, 9:11.
Yatiru (^{1}*ya-ti-ru*) (594), 364:4.

^{d}Zababa-šar-uṣur (^{1d}*za-ba$_{4}$-ba$_{4}$-*LUGAL.URÙ) (591) desc. of *Nadna-aplu*, wit., 358:12.
Zabidā (^{1}*za-bi-da*(-*a*))
1. *a.* of *^{d}Nergal-ina-tēšî-ēṭir*, 33:2.
2. *a.* of *^{d}Nabû-nāṣir*, 49:5; 59:3; 75:7.
Zākir (^{1}*za-kir*)
1. f. of *^{d}Nabû-erība*, 287:6.
2. *a.* of *Amēl-^{d}Nanā*, 110:3.
Zannea (^{1}*za-an-ni-e-a*) a. of *^{d}Nabû-bēlšunu* and *^{d}Marduk-aḫ-iddin*, 21:16.
Zēr-Bābili (^{1}NUMUN.TIN.TIR.KI)
1. (603) s. of *Šum-iddin*, 47:1.
2. (597) desc. of *^{h}Rē'û*, 317:4.
3. (589) s. of *^{d}Nabû-ušallim*, desc. of *^{h}Rē'û*, wit., 361:14.
4. f. of *Mušēzib-^{d}Bēl*, desc. of *Attabani*, 8:2.
5. *a.* of *Ina-ṣilli-^{d}Bēl*, 40:7; 143:12.
Zēr-ibnî
1. (^{1}NUMUN-*ib-ni*) f. of *^{d}Nabû-balāṭsu-iqbî*, desc. of *Nūr-^{d}Papsukkal*, 327:11.
2. (^{1}NUMUN.DÙ) *a.* of *^{d}Nabû-kēšir*, 159:9.
Zēr-iqīša (^{1}NUMUN.[BA-]*šá*) (594) desc. of *Aḫḫēšā*, 320:12.
Zēr-ukīn (^{1}NUMUN.GUB)
1. (586) s. of *^{d}Nabû-lē'î*, 83:5.
2. f. of *Mušibšî*, desc. of *Kidin-^{d}Marduk*, 7:14.

120. Possibly *Ku*-[X.X.X].

3. f. of ^{d}*Nabû-gāmil*, 41:17.
4. f. of *Tukulti-^{d}Marduk*, desc. of ^{h}*Atkuppu*, 5:14.
5. *a.* of *Bēlšunu*, 51:3.

Zēriya
1. (^{1}NUMUN-*iá*) (605) *a.*'s name broken, 29:9.
2. (^{1}NUMUN-*ya*) (600) s. of *Iddin-^{d}Marduk*, 12:2.
3. (^{1}NUMUN-*iá*) (599) s. of [X-]*gu*-[X.X.X], desc. of *Šigūa*, 276:5.
4. (^{1}NUMUN-*iá*) (593? — RN missing) s. of ^{d}*Bēl-aḫ-iddin*, 270:2.
5. (^{1}NUMUN-*iá*) (592) desc. of *Balāṭu*, 108:3.
6. (^{1}NUMUN-*iá*) (592), 353:3.
7. (^{1}NUMUN-*iá*) (591) desc. of *Balāṭu*, 360 ii 6.
8. (^{1}NUMUN-*iá*) (591) desc. of *Rīmūt-^{d}Gula*, 360 iv 14.
9. (^{1}NUMUN-*ya*) (590) s. of ^{d}*Nabû-ēpir-la'*, 82:22.
10. (^{1}NUMUN-*iá*) (588), 179:5.
11. (^{1}NUMUN-*iá*) (588, possibly Nbp., 609) desc. of *Aḫḫē-lūmur*, 146:17.
12. (^{1}NUMUN-*ya*) (587) desc. of ^{d}*Nabû-aḫ-ēreš*, 142:6.
13. (^{1}NUMUN-*ya*) (586) desc. of ^{d}*Nanā-ēreš*, 39:2.
14. (^{1}NUMUN-*iá*) (583) *a.*'s name broken, 177:6.
15. (^{1}NUMUN-*ya*) (582) desc. of *Amēl-^{d}Ea*, 234:4.
16. (^{1}NUMUN-*ya*) (521) desc. of ^{d}*Bēl-ēreš*, br. of ^{d}*Nabû-aḫḫē-iddin*, 294:6.
17. (^{1}NUMUN-*iá*) (521) desc. of ^{d}*Nanā-ēreš*, 300:28.
18. (^{1}NUMUN-*ya*) f. of ^{d}*Marduk-šum-ibnî*, desc. of *Dabibi*, 18:11.
19. (^{1}NUMUN-*iá*) *a.* of *Gimillu*, 193:3, 7.
20. (^{1}NUMUN-*ya*) *a.* of *Gimilli*, 360 v 25.
21. (^{1}NUMUN-*iá*) *a.* of *Kalbā*, 152:19.

Zērūtu (^{1}NUMUN-*tú*)
1. (594), 10:9.
2. (593) (^{1}NUMUN-*ú-tu*) s. of *Bulluṭa*, 41:3.
3. (590) desc. of ^{d}*Šamaš-erība*, 148:3.
4. (584) s. of ^{d}*Šamaš-erība*, 257:2.
5. f. of ^{d}*Marduk-šum-uṣur*, 115:23.
6. f. of *Rēmūtu*, 15:2.
7. (^{1}NUMUN-*ú-tu*) *a.* of ^{d}*Bēl-aḫḫē-erība*, 196:4.

Zigga (^{1}ZÌG.GA) (521) s. of ^{d}*Nabû-nāṣir*, wit., 291:16.

Zi'iri (^{1}*zi-'-i-ri*) (591) desc. of ^{d}*Nabû-zēr-ibnî*, wit., 358:10.

Partially broken names (beginning destroyed)

[X.]A, f. of *Nadna-aplu*, desc. of *Kurû*, 22:1.

[X.]⸢X.⸣A, *a.*, desc.'s name broken, 48:2.

⸢X.⸣BA.⸢X.X⸣, *a.* of ^{d}*Ištar-šum-ēreš*, 65:5.

⸢X.⸣DA.[X] (590), 171:4.

[X.X]⸢X.⸣GI, *a.* of ^{d}*Bēl*-[X.X], 142:21.

[X.X.X.]GÍD.DA?.É, f. of ⸢X-⸣*zēr*-⸢X⸣, 14:2.

⸢X.GIŠ⸣ (589) desc. of LÚ ŠU.[X.]AN, 239:2.

[X]LÚ *na-qid-di*, f. of ^{d}*Inninna-šum-uṣur*, 311:5.

[^{d}X-]*aḫḫē-erība*, f. of ^{d}*Nabû-šum-iddin*, 14:17.

[^{d}X-]*aḫḫē-iqīša* (584) s. of *Eṭir-^{d}Marduk*, desc. of *Egibi*, 6:21.

⸢X-⸣*ba*, f. of ^{d}*Nabû-šum-ibnî*, 28:13.

[^{d}]⸢X-]*bāni-aḫ* ([^{1d}][X.]DÙ.ŠEŠ) (587), 142:1.

[X.X.X-]^{d}*Bēl* (588) desc. of ^{d}*Nabû-aḫḫē-iddin*, 226:4.

[X.X.X.X.X.X.X-]^{d}*Bēl* (591), 360 iv 18.

⸢X.X-⸣*bi*, f. of ^{d}*Nabû-lē'ī*, 45:1.

⸢X-*e*-X.X⸣, *a.* of ^{d}*Nabû-šum-ibnî*, 61:2.

⌈X.X.⌉[X-]*Eanna* (592), 174:5.
[dX-]*ēpuš* ([1dX.]DÙ-*uš*) *a.* of *Balāṭsu*, 172:4.
[dX-]*ēreš* (562), 9:10.
[dX-]*ēṭir* ([1dX.]SUR) (584) s. of *Nadna-aplu*, desc. of *Saggiya*, 6:20.
[dX-]*ēṭir*, (1[dX.]SUR) *a.* of *dAnu-šum-ibnî*, 113:45.
[dX-]*gāmil* ([1dX-]⌈*ga*-⌉*mil*) (586) s. of *dBēl-ukīn*, 155:5.
[X-]*gu*-[X.X.X], f. of *Zēriya*, desc. of *Šigūa*, 276:5.
⌈X-⌉*ḫu*?-⌈X⌉ (590), 171:3.
[X-]*ibnî* ([1X.]DÙ) (602) desc. of 1⌈KU.⌉ [X.X.X], 279:8.
d[X.X-]*ilī* (1d[X.X]DINGIR.ME) (600) s. of *Šumā*, 115:5.
[X.X-]*im*?-d[X.X] (588, possibly Nbp., 609), 146:46.
⌈X.X.X-*iq-bi*⌉ (602), f. and a.'s names broken, 17:10.
[X.X.X-]*it* (593) s. of *dNabû-nāṣir*, 235:4.
⌈X.X-⌉*ki*-*dEa*, *a.* of *dNabû-ēpuš*, 234:6.
[X-]*dMarduk* (589), 204:1.
⌈X.X-⌉*dMarduk* (522) s. of *Šum-ukīn*, desc. of *Attabani*, wit., 8:10.
⌈X-⌉*dNabû*-[X.X.X.X] (589), 169:5.
[X-]*dNabû*-⌈X.X⌉, *a.* of *Arad-dInninna*, 146:27.
[dX-]*nāṣir*, f. of *dNabû-zēr-ibnî*, desc. of *hPūṣāya*, 3:14, 17.
[X.X-]*dNergal* (586) s. of *Saggillu*, 155:4.
[dX-*r*]*i-iḫ-ti-ú-ṣur* (586), 152:4.
[X.X-]*dSîn*, probably an ancestor, 113:17.
[X.X-]*ṣigil* (604) desc. of *Balaṭ*, 52:10.
[X.X-]*ši*, *a.* of *dBēl-ēpuš*, 310:7.
⌈X-⌉*šu*, *a.* of *dNanā-iddin*, 146:10.
⌈X-*šunu*⌉ (603) desc. of *dNabû-ušēzib*, 45:2.
d[X-]*šum-ibnî* (588) s. of *Idūa*, wit., 15:10′.
d[X-]*ušallim* (591) s. of *dBēl-nibšari*, a.'s name broken, 20:3.
[X.X.X-]*ušallim*, f., son's name broken, 115:17.
d[X-]*zēr-iddin* (582), 243:1.
[dX-]*zēr-ukīn* (591), 219:4.
⌈X-⌉*zēr*-⌈X⌉ (year broken) s. of 1[X.X.X.] GÍD.DA?.É, 14:1.
[X.X.]⌈X-⌉*zēr*, f. of *dBēl*-⌈X.X⌉, desc. of *Ekur-zākir*, 22:13.
[X.]⌈X.X-⌉*zēr*, f. of *dBēl-ušallim*, 29:12.

Broken Names

2:13; 6:16, 17, 18; 14:18; 15:10′; 17:11, 12, 13; 20:4, 11, 15; 21:11; 22:2, 3; 27:9; 28:3; 29:9, 10, 11; 38:3; 39:10; 43:3; 44:9; 48:2; 62:13; 75:5; 81:4; 84:4, 5; 107:2; 113:7, 33; 115:1, 3, 13, 17; 117:3′; 118:1; 126:20; 142:10, 11, 21, 22, 23; 146:31, 40, 41; 152:5, 7; 155:7; 169:3; 172:4, 5, 8; 177:6; 189:5; 202:3; 212:3; 227:15; 231:7, 8; 256:1′, 2′, 3′, 4′, 5′, 6′, 7′; 262:7; 275:10, 19; 307:6; 346:9; 359:11, 12, 13; 360 v 19.

GEOGRAPHICAL NAMES

Cities, Towns, Forts, Gates, Wharves, Regions

Abul ^{d}Adad (KÁ.GAL.^{d}IM), 41:14; 274:5.

Abul ^{d}Kanisurra ša qereb Uruk (KÁ.GAL ^{d}*ka-ni-sur-ra šá qé-reb* UNUG.KI), 2:2.

Ālu ša ^{d}Anu-aḫ-ēreš (URU *šá* ^{1d}60.ŠEŠ.KÁM), 287:19; 299:19.

Ālu ša ^{amel}šākin māti (URU *šá* LÚ *šá-kin* KUR), 18:12.

⌈*Ālu*⌉- [X.X.] ⌈X⌉ *ša Nadna-aplu massu*(?) (⌈URU⌉. [X.X.] ⌈X⌉ *šá* ^{1}SUM-*na*-A KUR-*šú*(?)), 37:19.

^{al}*Amānu*[121] (URU *a-ma-nu*), 358:18.

^{d}*Anu-aḫ-ēreš* in *ālu ša* . . . ; see sub *ālu* . . . .

^{al}*Asurrītum ša Bulta*(?) (URU *a-sur-ri-tum šá* ^{1}*bul-ta* [X?]), 37:2.

Asurrītum in ^{al}*Bāb Asurrītum* see sub *Bāb* . . . .

^{al}*Bāb Āli* (URU KÁ.URU), 300:21, 33.

^{al}*Bāb Asurrītum* (URU KÁ *a-sur-ri-tum*), 290:18.

Bāb Salīmu (É PN *šá ina* KÁ DI-*mu*), 336:10; 338:10.

Bābili (*ba-bi-lam*-KI), 172:11; (E.KI), *passim*; (KÁ.DINGIR.RA.KI), 303:2; (NUN.KI), 154:13; (TIN.TIR.KI), *passim*.

Barsippa (BAR.SIP.KI), 327:15; (BÁR.SÍP.KI), 336:21, 338:22, 357:21.

^{al}*Birat* (URU *bi-rat*), 43:1.

^{al}*Bīt-šaltu-īl* (URU É ^{1}*šá-al-tu*$_4$-DINGIR), 290:1.

Bitqa ša ^{d}Bēl-ēṭir (*bit-qa*/*qu šá* ^{1d}EN.SUR), 293:22; 294:19; 295:19; 296:18; 297:19; 298:21.

^{al}*Dūr Ugum* (URU BÀD *ú-gu-um*), 295:2.

Dūru ša Yatiru (⌈BÀD⌉ *šá* ^{1}*ya-ti-ru*), 364:4.

^{al}*Gadēti* (URU *ga-di-e-ti*), 286:2.

^{al}*Ḫannarabi* (URU *ḫa-an-na-ra-bi*), 7:5, 9.

Ḫirrāti (?) see sub X(-)*ḫi-ir-ra-ti* . . . .

Ḫirru (?) see sub X(-)*ḫi-ir-ra-ti* . . . .

^{al}*Ḫuṣṣēti* (URU *ḫu-uṣ*-⌈*ṣi-e-ti*⌉), 42:2.

Ḫuṣṣēti ša Baba (*ḫu-uṣ-ṣi-e-tú šá* ^{1}*ba-ba*), 31:15.

Ḫuṣṣēti ša ^{d}Bēl (*ḫu-uṣ-ṣi*!-[text: *ad*-] ⌈*tum*⌉ *šá* ^{d}EN), 28:14.

Kār-Eanna (KAR É.AN.NA), 6:5; 33:17; 287:2, 19 (KAR! É.AN.NA); 299:2, 19.

121. R. P. Dougherty, *AASOR* 5 (1925), p. 44, with reference to *GCCI* 2, 120:8 (dated at Uruk to Cambyses 2, 528 B.C.), suggests that ^{al}*Amānu* is in the region of Mt. Amanus, on the Syrian-Cilician border (see Honigmann, *RLA* 1, p. 92).

If this is correct, it may be that our text, 358, dated to 591 B.C., also comes from that region. Though Nebuchadnezzar is not mentioned in text 358 outside of the date, a *kizû ša šarri* and *rab būli*, two royal officials, are. Wiseman, *Chron.*, p. 74, line 25 (top), has Nebuchadnezzar marching "to the Hatti-land" in his eleventh year, 594 B.C. There is no record in the *Chronicle* extant for his fourteenth year, but it is conceivable that he was there also then.

However, it is more likely, in my opinion, that in both cases, the reference to ^{al}*Amānu* refers to some town in Southern Mesopotamia.

^{al}*Kār-Eanna*[122] (URU KAR É.AN.NA), 6:26.
Kār ^{d}*Nanā* (KAR ^{d}*na-na-a*), 325:4, 20.
Kullab[123] in *Kullabi ša qereb Uruk* (KI-*tim kul-la-bi šá qé-reb* UNUG.KI), 322:2.
Kumaru (KI-*tim ku-ma-ru šá qé-reb* KÁ.DINGIR.RA.KI) 303:2.
^{al}*Kuttāin* (URU *kut-ta-a-in*), 36:14.
Larsa (UD.UNUG.KI), 19:15.
Larsa (LÚ.UD.UNUG.KI-*ú-a*) person from Larsa, 360 i 15.
^{al}*Lasūtu*[124] (URU *la-su-tu*), 364:9.
^{al}*Nahallum* (URU *na-ḫal-lum*), 292:18.
^{al}*Namar Saparrāta* (URU *na-mar sa-par-ra-a-ta*), 359:15.
^{al}*Nāru Eššu* (URU ÍD-*eš-šú*), 288:18.
Nippur (EN.⌈LÍL.⌉KI) (reading doubtful), 320:14.
^{al}*Piḫat Ḫuṣētu ša Ḫašdia* (URU NAM *ḫu-ṣi-e-tum šá* ^{1}*ḫaš-di-iá*), 325:3.
Sippar (⌈UD.⌉KIB.⌈NUN.⌉KI), 313:1.
^{al}*Ṣimmir* (URU *ṣi-im-mir*), 304:2.
^{al}*Šakillatu* (URU *šá-kil-lat* [suburb of Uruk]), 291:19.
Šubat ḫurāṣi (DAG.KI.GUŠKIN), 45:4.
^{mat}*Tamtim* (KUR *tam-*⌈*tim-*KI⌉) in title: *šanû ša* . . . , 198:3.
Til Addaya in PN, LÚ *til ad-da-a-a*, 300:23.
^{al}*Udannu-*⌈KI⌉ (URU *ú-dan-nu-*⌈KI⌉), 138:4.
^{al}*Upia* (URU *ú-pi-ya*/*iá*), 30:20; 66:2; 360 i 25, 44′, 52′.
URU KUR.BAD 35:2, 18.
URU *ú*-[X X] 307:5.
Uruk (UNUG.KI), *passim.*
^{al}*Yadaqqu* (URU *ya-daq-qu*/*qa*), 203:3; 278:8.
^{mat}*Yāmanu* (KUR *ya-a-ma-nu*), 253:2.
Yatiru see sub *Dūru* . . . .
^{al}*Zamē* (URU *za-me-e*), 122:5.
X(-)*ḫirrāti* in *Kirû ša* X-*ḫirrāti* (GIŠ.ŠAR *šá* X(-)*ḫi-ir-ra-ti*), 41:18.

Doubtful

Bakātu (*i-ki-iṣ-ri ba-ka-a-ta*) (possibly *makātu*) meaning and reading unknown. Note "local name" (*al*(?)) *Makku* in *Ugar tamirti Ma-ak-ki-e UET* IV, p. 59b. Also *CAD baktu* p. 35. 146:35.
Bītu Šá- (É ^{1}*šá-*⌈X.X.⌉ [(X)] (perhaps *Ša-*^{d}*Nabû-šû*, mentioned as father/ancestor in line 8) GN where farmers produced barley and dates (?) 44:3.

122. See Cocquerillat, *Palmeraies*, plates 3a and 3b.
123. Cp. Boudou, *Or.* 36–38 (1929), p. 106.
124. Ebeling, *Neubab. Briefe*, p. 120 fn. For location see Cocquerillat.

ḪAL.ŠU/BA? 92:3.
URU KAL-*gu-gu* 54:12.
URU X.X.X.X 289:1.

Rivers, Canals, Seasonally Inundated Areas

$^{n\bar{a}r}$ ^{d}*Amurri* (ÍD ^{d}KUR.GAL), 153:2.
^{d}*Aška'īti* in *nāru ša* . . . ; see sub *nāru* . . . .
$^{n\bar{a}r}$*Asurrītu*[125] (ÍD *a-sur-ri-ti*/*tum*), 6:5, 11?; 291:3.
$^{n\bar{a}r}$*Banītu* (ÍD DÙ-*tú*), 153:3.
$^{n\bar{a}r}$*Barsippa* (ÍD BÁR.SIP.KI), 275:14.
$^{n\bar{a}r}$*Baru* (ÍD *ba-ru*), 6:4.
^{tamirtu}*Bīt Bēlti* (GARIN É.^{d}GAŠAN), 325:20.
$^{n\bar{a}r}$*Bitqa* (ÍD *bit-qa*), 296:2; 297:2; 300:1.
$^{n\bar{a}r}$*Eššu* (ÍD *eš-šú*), 275:11.
^{tamirtu} ^{d}GIL.ŠAR, 325:12.
$^{n\bar{a}r}$*Ḫarri ša Gubbā* (ÍD *ḫar-ri šá* ^{1}*gub-ba-a*), 152:14, 20.
$^{n\bar{a}r}$*Ḫarri ša* ^{d}*Nanā* (ÍD *ḫar-ri šá* ^{d}*na-na-a*), 348:11 f.
$^{n\bar{a}r}$*Ḫarri ša Šumā* (ÍD *ḫar-ri šá* ^{1}MU-*a*), 9:16, 20 f.
$^{n\bar{a}r}$*Ḫarri ša* . . . (ÍD *ḫ*[*ar-ri šá* . . .]), 3:3.
$^{n\bar{a}r}$KIL-*ḫi-ru* (ÍD KIL-*ḫi-ru*), 300:12.
^{tamirtu}KU.⌈X.GI⌉, 314:1.
^{tamirtu}*Naḫallum* (GARIN *na-ḫal-lum*), 289:18.
^{tamirtu}*Naṣibātu* (GARIN *na-ṣi-*⌈*ba-*⌉*la-tú*), 340:4.
nāru ša ^{d}*Aška'īti* (ÍD *šá* ^{d}*áš-ka-i-ti*), 31:2.
$^{n\bar{a}r}$*šār* ^{d}*Bēl-lišīḫu* (ÍD IM.^{d}EN-*li-ši-ḫu*),[126] 325:5.
$^{n\bar{a}r}$*šarri* (ÍD LUGAL), 6:4.
$^{n\bar{a}r}$*takkiri* (ÍD *tak-ki-ri*), 298:2.

125. For location, see Cocquerillat, *Palmeraies*, plates 3a and 3b.
126. Possibly *-li-ši-ri*?

CONCORDANCE OF MUSEUM NUMBERS

Museum Number	*Text*
YBC 3422	30
YBC 3430	169
YBC 3436	55
YBC 3437	162
YBC 3440	187
YBC 3442	34
YBC 3542	313
YBC 3697	340
YBC 3700	289
YBC 3701	26
YBC 3714	13
YBC 3733	4
YBC 3735	348
YBC 3736	295
YBC 3790	291
YBC 3792	302
YBC 3793	314
YBC 3799	297
YBC 3806	293
YBC 3820	31
YBC 3825	294
YBC 3854	357
YBC 4003	126
YBC 4010	40
YBC 4025	300
YBC 4027	325
YBC 4044	338
YBC 4045	288
YBC 4049	286
YBC 4050	290
YBC 4053	337
YBC 4057	336
YBC 4058	296
YBC 4061	274
YBC 4066	35
YBC 4071	9
YBC 4077	298

Museum Number	*Text*
YBC 4093	292
YBC 4103	32
YBC 4108	315
YBC 4110	36
YBC 4123	361
YBC 4125	299
YBC 4170	113
YBC 4175	166
YBC 4189	360
YBC 6854	329
YBC 6864	250
YBC 6866	236
YBC 6875	266
YBC 6886	57
YBC 6891	182
YBC 6892	239
YBC 6893	263
YBC 6896	264
YBC 6898	131
YBC 6899	280
YBC 6904	330
YBC 6915	87
YBC 6936	2
YBC 6938	301
YBC 6940	322
YBC 6944	303
YBC 7053	14
YBC 7362	18
YBC 7365	19
YBC 7386	287
YBC 7398	28
YBC 7400	37
YBC 7410	119
YBC 7424	3
YBC 8778	123
YBC 8787	284
YBC 8789	97

Museum Number	*Text*
YBC 8791	221
YBC 8794	58
YBC 8795	157
YBC 8797	285
YBC 8799	332
YBC 8801	163
YBC 8802	159
YBC 8805	109
YBC 8808	105
YBC 8810	138
YBC 8811	225
YBC 8812	66
YBC 8814	354
YBC 8816	23
YBC 8817	140
YBC 8820	130
YBC 8822	51
YBC 8824	89
YBC 8826	222
YBC 8827	62
YBC 8828	120
YBC 8830	262
YBC 8832	84
YBC 8837	310
YBC 8860	38
YBC 9050	201
YBC 9059	49
YBC 9065	102
YBC 9073	208
YBC 9123	22
YBC 9127	79
YBC 9131	29
YBC 9139	5
YBC 9145	226
YBC 9150	358
YBC 9152	327
YBC 9157	257

Museum Number	*Text*	*Museum Number*	*Text*	*Museum Number*	*Text*
YBC 9160	323	YBC 9360	335	YBC 9456	161
YBC 9163	8	YBC 9361	48	YBC 9458	346
YBC 9164	44	YBC 9363	249	YBC 9459	353
YBC 9166	275	YBC 9367	331	YBC 9461	272
YBC 9168	151	YBC 9369	112	YBC 9462	273
YBC 9175	341	YBC 9375	67	YBC 9463	135
YBC 9177	33	YBC 9376	86	YBC 9464	326
YBC 9182	11	YBC 9377	98	YBC 9465	110
YBC 9183	12	YBC 9378	70	YBC 9468	195
YBC 9198	24	YBC 9381	183	YBC 9473	77
YBC 9205	7	YBC 9382	204	YBC 9474	210
YBC 9207	317	YBC 9383	150	YBC 9481	72
YBC 9234	364	YBC 9384	342	YBC 9482	80
YBC 9241	27	YBC 9388	365	YBC 9483	267
YBC 9245	320	YBC 9389	344	YBC 9484	235
YBC 9261	321	YBC 9390	167	YBC 9485	121
YBC 9262	122	YBC 9391	190	YBC 9487	179
YBC 9272	253	YBC 9392	260	YBC 9488	223
YBC 9275	230	YBC 9396	255	YBC 9492	111
YBC 9279	193	YBC 9401	281	YBC 9493	170
YBC 9283	10	YBC 9404	17	YBC 9495	52
YBC 9287	306	YBC 9405	356	YBC 9500	366
YBC 9288	203	YBC 9408	245	YBC 9501	228
YBC 9289	316	YBC 9409	350	YBC 9504	311
YBC 9295	149	YBC 9412	158	YBC 9505	192
YBC 9303	312	YBC 9413	132	YBC 9506	211
YBC 9305	308	YBC 9415	108	YBC 9508	276
YBC 9307	283	YBC 9416	339	YBC 9512	174
YBC 9311	318	YBC 9419	95	YBC 9514	363
YBC 9312	16	YBC 9421	71	YBC 9515	194
YBC 9321	61	YBC 9422	269	YBC 9518	351
YBC 9322	369	YBC 9425	252	YBC 9519	319
YBC 9329	328	YBC 9426	181	YBC 9522	233
YBC 9331	241	YBC 9427	56	YBC 9528	349
YBC 9334	83	YBC 9429	209	YBC 9529	175
YBC 9336	279	YBC 9430	78	YBC 9532	50
YBC 9340	232	YBC 9433	114	YBC 9534	304
YBC 9342	254	YBC 9435	324	YBC 9538	347
YBC 9346	368	YBC 9439	237	YBC 9546	277
YBC 9348	154	YBC 9440	196	YBC 9552	345
YBC 9349	278	YBC 9443	94	YBC 9554	220
YBC 9350	216	YBC 9450	176	YBC 9555	91
YBC 9354	134	YBC 9451	307	YBC 9558	224
YBC 9357	185	YBC 9454	103	YBC 9561	139
YBC 9359	178	YBC 9455	367	YBC 9562	15

Museum Number	*Text*	*Museum Number*	*Text*	*Museum Number*	*Text*
YBC 9563	88	YBC 9643	42	NBC 4698	145
YBC 9565	148	YBC 9646	246	NBC 4699	189
YBC 9568	125	YBC 9649	54	NBC 4700	234
YBC 9569	261	YBC 9653	362	NBC 4701	85
YBC 9572	20	YBC 9654	359	NBC 4708	218
YBC 9573	343	YBC 9659	155	NBC 4715	215
YBC 9575	251	YBC 9663	136	NBC 4721	124
YBC 9579	227	YBC 11315	219	NBC 4726	248
YBC 9581	104	YBC 11500	238	NBC 4727	191
YBC 9584	305	YBC 11511	240	NBC 4728	63
YBC 9586	137	YBC 11514	214	NBC 4740	168
YBC 9587	309	YBC 11517	205	NBC 4746	153
YBC 9589	258	YBC 11527	188	NBC 4752	118
YBC 9591	352	YBC 11665	202	NBC 4760	206
YBC 9592	69	YBC 16299	117	NBC 4768	198
YBC 9595	242	YBC 16300	256	NBC 4770	43
YBC 9596	128			NBC 4785	39
YBC 9597	21			NBC 4788	200
YBC 9598	165	NBC 4605	115	NBC 4803	46
YBC 9599	164	NBC 4614	143	NBC 4807	76
YBC 9600	334	NBC 4615	96	NBC 4809	82
YBC 9602	60	NBC 4617	99	NBC 4813	1
YBC 9610	129	NBC 4628	73	NBC 4814	180
YBC 9612	68	NBC 4629	127	NBC 4816	106
YBC 9613	141	NBC 4633	156	NBC 4822	74
YBC 9615	101	NBC 4634	268	NBC 4823	152
YBC 9616	92	NBC 4635	64	NBC 4825	173
YBC 9618	259	NBC 4643	65	NBC 4853	6
YBC 9620	177	NBC 4644	271	NBC 4886	45
YBC 9622	213	NBC 4647	244	NBC 4887	53
YBC 9623	93	NBC 4648	116	NBC 4901	184
YBC 9624	100	NBC 4654	243	NBC 4902	172
YBC 9625	265	NBC 4659	197	NBC 4922	144
YBC 9626	355	NBC 4660	81	NBC 4923	146
YBC 9627	229	NBC 4661	270	NBC 4924	41
YBC 9629	212	NBC 4662	90	NBC 4931	247
YBC 9630	207	NBC 4668	160	NBC 4947	217
YBC 9632	199	NBC 4671	282	NBC 6129	75
YBC 9633	333	NBC 4677	171	NBC 6176	25
YBC 9634	47	NBC 4682	142	NBC 6180	231
YBC 9635	133	NBC 4687	186	NBC 8354	147
YBC 9637	59	NBC 4691	107		

Tablets Copied by Dougherty (Arranged According to Text Number)

RPD	*Text*
1	286
2	287
3	288
4	289
5	290
6	291
7	292
8	293
9	294
10	295
11	296
12	297
13	298
14	299
15	300
16	301
17	302
18	303
19	304
20	305
21	306
22/23	307
24	308
25	309
26	(YBC 8822 see 51)
27	310
28	311
29	312
30	313
31	314
32	315
33	316
34	317
35	318
36	319
37	320
38	321
39	322
40	323
41	324
42	325
43	326
44	327
45	328
46	329
47	330
48	331
49	332
50	333
51	334
52	335
53	336
54	337
55	338
56	339
57	340
58	341
59	342
60	(YBC 9369 see 112)
61	343
62	344
63	345
64	346
65	347
66	348
67	349
68	350
69	351
70	352
71	353
72	354
73	355
74	356
75	357
76/77	358
78	359
79	360
80	361
81	362
82	363
83	364
84	365
85	366
86	367
87	368
88	369

COMMENTS AND COLLATIONS TO COPIES AUTOGRAPHED BY RAYMOND PHILIP DOUGHERTY

286:2f. Space of two lines.

286:14 End:  (*ú* correctly copied)

287:3 Beginning, read: 

287:19 Read:  ($^{\mathrm{1d}}$60.ŠEŠ.KÁM)

288:2f. Space of ½ line.

288:8 *ina* UGU-*ḫi* 1-*it rit-tum* ≪1-*it rit-tum*≫ . . . (copy correct; dittography of ancient scribe)

288:13f. Space of ½ line

289:1 End: The geographical name seems to be written over an erasure; despite several collations, I can get no coherent reading: 

289:1f. Space of ½ line

289:6–10 There should be shading at the end of these lines to indicate the broken signs.

289:7 End should read:  (⸢36⸣[GUR . . .])

289:13 End:  (*šis-sin-nu-šú* $^{\mathrm{1d}}$AG-⸢*muk-ki*-⸣[*e-lip e-ṭir*])

289:13f. Space of one line

289:14 End: *ú*-sign actually written thus:  ; Traces of verticals not visible

290:2 End: sic.

290:8 Read: 

290:11 For RPD's  , read: 

290:13 Read:  . . .

290:15 End: (See note to 289:14, above.)

290:15f. Space of ½ line

291:2 Read: GIŠ.GIŠIMMAR *za-ru-tu* (*za* written over erasure)

291:6 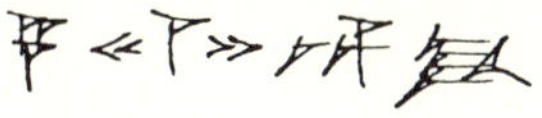 . . . (upright error of ancient scribe)

291:8  error of ancient scribe for 

291:9 End:  error of ancient scribe for 

291:14f. Space of one line

291:16 Beginning, read:  ([1]*zìg-ga*)

291:19 The month, a badly written KIN, is as copied, except without shading.

292:5 End: The reading ^{d}AG-(X-)*bi-na-an-ni* (?) is possible on the assumption that the name is written over partially erased signs:  (⌈*bi-na-an-ni?*⌉)

292:13f. Space of one line

292:14 End, read: 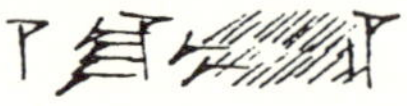 ([1]*šu-⌈la-a*⌉)

292:18 (See note to 291:19, above.)

293:1 End. There is an erasure visible: 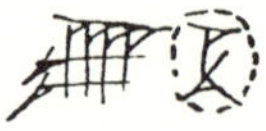

293:16 End. sic.

294:15 End, error of ancient scribe for:  ([1]*mi-ṣir*)

295:2f. Space of one line

295:5 End, read:  (dittography of ancient scribe)

295:14f. Space of one line

296:2f. Space of ½ line

296:13 Following 1 GUR: an erasure of two signs: 

297:3 Beginning, read: 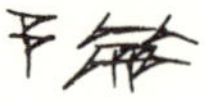

297:7  is erasure

297:16f. RPD omitted line:  (rest of line blank)

297:20 Read: 

298:2f. Space of ½ line

299:1 Beginning: 

299:1 End:  (?)

299:2 Read: 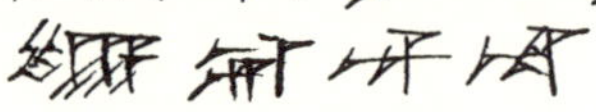

299:3 Read:  (42 GUR . . .)

299:8 End, read: 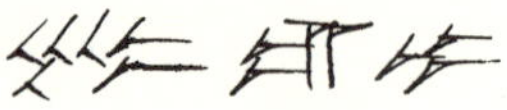 °sic

299:13 End, read: 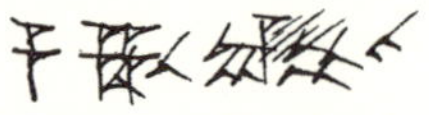 (*šá ḫa-*⌈X-X⌉)

299:15 Read: 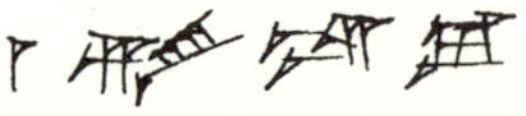 . . .

299:20  Trace of month-sign visible at beginning of line

300:7 End, read: 

300:22 End:  (copy correct)

300:25 ^{1d}UTU.MU.A ≪^{1d}UTU.MU≫ A ^{1d}AG.KAL (copy correct; dittography of ancient scribe)

300:31 End, read: 

300:37 Partially destroyed sign: 

300:38 End, read: 

301:16 Begins thus: 

303:2  (*ku*-⌈*ma*-⌉*ru*)

303:3 

303:9 Beginning: 

303:10f. Ruling appears between lines 10 and 11.

303:25 End, read:  (*kàs-pa*)

303:27f.; 28f. Ruling appears after line 27 and line 28.

303:39 End, read: 

305:9 Note traces: 

306:7–9 Beginning: space for one destroyed sign

306:7 Read:  (⌈*dùr*⌉)

307:6 End: 

307:9f. RPD omitted two lines:

9.
10.
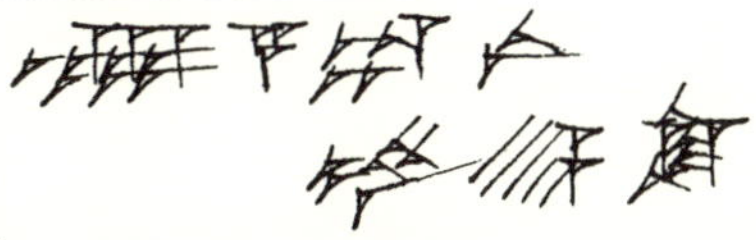

308:2  : SU over erasure

309:4 RPD normalized  ; original has: 

310:2 End:  (*-it*)

310:7 Beginning, read:  . . .

311:3 End, read: 

311:5 After break:  (?)

311:16  (UD.⌈16.⌉KÁM)

314:7 Beginning, note trace:  (⌈30⌉)

314:8–10 Shading should be extended to the right.

314:12 Beginning, note traces:  (⌈20⌉)

314:16 Beginning: The sign is not IGI (), but *ù* ()

314:17 End: ¹*mu-še-zib*-DINGIR is correct; nothing follows.

315:4 Read: 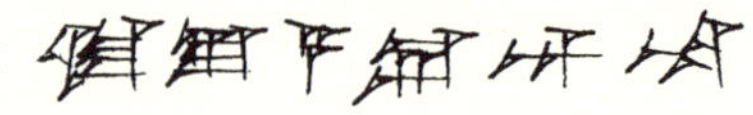 (*šá* omitted by RPD)

315:7 Beginning: The first sign is a *ya* over an erasure.

315:10 Read:  (¹ᵈEN.⌈NIGIN-*ir*⌉)

315:13 Read:  (UD.14.KÁM)

317:2 End: 

317:5 Read: 

317:7 End:  (UD.⌈29.⌉[KÁM])

319:3 Reading is probably:  (*ib-bak*-⌈*kà*⌉(⌈GA⌉)-*am-ma*). There may be two vertical lines in the GA-sign; even under the microscope it is hard to tell.

319:11 End, read: 

320:5 For the fourth sign I see only:  (-⌈*su*⌉).

320:5 End, perhaps:  (¹ᵈEN-*e*-⌈*ṭir*⌉)

320:14 Read: 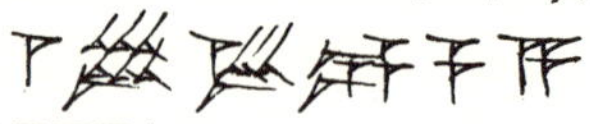 (¹ŠEŠ.MEŠ-*e-šá-a*; omission of "*e*" error of RPD)

321:2 Read:  (⌈MU.⌉6.KÁM)

321:4 End, read:  (⌈*ip-ru-us*?⌉)

322:9 The third sign is not LUGAL (), but *rap*- ().

322:10 Read:  . . . (RPD omitted first "*a*")

322:13 Second sign from end:  (*it*-)

322:25 End: 

Original reads: SAL *ḫa-am-mi-li*-⌈DINGIR⌉ which is clearly an ancient error for: SAL *ḫa-am-ma-a*.

322:33 For  , read: 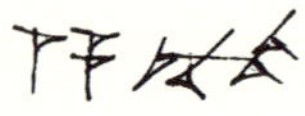 (¹GAR.NUMUN; error of RPD)

323:4 End: 

(65 GUR 3 PI 2 BÁN ⸢ŠE.⸣BAR)

323:5 Beginning: 

323:10 Beginning:  ([*ina* GUB-*z*]*u*)

323:14 Beginning:  ([¹*n*]*a-din*)

324:2 End: The signs *ina* NÍG.GA actually form line 3 of a five-line text. RPD may have been trying to save a line so that the two columns of this plate would end evenly. I have kept RPD's line count.

325:2 Damaged sign is *-as-*, as copied.

325:6 For  read: 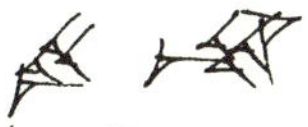 (LÚ.ÌR)

325:8 The second sign is  , an erasure.

Read: *ù* (erasure) 10 ERÍN . . .

325:16 Beginning:  (⸢23?⸣)

325:16 Read:  . . .

(¹ᵈAG.KÁM ⸢X⸣ 60 . . .)

325:19f. Ruling appears between lines 19 and 20.

325:24f. Ruling appears between lines 24 and 25.

327:3 End: For RPD's 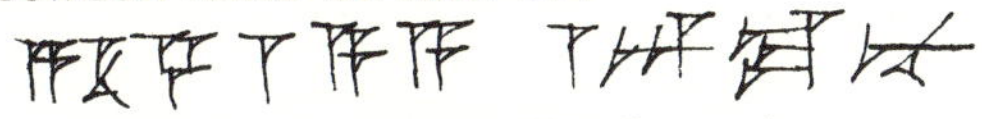

(A-*šú šá* ¹A-*a* ¹DINGIR-*ba-nu*)

read: 

(A-*šú šá* ¹A-*a* A ¹DINGIR-*ba-nu*)

328:4 Read:  (MU.⸢11.⸣[KÁM ᵈA]G . . .)

329:6 End:  (LAḪ₄)

330:7 End: For RPD's  read: 

331:9 Line is actually on Right Edge. Signs are as copied with the addition of: 

332:4 Beginning:  (ŠUK)

334:1 End:  (KIN)

335:3 End:  (¹ᵈ*na-na-a*-⸢KÁM⸣)

336 and Duplicates; 336 (YBC 4057) finely written, black;

338	338 (YBC 4044) poorly written, white.
336:4	The sign following *mi-* is an erasure.
336:21 and 338:22	Read:  (UD.17.KÁM; RPD error in both copies)
338:11	 (*u* ⸢*mim-mu-šú šá* URU *u*⸣ . . .)
338:12	 (^{1}MU-⸢*a*⸣ . . .)
338:12	 ([K]Ù.BABBAR-*šú*)
337:8f.	Ruling appears between lines 8 and 9.
337:16	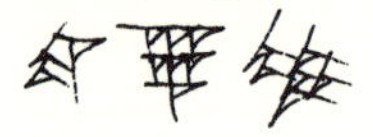 (<UD.> 7.KÁM; omission of ancient scribe)
339:4	Third sign is  (read: ^{1}*ta-ba-la-a-a*)
340:5	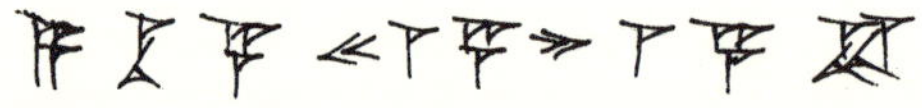 (Dittography error of ancient scribe)
340:6	Read: 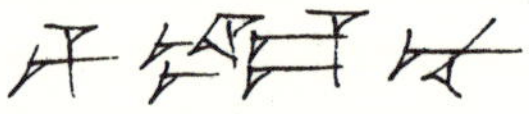 (error of RPD)
341:2	Read: 25½ [GÍN] ⸢*ku*-⸣*lum*
343:4	Read: 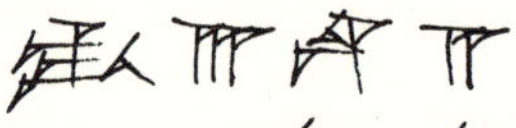 . . .
343:6	End, read: 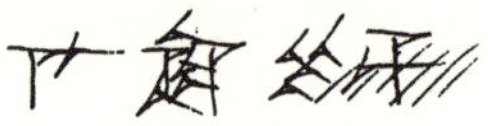 (LÁ-*ṭi* ŠE.BAR)
343:15	Beginning: 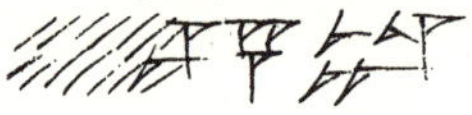 . . . ([^{d}A]G.NÍG.DU.URÙ)
344:2	Read: *šá* KI.NE.NE <*šá*> *a-n*[*a*] (error of RPD)
345:11	Read: ITI.ŠE UD.6.KÁM ( is error of RPD)
346:5–8	Show shading at beginning of lines that extends into first cuneiform wedges.
348:1	End, read:  (⸢.SI.SÁ⸣)
348:22	End, read:  (LÚ.ŠID.⸢^{d}MAŠ⸣)
351:10	Read: KÁ.DINGIR.<RA.> KI (omission of RA error of ancient scribe)
354:1	Read: *šá* ⸢*a*-⸣[*na*] ^{1} . . .
354:6	Note collation of month:  (ITI.⸢ZÍZ⸣)

356:5 After cleaning of surface of tablet, day definitely appears to be  (18) not  (15).

357:4 Fourth sign is  (BA).

357:11 Read:  . . .
ina pi-i šá [1]MU-*a* A-*šú šá* . . . (over erasure)

357:19 Beginning, read: [1]⌈BA-⌉*šá-* . . . (BA over erasure)

358:3 Read: . . . UDU.ḪI.A *šá* LÚ . . . (omission of *šá* error of RPD)

358:9 Read:  (LÚ *ki-zu-*⌈*ú*⌉ . . .)

358:11 Beginning, read:  . . . ([1][*na-*]*ṣir-*'-DINGIR; upright before PN preserved)

359:9 Beginning, read trace of ⌈LÚ⌉: 

359:10 Beginning, read traces:

[[1d]A]G.⌈ŠEŠ⌉.ME.GI

359:11 Beginning, read trace: 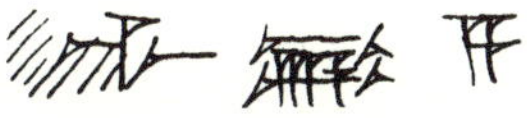
([. . . [1]*ma*]*r-duk-a*)

359:12 Beginning, note trace:  (⌈X⌉)

359:13 Beginning, note traces: 

359:15 For  read  (error of RPD)

360 i 8 Read: 
(omission of 1 error of RPD)

360 i 10 RPD skipped this line: 

360 i 18 End, read: 

360 i 22 Broken sign is KAR over erasure.

360 i 26ff. On the original there is a break here of about 13 lines (27′–39′) which RPD apparently shortened on his copy.

360 i 53′ End, read:  (UD.16.[+X? KÁM]; error of RPD)

360 i 54′f. Ruling appears after line 54′.

360 ii 15f. Two erased lines on original.

360 ii 19 Read: 
(omission of 1 error of RPD)

360 ii 23 — End, read: 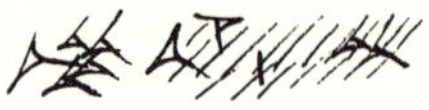 (MU.⸢14.KÁM⸣)

360 ii 37′ — End, note two verticals: 

360 ii 38′f. — Ruling appears after line 38′. The bottom eleven lines of column ii on the original are blank (not shown on copy).

360 iii 5 — End, note trace of K[I]: 

360 iii 6 — End, note trace of K[Ù]: 

360 iii 10 — End, note trace of *t*[*i*]: 

360 iii 14 — End, note trace of ⸢BÁRA⸣: 

360 iii 16 — Read: 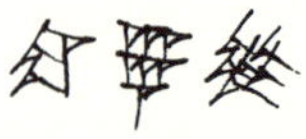 (UD.7.KÁM)

360 iii 22ff. — The size of the break here, unlike that at i 26ff., above, is correctly drawn. There is a break of 5 lines (23′–27′ are completely destroyed); however, RPD omitted traces of line 28′: 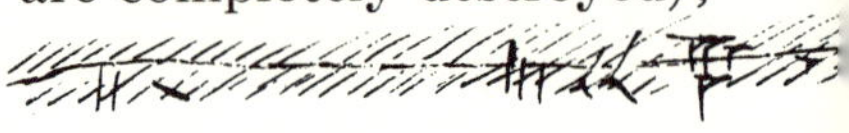

360 iii 32′ — Beginning, read:  . . .
(KÙ.BABBAR omitted in error by RPD)

360 iii 38′ — Read:  (KUŠ.TAB.BA)

360 iii 41′ — Beginning, read:  (⸢^{1}GAR.⸣MU . . .)

360 iii 43′f. — Ruling appears after line 43′.

360 iv 8 — Read: IGI ^{d}*na-na-a* (omission of DINGIR error of RPD)

360 iv 19 — End, read:  (⸢X X X⸣[X])

360 iv 41 —  ([TIN.TI]R.KI)

360 iv 42 — End, traces:  (⸢X X X⸣)

360 iv 52f. — Ruling appears after line 52.

360 v 19 — End, traces:  (^{1}[X.X⸣)

360 v 20 — End, traces:  (*it-ta-*⸢*šu-ú*⸣)

360 v 31 — Read:  . . . (^{1}A-*a* A ^{1d} . . .;
omission of third "A" error of RPD)

360 v 50f. — Ruling appears after line 50.

360 vi 10 — For RPD's 
read  (*šá ina* UD-*me*)

360 vi 20 — End, read: 

360 vi 21 RPD omitted line:

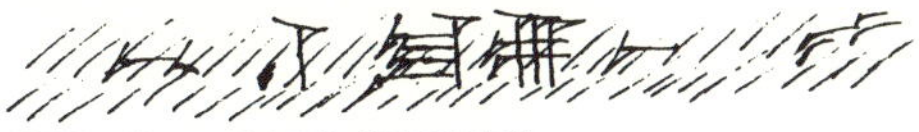

(⌈X *šu-ú*? X⌉ [X]⌈X⌉)

360 vi 27 RPD omitted line:

(*ina* ŠE.BAR-*šú-nu šá* ITI.ŠE *u* ITI.BÁRA)

360 vi 34f. Ruling appears after line 34.

361:23 For RPD's  (*šu*) read  (*ku*: *za-ku-ú*)

362:1 End, read: 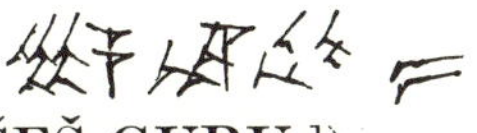 ^{D} sic

(SUM-⌈*na*-ŠEŠ GURU$_{9}$⌉)

362:11 For RPD's  read:  (^{1}ÌR-*a*)

362:12 The PN at the end of the line is:  (^{1}*tal*-⌈*li*⌉)

362:21 For RPD's  (*šu*) read  (KU)

362:23 For RPD's  (*šu*) read  (KU)

362:25 End, add shading at damaged ⌊KI⌋ sign.

362:30 The month is ITI.ZÍZ.

362:30–31 RPD's note appended here read: "Add two lines to 6927." However, the lines in question are actually the Upper Edge of 9653.

363:2 End, note trace: 

363:6 The second sign from the end is 

363:9 The reading of this line is:

^{1}*ina-qí-bi*-^{d}AG -*liš-lim* A ^{1d}AG.MU.GUB.

363:10 Read: ^{1d}INNIN.ŠEŠ.URÙ ⌈A⌉ . . .

363:11 The fifth sign is  .

363:13 The day is not UD.16.KÁM, as copied, but UD.19.KÁM.

364:5 Beginning, read: 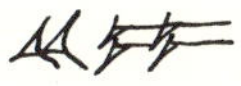 (24 GUR)

364:8 End: There is a break where *šá* probably stood originally.

364:11 The day is not UD.25.KÁM, as copied, but UD.⌊28⌋KÁM

().

365:2 Third sign from end is  , a poorly written *lu*. Read: *u* ⌈*dul*-⌉*lu* LÁ-*e*.

368:4 End, date is: UD.22.KÁM MU.14.[KÁM].

368:5 Beginning, read: ^{ld}AG . . . (RPD omitted )

368:6 Trace of TI[R] visible: 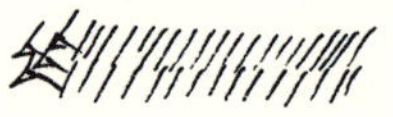 .

PLATE I

1

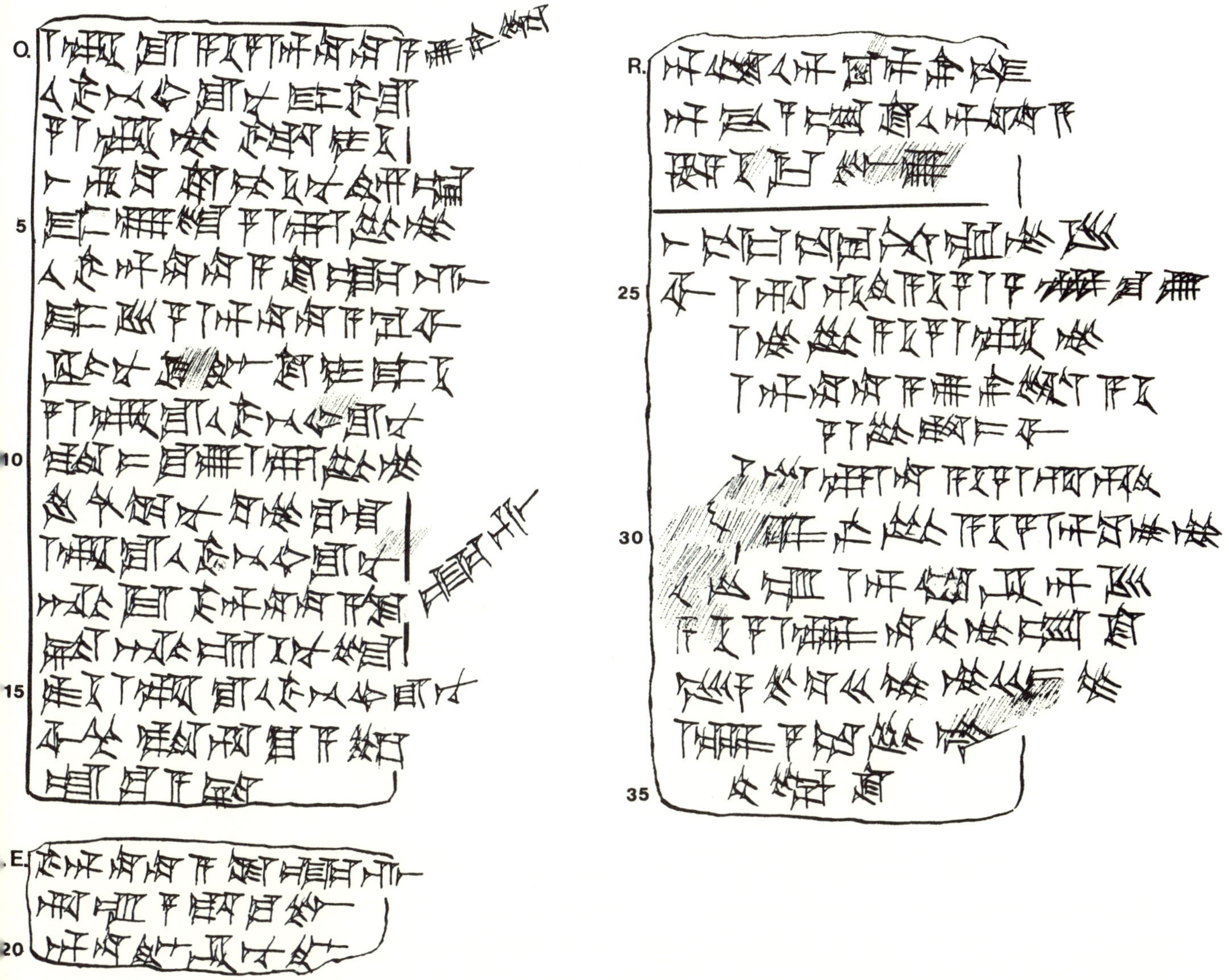

2

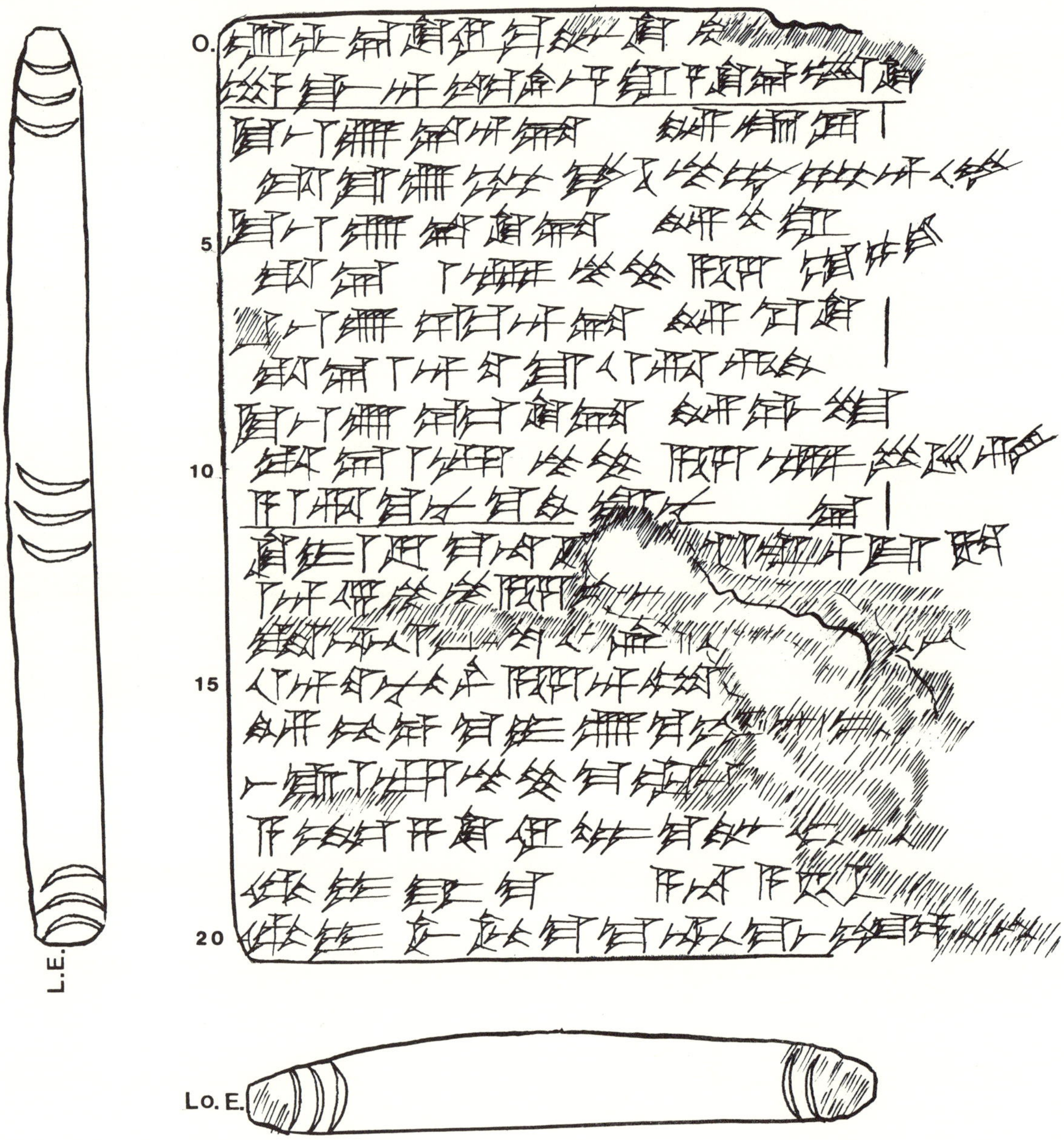

over erasure

sic, for

2

R.

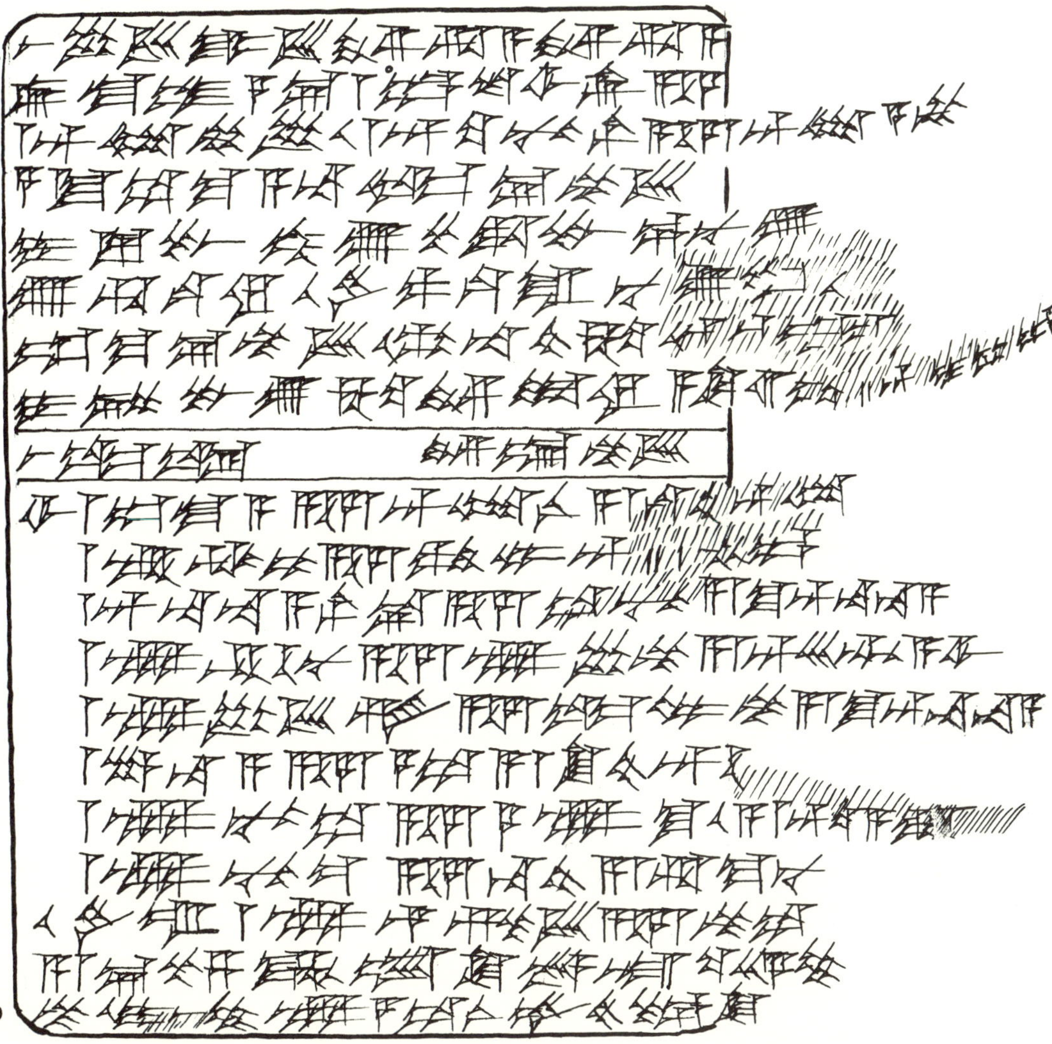

R.E.

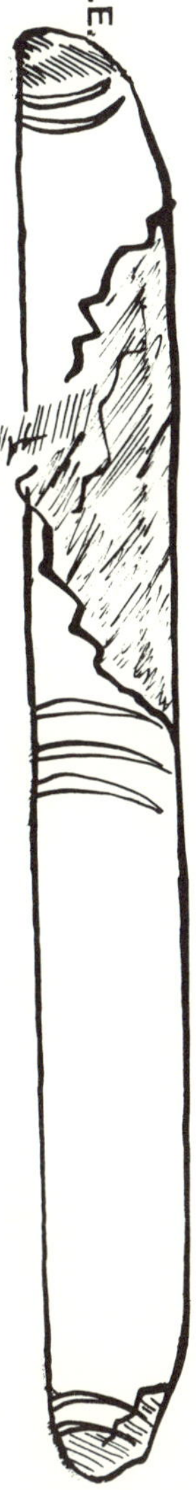

U.E.

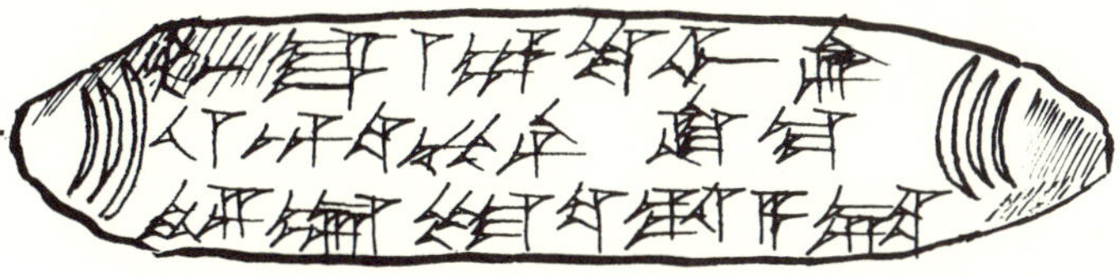

3

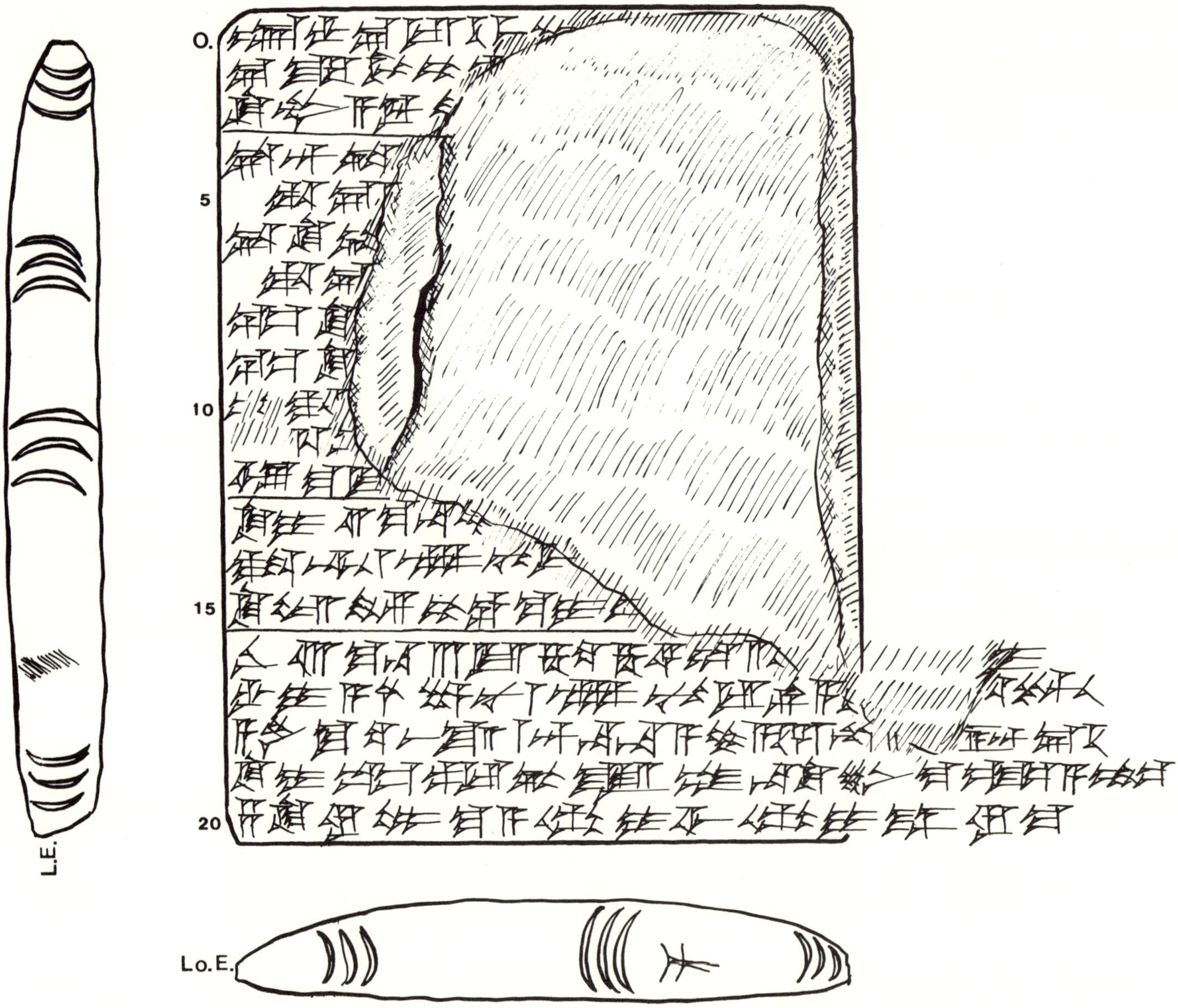

3

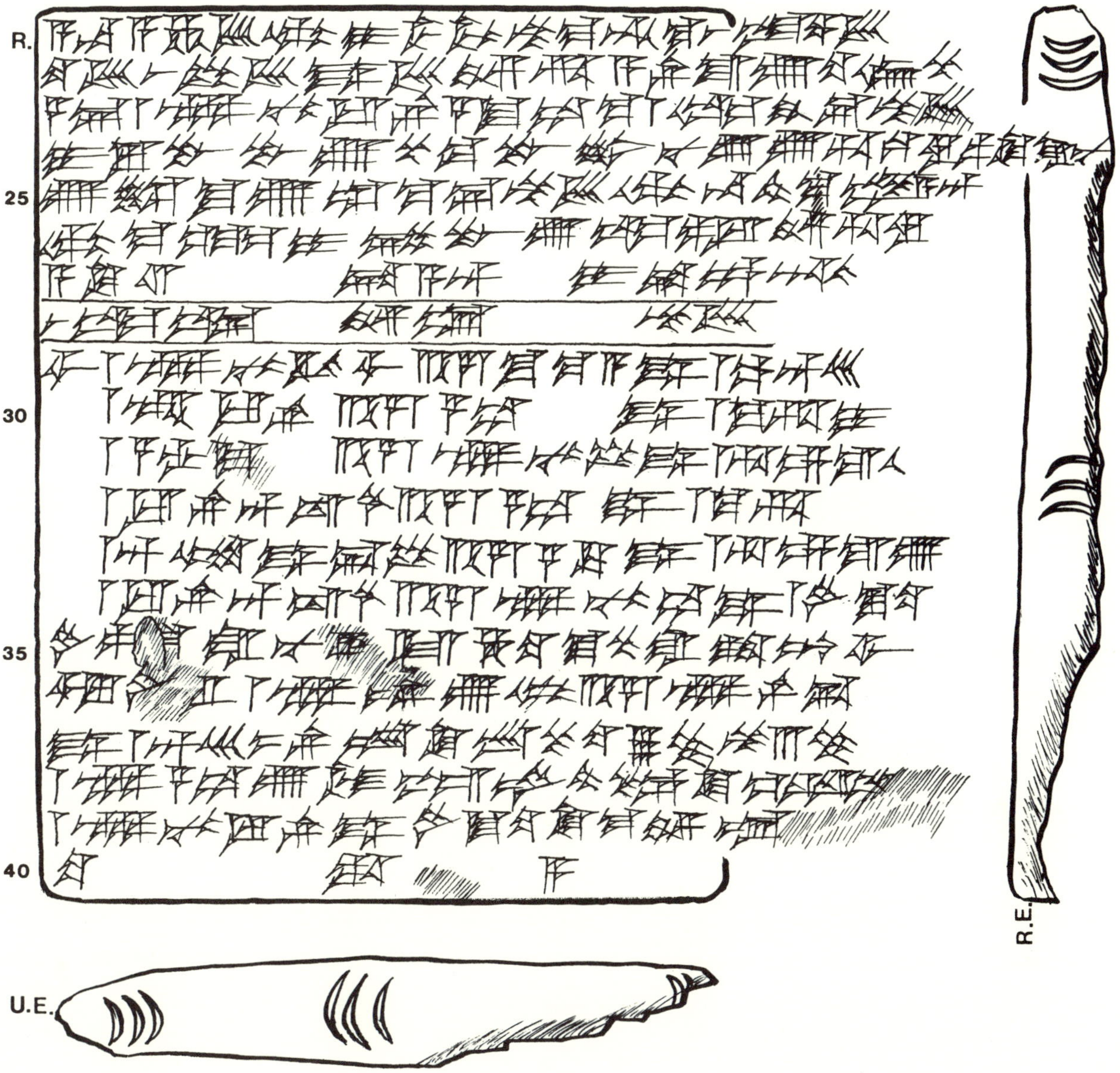

PLATE VI

4

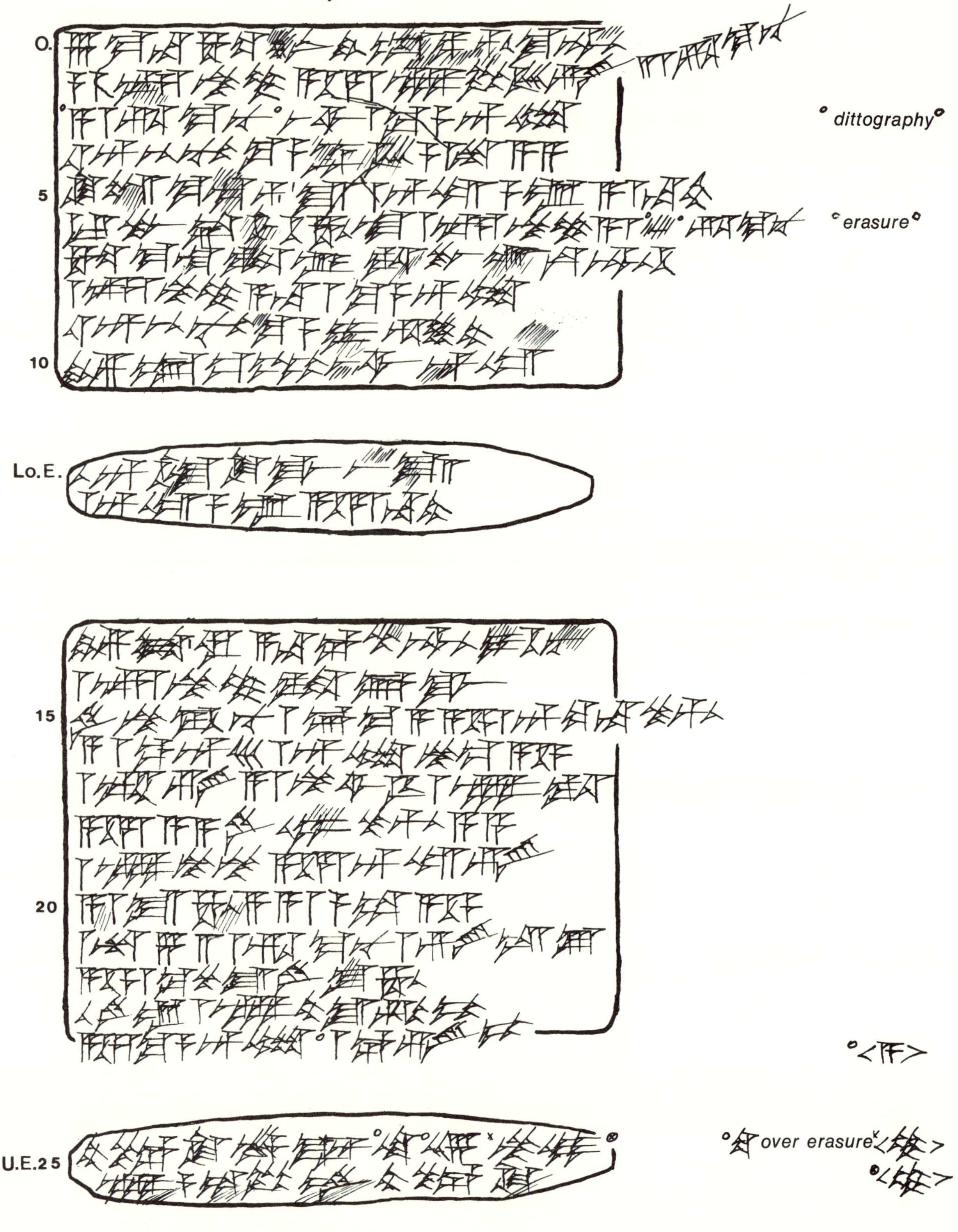

5

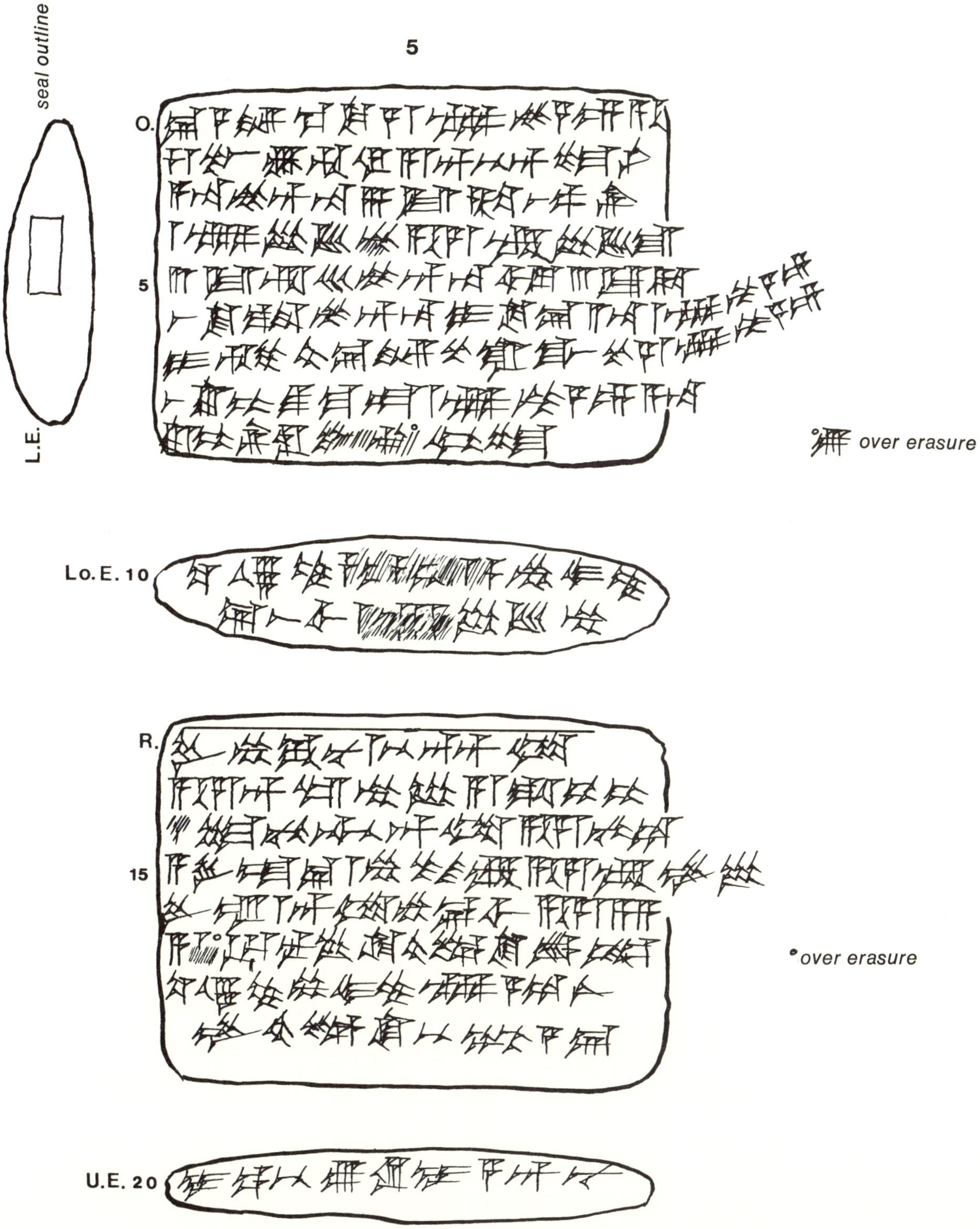

6

O.

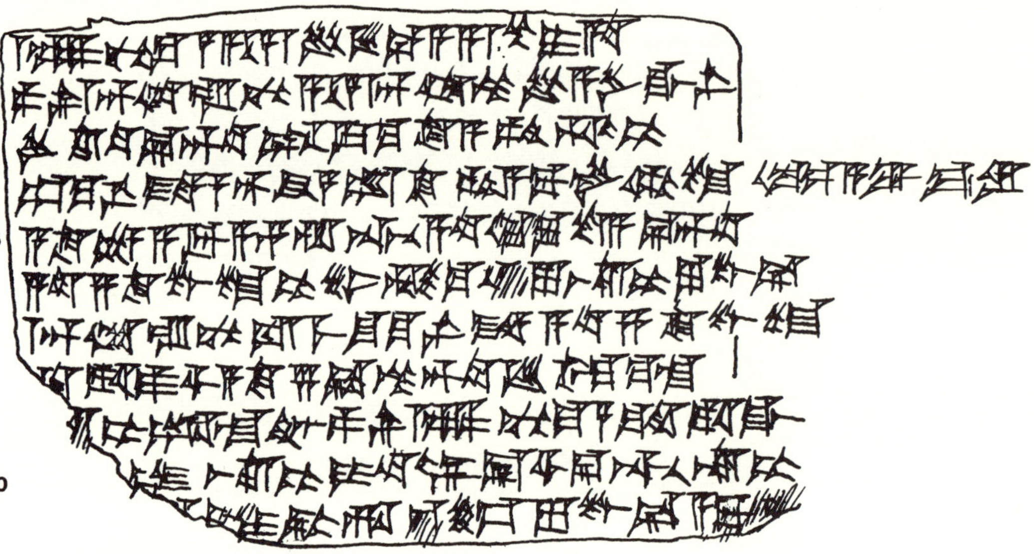

Lo. E.

R.

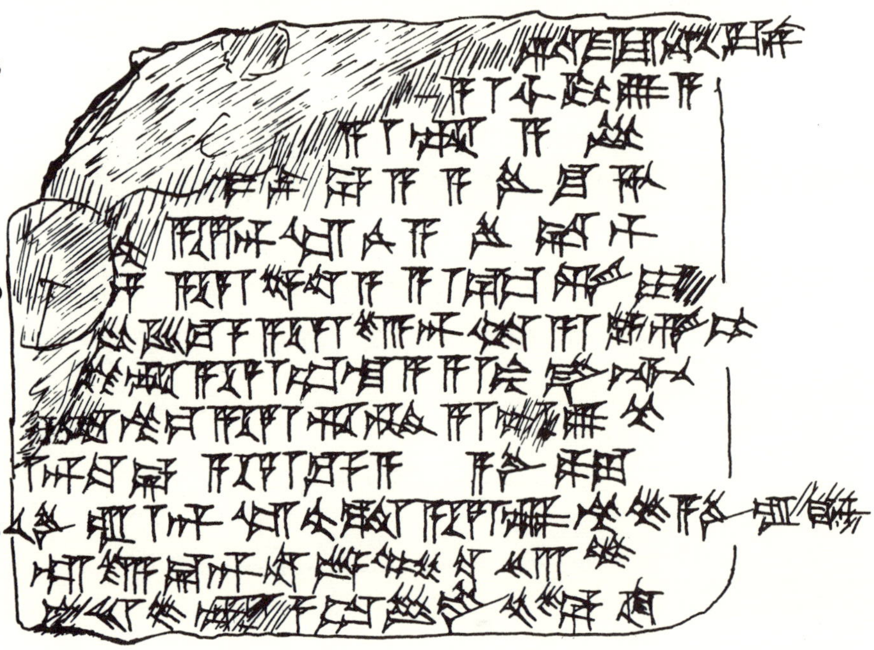

7

O.

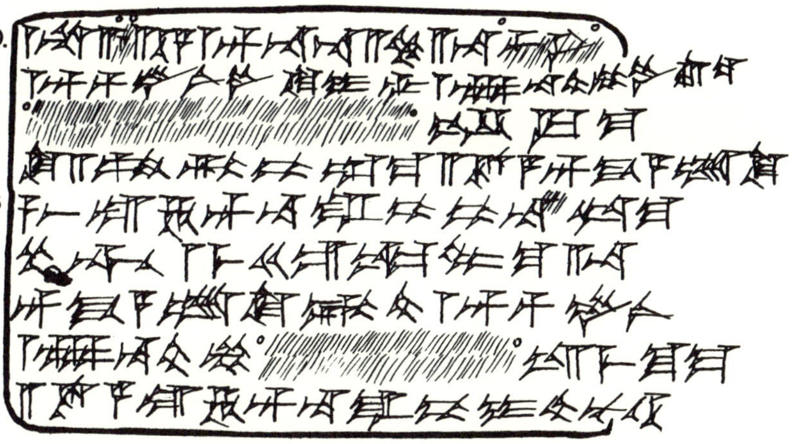

° erasure

° erasure

° erasure

Lo.E.

R.

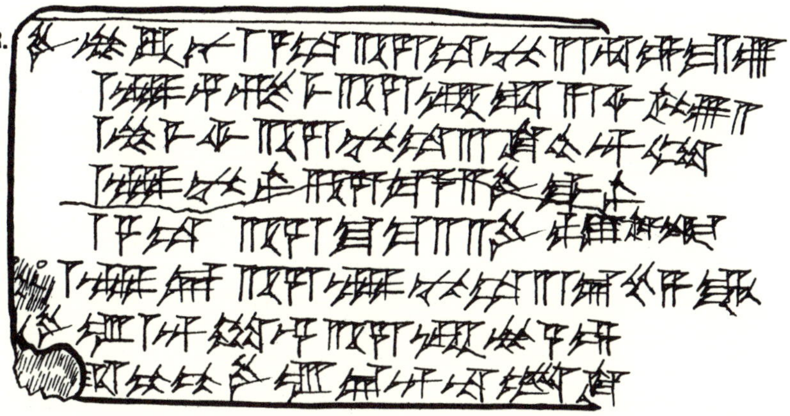

° erasure

U.E.

8

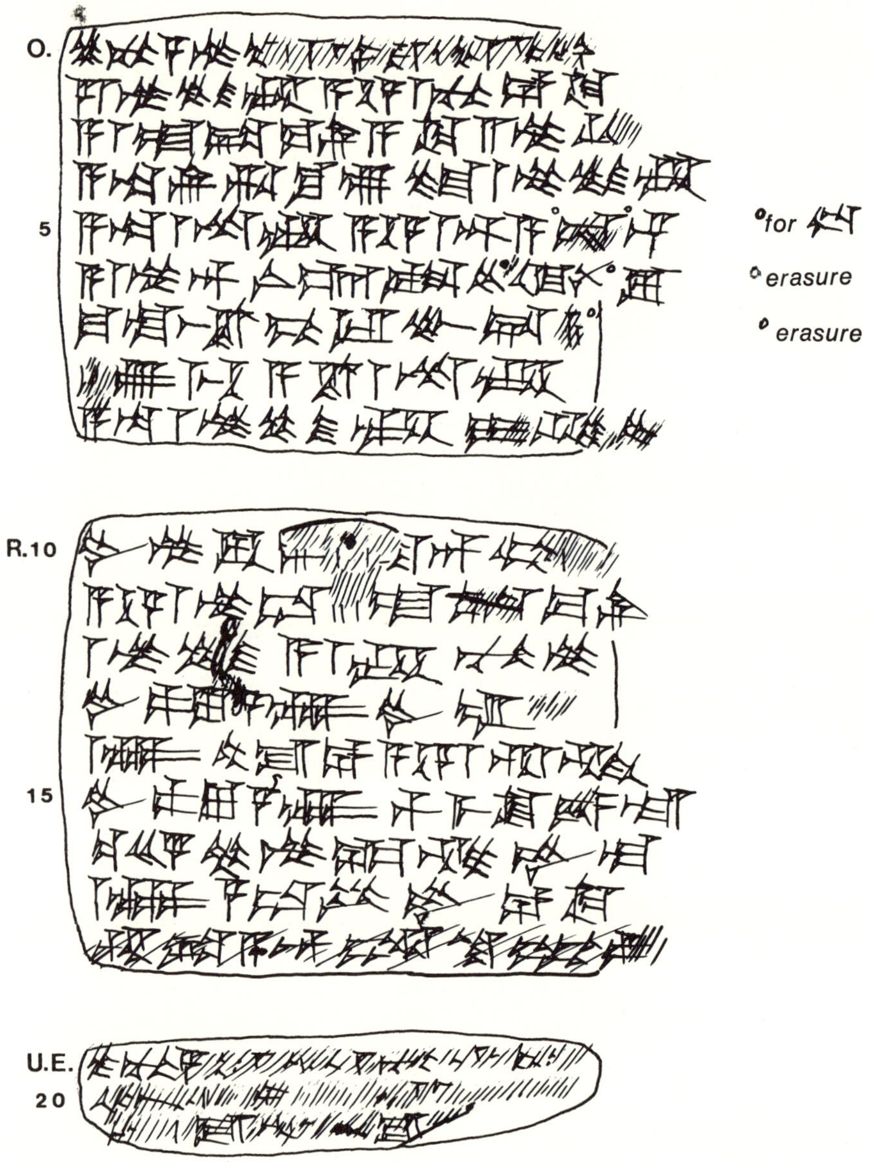

9

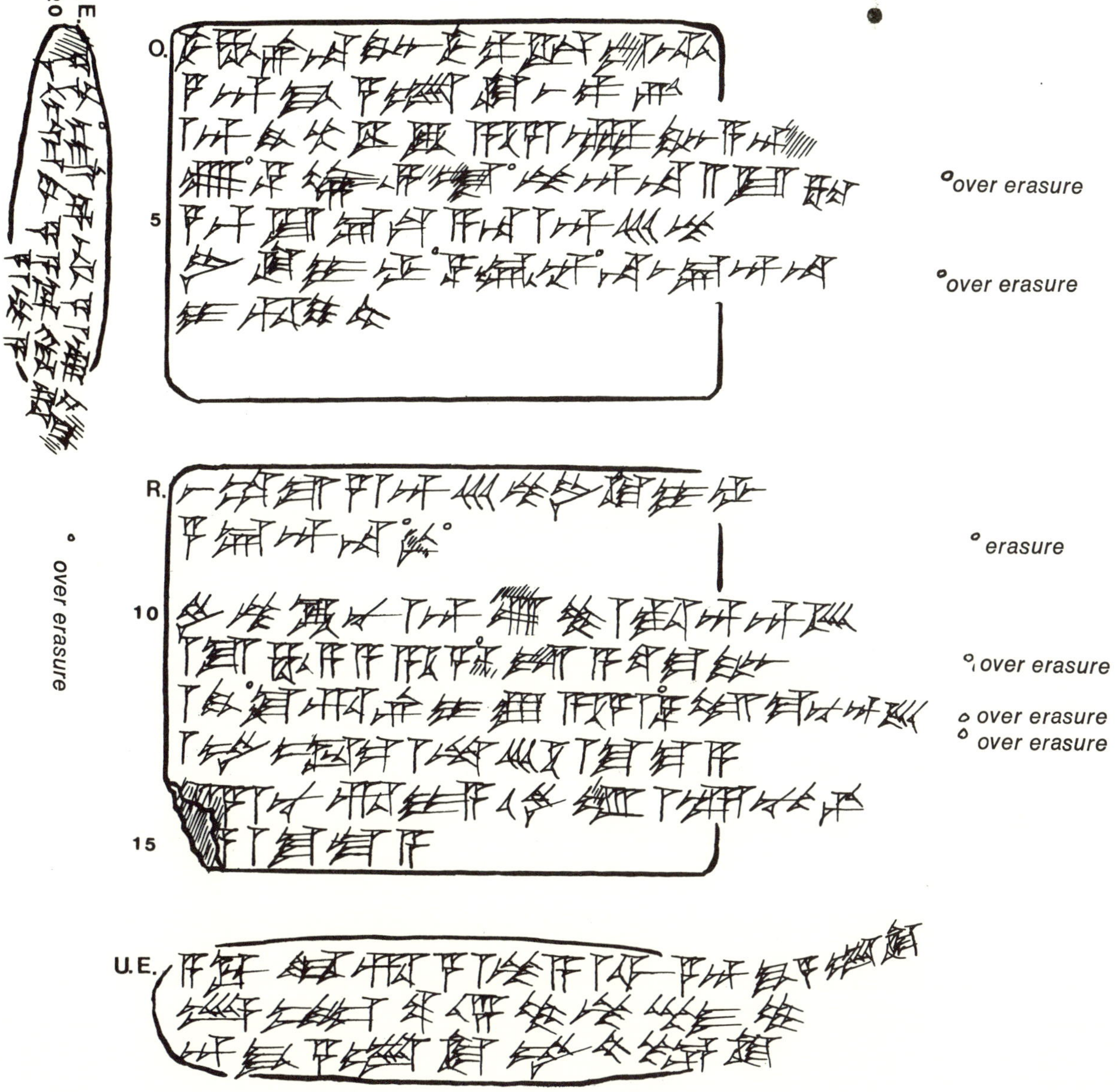
L.E.
20
over erasure
O.
5
over erasure
over erasure
R.
10
15
erasure
over erasure
over erasure
over erasure
U.E.

10

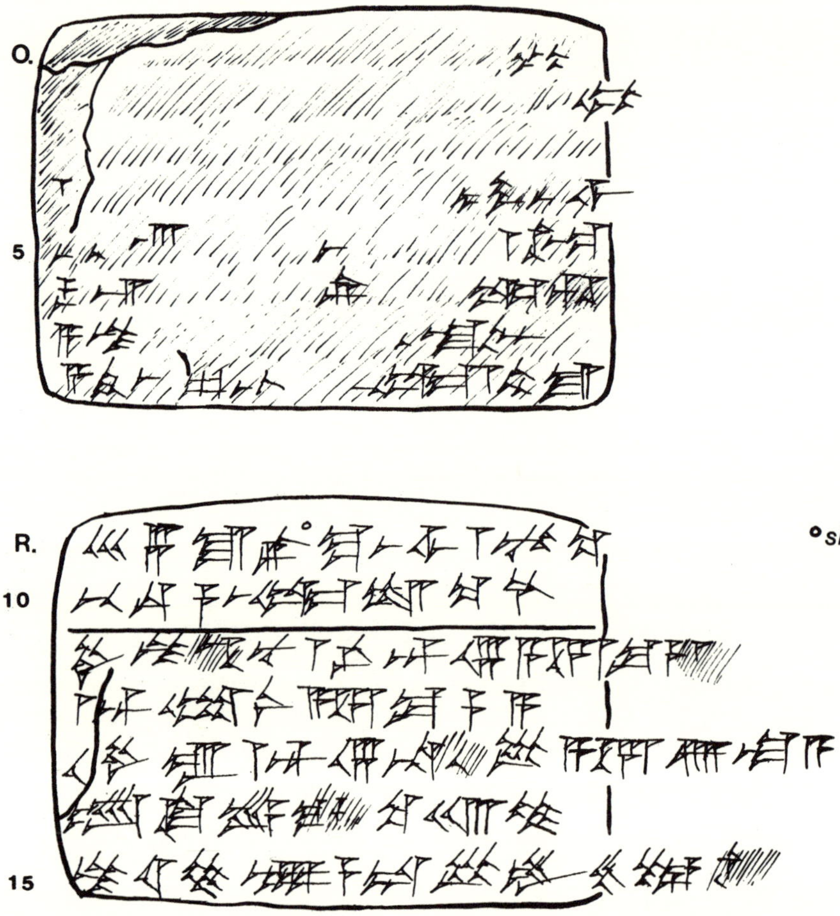

°*sic, for*

11

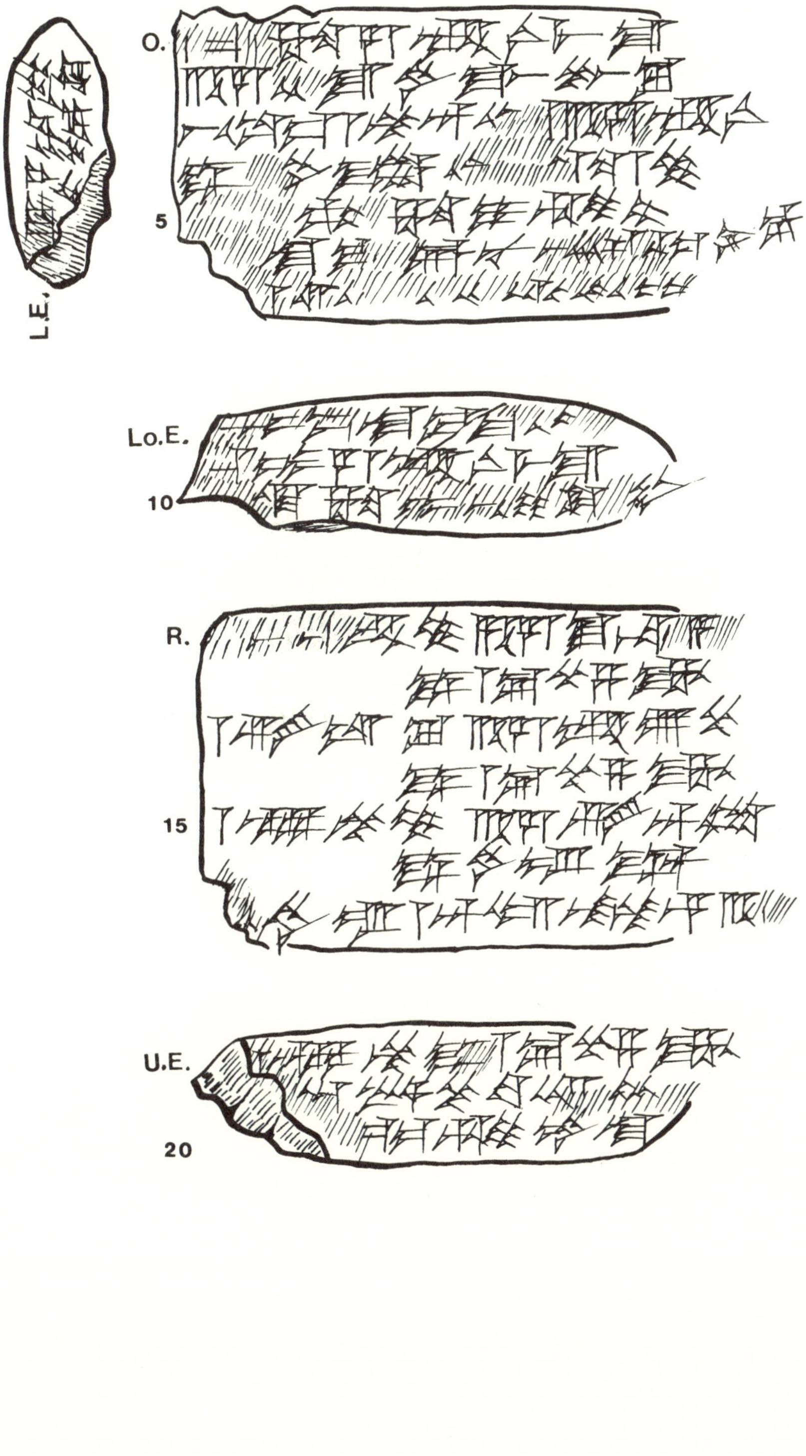

12

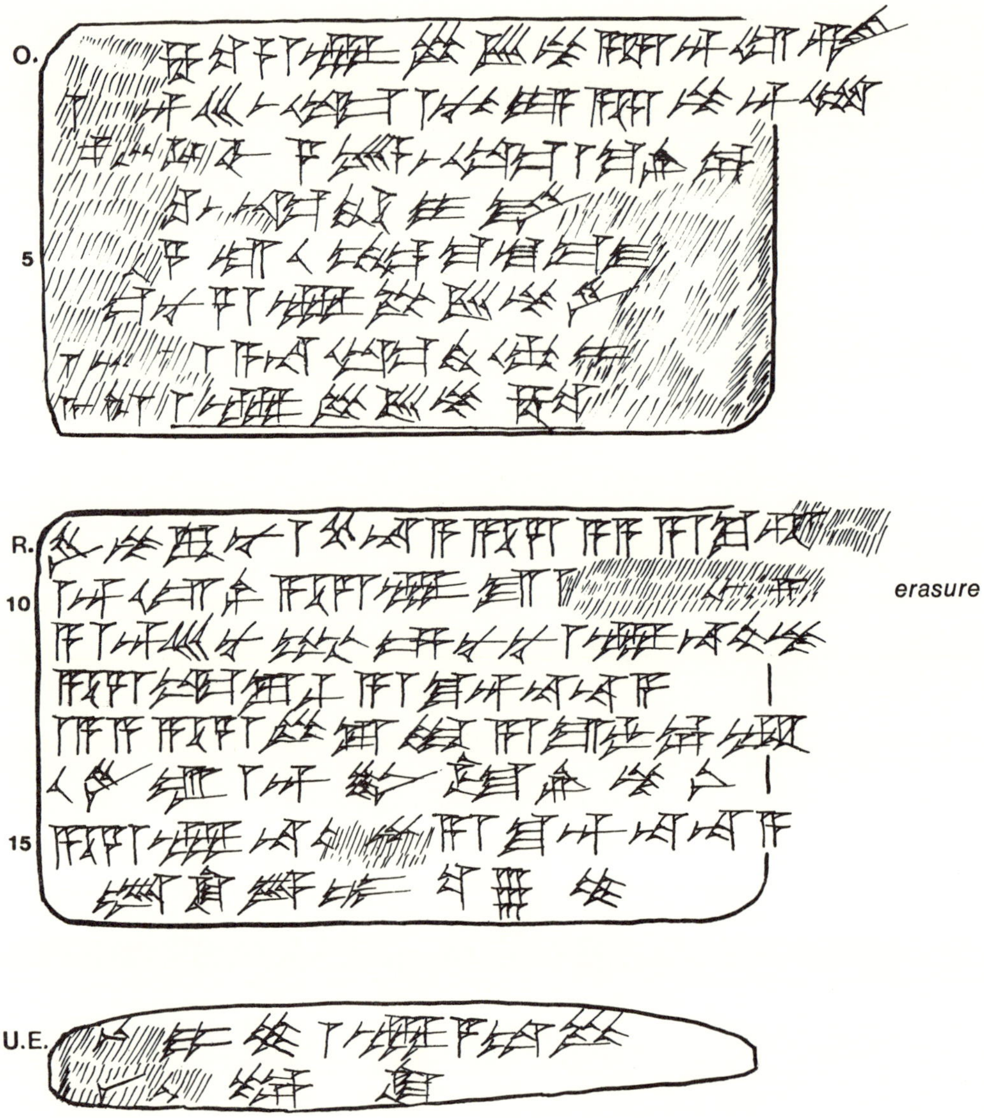

13

O.

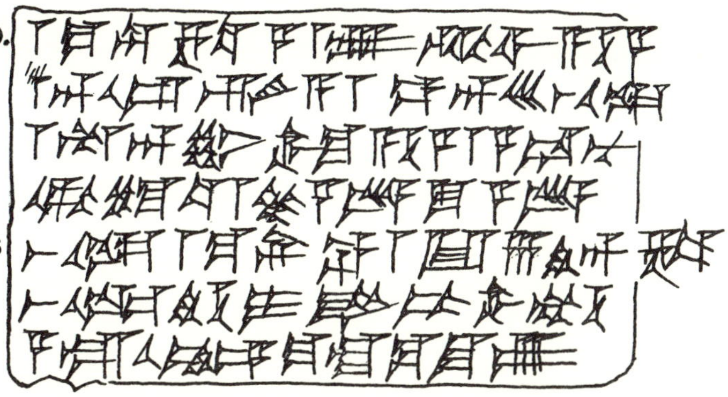

Lo.E.

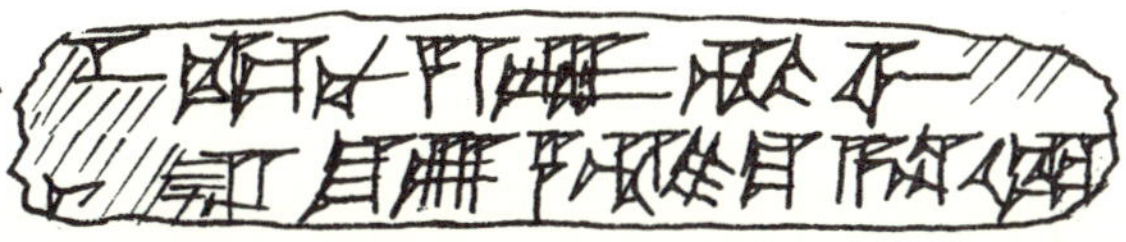

R.

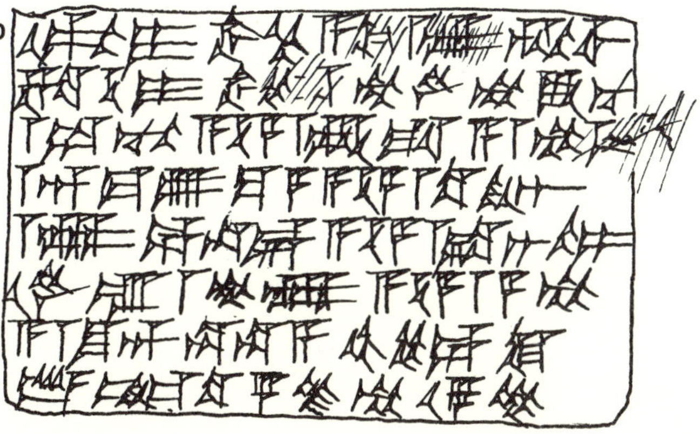

U.E.

14

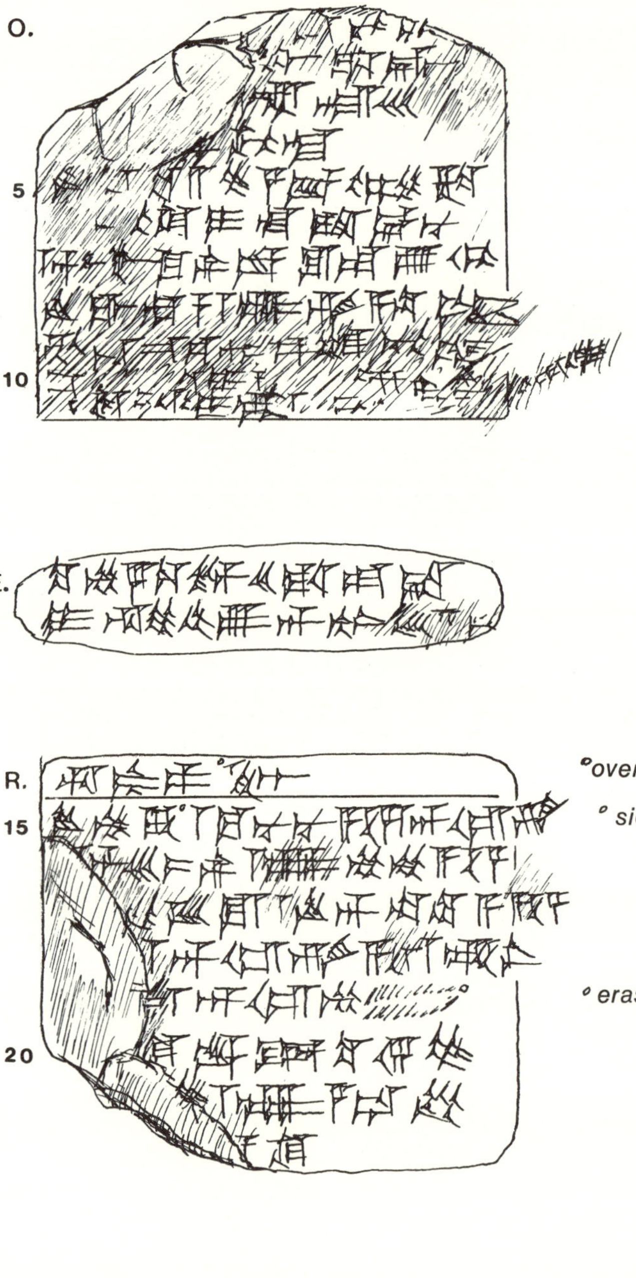

15

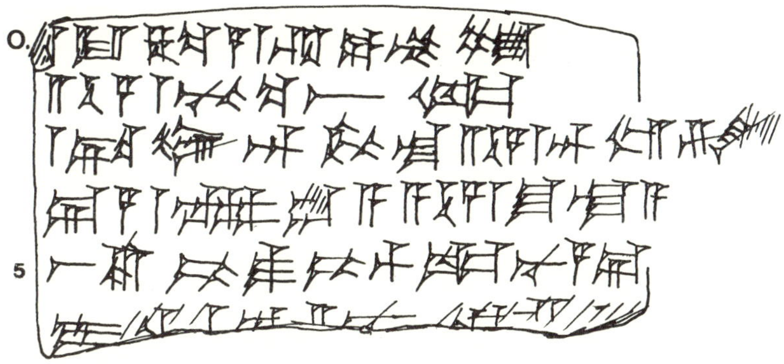

about 3 lines broken away

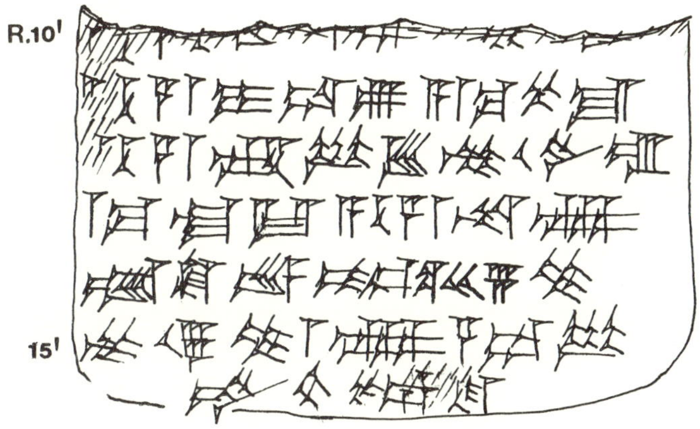

16

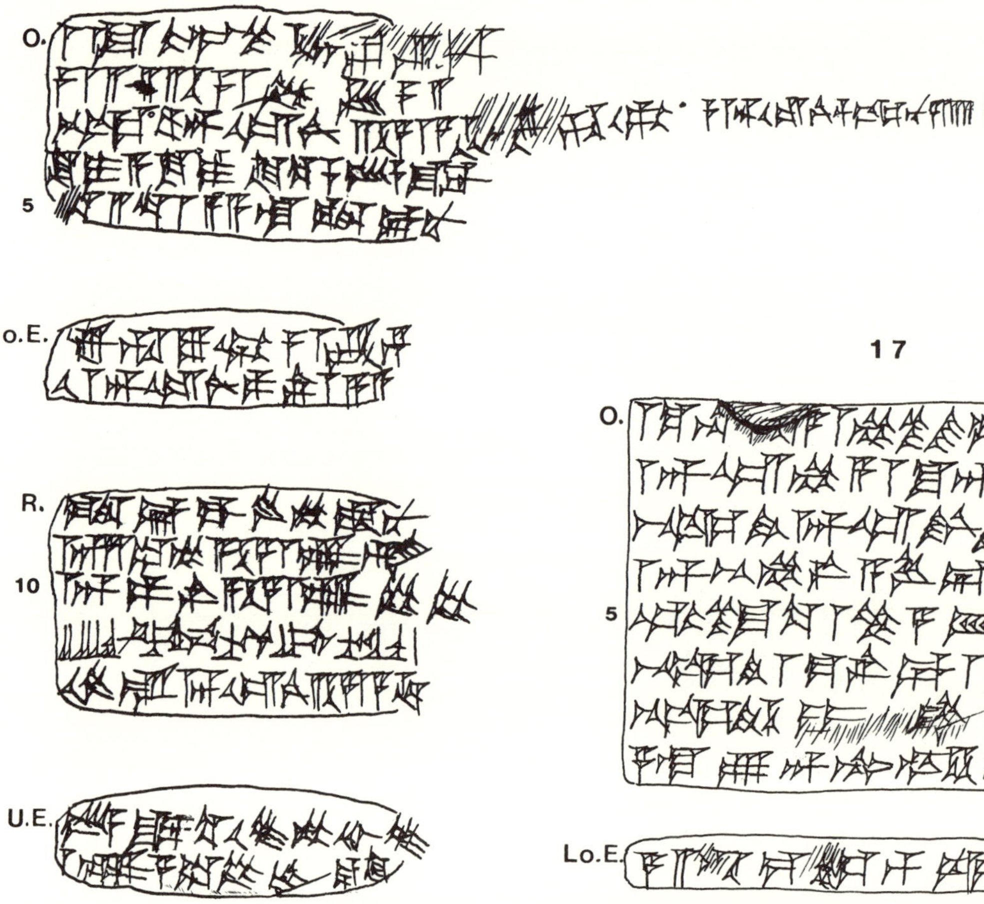

ᵃover erasure

(text continues on R. line 11)

ᵇover erasure

ᶜover erasure

17

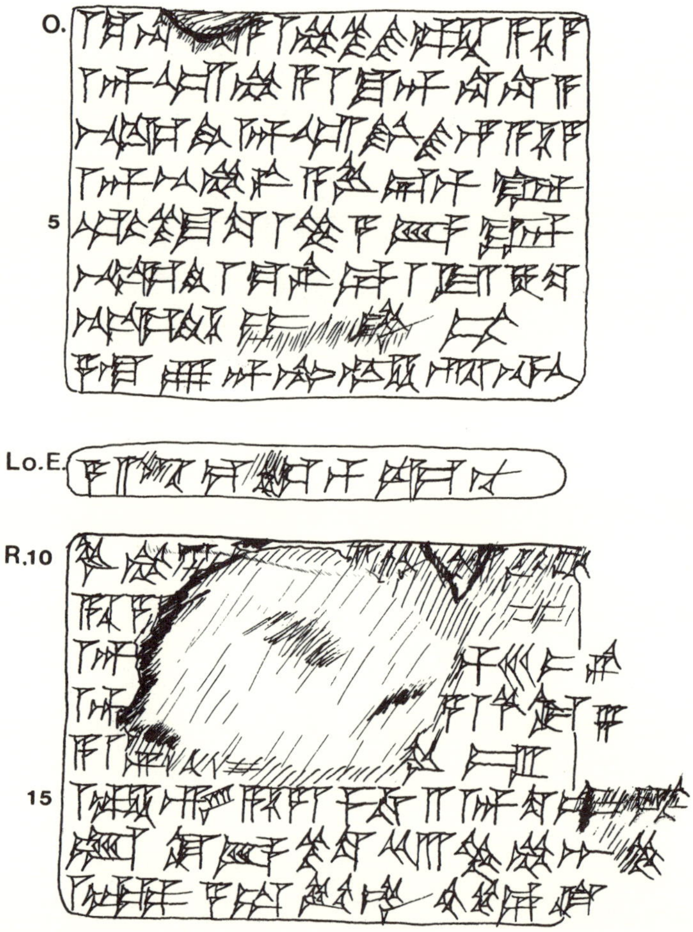

18

O.

R.

U.E.

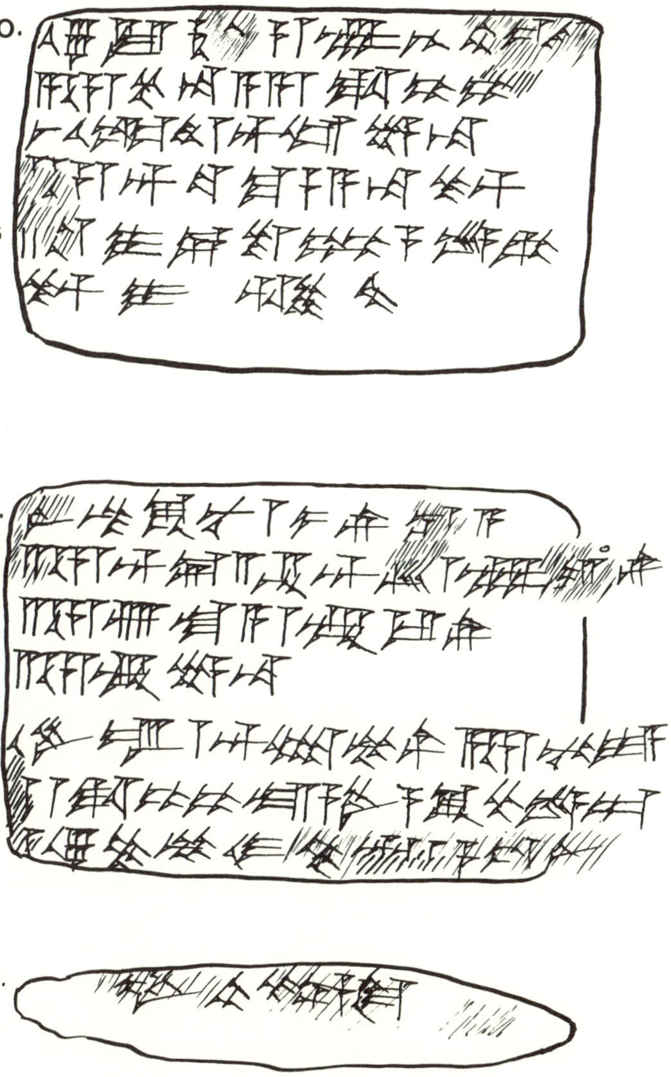

sic, for

PLATE XX

19

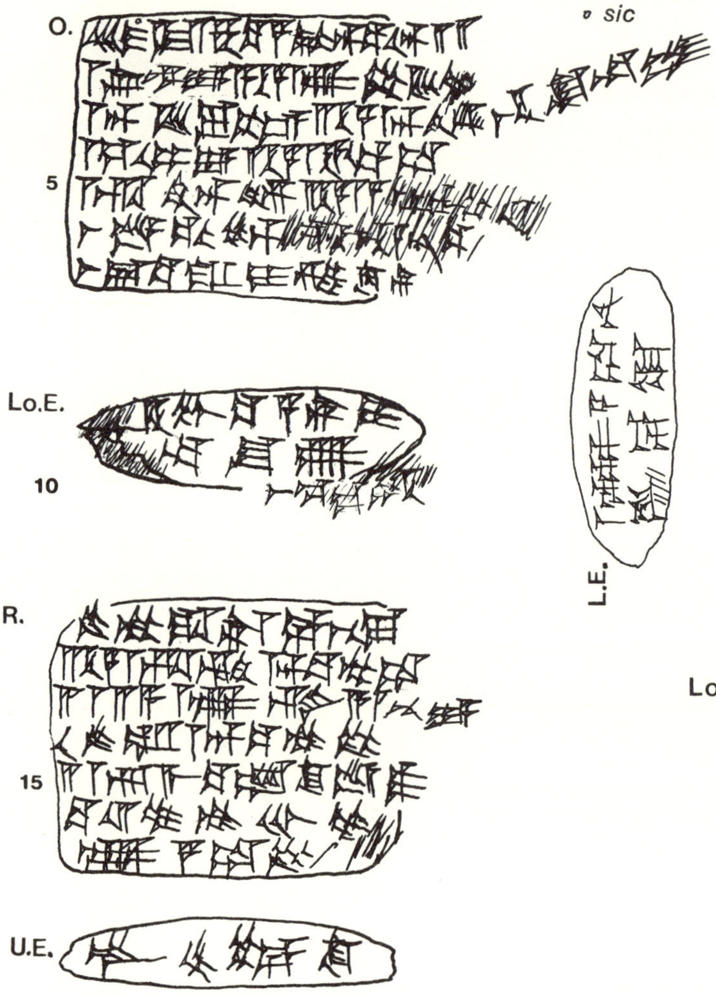

20

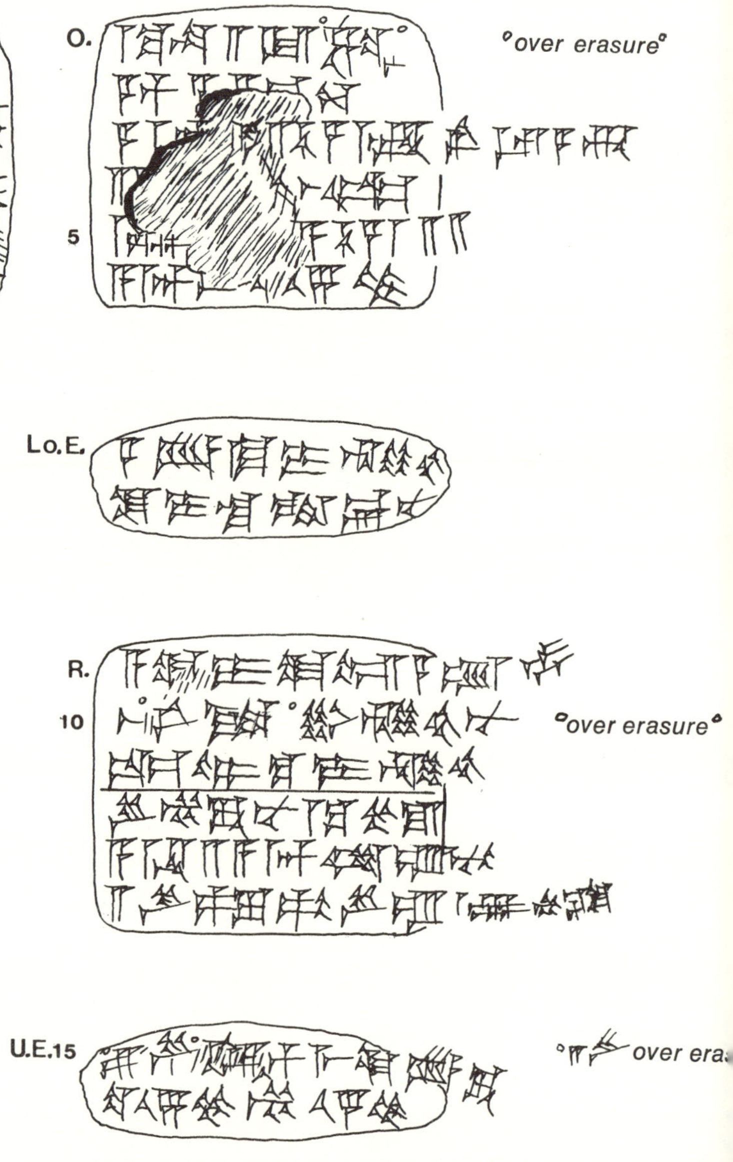

21

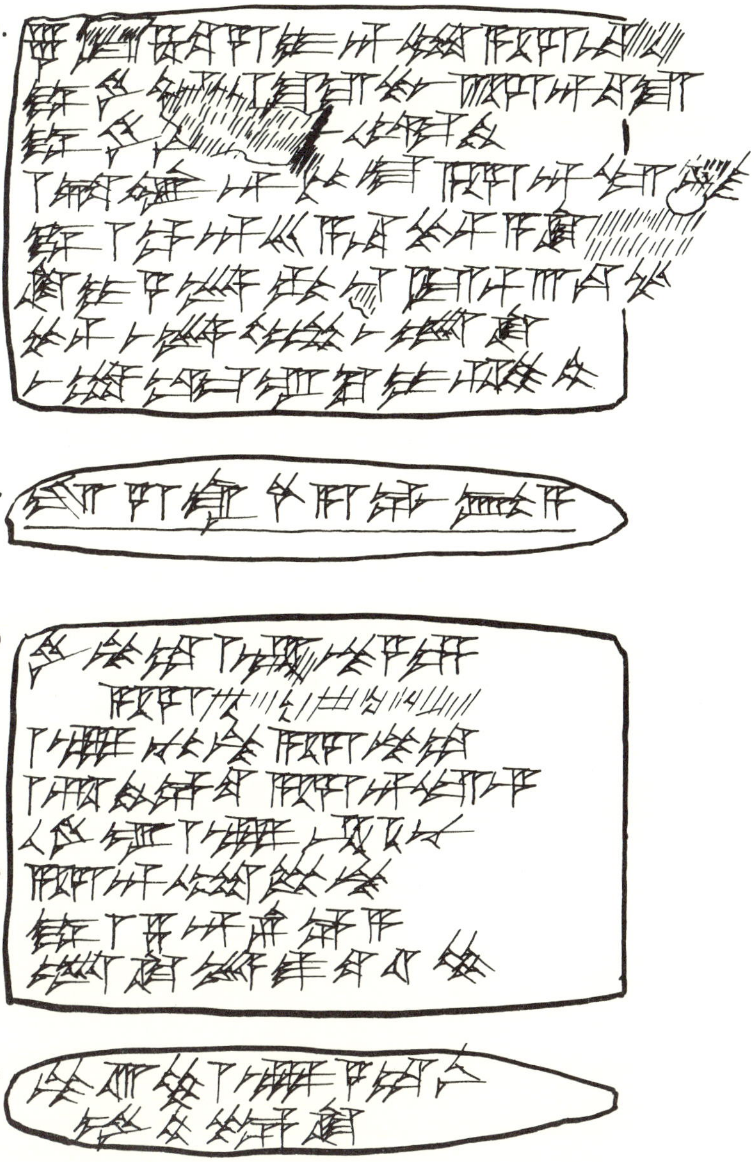

O. 5 Lo.E. R.10 15 U.E.

22

O.

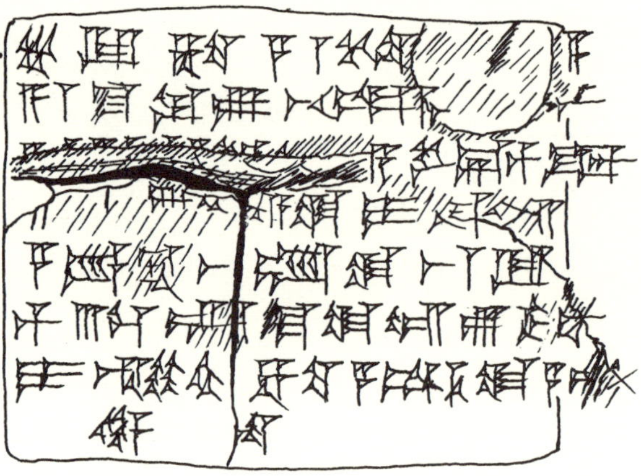

R.

U.E.

23

O.

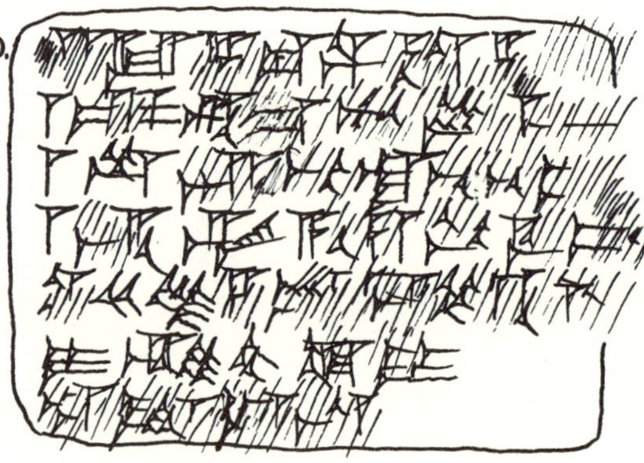

Lo.E.

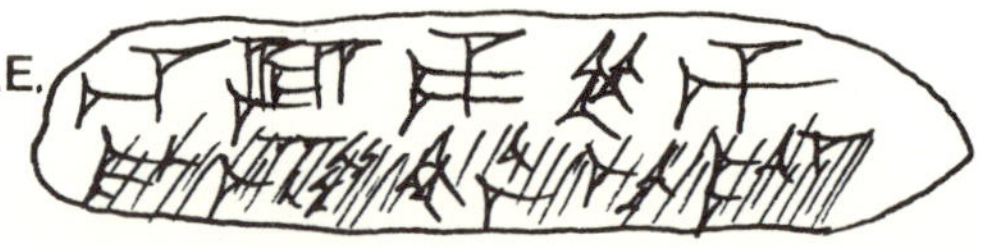

R.10

wri
over e

U.E.

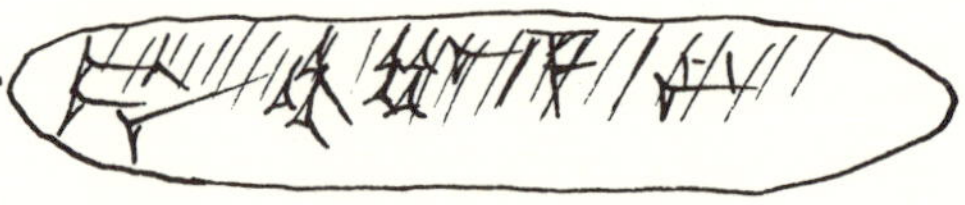

24

O.

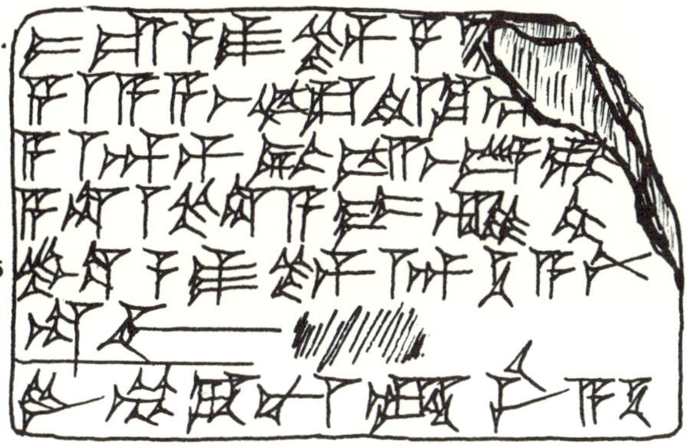

L.o.E.

R.

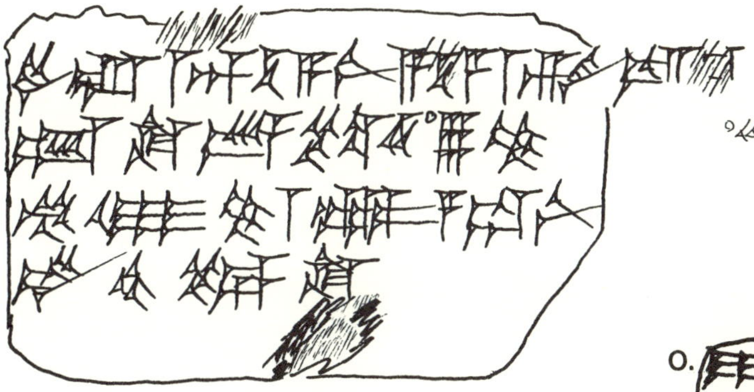

⁹ over erasure

25

O.

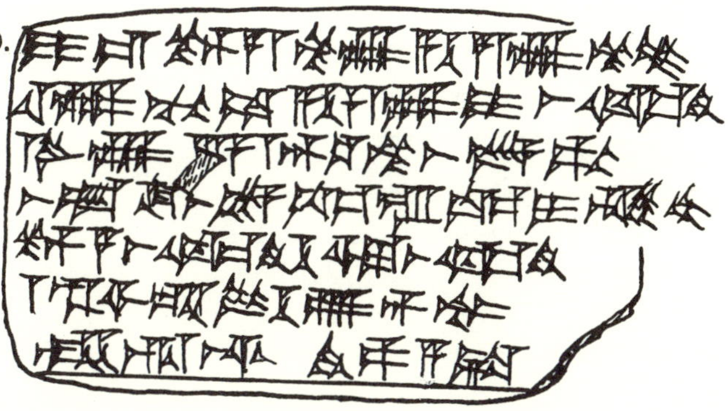

R.

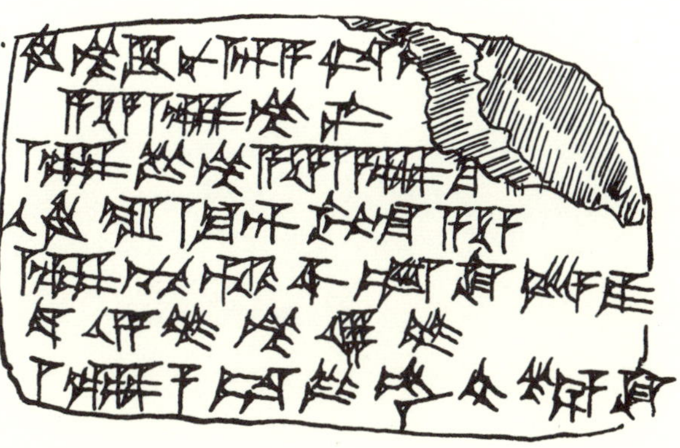

26

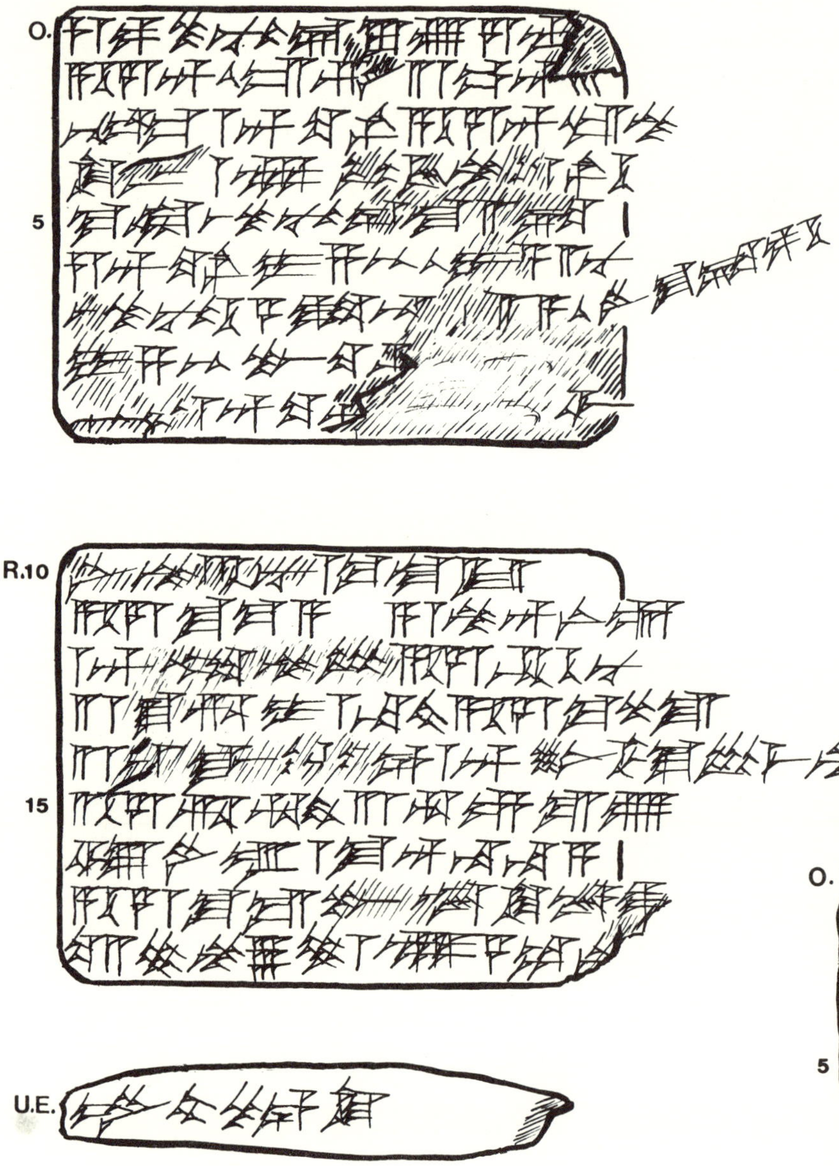

27

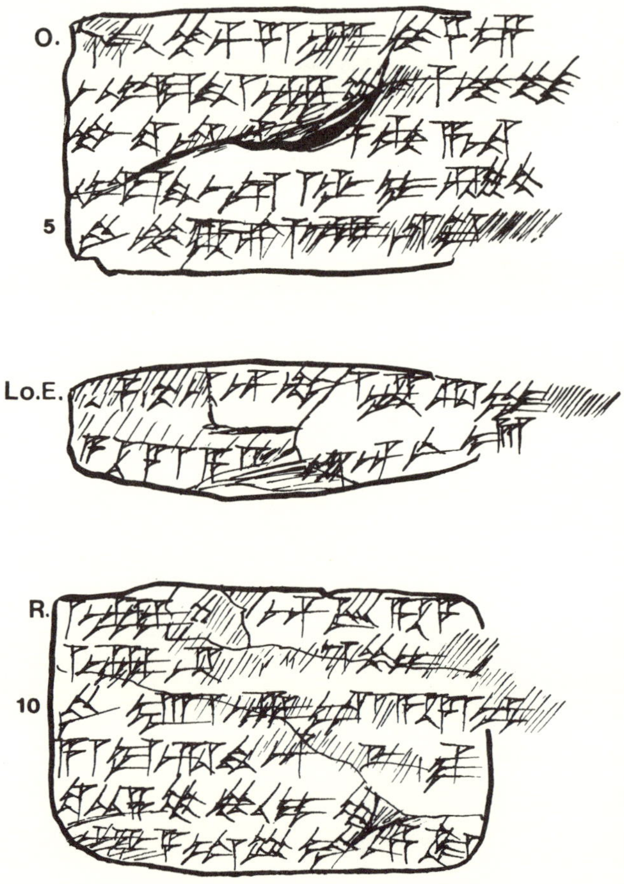

28

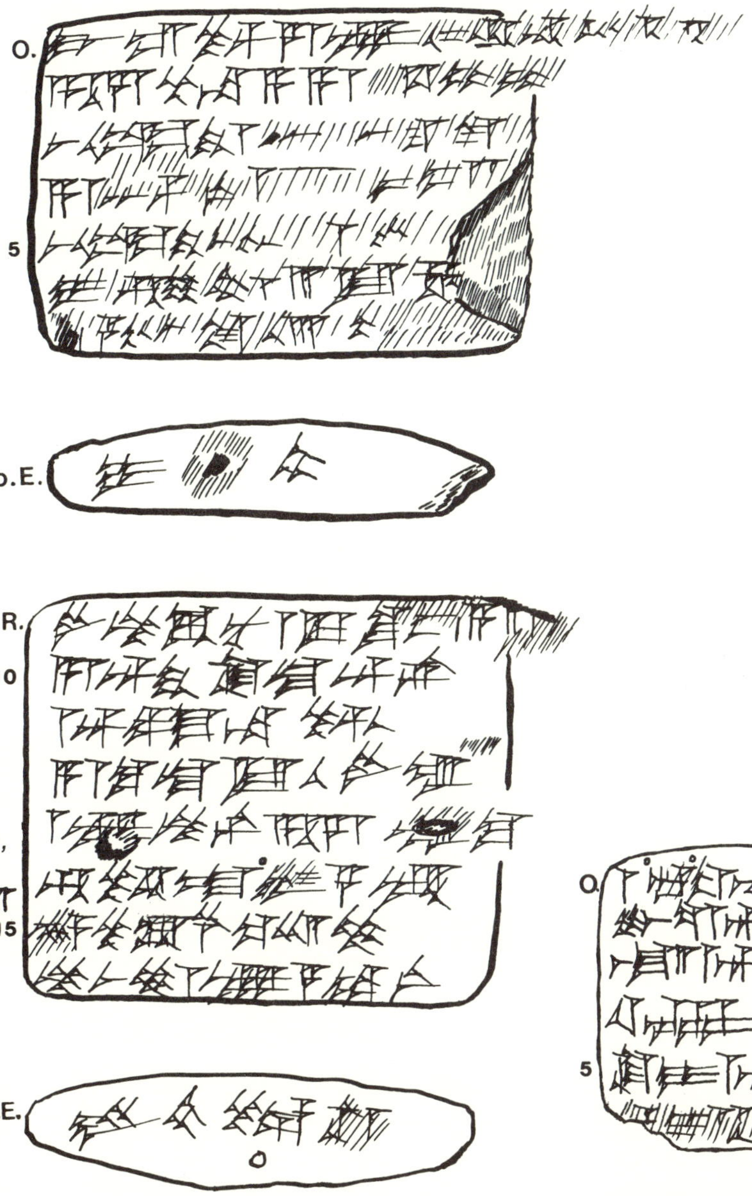

29

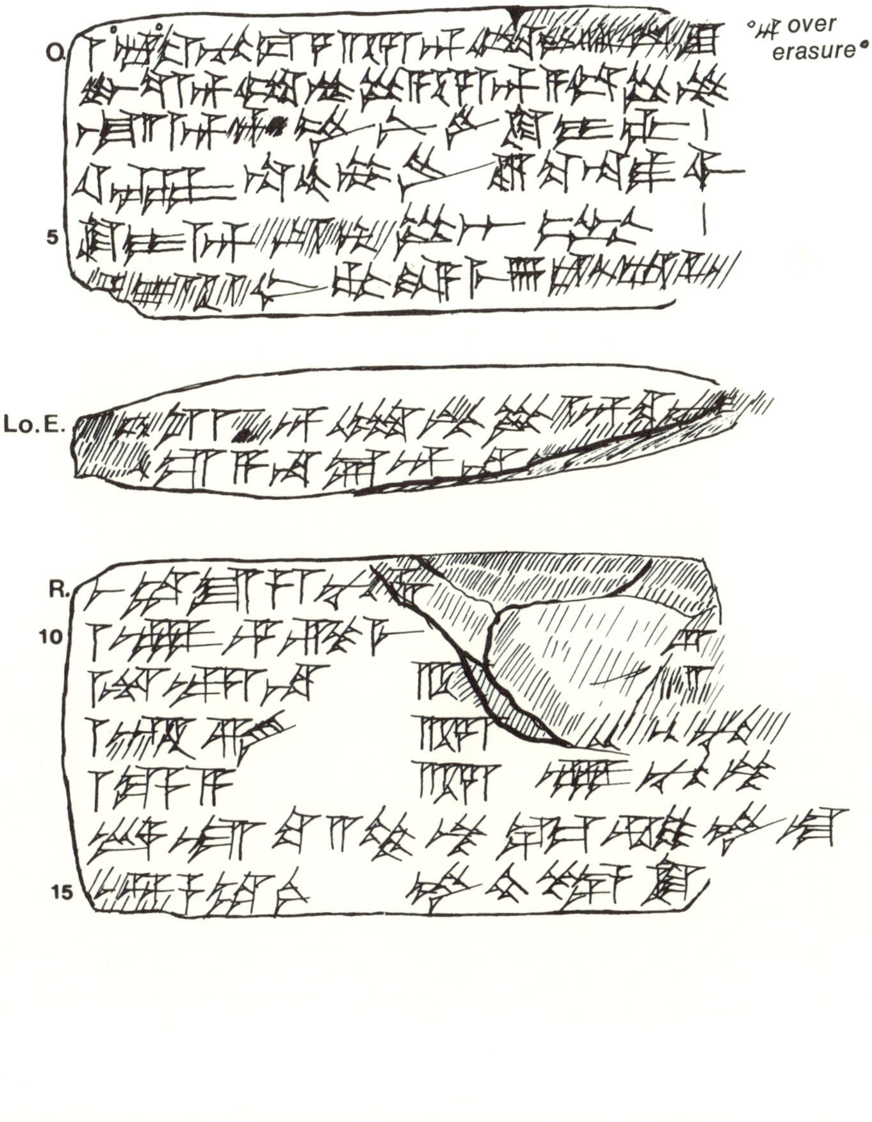

PLATE XXVI

30

O.

Lo. E.

R.

U.E.

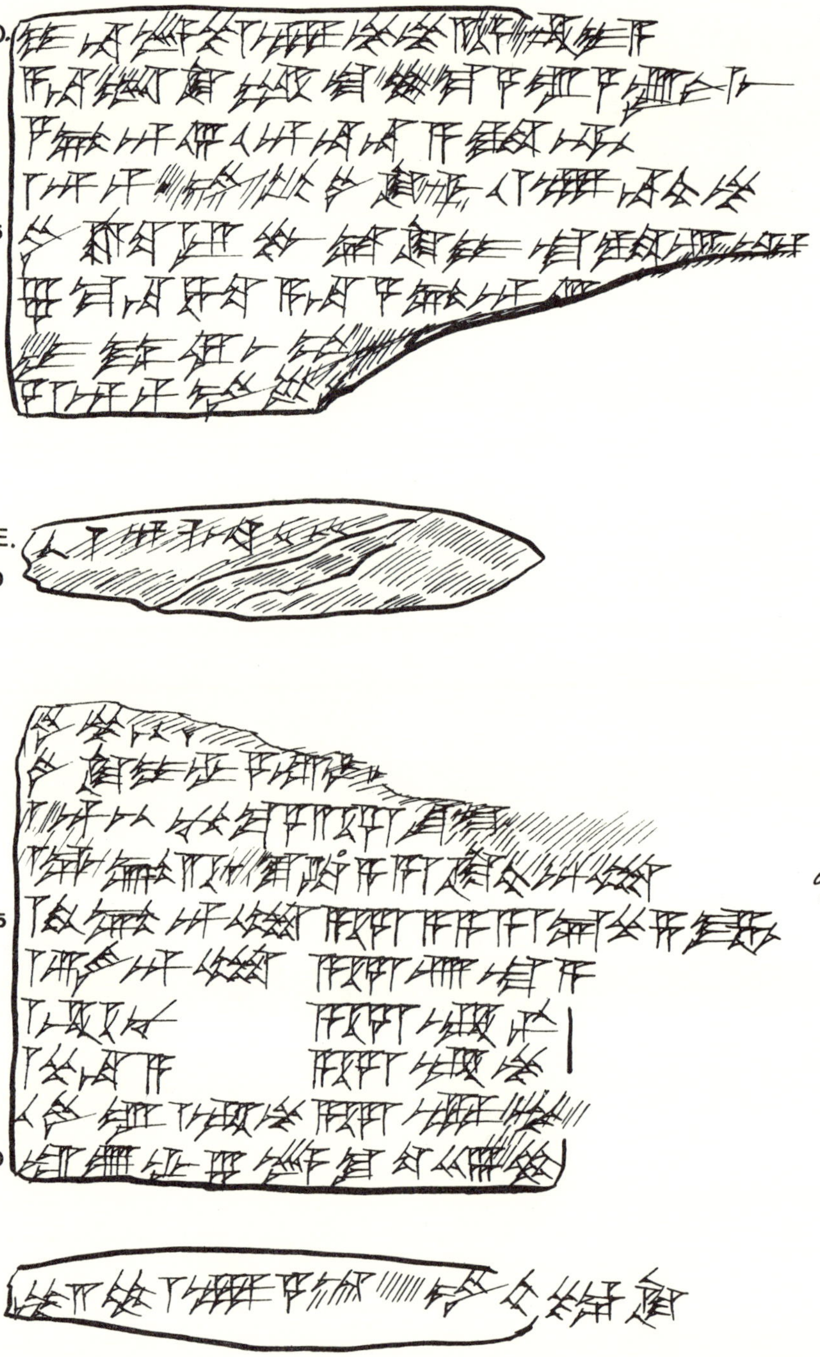

over erasure

31

O.

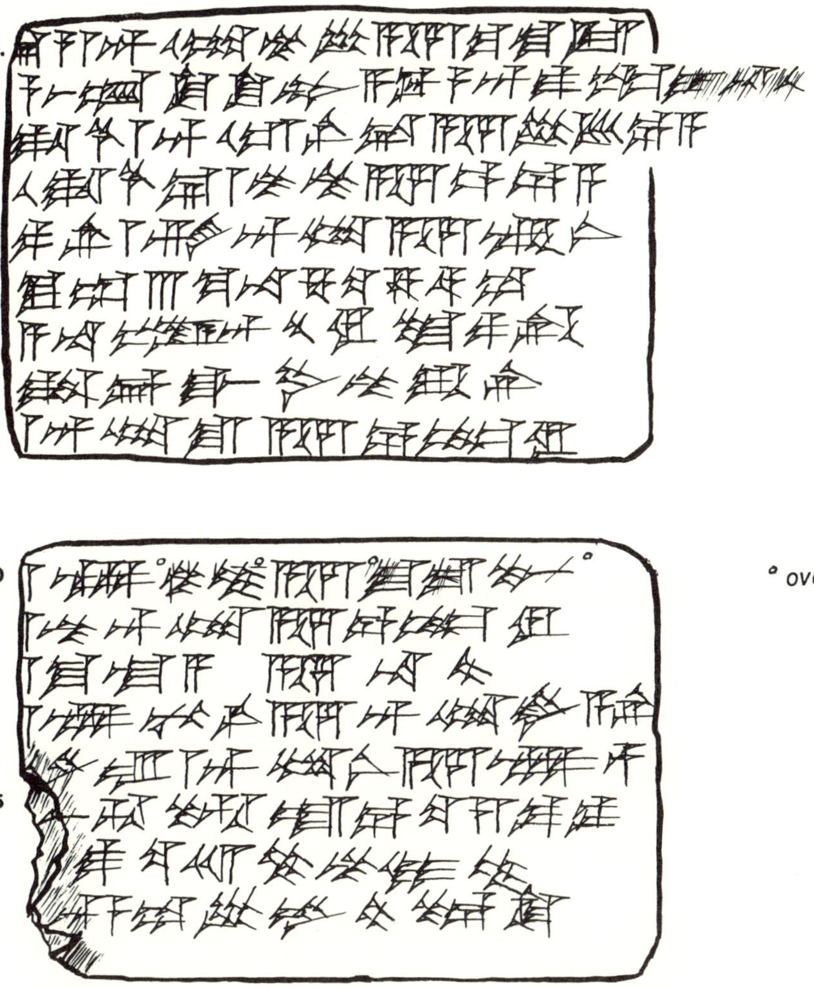

R.

° over erasure

PLATE XXVIII

32

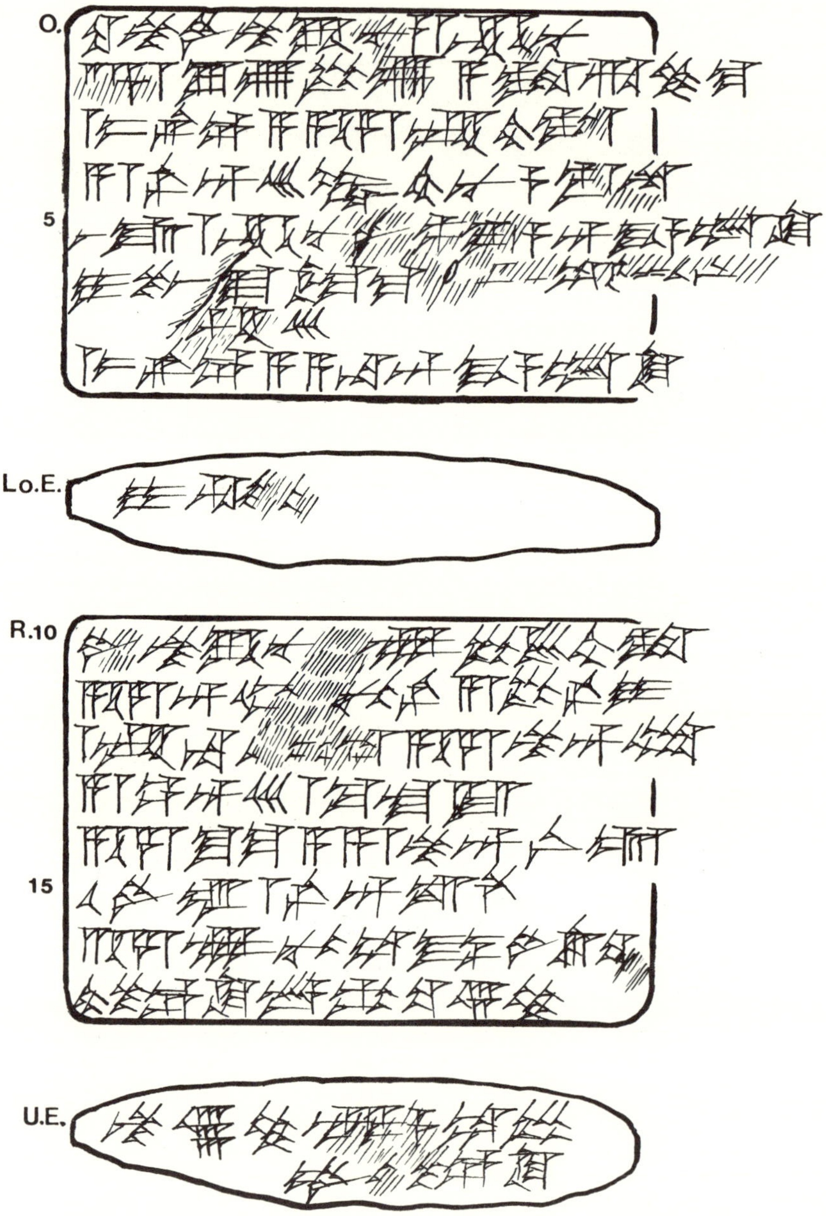

33

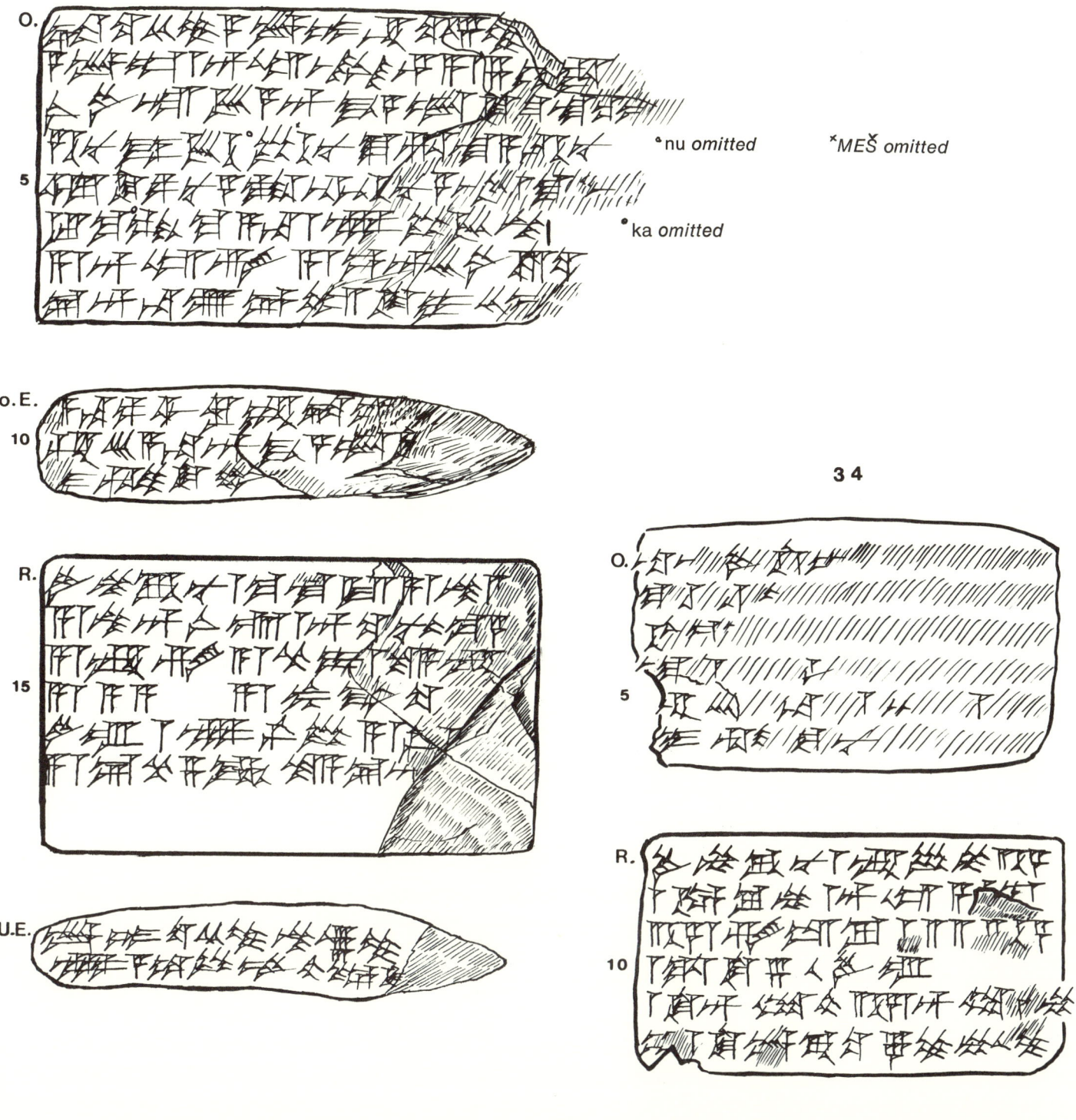

O.

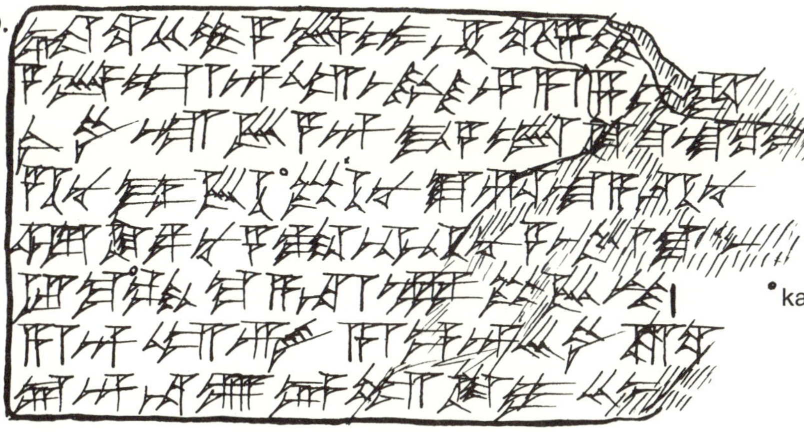

°nu *omitted*

ˣMEŠ *omitted*

°ka *omitted*

Lo.E.

R.

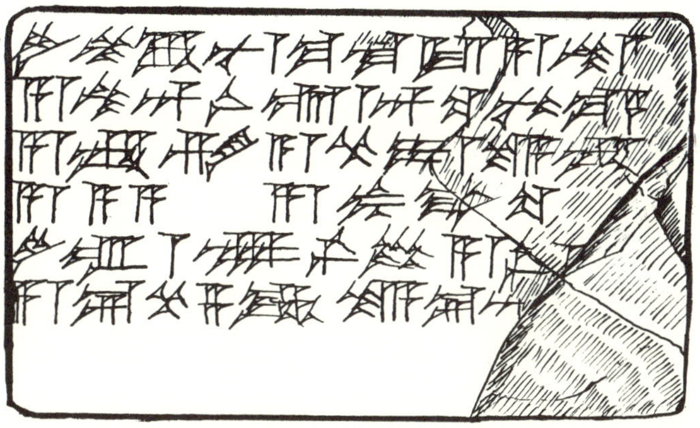

U.E.

34

O.

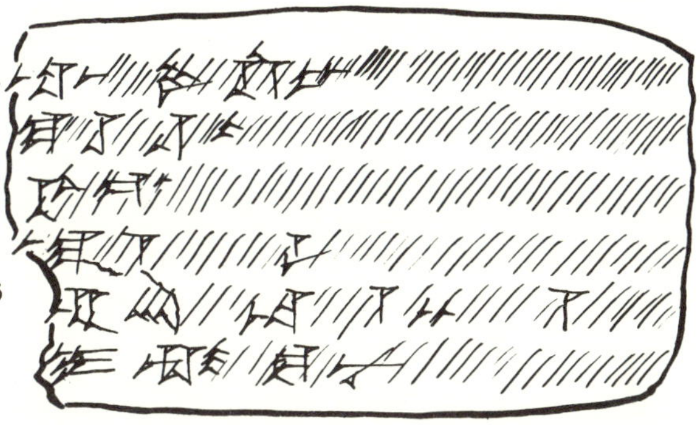

R.

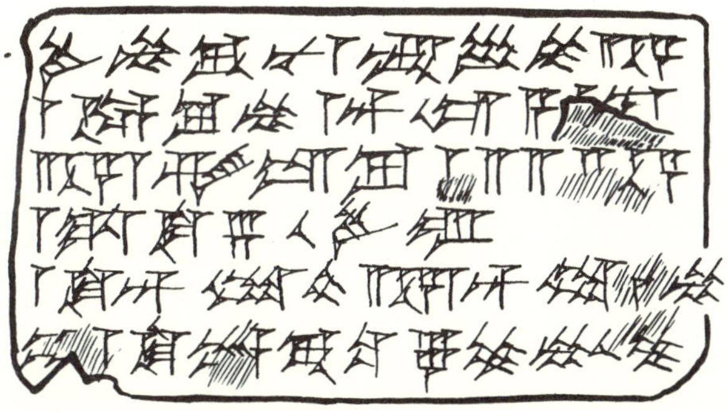

U.E.

35

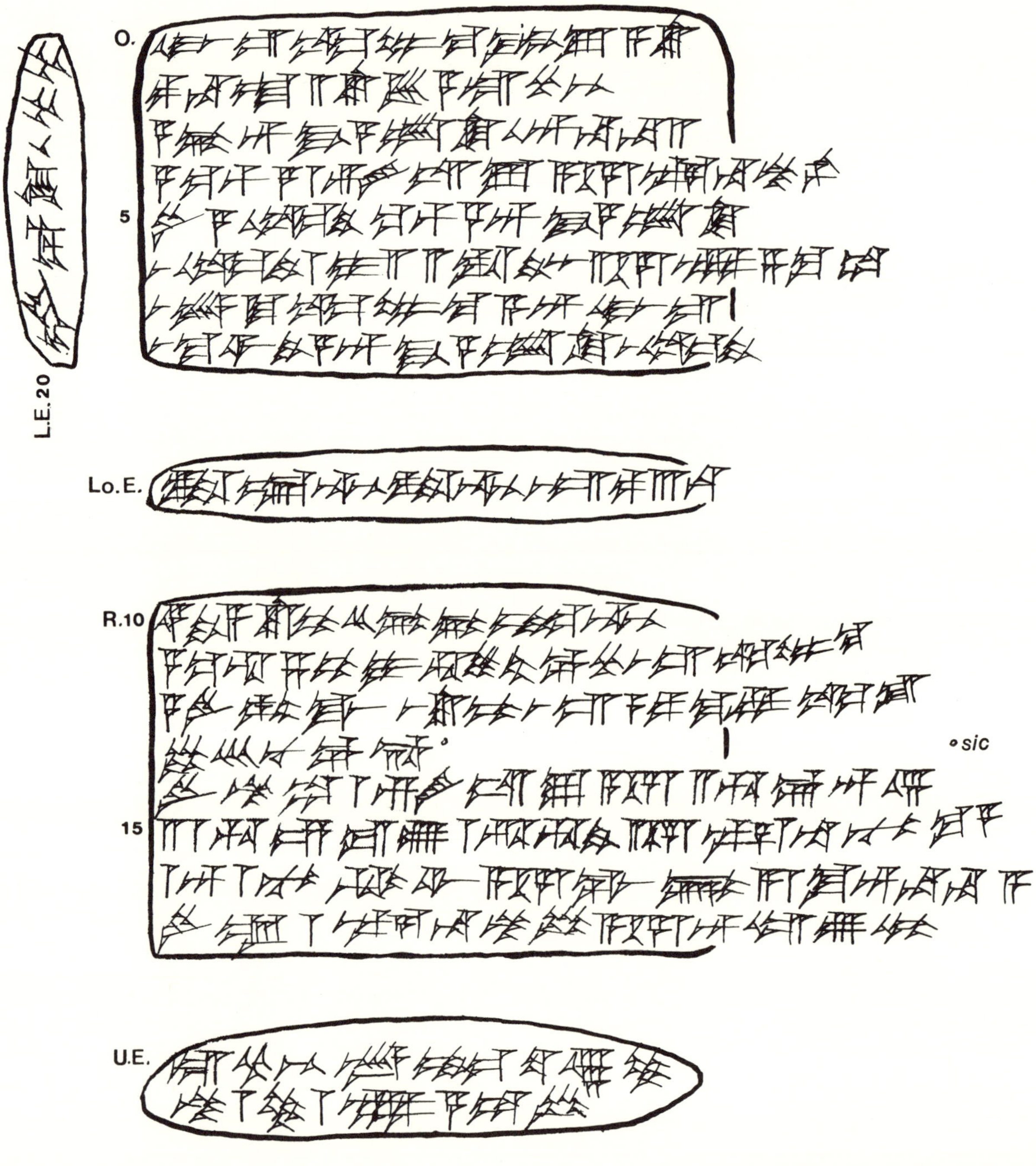

36

O.

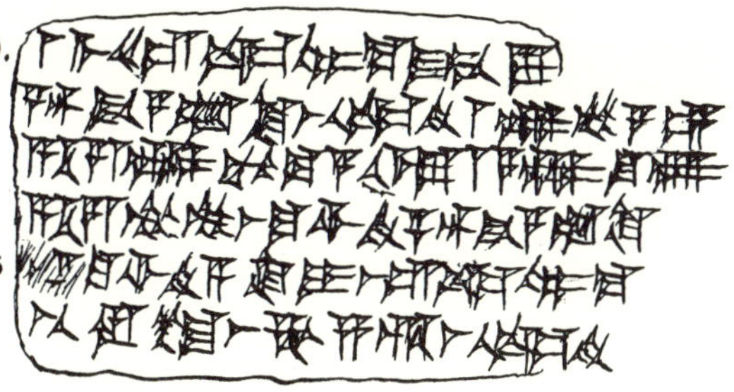

Lo.E.

R.

∘ *dittography*

U.E.

37

O.

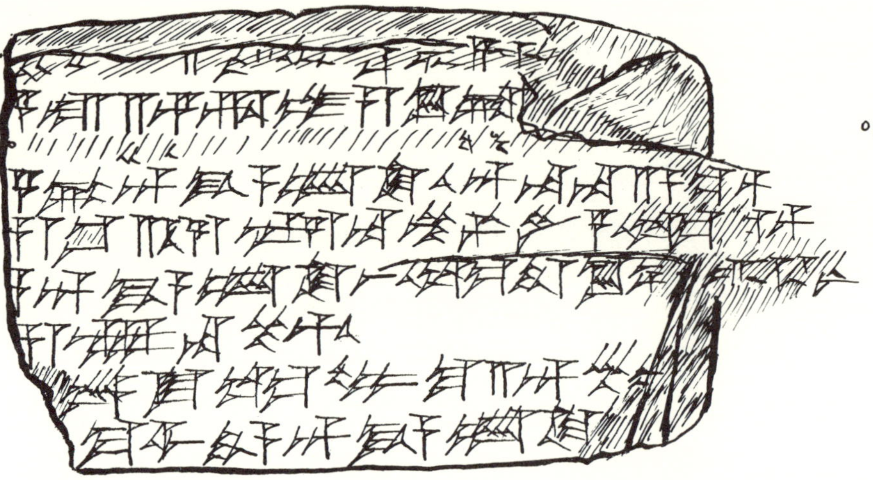

°erased half line°

Lo.E.

R.

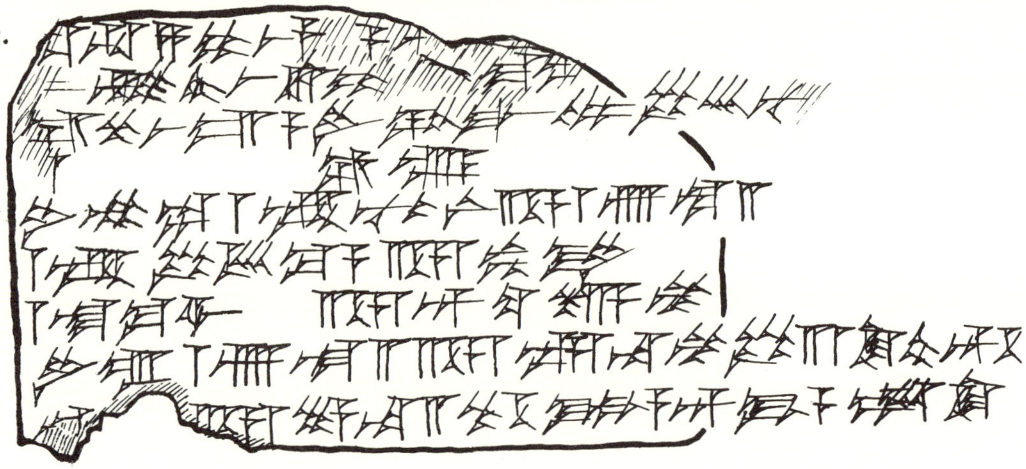

U.E.

38

O. R. U.E.

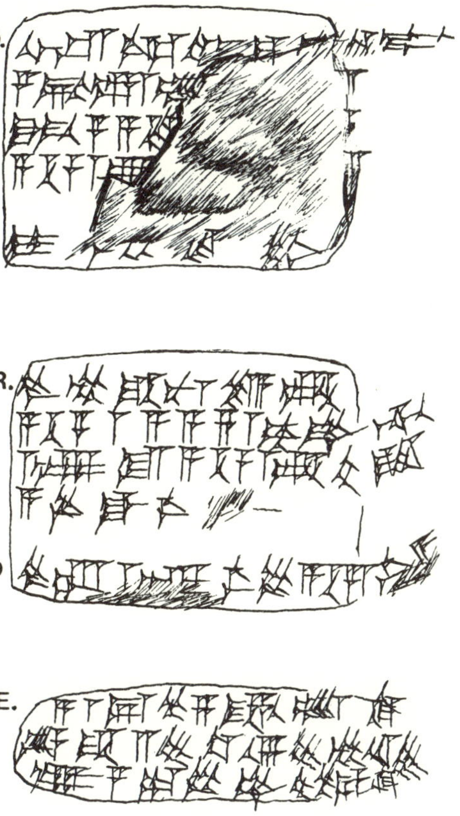

39

O. Lo.E. R.10

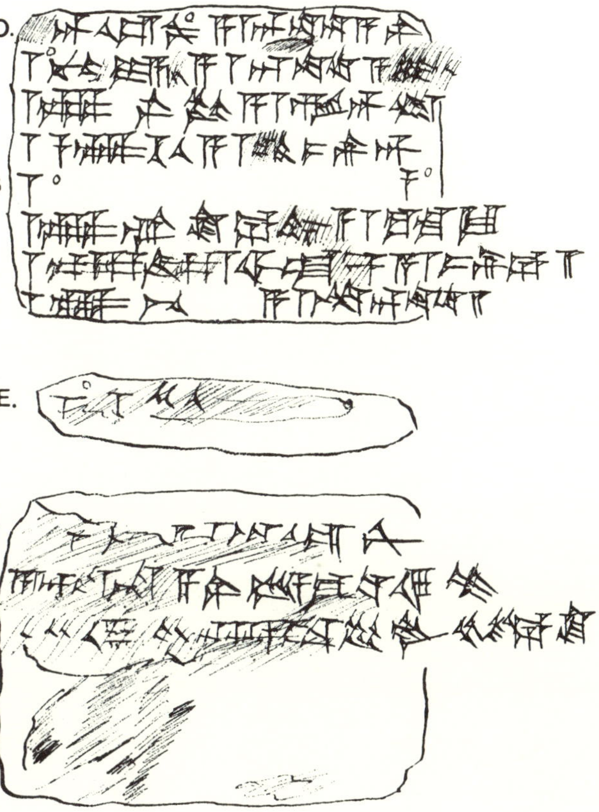

°over erasure
°over erasure

°erasure°

°erasure

40

O.

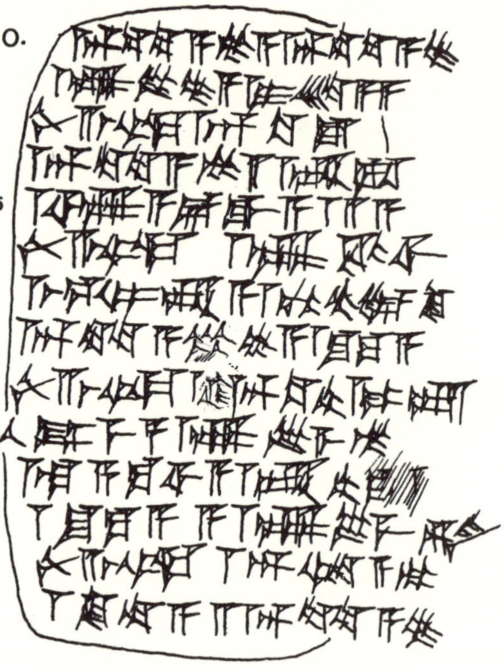

R.

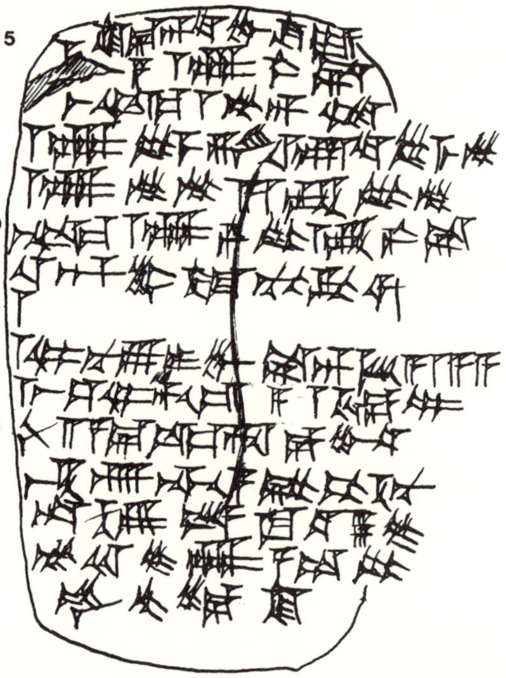

41

O.

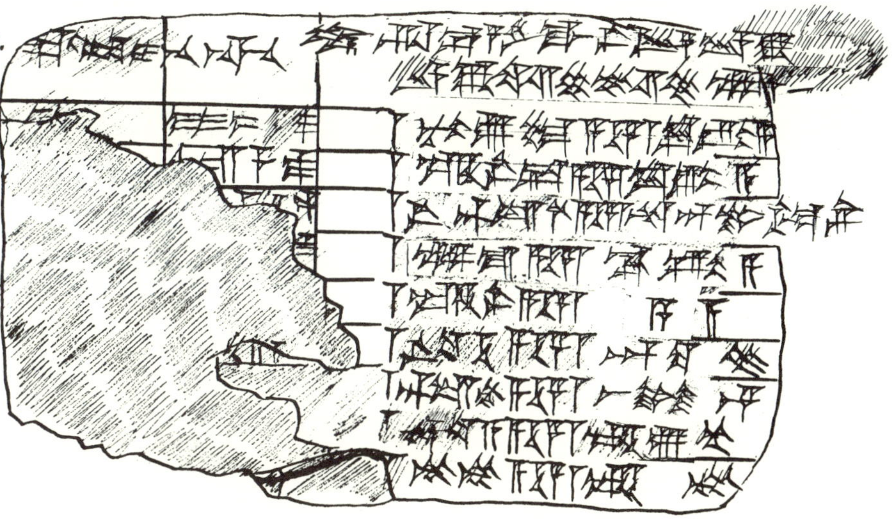

Lo.E.

R.

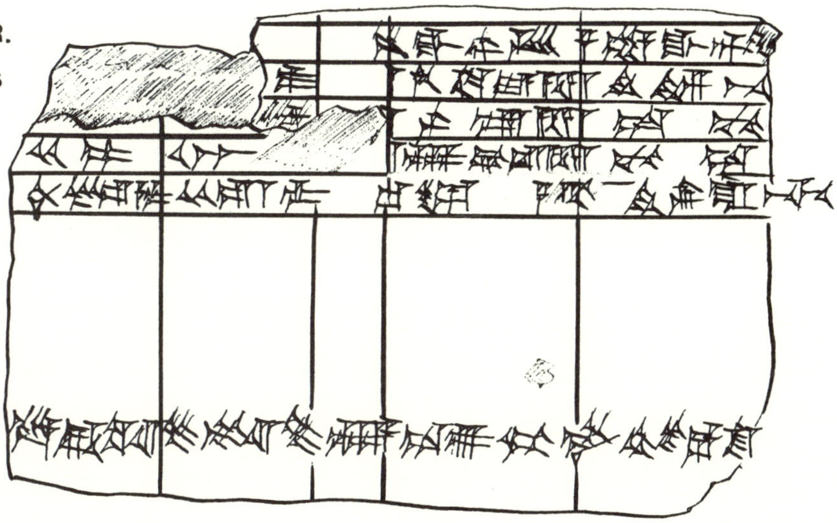

42

U.E.

O.

5

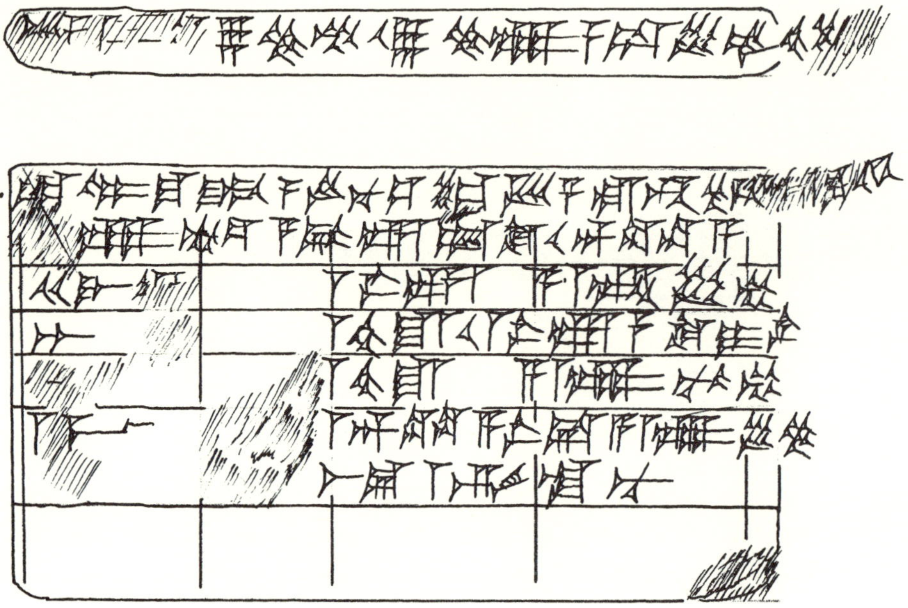

Reverse Uninscribed

43

O.

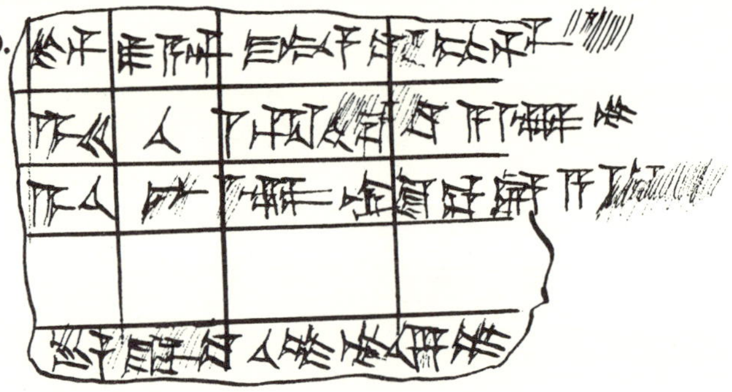

U.E.5

R.

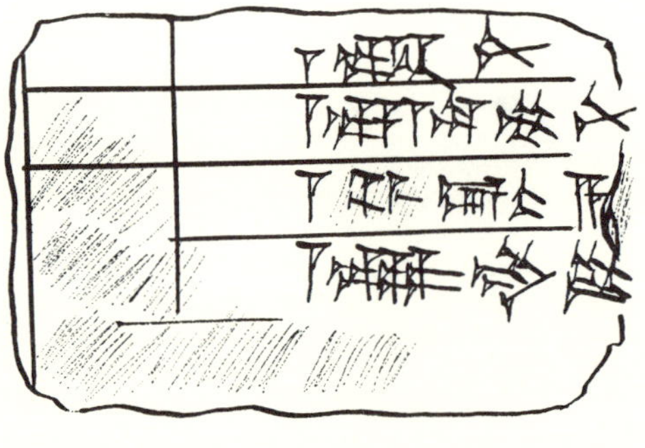

44

U.E.

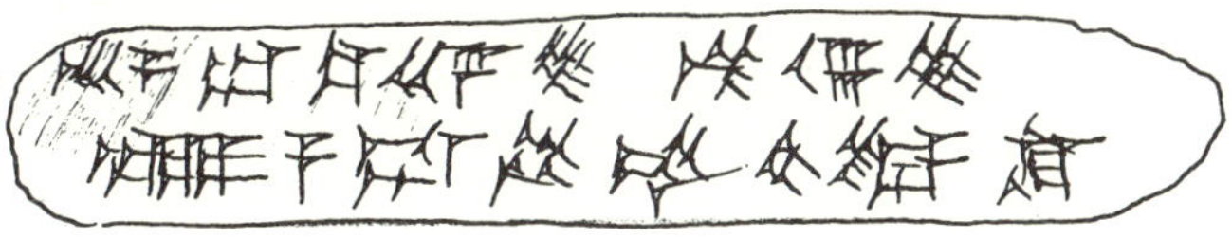

O.

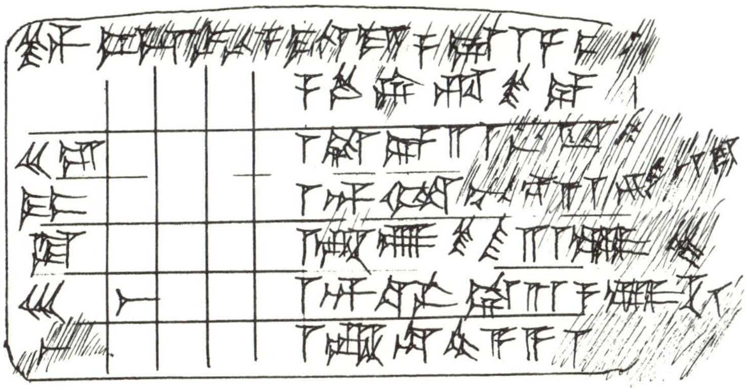

Reverse Uninscribed

45

O.

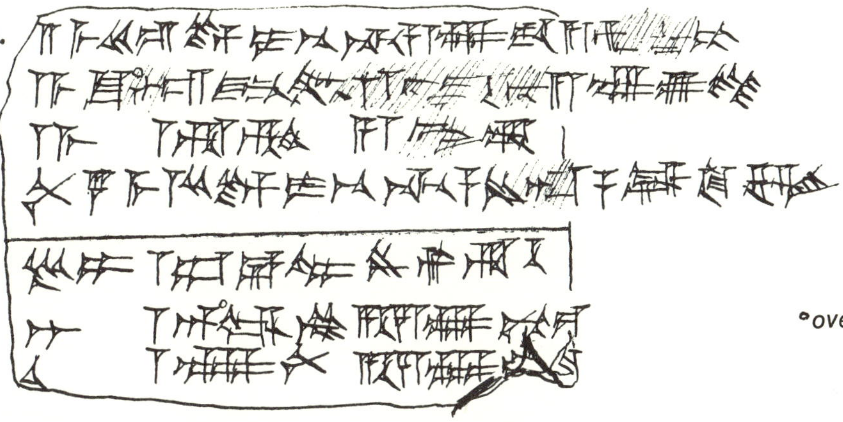

° erasure

°over erasure

Lo.E.

°over erasure

R.

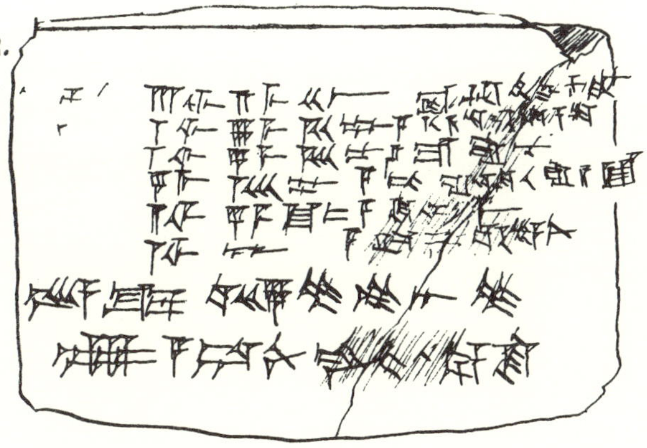

46

O.

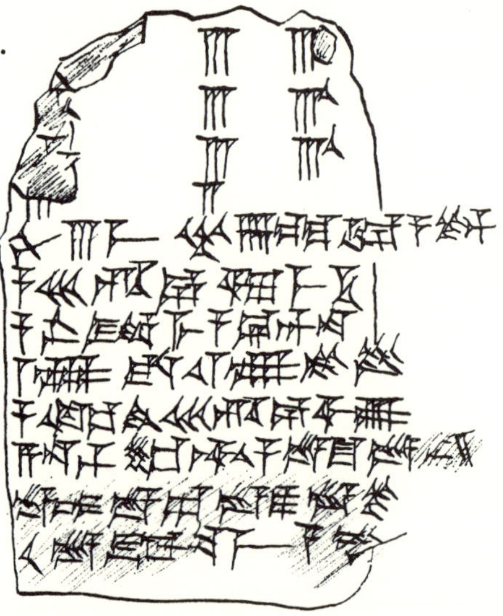

R.

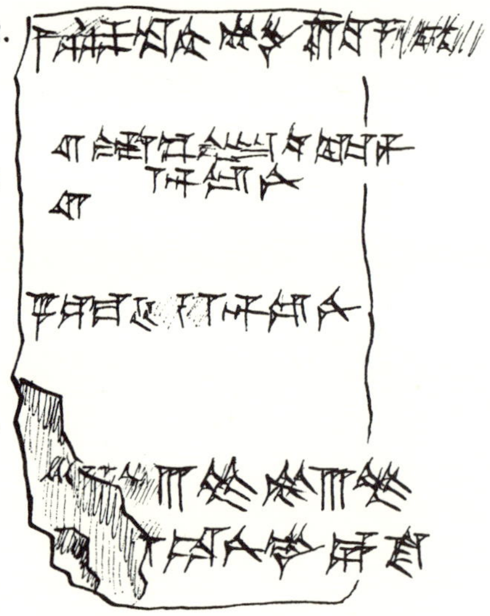

47

O.

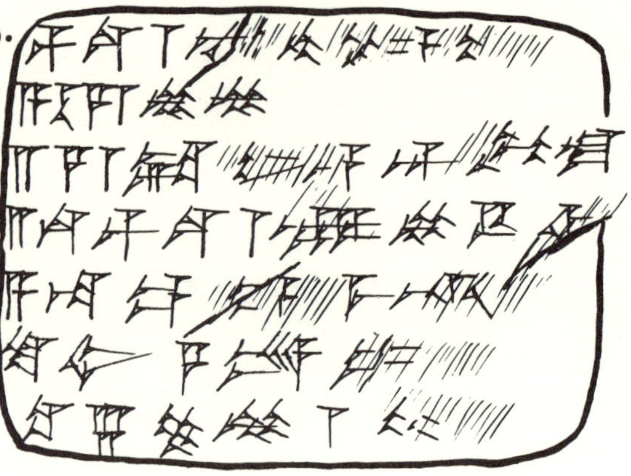

R.

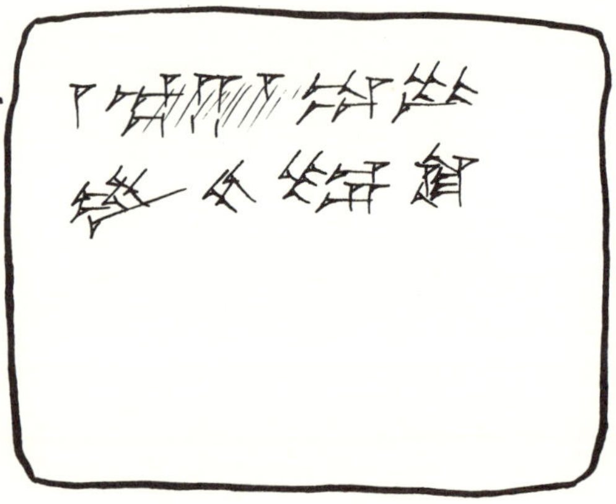

48

O.

R.

49

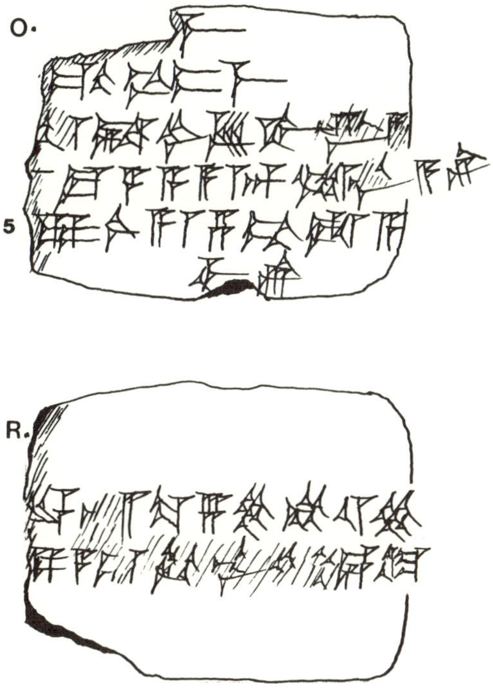

50

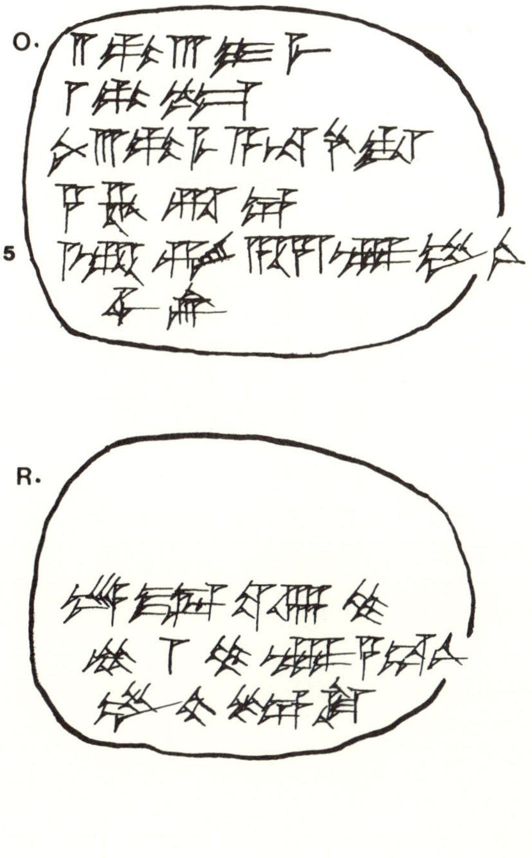

51

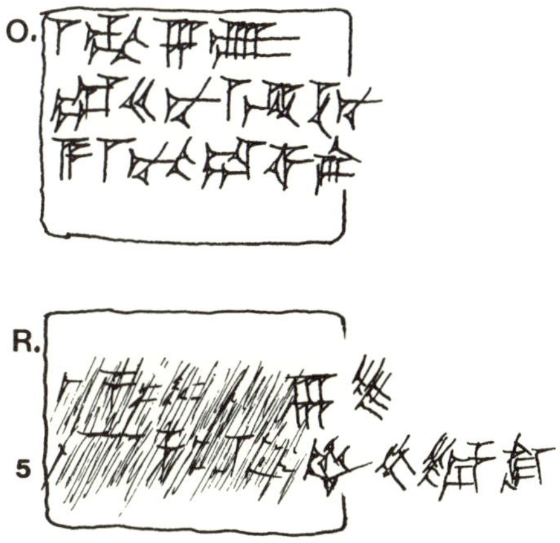

52

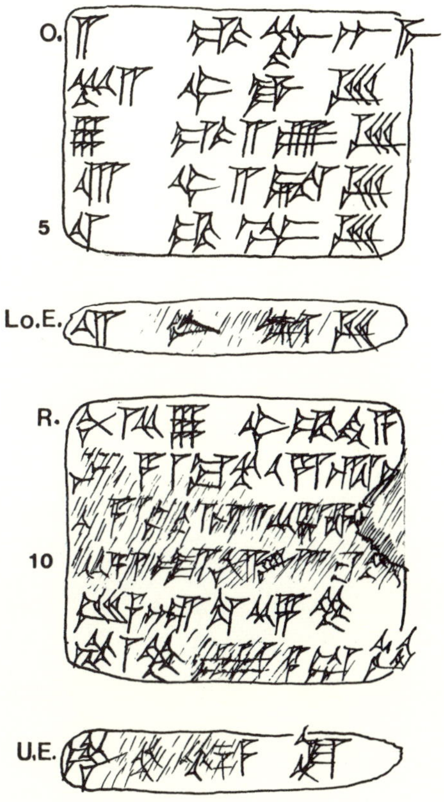

53

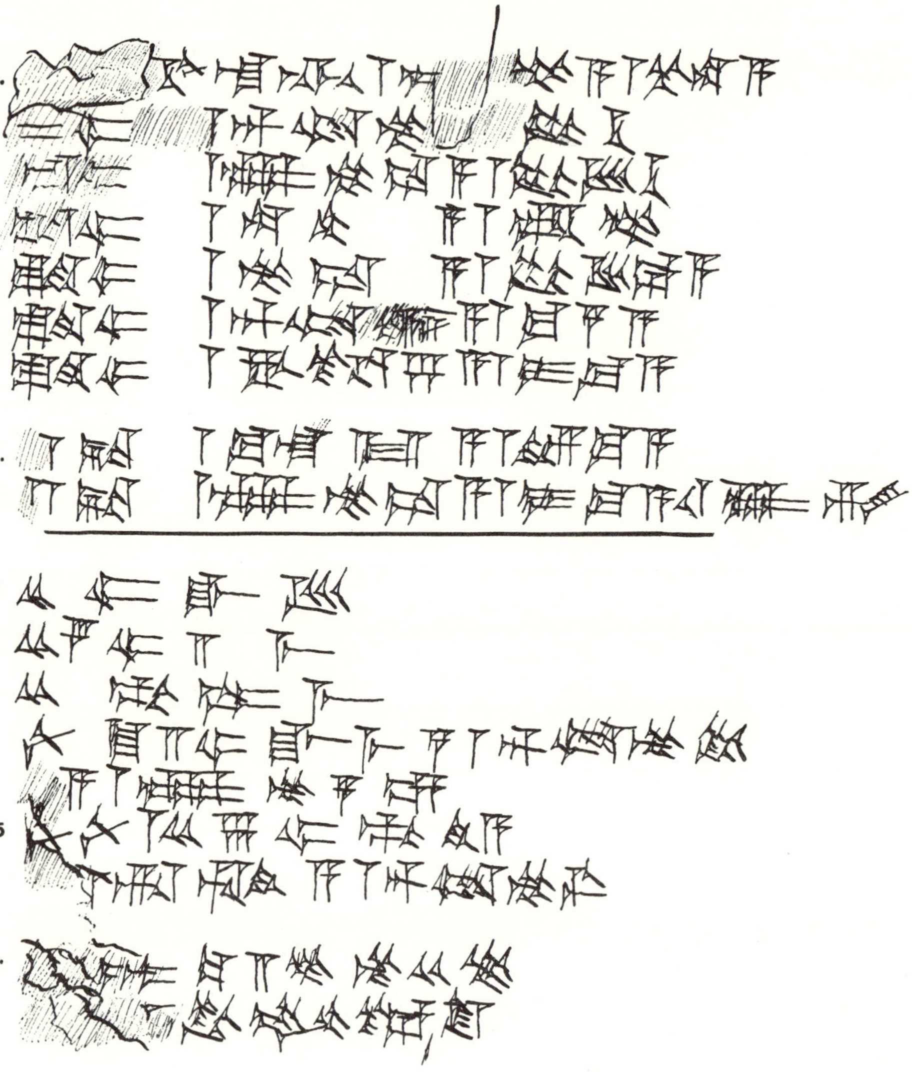

O.
5
Lo.E.
R.10
15
U.E.

54

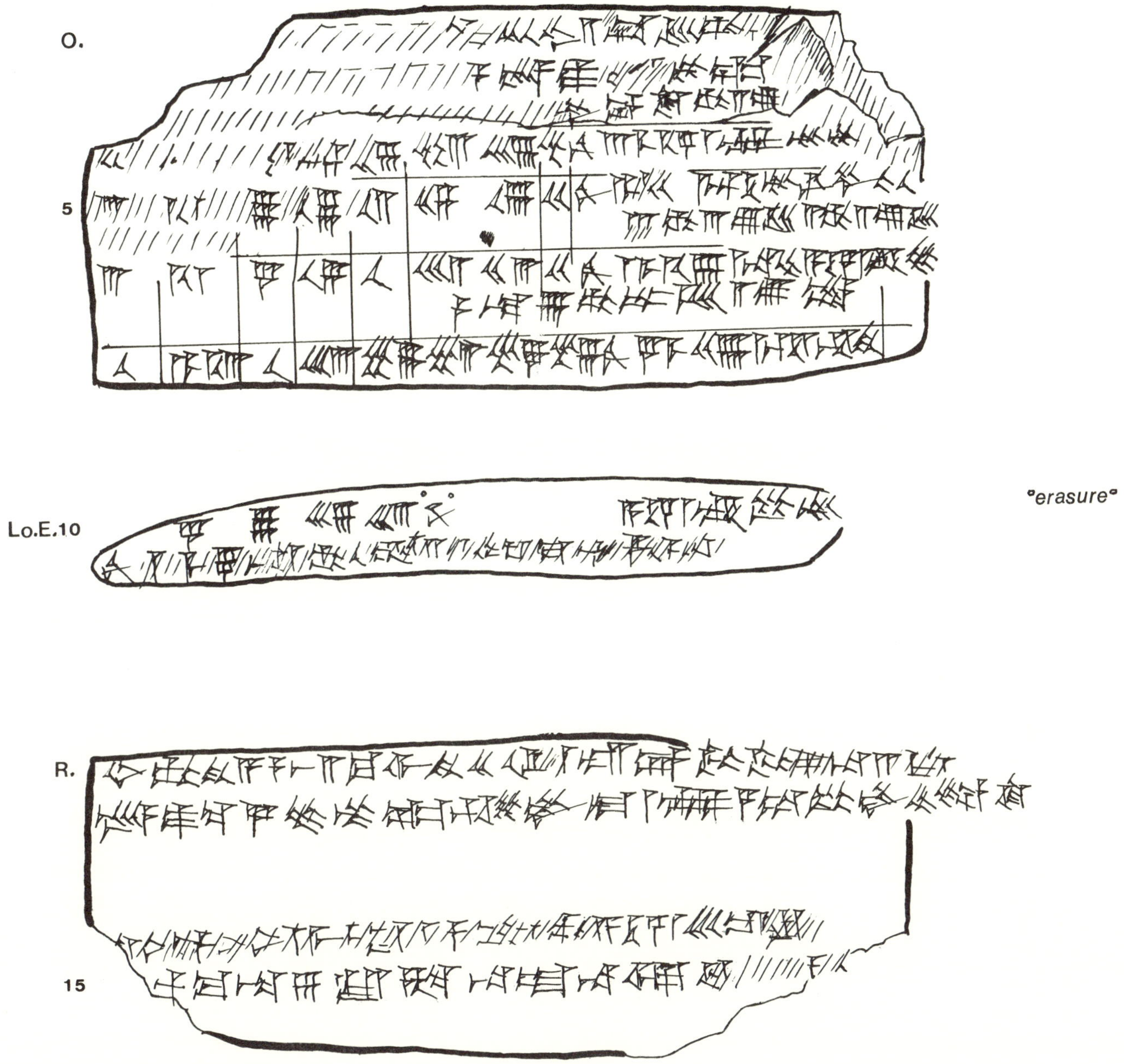

55

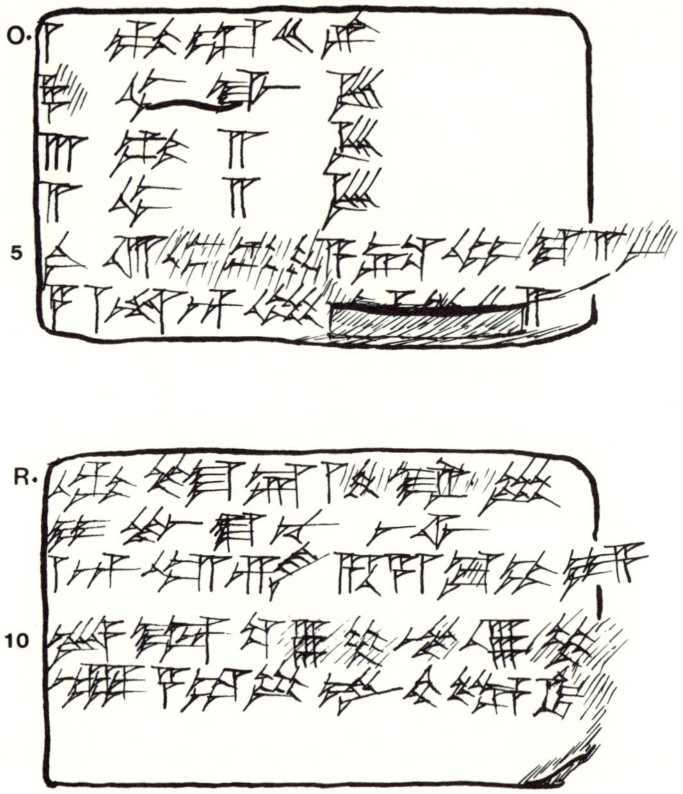

56

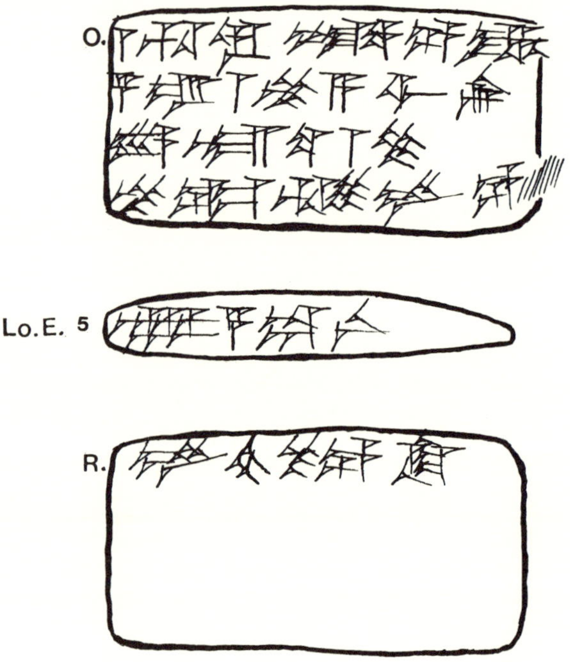

57

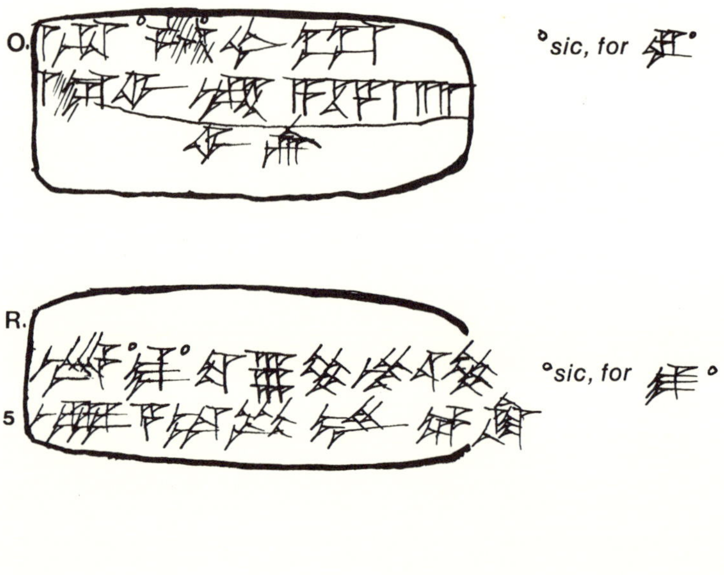

58

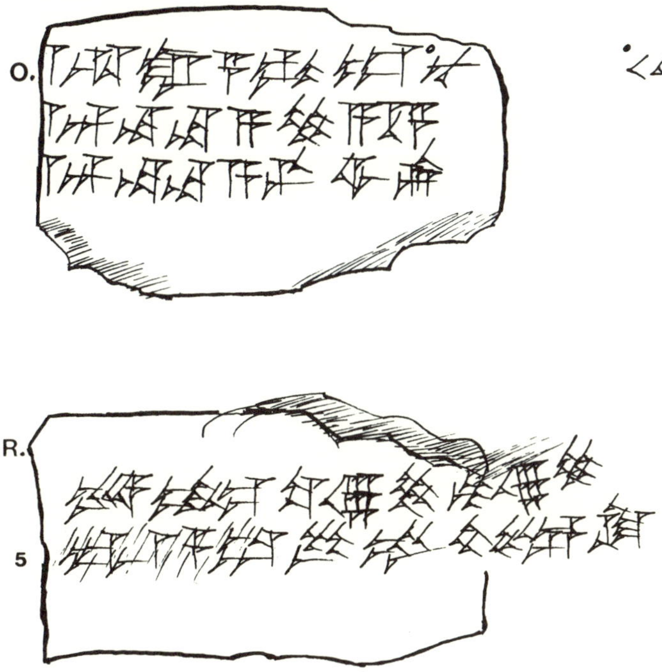

(omitted by scribe)

59

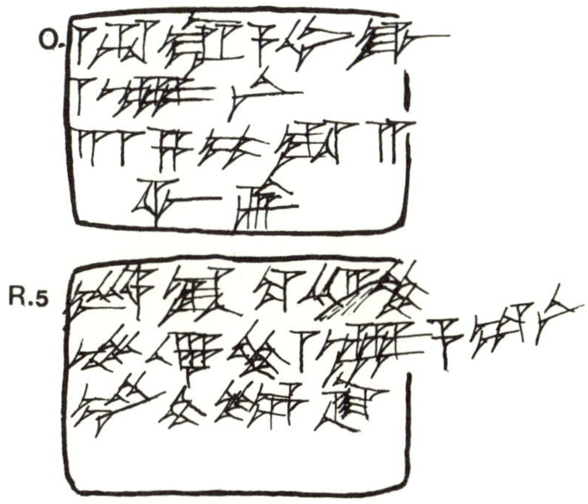

60

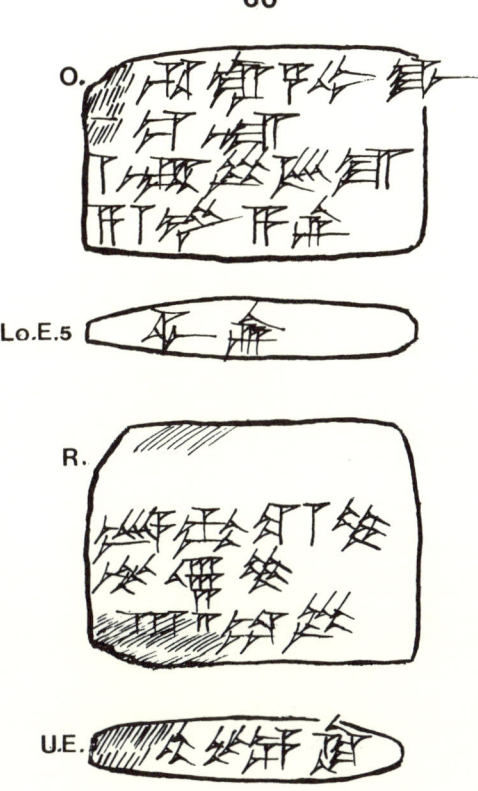

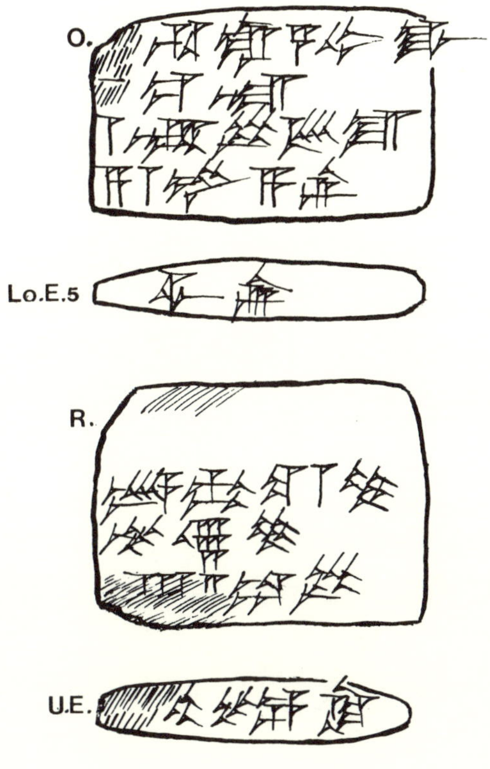

61

O.

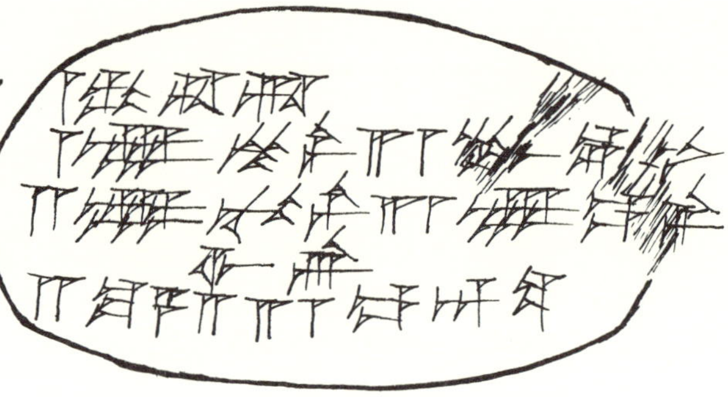

R.

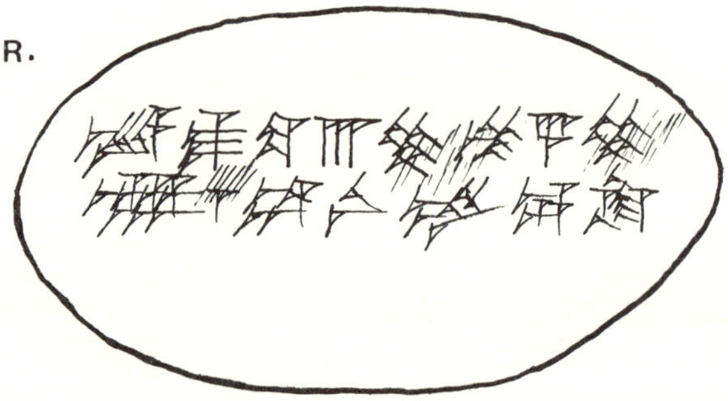

62

O.

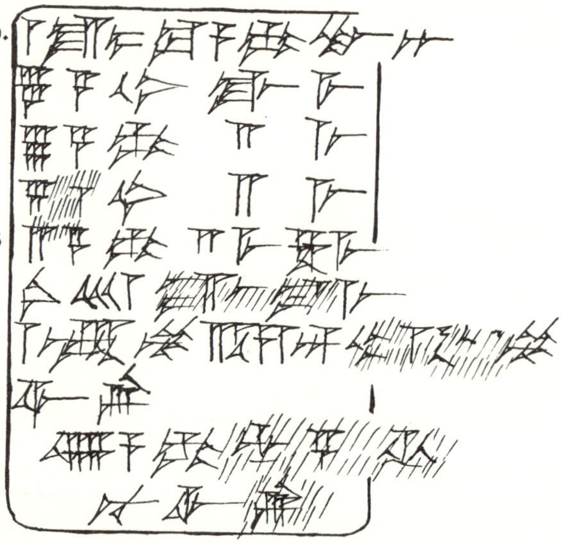

R.

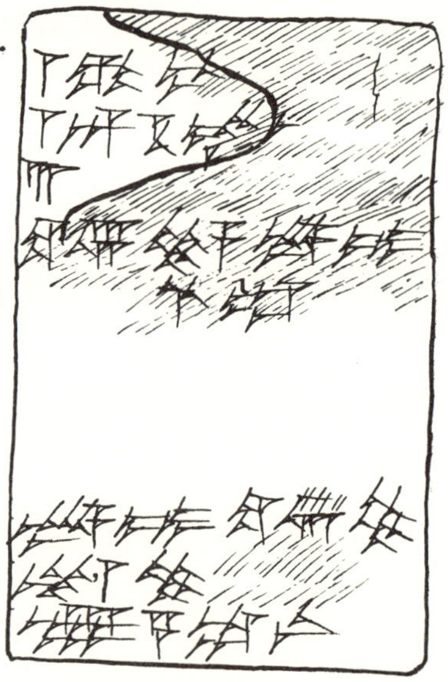

U.E.

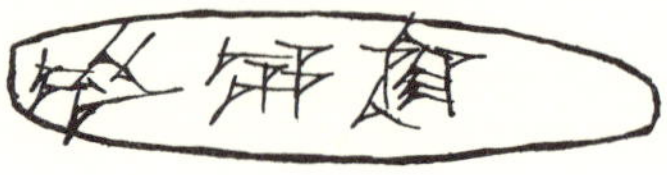

63

O.

R.

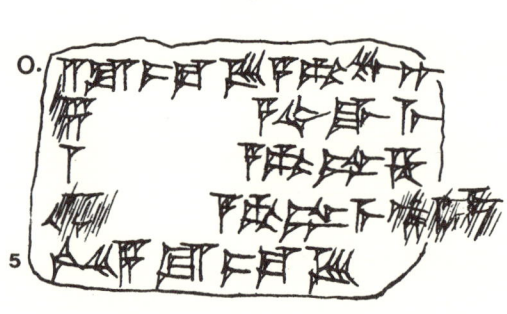

64

O.

R.5

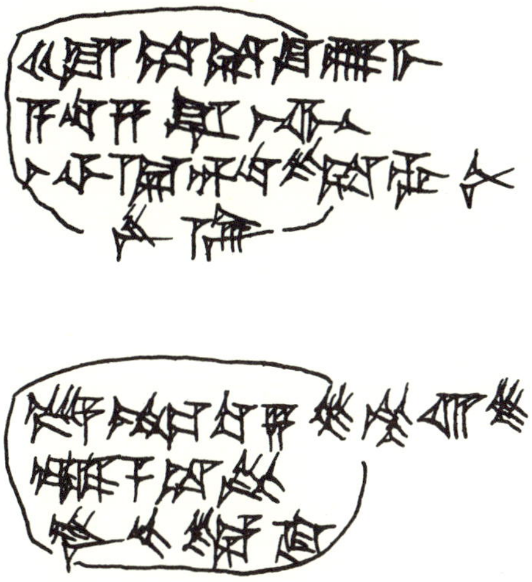

65

O.

5

R.

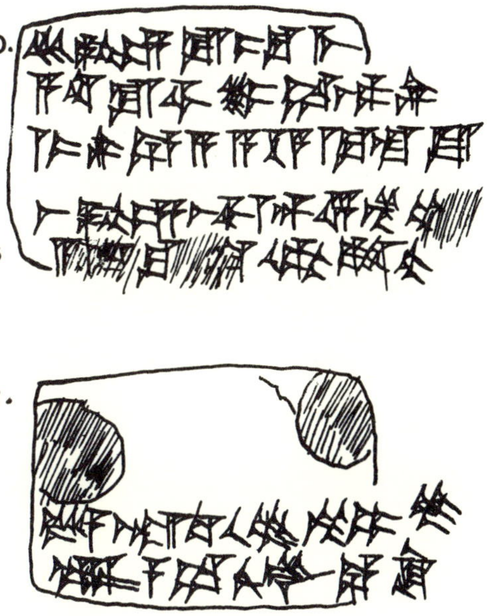

66

O.

Lo.E.5

R.

10

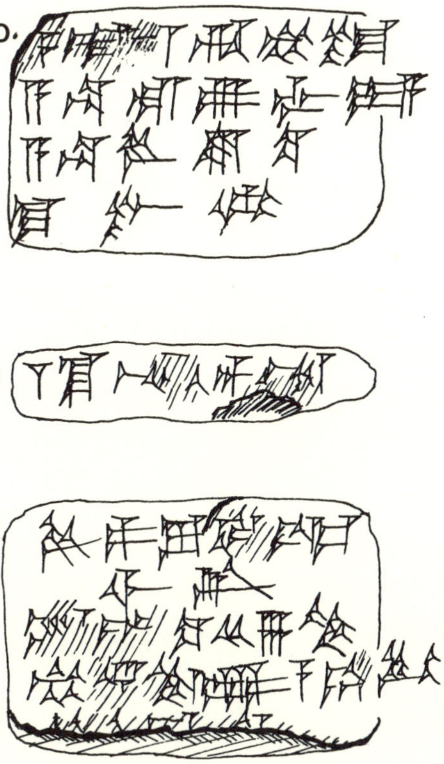

67

O.

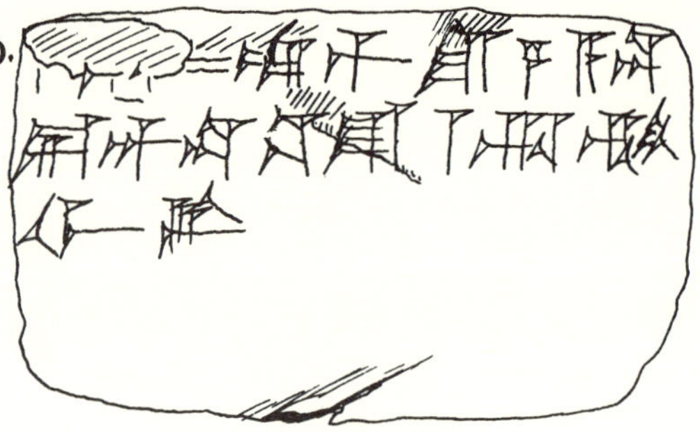

R.

68

O.

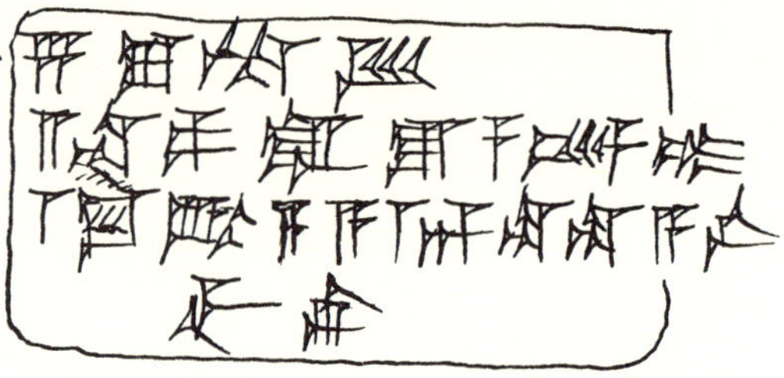

R.

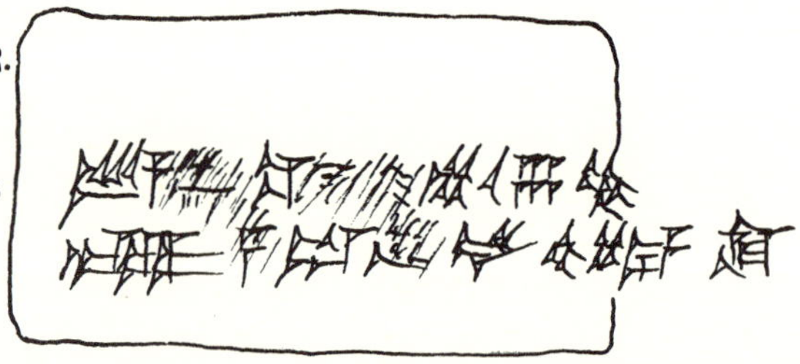

69

O.

° over erasure

Lo.E.

R.

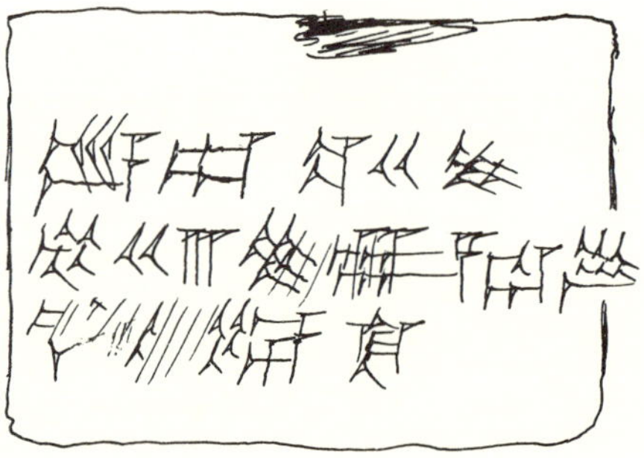

70

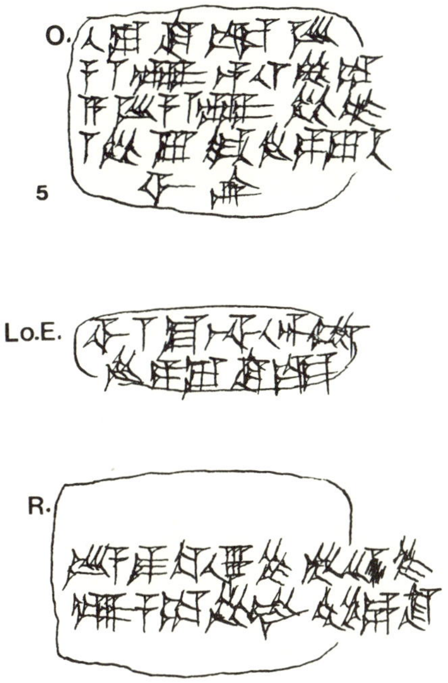

72

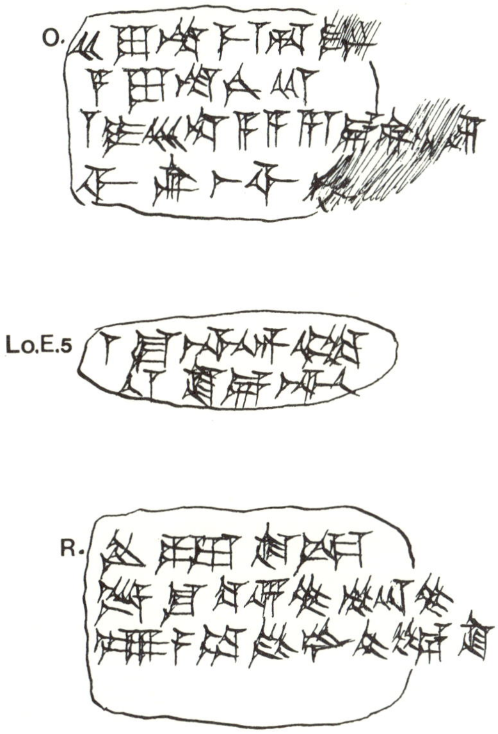

71

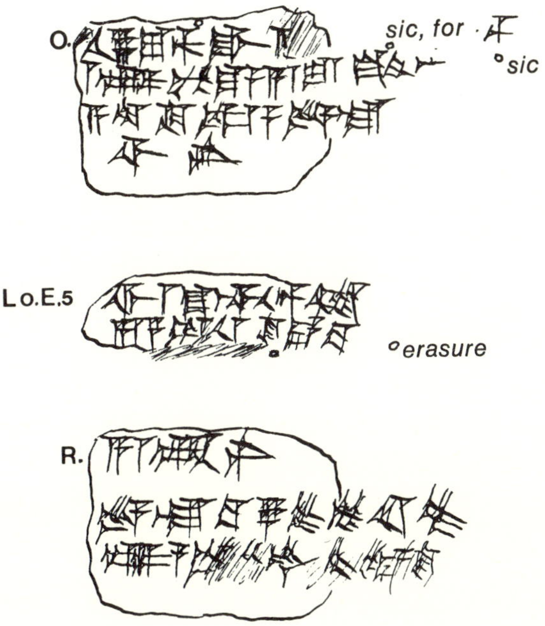

73

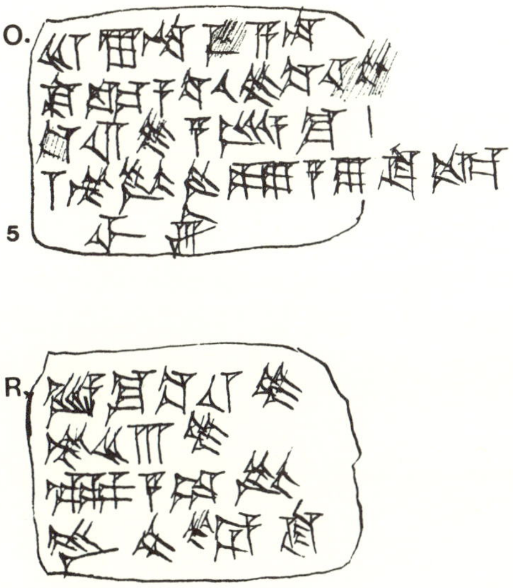

75

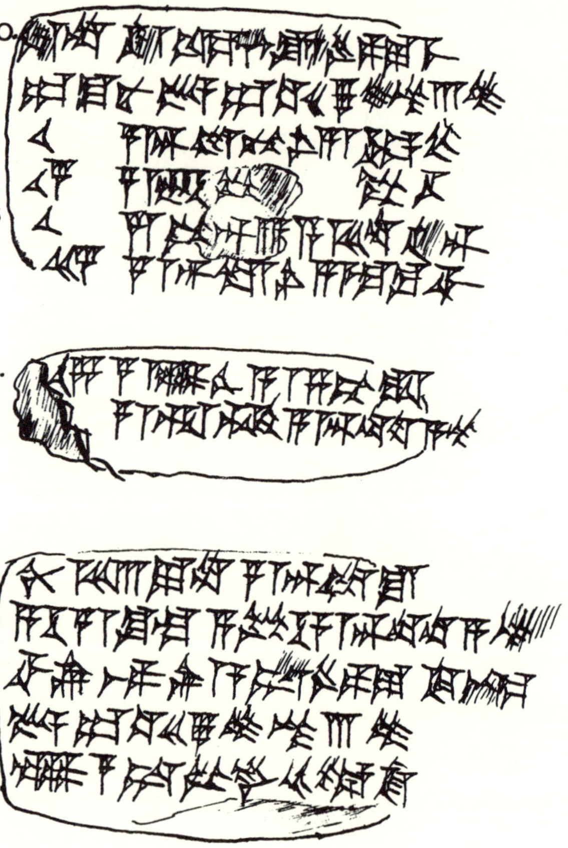

74

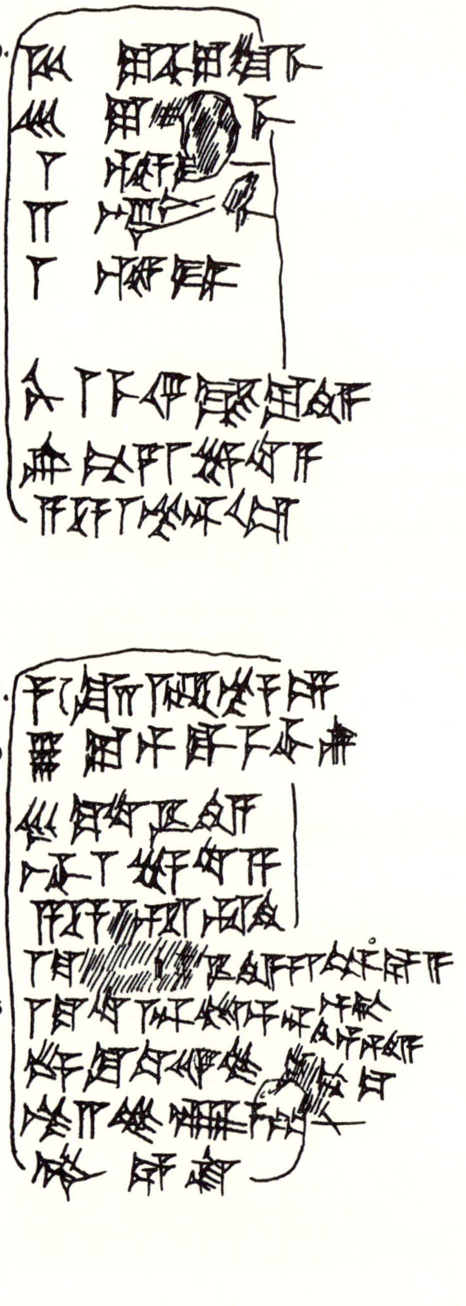

[a] over erasure

76

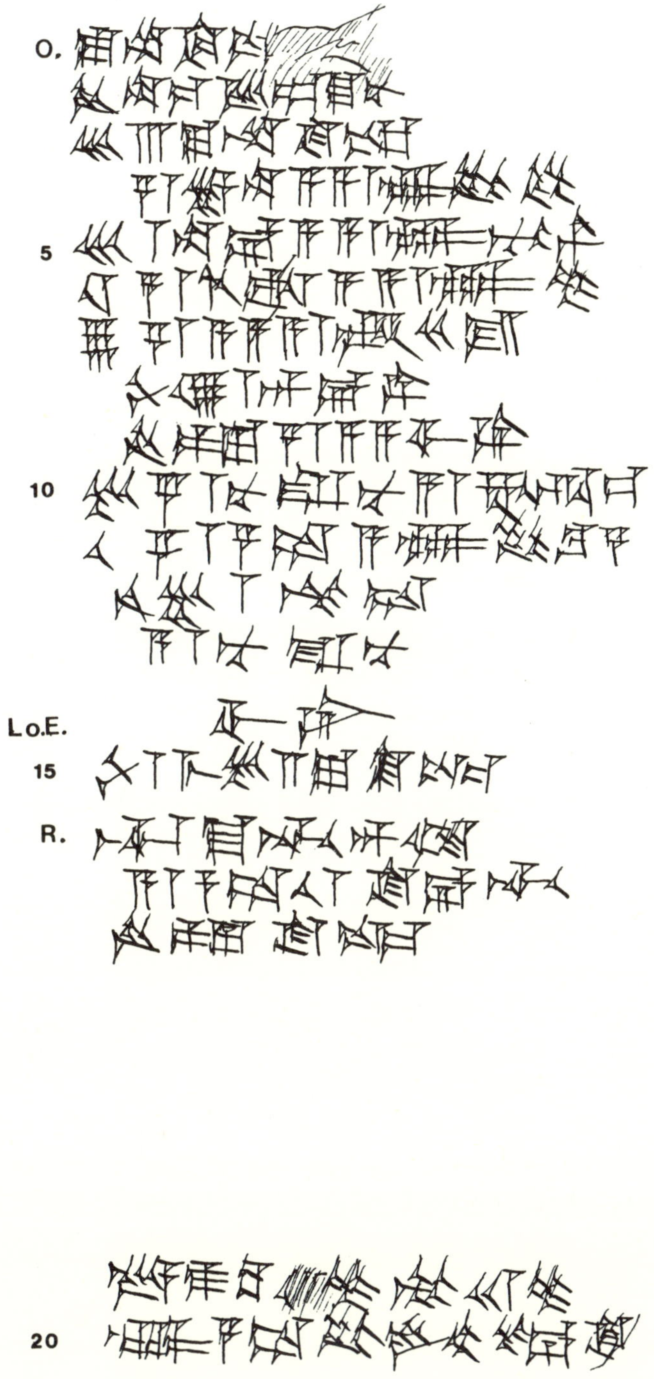

77

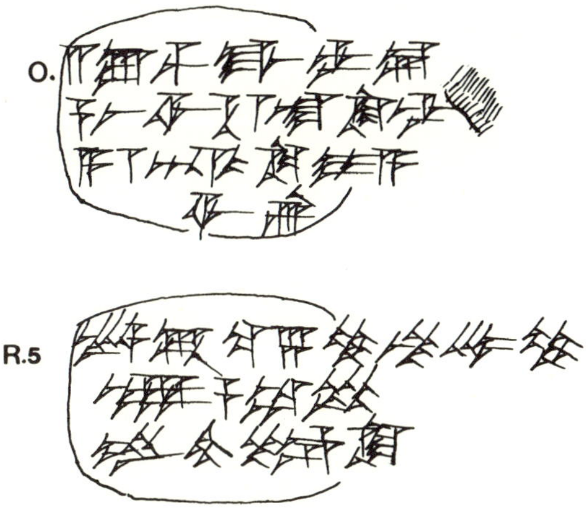

78

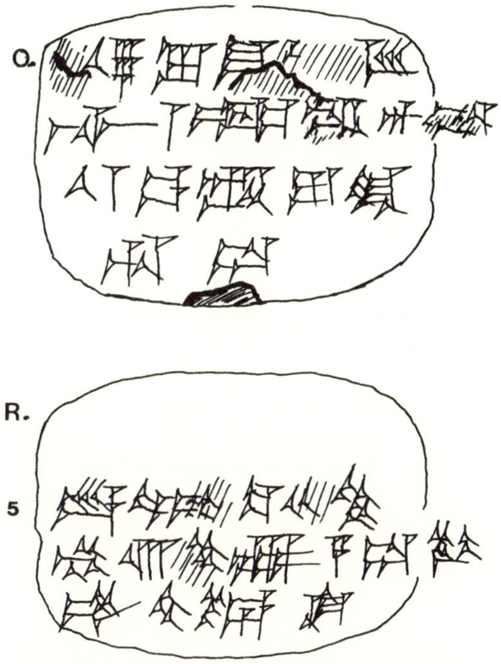

PLATE L

79

O.

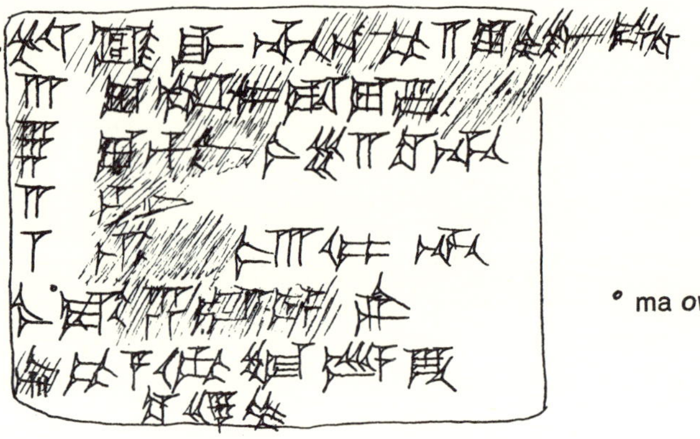

° ma over erasure

Lo.E.

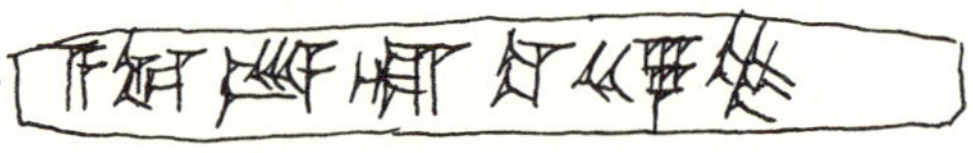

R.

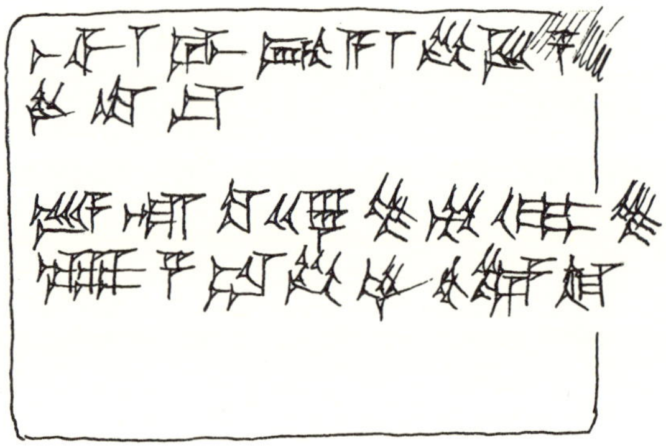

80

O.

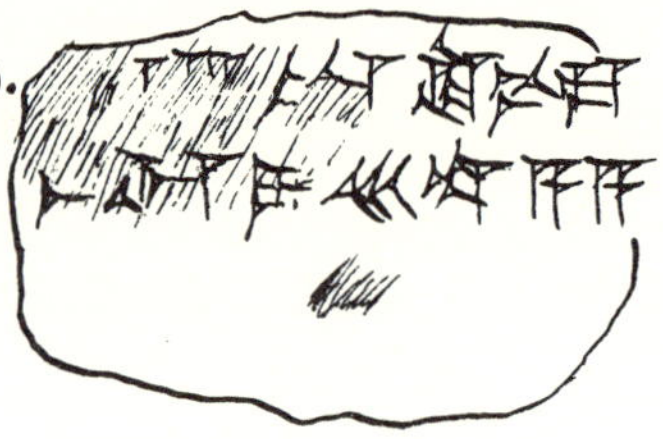

R.

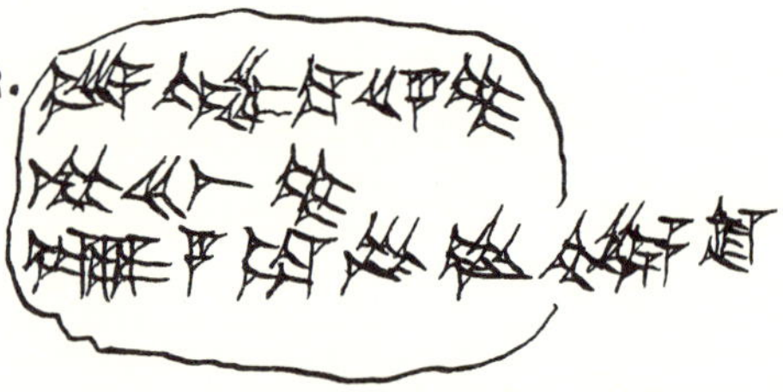

81

O.

Lo.E.

R.

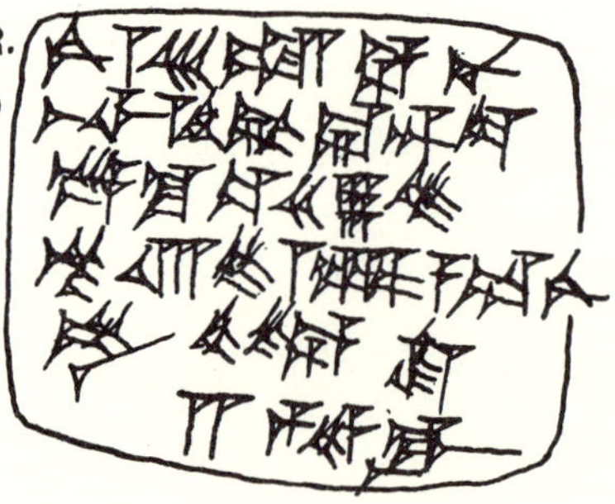

83

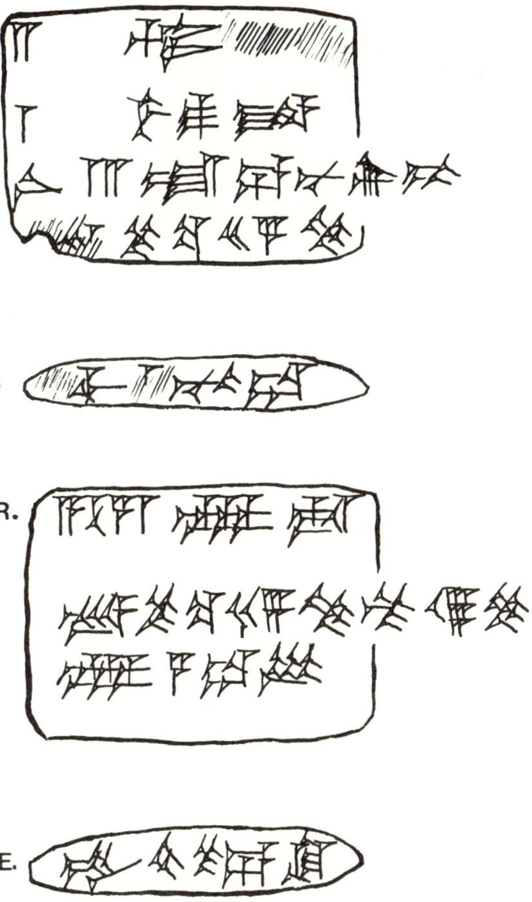

O. Lo.E. R. U.E.

82

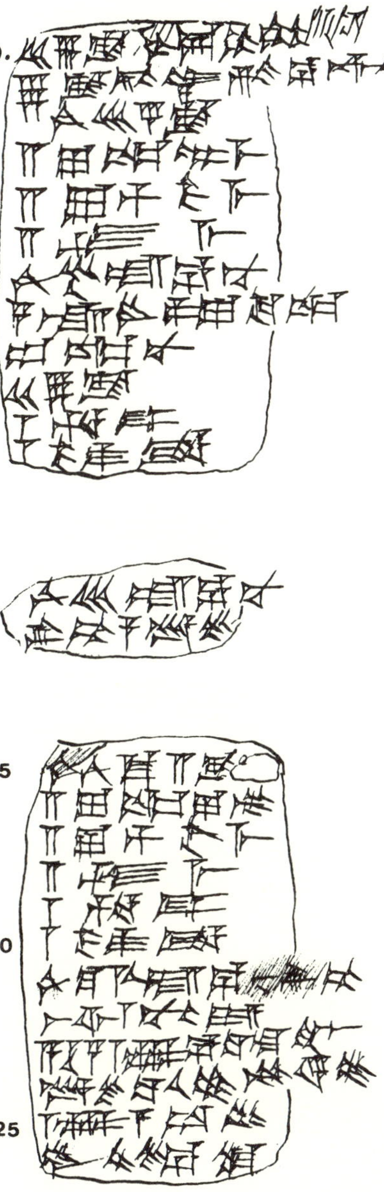

O. Lo.E. R.

°erasure

84

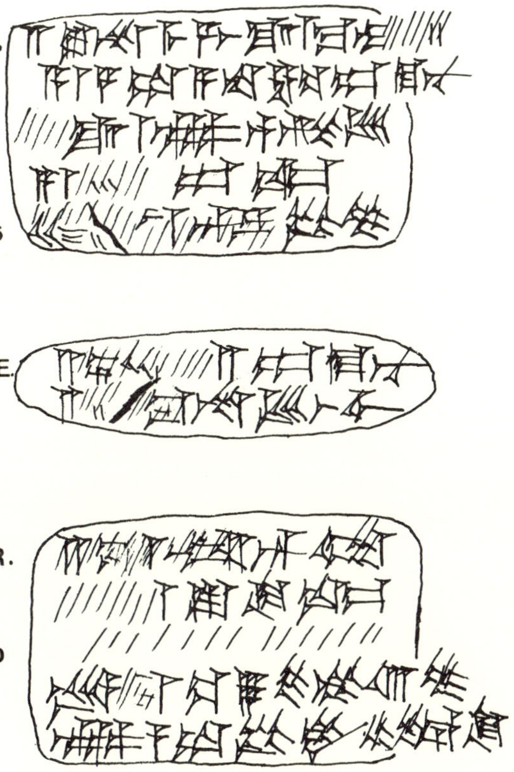

O. Lo.E. R.

85

O.

R.

U.E.

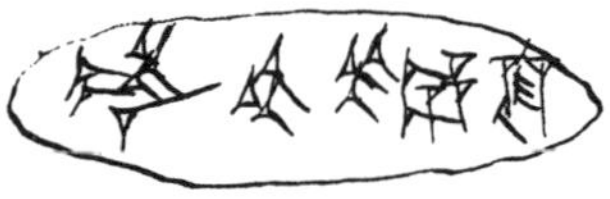

86

O.

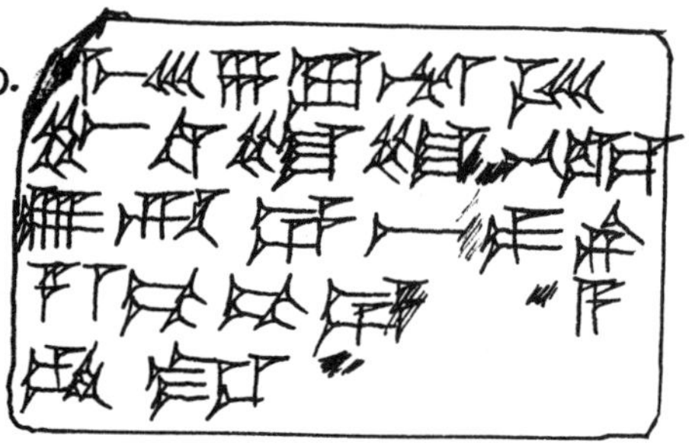

R.

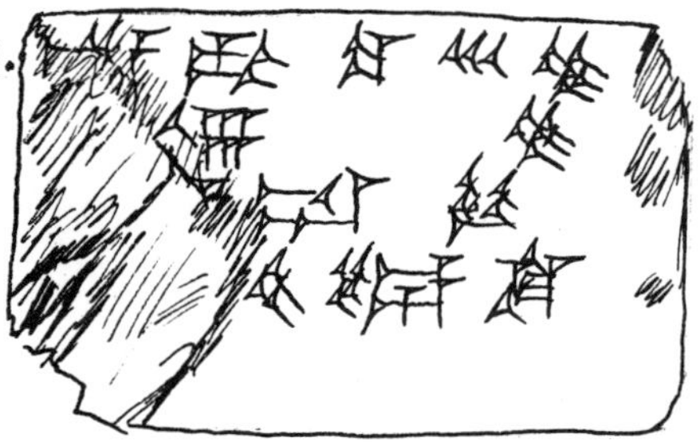

87

O.

R.

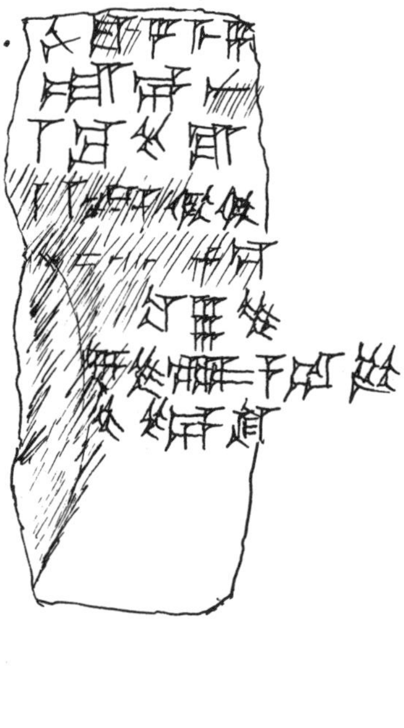

88

O.

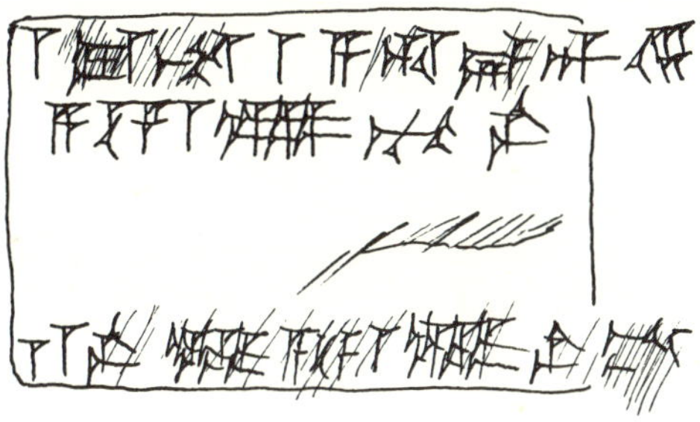

Lo.E.

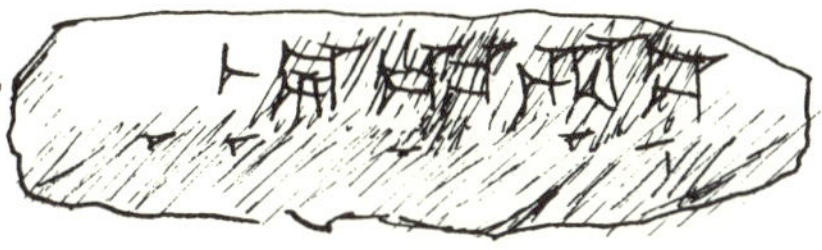

R.

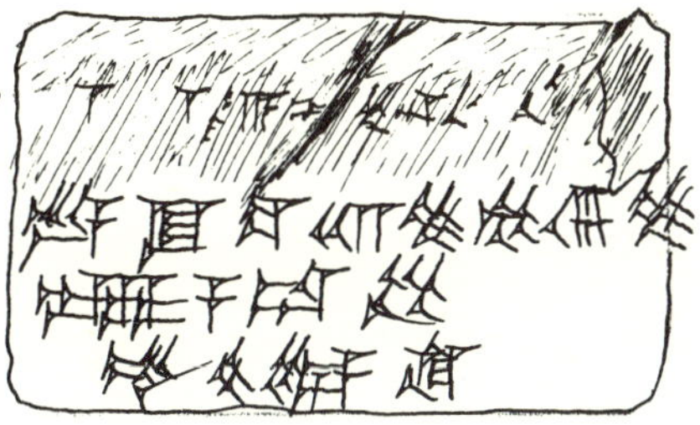

89

O.

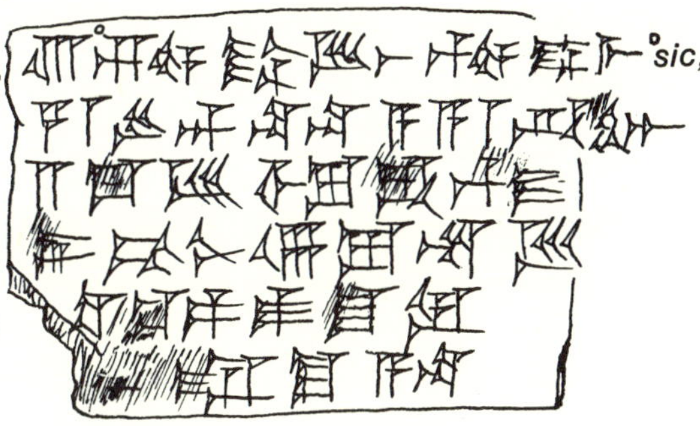

sic, for

Lo.E.

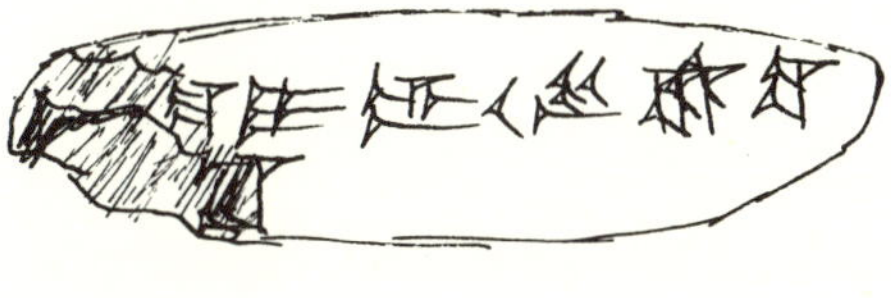

R.

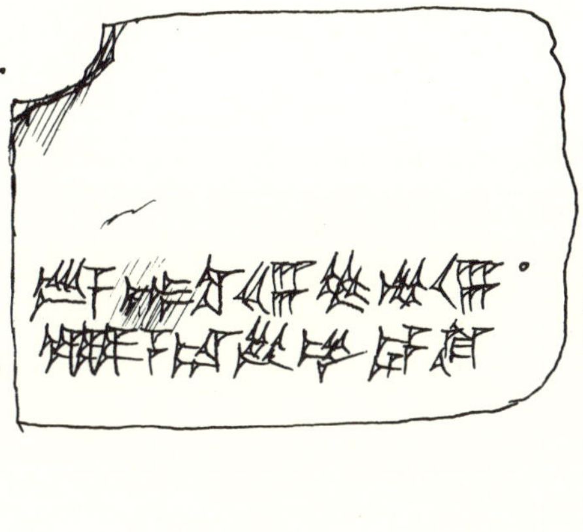

Scribe omitted KÁM since line 2 of obverse intruded here.

90

O.

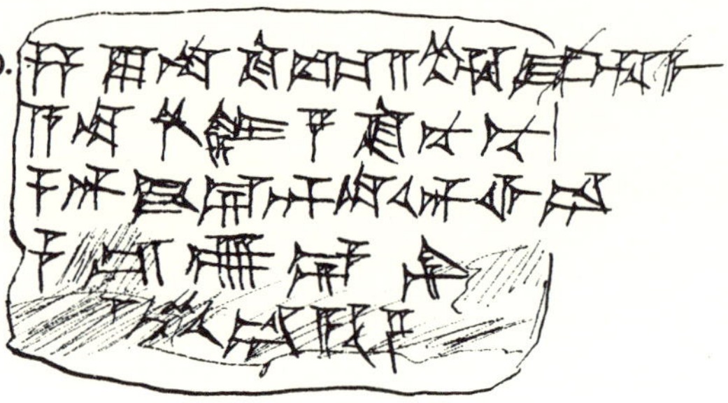

Lo.E.

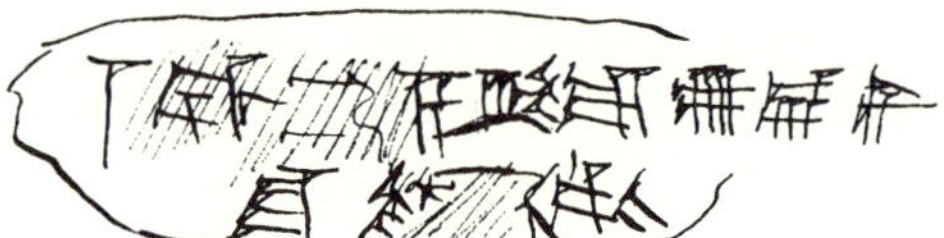

R.

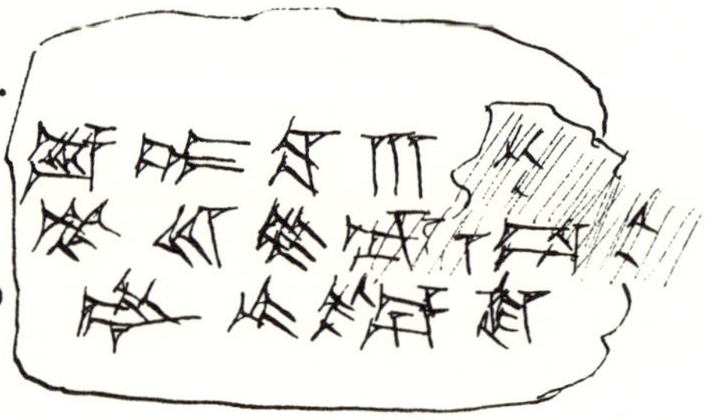

91

O.

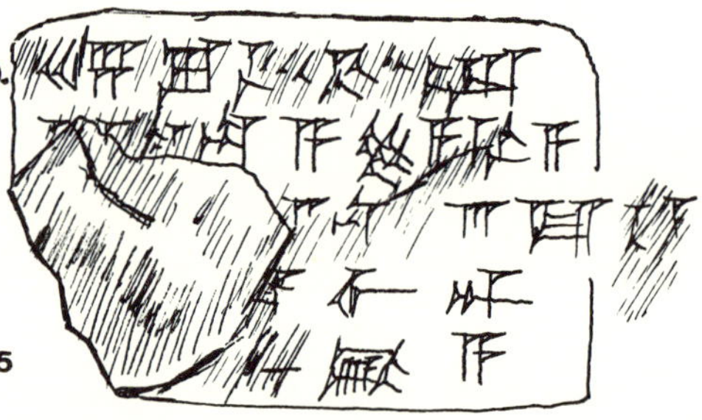

R.

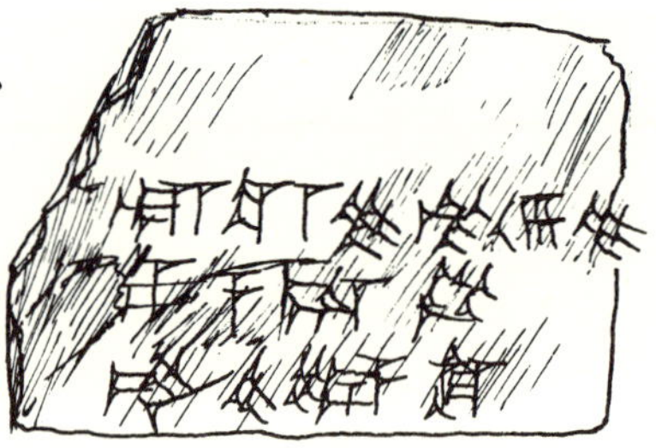

92

O.

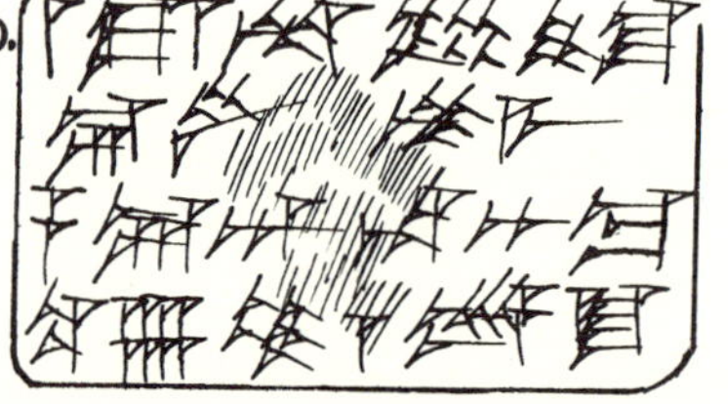

Lo.E.

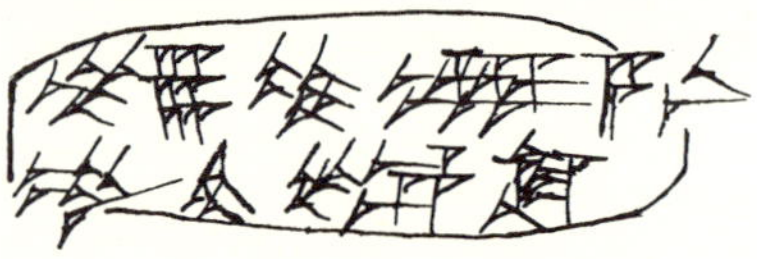

Reverse Uninscribed

93

O. 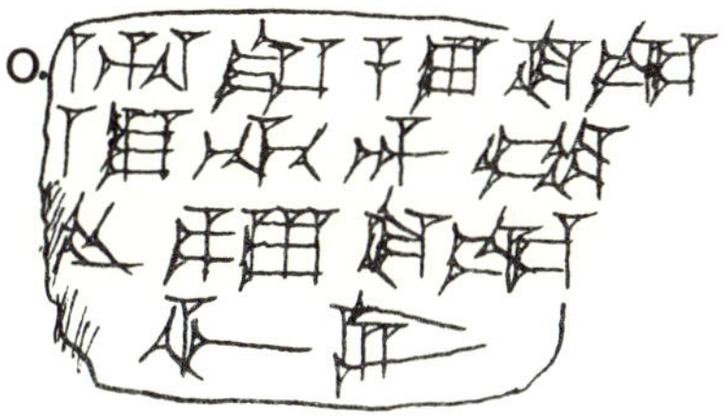

R.
5 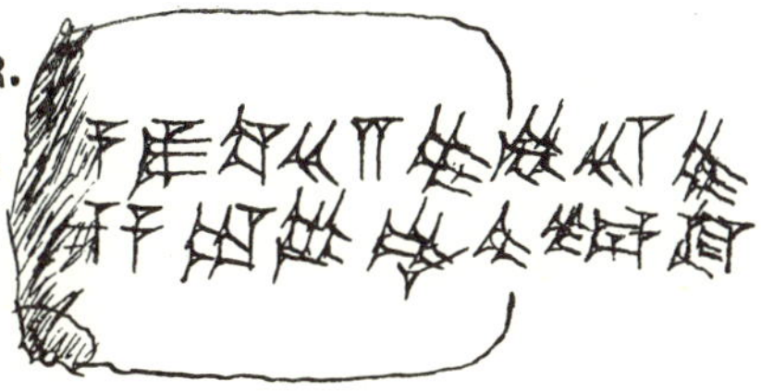

95

O. 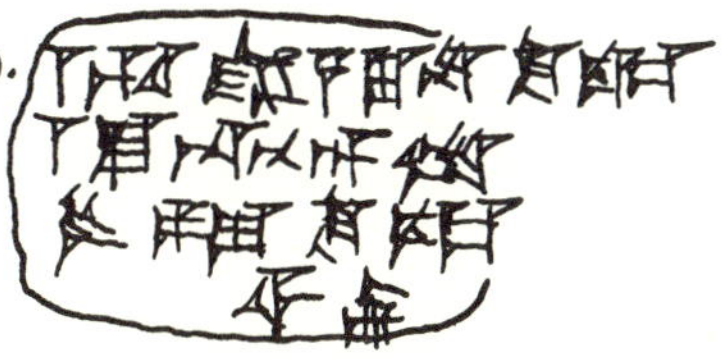

R. 5 

U.E. 

94

O. 

R.
5 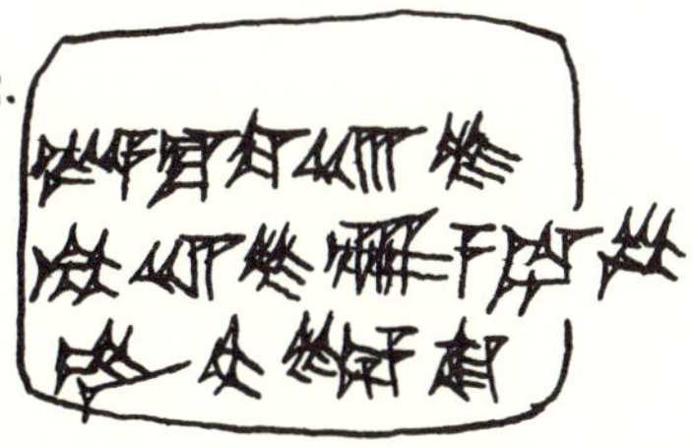

96

O. 

R.
5 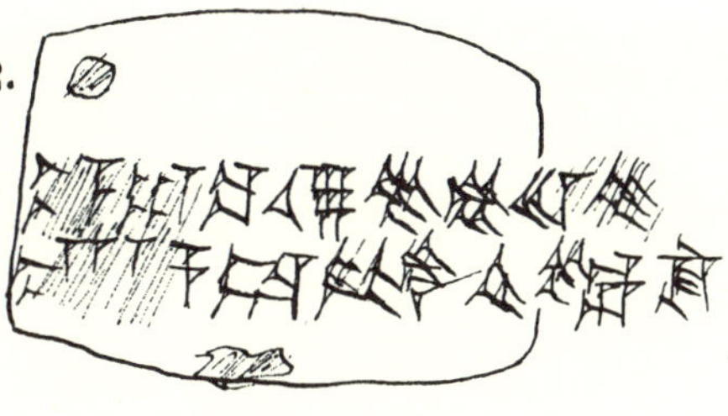

97

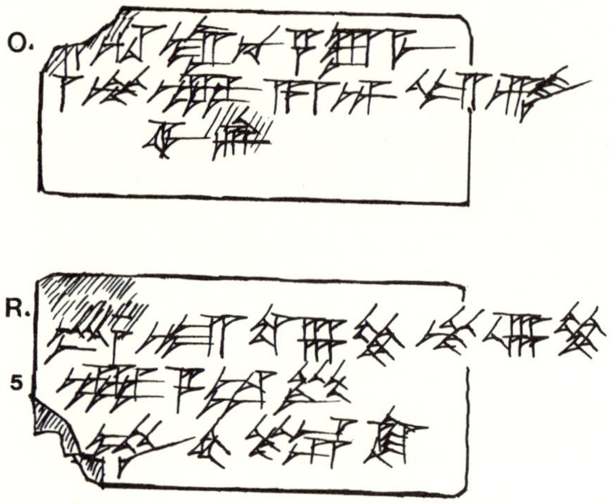

98

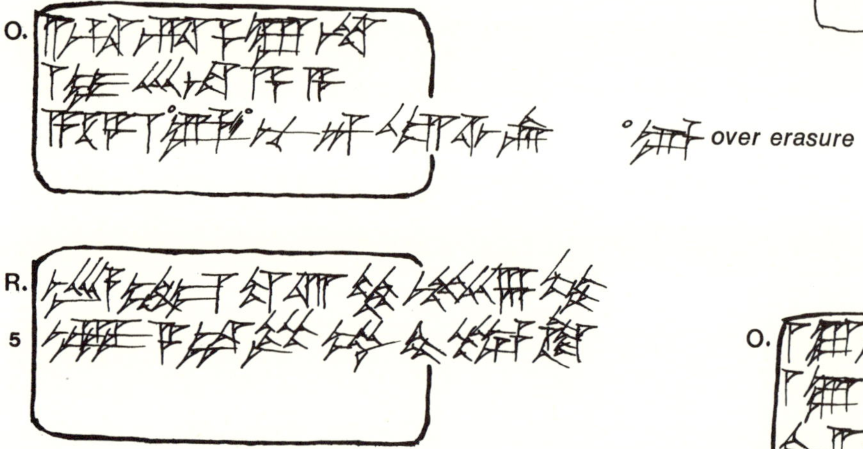

99

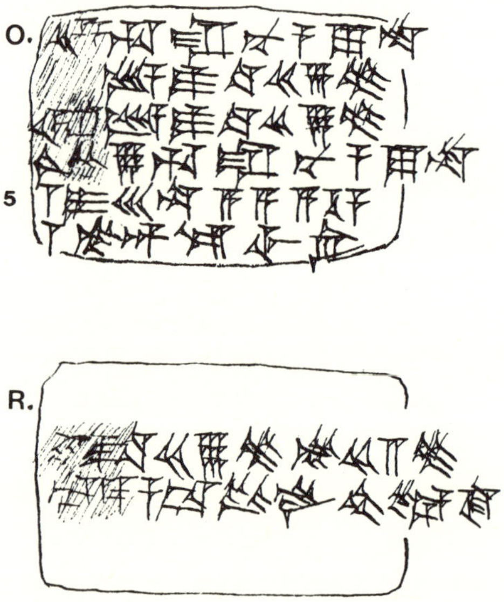

100

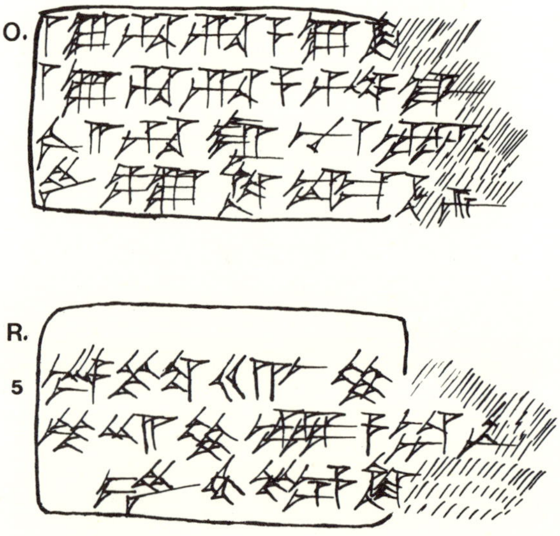

101

O.

R.

5

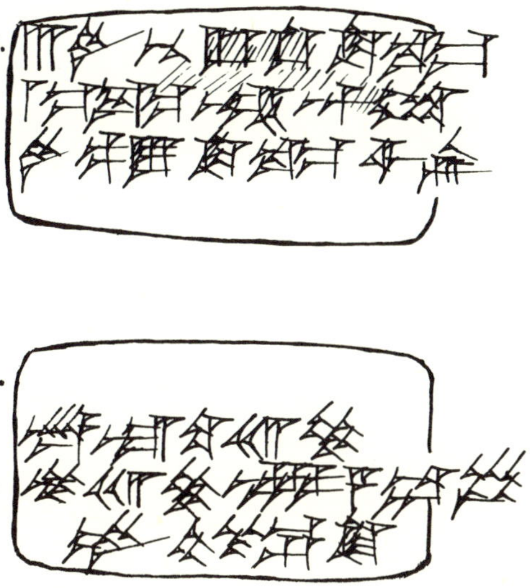

103

O.

Lo.E.

5

R.

U.E.

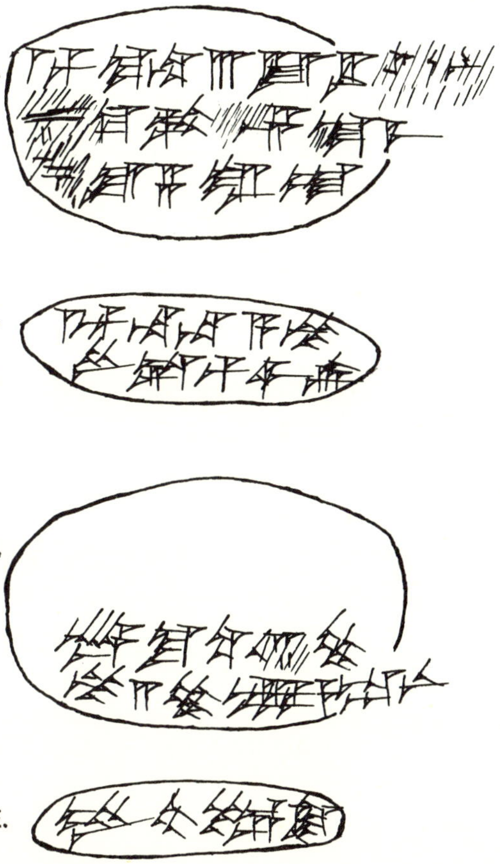

102

O.

R.

5

U.E.

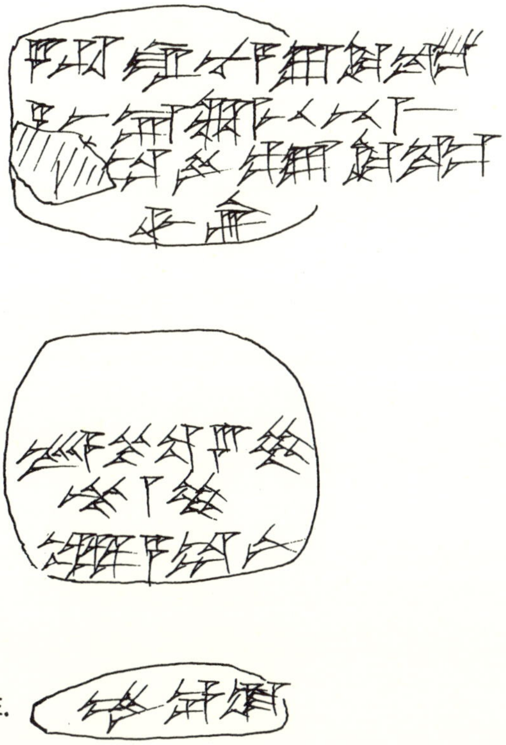

104

O.

Lo.E.5

R.

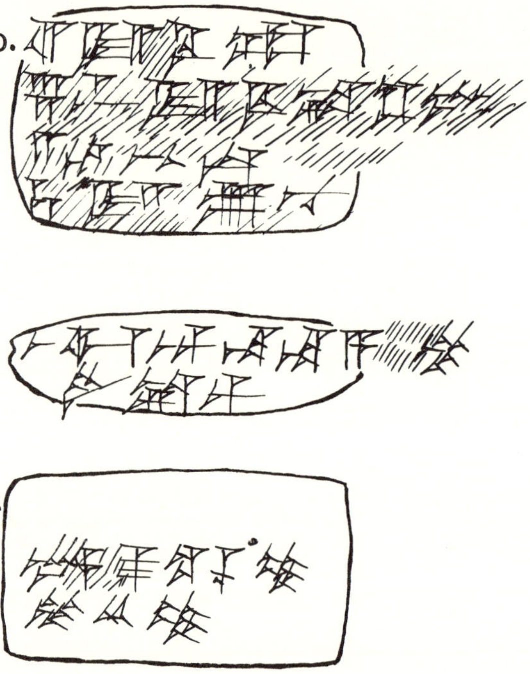

° over erasure

105

O.

5

R.

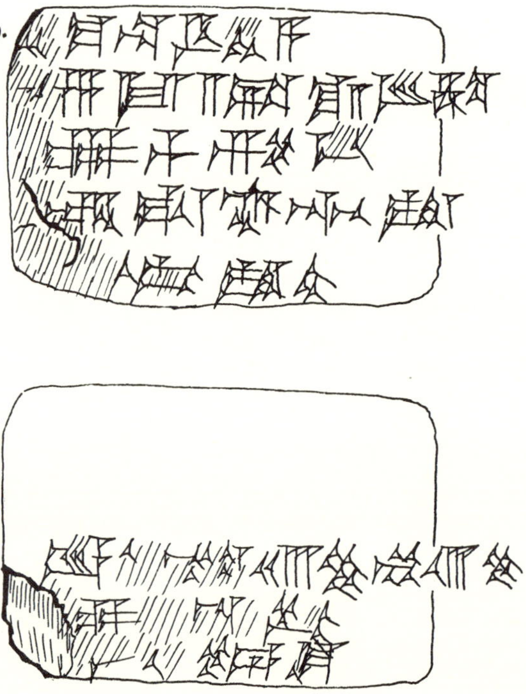

106

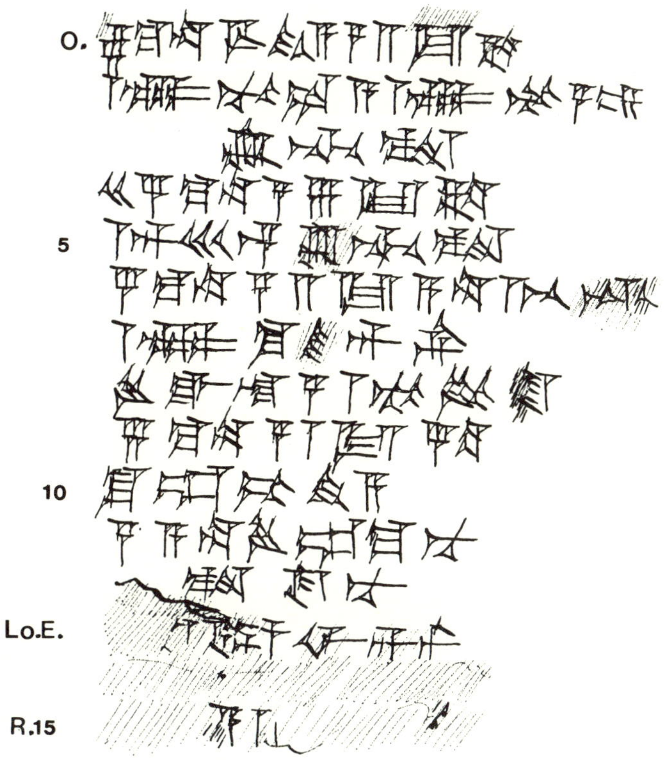

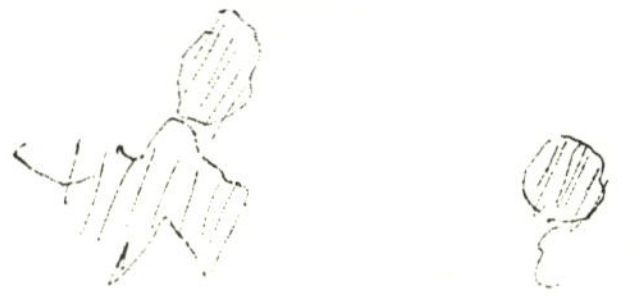

107

O.

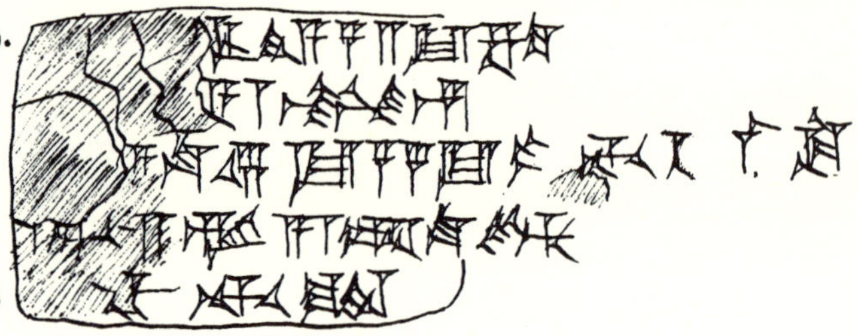

5

Line continues on Reverse.

R.

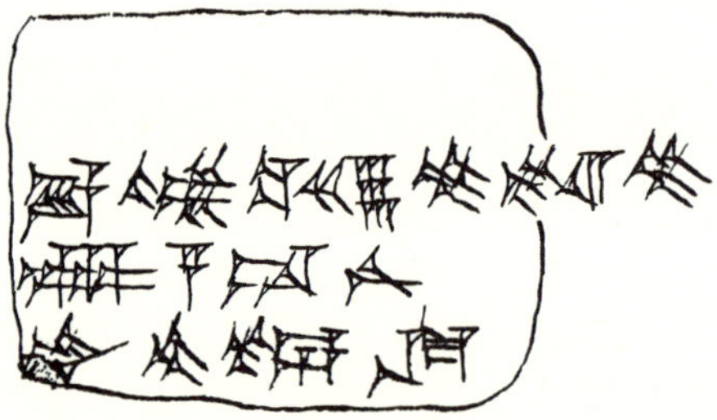

108

O.

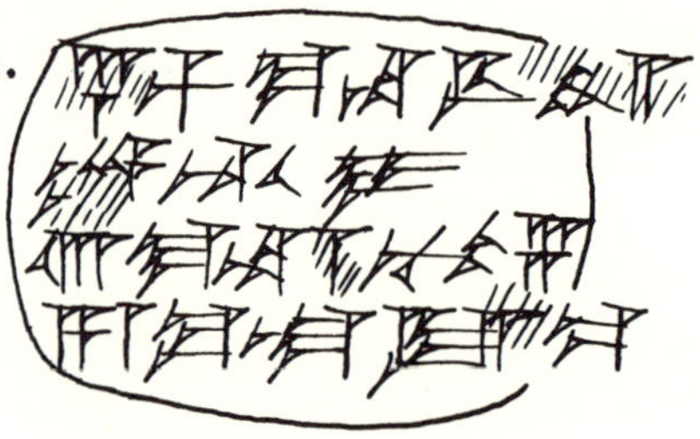

R.5

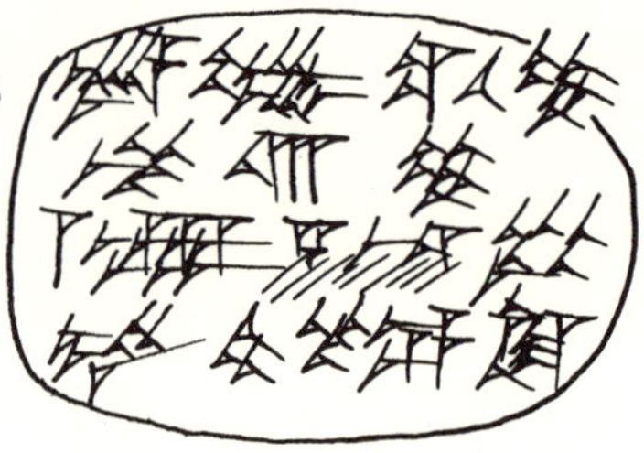

109

O.

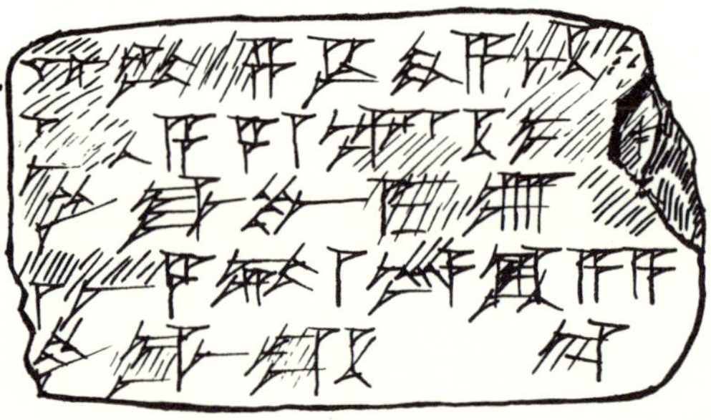

5

Lo.E.

R.

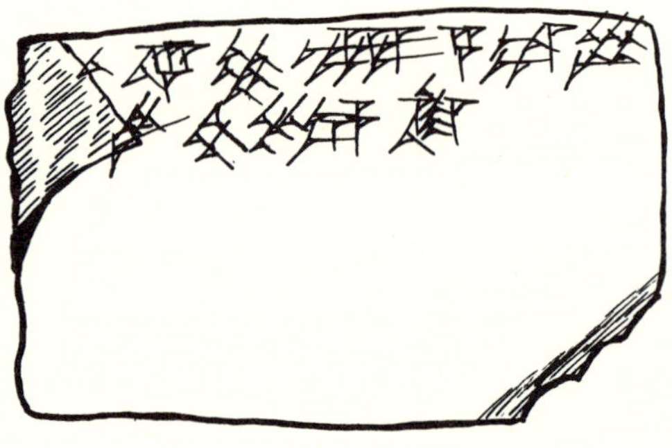

110

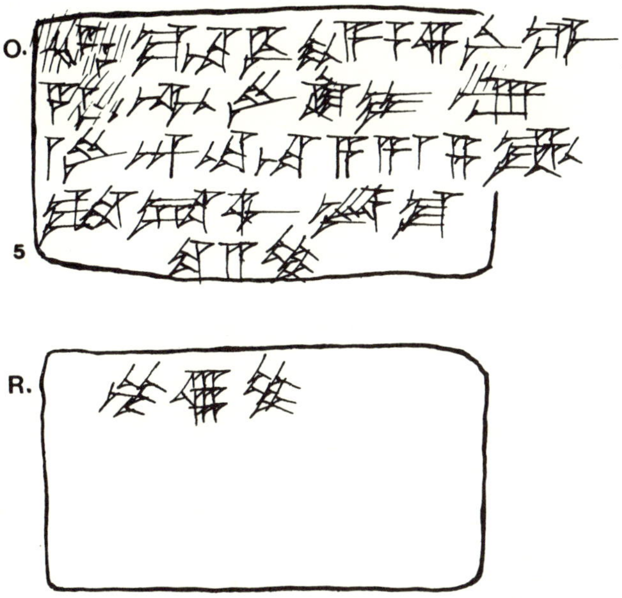

111

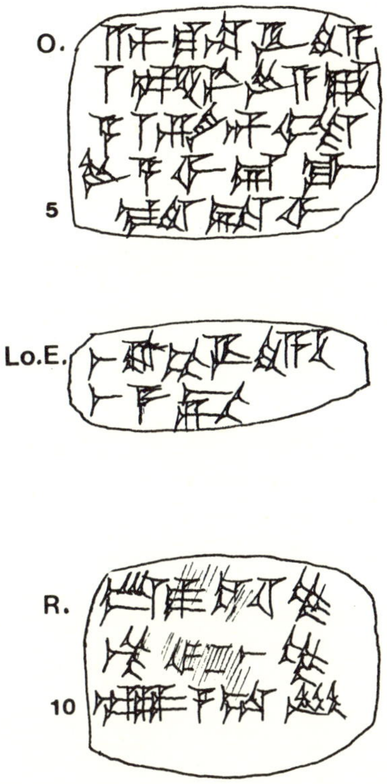

112

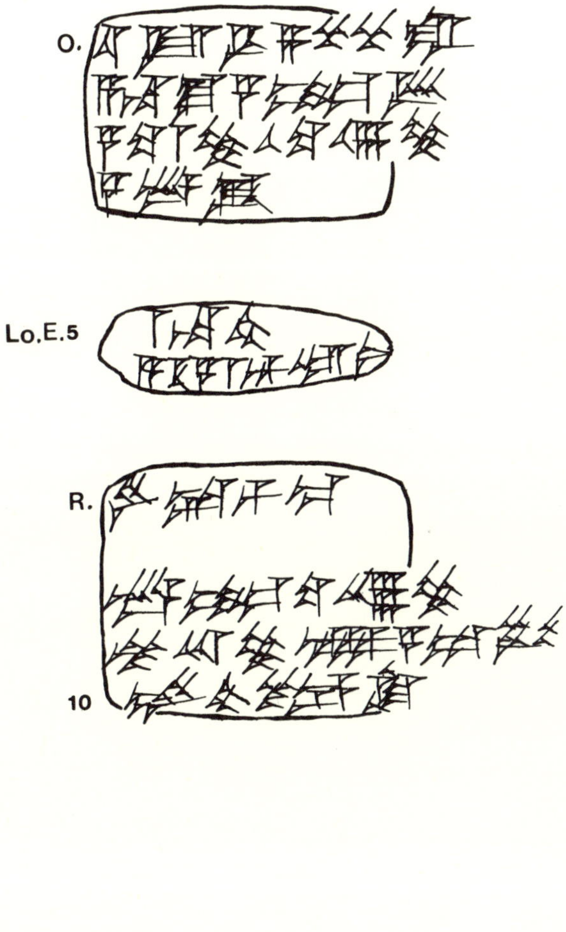

113

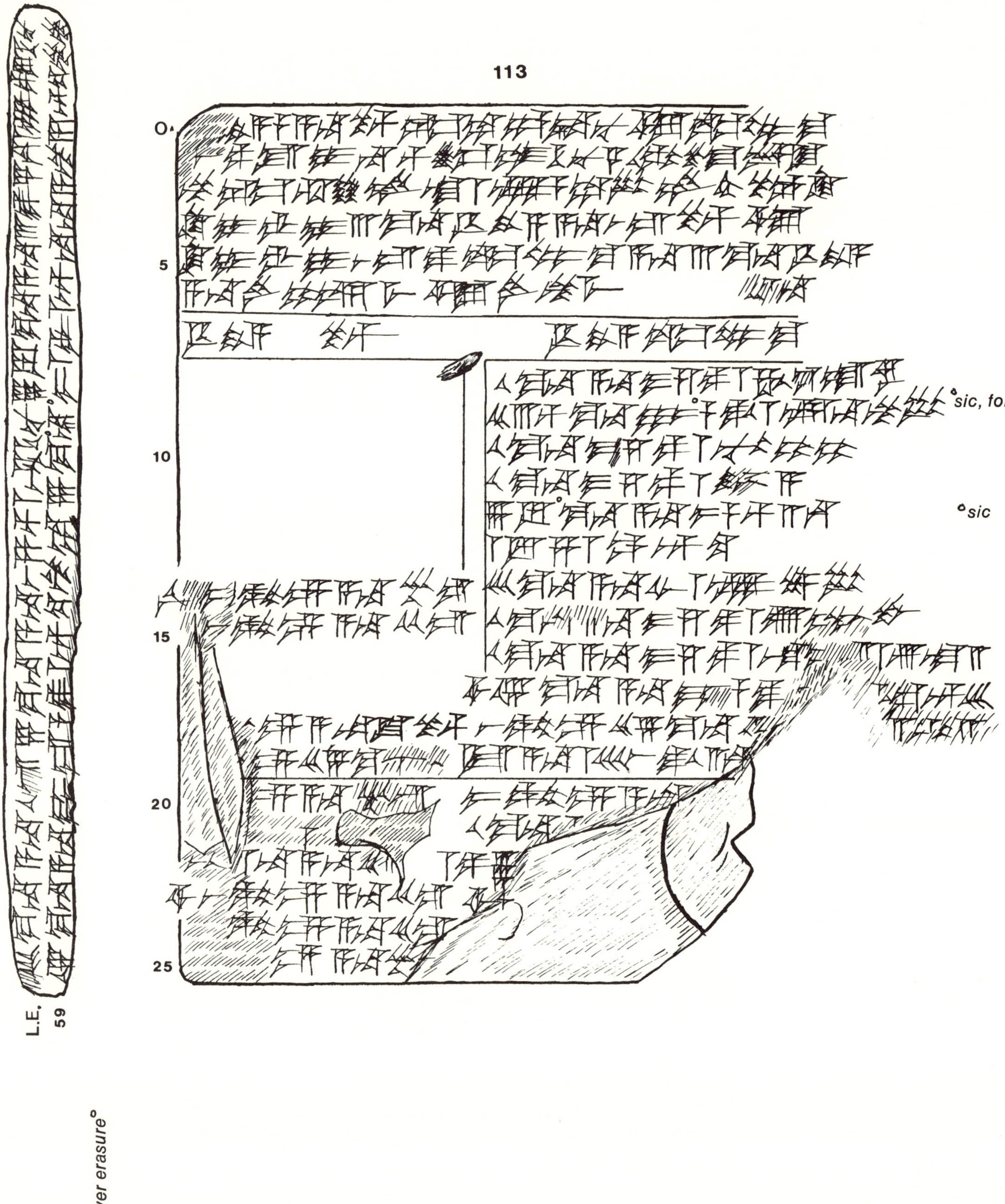

°over erasure°

113

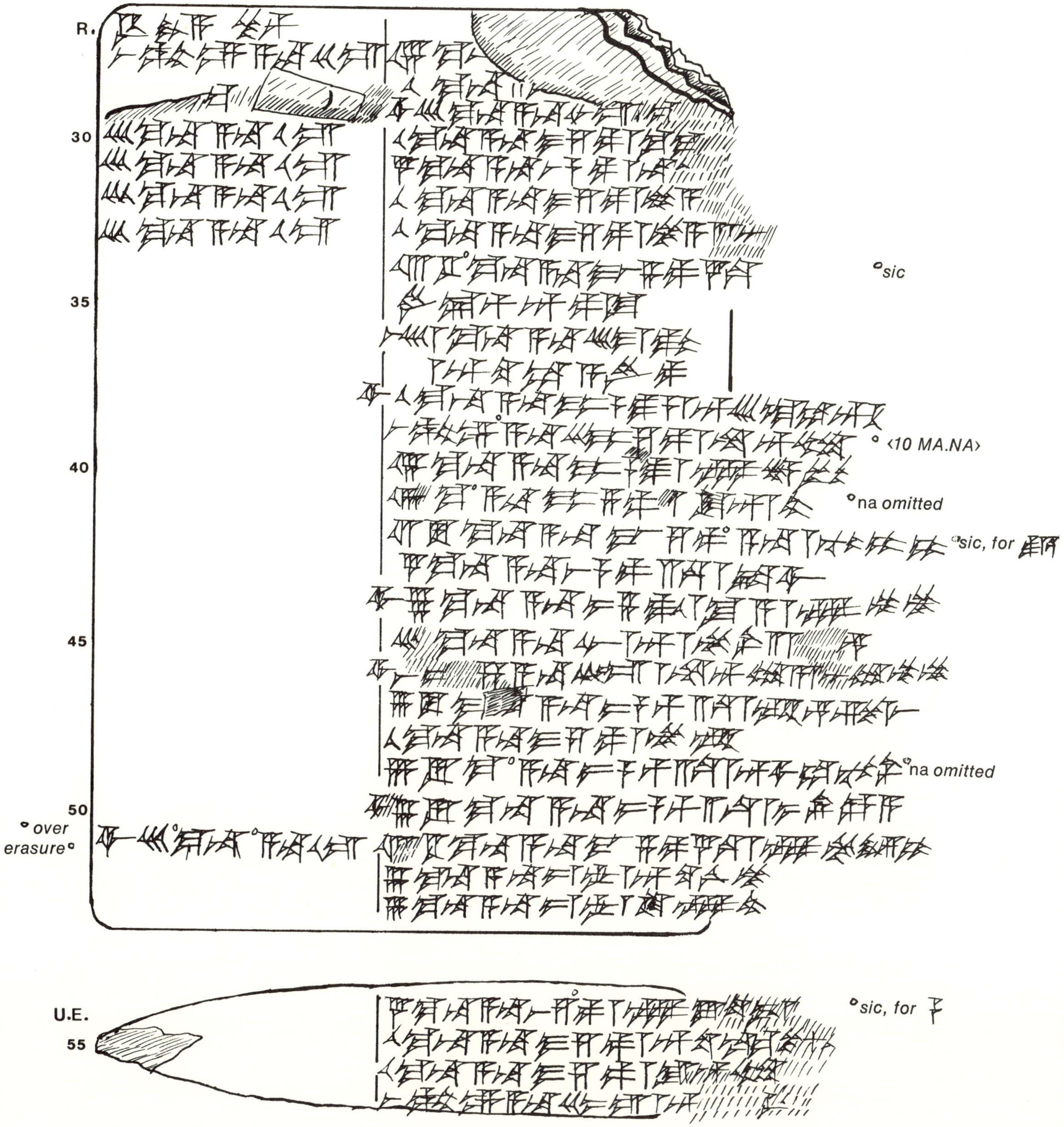
R.
°sic
° <10 MA.NA>
°na omitted
°sic, for
°na omitted
°over erasure°
U.E.
°sic, for

115

O.

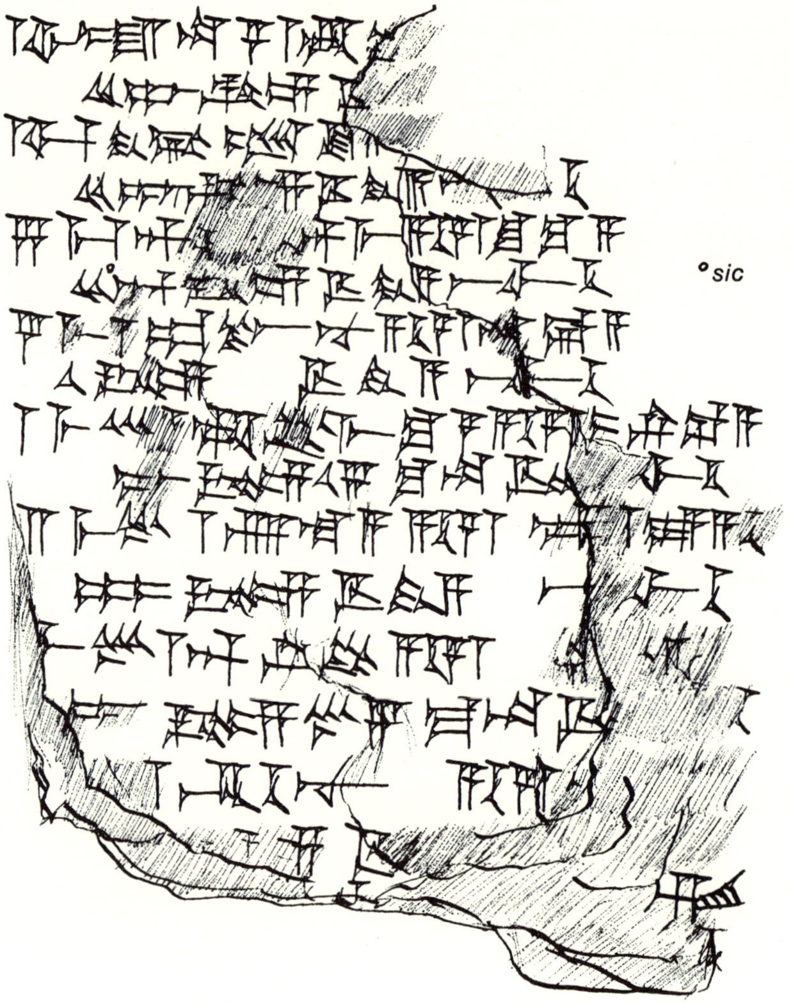

° sic

114

O.

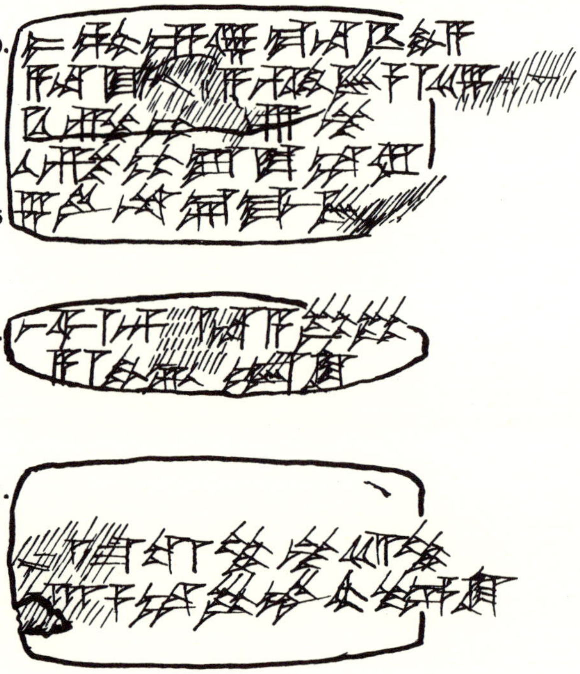

Lo.E.

R.

115

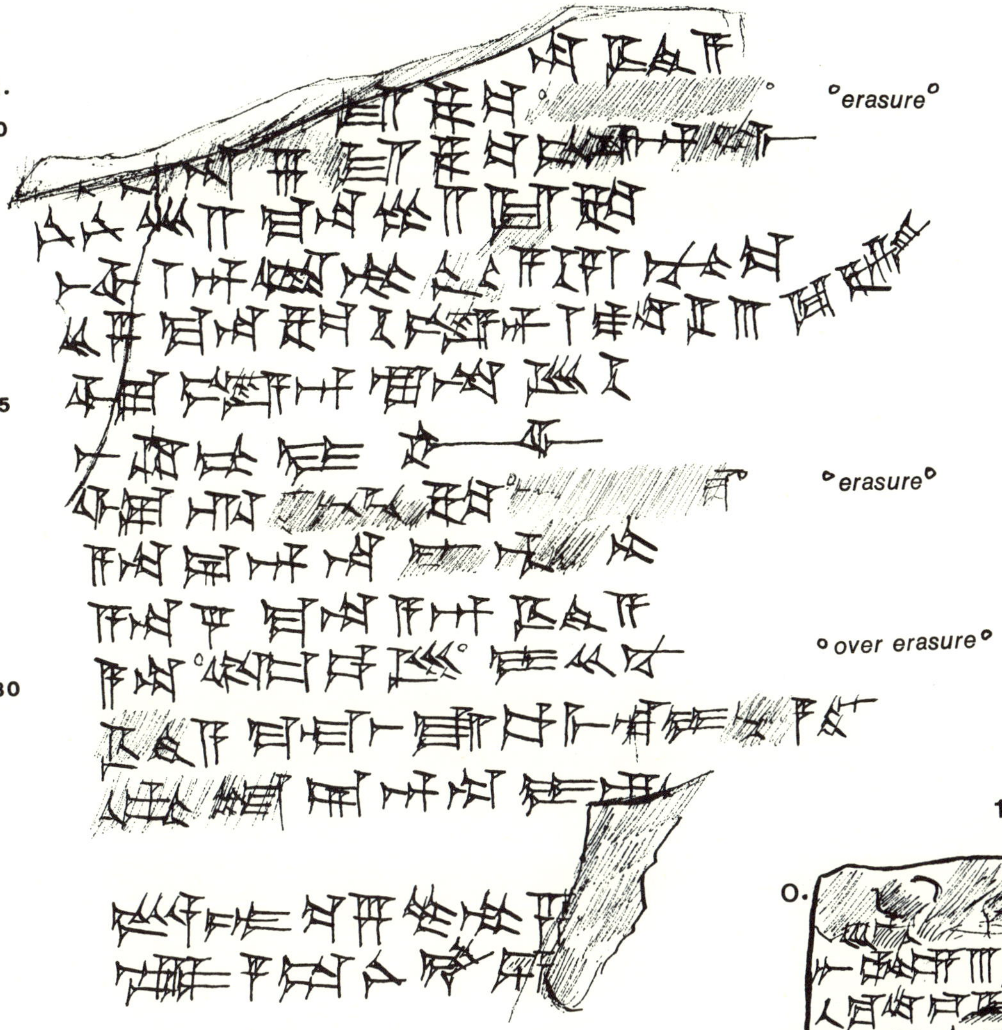

116

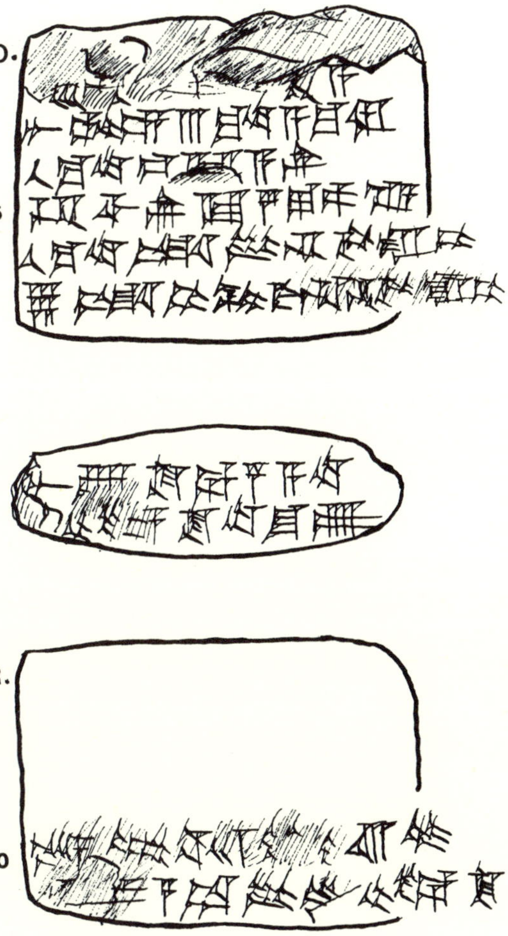

117

O.

118

O.

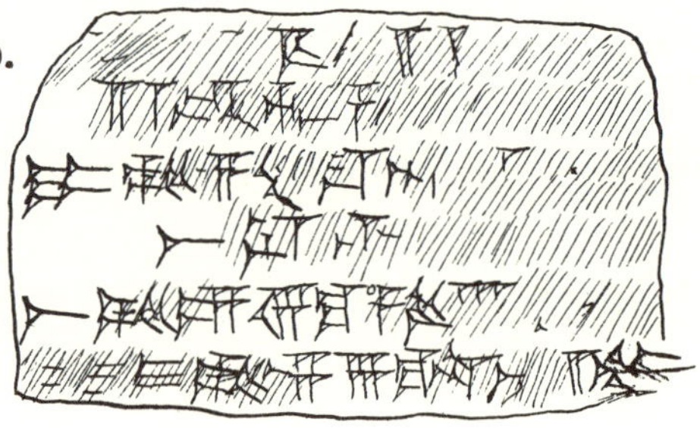

° na *omitted*

R.

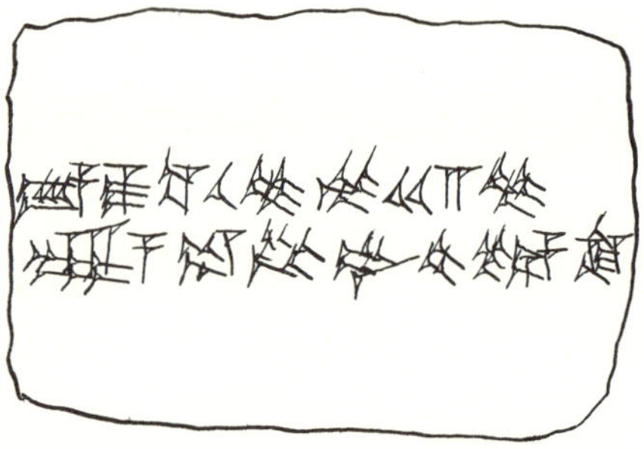

119

O.

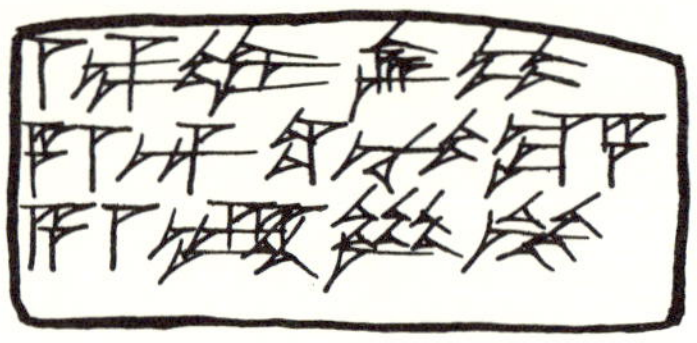

R.

U.E.

120

O.

R.

121

O.

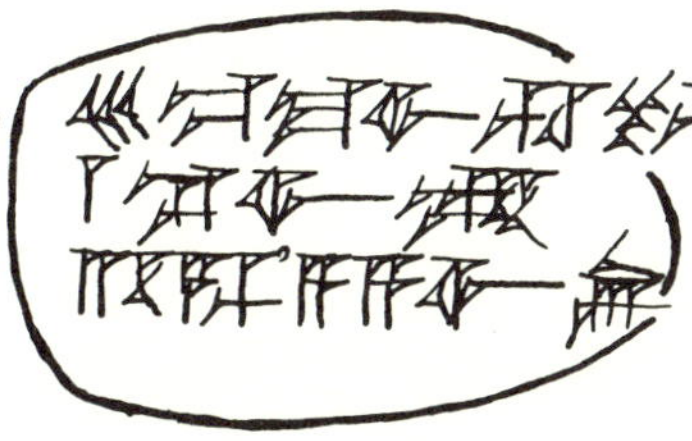

° over erasure

R.

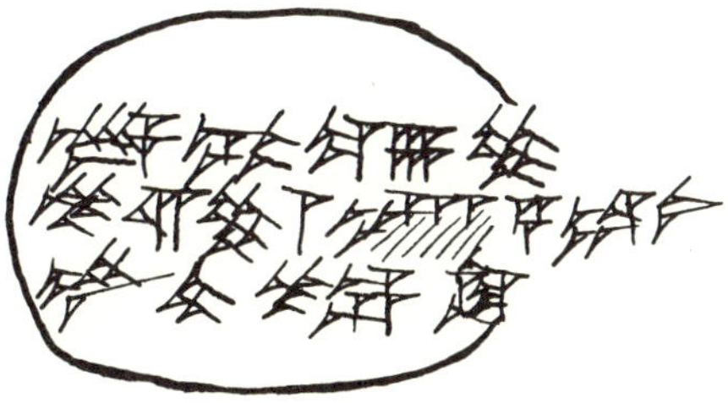

122

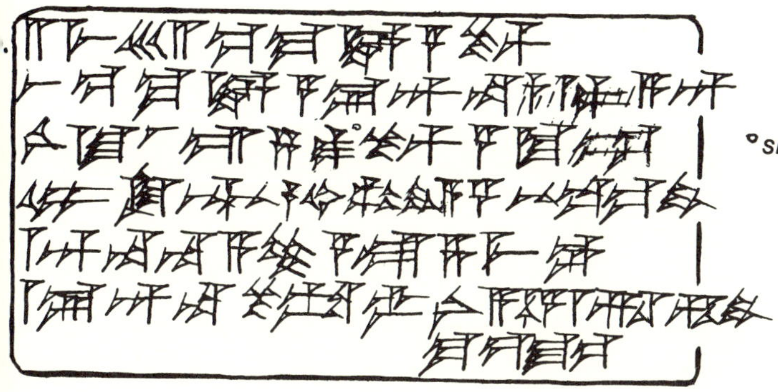

° sic

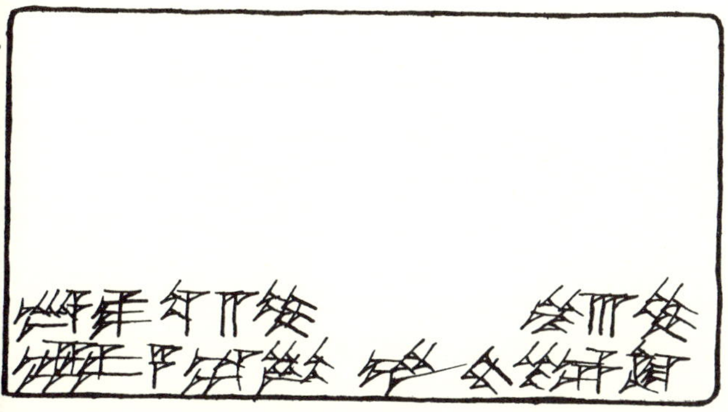

123

O.

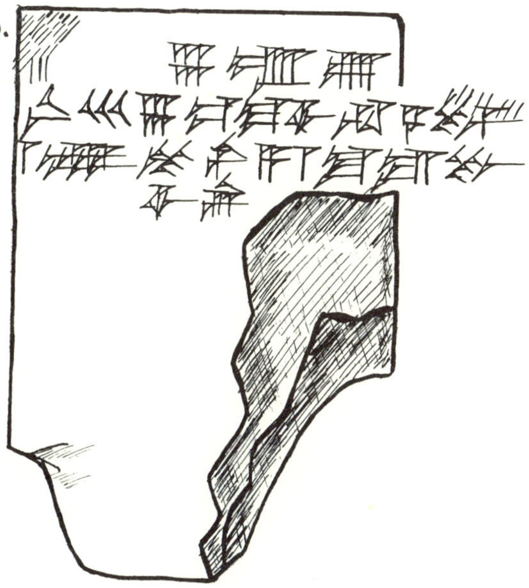

R.

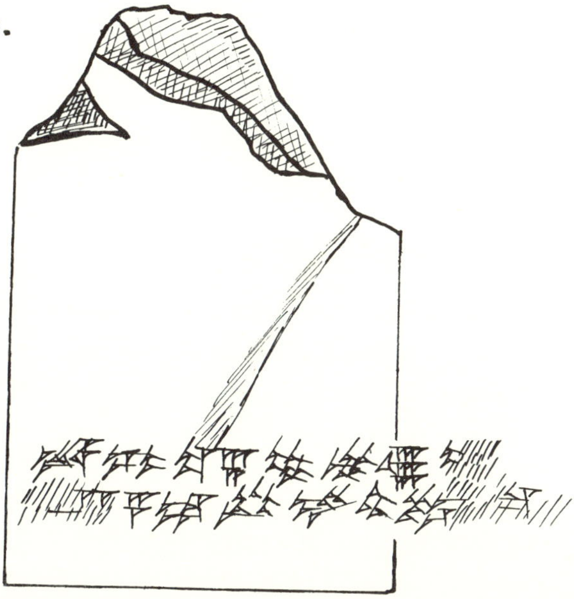

124

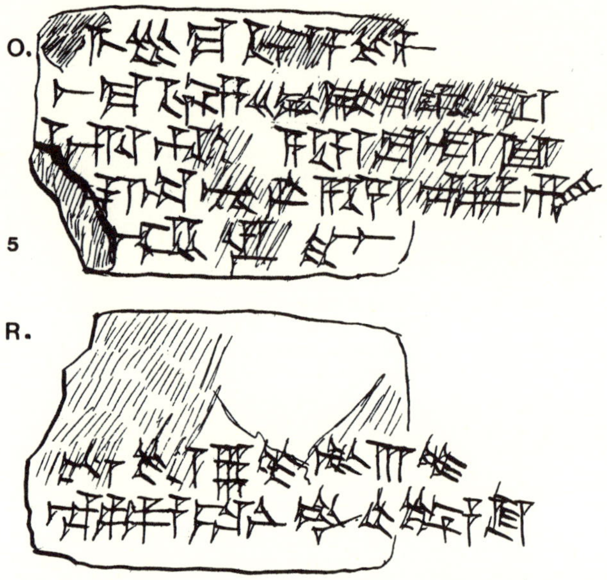

125

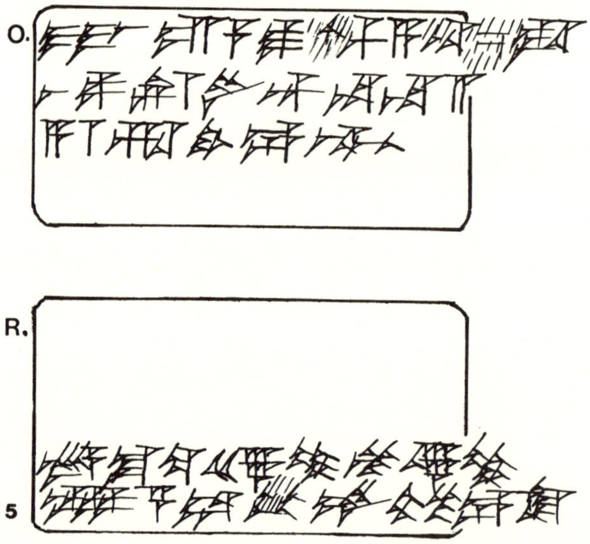

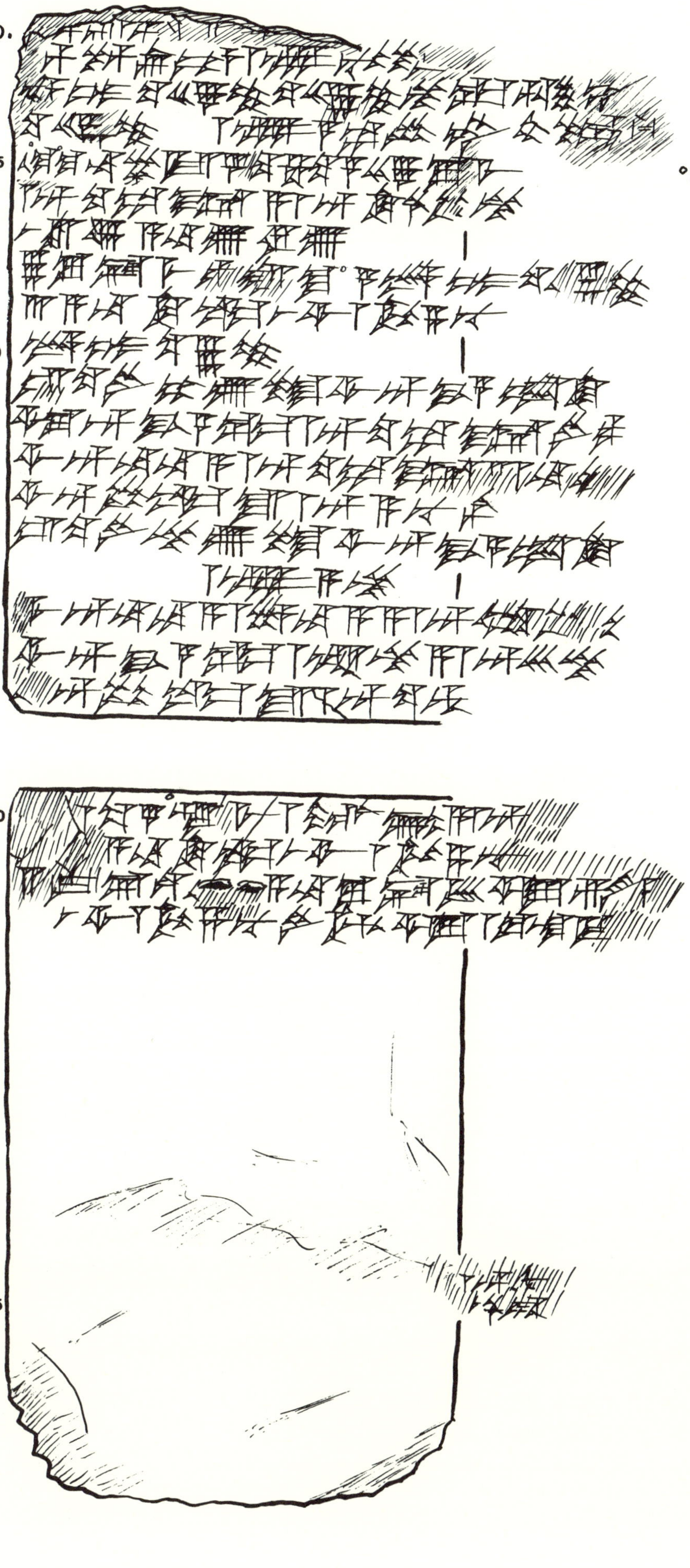
O.
°dittography°
°sic
R.20
°sic

127

O.

over erasure

R.5

128

O.

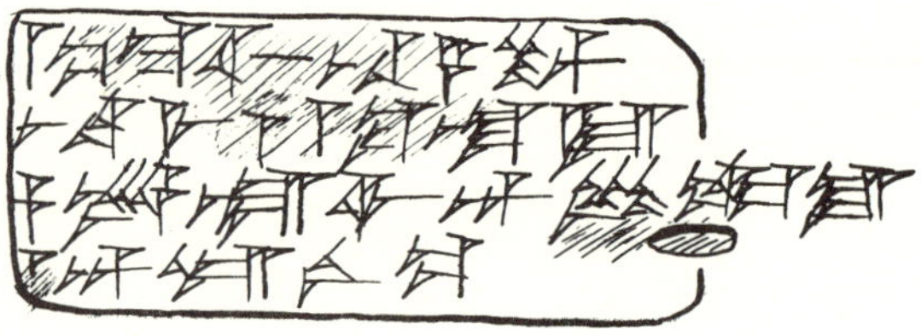

R.5

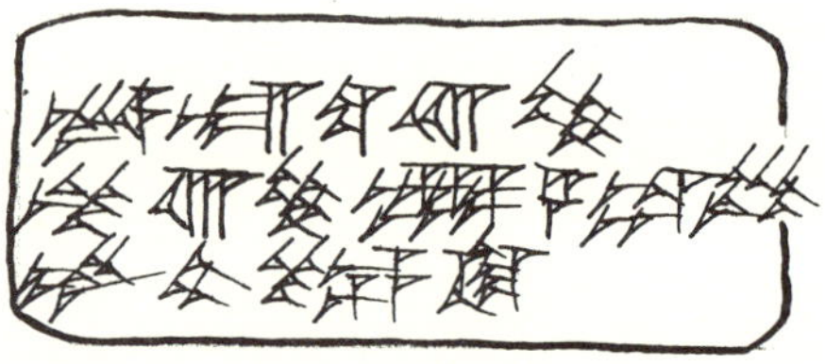

129

O.

R.

5

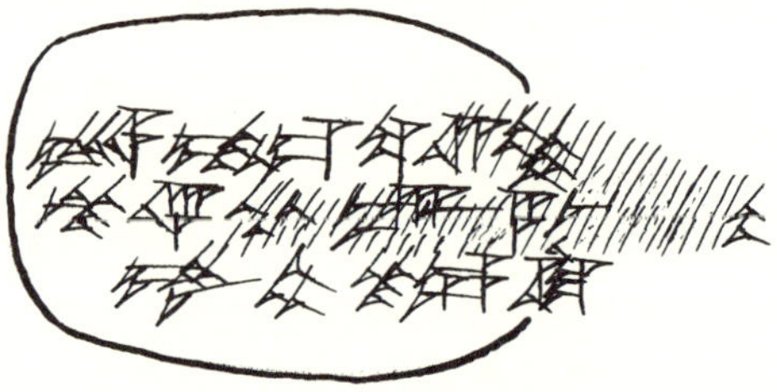

130

O.

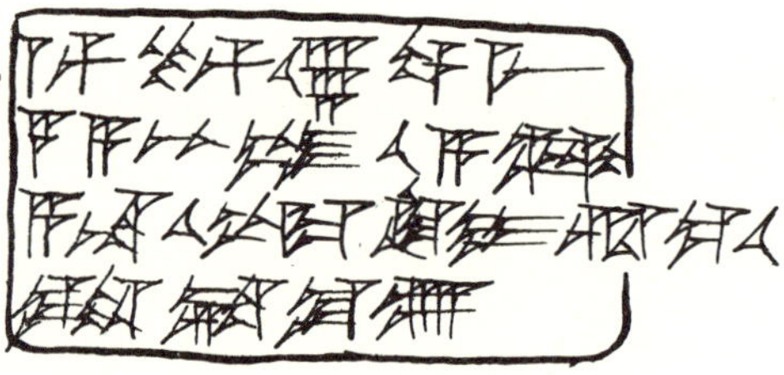

R.

5

131

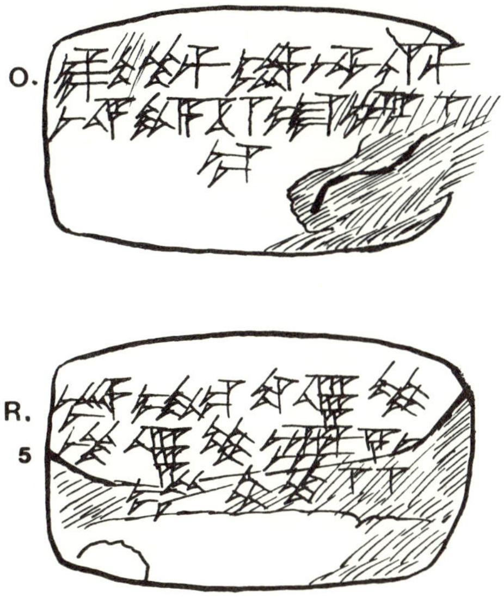

133

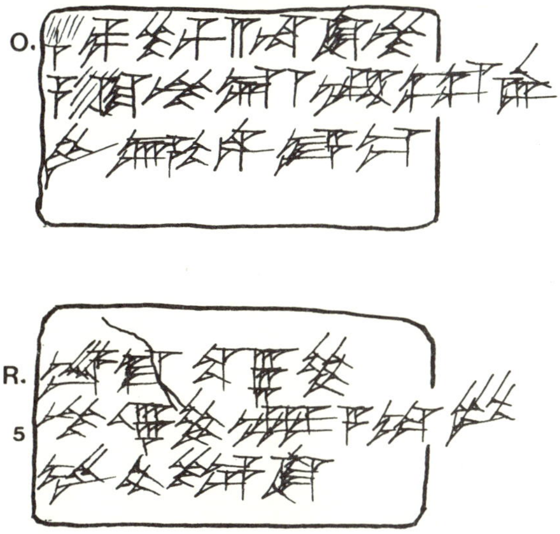

132

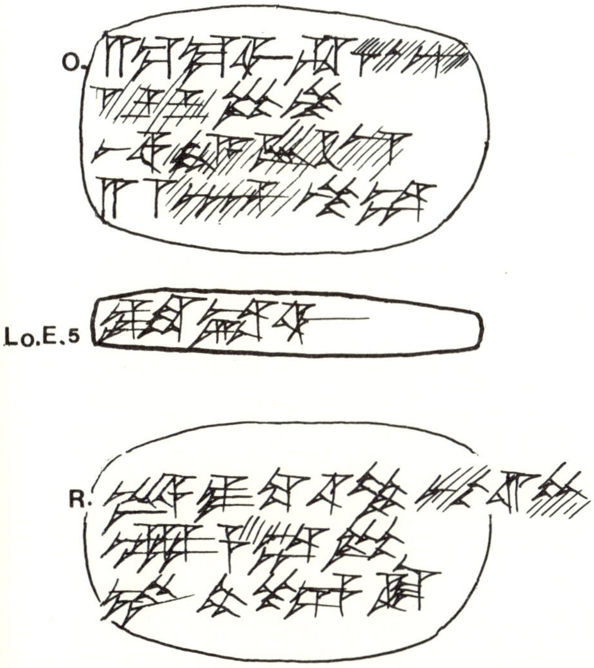

134

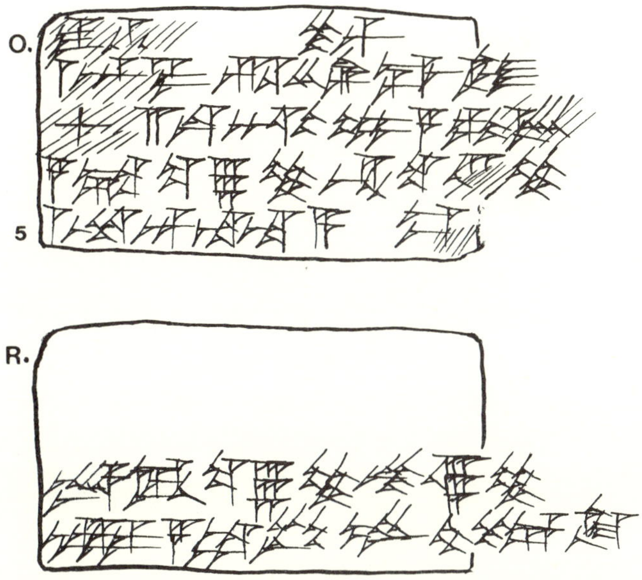

135

O.

Lo.E.

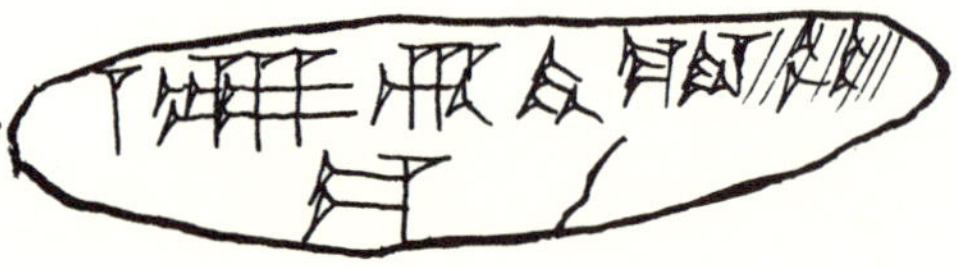

R.

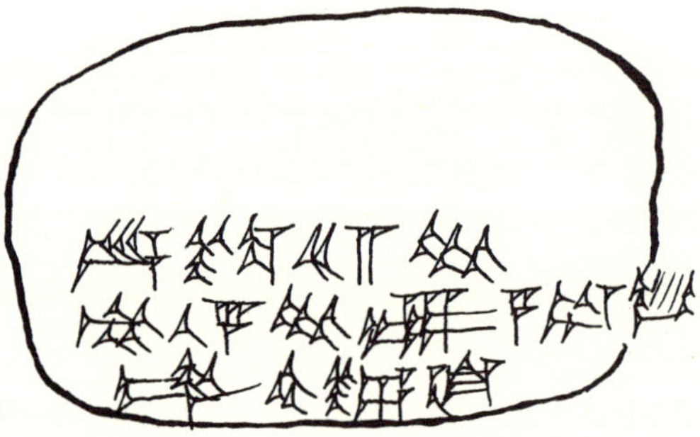

136

O.

R.

137

O.

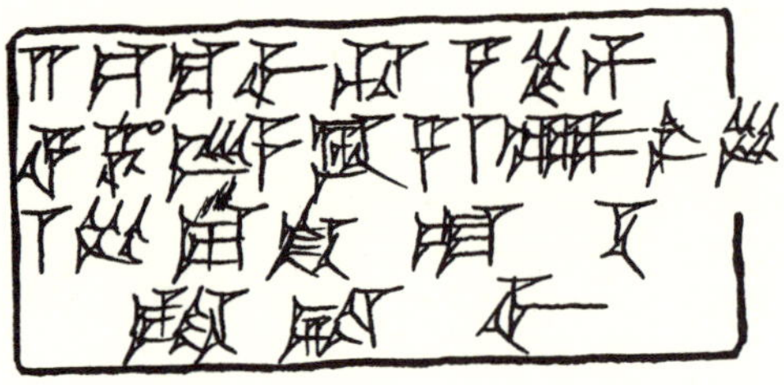

° over erasure

R.

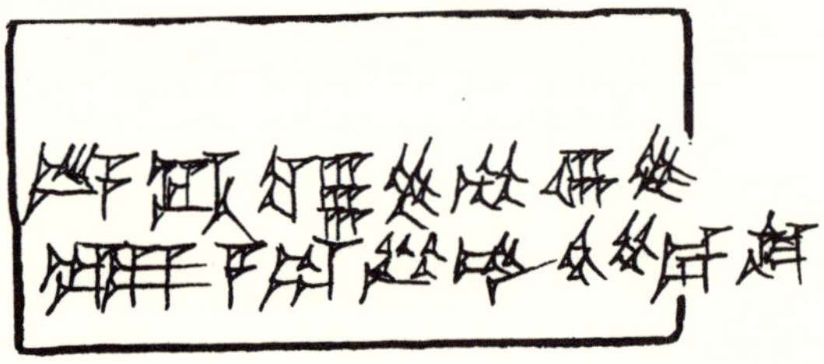

138

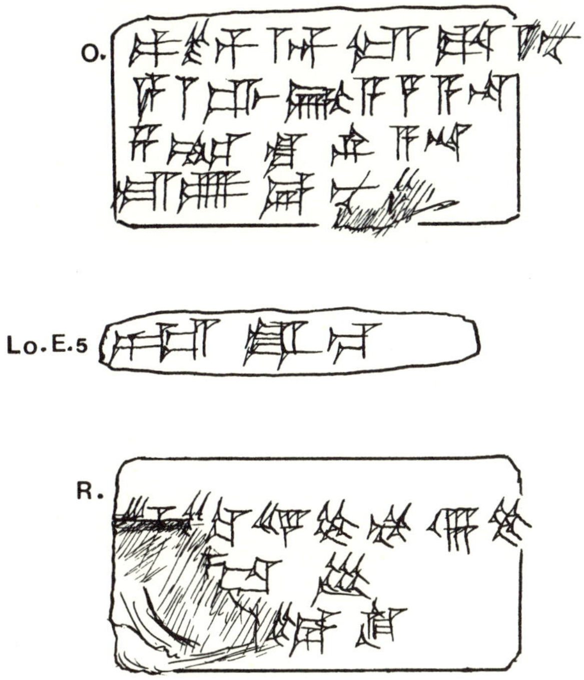

140

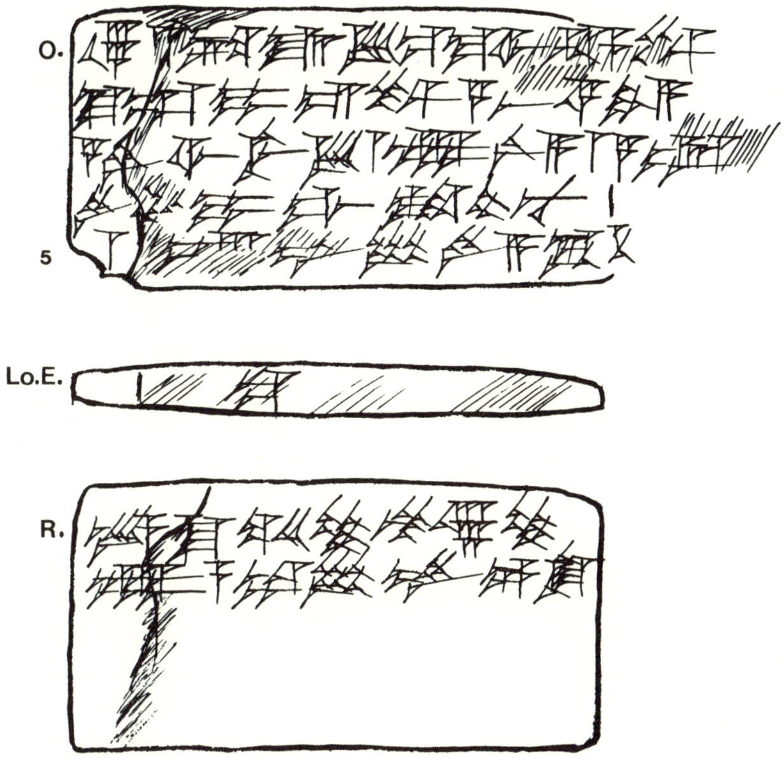

139

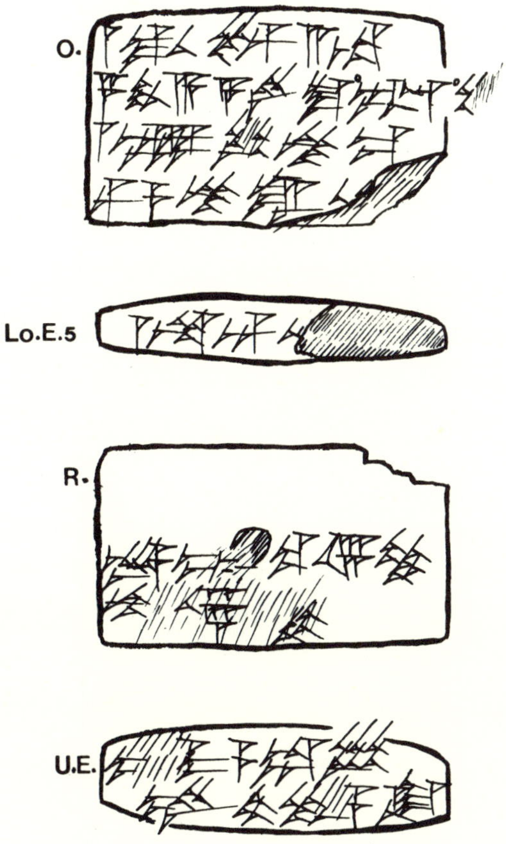

° *sic*

141

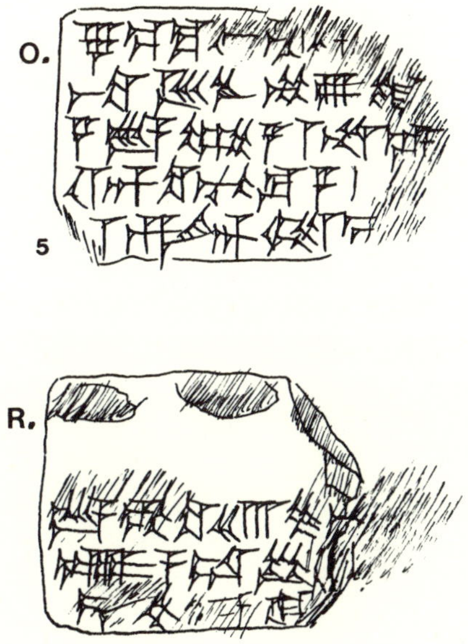

142

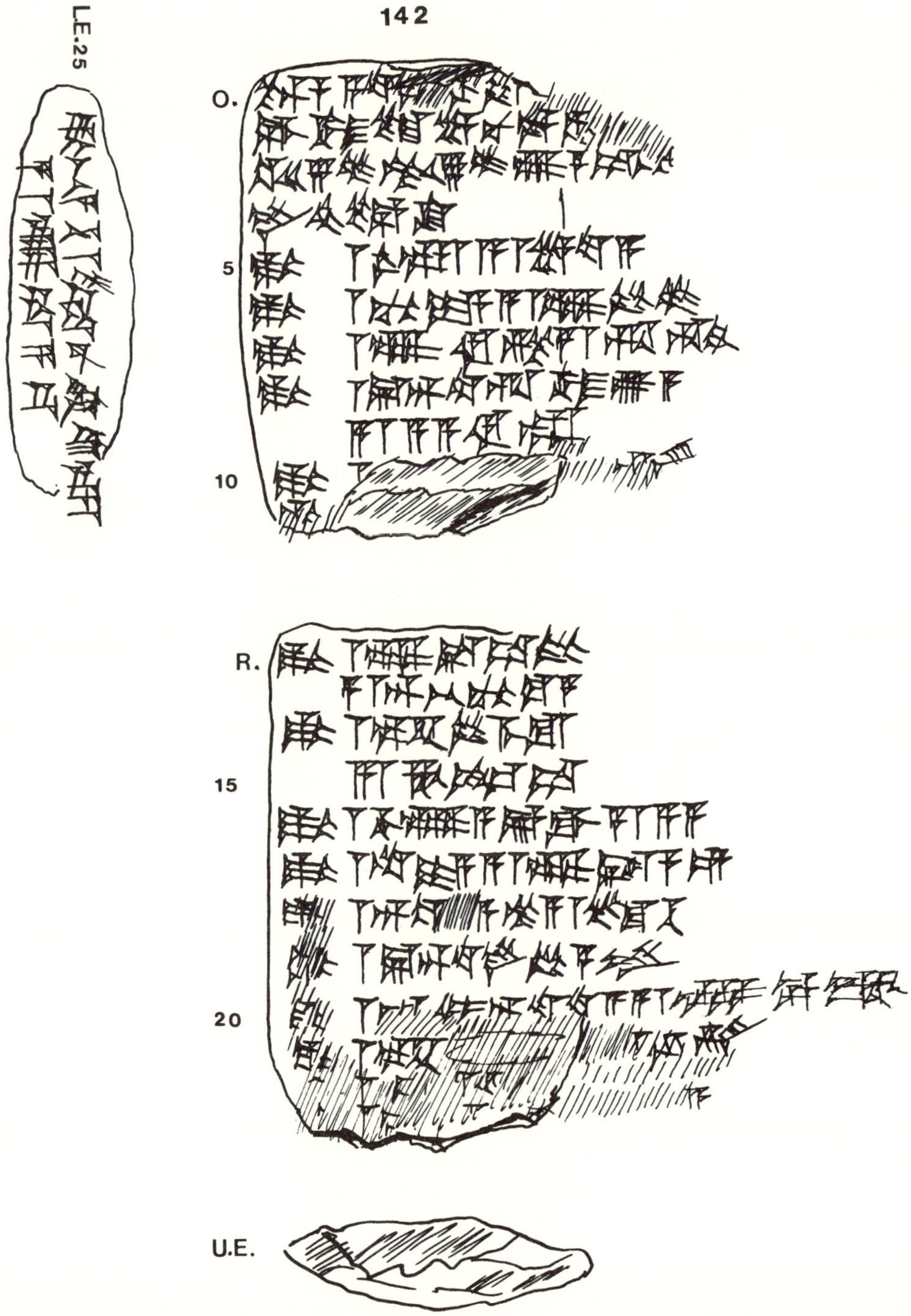

143

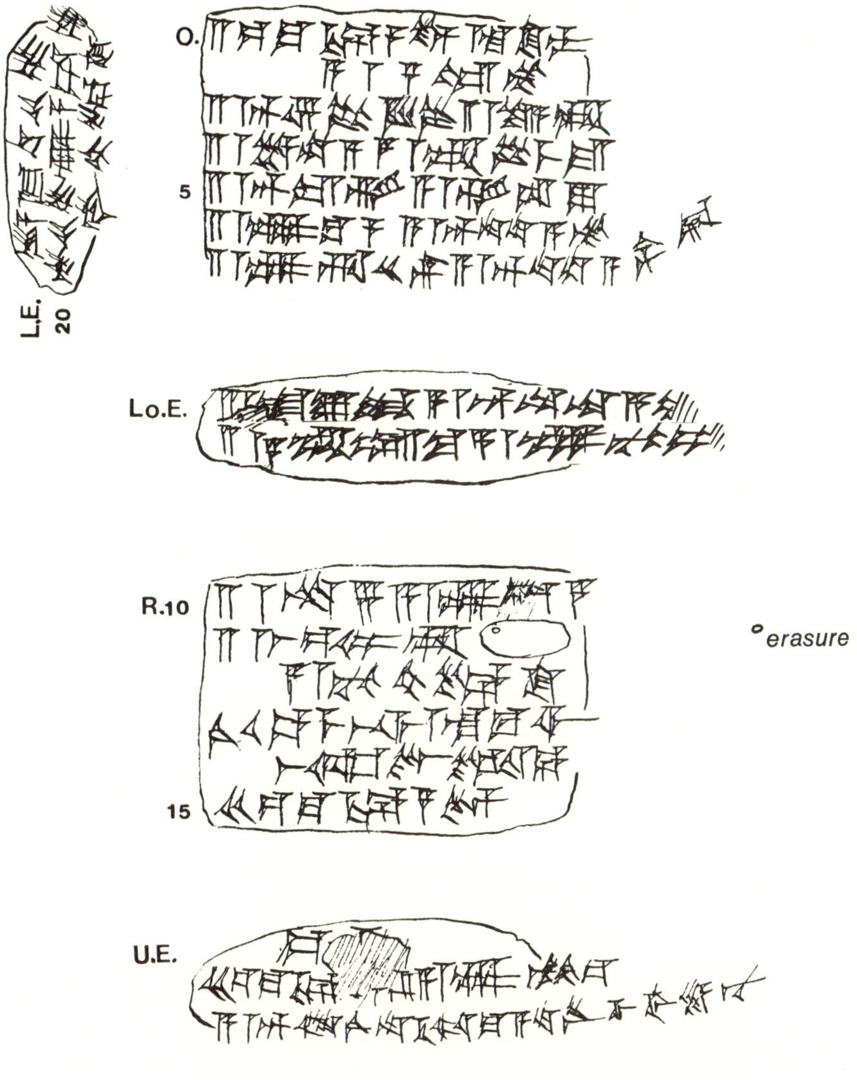

144

O.

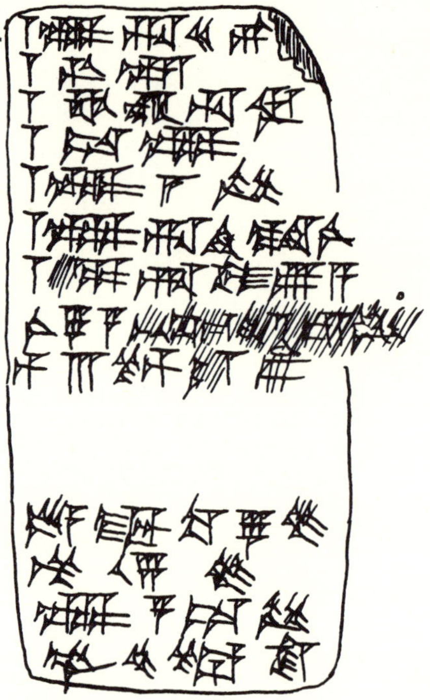

°sic, for 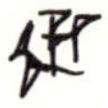

Reverse Uninscribed

145

O.

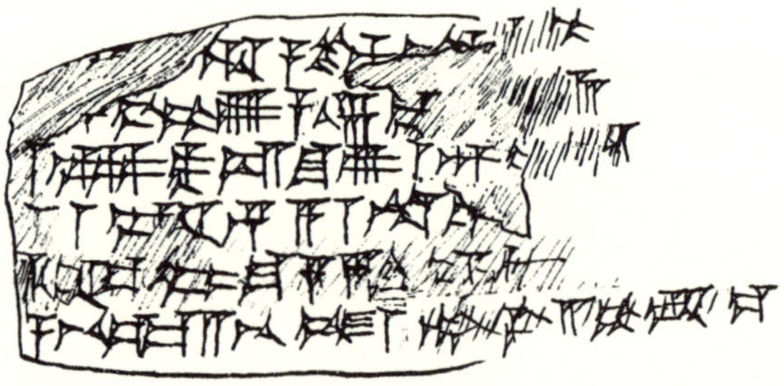

R.

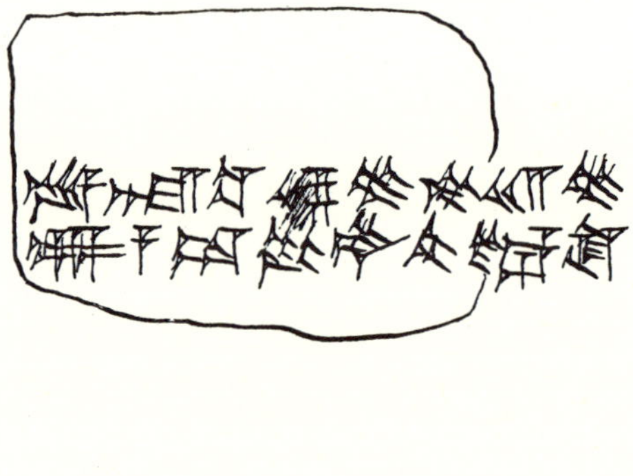

146

O.
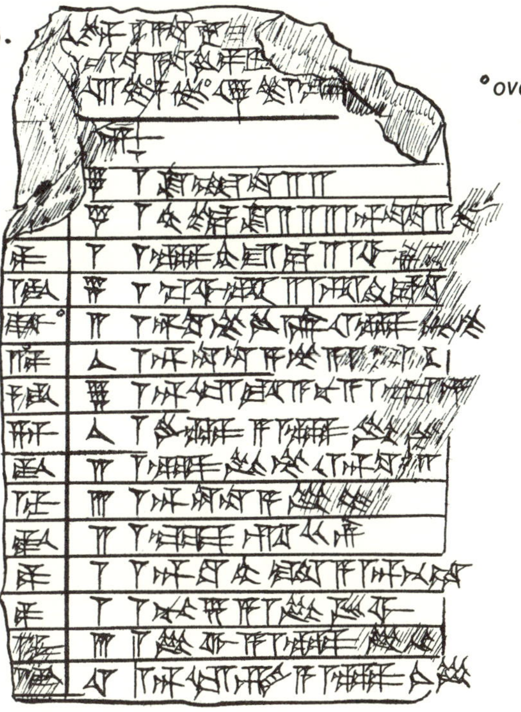

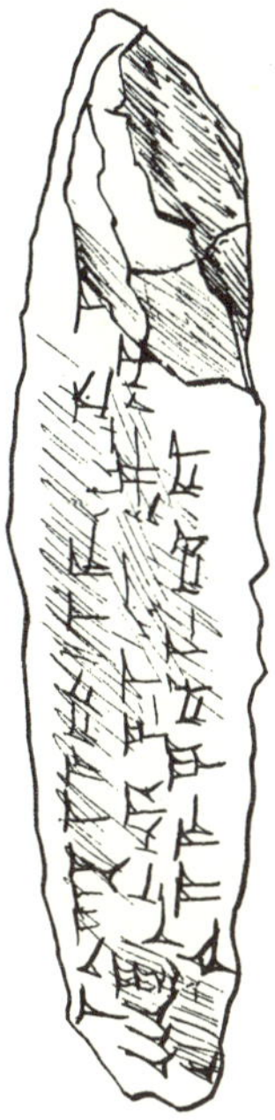
L.E. 45

Lo.E. 20
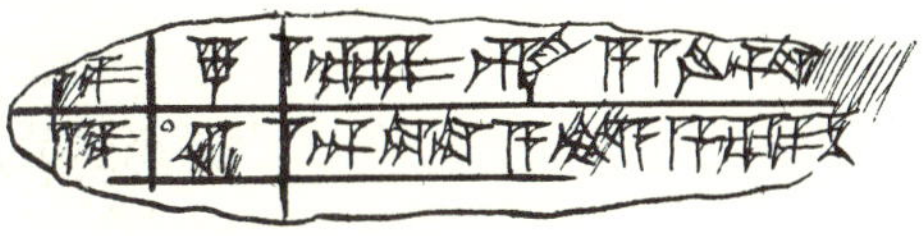

R.
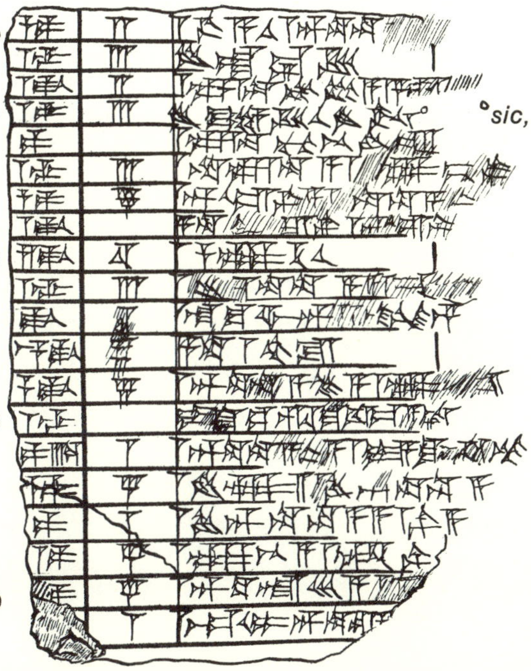

U.E.

147

O.

5

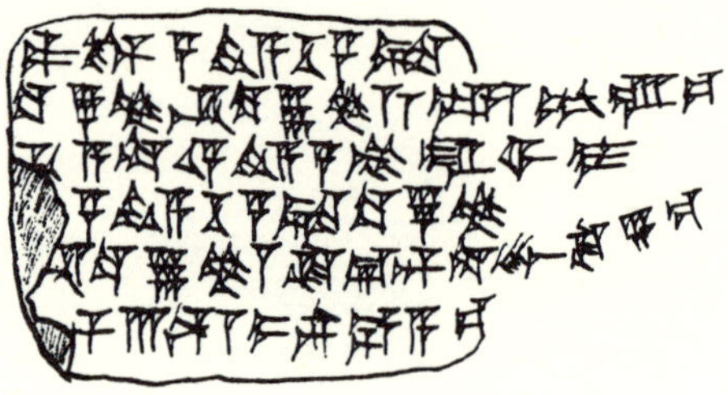

R.

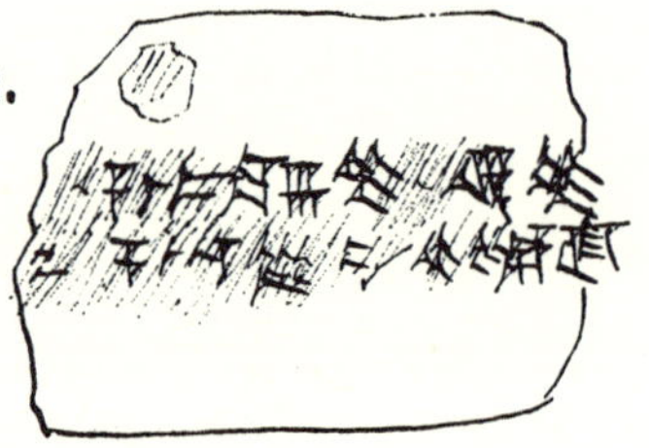

148

O.

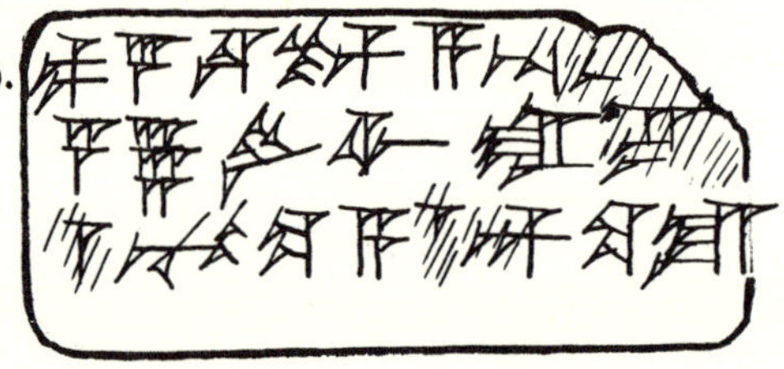

R.

5

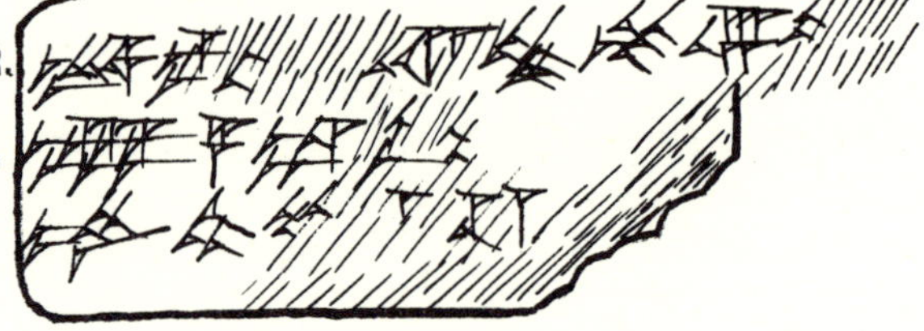

149

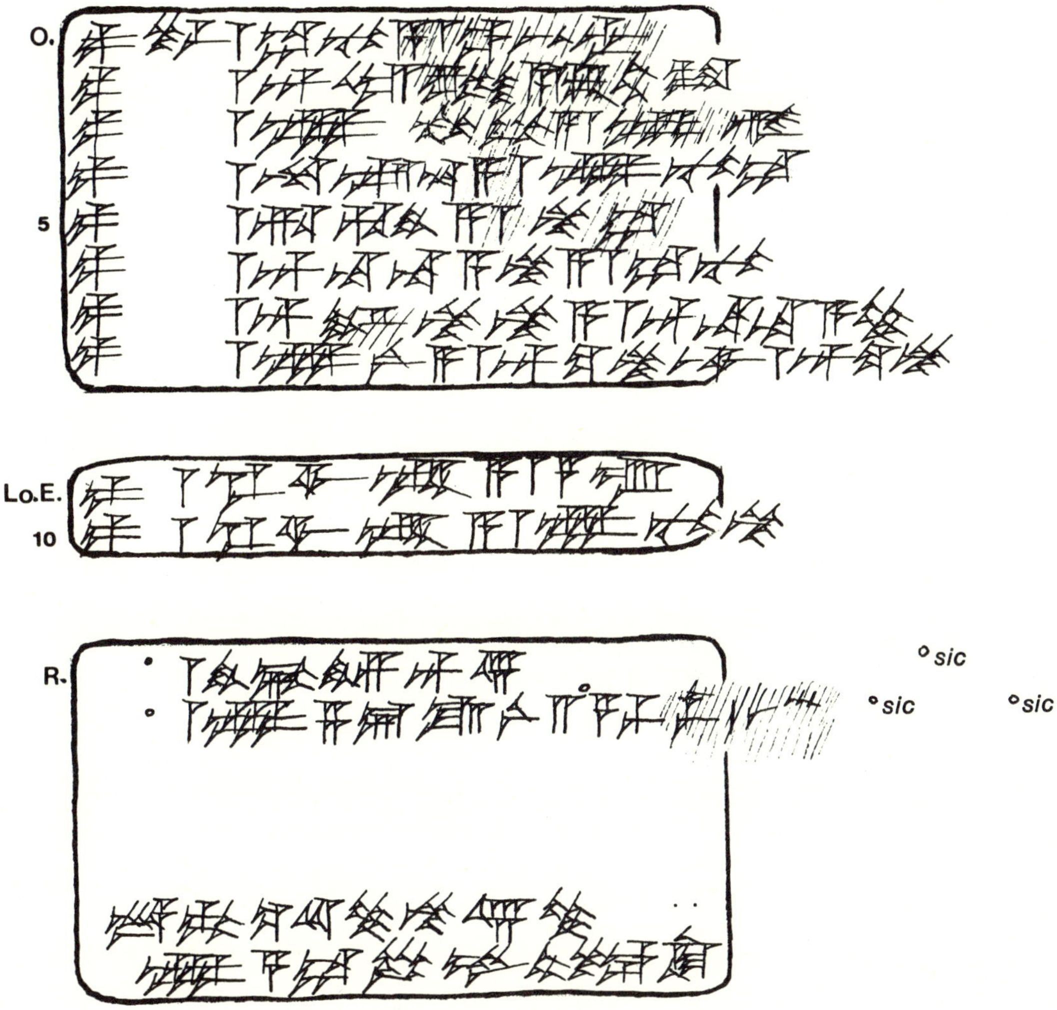

150

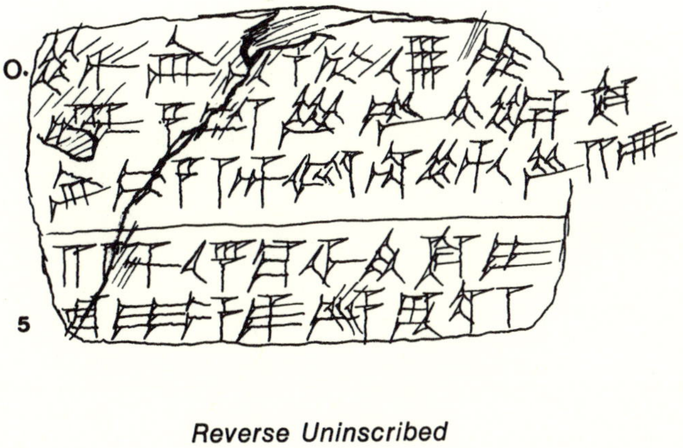

Reverse Uninscribed

151

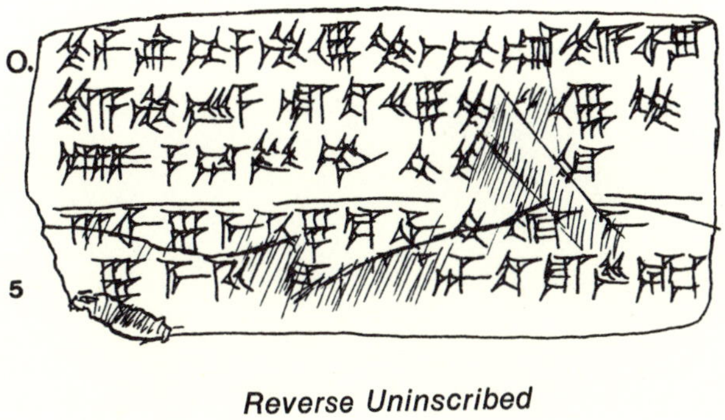

Reverse Uninscribed

152

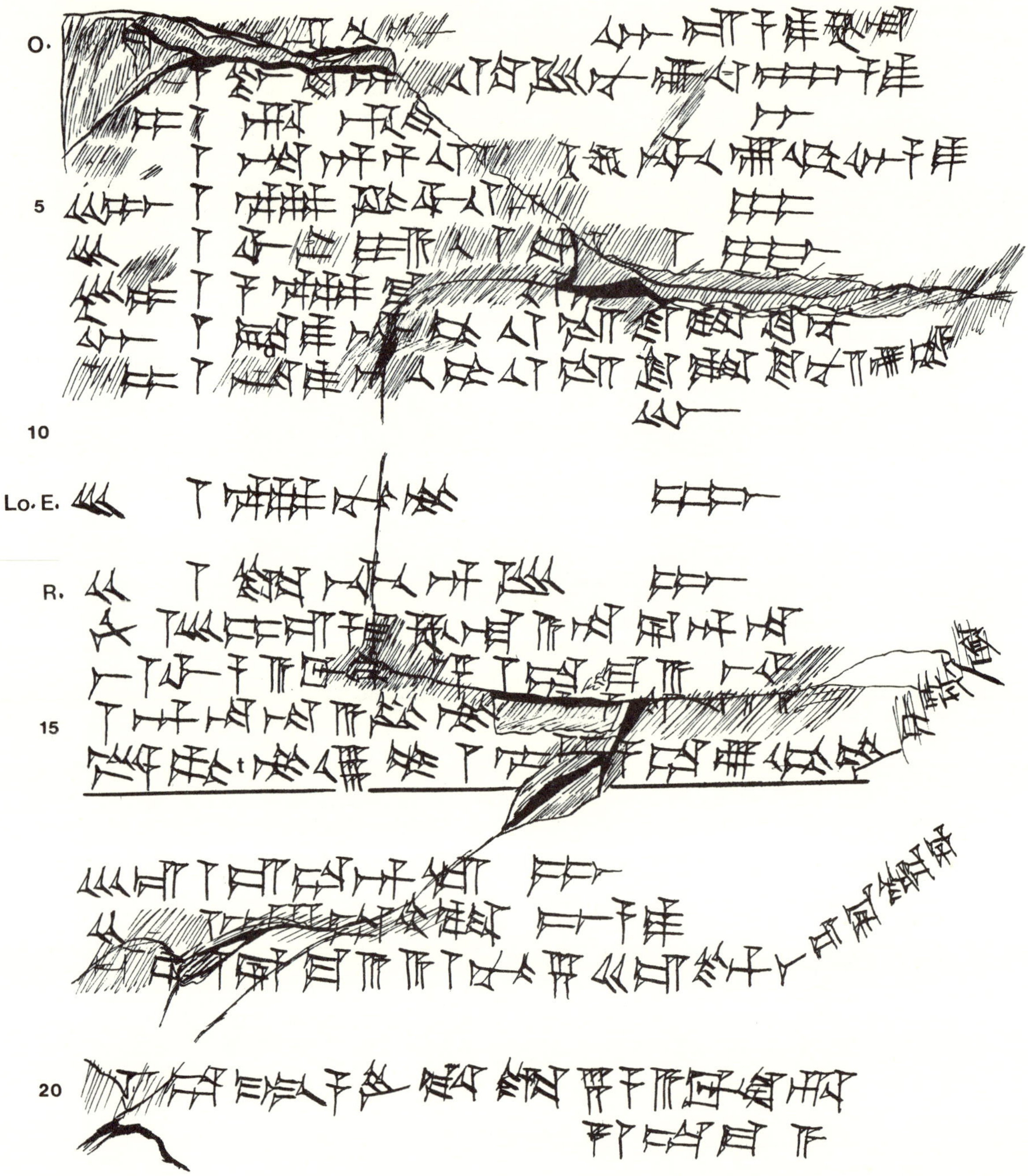

PLATE LXXXI

153

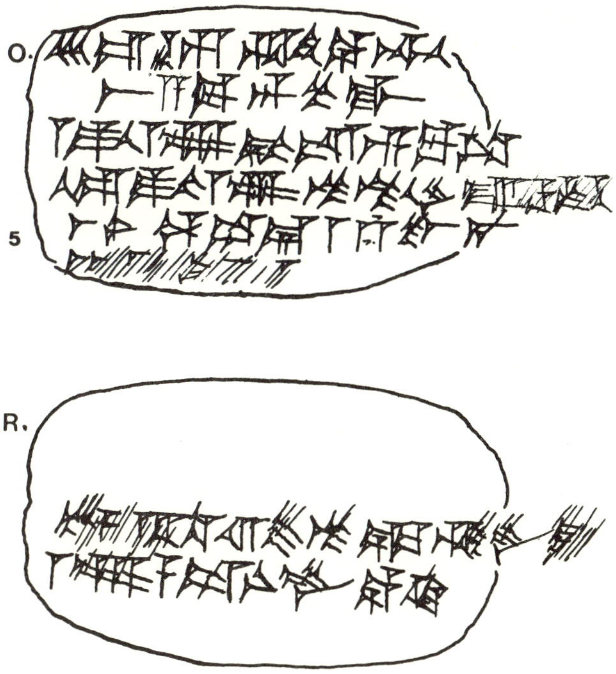

154

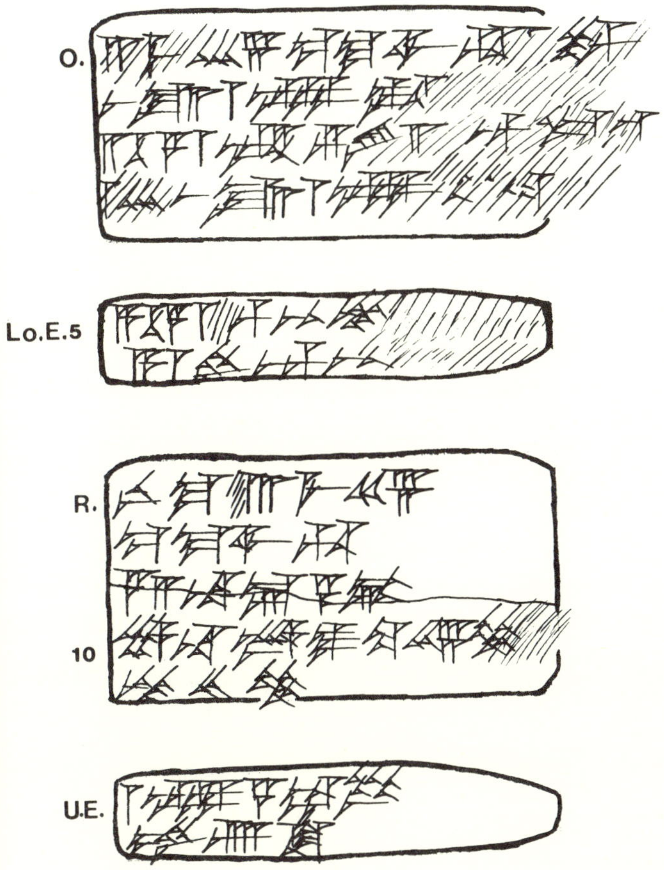

155

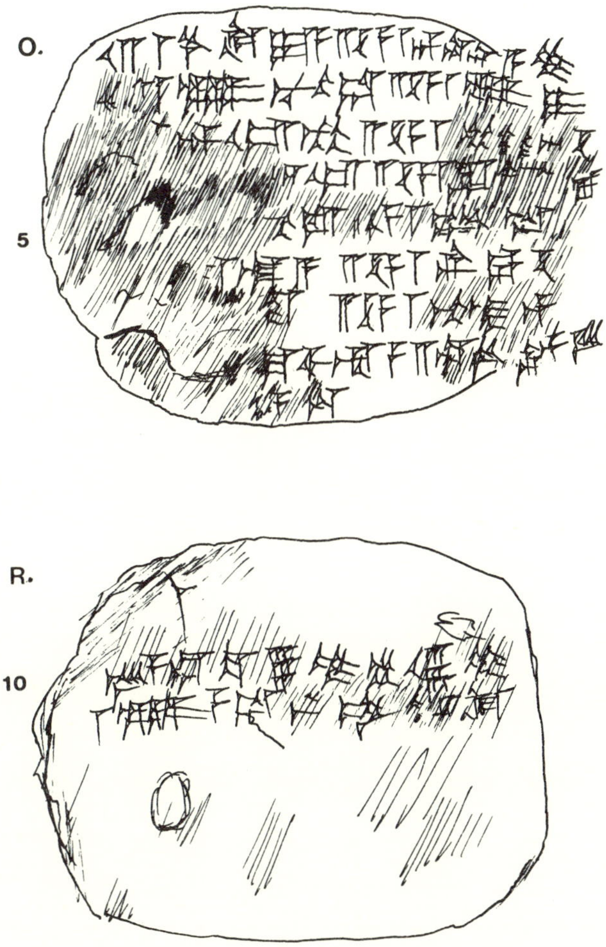

156

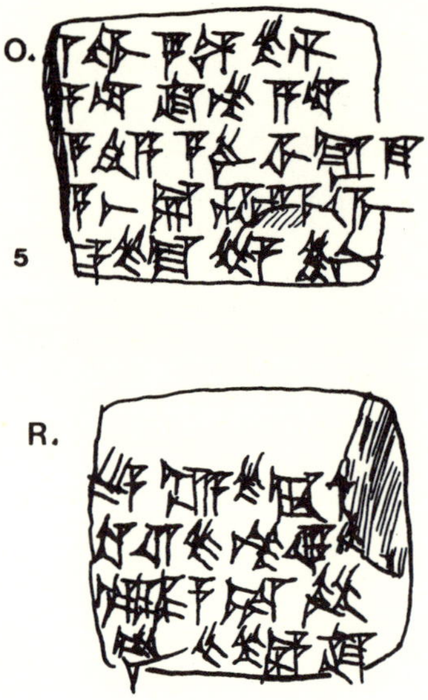

157

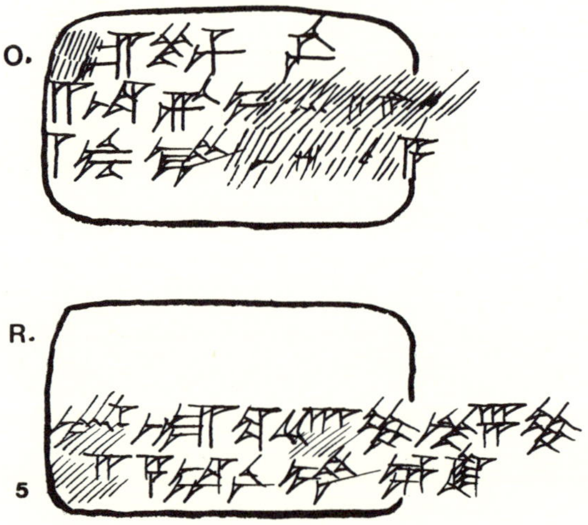

158

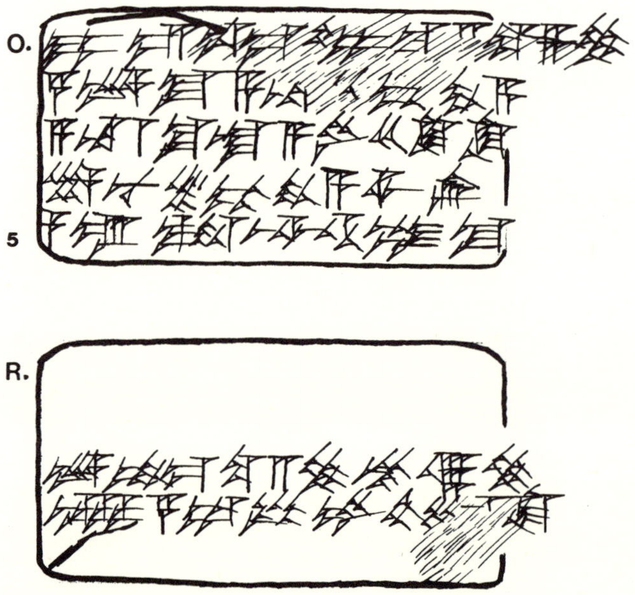

159

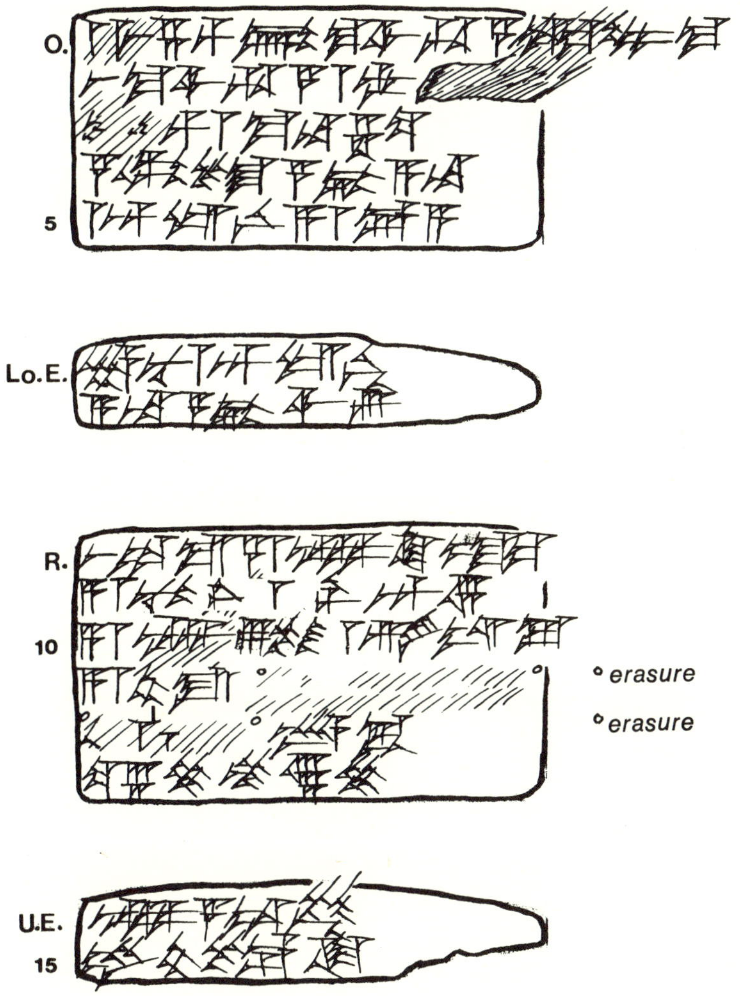

160

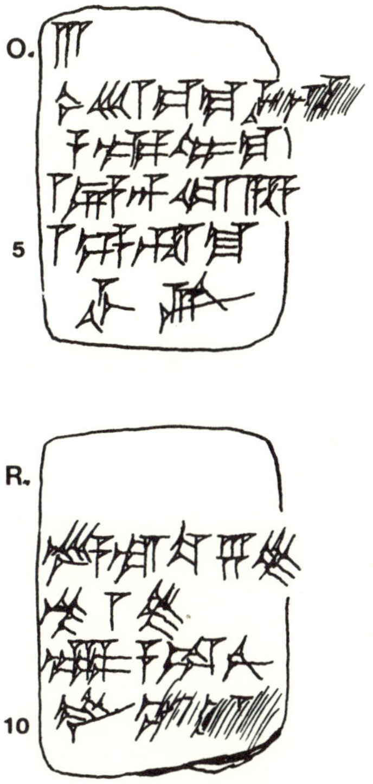

161

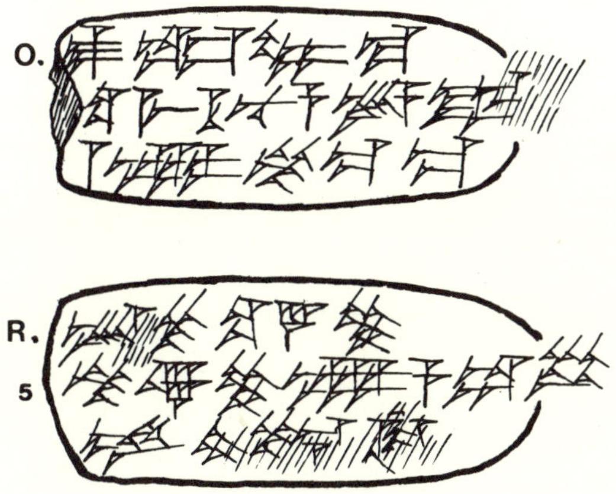

162

O.
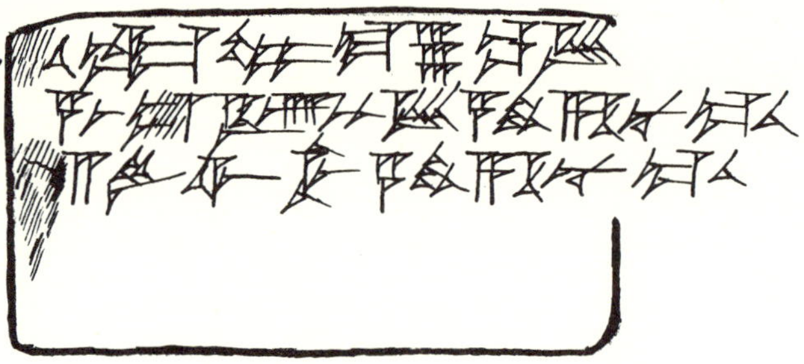

R.
5
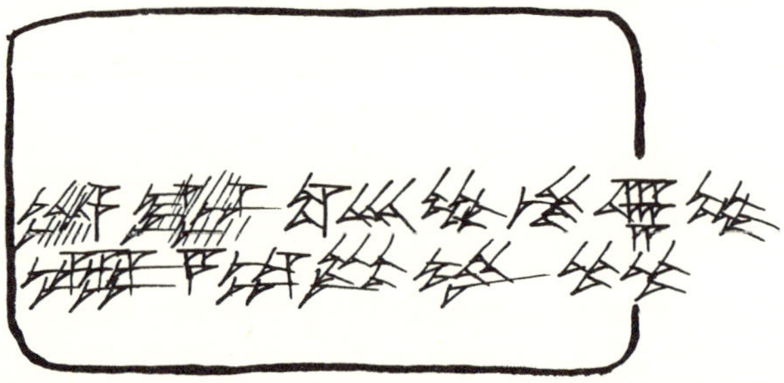

164

O.
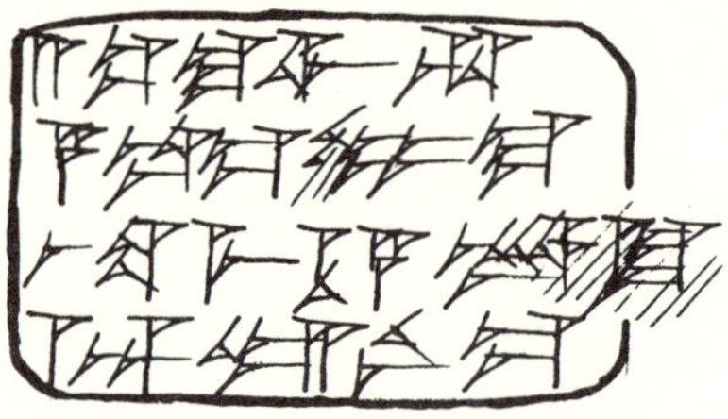

Lo.E.5

R.
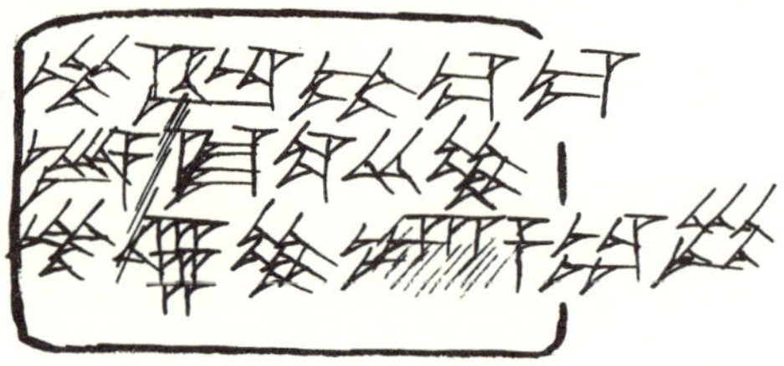

U.E.

163

O.
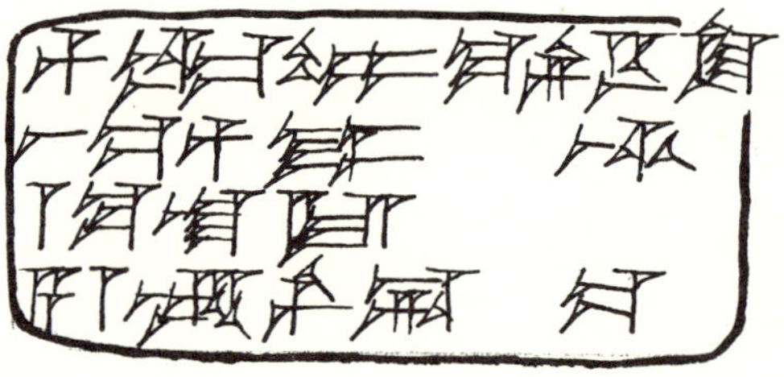

R.5
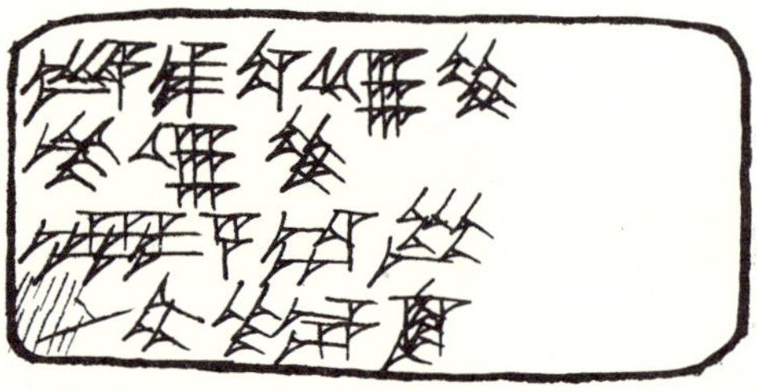

165

O.

Lo.E.5

R.

166

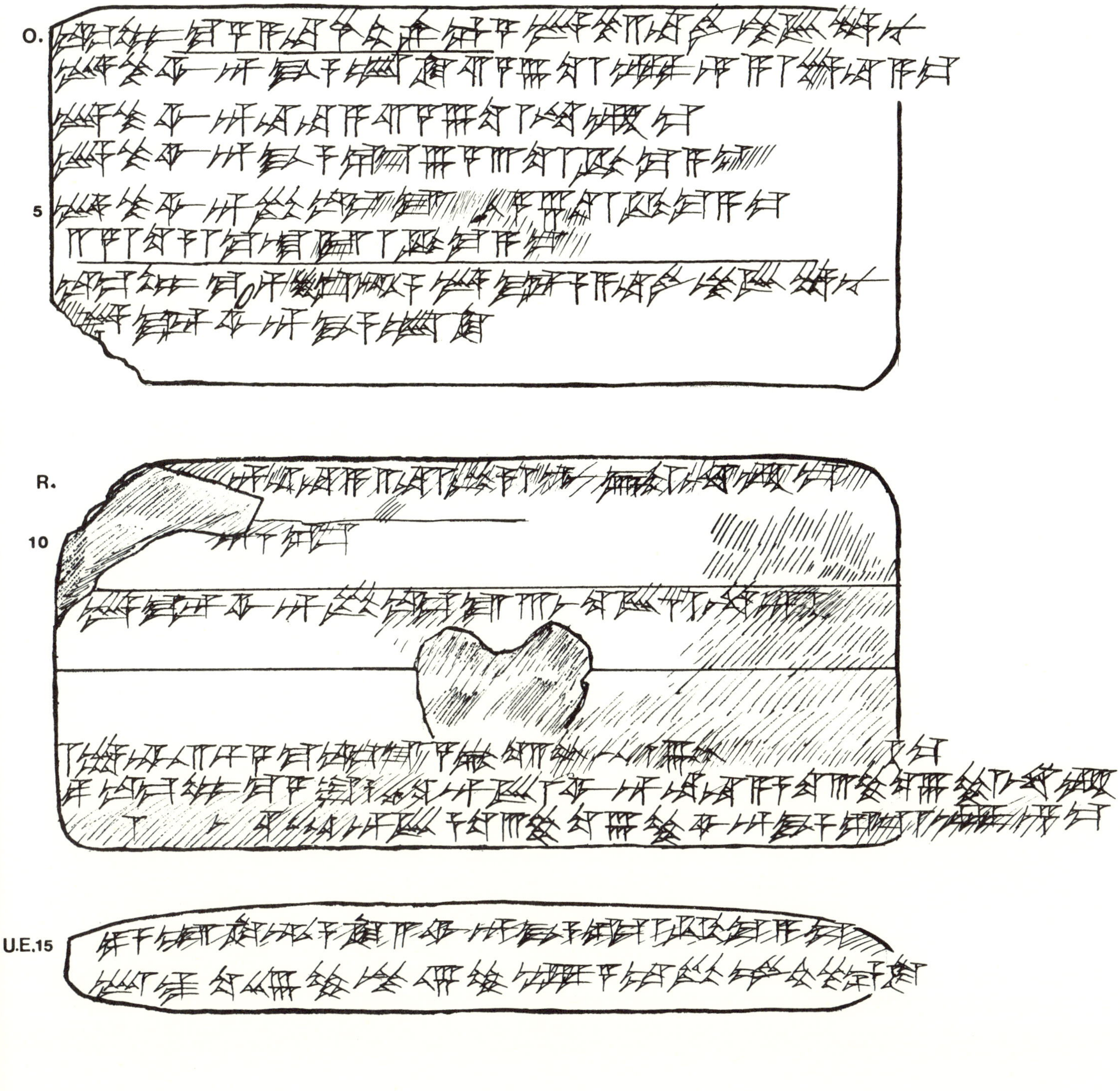

167

O.

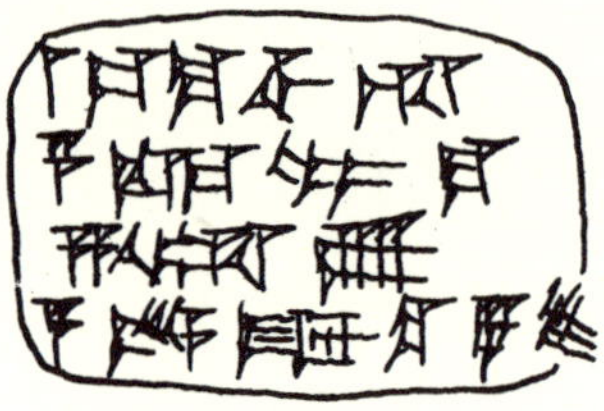

Lo.E. 5

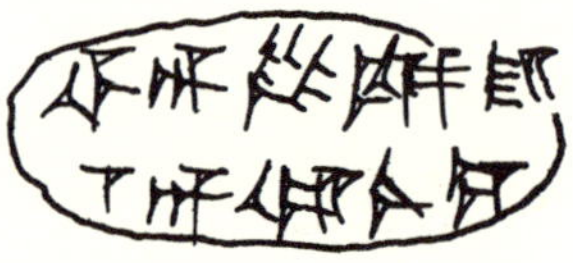

R.

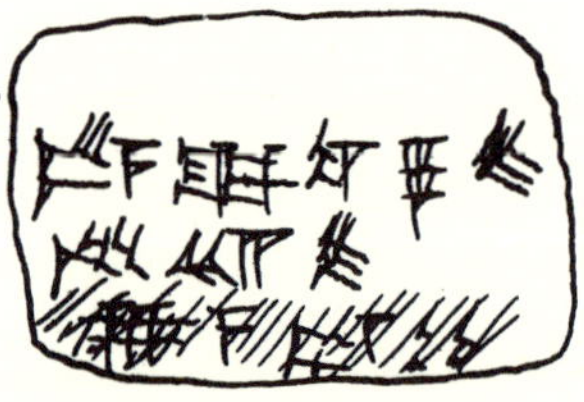

U.E. 10

168

O.

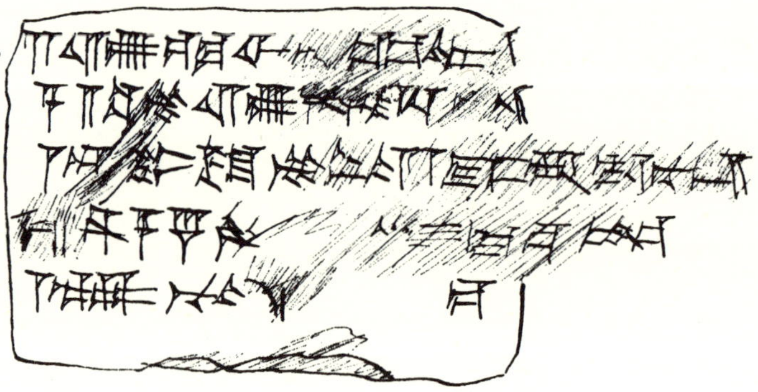

R.

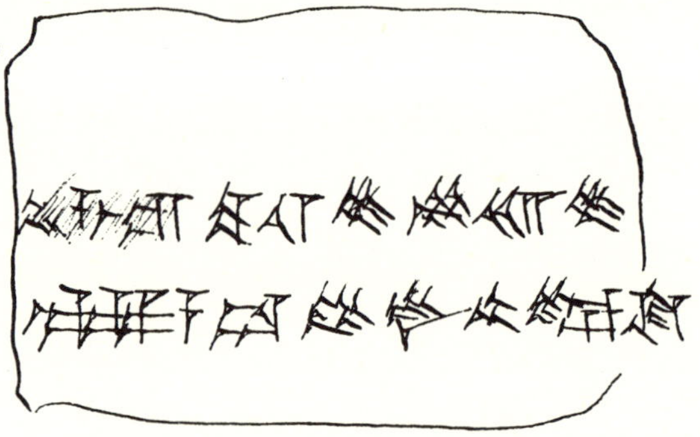

170

O.

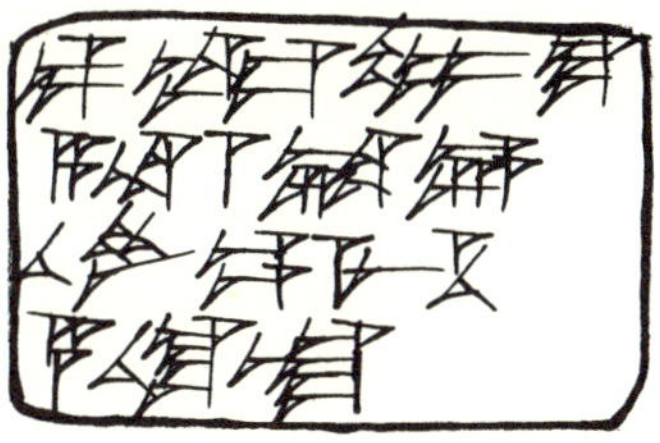

Lo.E.

R.

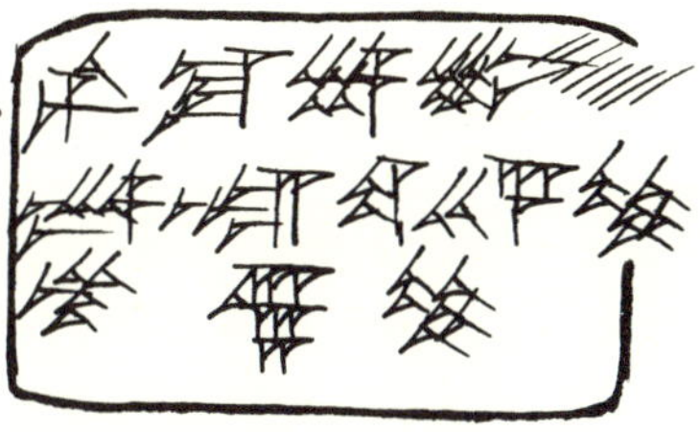

U.E.

169

O.

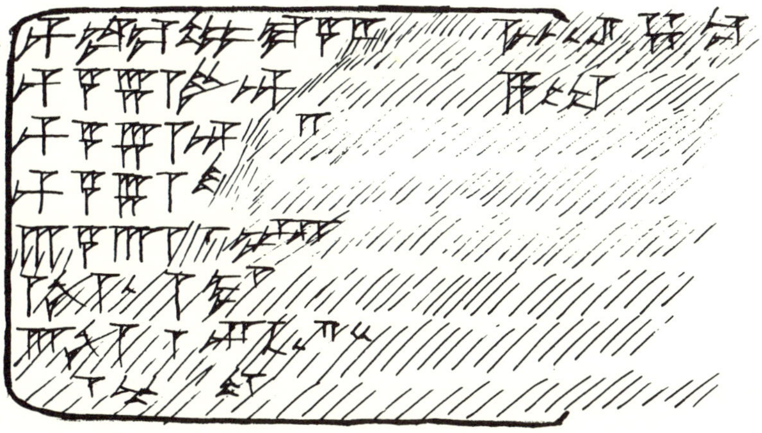

R.

171

O.

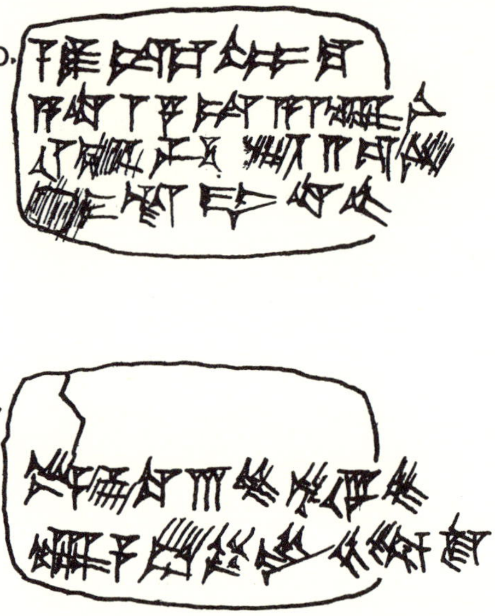

R.

172

U.E.

O.

R.

173

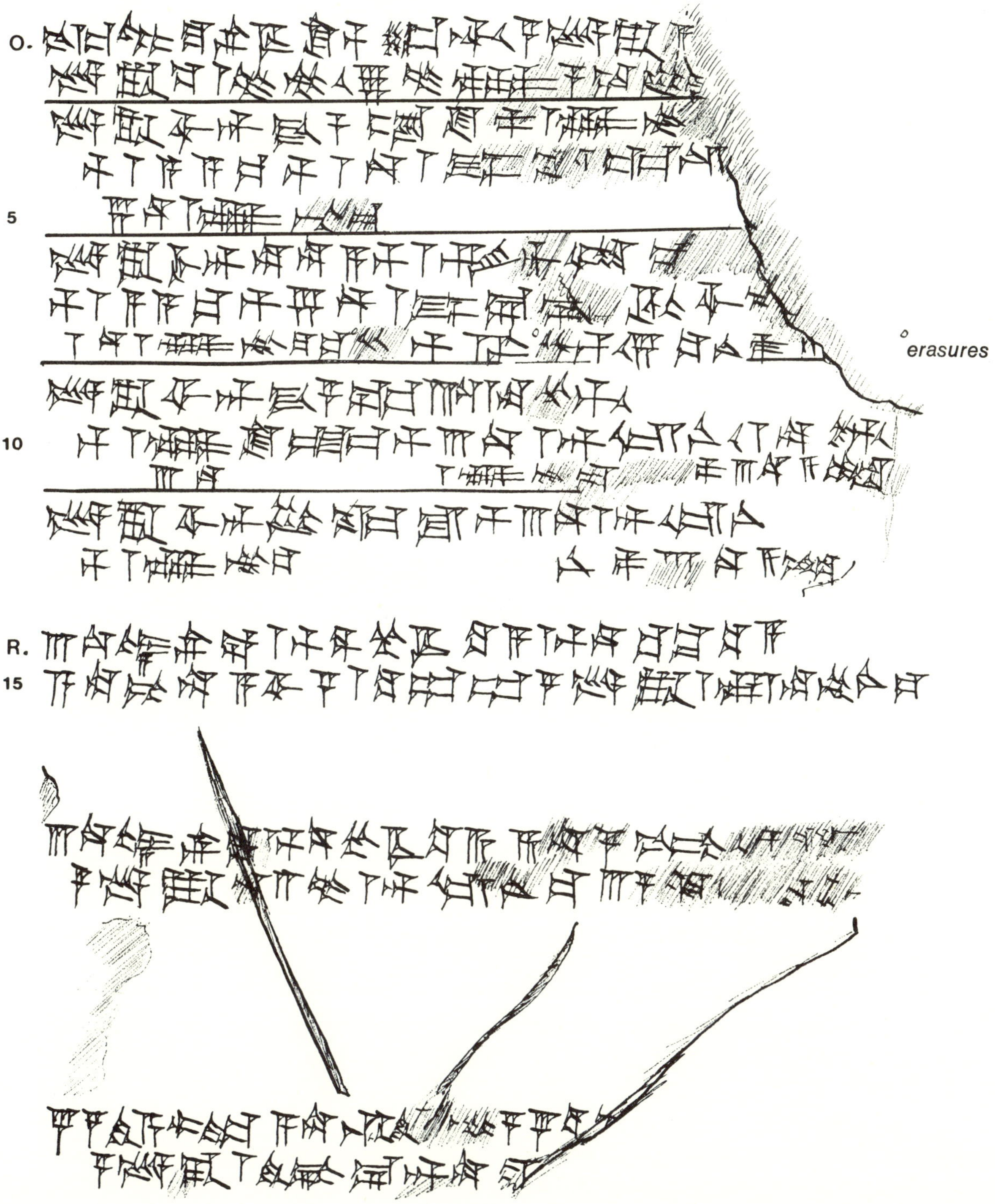

174

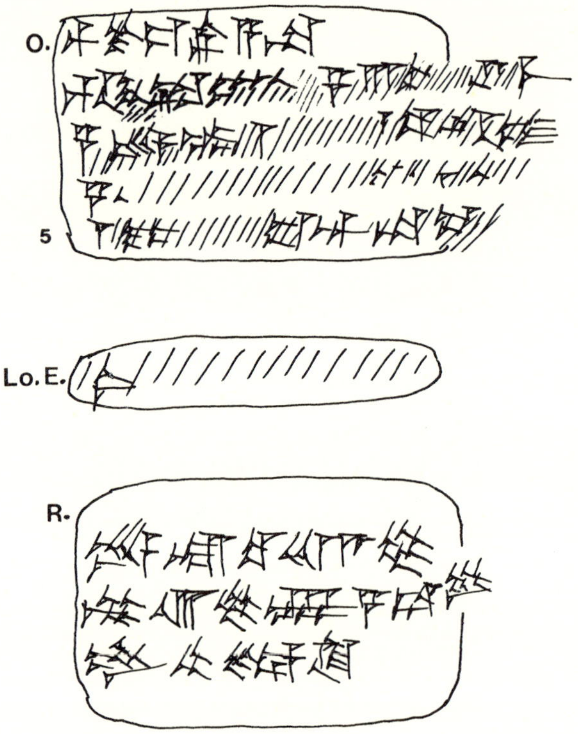

175

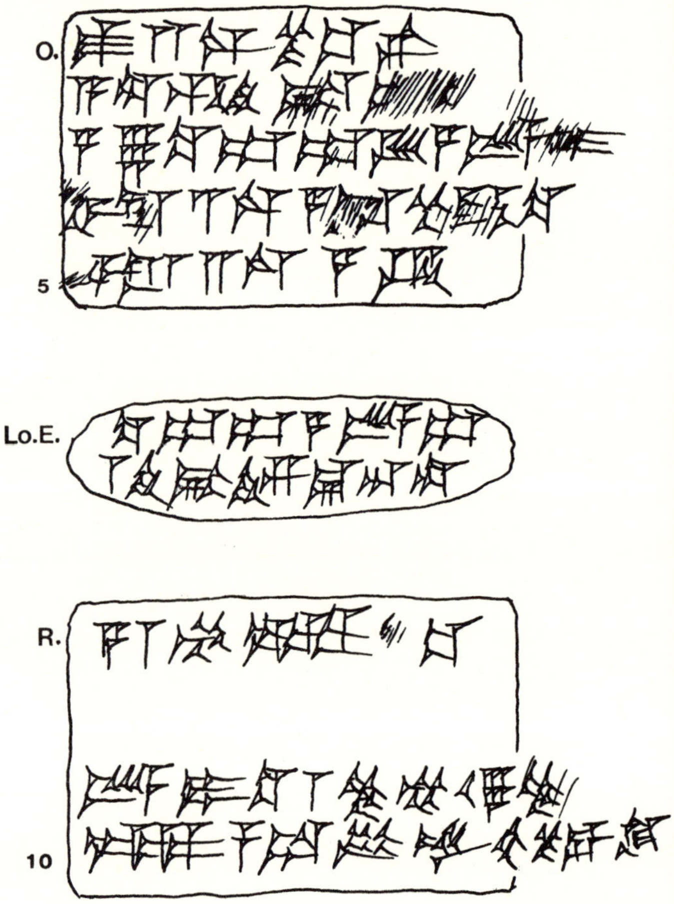

176

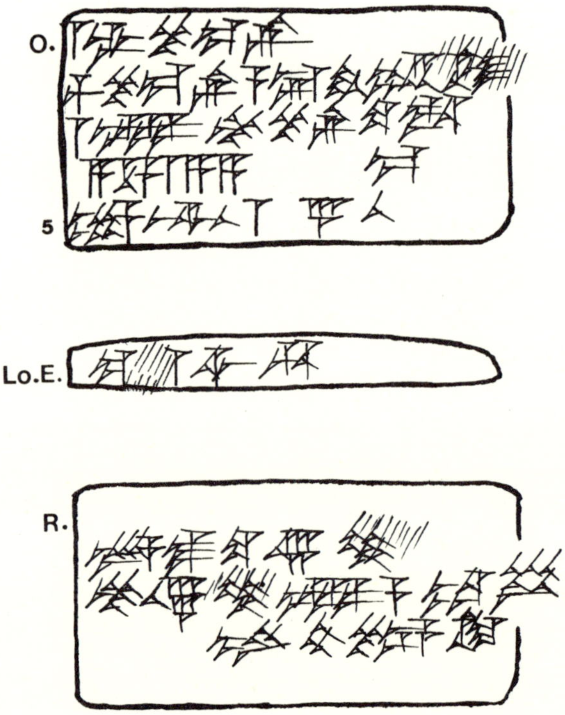

177

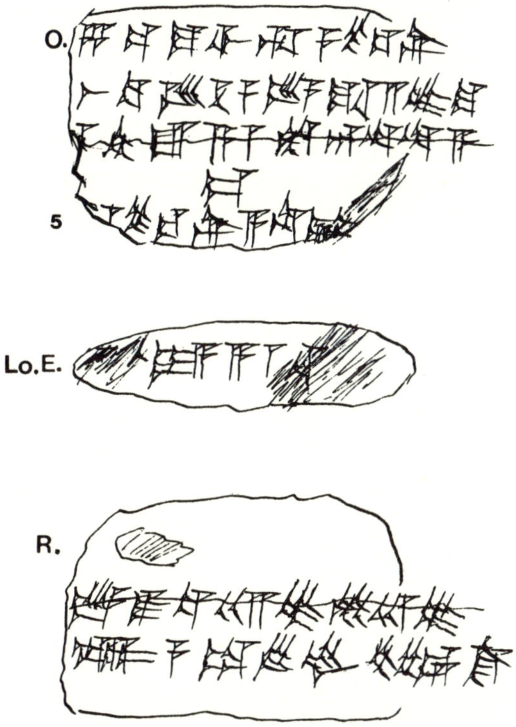

178

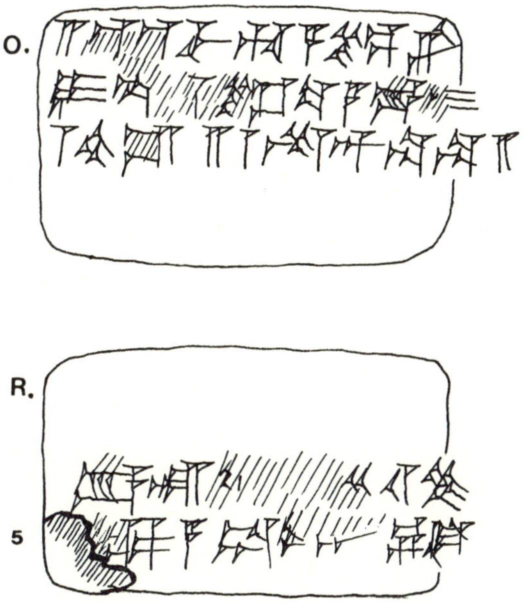

179

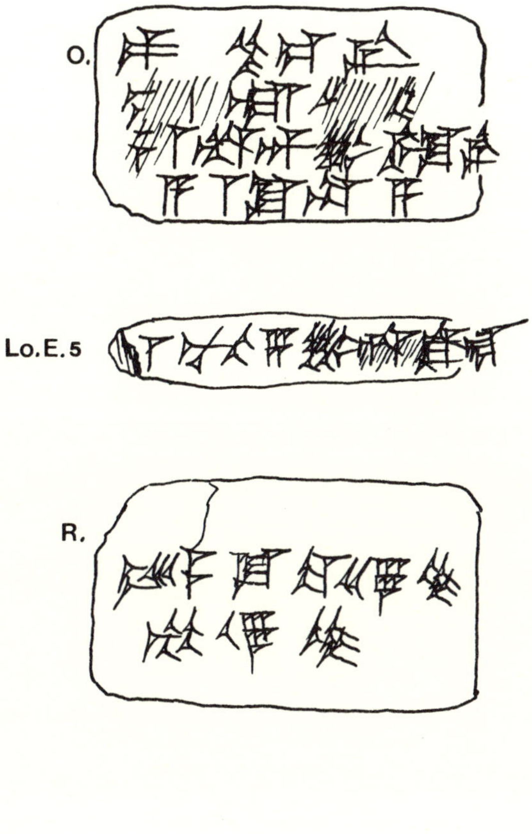

180

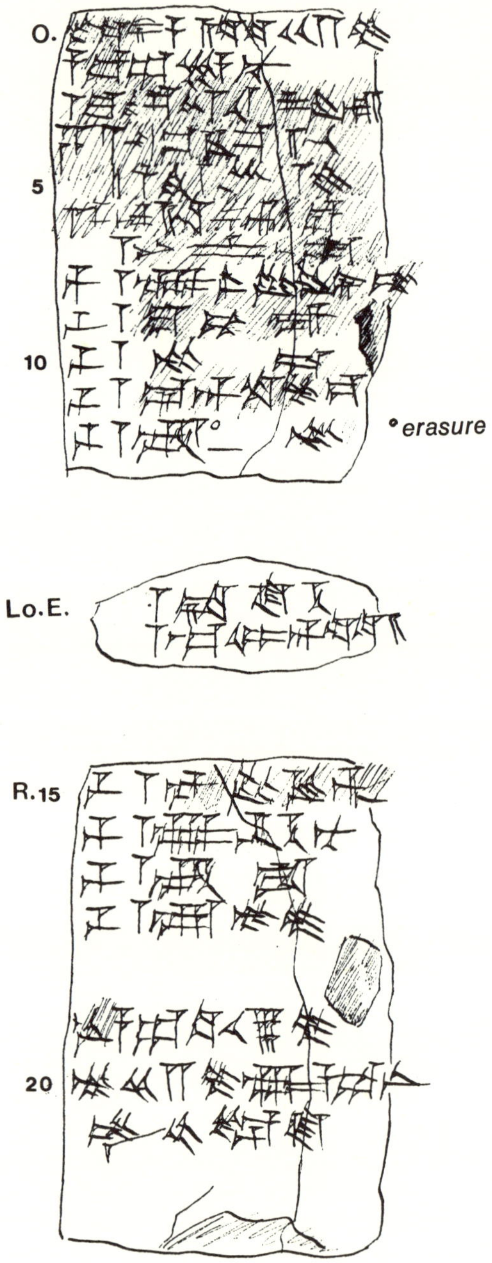

181

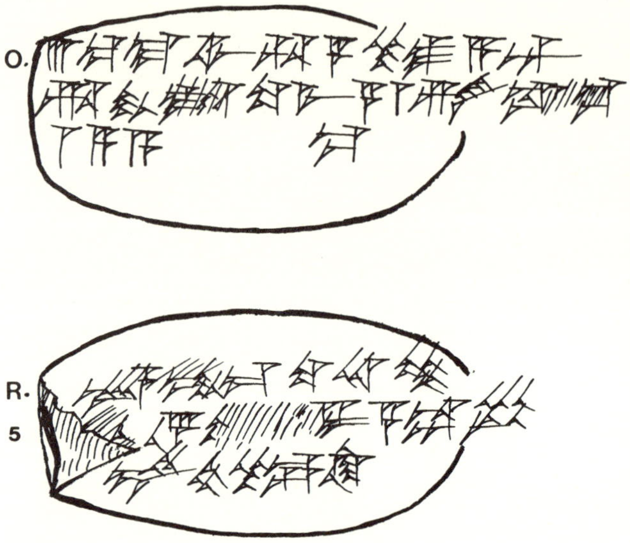

182

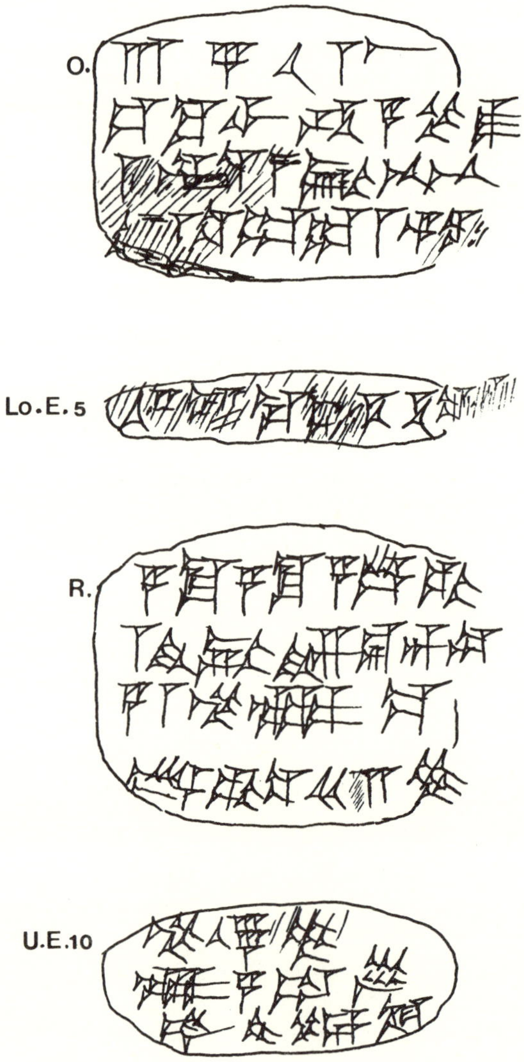

183

O.

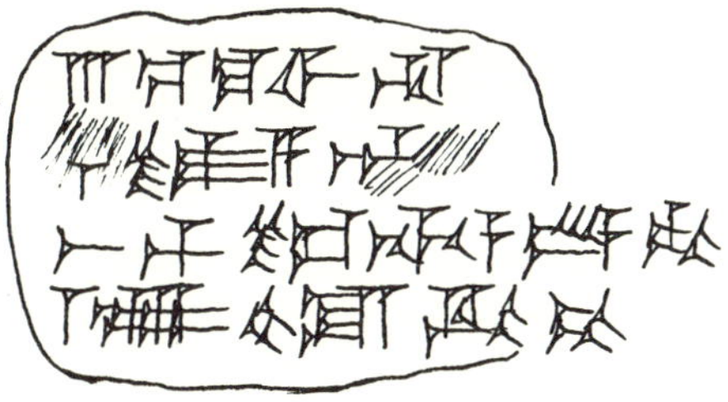

Lo.E. 5

R.

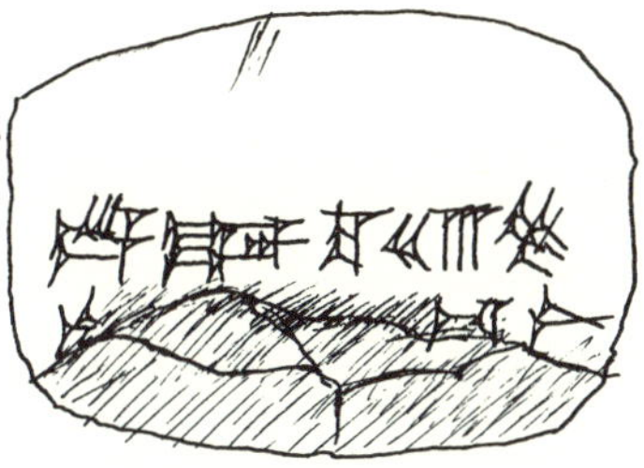

184

O.

5

R.

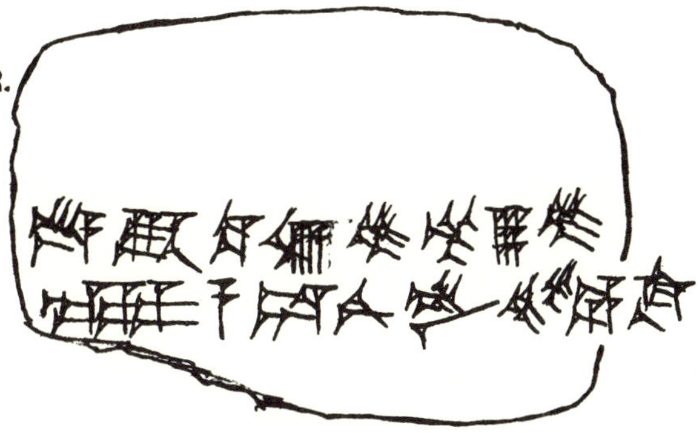

185

O.

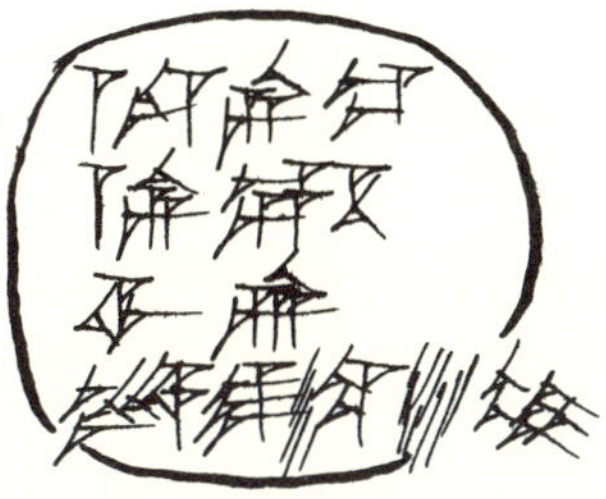

Lo.E.5

R.

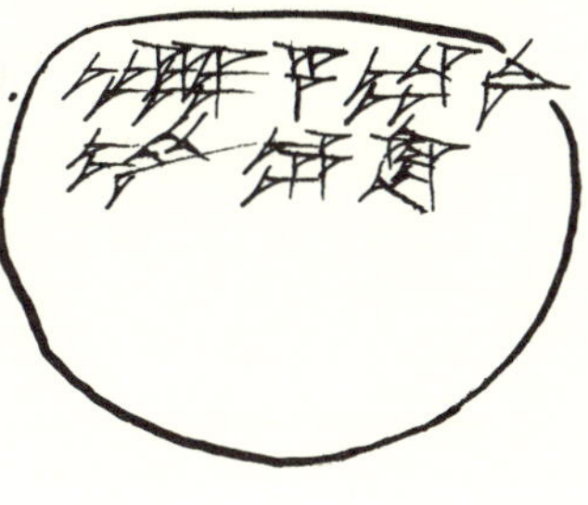

186

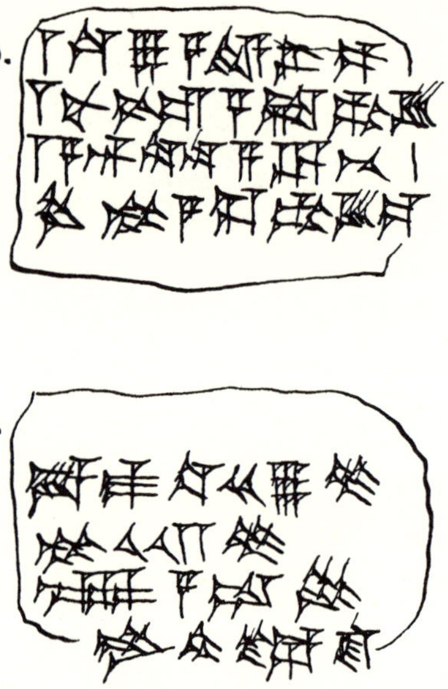

187

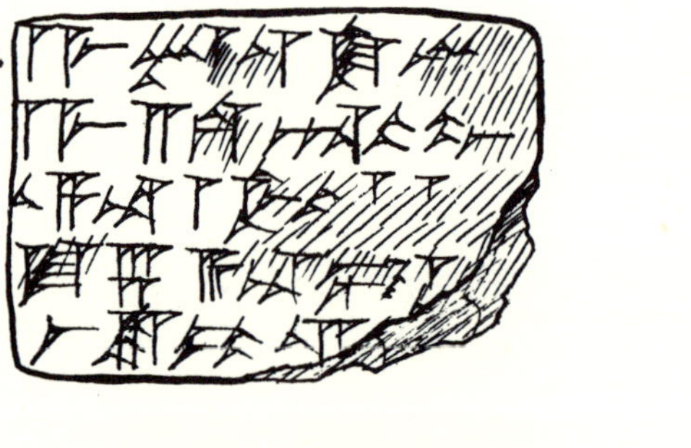

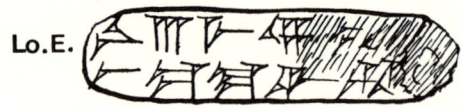

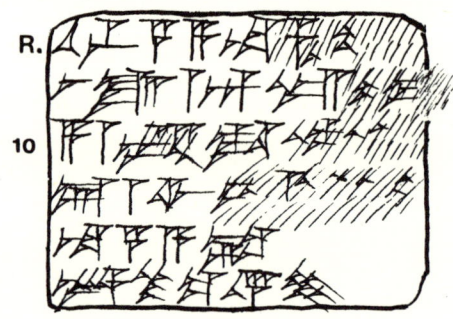

188

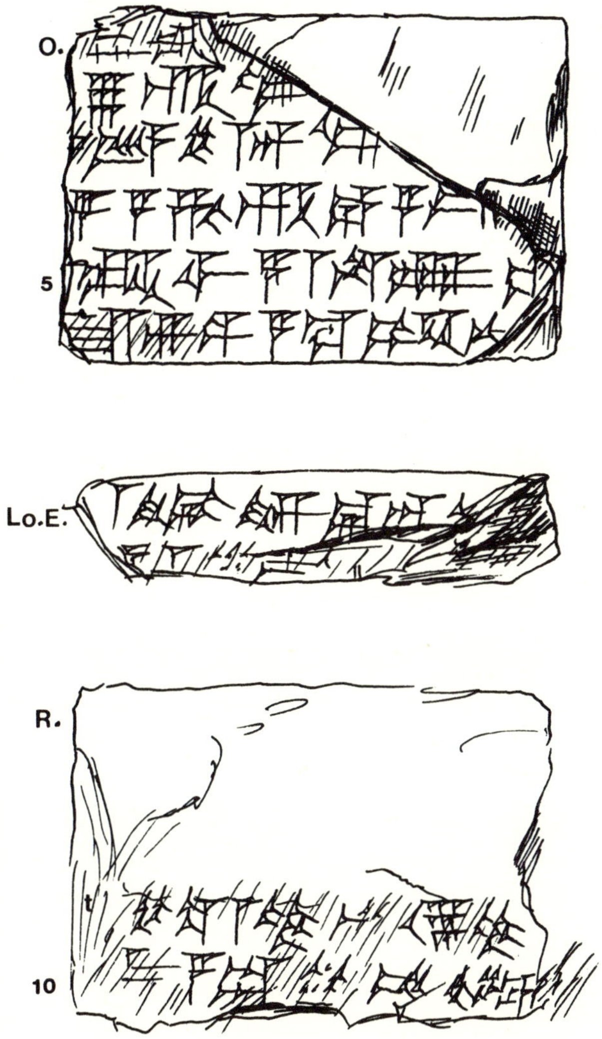

189

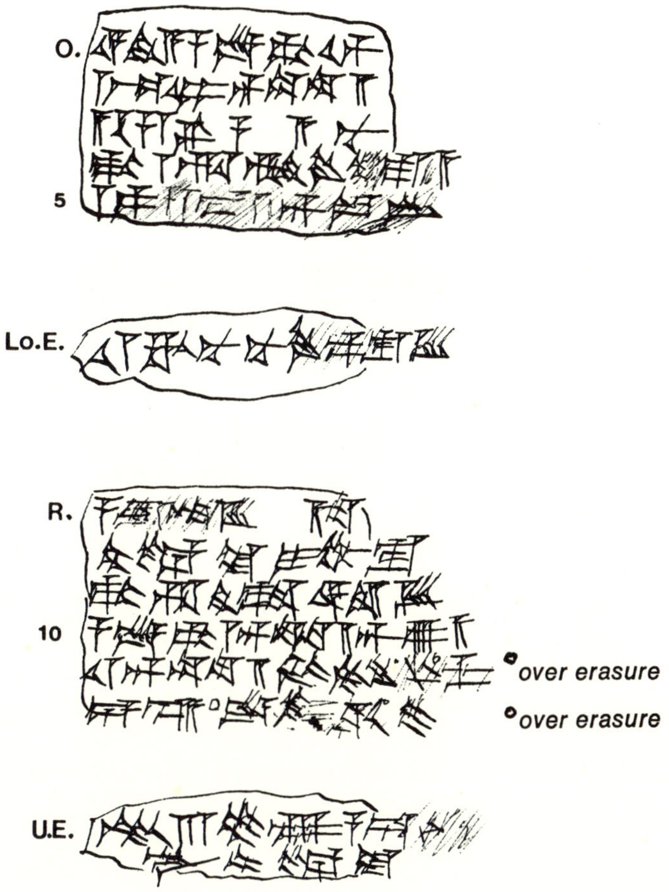

190

O.
R.

191

O.
R.

192

O.
R.

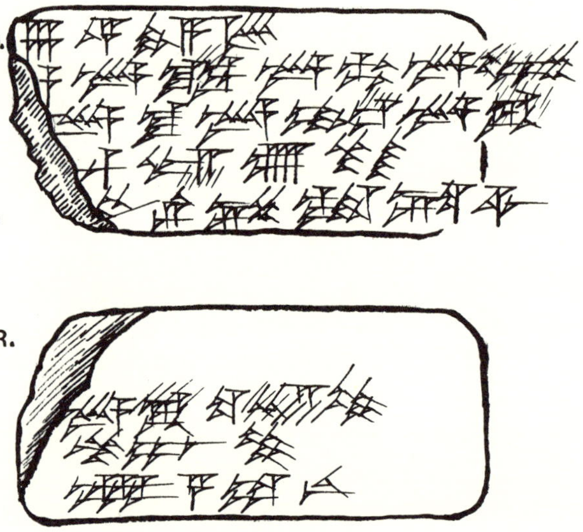

193

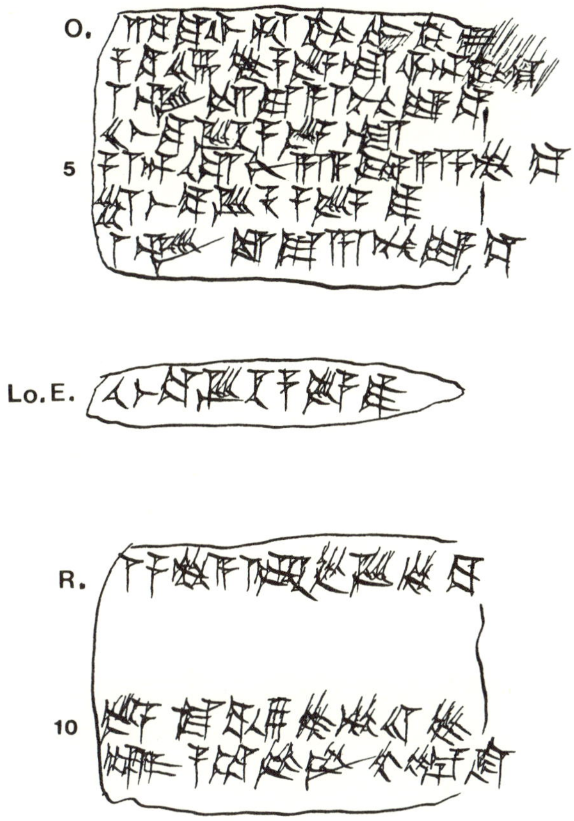

194

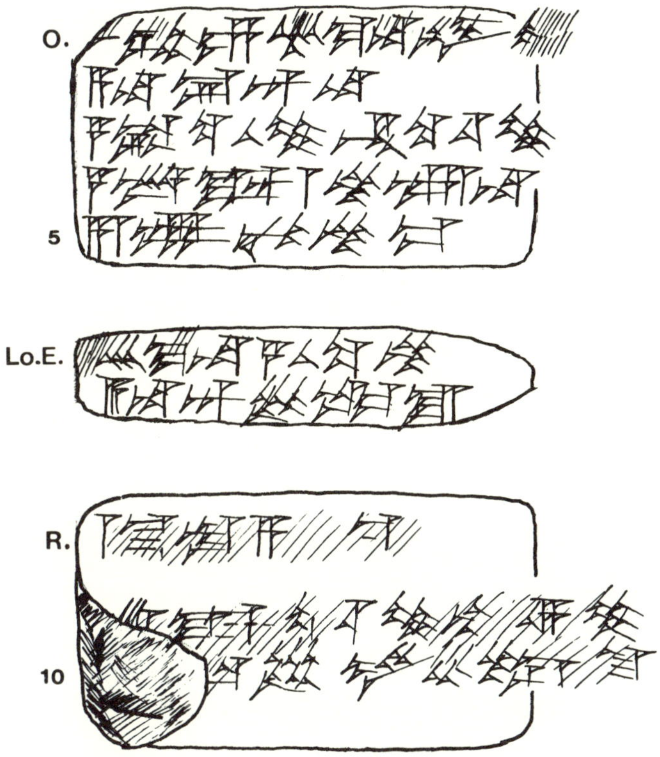

195

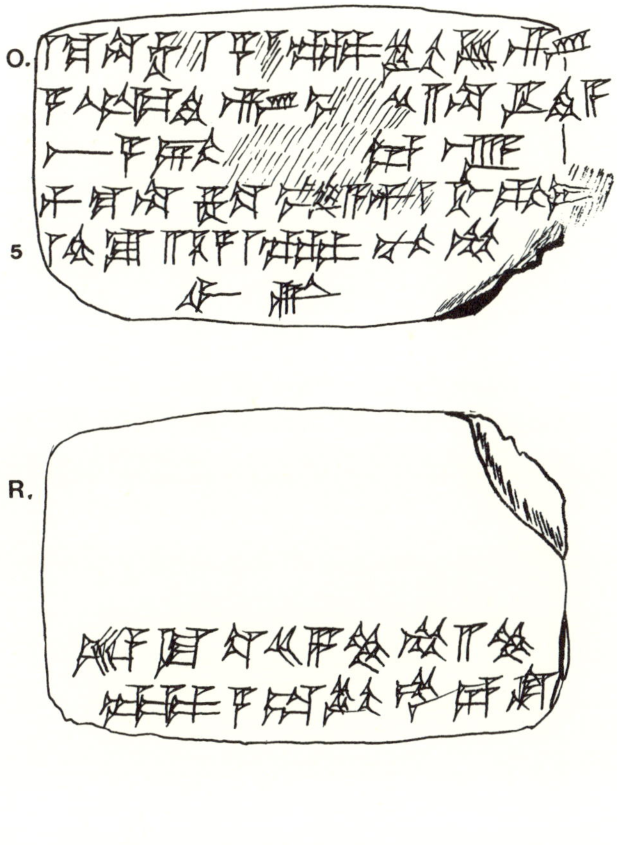

196

O. 5

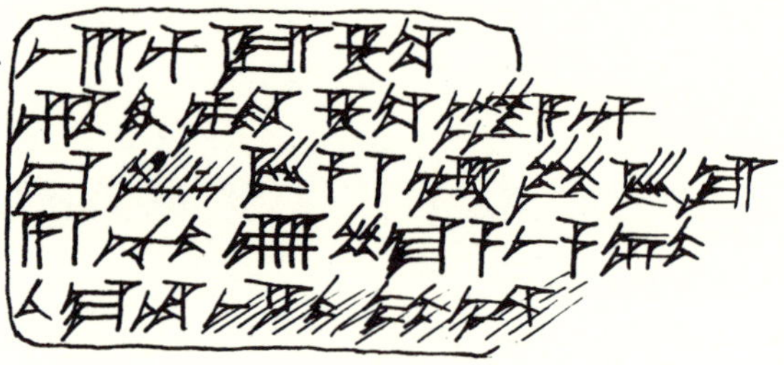

Lo.E.

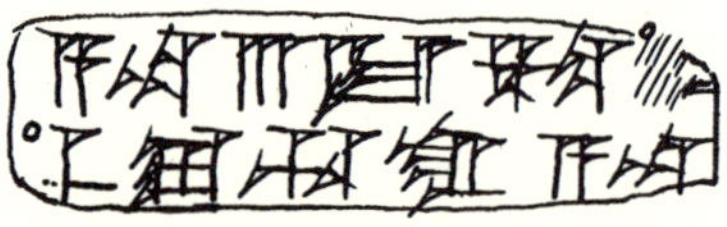

erasure

° *over a horizontal wedge*

R. 10

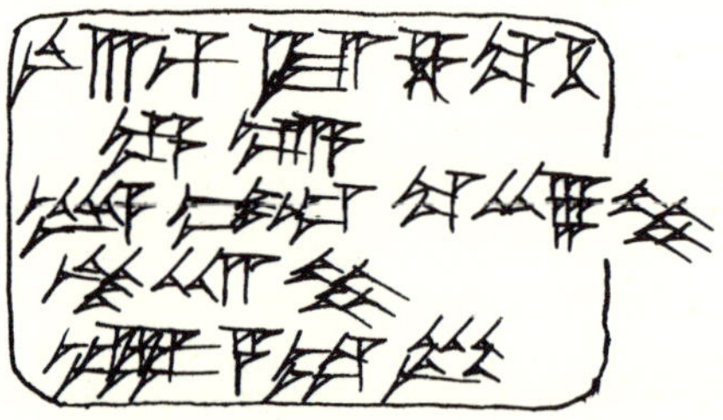

U.E.

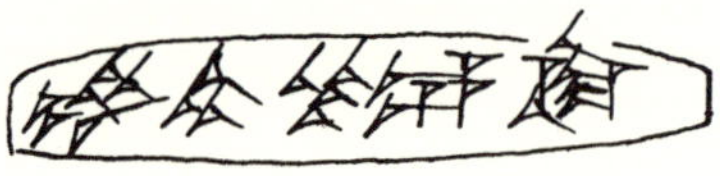

197

O. 5

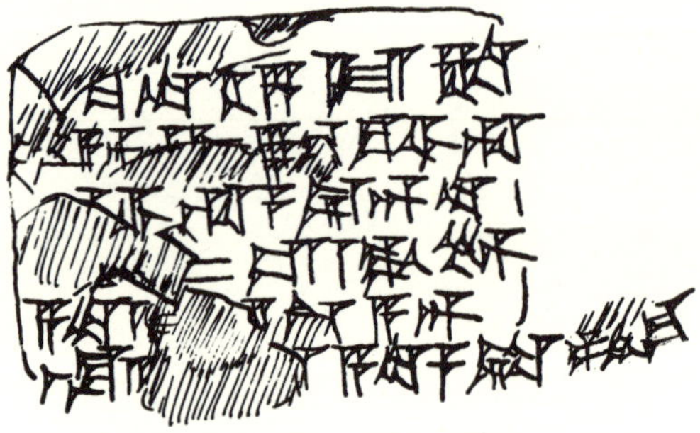

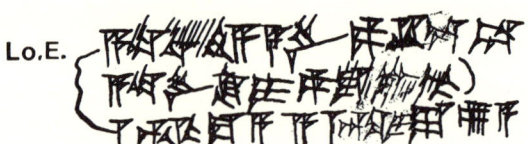

Lo.E.

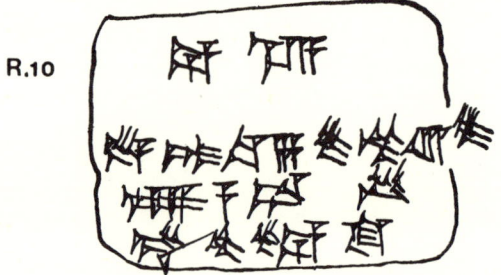

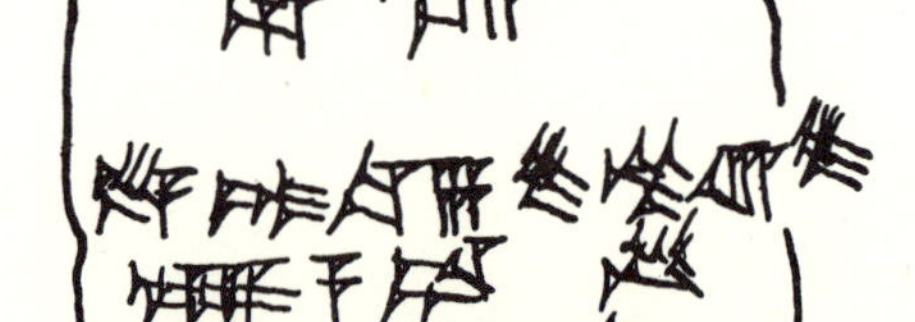

R.10

198

O.

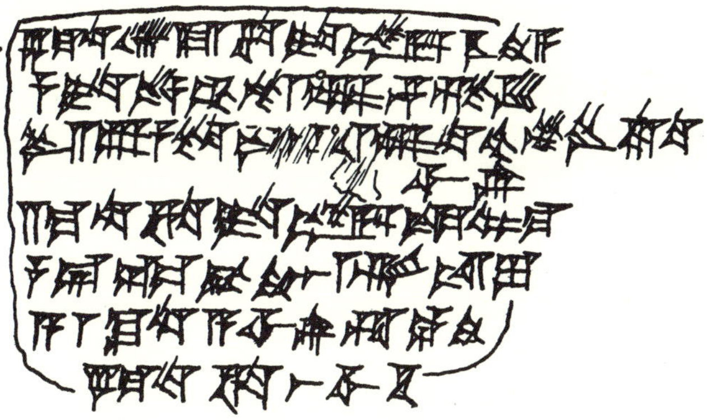

over erasure

R.

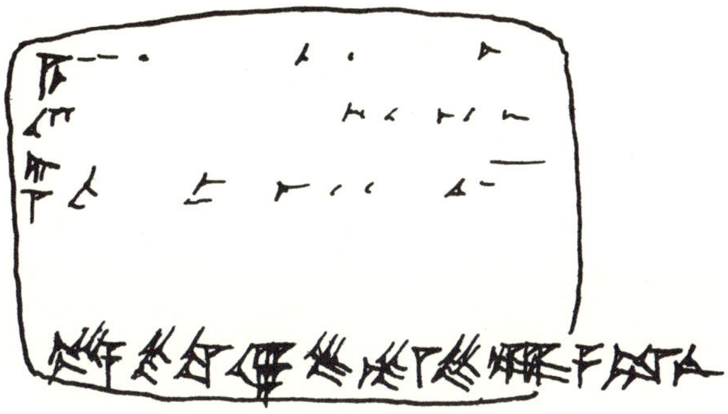

erasure

erasure

erasure

erasure

U.E.

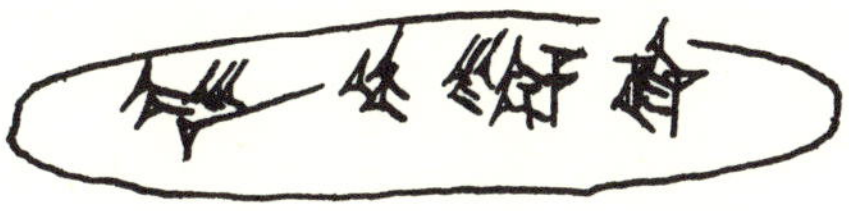

199

O.

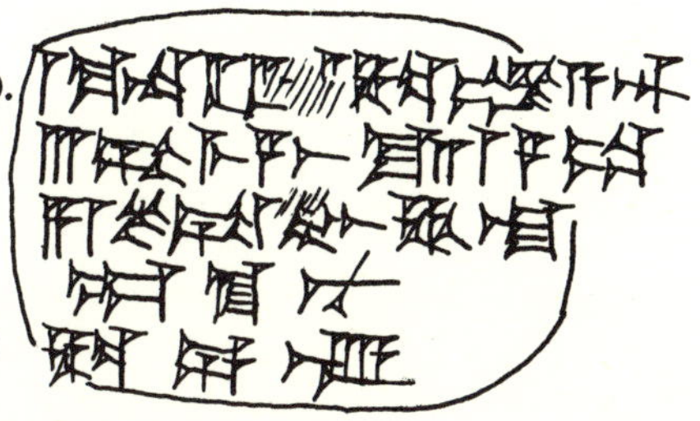

R.

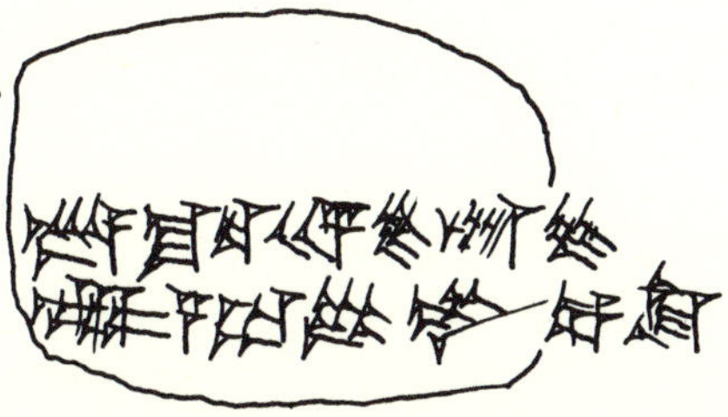

PLATE C

200

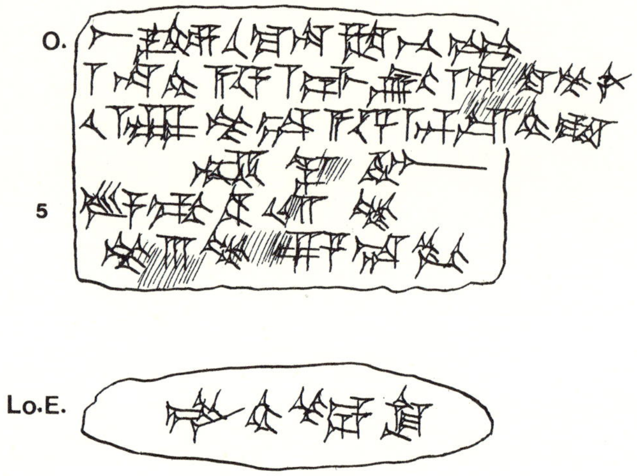

Reverse Uninscribed

201

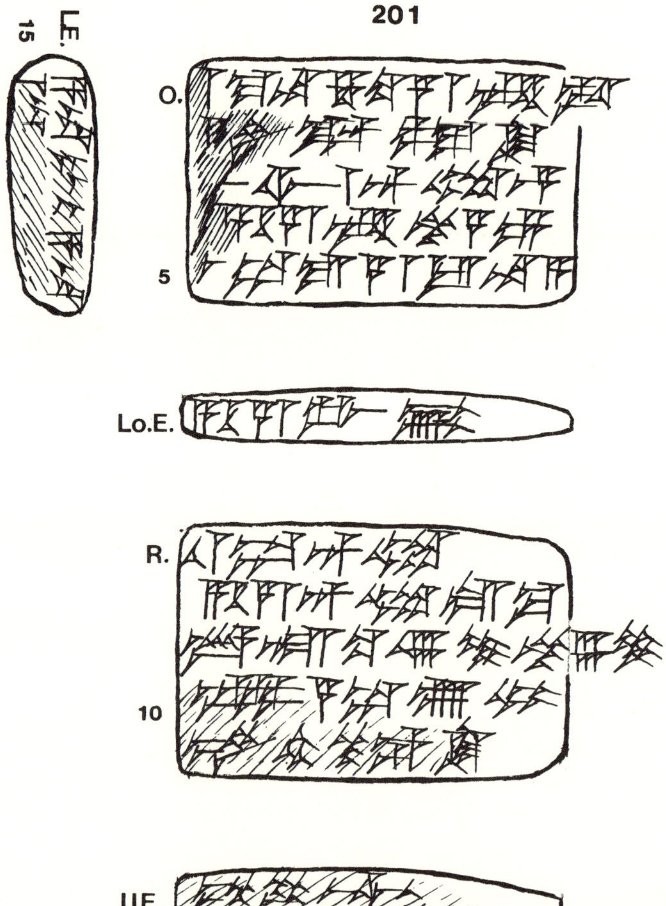

202

O.

lines 4, 5 broken away

R.
6'

U.E.

203

O.

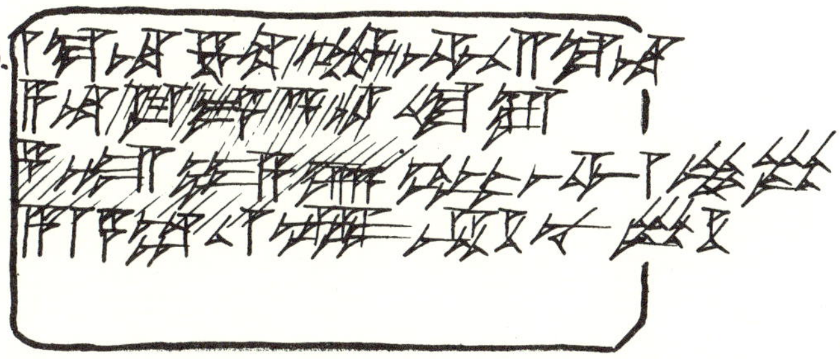

R.
5

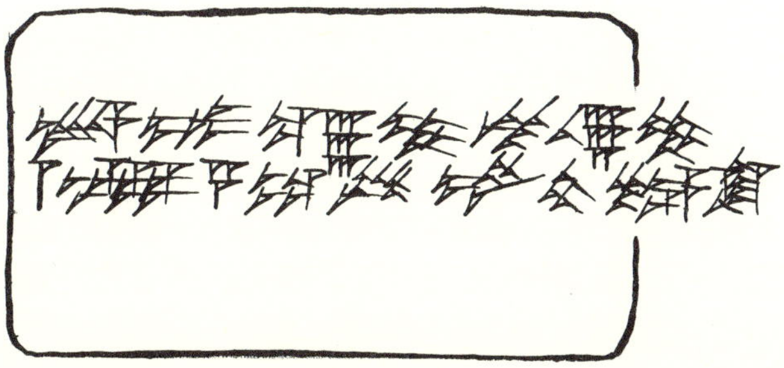

PLATE CII

204

O.

R.

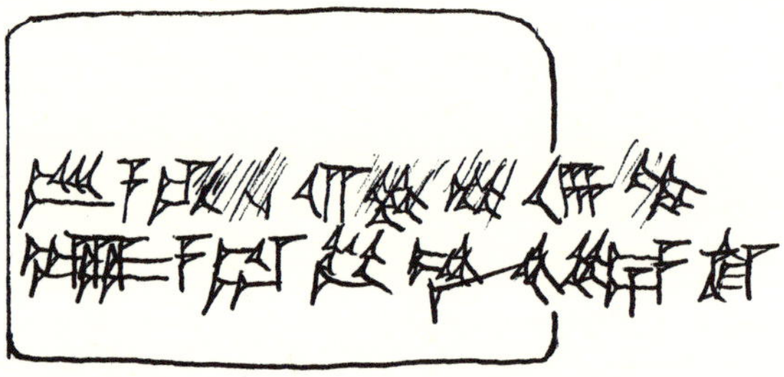

205

O.

 over erasure

R.

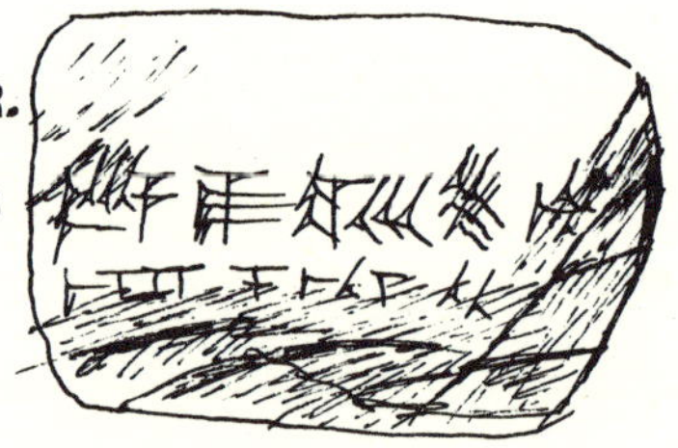

206

O.

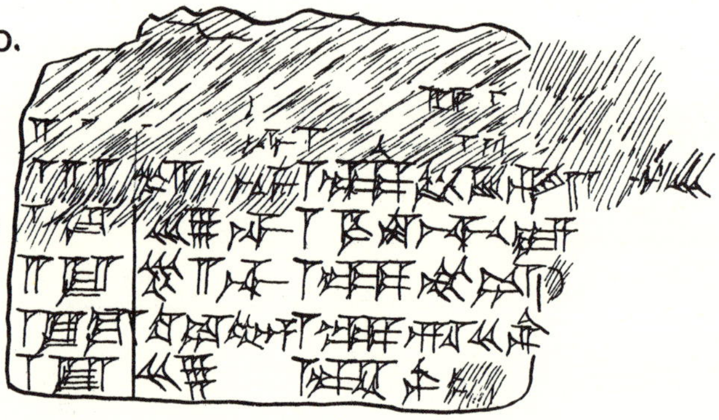

R.

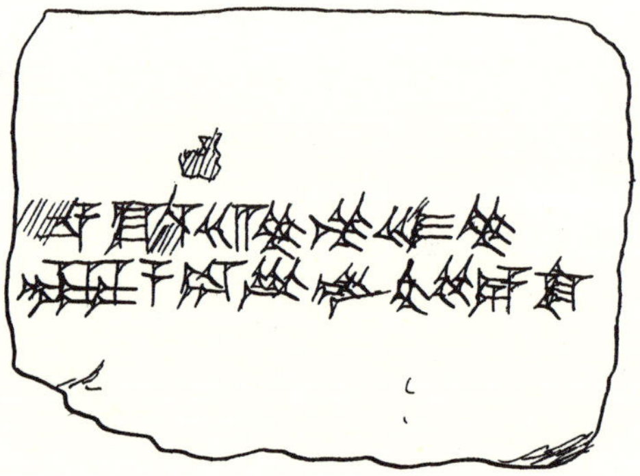

207

O. °sic

5 °sic °sic

R.

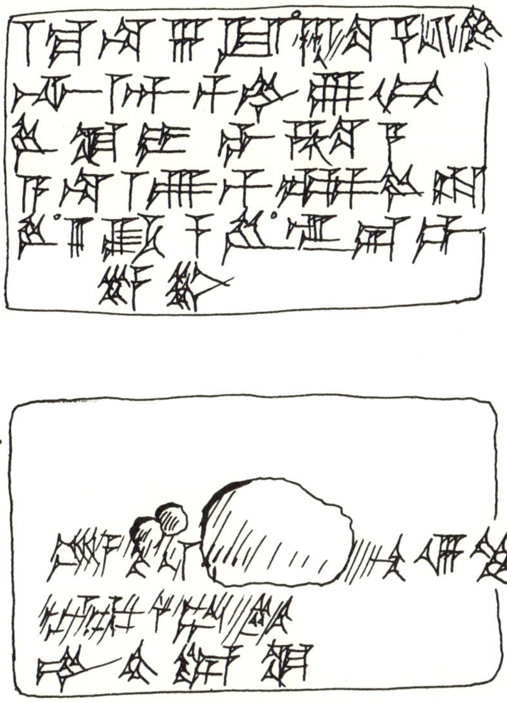

208

O.

Lo.E.5

R.

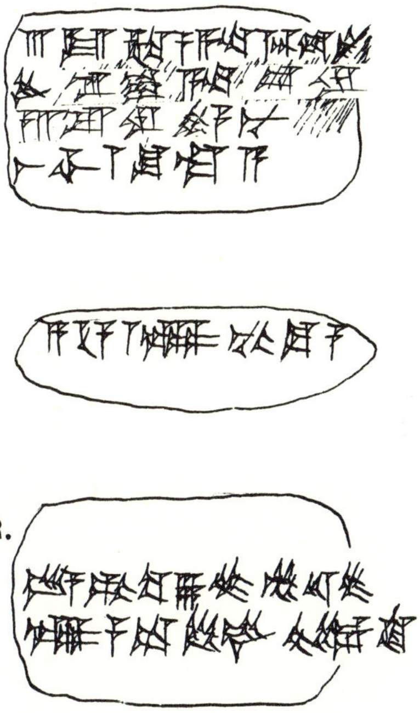

209

O.

5

Lo.E.

R.10

15

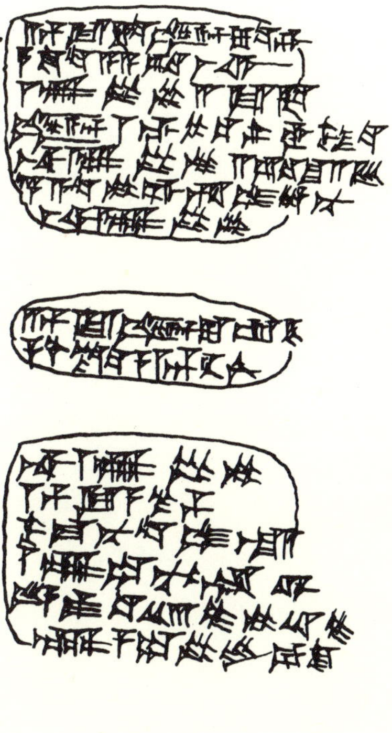

210

O.

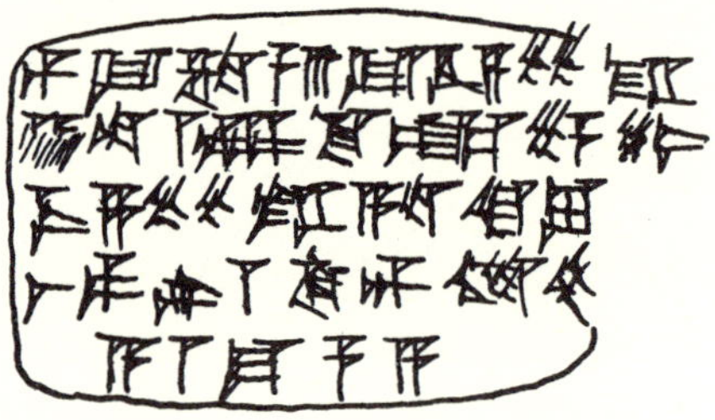

R.

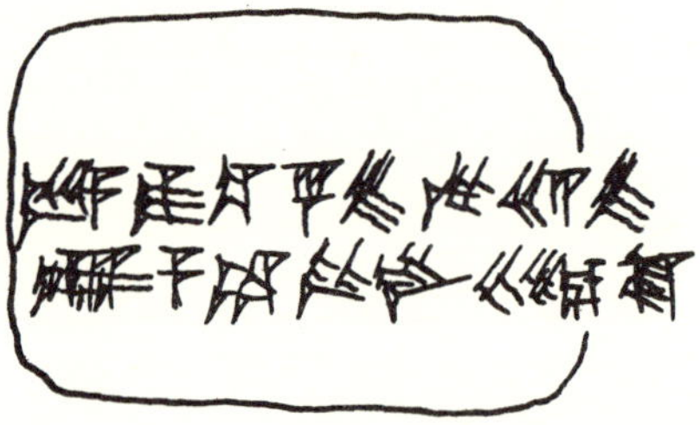

211

O.

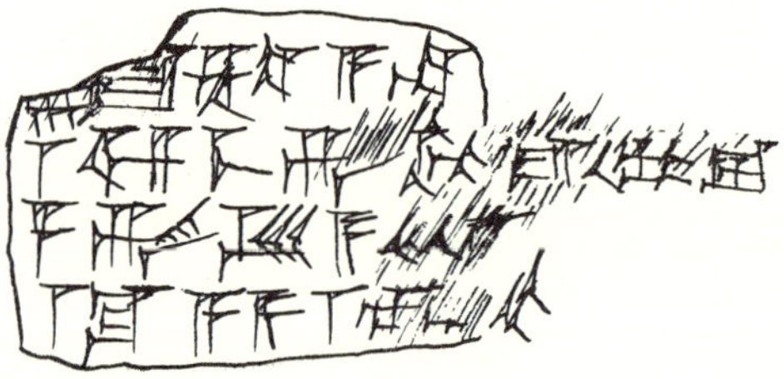

Lo.E.

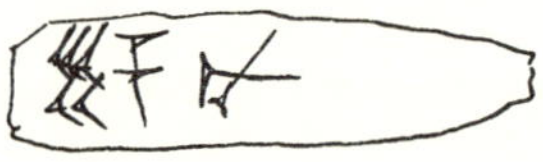

R.

U.E.

212

O.

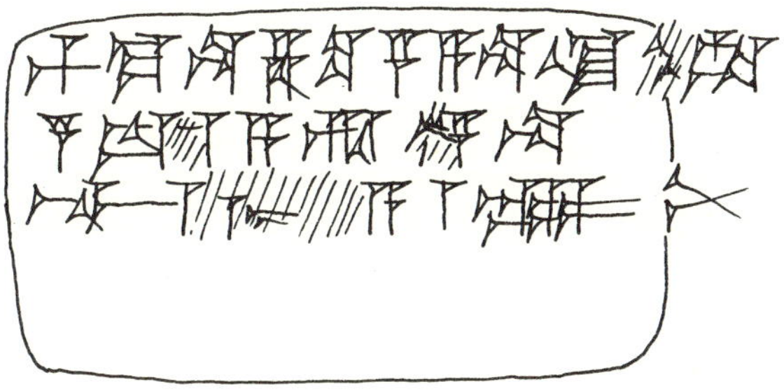

R.

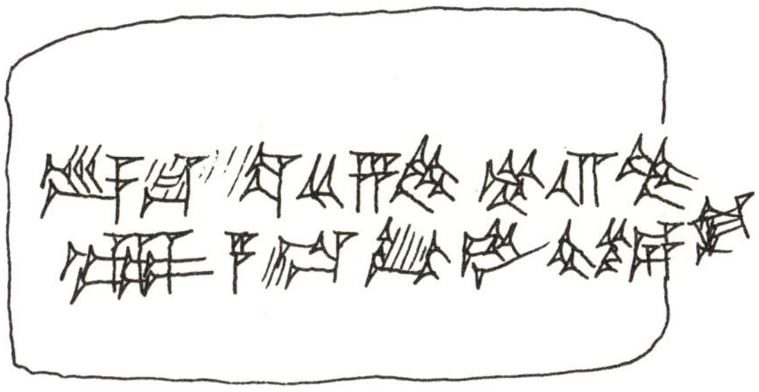

213

O.

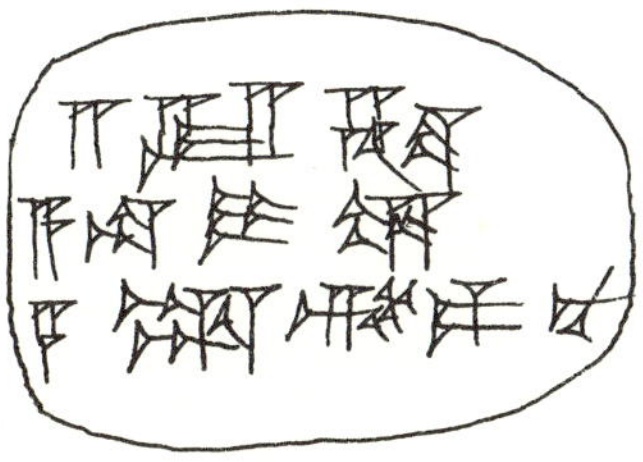

Lo.E.

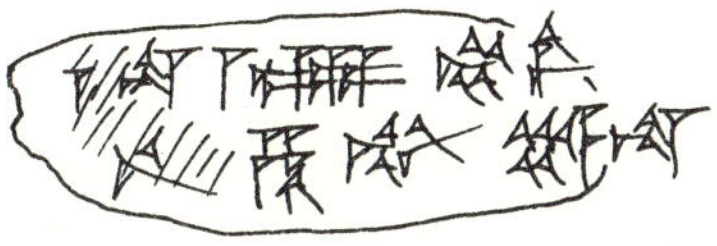

R.

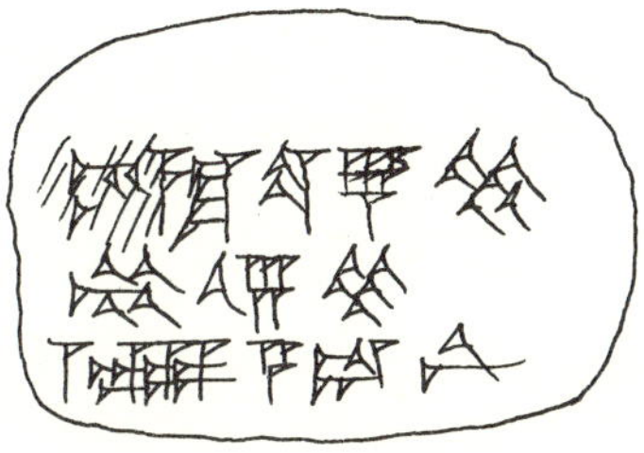

U.E.

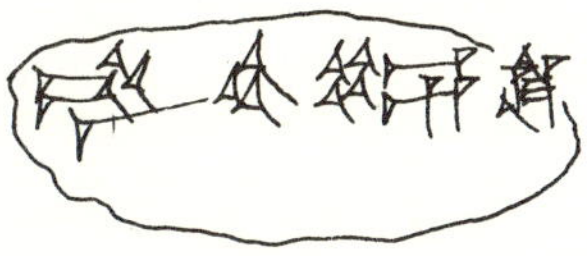

214

O.

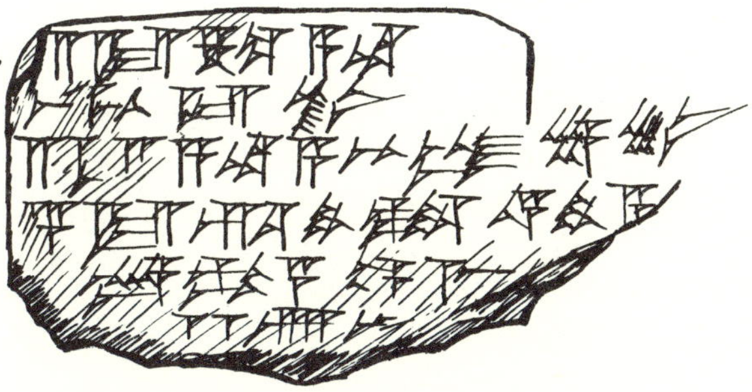

R.

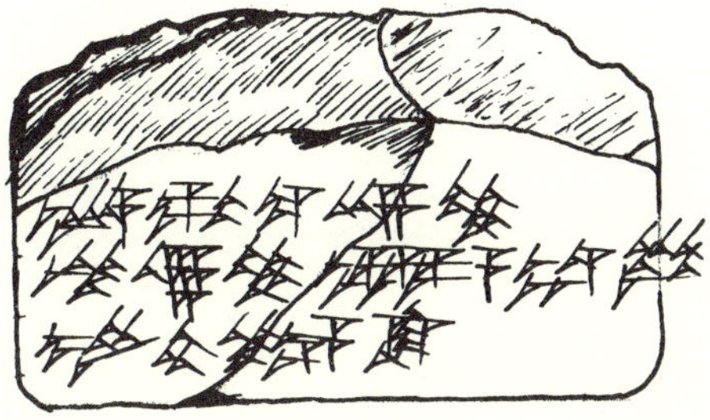

215

O.

R.

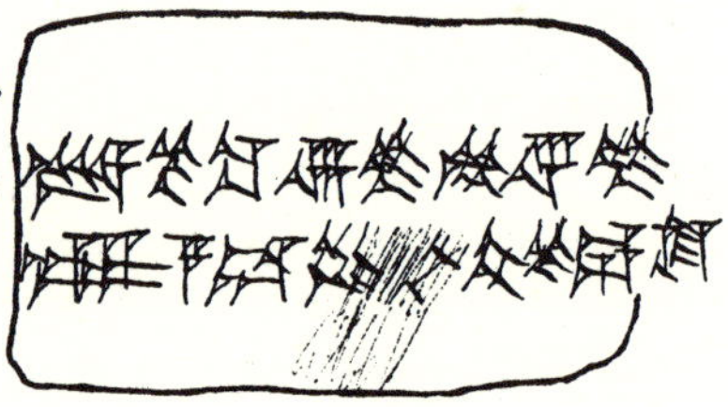

216

O.

R.

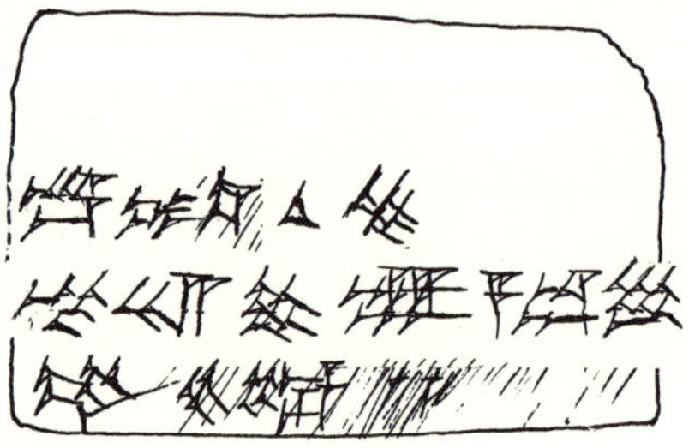

217

O.

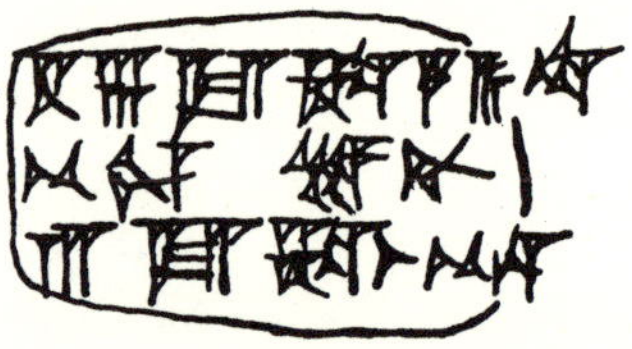

Lo. E.

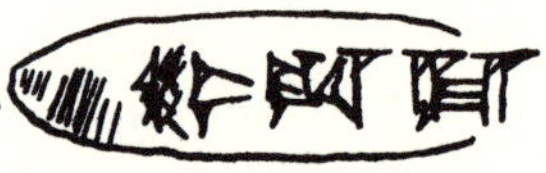

R.

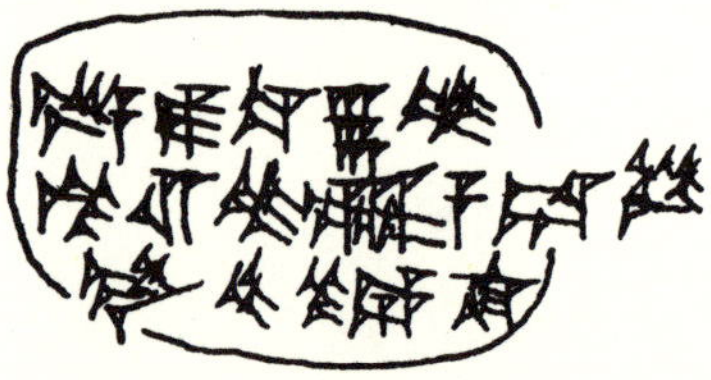

218

O.

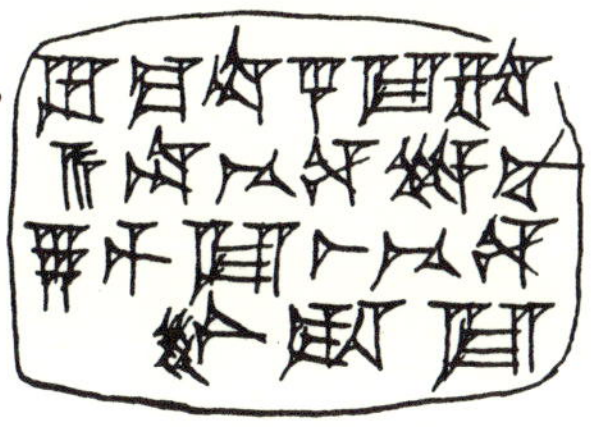

R.

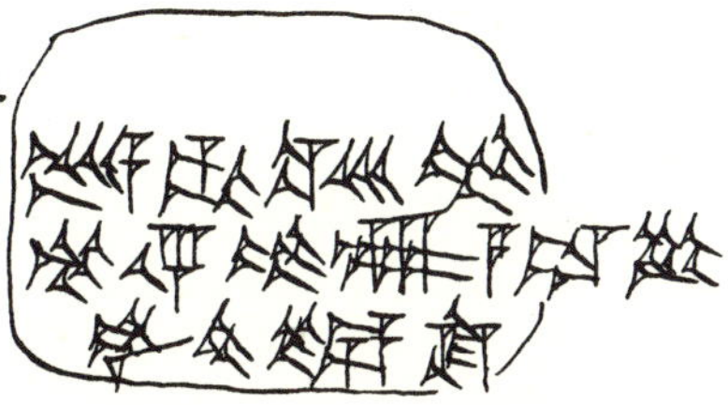

219

O.

Lo.E.

R.

220

O.

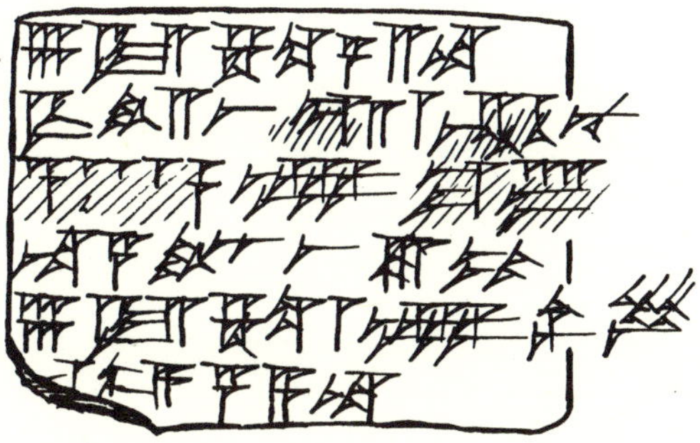

Lo.E.

R.

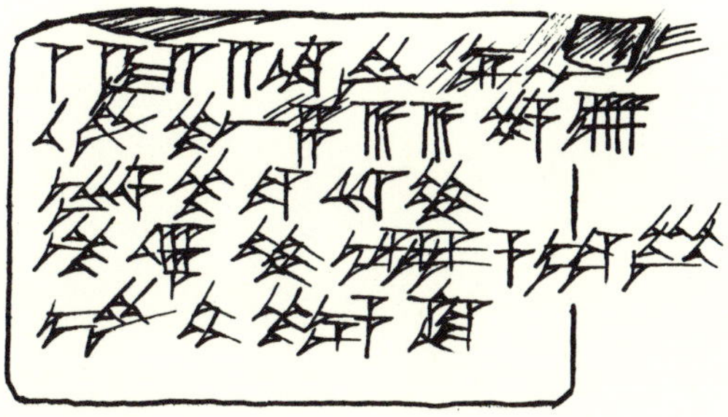

221

O.

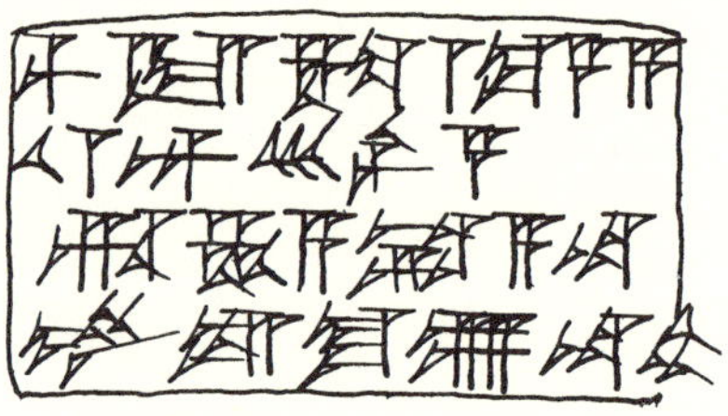

Lo.E.5

R.

U.E.10

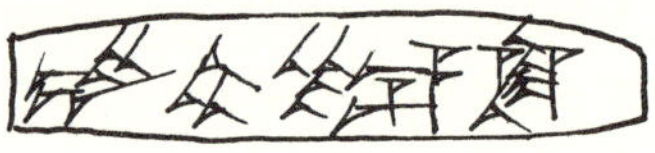

222

O.

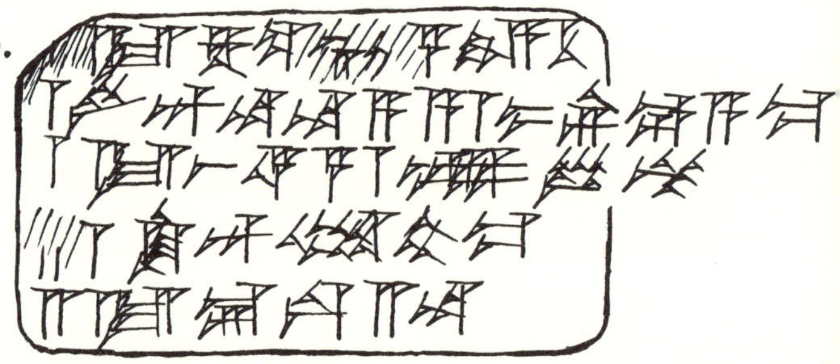

Lo.E.

R.

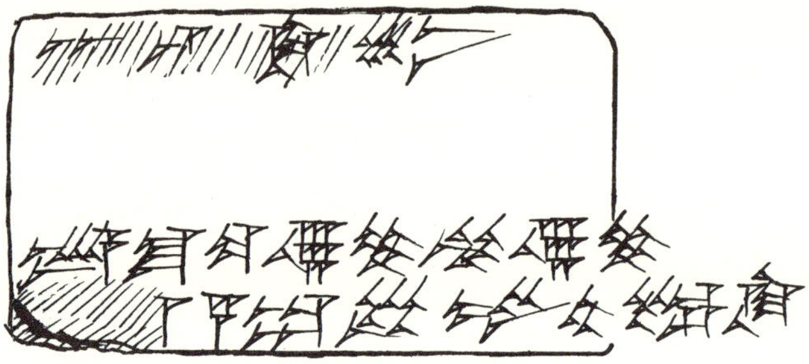

223

O.

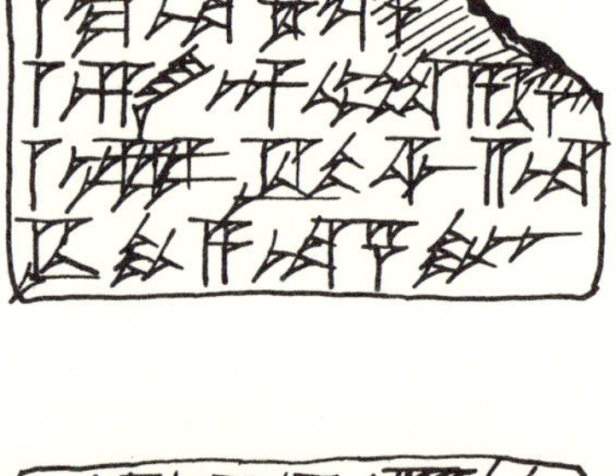

R.5

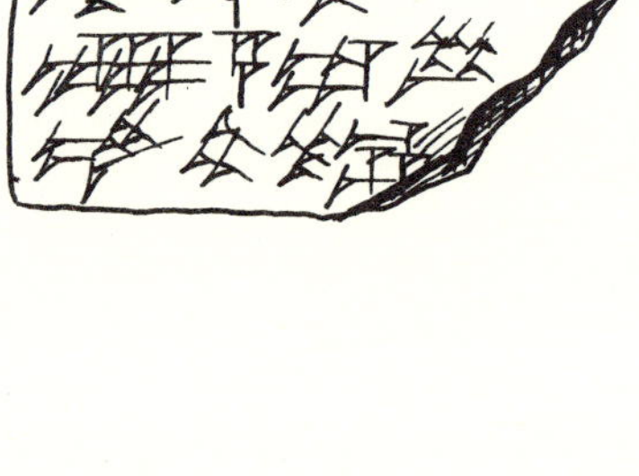

224

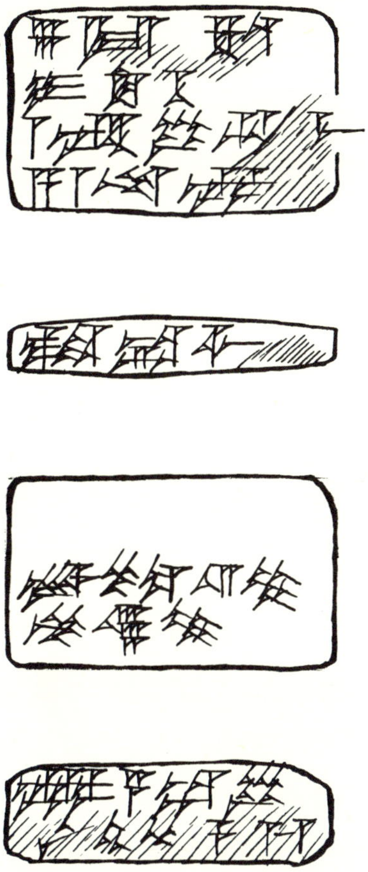

225

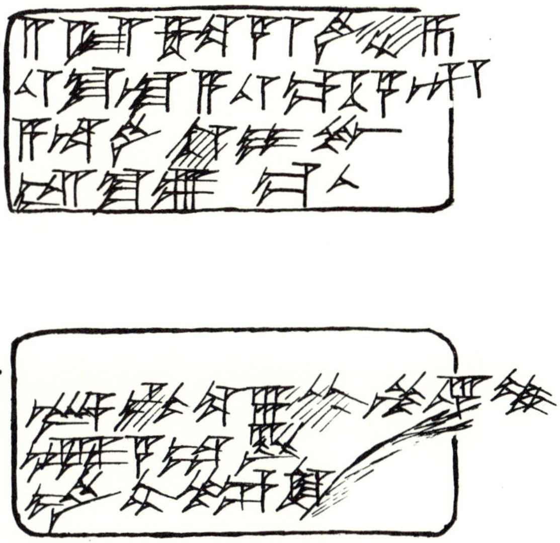

226

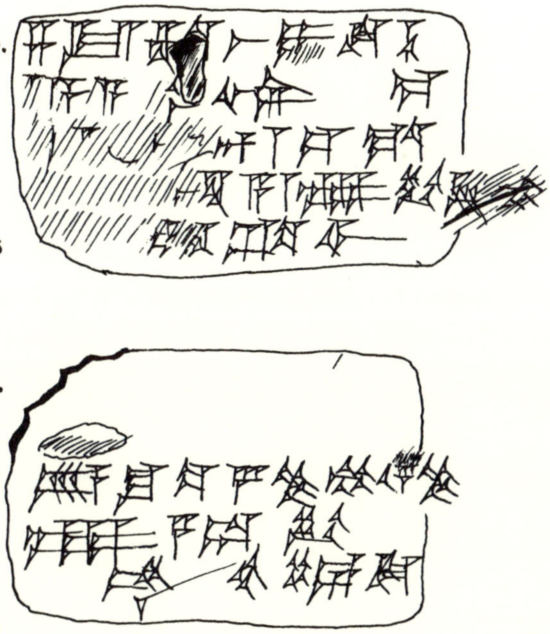

227

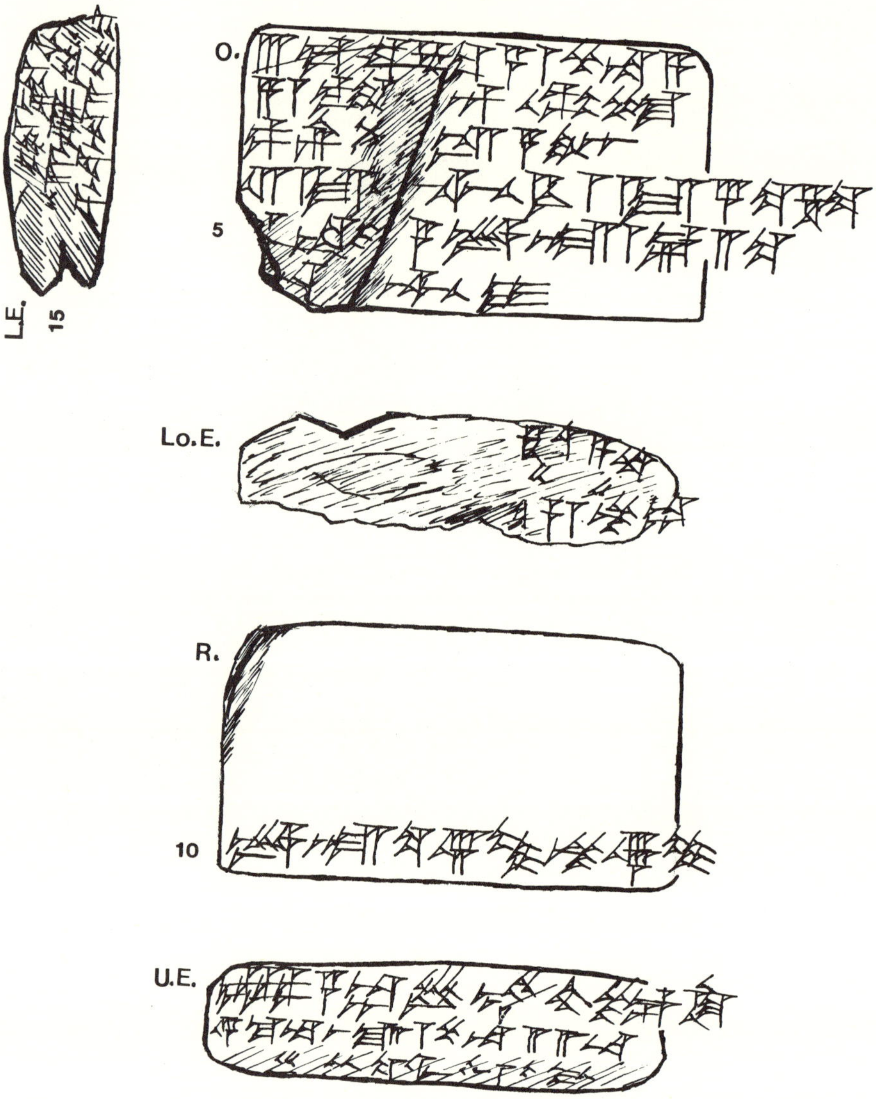

228

O.

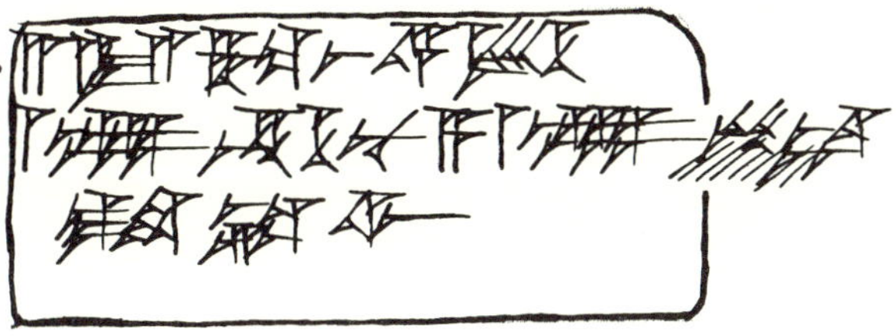

R.

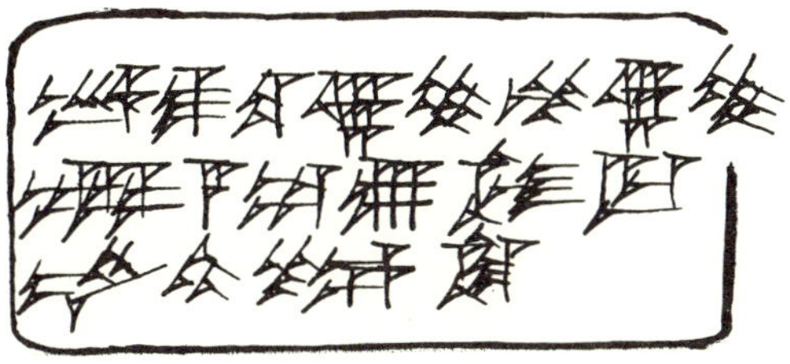

229

O.

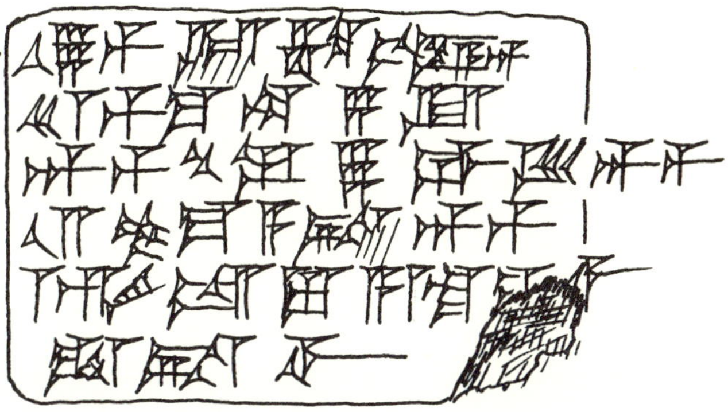

R.

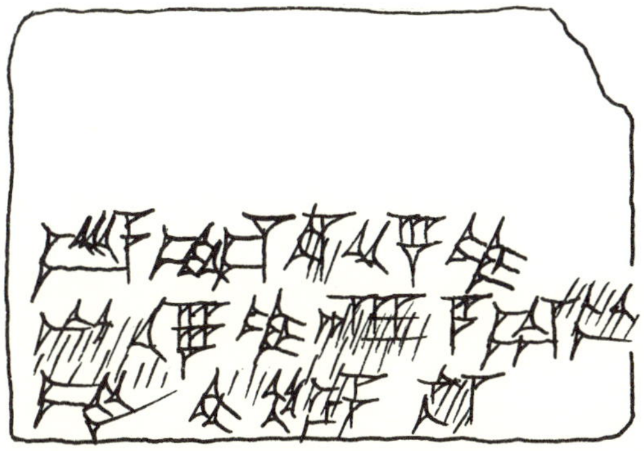

230

O.

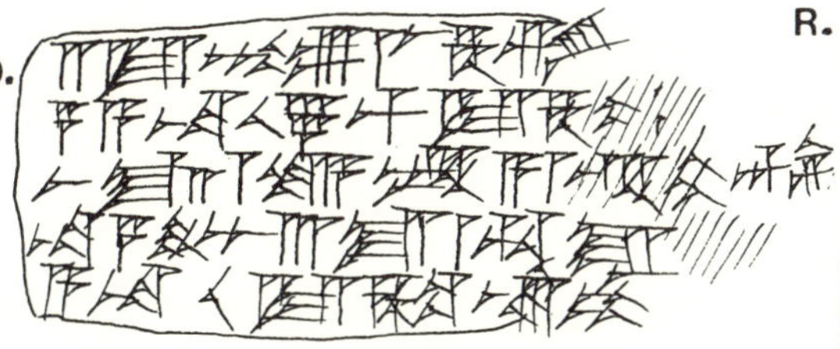

Lo.E.

R.

231

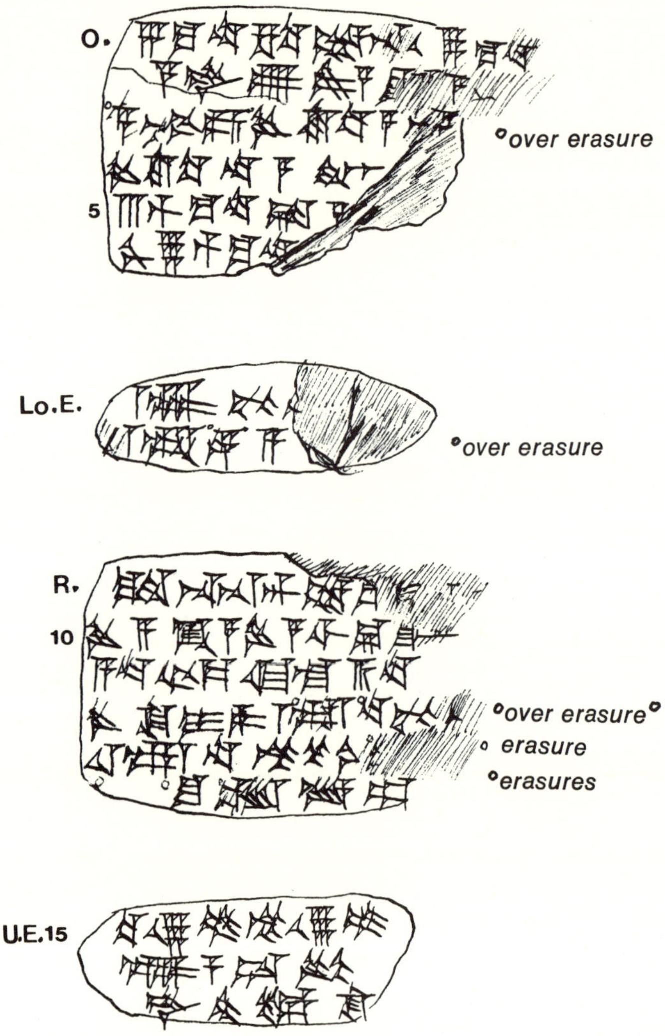
O.
5
°over erasure
Lo.E.
°over erasure
R.
10
°over erasure°
° erasure
°erasures
U.E.15

232

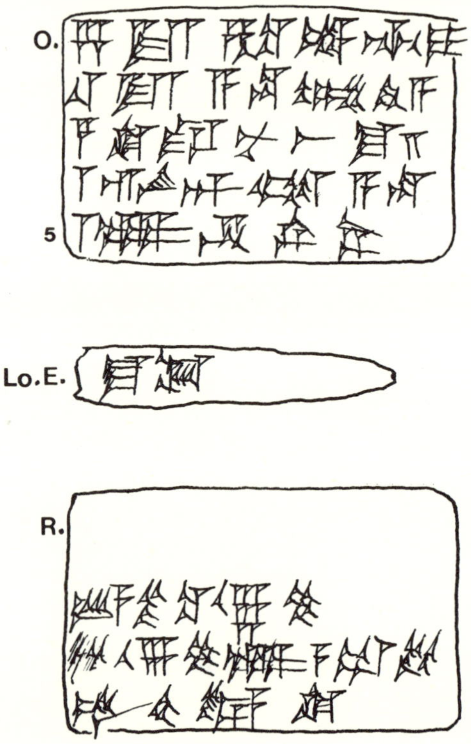
O.
5
Lo.E.
R.

233

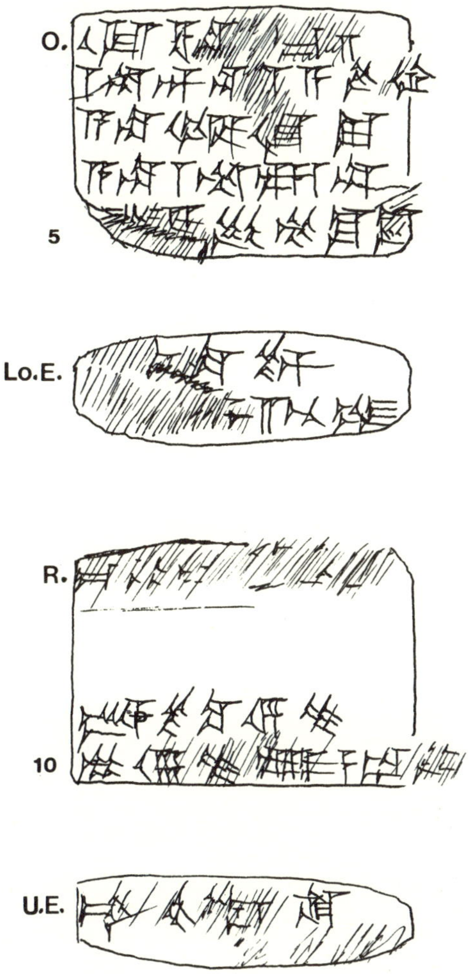

234

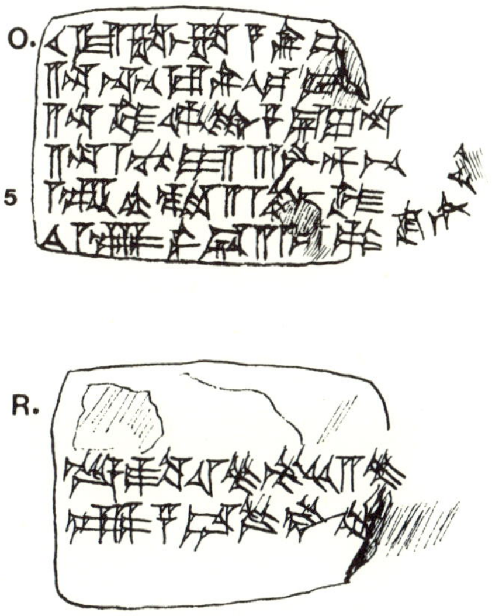

235

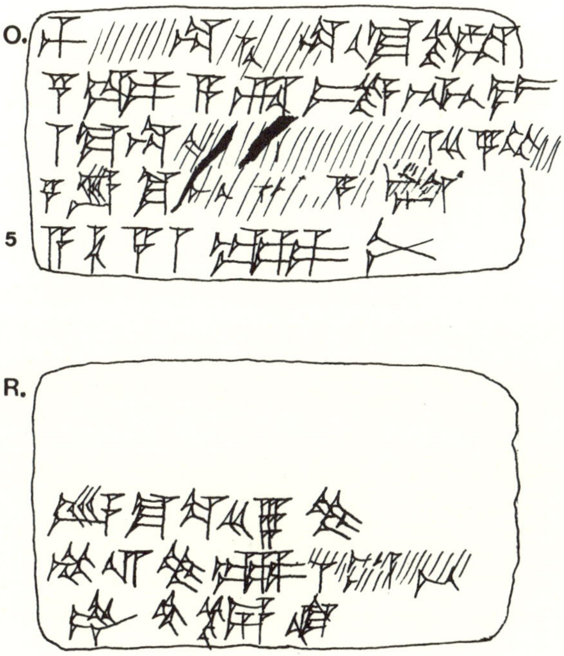

* over erasure

236

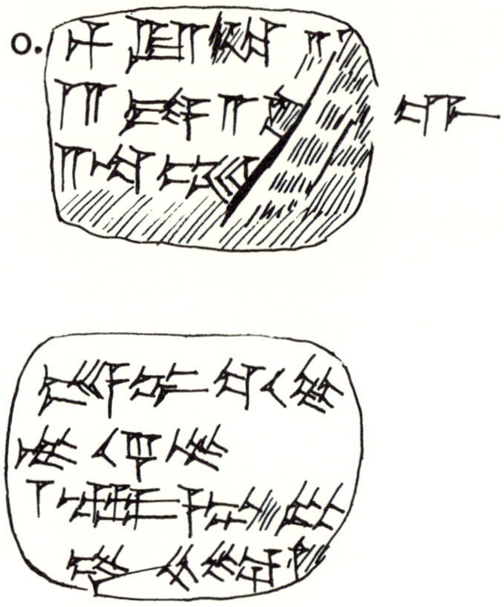

237

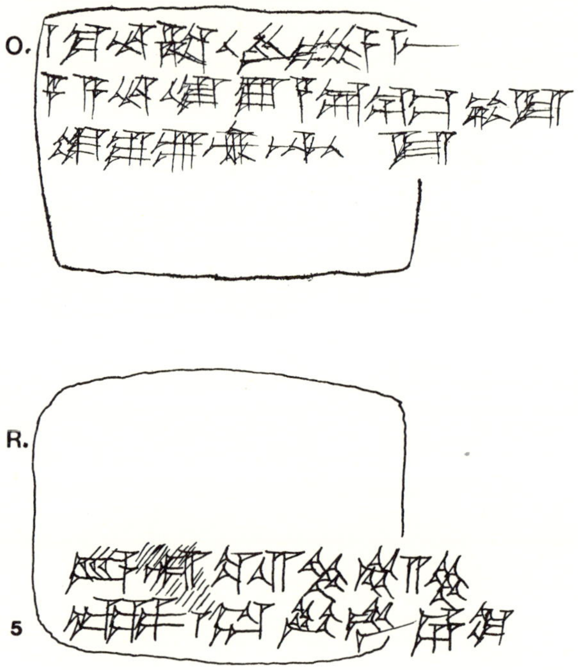

238

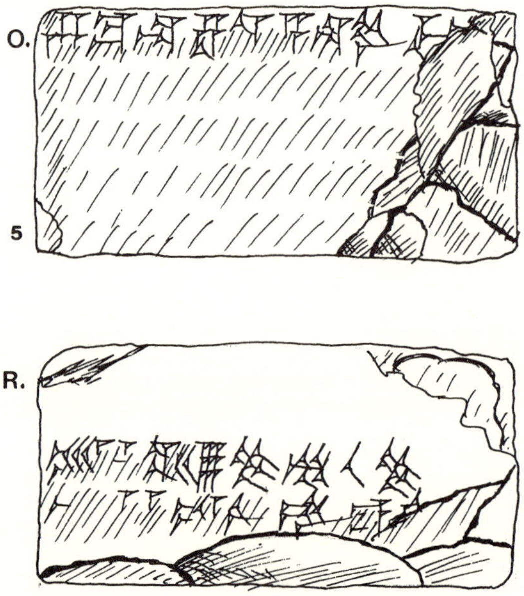

239

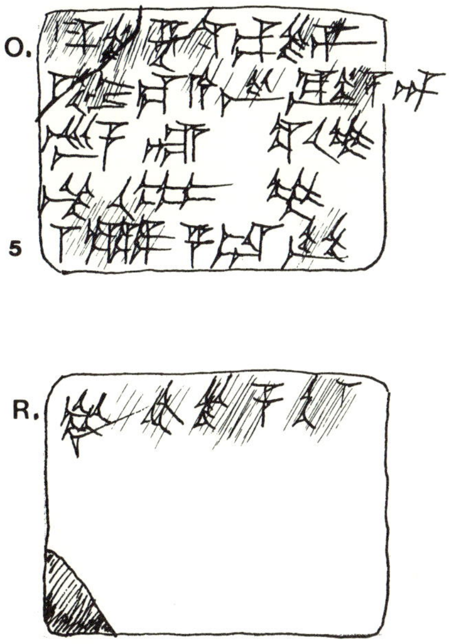

240

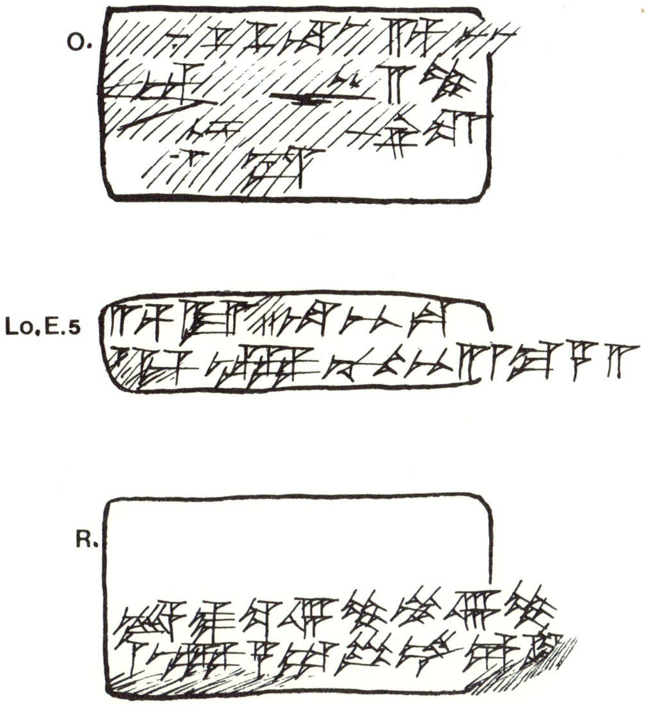

241

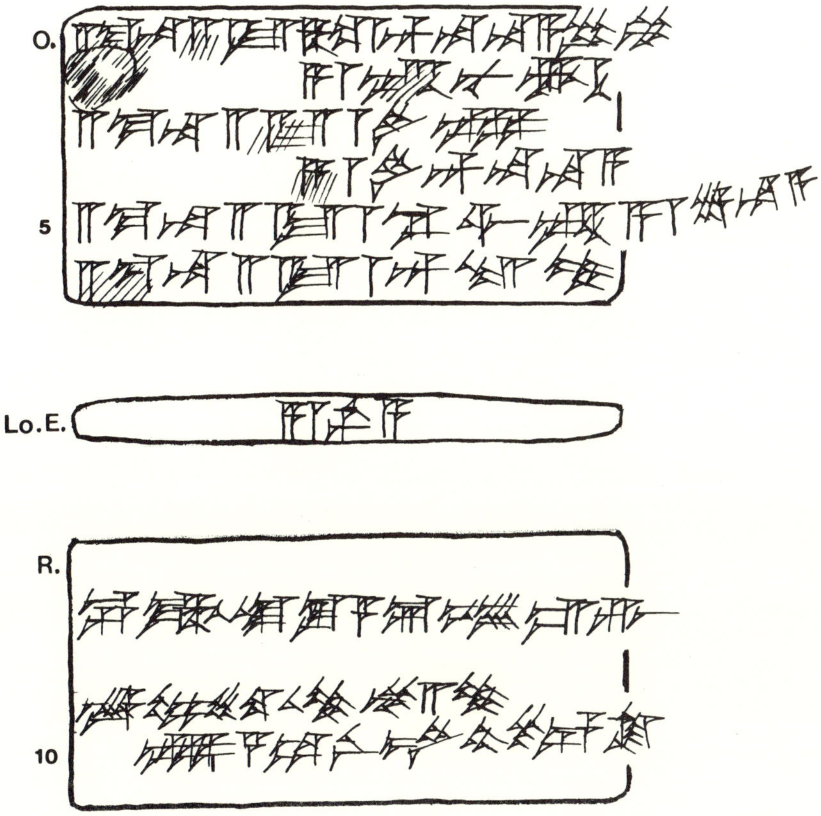

242

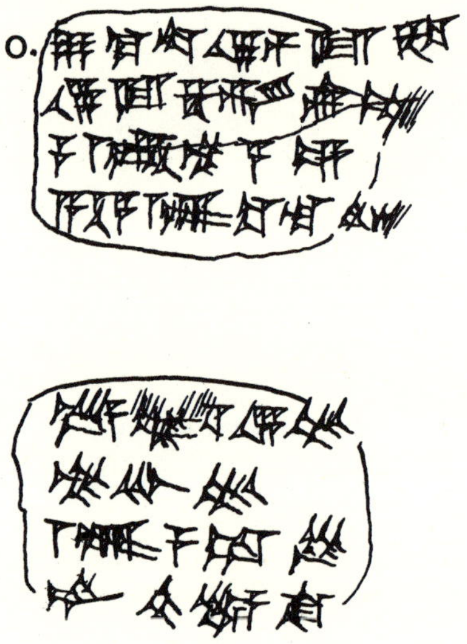

243

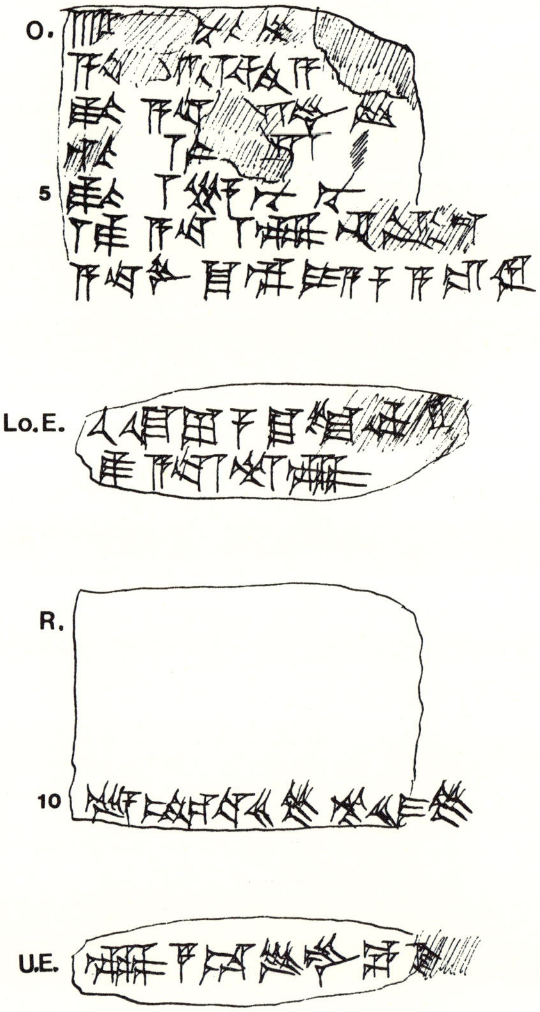

244

O.

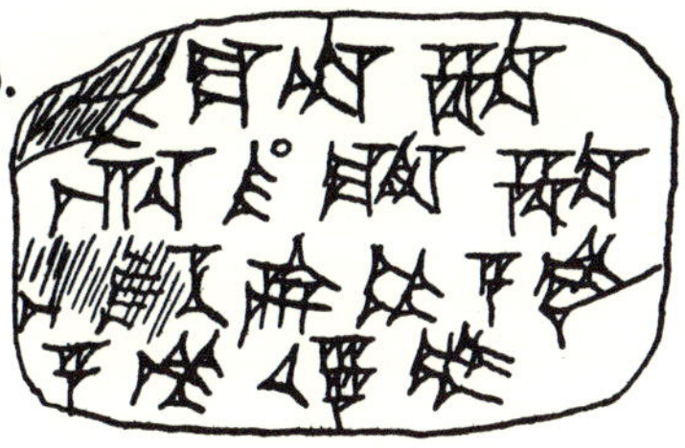

°sic, for 

Lo.E.

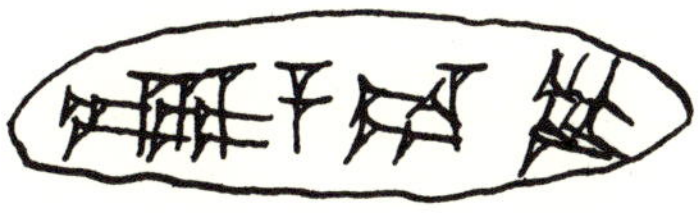

R.

245

O.

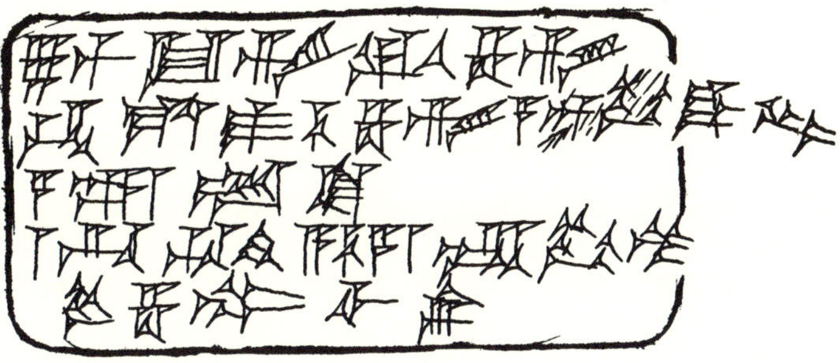

R.

246

O.

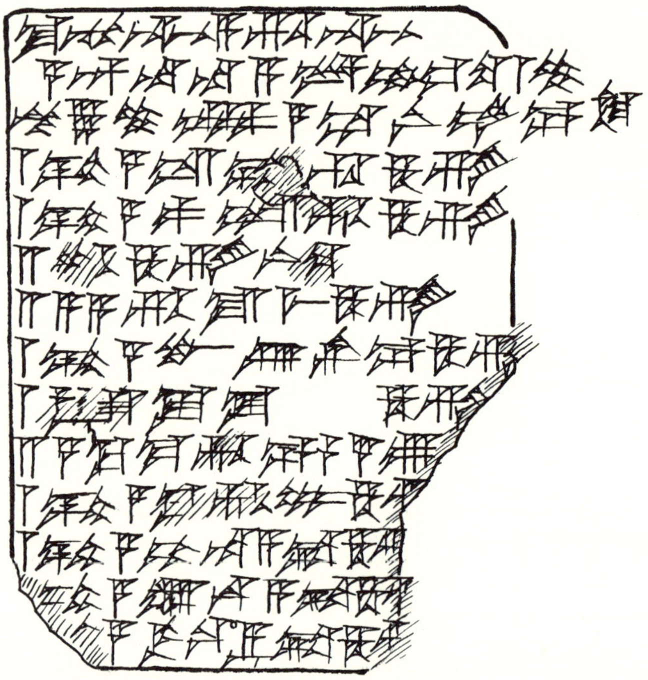

R. 15

° over erasure

° sic

247

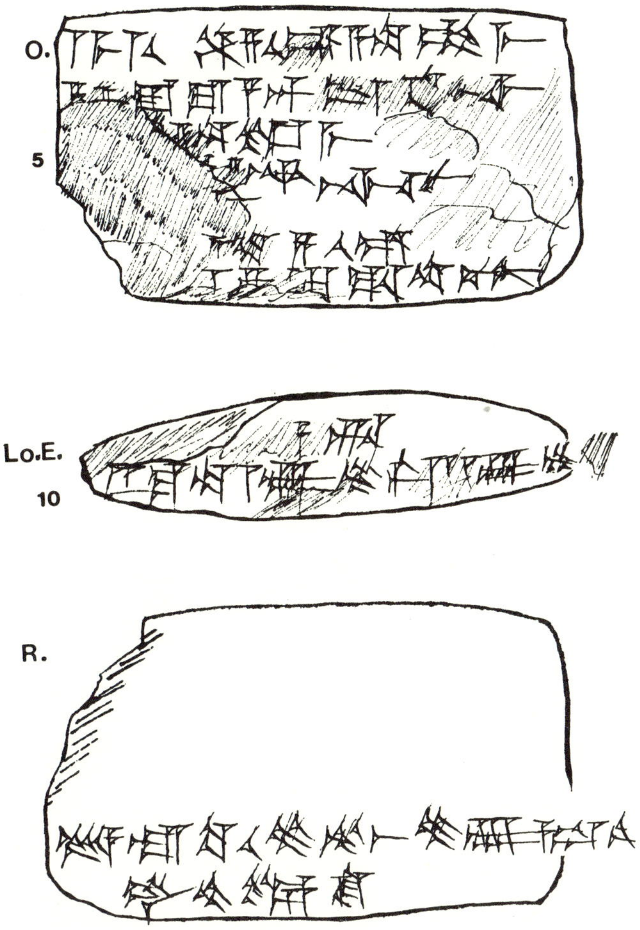

248

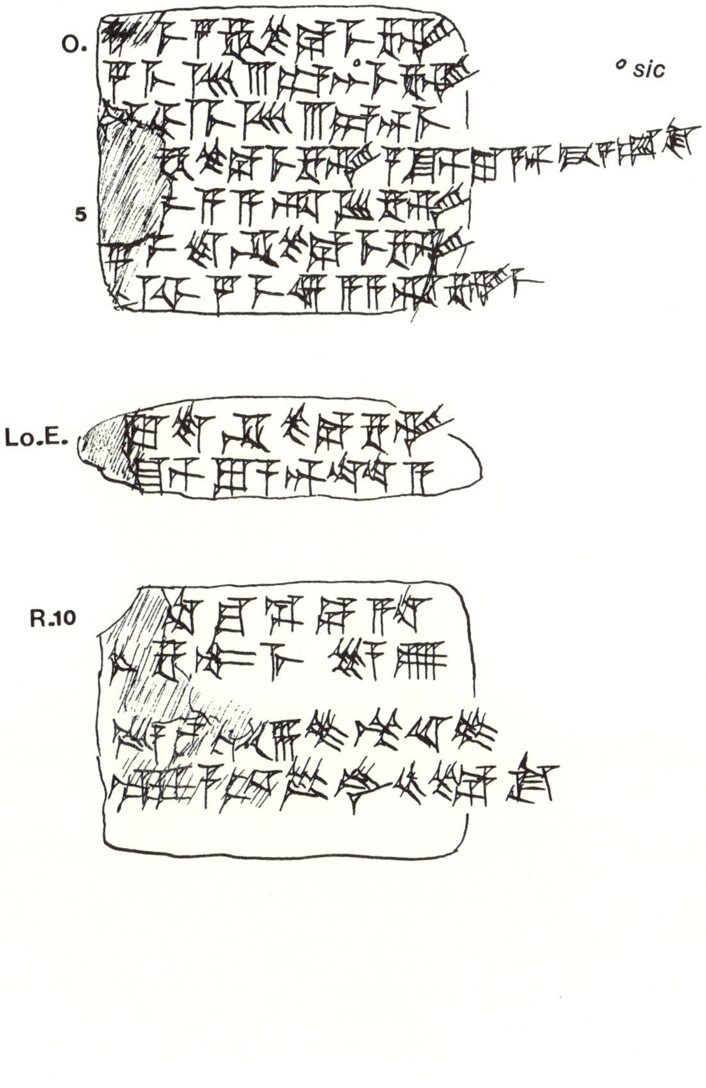

249

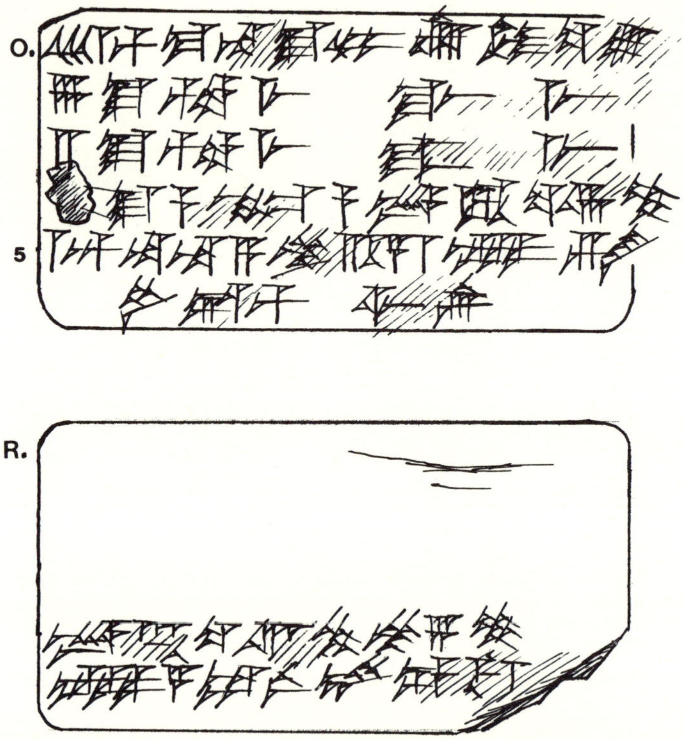

250

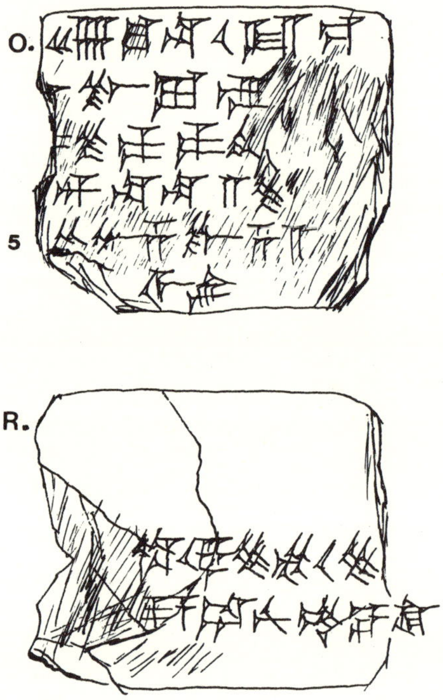

251

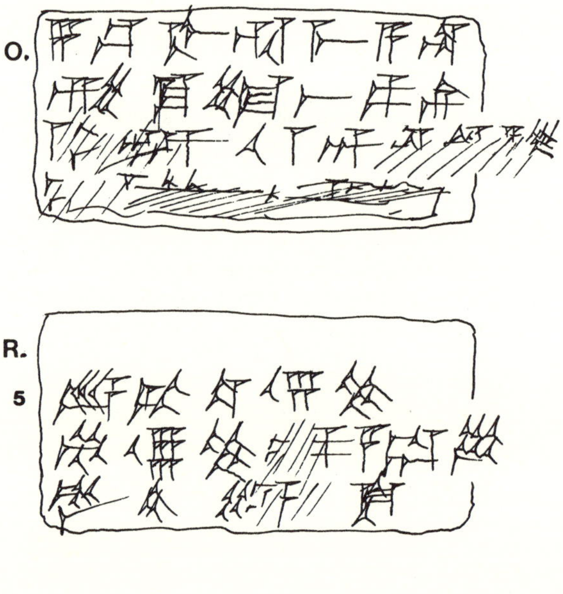

252

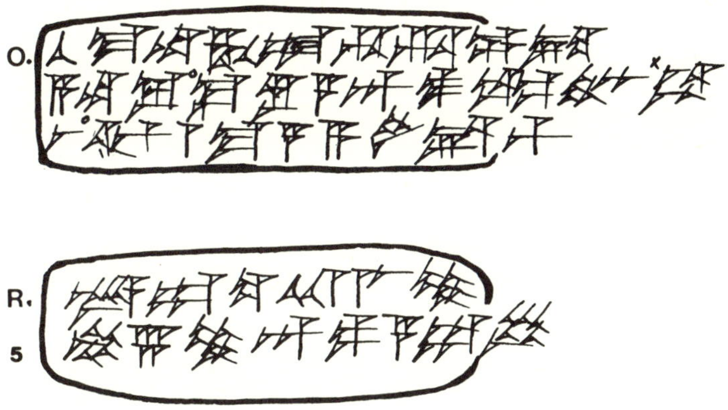

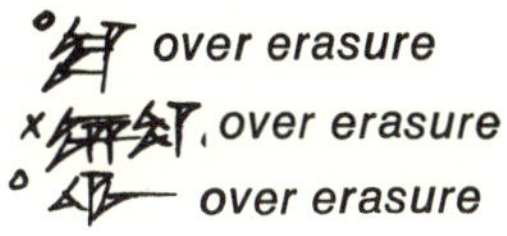

253

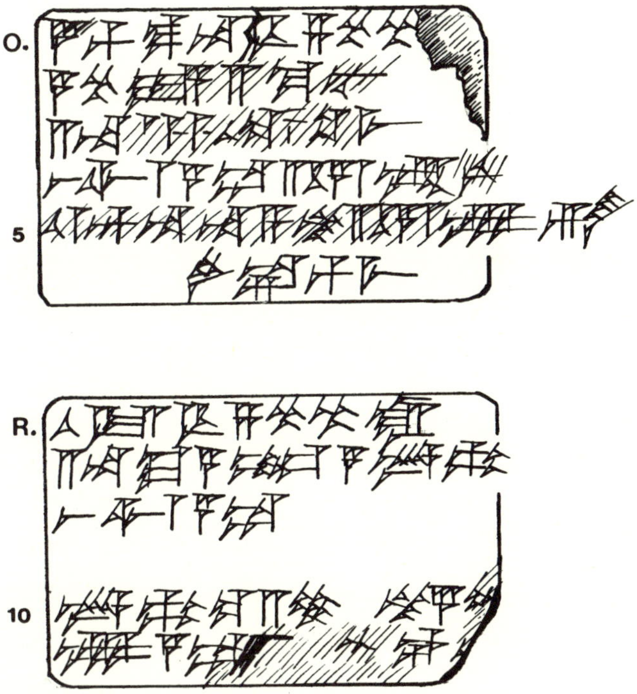

254

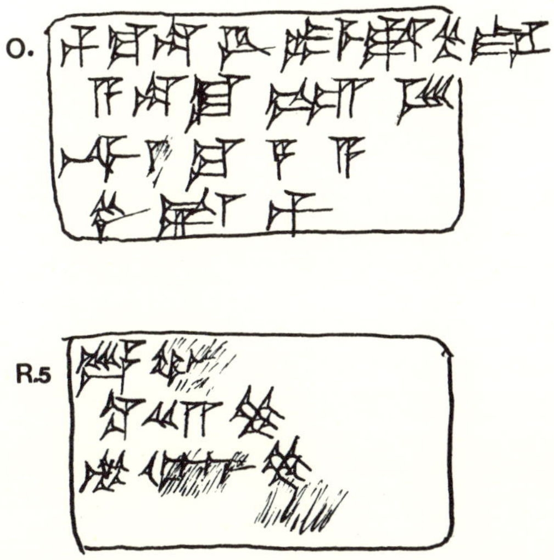

255

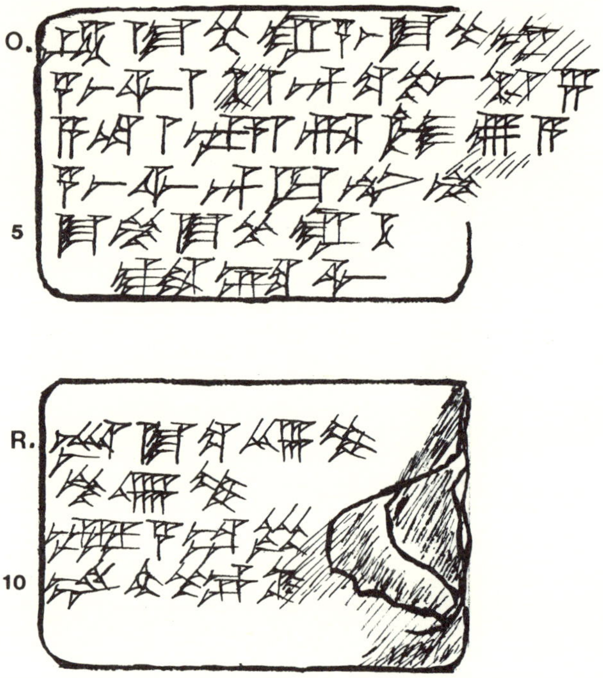

256

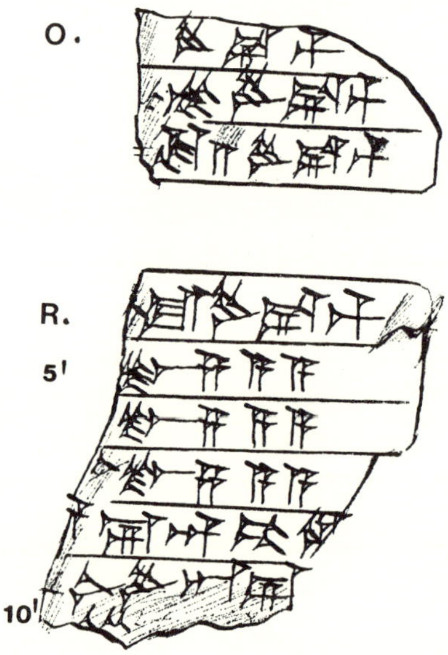

257

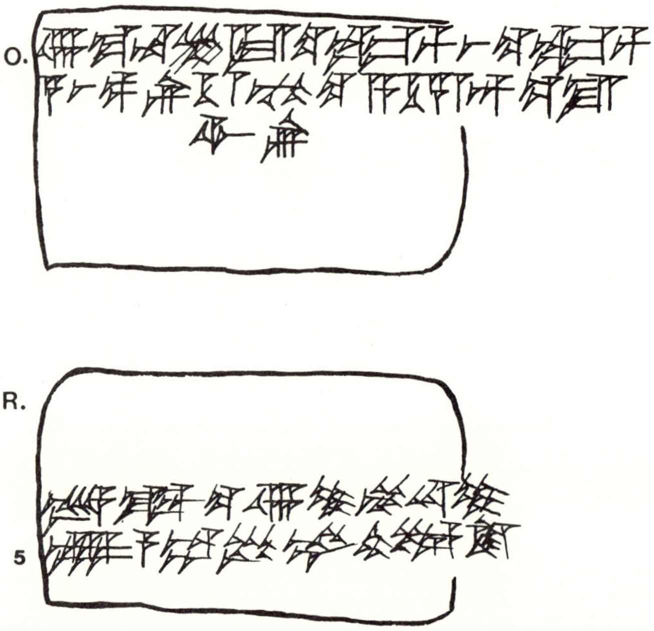

258

O.

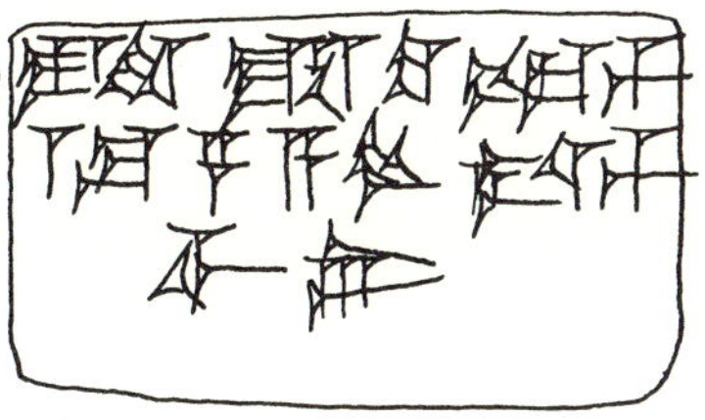

R.

259

O.

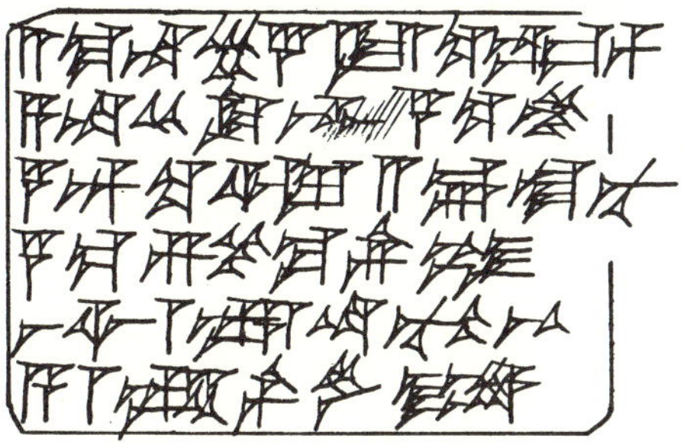

R.

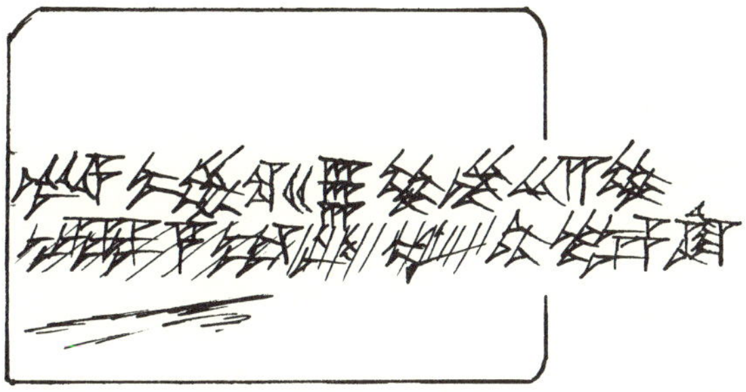

260

O.

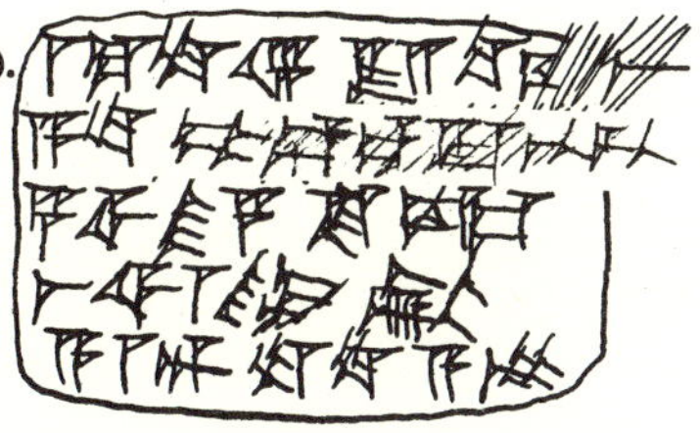

Lo.E.

R.

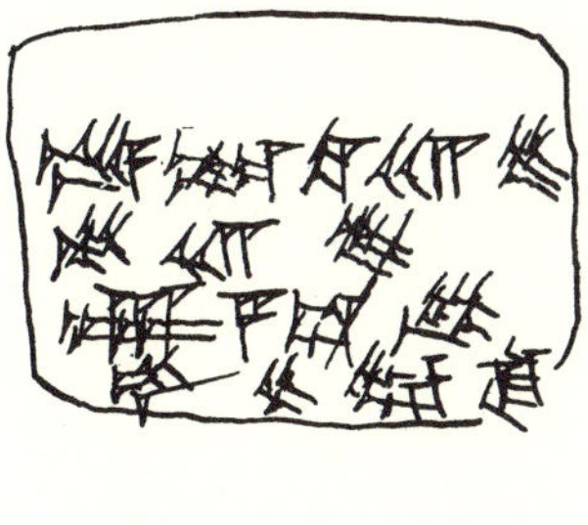

261

O.

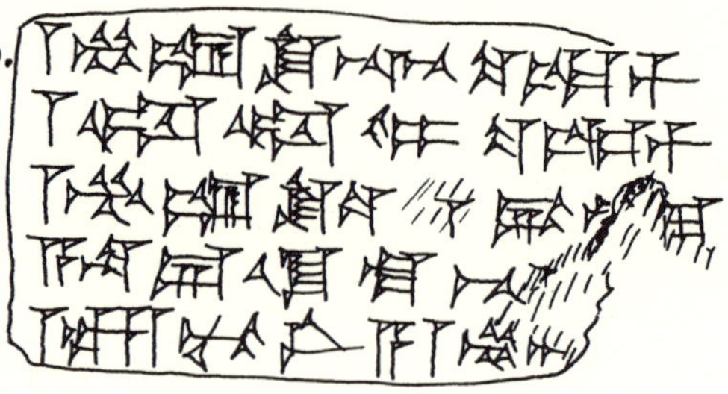

R.

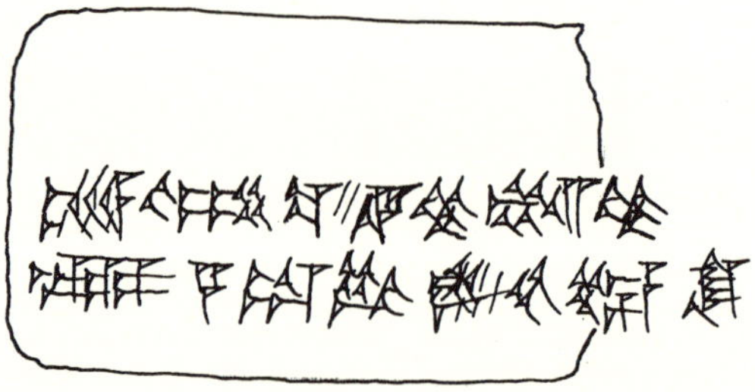

262

O.

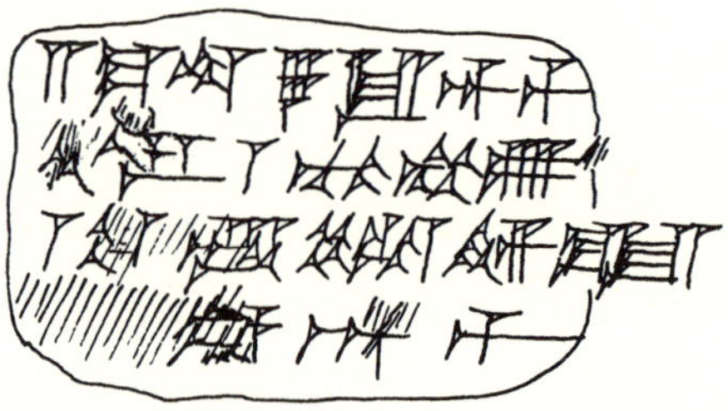

Lo.E.5

R.

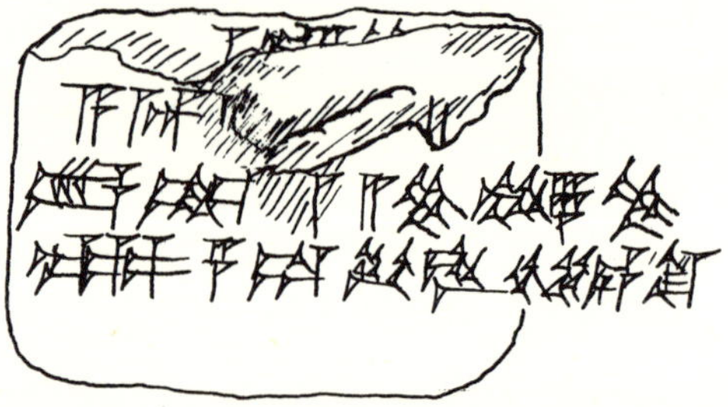

263

O.

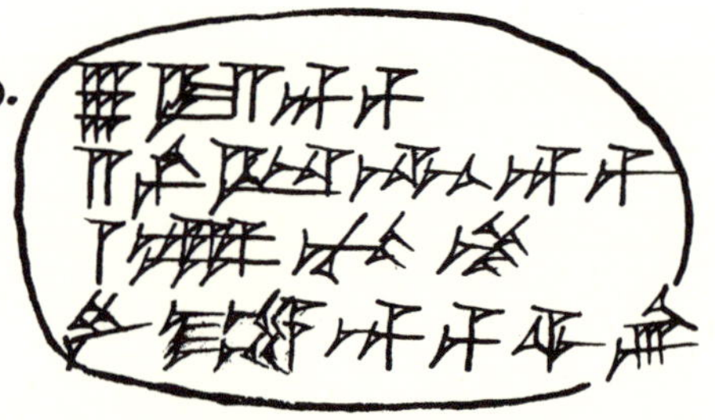

R.

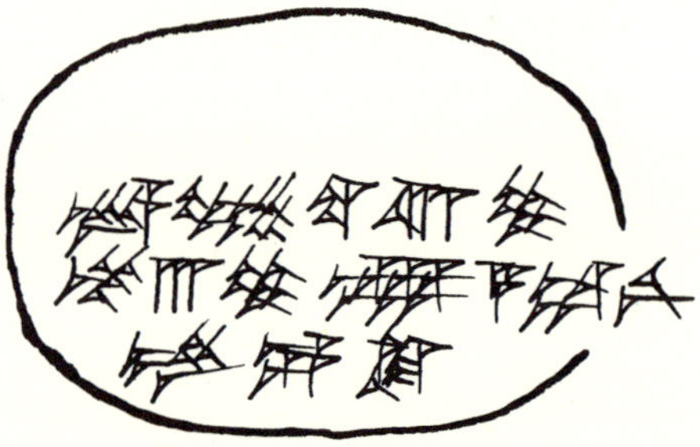

264

O.

Lo.E.5

R.

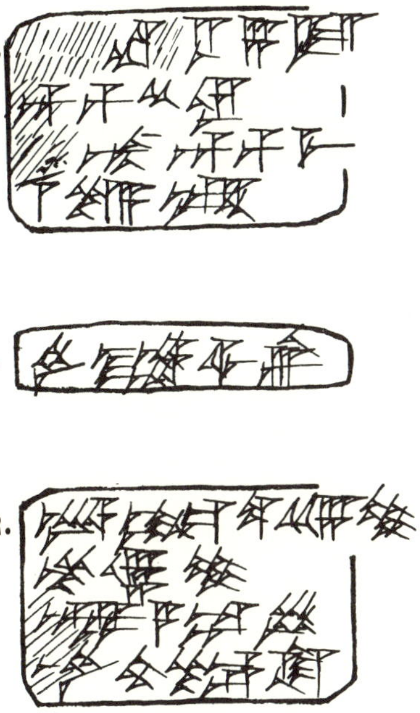

265

O.

Lo.E.5

R.

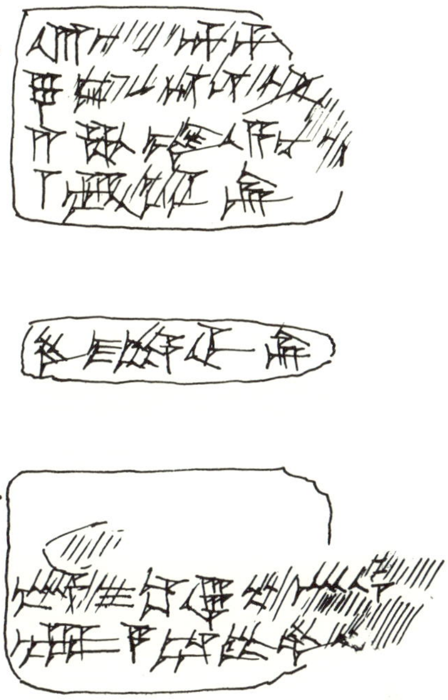

266

O.

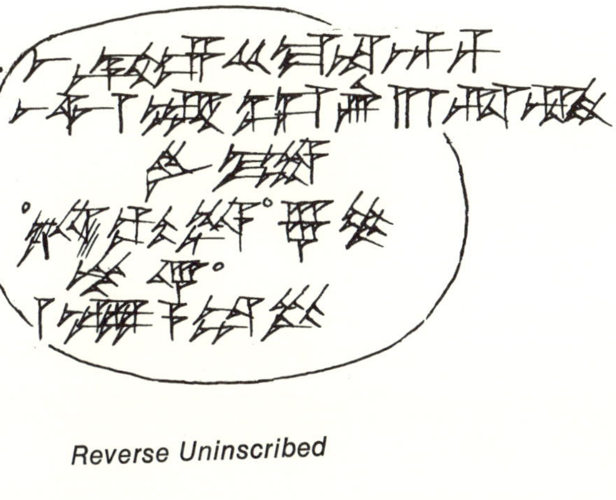

Reverse Uninscribed

°error for 

°  *omitted*

267

O.

R.

269

O.

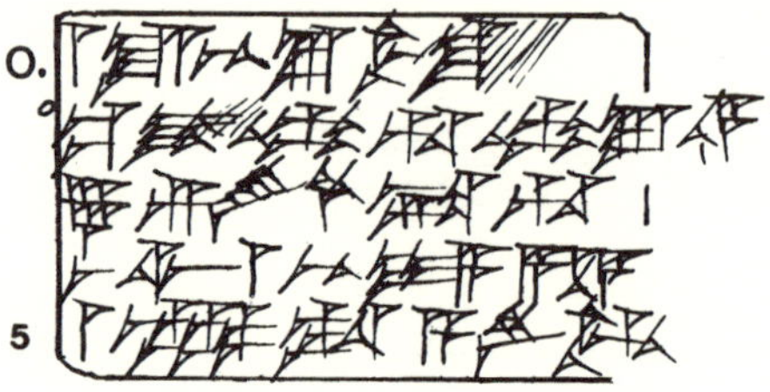

°over eras

R.

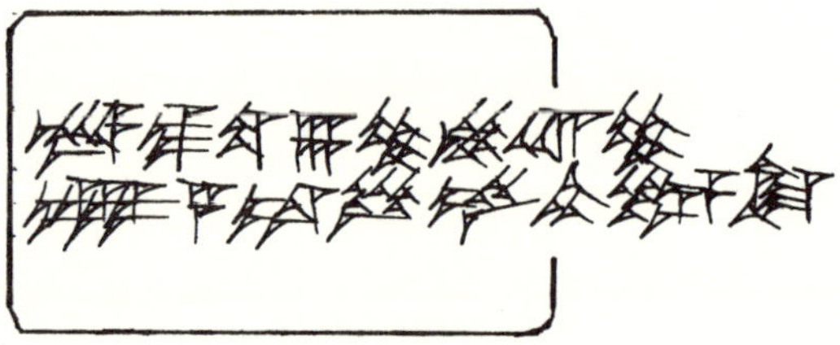

268

O.

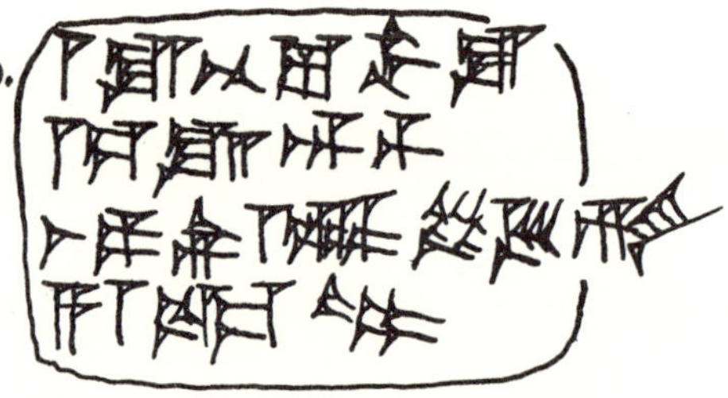

R.

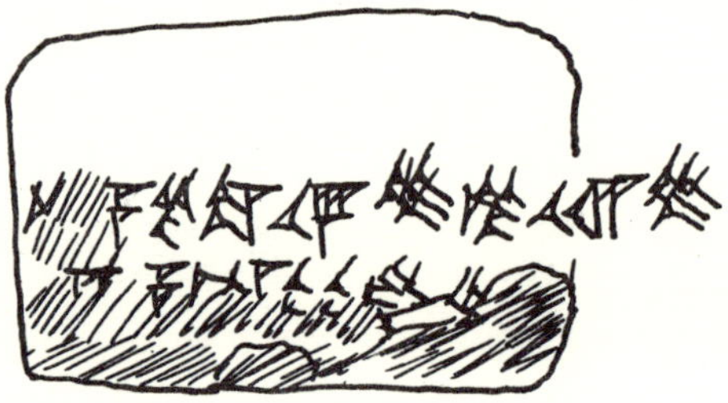

270

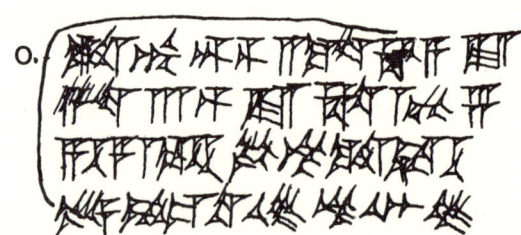

O.

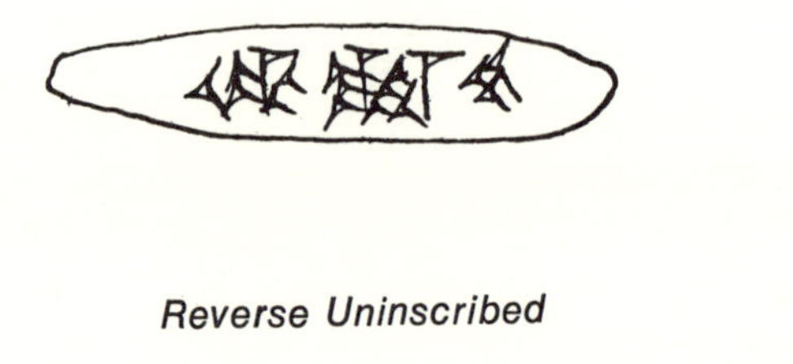

Lo.E.5

Reverse Uninscribed

271

O.

Lo.E.

R.

272

O.

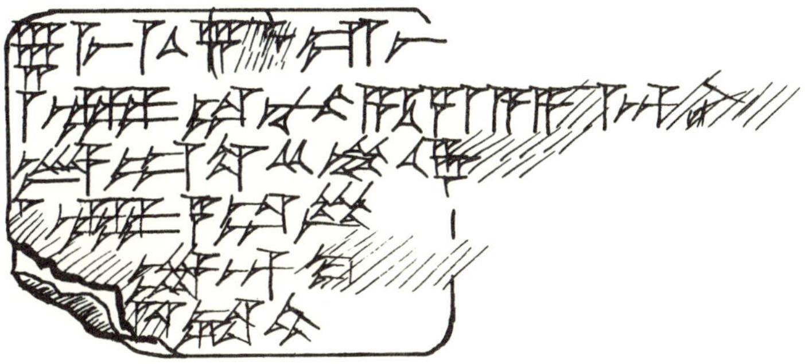

Reverse Uninscribed

273

O.

Lo.E.

R.

U.E.

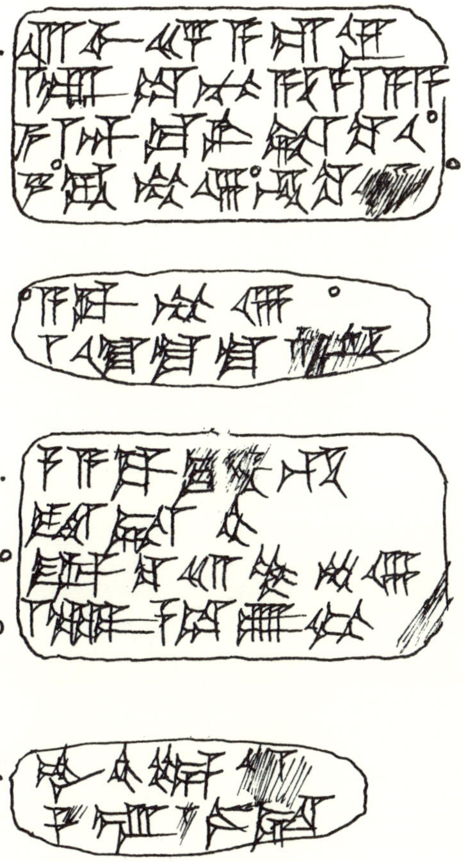

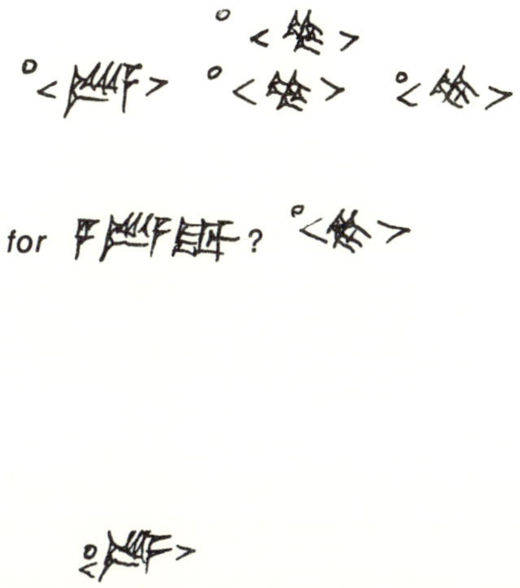

274

O.

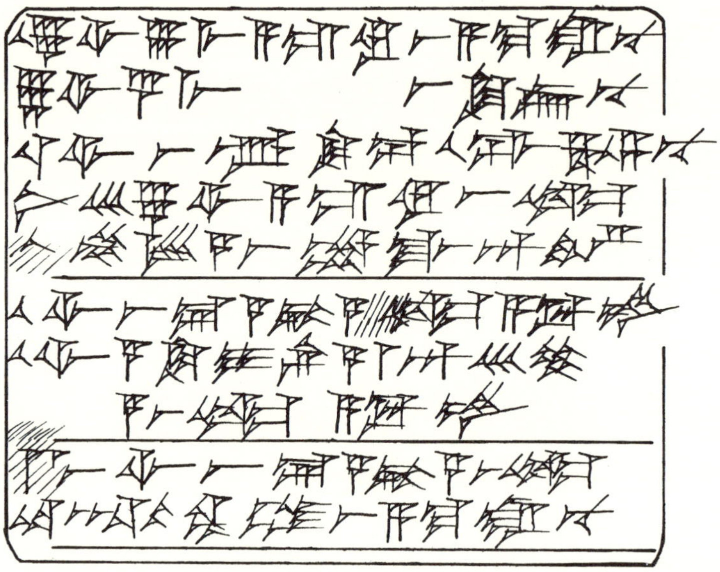

Lo.E.

R.

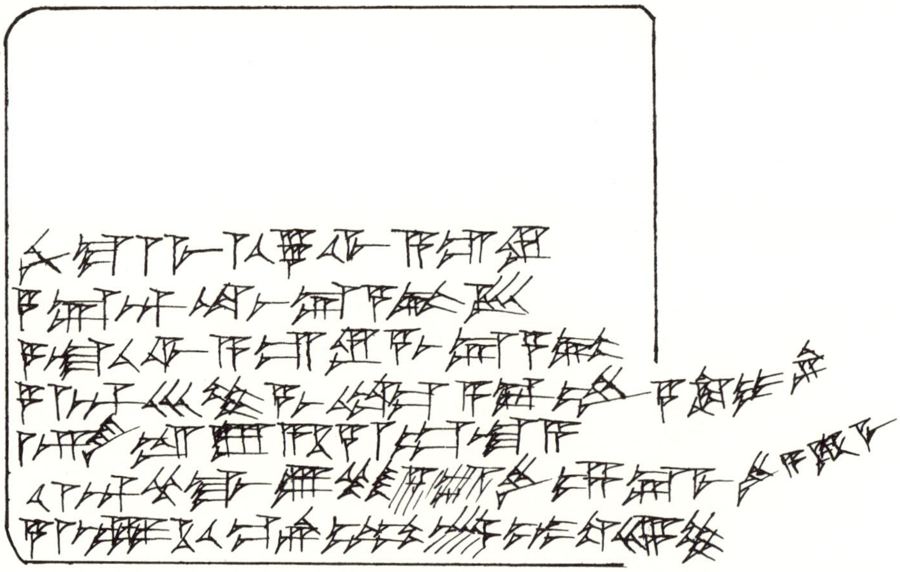

U.E.

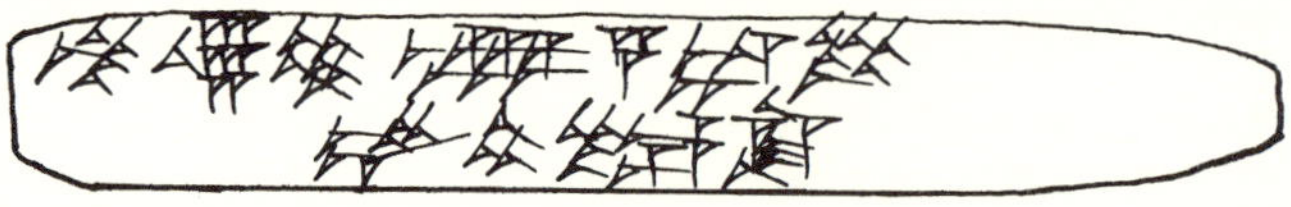

275

O.

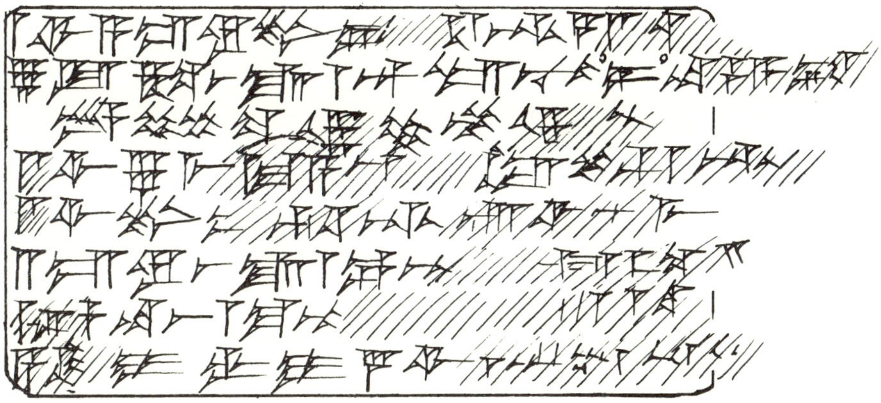

° sic, for DÙ °

Lo. E.

R.

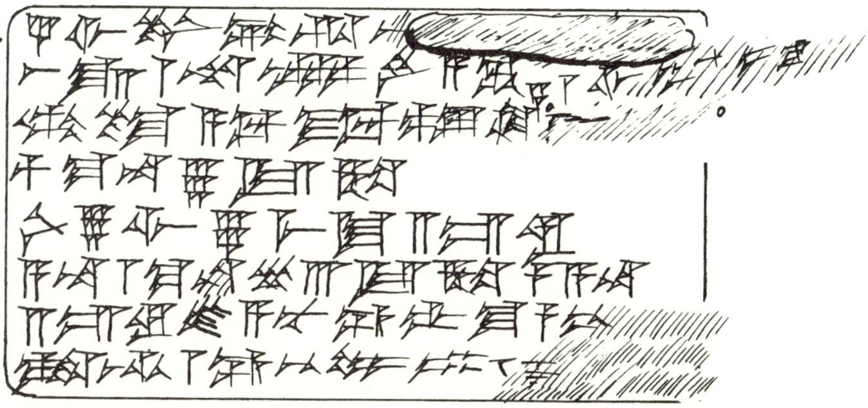

° erasure °

U.E.

° sic, for SIG_4 «UD.X.KÁM»

276

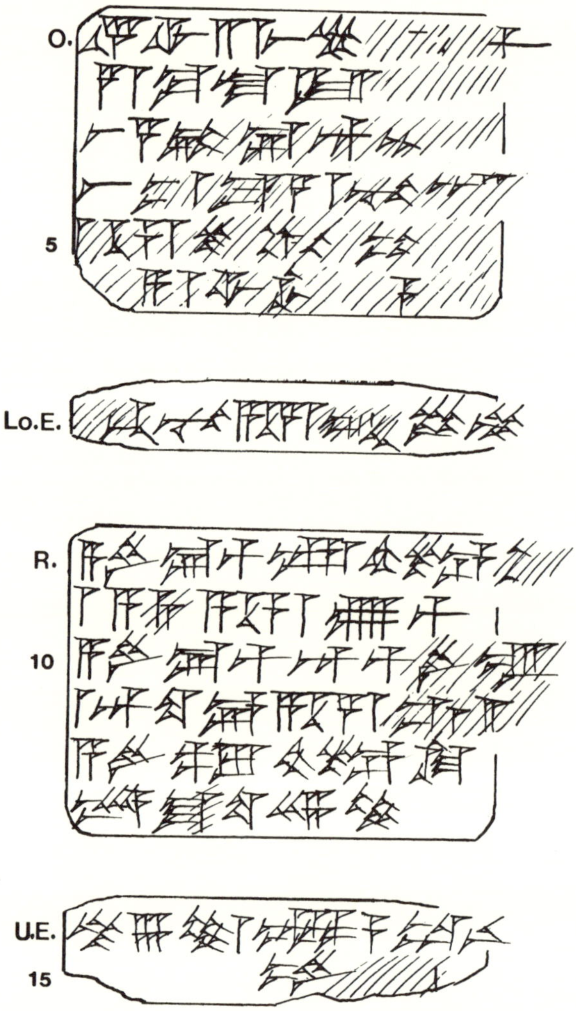

277

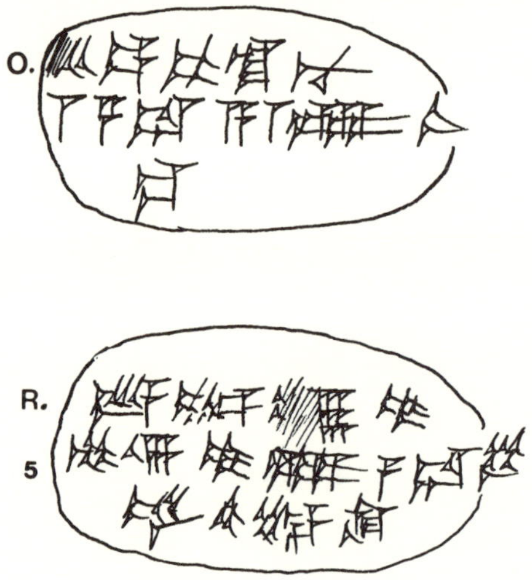

278

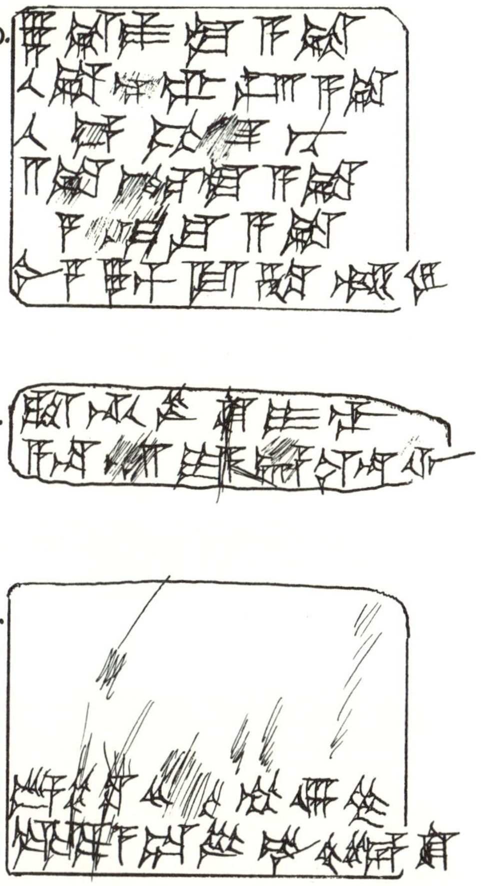

279

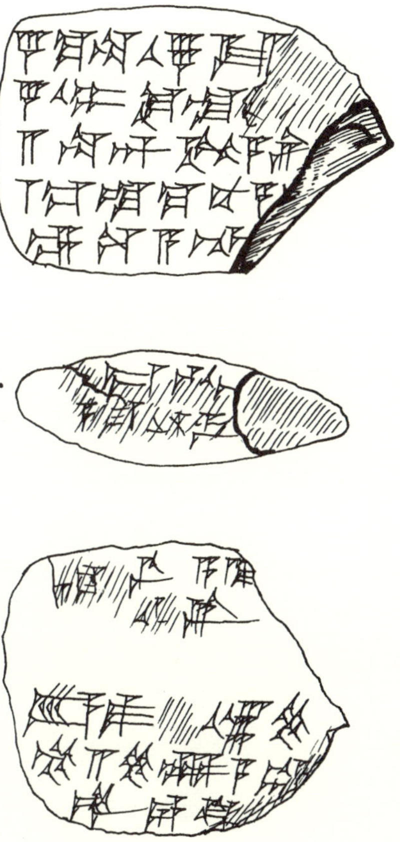

280

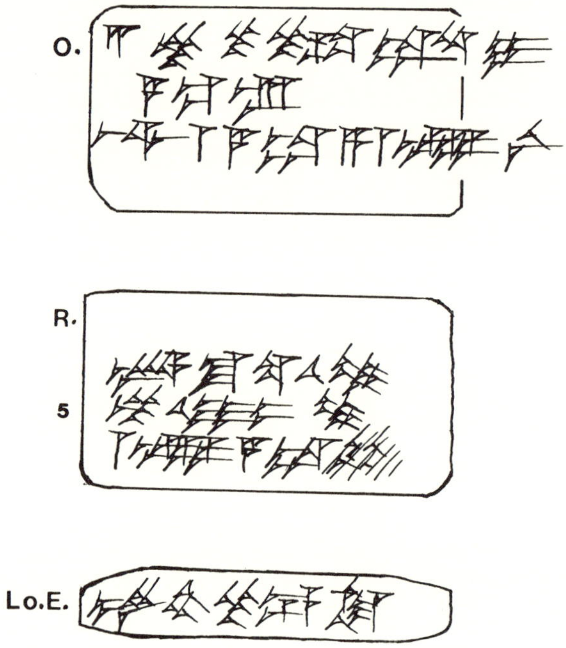

281

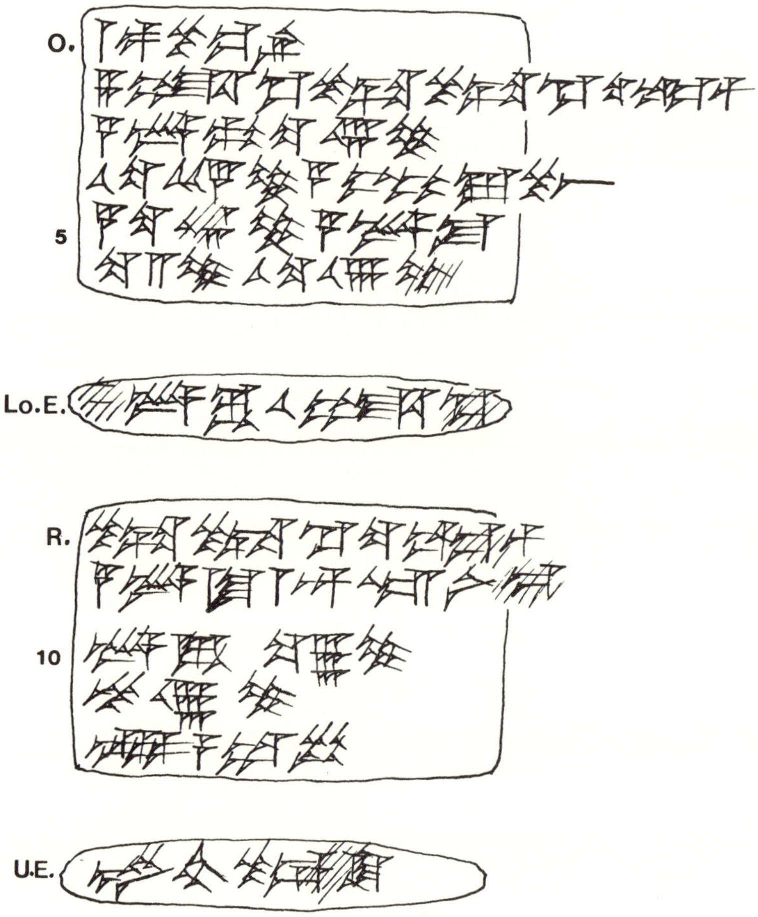

282

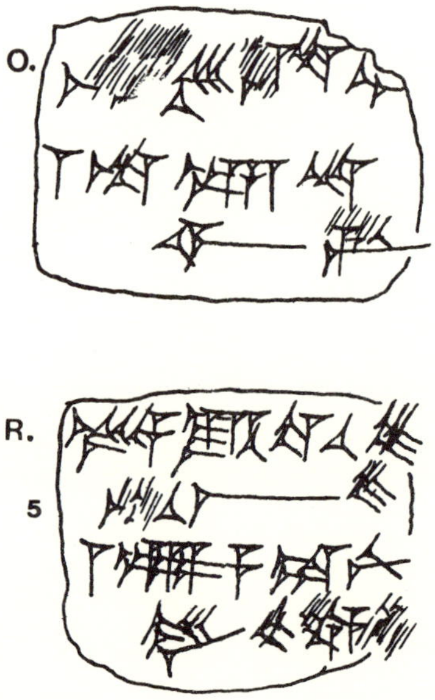

283

O.

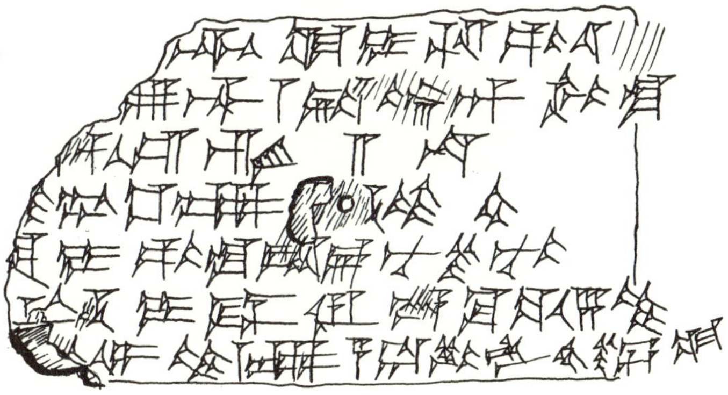

Reverse Uninscribed

Seal impression in lower right corner?

284

O.

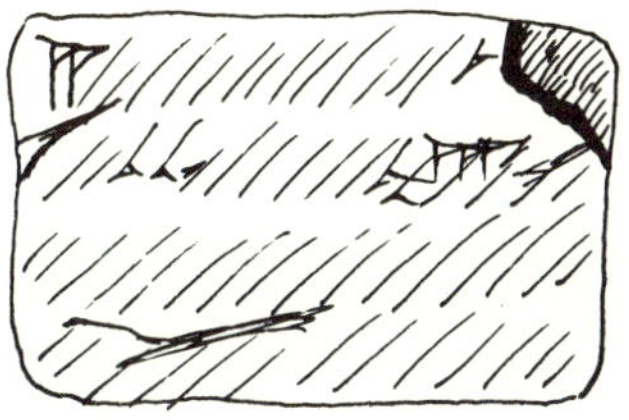

R.

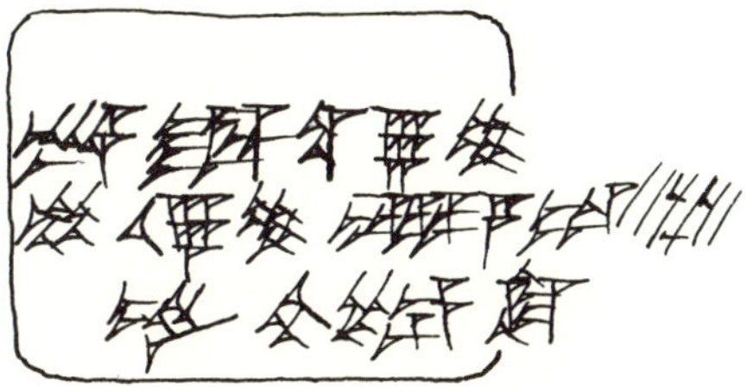

285

(obverse destroyed)

R.

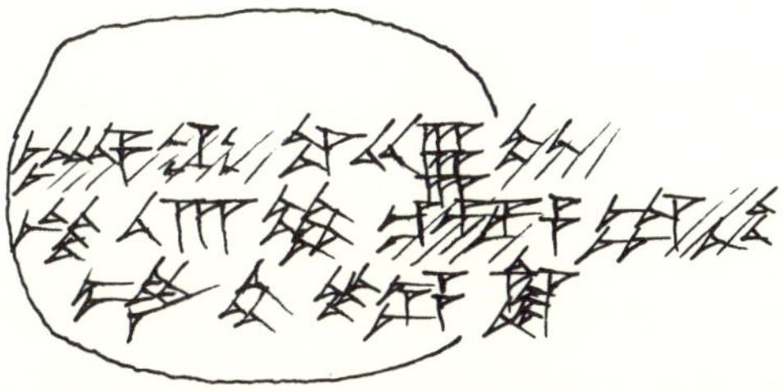

286

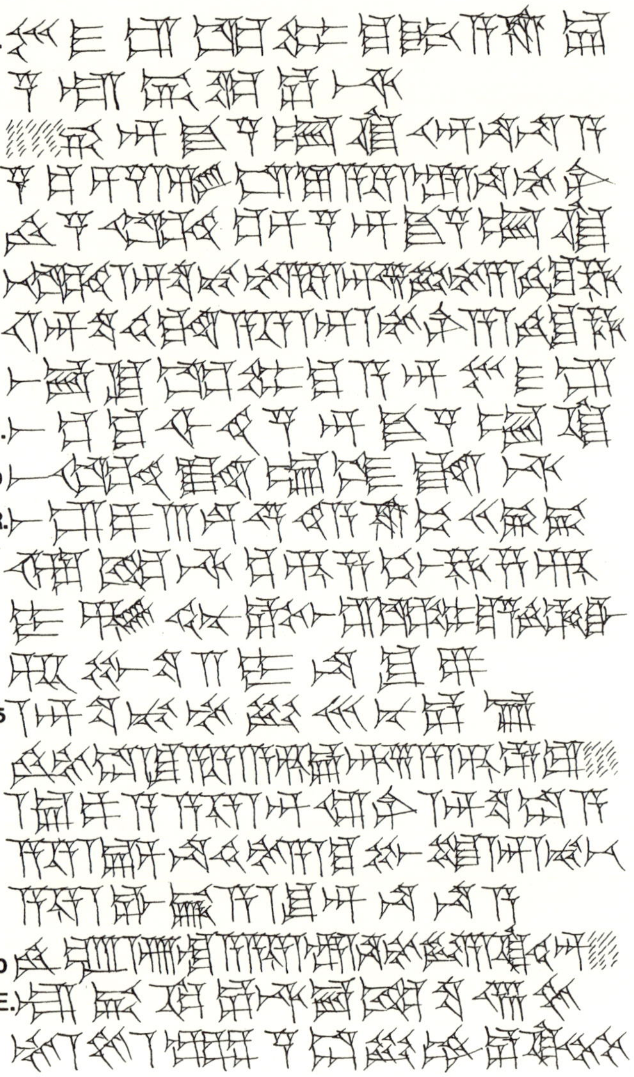

287

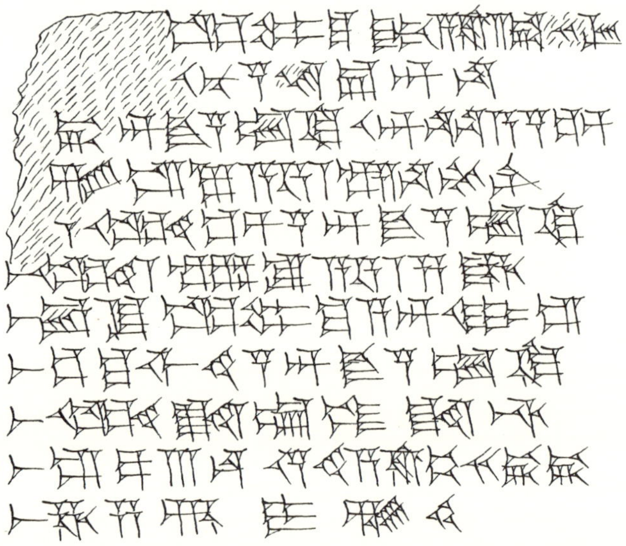

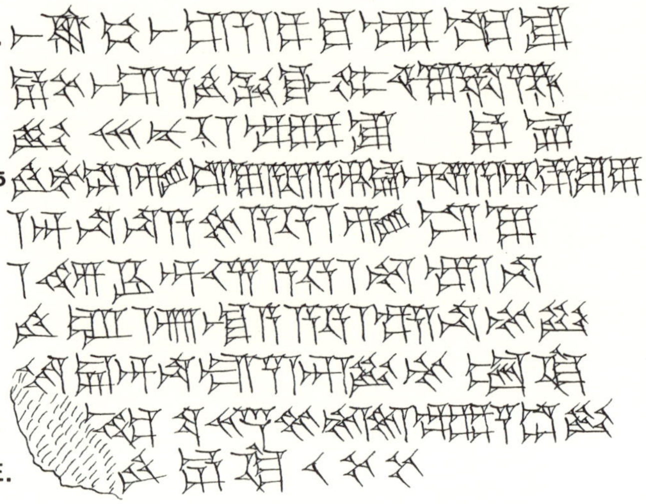

288

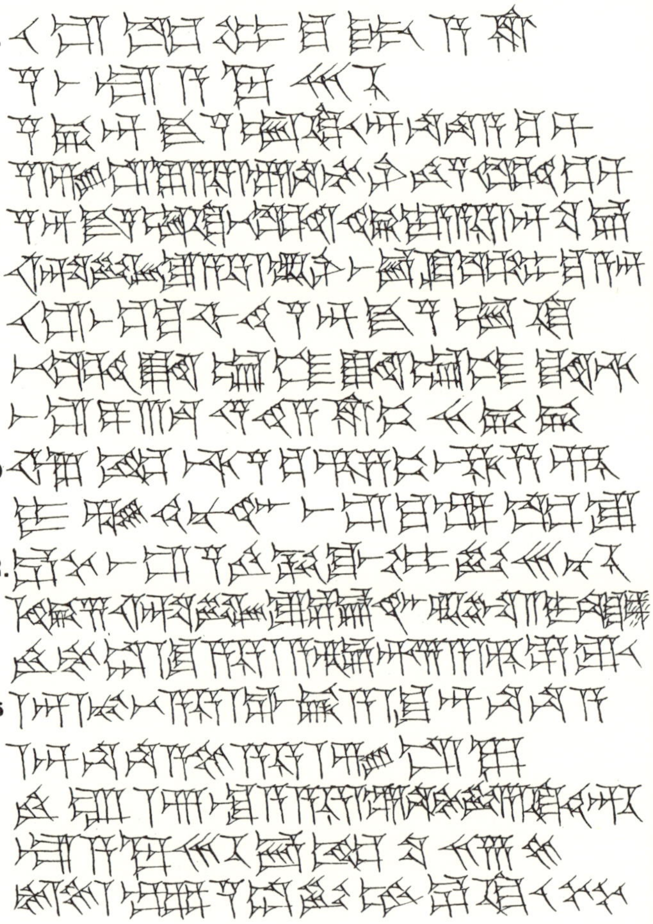

289

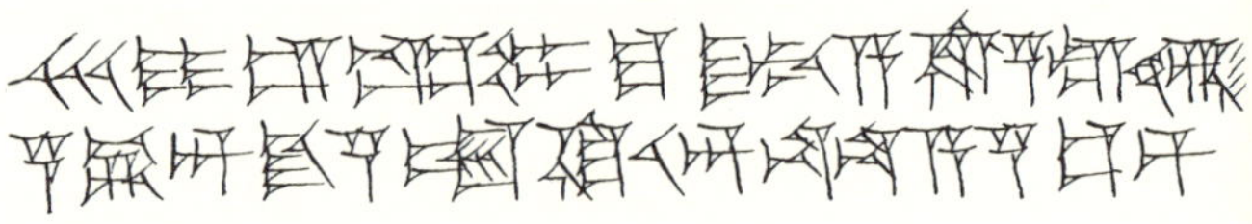

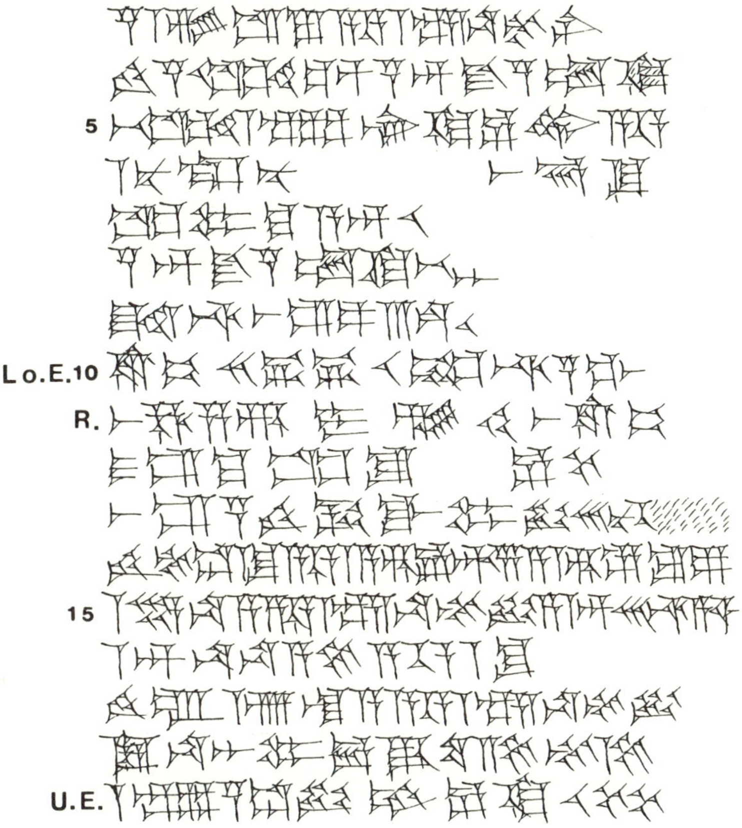

290

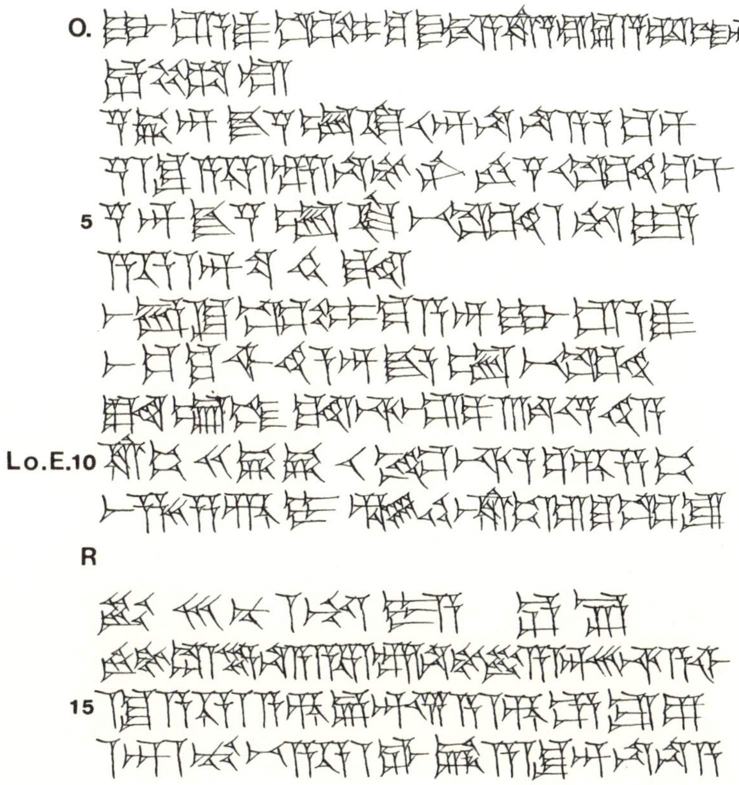

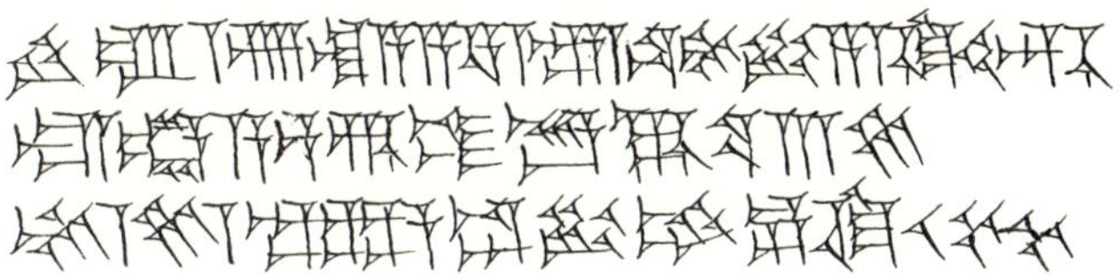

291

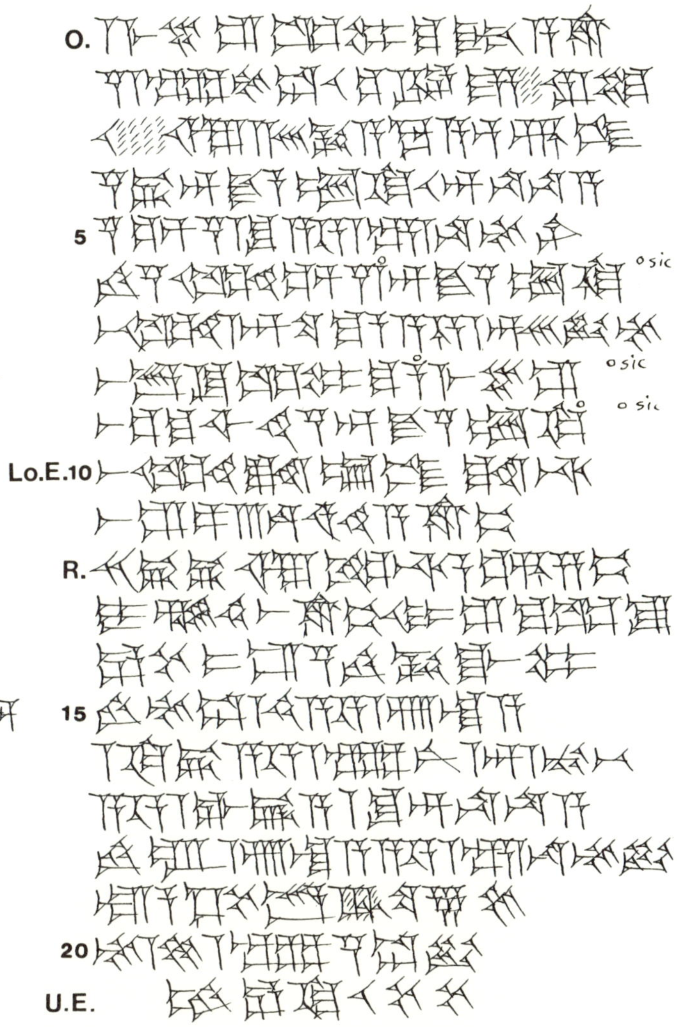

292

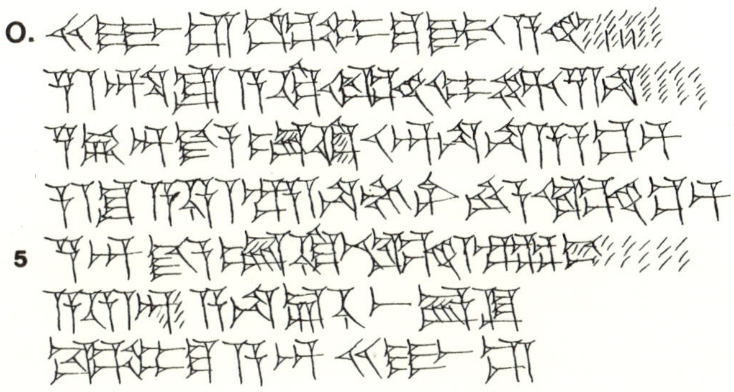

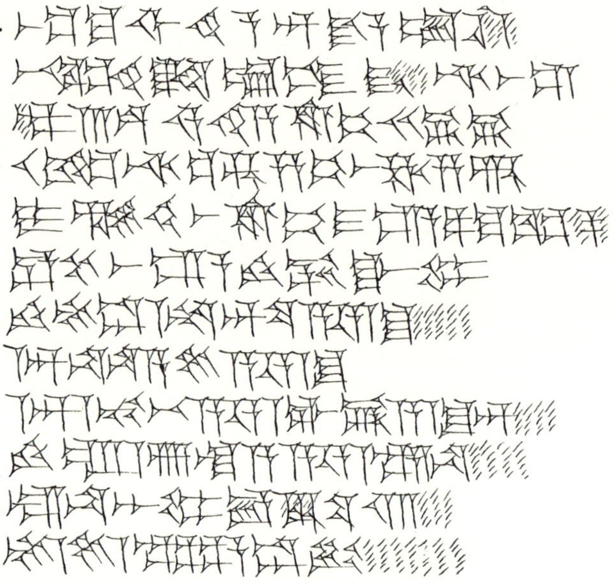

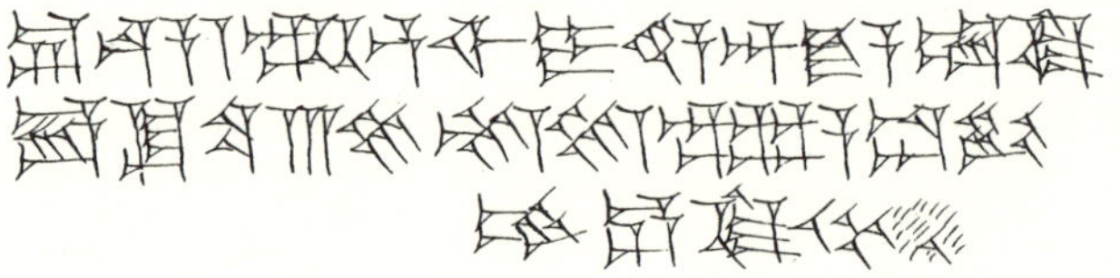

293

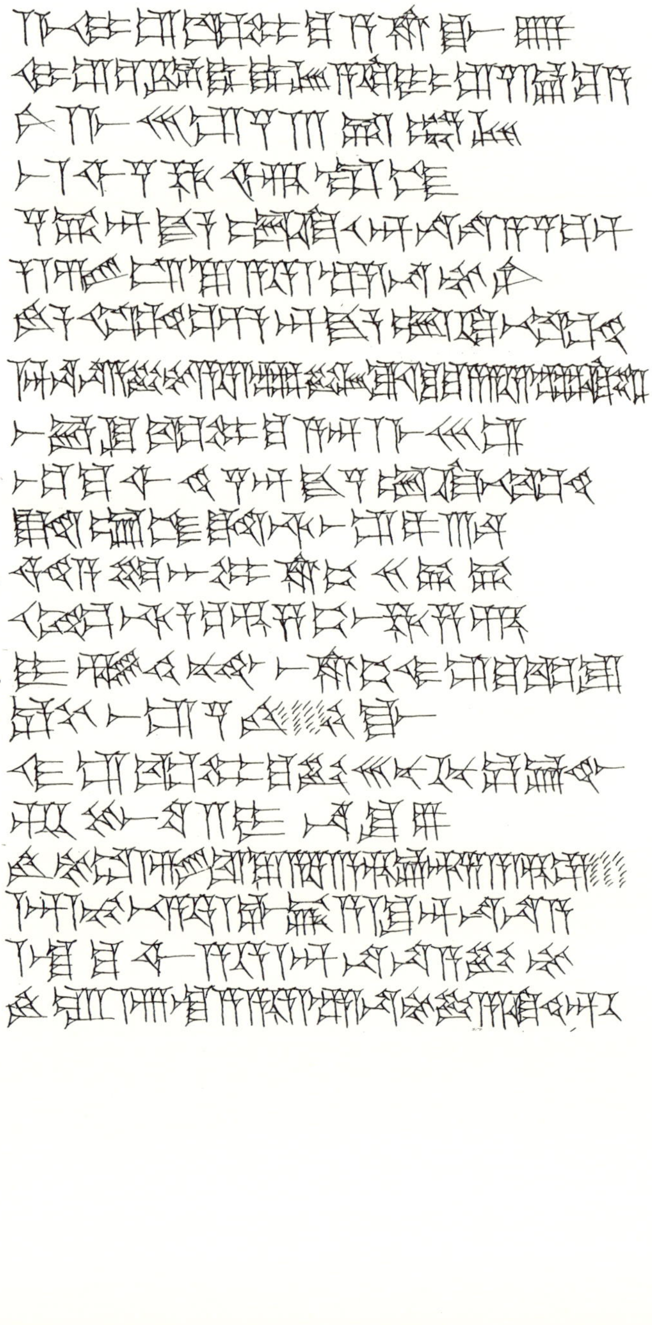

294

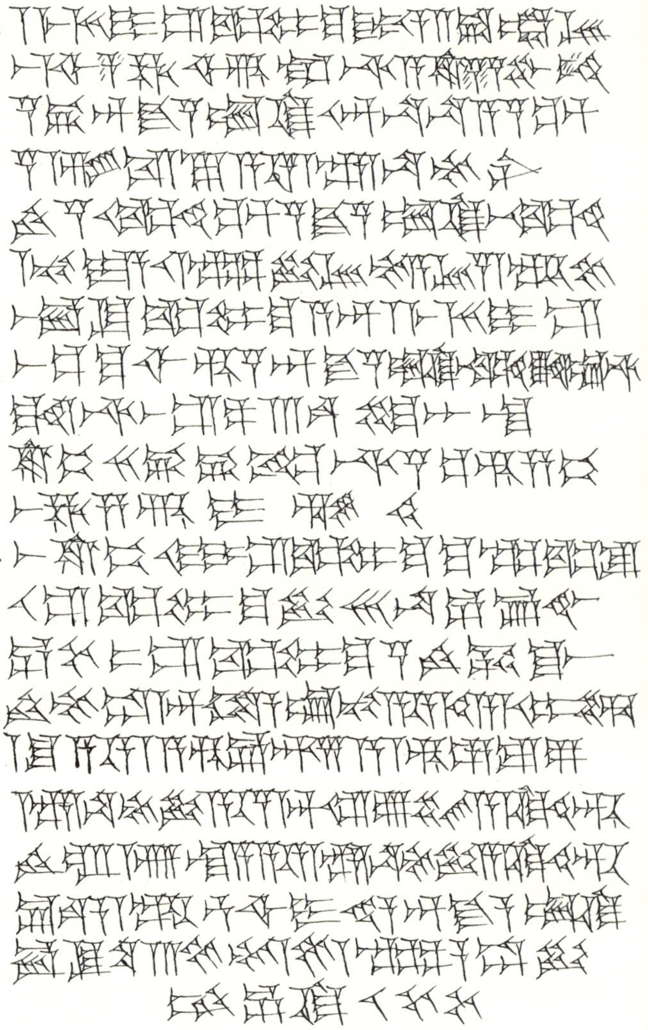

295

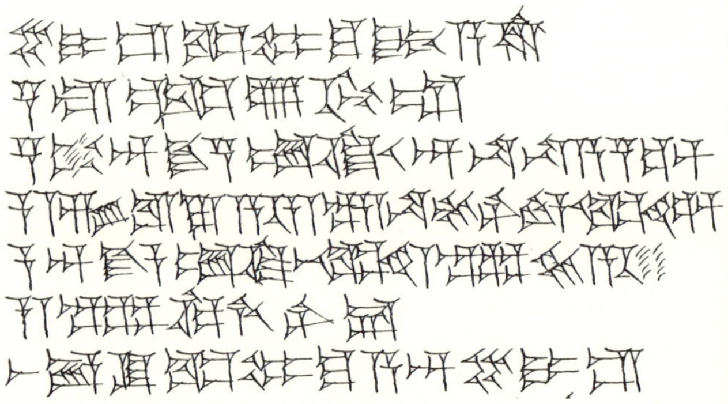

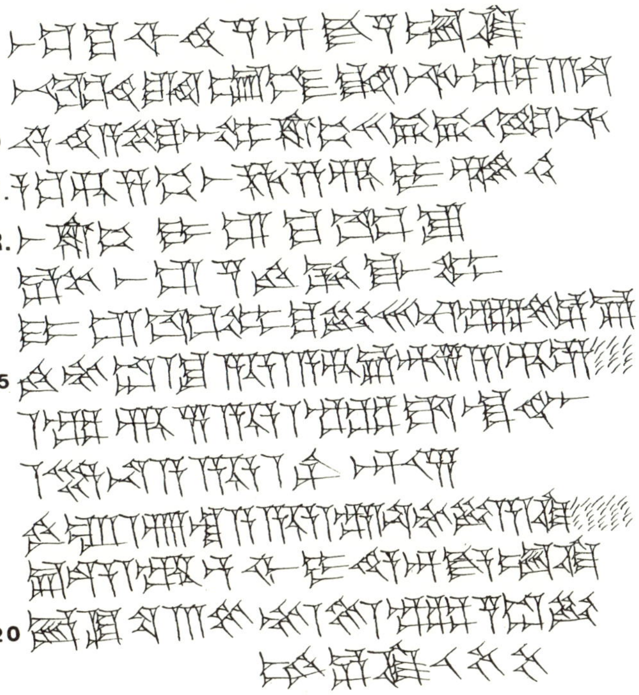

297

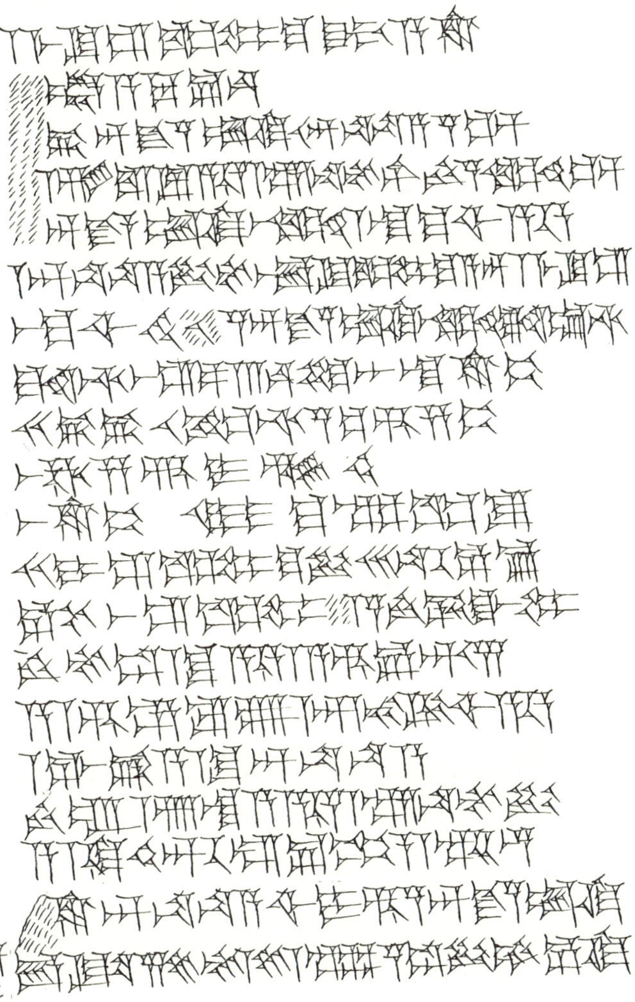

296

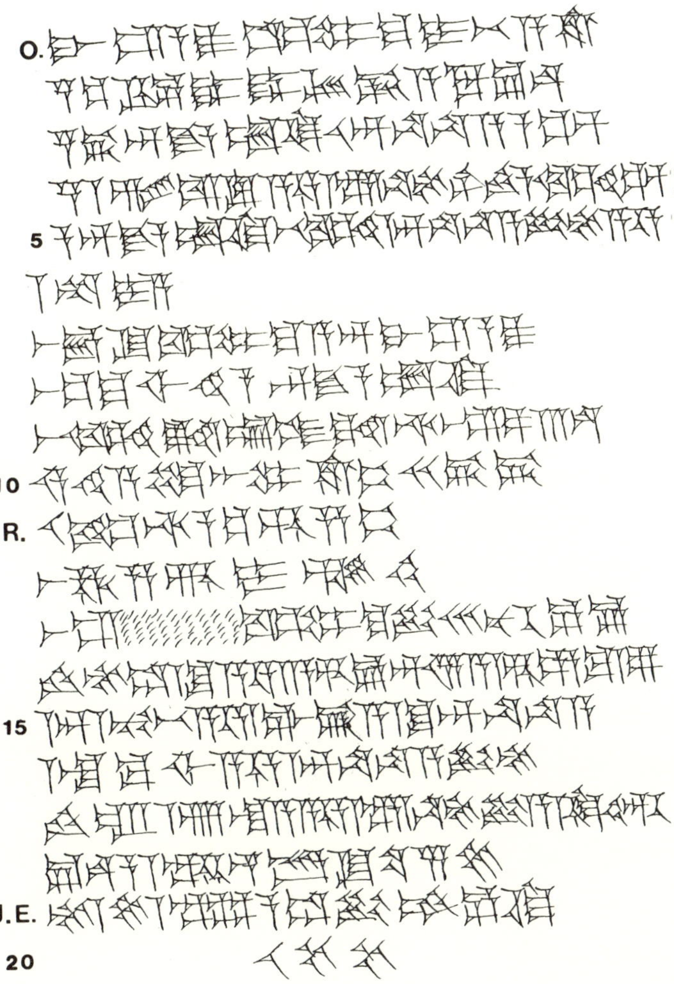

298

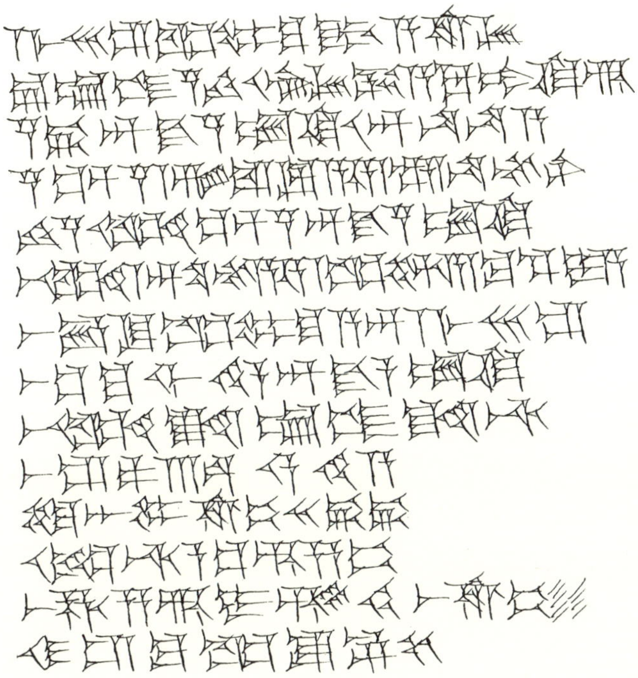

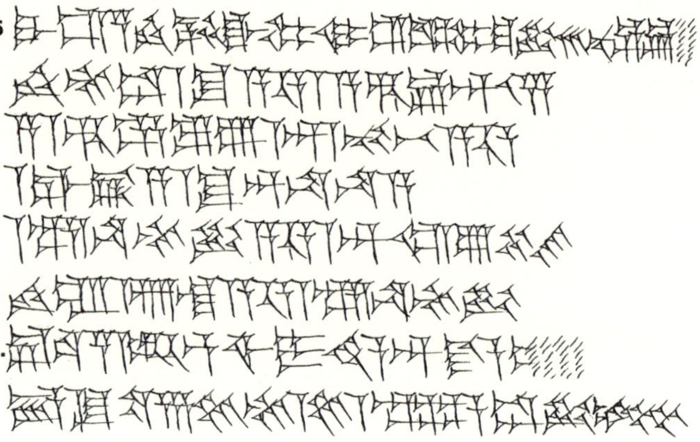

299

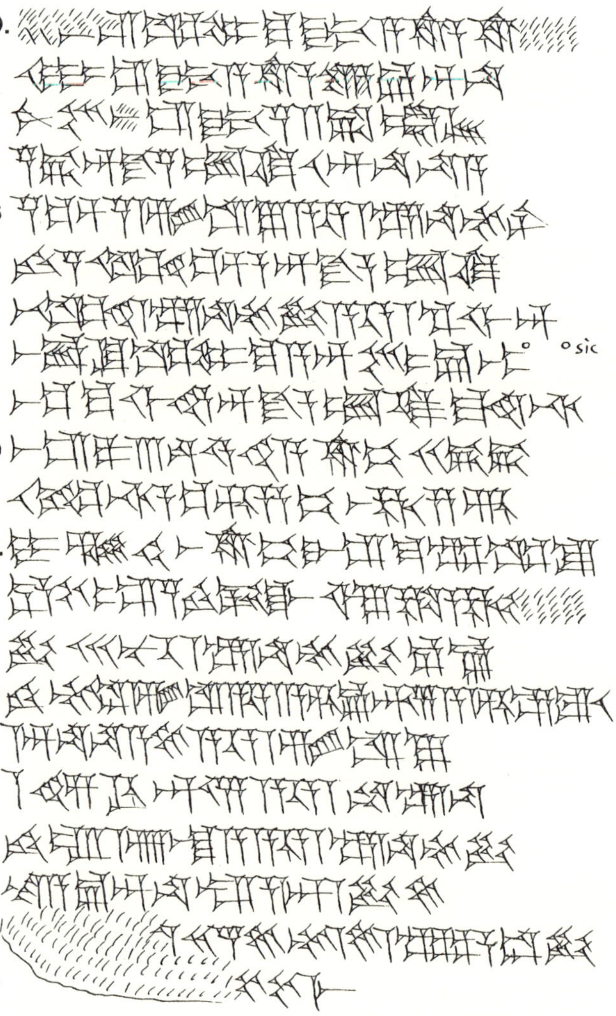

300

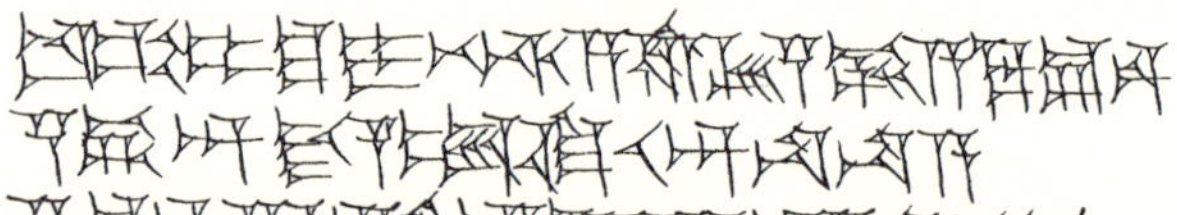

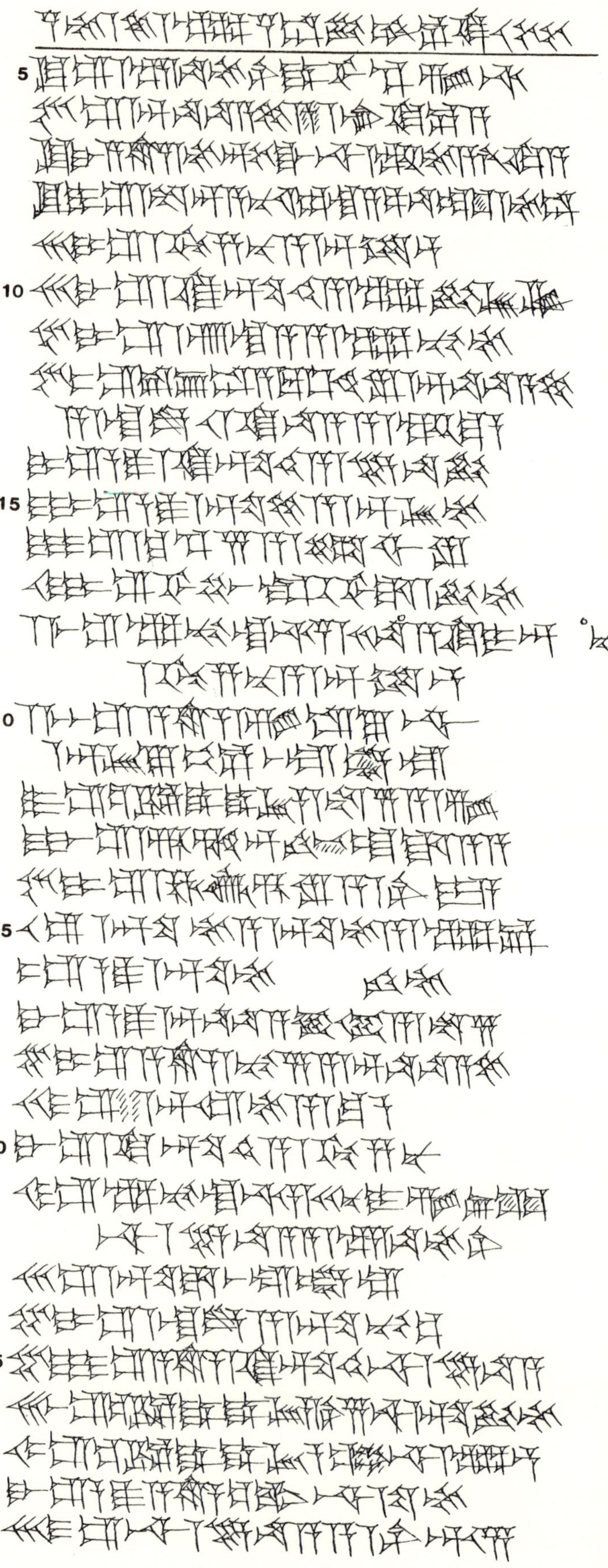

301

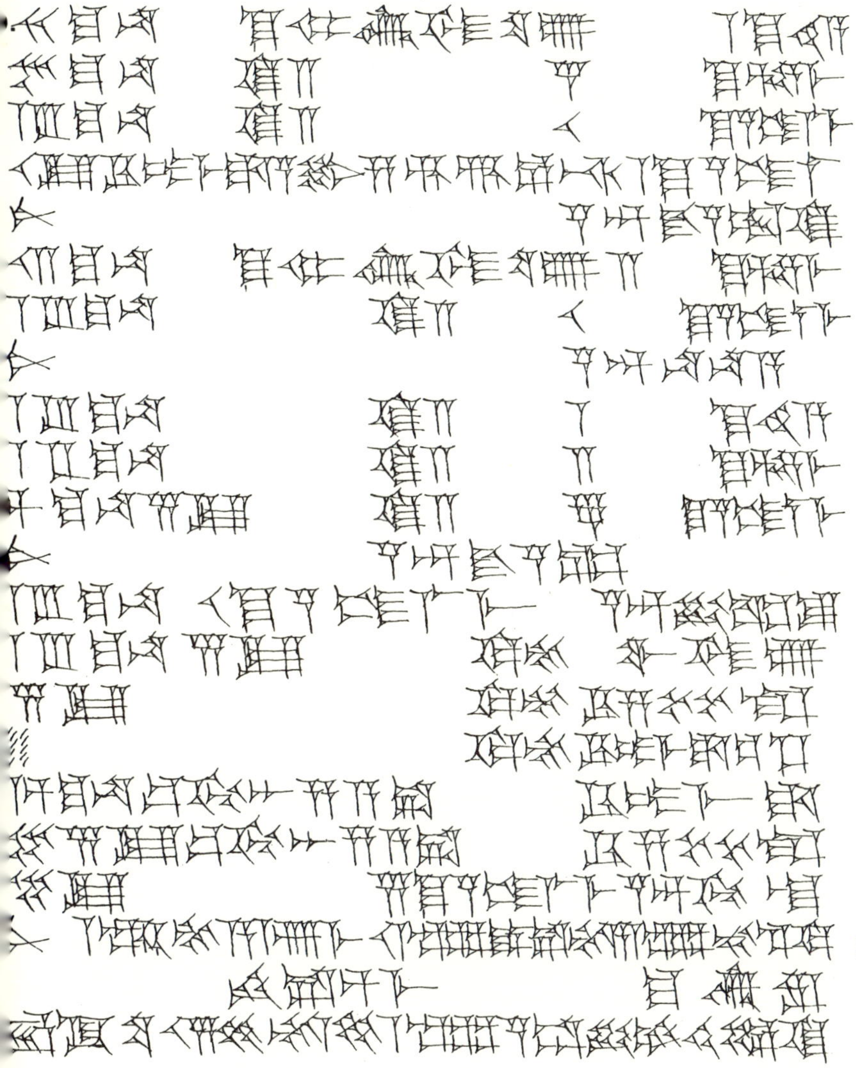

302

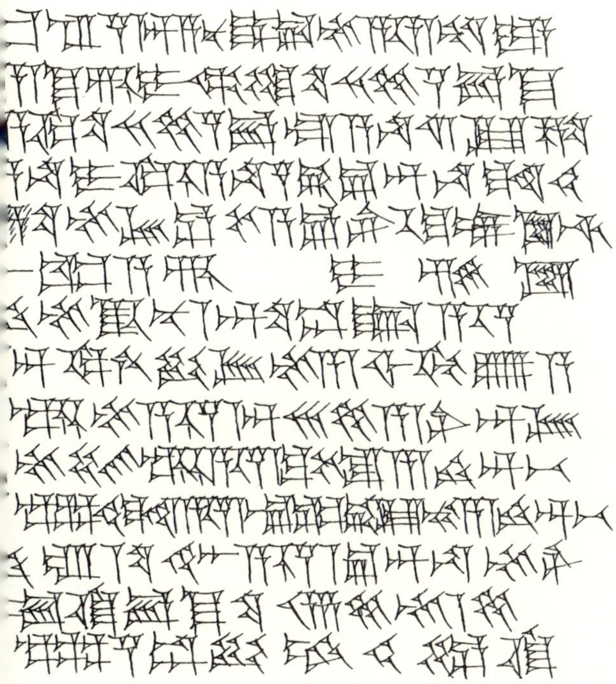

303

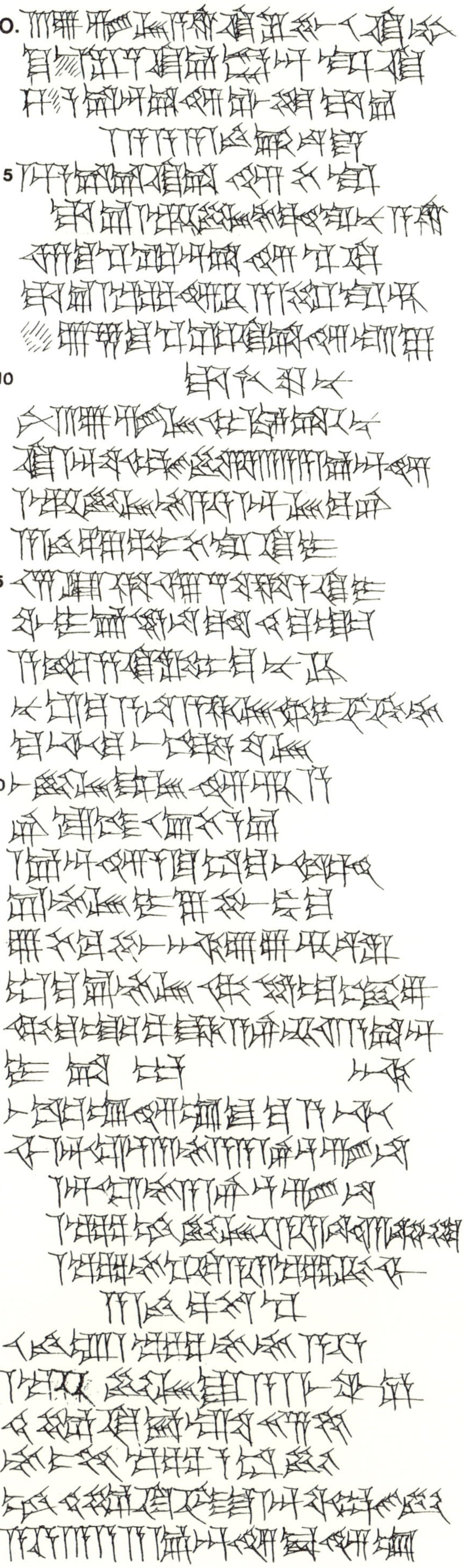

PLATE CXL

304

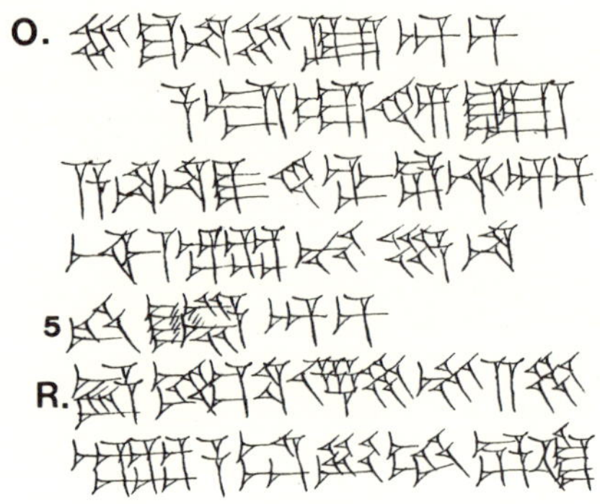

305

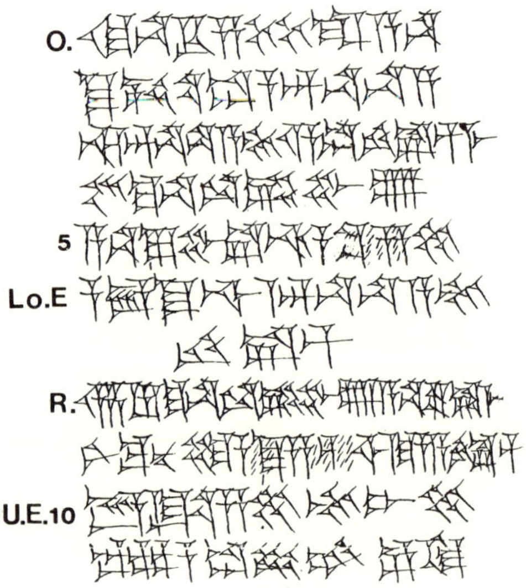

306

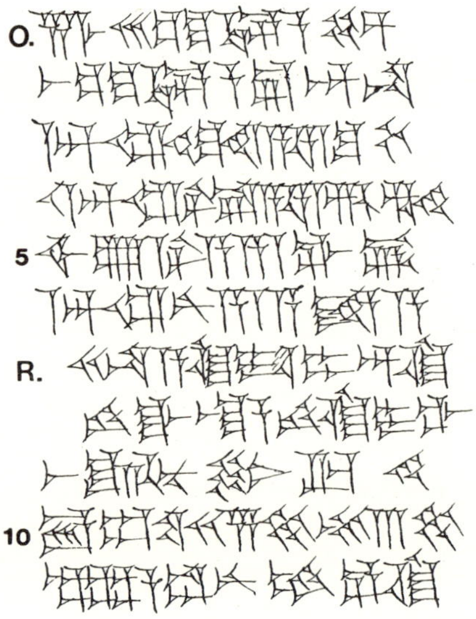

307

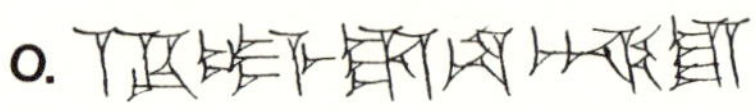

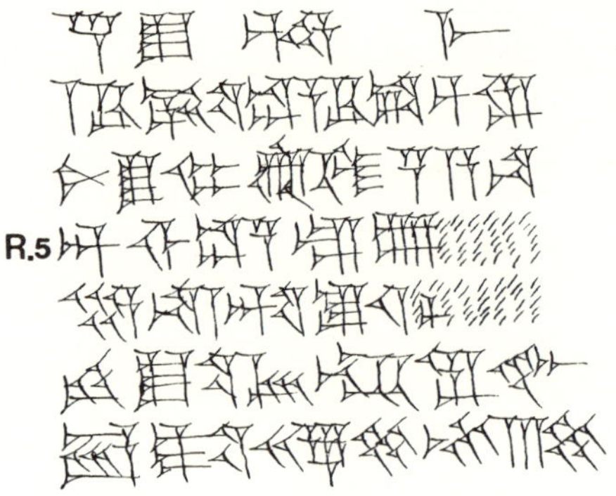

308

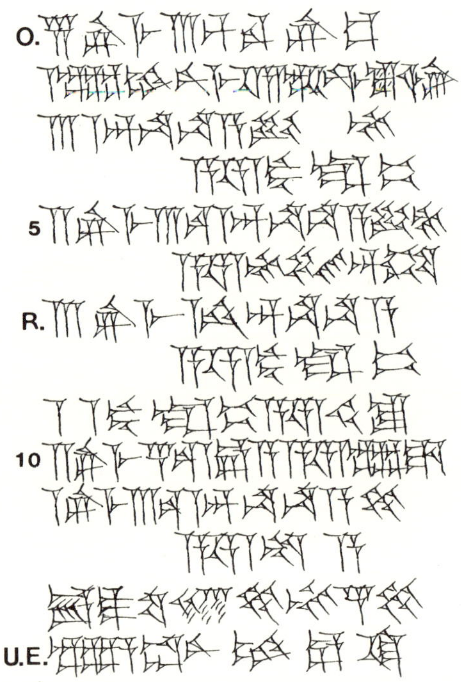

309

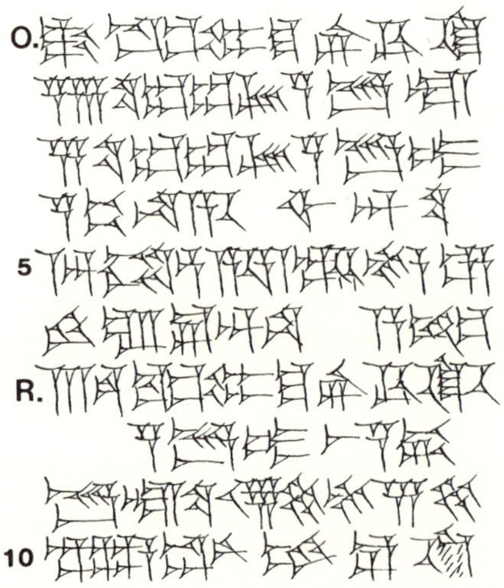

310

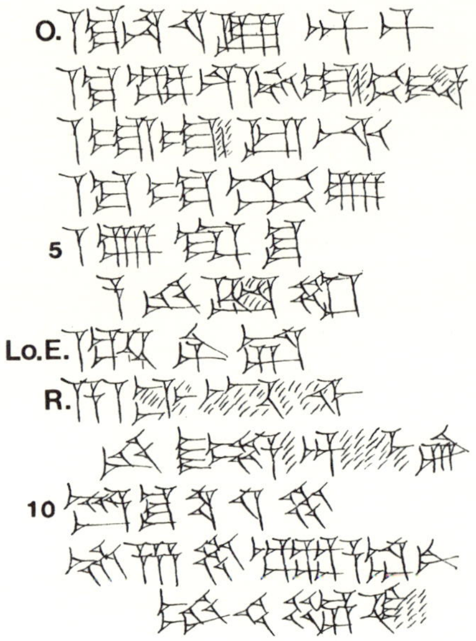

311

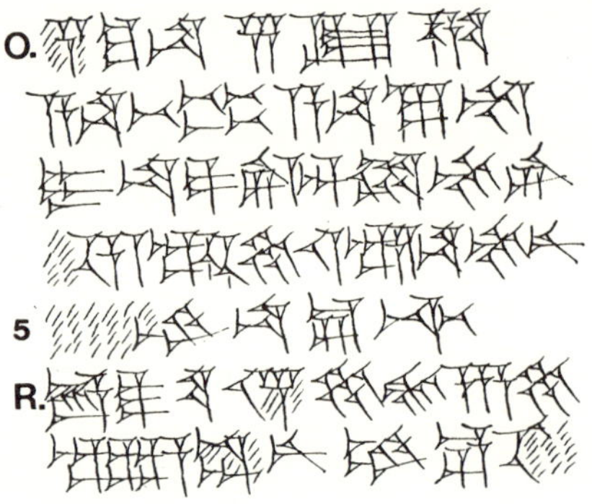

312

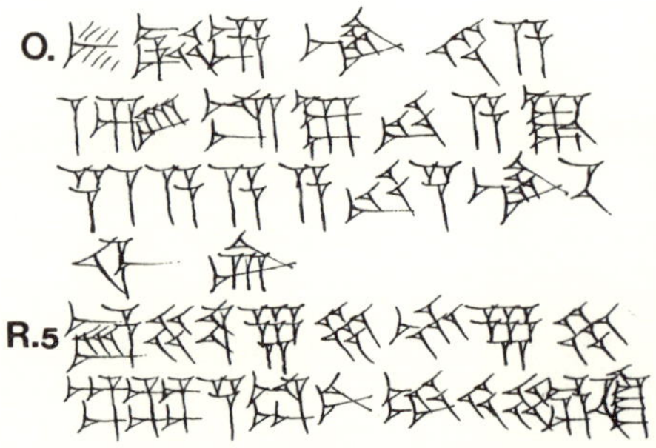

313

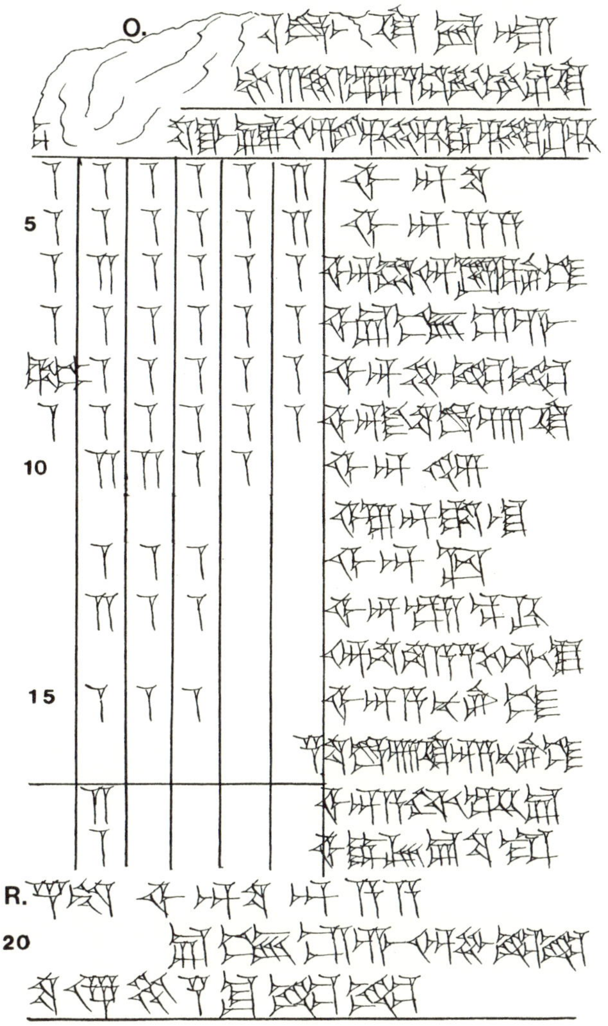

314

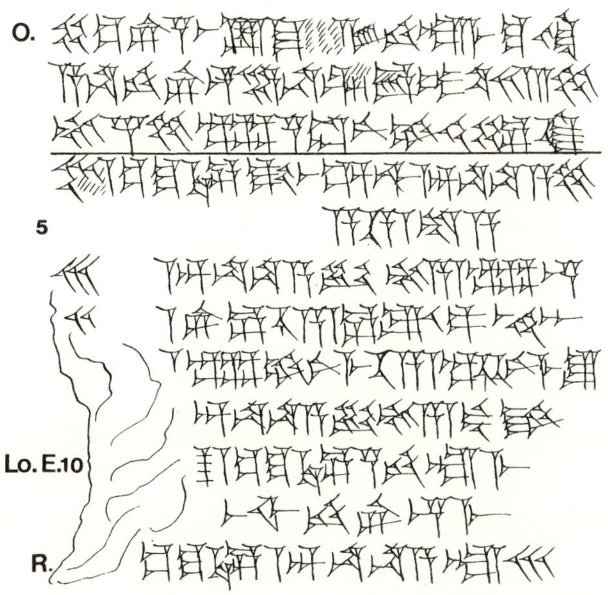

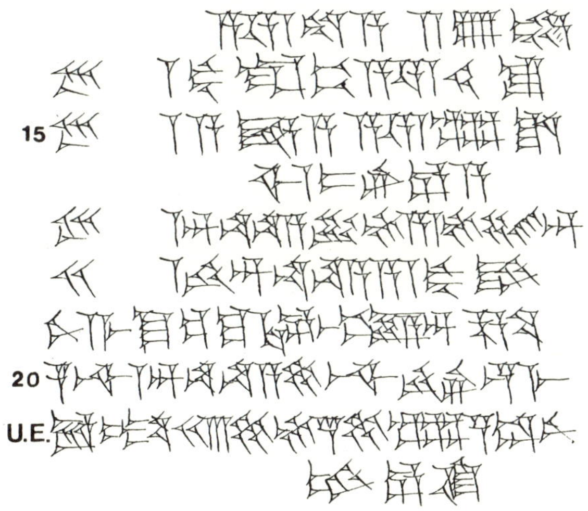

315

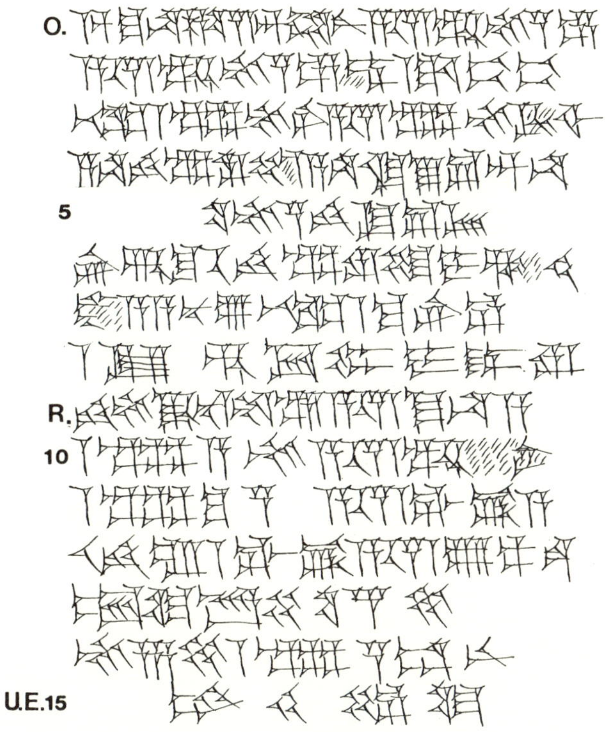

316

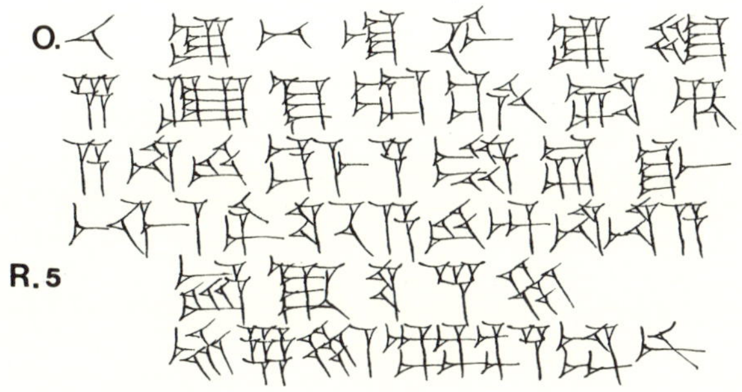

317

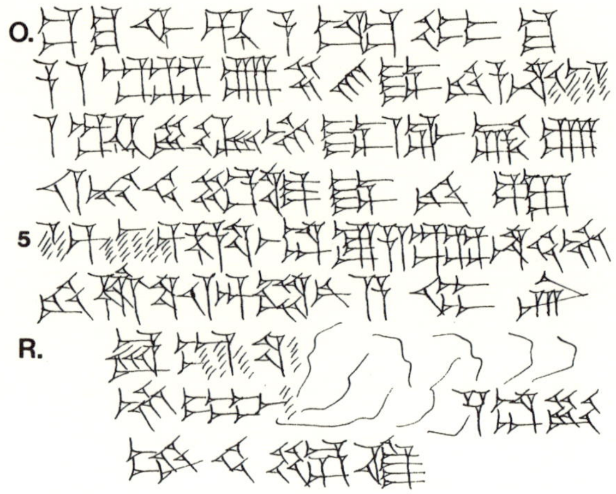

318

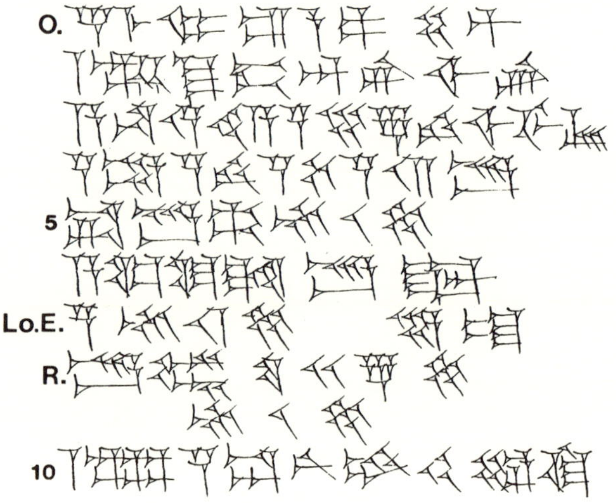

319

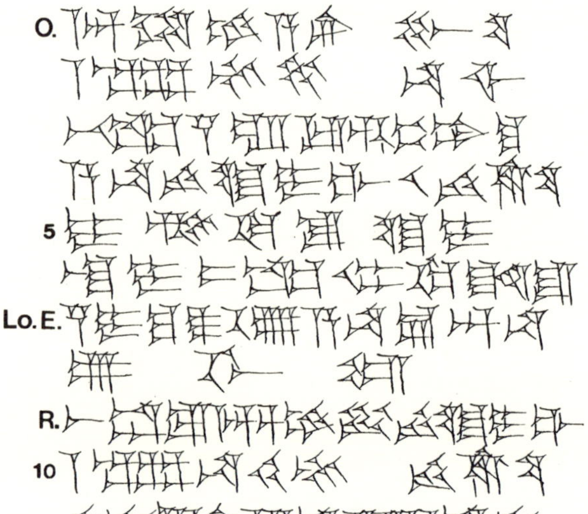

320

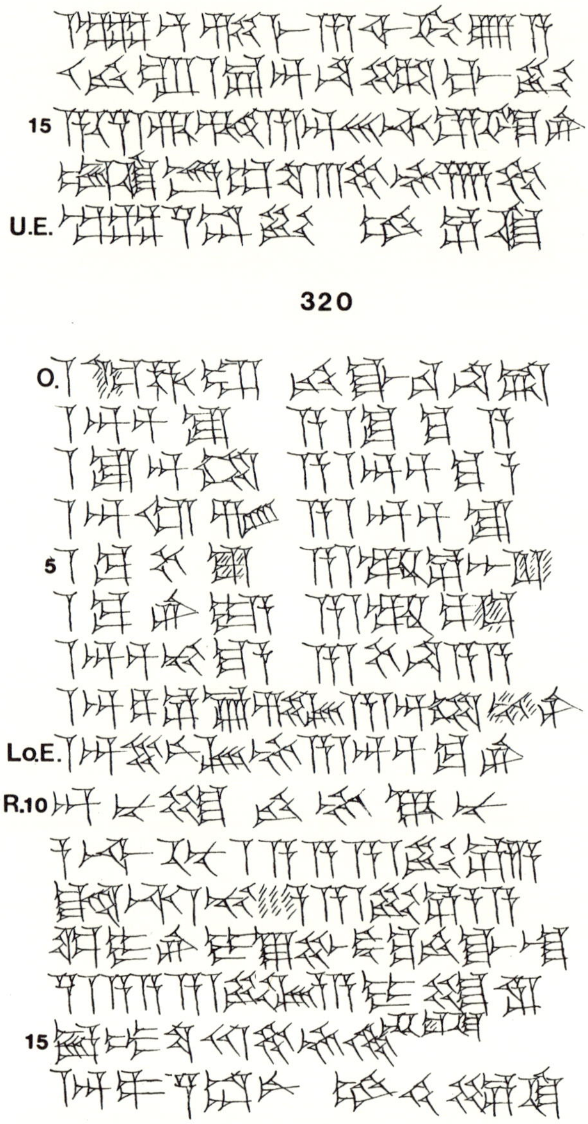

321

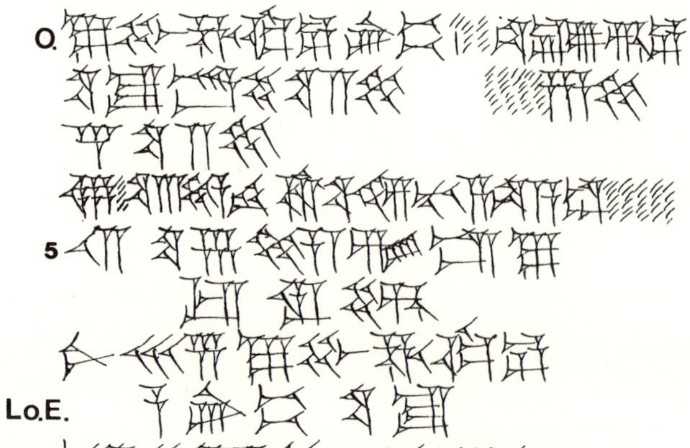

322

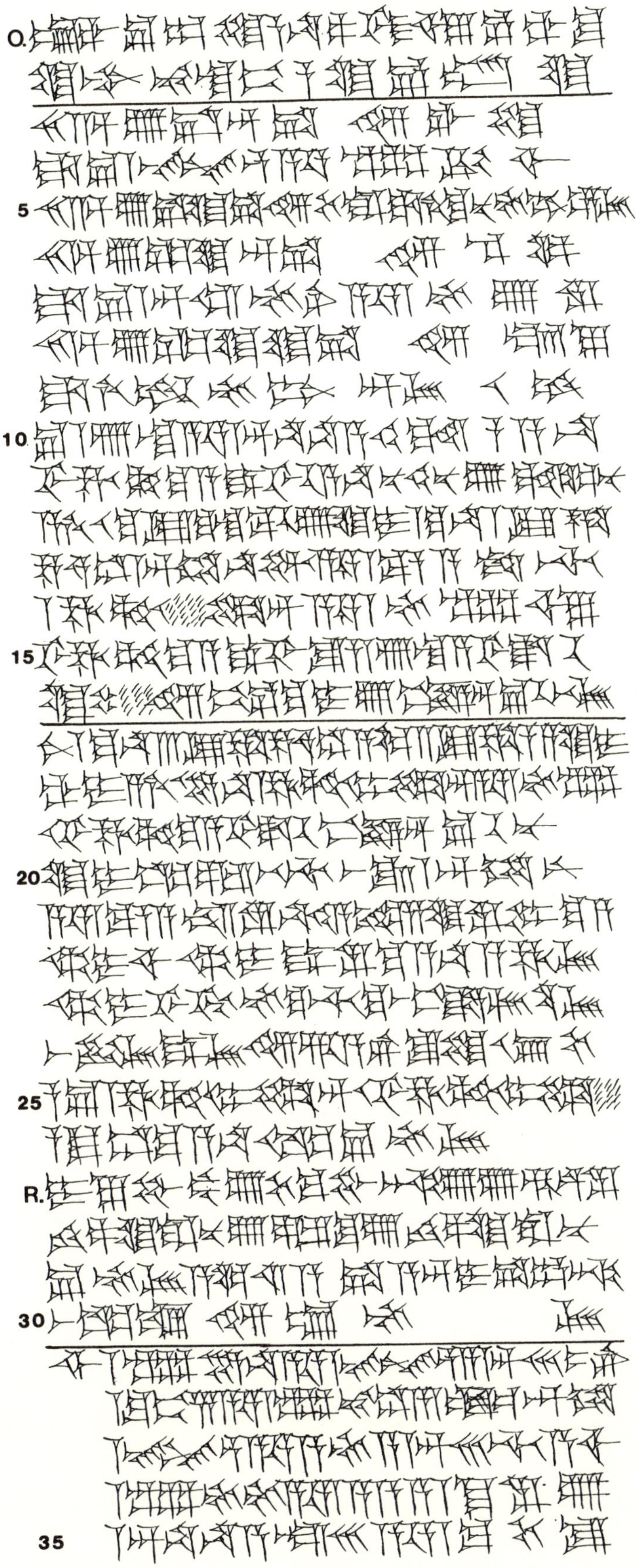

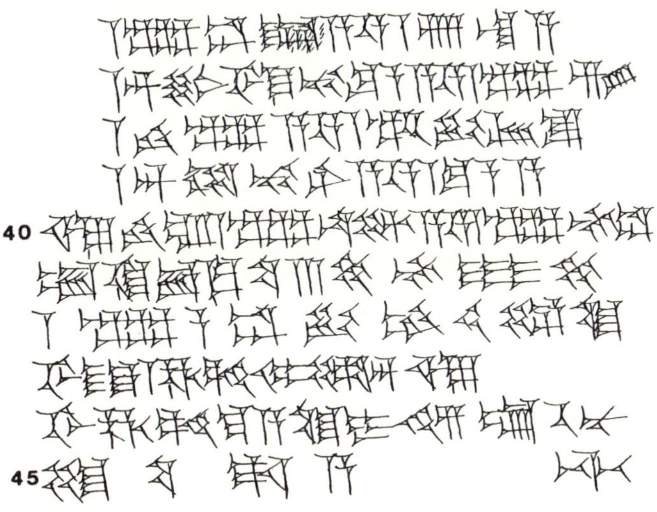

323

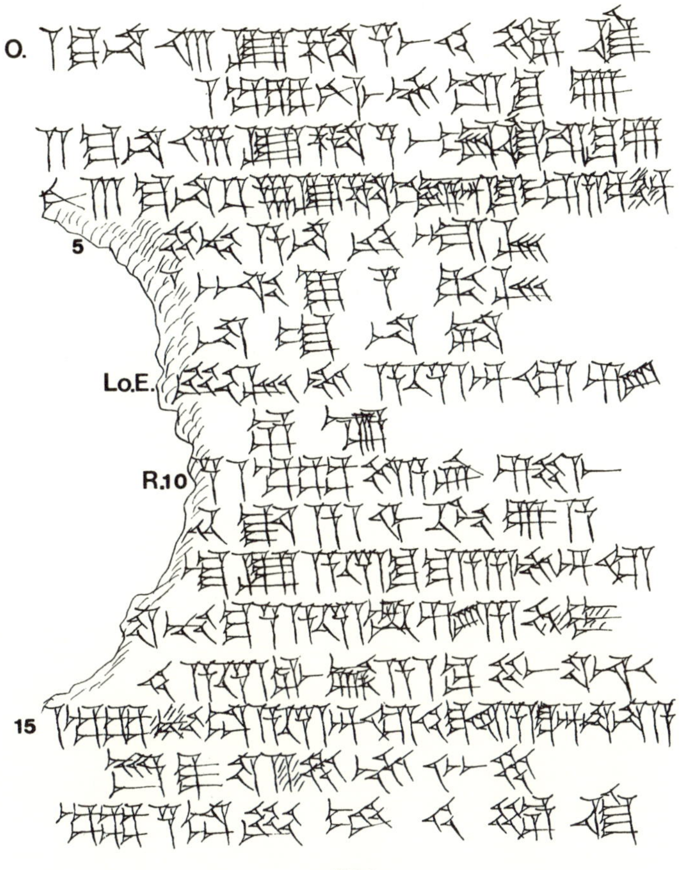

324

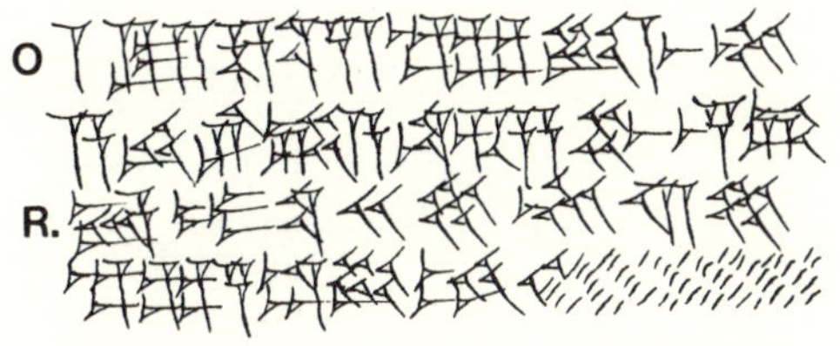

325

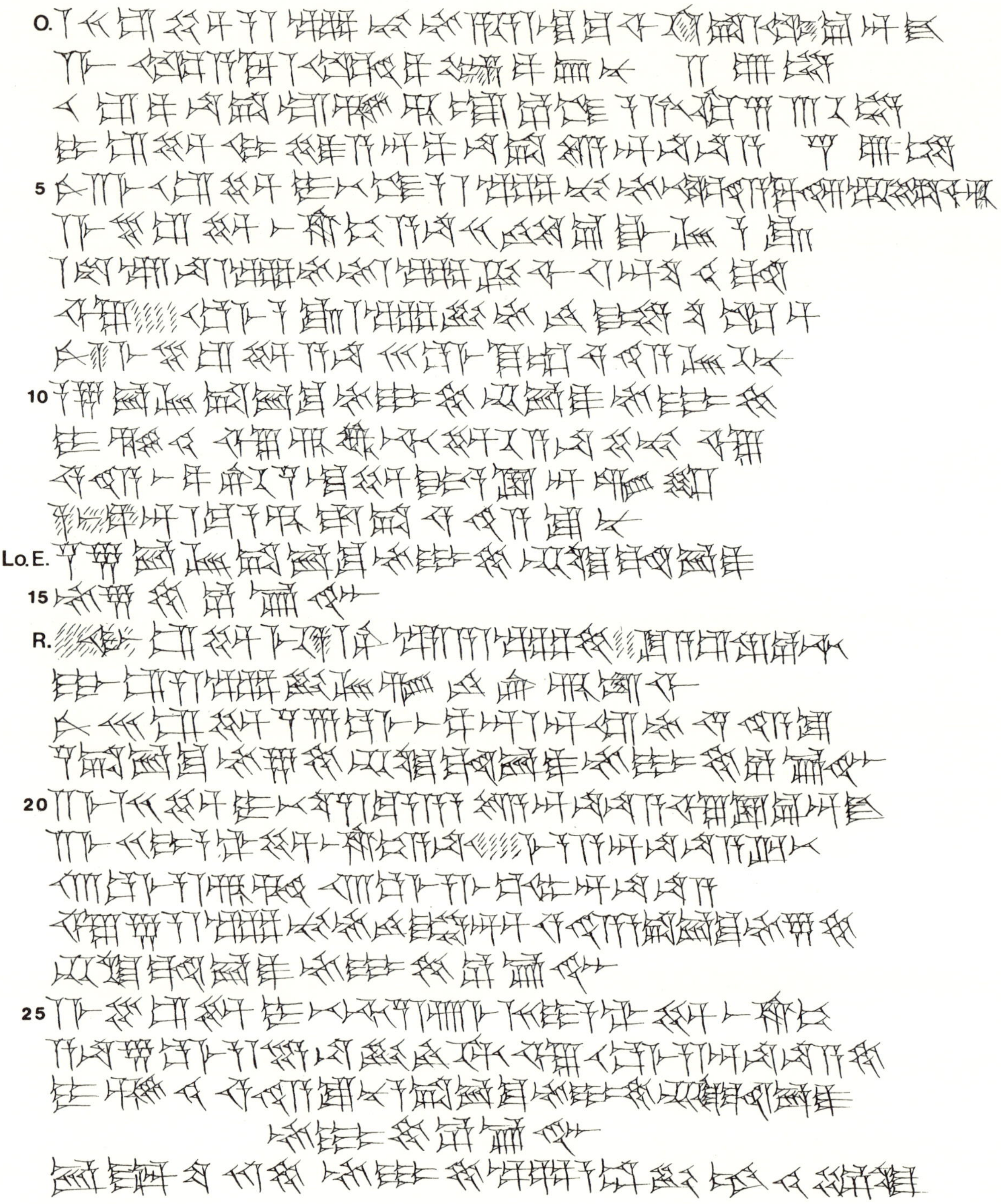

326

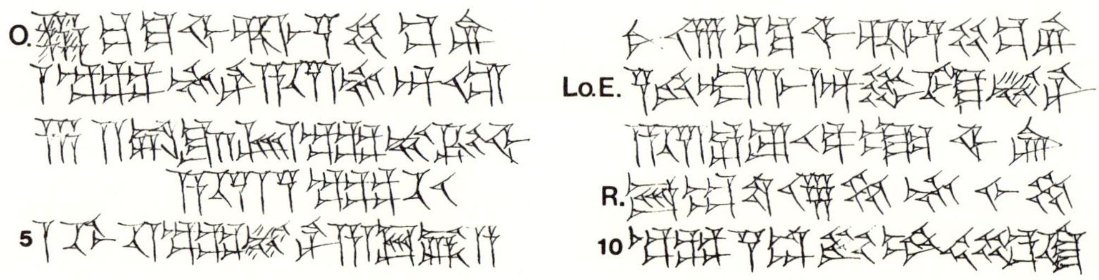

327

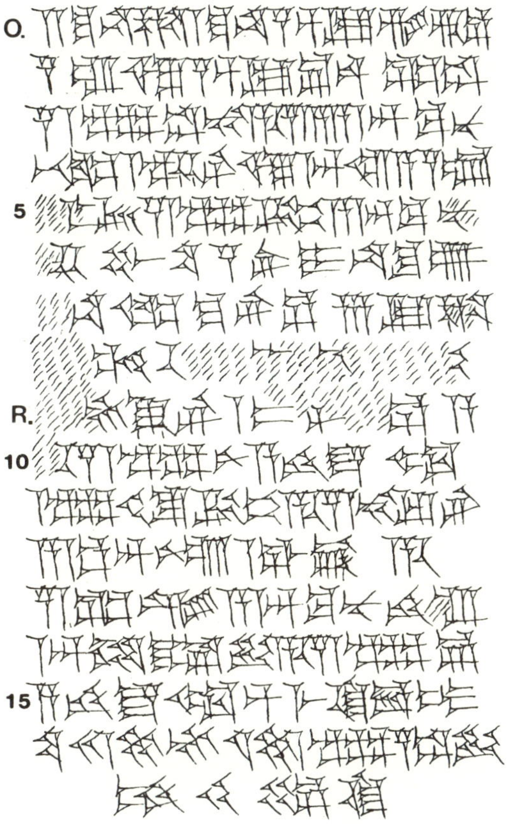

328

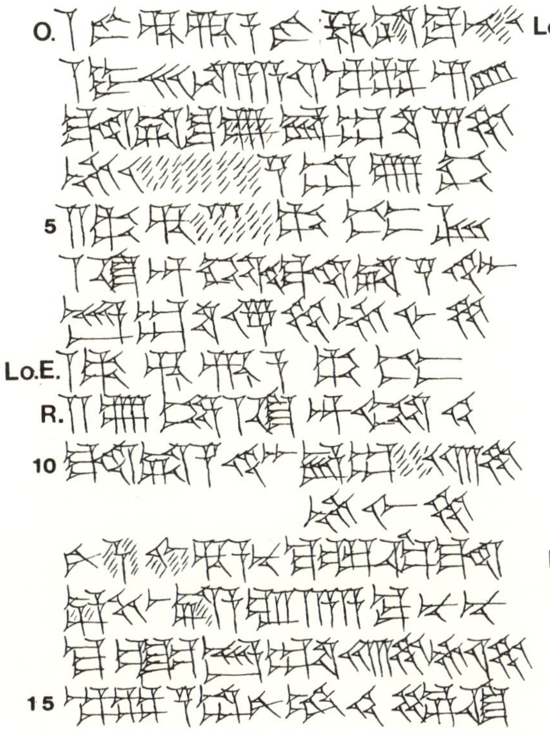

329

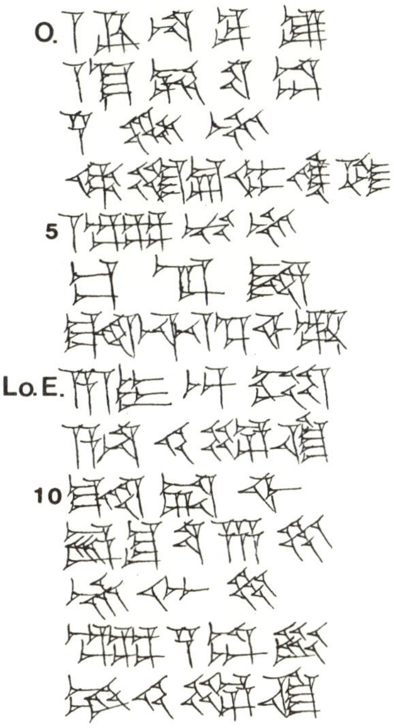

330

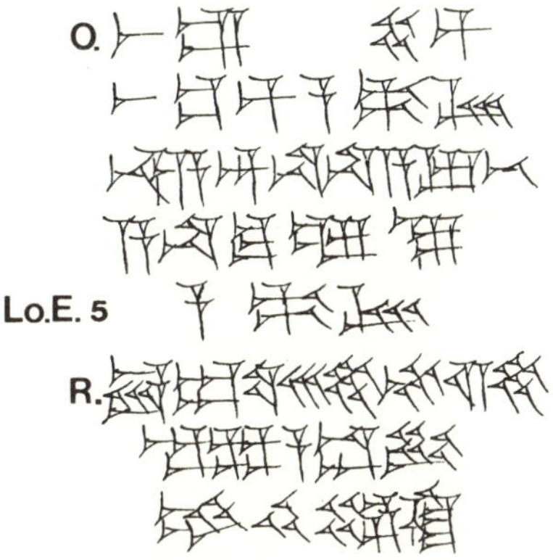

331

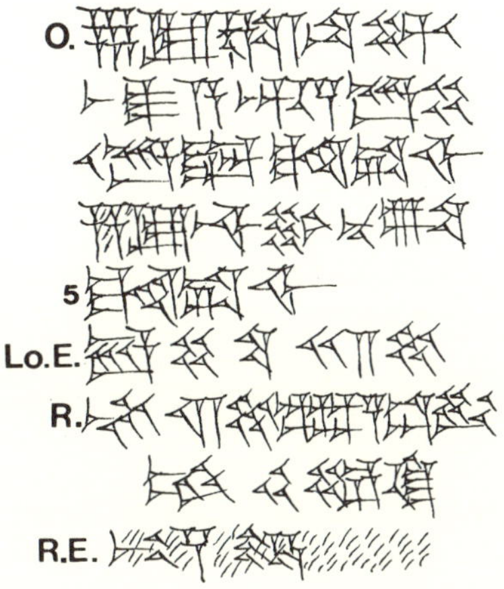

332

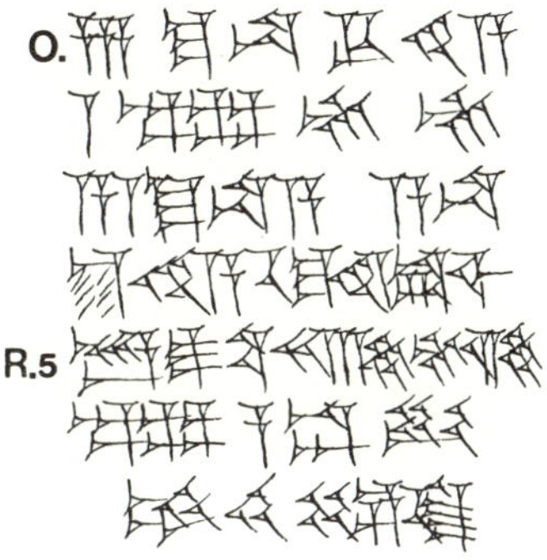

333

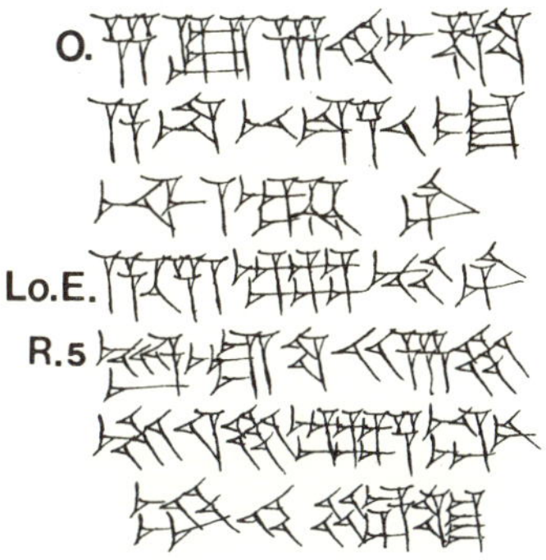

334

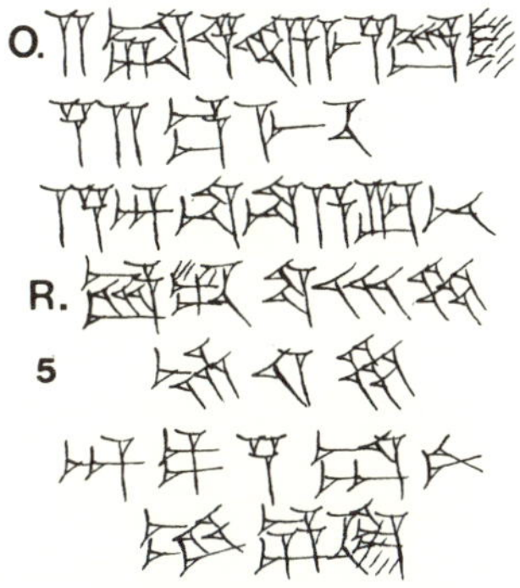

335

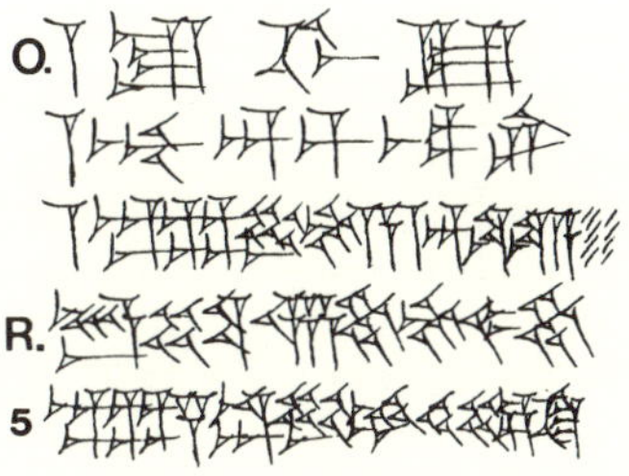

PLATE CXLVI

336

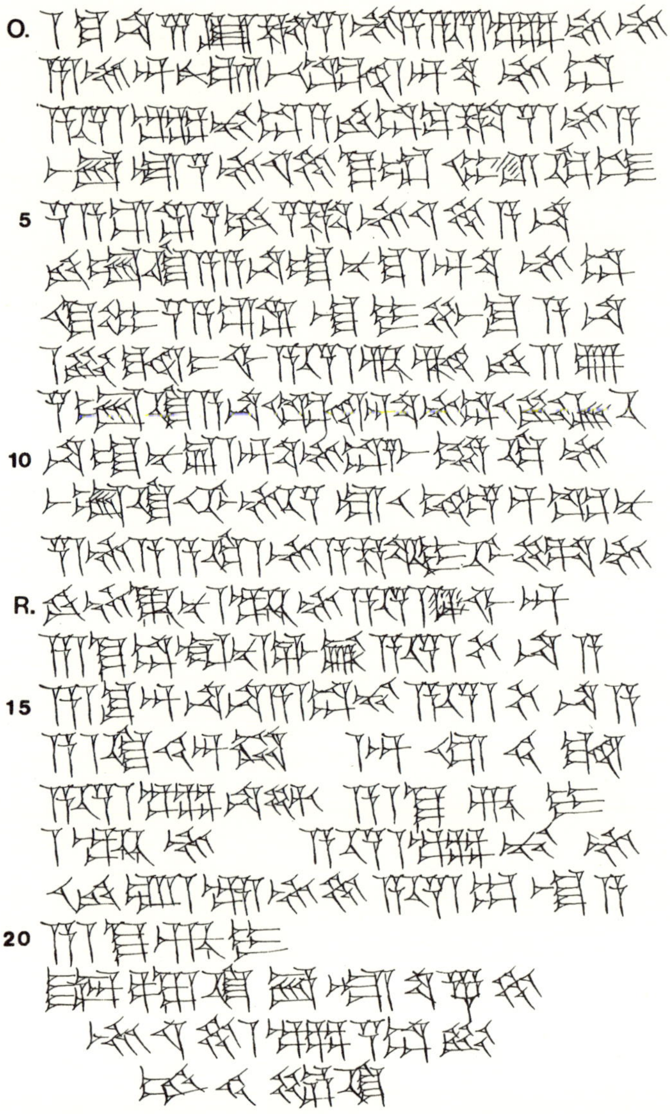

338

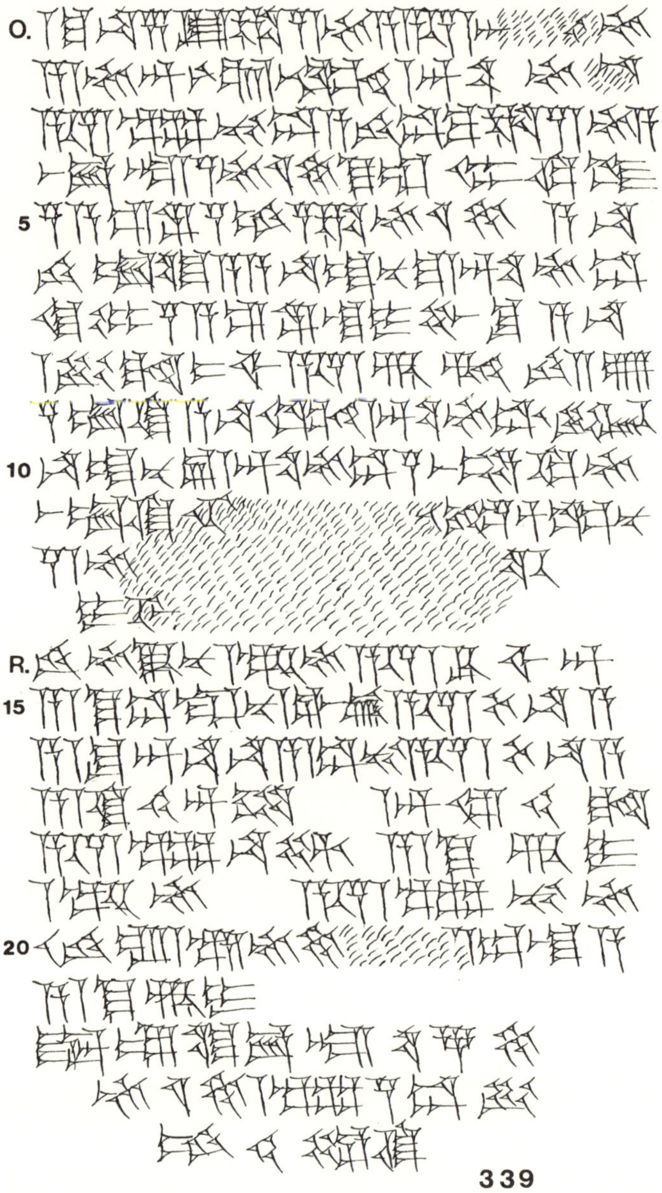

337

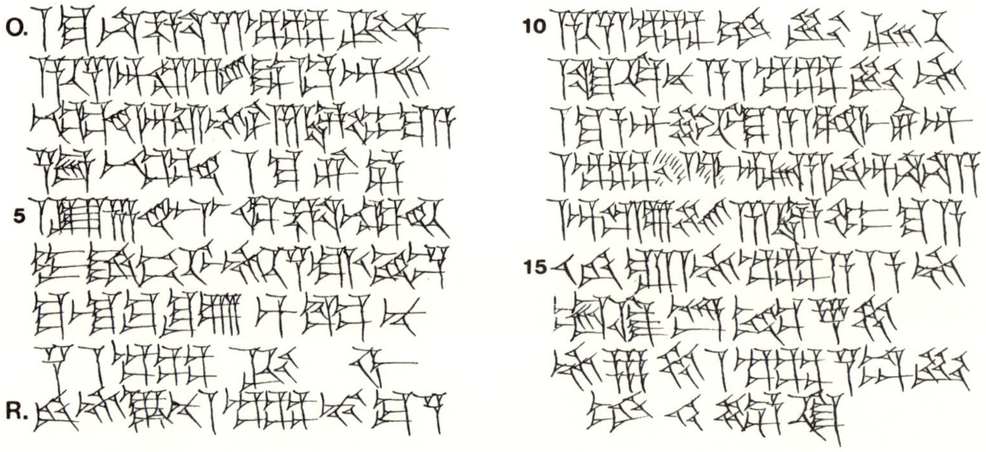

339

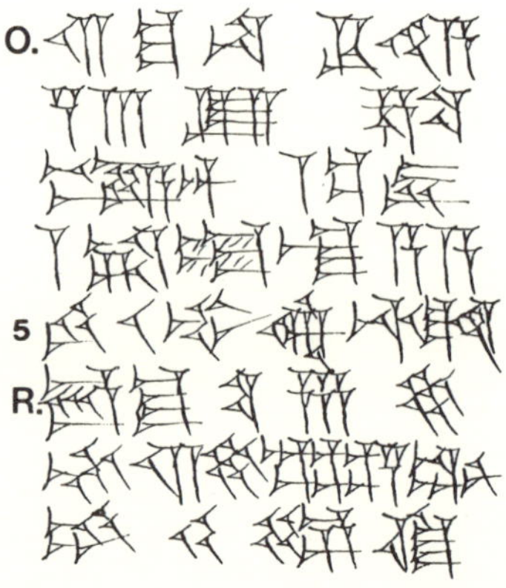

340

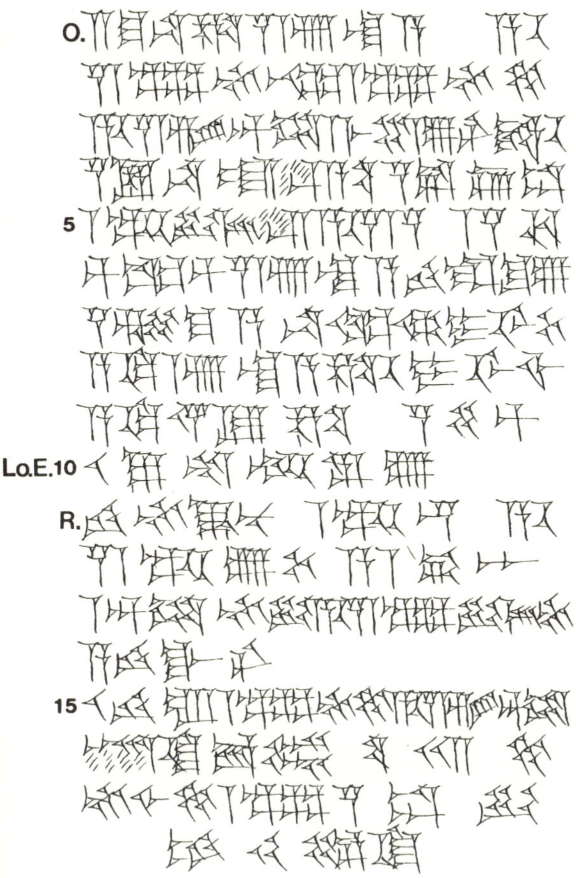

341

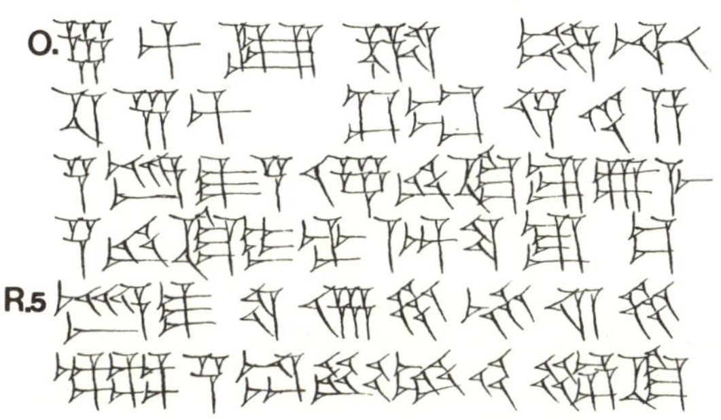

342

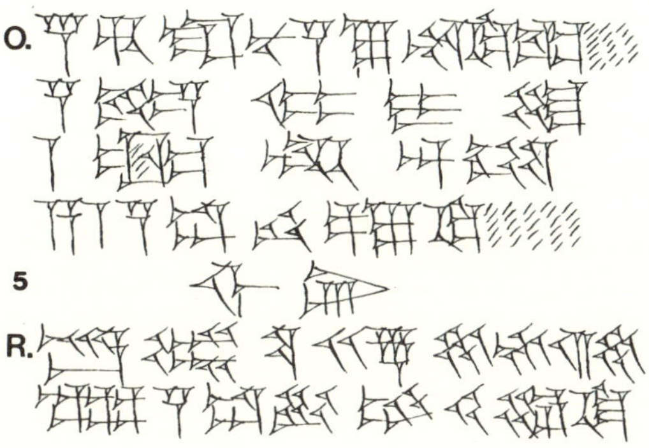

343

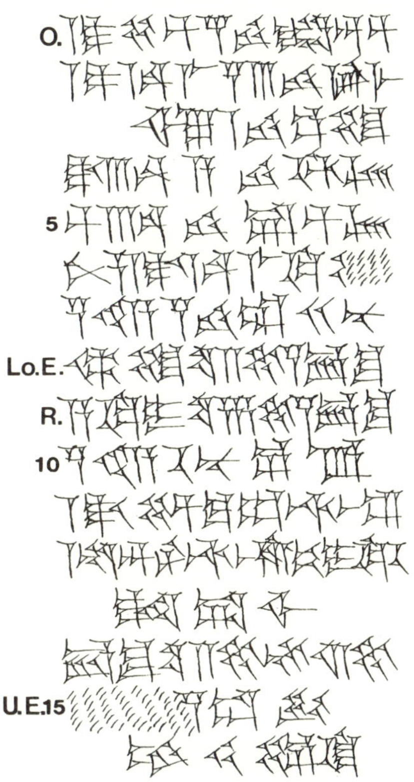

344

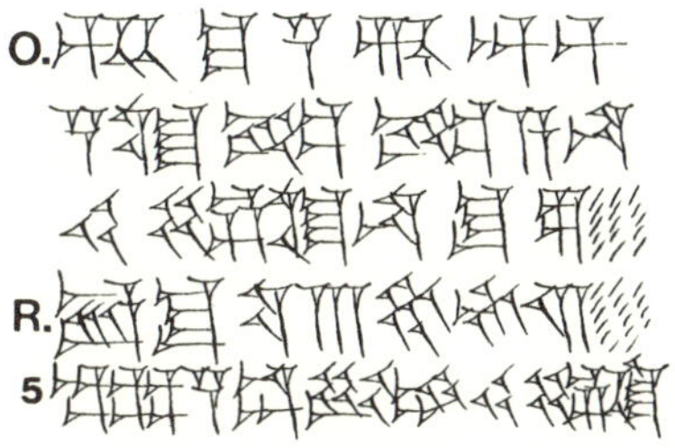

345

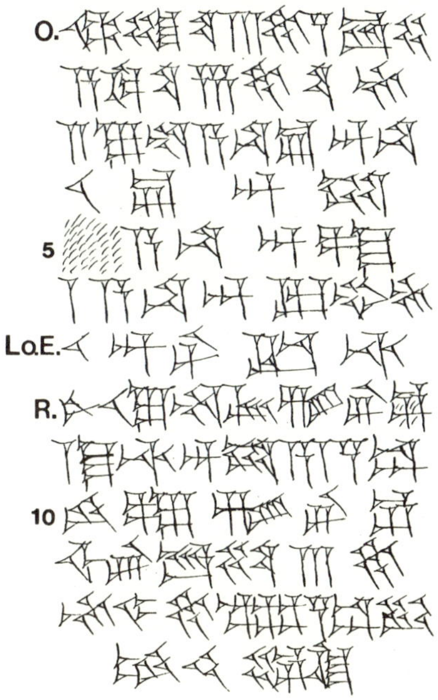

346

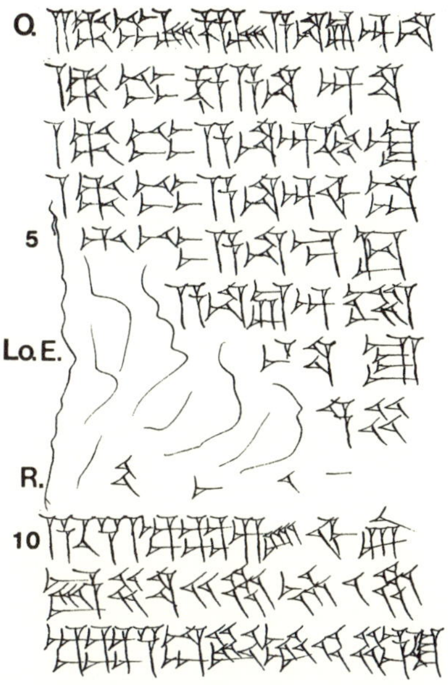

347

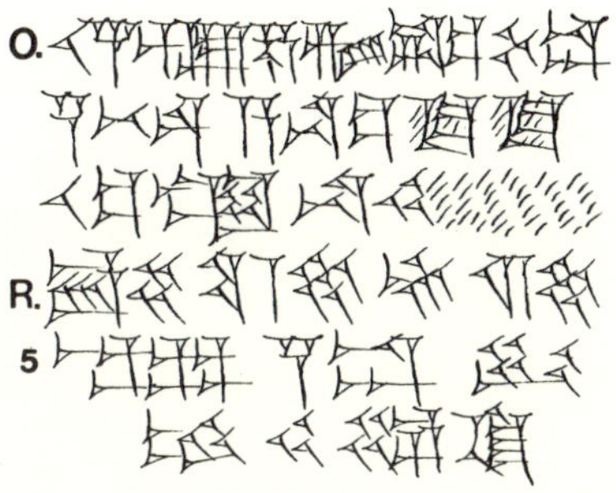

348

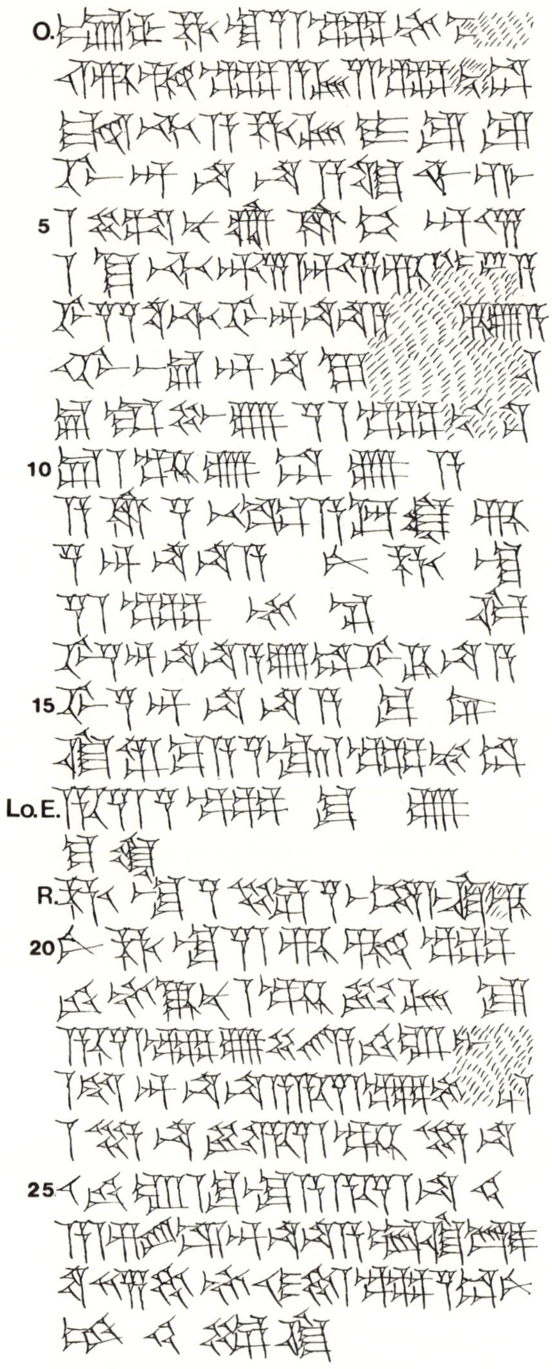

349

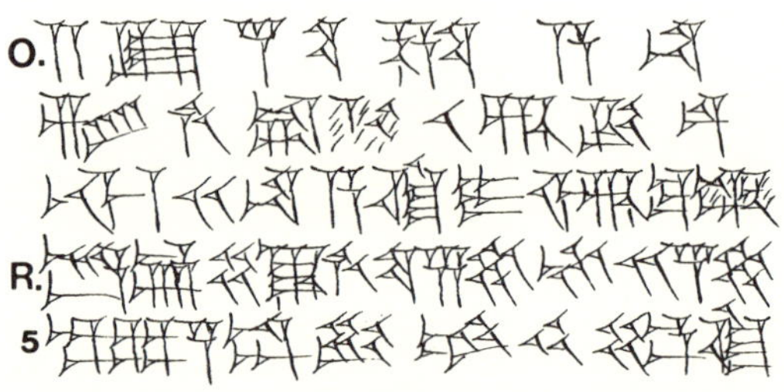

350

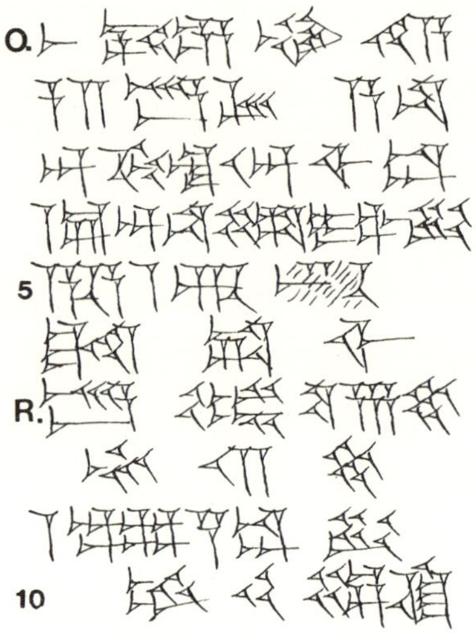

351

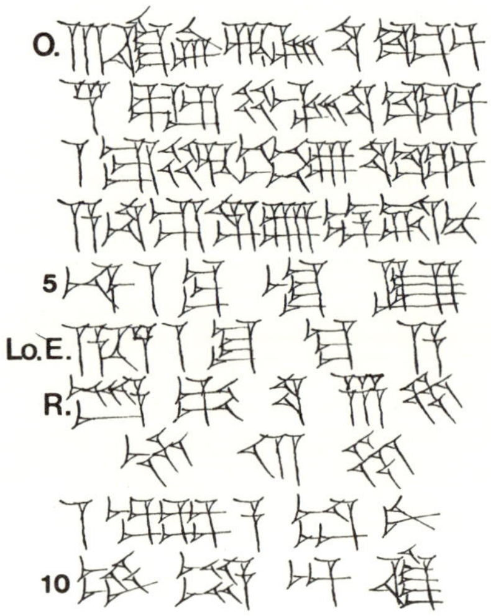

352

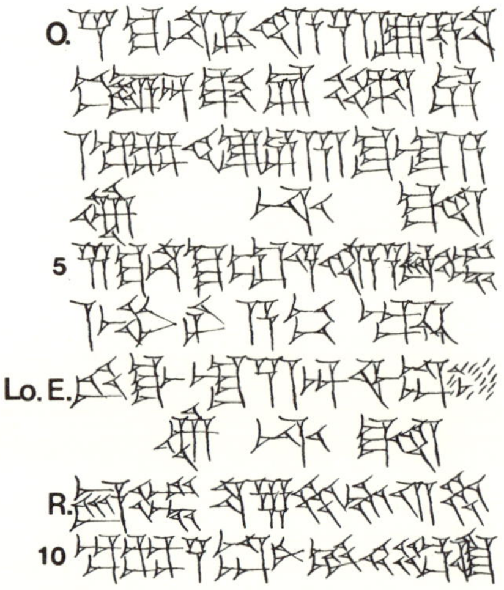

353

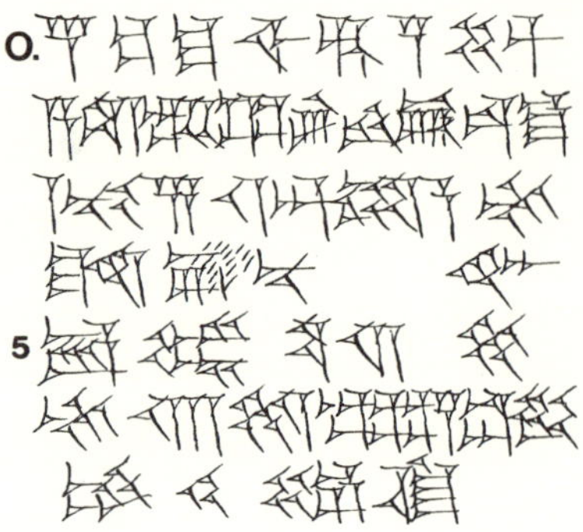

354

355

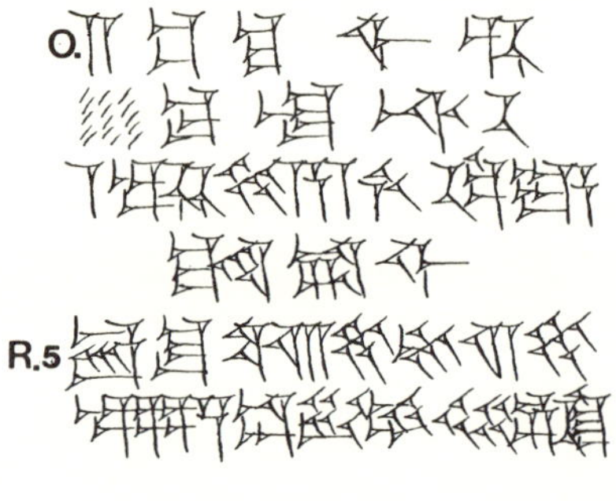

356

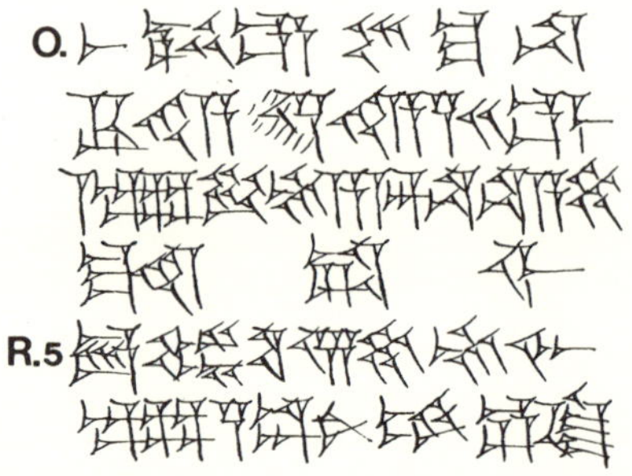

357

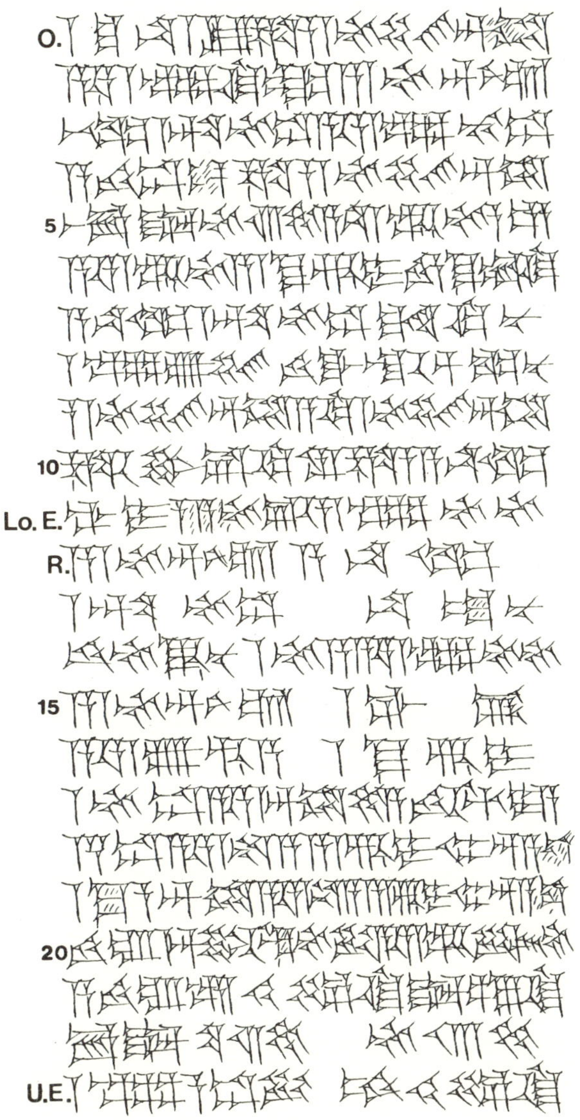

358

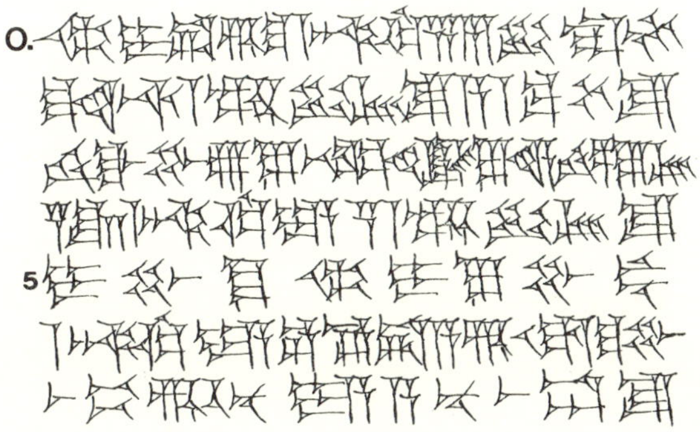

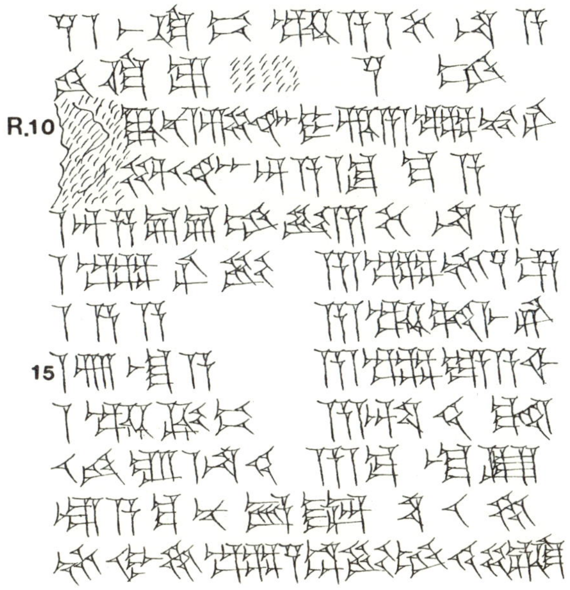

359

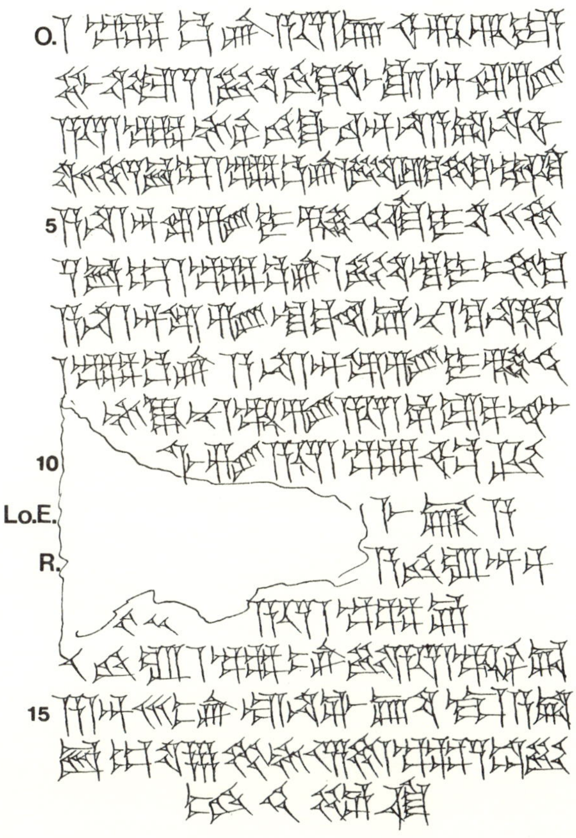

360

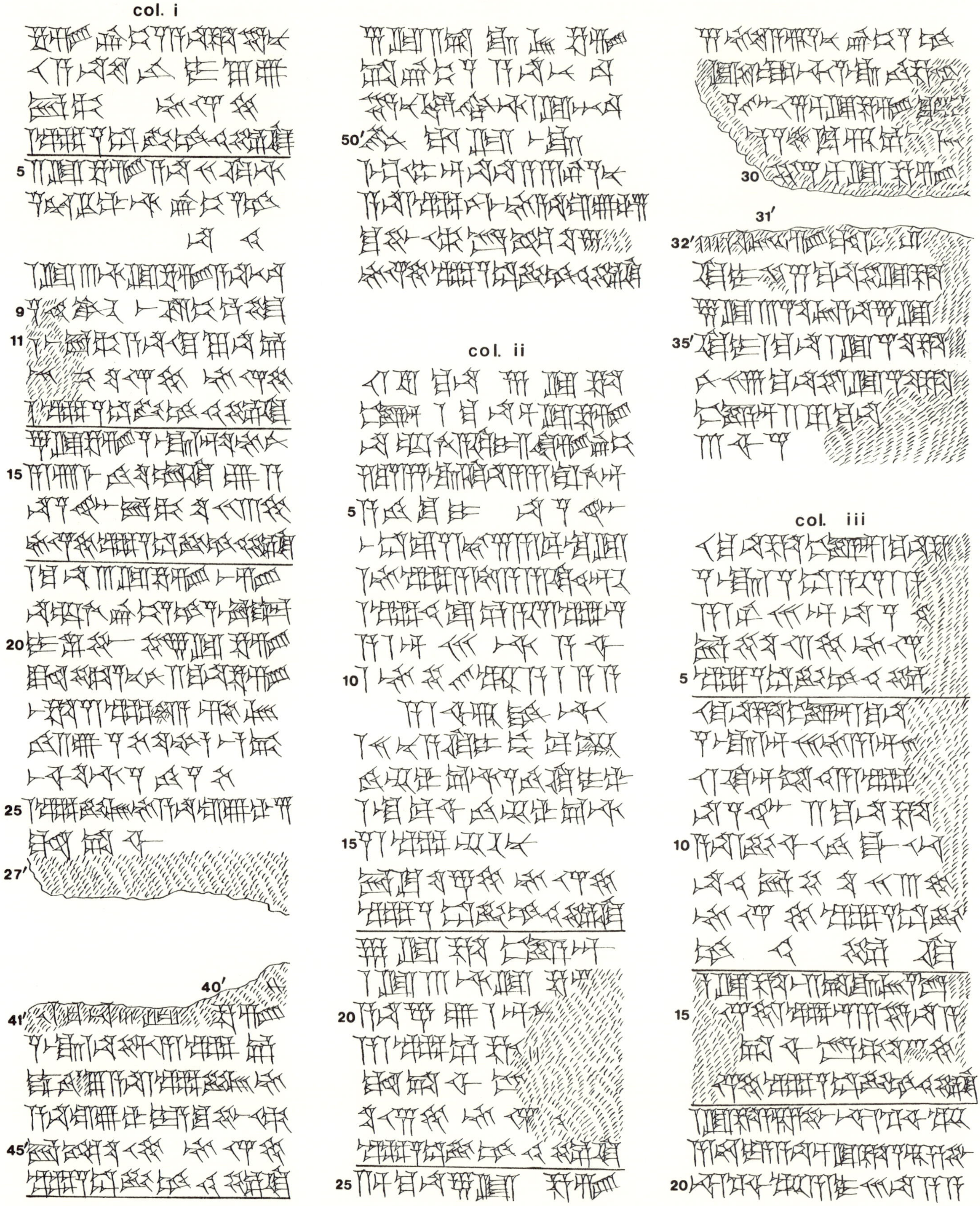

360 CONTINUED

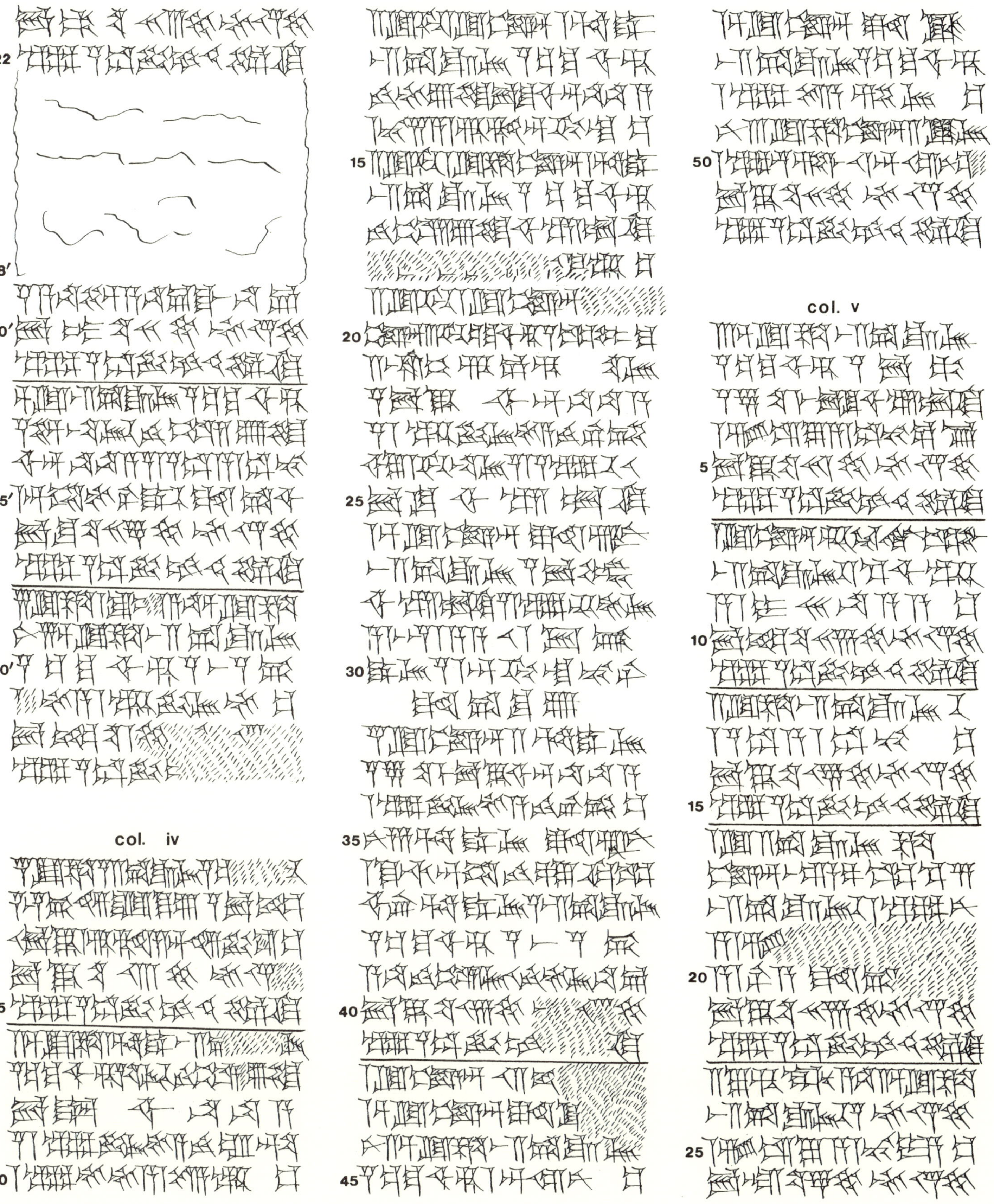

360 CONTINUED

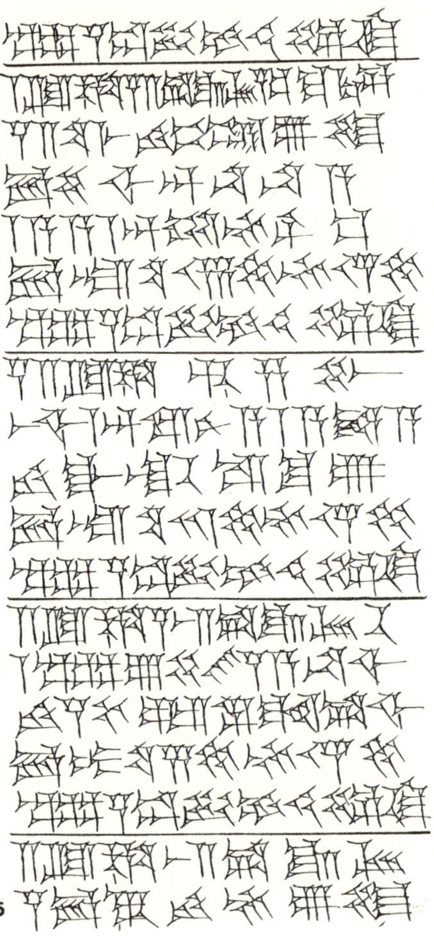

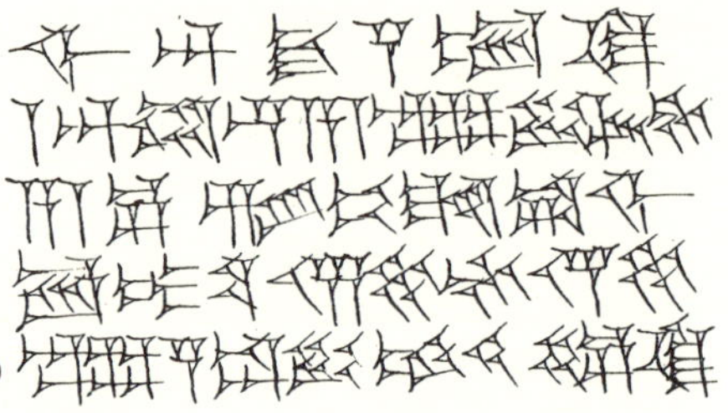

col. vi

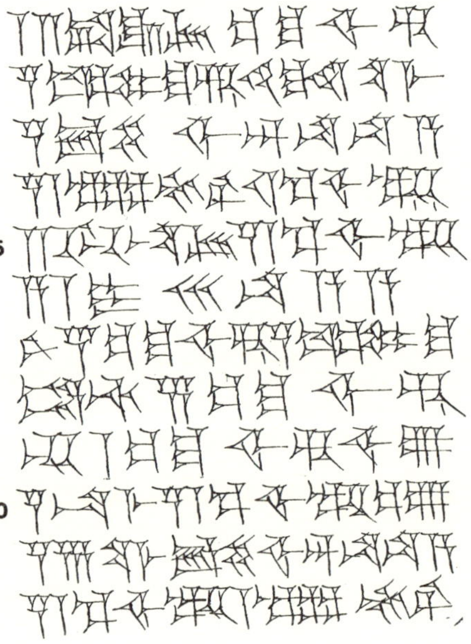

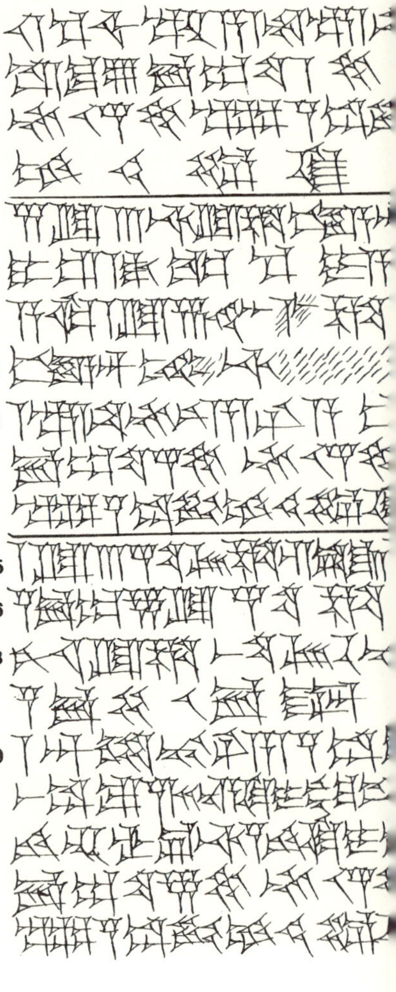

361

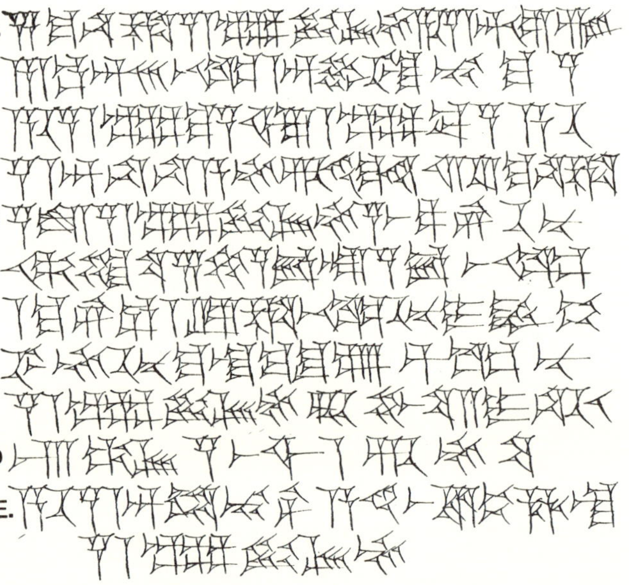

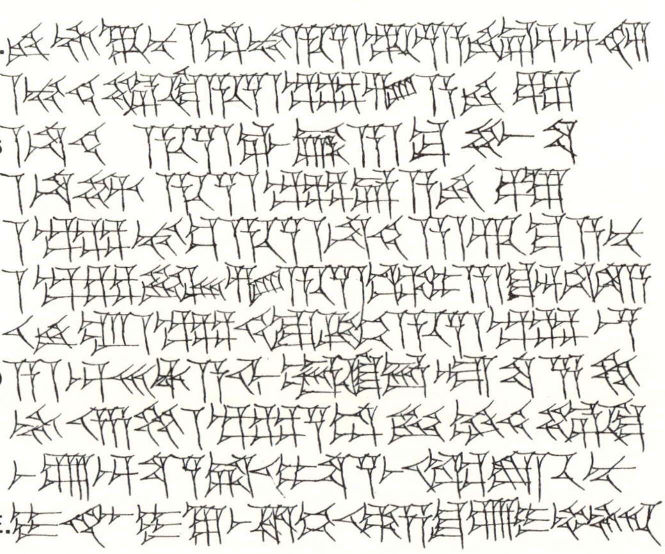

362

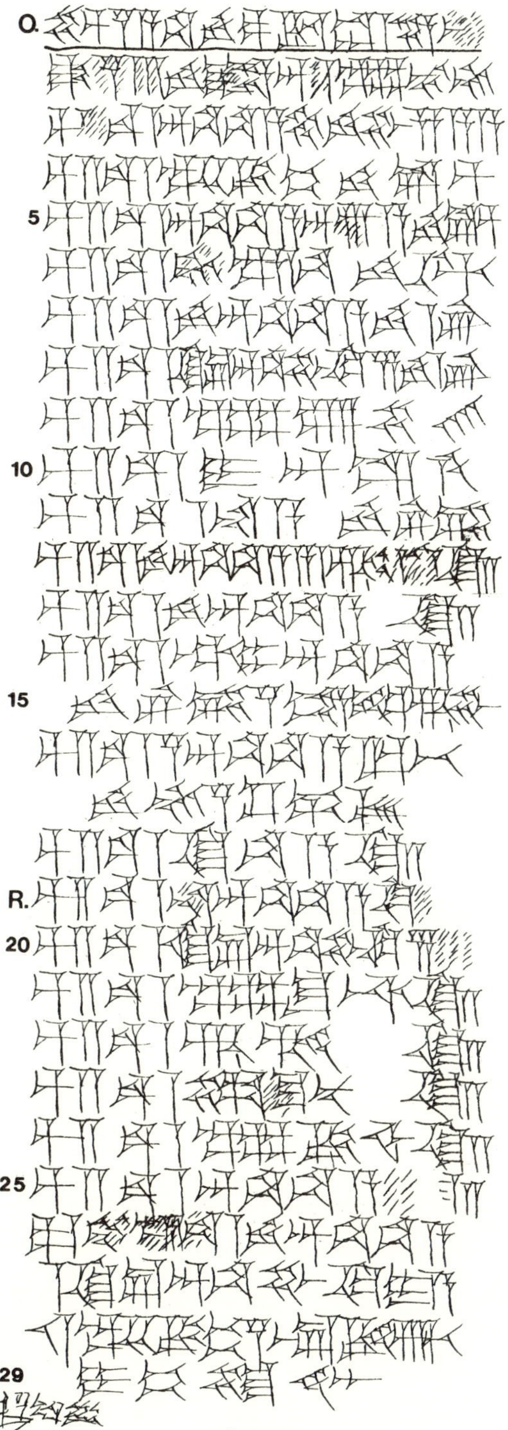

363

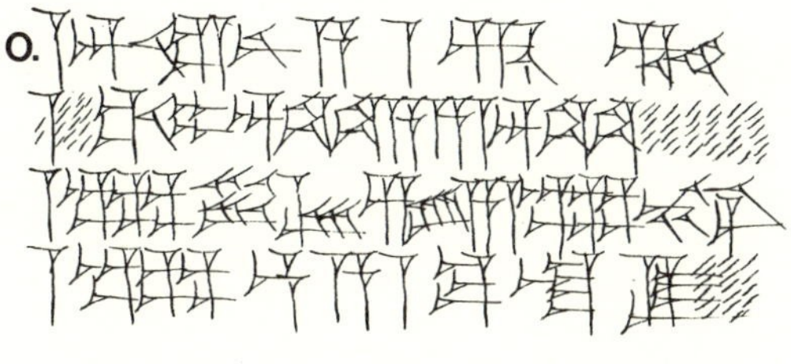

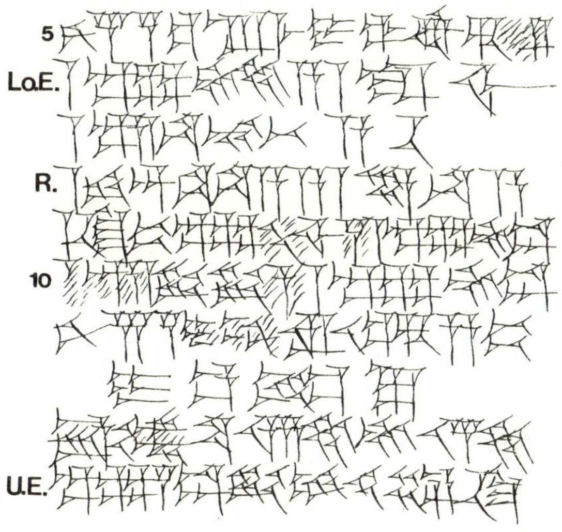

364

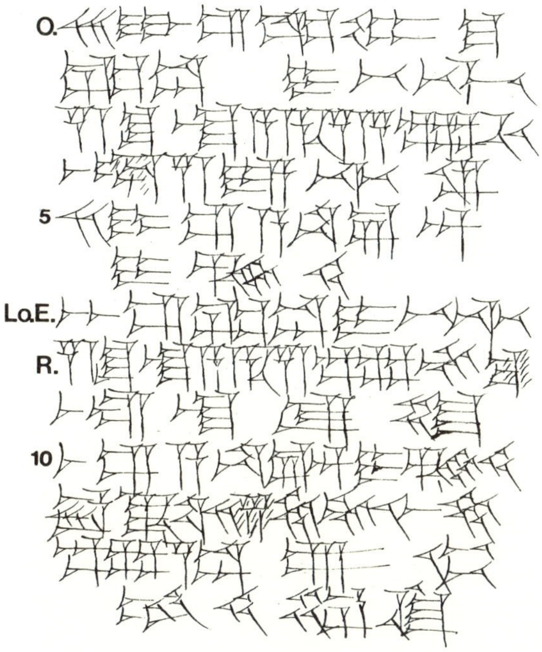

365

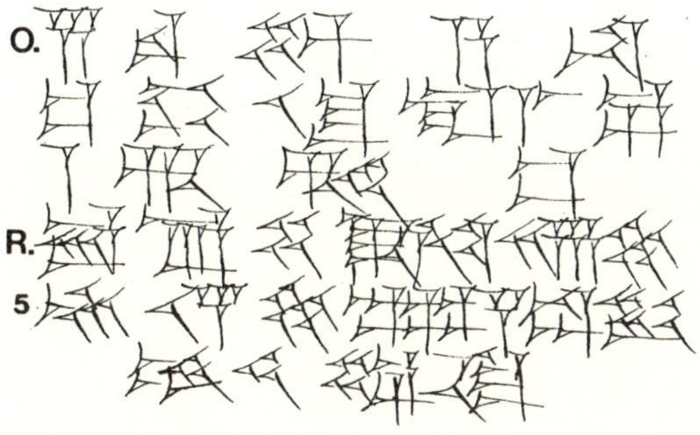

366

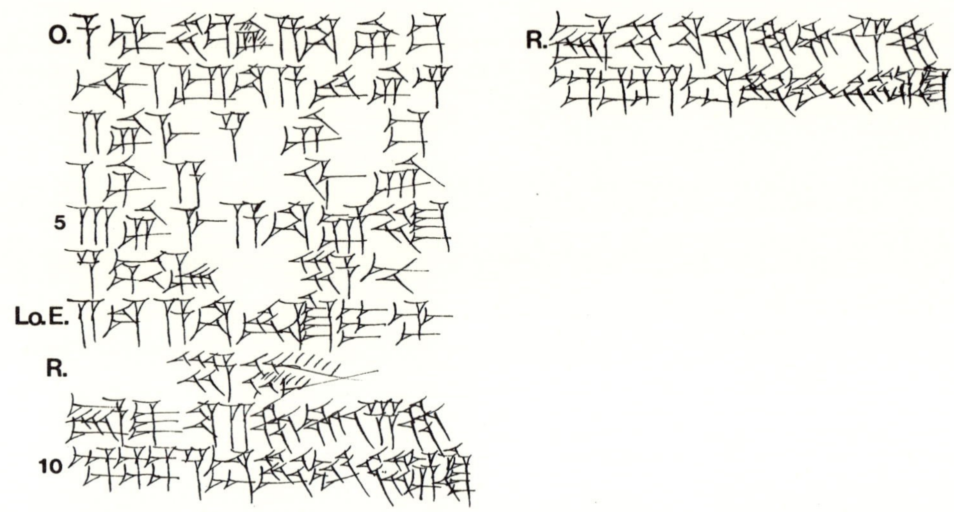

367

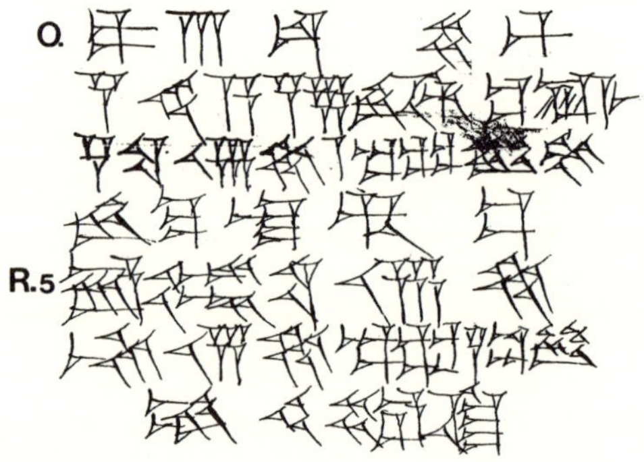

368

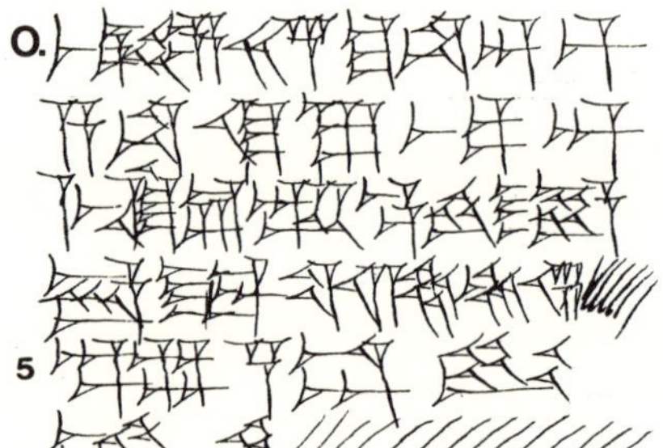

369

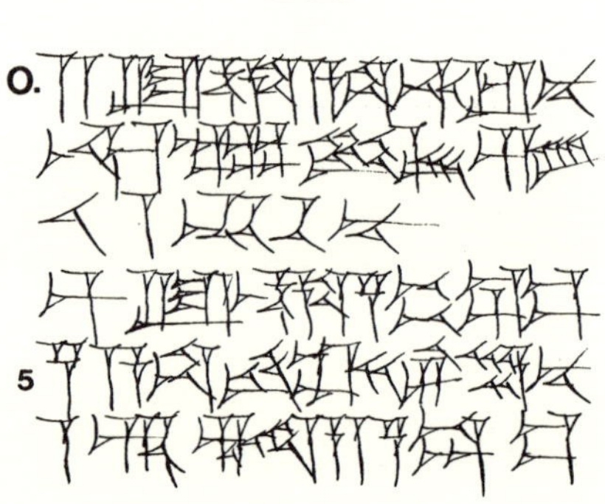